Managing Risk in the Financial System

Managing Risk in the Financial System

Edited by

John Raymond LaBrosse

Patterson & LaBrosse Financial Consultants Ltd., Canada and Honorary Visiting Fellow, School of Law, University of Warwick, UK

Rodrigo Olivares-Caminal

Centre for Financial & Management Studies (SOAS), University of London, UK

Dalvinder Singh

School of Law, University of Warwick, UK

Edward Elgar

Cheltenham, UK • Northampton, MA, USA

Published by
Edward Elgar Publishing Limited
The Lypiatts
15 Lansdown Road
Cheltenham
Glos GL50 2JA
UK

Edward Elgar Publishing, Inc.
William Pratt House
9 Dewey Court
Northampton
Massachusetts 01060
USA

A catalogue record for this book
is available from the British Library

Library of Congress Control Number: 2011924313

MIX
Paper from responsible sources
FSC® C018575
FSC www.fsc.org

ISBN 978 0 85793 381 2

Typeset by Servis Filmsetting Ltd, Stockport, Cheshire
Printed and bound by MPG Books Group, UK

Contents

List of contributors viii
Foreword: The 2010 Banking Law Symposium on Managing Systemic Risk by Charles Enoch x
Special Address: The deposit insurer's role in transitioning from a government deposit guarantee by Jean Pierre Sabourin xix
Preface: It has been 'A Hard Day's Night' by John Raymond LaBrosse, Rodrigo Olivares-Caminal and Dalvinder Singh xxix
Acknowledgements xlvi

PART I SYSTEMIC RISK

1. Investor behaviour in the period before the 2007–08 financial crisis 3
   Richard J. Rosen
2. The nature of systemic risk 19
   Jack Selody
3. The government as guarantor of last resort: benefits, costs and the case for premium charges 32
   Sebastian Schich
4. The Troubled Asset Relief Program: has forbearance as far as the eye can see saved the US economy? 55
   Gillian G.H. Garcia
5. Why is the Canadian banking system so remarkably stable? A comparative analysis with the US 81
   Jean Roy, Rima Turk-Ariss and Yenni Redjah
6. Systemic contingent claim analysis – a model approach to systemic risk 93
   Dale F. Gray and Andreas A. Jobst
7. Tax and the city: the UK's proposals for a bank levy 111
   John Snape

PART II SOVEREIGN DEBT

8. Iceland's financial disaster and its fiscal impact 133
Arnór Sighvatsson and Gunnar Gunnarsson
9. The Greek tragedy: is there a *Deus ex Machina*? 155
Ioannis Kokkoris, Rodrigo Olivares-Caminal and Kiriakos Papadakis
10. Restructuring a nation's debt 168
Lee C. Buchheit and Mitu Gulati

PART III ADDRESSING THE PROBLEM OF 'TOO-BIG-TO-FAIL'

11. Firm stability and system stability: the regulatory delusion 181
Geoffrey Wood with Ali Kabiri
12. 'Living wills': putting the caboose before the engine and designing a better engine 194
George G. Kaufman
13. Finding a solution to the 'too-big-to-fail' problem 208
Arthur E. Wilmarth, Jr.
14. 'Too-big-to-fail' – can alternative resolution regimes really remedy systemic risk in large financial institutions' insolvency? 233
Jens-Hinrich Binder
15. To divest or not to divest: that is the question . . . 248
Ioannis Kokkoris

PART IV CROSS-BORDER ISSUES

16. Resolving large complex financial institutions within and across jurisdictions 271
Robert R. Bliss and George G. Kaufman
17. From consolidated supervision to consolidated resolution 308
Rosa M. Lastra and Rodrigo Olivares-Caminal
18. Creating an EU-level supervisor for cross-border banking groups: issues raised by the US experience with dual banking 333
Larry D. Wall, María J. Nieto and David G. Mayes

PART V PRUDENTIAL REGULATION

19. Capital and liquidity reform – a new global agenda 351
George A. Walker

20. Basel II to Basel III: a great leap forward? 374
Imad Moosa

PART VI COUNTRY CASE STUDIES

21. The US architecture of bank regulation and supervision: recent reforms in their historical context 399
Dalvinder Singh
22. An evaluation of the Canadian financial safety net during the global financial crisis 416
John Raymond LaBrosse and James F. McCollum
23. Financial safety net reform in Nigeria 434
Ganiyu Ogunleye
24. Islamic deposit insurance system: the Malaysian model 442
Khairuddin Hj Arshad
25. Managing financial risk: the precautionary principle and protecting the public interest in the UK 449
John F. McEldowney

Index 473

Contributors

Jens-Hinrich Binder, University of Freiburg, Germany

Robert R. Bliss, Wake Forest University, USA

Lee C. Buchheit, Cleary Gottlieb Steen & Hamilton LLP, USA

Charles Enoch, International Monetary Fund

Gillian G.H. Garcia, Gillian GH Garcia Associates, USA

Dale F. Gray, International Monetary Fund

Mitu Gulati, Duke University, USA

Gunnar Gunnarsson, Central Bank of Iceland, Iceland

Khairuddin Hj Arshad, Malaysia Deposit Insurance Corporation, Malaysia

Andreas A. Jobst, International Monetary Fund

Ali Kabiri, University of Westminster, UK

George G. Kaufman, Loyola University Chicago, USA

Ioannis Kokkoris, University of Reading, UK

John Raymond LaBrosse, Patterson & LaBrosse Financial Consultants Ltd, Canada

Rosa M. Lastra, Queen Mary, University of London, UK

David G. Mayes, University of Auckland, New Zealand

James F. McCollum, JF McCollum and Consultants, Canada

John F. McEldowney, University of Warwick, UK

Imad Moosa, RMIT, Australia

María J. Nieto, Banco de España, Spain

Ganiyu Ogunleye, Jaffa Consulting, Nigeria

Rodrigo Olivares-Caminal, Centre for Financial & Mangement Studies (SOAS), University of London, UK

Kiriakos Papadakis, Decidendi Consultants, Greece

Jean Pierre Sabourin, Malaysia Deposit Insurance Corporation, Malaysia

Yenni Redjah, HEC Montreal, Canada

Richard J. Rosen, Federal Reserve Bank of Chicago, USA

Jean Roy, HEC Montreal, Canada

Sebastian Schich, OECD

Jack Selody, Bank of Canada, Canada

Arnór Sighvatsson, Central Bank of Iceland, Iceland

Dalvinder Singh, University of Warwick, UK

John Snape, University of Warwick, UK

Rima Turk-Ariss, HEC Montreal, Canada

George A. Walker, Queen Mary, University of London, UK

Larry D. Wall, Federal Reserve Bank of Atlanta, USA

Arthur E. Wilmarth, Jr., George Washington University, USA

Geoffrey Wood, Cass Business School, City University London, UK

Foreword

The 2010 Banking Law Symposium on Managing Systemic Risk

Charles Enoch[1]

The symposium covered a great deal of ground. Given the severity of the recent crisis and the need for a massive response, there will continue to be debate for some time. Many of the issues raised are fundamental and still controversial. One can divide the discussion into a number of broad topics. Some of them – such as the future of bank regulation – aim at limiting the occurrence of systemic crisis in the future as well as its consequences; others – for instance the explosion in the size of central bank balance sheets – are amongst the by-products of the handling of crisis, and may or may not have consequences that would need to be addressed later.

The macroeconomic aspects are the most visible and immediate sign of the global banking crisis, with the world having fallen into the deepest recession since the 1930s, and still struggling to recover. The long period of uninterrupted growth backed by the 'great moderation' came to an abrupt end in 2008. Massive Keynesian-type fiscal expansion was carried out in response pretty much everywhere, to avoid a recession that would lead to something even worse. In some places, such as the US, the stimulus was illuminated with high media visibility; in others, such as China, the stimulus was introduced relatively quietly. The public emphasis was on 'shovel ready' projects, rather than well-planned overall programmes. Whilst the stimuli were introduced pretty much by consensus at the time, now there is much less certainty as to what needs to be done – and indeed even whether those who pushed the stimulus were right to do so. Should the stimulus be reined in now, or would that jeopardize the still anaemic growth? Perhaps this is one of many areas where one size might not fit all, and policies that are appropriate in one place may not be appropriate universally.

While demand-enhancing stimulus was an initial response to the global crisis, as one goes forward and policymakers consider how to encourage sustainable medium-term growth, there is a particular focus on structural factors. Amongst these are some quite fundamental issues concerning the optimal size of the banking sector. Those suggestions lead to widely diverging policy recommendations, for instance as regards increasing taxes on the banking sector. On the one side, there are concerns that if taxes are imposed this may reduce the sector's willingness or ability to lend, and hence its potential to revive economic growth. In much of the world credit growth is weak, despite direct fiscal support into the banking sector, and further taxes on the banking sector might be considered likely to cripple it further, hence also jeopardizing economic growth. On the other side, however, are those who argue that the various 'bail-out' facilities, whether fiscal, monetary, or structural such as the provision of guarantees, are at present not fully financed by the banking sector. They represent a subsidy to the sector, which therefore is larger than would be optimal from a social cost–benefit point of view. If this subsidy were countered by taxes, it would at least partially address the negative externalities of systemic risk.

When considering the handling of the banking sector, it has been recognized that policymakers in the past have been defective in defining what precisely the banking sector is. Beyond the core issue of deposit taking there is a spectrum of financial activities and institutions (e.g. shadow banking systems; investment banks; insurance companies) that in many ways raise similar issues of safety and soundness, but that traditionally have been more or less excluded from the perimeter of prudential regulation. For instance, there was pervasive 'shadow banking' hiding the true leverage of banks; there were financial institutions such as AIG taking large amounts of credit risk from the banking sector via guarantees and contingent contracts so that its problems were considered systemic. And, if these institutions are so interconnected with the deposit-accepting banks that it is not possible to separate their handling from that of the banking sector, should one instead create narrow banks – or rigid firewalls within banks – so that what is within the narrow bank or the firewall cannot be contaminated by high risk-taking financial activities? But would narrow banking make the cost of credit too high? Would it lead to risk again moving beyond the regulatory perimeter, potentially resulting in further threats to financial stability?

As well as questions regarding the perimeter of the banking sector, there are issues concerning the optimal size of the banks. At the outset of the crisis, the authorities in several countries – in particular the US and the UK – pressed what appeared to be strong banks, such as Bank of America and Lloyds TSB, to take over weaker banks. This has been in other countries a fairly standard supervisory response to banking problems that are thought to be not systemic. In some cases the authorities offer protection to the 'white knight' bank, for instance limiting its liability in the event the loan book it is acquiring turns out to be worse than anticipated. In the great recession of the global financial crisis, however, it quickly became apparent that the 'white knight' banks were themselves under water, if not originally then certainly very shortly afterwards. Bank of America acquired Wachovia with the support of the regulators, but soon required government infusions. In the UK, Lloyds TSB was encouraged by the regulators to take Halifax Bank of Scotland, but almost immediately thereafter was seen to be deeply distressed and still remains with substantial government equity.

The rationale for pushing a takeover of a weaker bank by a stronger one is in principle clear: the performing assets and liabilities of the weaker bank remain within the banking sector, and will be managed by a stronger institution within the sector – this should limit the public costs compared to the takeover of the entire weaker bank by the public sector, even if the public sector has to financially help the acquiring bank, in one form or another, in order to persuade it to undertake the takeover. On the other hand, even in the best of conditions, mergers between – or takeovers of – financial institutions may not turn out well; when the merger or takeover is being undertaken at speed in conditions of turmoil, prospects of success are potentially going to be dim. There will be second-guessing of any takeover decision if it starts to go badly, and questioning of who knew what when and what did they do about it. Bank of America executives are being questioned closely by shareholders about the details of their takeover of Merrill Lynch. On the other side, if, notwithstanding these initial challenges, the takeover nevertheless works out well for the acquiring bank, this causes its own difficulties. A banking system that has gone through a process of strong banks taking over weak banks with official support will be a more concentrated system, with all the attendant issues: such a system may be subject to oligopolistic power, with resulting costs to the consumers; and if banks in such a system run into difficulties, there is greater likelihood that such banks would be 'too-big-to-fail'. Even worse, particularly for a small country, if such a process has gone on far enough, individual institutions might become 'too-big-to-save', with potentially catastrophic implications for the country as a whole, and potentially for the global financial system. An alternative model, practised in Sweden and to some extent in Asia in the 1990s, involved the state taking over the weak institutions for a while, restructuring them under government auspices, generally through having such banks unload their bad assets into a dedicated asset-resolution agency, and ultimately selling the cleansed institution back to the private sector – in many cases much smaller than they were at the time that they went into crisis. There were few proponents of such an approach during the present crisis, perhaps because finance is now much more complicated, and it is not clear where governments might find the substitute managements that could fully understand the business and turn it around, and because at this point there were too many institutions for the governments to swallow. Also, while the active breaking-up of large banks was discussed at the outset of the crisis from the financial stability perspective, this debate now seems, particularly in the European Union, to be in the hands of the competition authorities.

With the wide variety of orthodox and heterodox measures that have been employed, often in haste, to stimulate the economy and protect weak financial institutions, there is naturally a focus on countries' fiscal position. In virtually all countries, there has been a major deterioration in the fiscal stance. In the European Union, for instance, only five of the 27 member countries are now not subject to the excessive deficit procedure: within the euro area, only Finland and Luxembourg are not in breach. Beyond the headline fiscal position, however, there is uncertainty as to what the fiscal position actually is. Guarantees, for instance, have been widely used in the crisis; the potential liability that arises is not included in headline fiscal measures. Also, institutions outside the central government have been brought in to help effect the stimulus – most particularly the central banks. Central bank balance sheets have expanded multiplicatively, and in some cases central banks have intervened directly to support institutions. Central banks have also compromised their earlier standards on the quality of the assets that they have assumed. In the event that those assets lose value or fail to perform, the central bank – or other agency – will itself make losses of a fiscal nature. Quasi-fiscal activities may be less immediately apparent on the fiscal balance sheets, but of themselves create contingent fiscal liabilities that may ultimately lead to pressures to recapitalize one or more troubled central banks at a time when governments are already under fiscal pressure. Early recognition of such liabilities is important for appropriate policy formulation. Late recognition may cause a loss of credibility in the government more generally, particularly if the overall economic and financial situation still remains fragile.

Moral hazard will be a pervasive and long lasting result of the measures introduced in the face of the global financial crisis. Banking sector activity is determined by the balance between risks and rewards. If risks are not fully assessed, activity may be reckless. If risks are essentially removed, absent anything else, reckless behaviour seems assured. The blanket guarantees on deposits, and the reductions on interest rates and provision of quantitative easing, together with forbearance and the provision of capital without the state taking full equity control, have served to reduce the role of risk in mitigating reckless behaviour. Moreover, even if some of these measures are quickly reversed – for instance, the blanket guarantee has a notional time limit or a quantitative limit, and some banks have already paid, or are in the process of paying, back the direct public capital infusions – it is not credible that for the foreseeable future 'next time' governments and central banks will not provide the same protection. Traditionally moral hazard is addressed by distinguishing between saving an institution and saving those responsible. The institution may at least partially survive, but managers will quickly be replaced; shareholders and unsecured creditors will be wiped out, or at any rate have their stakes substantially reduced; and any malfeasance will be investigated and prosecuted; meanwhile, regulatory reform serves to avoid a recurrence of such behaviour in the future. Views differ as to the extent to which measures taken so far will serve to mitigate moral hazard, and indeed even how serious the moral hazard problem is. Regulatory reform is coming, although it is not clear at this stage how extensive it will be. In most of the financial institutions requiring the largest infusions, shareholders – although not wiped out – have lost substantial amounts of equity value; in many institutions management has been largely replaced, but unsecured creditors have been bailed out for the most part. In the US and elsewhere, banks had to undergo stress tests to establish whether they were adequately capitalized; and where they were not would have had to take action to replenish their capital. On the other hand, however, low interest rates and quantitative easing have enabled many of these institutions rapidly to make a come-back, showing high profitability while the overall economy stays weak; and key staff are again being paid large bonuses to avert their departures. Oxford students are being enticed once again with huge salary offers, implying that banks' behaviour may not have changed from before, or indeed may even be considered to have been validated. Moral hazard undermines the core principles of the market economy; addressing the present enhanced level of moral hazard is likely to be critical for the sustainability of the post-crisis economy. An exit strategy from the moral hazard conjuncture should be a priority.

Much has been made, in this symposium and more widely, of the role of institutions. Much has been made of the contrast between Canada and other industrial countries. Canada has one institution per function: a central bank; a banking supervisor; a financial consumer protection agency; and a deposit insurer. It also has separate provincial securities supervisors. Other countries have functions combined within institutions, hence arguably causing confusion about objectives and reducing the overall quality of decision-making and economic and financial management. On the other hand, separation of institutions by function does not necessarily mean that the resultant structure will be successful. The Bank of England, for example, progressively lost its various functions and objectives over the past 15 years, so that it finally focused solely on operating monetary policy, while prudential regulation and supervision as well as debt management were taken away. Overall, it is not clear that the Financial Services Authority (FSA) managed oversight of the banking sector better than an unreformed Bank of England might have done. In short, the quality of institutions clearly matters, but it is not obvious that one system of institutions is necessarily better than another: any particular one might work well, but any might mess up. Moreover, the process of changing a country's system of institutions is itself disruptive and may cause additional problems, particularly during the transition. In any case, even if there is one institution per function, if they coordinate properly, as soon as they take into account the perspectives of their partner institutions in such coordination, they will themselves be facing more than one objective.

Amongst the various institutions there is at present a close focus on the role of the regulators. There are serious concerns that the crisis was caused in part by industry capture – for example, that the regulators fell too far under the spell of the institutions that they were meant to regulate. Such behaviour could be ascribed to the pervasive culture that the most successful bankers were 'masters of the universe', responsible for economic growth and innovation in a rapidly-changing economy, and not to be easily challenged by ponderous bureaucrats. Neither at the most senior level amongst the regulators nor amongst the common foot soldiers would there be much incentive to try to pull away the punch bowl as the party gets into full swing, and although there were a number of whistle blowers they could not make themselves heard. No doubt to some extent the aura of bankers' invincibility is gone, and regulators will be more confident in standing in the way of a banker's deviant behaviour. On the other hand, with economies very fragile and strong official pressure on banks to lend more on the back of official guarantees, regulators may be conflicted in taking strong positions against the banks. In order to encourage them, there are some ideas on how to stimulate increased accountability amongst the regulators, for instance public disclosure in close to real time on their interactions with the banks. Beyond this, there is recognition that there might be an underlying flaw in having regulators focus solely on risks in individual banks. As the recent crisis has shown, risks may rather be systemic and result from contagion across interconnected institutions. Prudential supervision of individual institutions is being complemented by systemic or macro-prudential supervision, which might not be hosted by the same set of regulators or indeed even the same regulatory institutions.

There was little agreement at the symposium on the relative merits of determinism or flexibility in addressing the crisis. Prompt corrective action was intended to be the deterministic policy response to the handling of the US savings and loans collapse in the 1980s, when it was perceived that the ultimate costs of the collapse were much higher than if the regulators had intervened more quickly. In the present crisis, however, in spite of the large social cost, supervisors, particularly in Europe, still resist the adoption of prompt corrective action and early intervention. Moreover, the high integration of financial markets demands early recognition of financial problems and increasing coordination to avoid contagion, both in normal times and in crisis situations. Thus even more than in earlier crises, the pre-setting of deterministic rules could be argued to be critical to reduce overall costs. On the other hand, the present crisis is different from all those before, so rules based on 'fighting the last war' may not be helpful.

While managing the crisis in a single country would be complicated enough, the situation becomes even more difficult given the international character of large cross-border banks and the many sovereign interactions. Many of the main institutions involved are active in many countries; indeed, some institutions no longer have a clear national parentage. There are important asymmetries in the importance of some of these institutions across the countries in which they operate. While an institution may be barely systemic in its home country, it may have a dominant presence in countries where it operates. In a crisis situation the institution may show home country preference, withdrawing disproportionately from the 'peripheral' countries of its activities. At the outset, there were no clear rules as to how such situations should be resolved, although considerable work has been undertaken, both at the Bank for International Settlements and in the European institutions, to have a framework under which countries can cooperate. Nevertheless, there remains severe discomfort. The UK and the Netherlands used an array of weapons to seek that their nationals were compensated for the collapse of an Icelandic bank in which they had deposits. Going forward, nobody is suggesting that citizens should not be permitted to deposit in an overseas bank; but there is plenty of ongoing work to ensure that in future it will be clear what are the respective responsibilities if another international bank failure causes problems in countries outside its home base. The complexity of the large cross-border banks makes their reorganization and winding-up so complex that it is an invitation for governments to rescue banks. In the absence of an international bank resolution authority and international harmonization of bank reorganization and winding-up procedures, 'living wills' are contingency plans under which banks specify in advance how they are to be treated if they approach failure – hence seeking advance preparation for resolution even before the background to the resolution is known. Having such a framework in place in advance may well be a useful protection against confusion and knee-jerk reactions in the event of a crisis. But one cannot foresee all states of the world, and however precisely a 'living will' may have set out a course to be followed, there presumably still needs to be some flexibility in how it will be applied in reality – and its success in terms of limiting the cost of resolving failed banks is very much dependent on the national institutional frameworks for supervision and the resolution of failed banks.

In this environment international coordination and the role of international institutions comes to the fore. Hong Kong, Malaysia and Singapore are reportedly coordinating over their plans to exit from their crisis measures. This no doubt is helpful. But an interesting question then arises as to where are the limits of coordination. For instance, could the rest of ASEAN be included in this coordination framework? Probably every country wants to be the last member into a coordination club – happy to get the benefits from association with a 'stronger' country, but they may be reluctant to share with one that is perceived to be 'weaker'. Beyond these informal groupings there are the established international financial institutions such as the International Monetary Fund (IMF) and the collectives of subsets of the Fund's membership. The present crisis has led to some creativity as regards these. The former Financial Stability Forum, established after an earlier crisis, has morphed into the Financial Stability Board, with an enhanced mandate, while the G-20 seems to have become a key strategy-defining body. Meanwhile, the IMF focuses also on its own internal governance in order to address issues of legitimacy as it comes to the centre in handling the present crisis.

So, is the global financial crisis over? Views differ, and the issue can only be resolved ex post. Certainly the momentum for significant reform seems to have diminished, at least for the moment, perhaps because the focus shifts towards the need for fiscal retrenchment. Most likely the answer depends on the answers to the questions being addressed earlier, in particular that of macroeconomic prospects. If growth does not falter, the worst may well be behind us, and the momentum for serious reform may flag, although the possible emergence of new sovereign problems suggests caution as regards any early declaration of victory.

The symposium looked also briefly at possible overarching solutions to problems of over-indebtedness and macroeconomic imbalances. Clearly the IMF has a revived role, but there was also interest in private solutions that have been put forward, such as bond contracts. More fundamental would be asset sales. When lending to the UK in 1976, the IMF required that the UK begin to sell off then-state owned British Petroleum (BP). Much earlier, Charles II had progressively sold off the territories he had acquired as a dowry when he married Catherine of Braganza: so England lost Tangier and Dunkirk. In the Latin American banking crisis of the 1980s, the wags said that Brazil should 'sell off the Matto Grosso' to pay its debts; similar types in Germany are saying that Greece should sell some of its islands. This of course will not happen – but it indicates the desperation of creditors in dealing with a country that might be close to insolvency.

Next time there is a global financial crisis, its handling will have to be different. Unless the authorities show particular imagination, or demonstrate greater up-front accountability, there are likely to be fewer instruments available. The public will be less trusting of a US Treasury Secretary announcing that he needs USD700 billion or else the economy will collapse. And, in the next few years at least, there will be far less fiscal space available for governments to try to spend their way out of trouble.

Finally, what is the conclusion? Overall, one can be cautiously optimistic. Countries are likely to be able to muddle through, or to be able to receive help if they cannot. Some things were learned from the last crisis which prevented this crisis becoming even more serious; more will be learned this time. Recovery and resolution funds, greater powers for regulators, heightened transparency and accountability, and much better coordination are all ideas that are being further developed, and all are likely to have a role to play in safeguarding the exit from the present crisis and reducing the risk of a crisis in the future.

NOTE

1. The views expressed are those of the author and should not be attributed to the International Monetary Fund, its Executive Board, or its Management. I am grateful for comments from Gillian Garcia and María Nieto.

Special Address

The deposit insurer's role in transitioning from a government deposit guarantee

Jean Pierre Sabourin[1]

It is an honour for me to participate once again in this prestigious symposium and I appreciate the opportunity to be here today to speak to this distinguished group. Many thanks to Ray LaBrosse and the organizers of this symposium for this kind invitation. Having seen and participated in the success of last year's symposium, the Malaysia Deposit Insurance Corporation, or otherwise known as MDIC, is, once again, proud to be a co-sponsor of this symposium.

What a difference a year makes! This time last year, the global economy was mired in the depth of the worst recession since the Great Depression. Fast forward one year, recent months have brought better economic news with traces of more sustaining growth becoming more visible. At the time of writing, the healing of financial conditions along with gradually building public confidence remains supportive to keep the recovery going. As the dust settles, I hope we can now better see the proximate causes of the crisis and solutions to these problems. Hence, it is good for us to reconvene in Warwick at a time of recovery from the financial crisis.

This year's symposium on managing systemic risks, and the topics being discussed, is of great importance to all of us here who share a common interest in fostering the stability of the financial system. Indeed, with global financial risks now receding, this is an opportune time for us to come together to reflect and discuss pertinent issues on managing and preventing systemic risks. In line with the theme of the symposium, my remarks today are on a deposit insurer's role in transitioning from a government deposit guarantee (GDG).

It is indeed fact that the implementation of extraordinary measures, including the introduction of GDG, have helped to prevent the global economy from sinking further into an economic abyss. However, while necessary to avert an economic disaster of this proportion, such support measures can distort financial efficiency and erode market discipline.

More perversely, they encourage moral hazard and substantially distort incentives. In fact, the current crisis has generated what I believe to be the 'mother of all' moral hazard! The general public and 'too-big-to-fail' financial institutions are again being conditioned to believe that the government would always step in with a blanket guarantee or bail them out whenever risks materialize. It also leaves no doubt that such distortions could encourage banks to continue taking excessive risks in the future. This would, eventually, sow the seeds for future crises.

Hence, given their nature, a clear message needs to be sent to explain that such measures are temporary. Measures should also be implemented to mitigate 'too-big-to-fail' expectations and conditions to always step in to help. And, it is prudent economic management if they are unwound as soon as conditions return to normal. Correct timing to unwinding is, therefore, crucial. Pre-conditions for exit would require that economic conditions are stable and improving and that the banking system, underpinned by strong prudential regulation and supervision, is safe and sound. Also, it should be carried out at a time when consumer sentiment is up and depositors have a 'feel good' sense about the general economic conditions, their income and job prospects. Now that we are on a bit of firmer ground, the issue of 'when' and 'how' to pull back the unorthodox measures should definitely heat up. For deposit insurers, I believe the stage is now set, especially for some of us with a 2010 year-end deadline, to start planning, if we haven't, for an exit from these measures. The challenge, therefore, is to formulate and execute a well-planned, highly coordinated and comprehensive exit strategy to a credible alternative that would not destabilize depositors' confidence and the financial system. This serves as the broad objective for any exit strategy. In other words, the transition must be a non-event in the eyes of the public. To achieve this, how can we revert to an explicit deposit insurance scheme while, at the same time, being able to promote and enhance public confidence?

I must concede that this is a tall order. And, there remain wider concerns that the general public has been conditioned to expect the government not to quickly remove benefits given to them. It is difficult but, with the right plan and strategies, not impossible. For deposit insurers, we will be held accountable in our ability to maintain confidence during the transition. This being one of our key functions, it is natural for deposit insurers to spend time and energy planning for the transition process.

I would like to share some thoughts on what we are working on in Malaysia and from my personal perspective as a seasoned deposit insurance practitioner for the last 35 years. I have organized my remarks into four sections. First, I will briefly review the actions taken by deposit insurers to mitigate the crisis, the pre-announced exit timelines and some preparatory actions taken recently by Australia, New Zealand, Hong Kong and Singapore. Second, I discuss Malaysia's preliminary thoughts about our exit strategy and look into our role in managing the transition. Third, I will highlight some desired principles that should promote a smooth transition. In the last section I provide some conclusions.

I. RECENT CRISIS MITIGATING ACTIONS BY DEPOSIT INSURERS

According to a joint survey by the International Association of Deposit Insurers and the International Monetary Fund released in September 2009 that had the aim to identify strategies to unwind temporary depositor protection, it was found that 46 jurisdictions adopted policies to enhance depositor protection during the crisis of which 28 jurisdictions opted to increase coverage levels ranging from 75 per cent to 400 per cent while 18 jurisdictions provided full or partial depositor guarantees.

Of the 25 jurisdictions that adopted either temporary full depositor guarantees or temporary increases in deposit insurance coverage levels, 18 jurisdictions have announced scheduled expiry dates, with the majority of timings falling between 2010 and 2011. The survey showed that eight jurisdictions, including four in Asia, will exit from guarantees between September to December 2010.

Some countries have recently taken preparatory steps towards such an exit. While still maintaining the guarantee for retail deposits, both Australia and New Zealand have announced the removal of wholesale funding from the government guarantee. In the UK, the 100 per cent deposit protection for customers of Northern Rock will soon be lifted. And, driven by the primary objective of protecting small depositors, both Hong Kong and Singapore have proposed to amend and enhance various features of their deposit insurance schemes. Key enhancements include raising the coverage limit and expanding the scope of coverage to replace the government blanket guarantee. In Hong Kong, the proposed coverage limit was raised substantially to HKD500 000 from HKD100 000 while Singapore proposes to raise theirs from SGD20 000 to SGD50 000. In addition, the Singapore Deposit Insurance Corporation will also expand their protection to include policyholders of the insurance industry. The Federal Deposit Insurance Corporation, meanwhile, will decide soon whether they will end a government guarantee for special deposit accounts in banks used by businesses. In Malaysia, we are looking into the features of an improved deposit insurance scheme that would meet public expectations, promote public confidence and maintain the stability of the financial system.

II. MDIC'S ROLE IN MANAGING THE TRANSITION

In the current context, an exit strategy is a strategic plan that guides the approach to unwinding the various extraordinary measures implemented to mitigate the effects of the financial crisis. There are three main areas which required orderly unwinding. They include the unwinding of monetary stimulus to anchor inflationary expectations, cutting back government fiscal support to banks and to the broader economy in a sustainable manner and third, transitioning from a government blanket guarantee to a limited deposit insurance system to minimize the risks associated with moral hazard.

The overarching objective in the unwinding process of these three areas is to maintain public confidence and financial system stability. I shall now outline Malaysia's plans to unwind the 'GDG'. And, since unwinding a blanket guarantee carries potential negative effects on depositor confidence, I believe the task to unwind a blanket guarantee is the trickiest of the three. As a deposit insurer, we are in frequent direct contact with depositors during a crisis. We, therefore, understand how fragile and irrational depositor confidence can be! Once confidence begins to erode, it can do so very rapidly. Many of the challenges that deposit insurers face while managing a transition arise from managing and meeting public expectations. This is the heart of the matter. If the general public has a concern with the exit plan, this may undermine their perception of the safety of their savings in the banking system. In turn, this may culminate into financial instability through bank runs. And internationally, mobile capital could head elsewhere.

In Malaysia, the implementation of the GDG in October 2008 was a preemptive measure to maintain financial system stability. Malaysian banks were well capitalized and the banking system was liquid. In Malaysia, we hear daily from depositors through our call centre operators and we go down to the ground to meet regularly with depositors through face-to-face meetings via our outreach programmes. We were, therefore, surprised when some depositors expressed concerns that the GDG was seen as a preliminary measure to address hidden banking system issues. This is an example of unexpected depositor perception that can arise anywhere even when a government deposit guarantee is put in place.

We were able to address depositor concerns and expectations early and effectively since they were limited to a very small group of depositors. From 2009, we have been monitoring the level of depositor confidence and their issues of concern arising from the implementation of the GDG. We maximized the direct contacts with depositors. Indeed, the face-to-face meetings were most useful as they provided opportunities for us to understand the pulse of depositors, their concerns and expectations. They enabled us to identify, at an early stage, the strands of concerns amidst the chatter and the noise of depositor talk. In this regard, depositors indicated a preference for a higher level of deposit insurance coverage. This was confirmed by a survey conducted by MDIC to gauge the level of deposits maintained with our member banks. Based on this survey, the level of deposits held by banks had grown significantly since the establishment of MDIC in 2005. By 2009, only 60 per cent of depositors would be covered in full under the RM60 000 deposit insurance limit.

As the deposit insurer, the MDIC is responsible for developing and recommending the exit strategy plan to the government in consultation with the Central Bank of Malaysia. Depositor expectations and other issues are incorporated into the strategic transition plan which we believe will maintain depositor confidence in the stability of the financial system, even after the GDG exit.

Suffice it to say that we consider a well-planned exit strategy as the pillar of a smooth transition. Our exit strategy plan outlines the objectives of the strategy, the timetable, contingency plans, and policies and processes to execute the exit plan. And there is a substantial amount of planning required if one is to exit the GDG in a manner that would promote and enhance public confidence. I am not at liberty to discuss the details of the financial consumer protection package which we have developed. What I will highlight is MDIC's role in managing the transition. They are as follows:

- Designing the financial consumer protection package to be implemented after the expiry of the GDG. This would involve developing an improved deposit insurance scheme to take into account MDIC's current deposit insurance limit and scope of coverage. This includes a recommendation on changes to the *MDIC Act*, new regulations and new coverage limits, if necessary, taking into consideration depositor sentiments. In my view when exiting from a GDG, it is important to provide for a higher limit and scope of coverage to create a 'feel good' sense among depositors and be adequate enough to meet their needs for the next few years. To be credible, in deciding by how much the present deposit insurance programme could be increased, it would generally be necessary to cover between 85 per cent to 95 per cent of depositors in full. In Malaysia, we plan to achieve a coverage limit that would slightly exceed the public's expectations. Therefore, we plan to cover a minimum of 95 per cent of all depositors in full while ensuring between 35 per cent to 45 per cent of deposits, in terms of value. It would not work if the new coverage is seen to be inferior to previous benefits, be it actual or perceived;

- Implementing a new Regulation to require banks to provide clearer product information to depositors. Conventional and Islamic banks would have to inform depositors on whether a deposit product is insured or not insured prior to a sale. This imposes new responsibilities on MDIC which will have to determine and inform the banks of the insurability status of all new deposit products prior to these products being offered for sale to bank customers. The objective is to provide depositors with knowledge of what *is* and what *is not* insured prior to making investment decisions;
- Developing and executing a communications plan. This would enable clear communication with the general public to ensure that they are fully informed about the new arrangements well before exit. Focus groups would also be conducted to assess depositors' acceptance of the proposed package; and
- Recommending the timing of the announcement of the financial consumer protection package. This is important for us. To maximize benefits, we would prefer that the announcement be made against a backdrop of good news.

III. SOME GENERAL FEATURES FOR AN EFFECTIVE EXIT PLAN

Having gone through the experience of developing an exit strategy plan, I would like to share some general features for an effective plan. I am aware that the challenges may differ from one country to another. Hence, there are no simple answers and there is no 'one size fits all' way of going about a plan.

Close cooperation and support between all relevant safety net players in planning and executing the exit plan is vital. Even with an effective transition strategy on paper, it would still not be effective if the implementation is not well coordinated.

First, it is the responsibility of all safety net players to work together to develop a comprehensive exit plan. Second, as separate and independent organizations, the roles of each agency need to be clearly understood as all agencies must know who is to do *what* and *when* to avoid unproductive overlap! This would also minimize the likelihood of agencies acting at cross purposes, and sending out conflicting signals and messages, which would not only seriously undermine public confidence, but, in turn, affect the credibility of the safety net players.

Clear communication of an exit plan with the general public is critical. A potential concern is that the exit strategy could cause confusion among depositors. Drawing from our own experience that even a GDG can bring unintended perceptions, it is important to understand depositor concerns and expectations through regular communications. Hence, it is the responsibility of the deposit insurer to mitigate this risk by communicating clearly the policy intentions of the exit plan and to explain the purpose for the direction taken. In other words, the plan has to be clear and needs to be constantly communicated to the general public. That is why the communication plan and strategy is a very important component of the transition package. In fact, this would be the most active phase of the entire transition.

An exit plan that is communicated early and regularly can bolster its effectiveness in a number of ways. First, it would ensure that the public is fully informed about the exit and its related timelines as well as the new or improved deposit insurance arrangements well before the exit. Second, if communicated early and effectively, depositors would be better prepared and would have enough time to adjust to the new circumstance ahead of the exit. This would ensure public acceptance of the new or improved deposit insurance system, which would, in turn, reduce market uncertainties. And the heavy costs of catching the public by surprise could be avoided.

What communications approach is best? The communications approach that we proposed to adopt is to position the financial consumer protection package as a 'good news' story by informing depositors of the benefits of the new features of a financial consumer protection package being implemented. In other words, we want to draw the attention of the public to the financial consumer package. It will also be positioned as giving depositors a sense of comfort and well being. This means informing the public that the package is in their best interests as it provides explicit benefits. For example, pointing out that blanket guarantees do not always benefit depositors in every aspect. They have attractions but also problems. Blanket guarantees do not specify a statutory timeline for depositors to be reimbursed, unlike statutory explicit limited deposit insurance systems. Also, an implicit government blanket guarantee would mean that any cost incurred does not fall on those who received the benefits. Hence, it is 'heads, the banks win, tails, the taxpayers lose'. Reverting to an effective deposit insurance system would eliminate that distortion.

i. One of the challenges we face is whether we should test public response to the proposed transition package. We are inclined to do this since the implications of missing the mark would be too costly.

To 'test the water', we proposed to put up 'trial balloons' to gauge public reaction to different coverage proposals. This could be a simple announcement to the press on the key features of the new depositor protection package, such as a proposed limit. At this time, we also plan to monitor closely the sentiments of the depositing public for any signs of public concern. Depositors may react by transferring their deposits to banks that are perceived to be 'too-big-to-fail' or take flight to quality. Depending on depositor reaction, deposit insurers may, if necessary, opt to scale up the transition package to converge with depositor expectations.

ii. Malaysia is an open economy with strong economic links to neighbouring jurisdictions which have also implemented similar government guarantees that are also scheduled to expire on 31 December 2010. There are, therefore, strong arguments for international coordination. Such arguments are magnified in the light of the recent crisis. Having seen the *ad hoc* actions taken to maintain public confidence during the crisis, I am mindful of the past mistakes of implementing measures without proper consideration of their long-term implications. When announcing the blanket government deposit guarantee, many jurisdictions did not put much thought into cross-border issues and repercussions, mitigating moral hazard and developing orderly plans on how to exit from such measures when their economies stabilized. This is a risky strategy. Such haphazard policy decisions must be avoided when developing and executing an exit plan.

This is, indeed, one area which I feel the importance is clearly underappreciated. Uncoordinated exits and inconsistent exit frameworks can lead to potential disruptions and erode public confidence. Countries with high cross-border banking and strong retail deposit flows are particularly vulnerable.

We look towards working with our neighbours in the region in three areas. There will be challenges, since not all deposit insurers have autonomy of operations. Nonetheless, the following are areas for cooperation:

- Sharing of information and experiences. There are definitely clear gains from the exchange of information as countries can then learn from one another. The information shared could help other jurisdictions in formulating their own exit policy decisions. Countries could share with each other relevant information such as the broad principles underpinning exit decisions and information on cross-border fund movements. More importantly, they could give prior notification on decisions and plans that are to be shortly implemented in other jurisdictions.

- Planning for synchronized exits for close financially linked countries to minimize competitive distortion, potential spillovers and arbitrage risks. One example is the tripartite agreement between Hong Kong, Singapore and Malaysia to exit at the same time. In an ideal scenario, all countries should exit at the same time. This would ensure a level playing field among financial institutions and minimize cross-border impact by avoiding harmful spill-over, competitive distortions and arbitrage opportunities.

  However, this is easier said than done. The difficulty here is country-specific circumstances, which influenced the timing of the exit of a jurisdiction. Circumstances such as the strength and robustness of a country's financial system and the state of the social and economic environment might vary from country to country. This is a key constraint to a common exit. But I think there is strength in numbers. And there are potential gains for all. By exiting together, there might be less to lose but more to gain!
- Implementing a consistent deposit coverage framework for closely linked countries. This could include roughly similar limits and levels of coverage, simultaneous announcements and implementation of policy changes.

iii. Another challenge is to have in place a contingent plan should economic conditions not be conducive for removing the blanket guarantee. This is necessary for two reasons. First, a back-up liquidity line may be needed from the central bank to ensure adequate liquidity in the banking system when there might be capital outflows following an exit from the GDG. Second, there are situations where delaying an exit may prove less destructive to the economy. In such an extreme case, policymakers may have no choice but to extend the blanket guarantee. If the transition strategy is well planned and well executed, I doubt that the contingent measures would ever be called upon. However, it is important to know in advance, from a strategic planning perspective, that such contingency plans are in place to deal with key risks, if necessary.

iv. We also plan to determine a sunset date for the public announcement of the new package. It is crucial to determine upfront the sunset date as it is the date that will kick-start the transition plan. Since the exit is timed for 31 December 2010, as in Malaysia's case, we will be looking at a sunset date of June 2010 as it requires some six months to prepare the action plans.

IV. CONCLUSION

Ladies and gentlemen, the above are the main features of Malaysia's approach to a smooth exit strategy to its GDG. The plan will be tested over the next few months. While certain areas will continue to be refined, we are hopeful that the exit strategy plan is robust to ensure a smooth exit. This has been a complex task for us since Malaysian depositors have only known MDIC for five years. While we have built our reputation and credibility with depositors over the last five years, the test is when the lapse of the GDG is a non-event in the eyes of depositors.

In the eyes of the public, MDIC is the organization which provides the GDG. This was a strategic decision to maintain MDIC's credibility and image. As we well know, the implementation of a blanket guarantee normally causes the deposit insurer to sit out on the sideline during the period of the blanket guarantee. In Malaysia's case, the government's blanket guarantee is designed to cover deposits over and above the statutory limit of RM60 000 provided by MDIC. As such, MDIC functions alongside the government blanket guarantee. We continue to maintain our deposit insurance relationship with depositors and through our on-going depositor awareness programmes during the blanket guarantee. Indeed, we have put in many hours building our relationship with depositors. With so much at stake, there is no room for error.

Thank you.

NOTE

1. Many thanks to Wai Keen, Lai and Kevin Chew for their research and contribution to these remarks.

Preface

It has been 'A Hard Day's Night'*

John Raymond LaBrosse, Rodrigo Olivares-Caminal and Dalvinder Singh

The sub-title to this part of the book could have been – *What have we learned since the demise of Lehman Brothers?* The question, however, could not actually have been that short as we would have needed to add something about the number of investment banks that had to convert to become US holding companies, the re-nationalization of Fannie Mae and Freddie Mac, the death and then resurrection of AIG, the collapse of the Icelandic banking system, the overhauls of financial regulation in the UK, US and much of Europe, the Greek debt tragedy, and of course, we would need to list the extraordinary measures that governments took around the world to prop up their banking systems through explicit guarantees that contributed to the ballooning of government fiscal deficits. Instead, we think that The Beatles' 1964 tune *A Hard Day's Night* is more appropriate. While some of us might remember the lyrics better than others, the words go a long way in describing the recent global financial crisis. For some, people have been '. . . *working like a dog*', or not working at all, trying to save their homes from a short sale or foreclosure. For others, they are finally seeing conditions in financial markets improving as low interest rates and quantitative easing are helping to boost the real economy and improving bank profitability; leading managers and traders to long for a return to large bonuses and the prospects of acquiring bargain-priced vacation homes in exotic locations. Perhaps it is not much more than a natural evolution of the capitalist system.

By and large, policymakers and regulators have not been '. . . *sleeping like a log* . . .' (as the song goes), as many of them have awoken with what seems to be a terrible hangover. Some of those mornings-after were brought about through bank managers taking excessive risks or an evaporation of confidence, while others are suffering after following advice or the spin of people like Bernie Madoff, R. Allen Stanford and Marc Dreier – fraud artists who were not 'playing by the rules'.[1] As well, central bankers had been warning about systemic risk issues for some time but the vagueness of the term and the low probability that a financial system would fail to function kept attention to the issue largely to gatherings of central bankers at meetings of the Bank for International Settlements (BIS) or around the board table of the International Monetary Fund (IMF).

The 2010 Banking Law Symposium held in April 2010 focused on the issue of managing systemic risk in detail. We have collected in this book research on the global financial crisis by leading scholars, policymakers and practitioners. It is clear from the analysis that there was no single cause of the crisis. If that were the case, dissection of the issues might be relatively straightforward. Instead, we are left with considering a number of issues and learning from mistakes that were made in our economic systems. David Harvey, the noted social theorist, for example, in his *You Tube* lecture on *The Crisis of Capitalism* suggests six points that should be considered.[2] First, he offers human frailty by picking up on points made by Alan Greenspan that investors were under delusions and greed played a key role in the behaviour of Wall Street. Second, there were institutional failures and regulators were found 'asleep at the switch' as the shadow banking system grew very large and outside their purview. Third, the capitalist system might well be inherently unstable and we need to remind ourselves of the teachings of Keynes. Fourth, there are deep-seated cultural differences noting that the Europeans saw the early stages of the crisis as '. . . having nothing to do with us' because the origins were linked to the US fascination for homeownership and the excesses caused by the deductibility of mortgage interest. Fifth, argument raised by Fox News that there was too much regulation and much of it was of the wrong sort. Lastly, a key issue that was missed was an understanding of systemic risk linkages between financial stability and government guarantees, regulation of the financial sector and sovereign risk.

PART I: SYSTEMIC RISK: '*TICKET TO RIDE*'

The first part of the Symposium started with a discussion of systemic risk. In his keynote remarks to the Symposium Jean Pierre Sabourin, a leading authority on deposit insurance, noted that the implementation of extraordinary measures, including blanket government deposit guarantees, has helped to prevent the global economy from sinking into an economic abyss. Such measures can lead, however, to inefficiencies, erode market discipline and encourage moral hazard by distorting incentives. What is often not considered, Sabourin noted, is charging banks for the privilege of the application of a full guarantee and plans to transition out of such guarantees are often left too late. What happens is that the banks will believe that governments will always step in to bail them out – 'too-big-to-fail'; an issue that was examined in great detail throughout the Symposium and one that will be on the minds of policymakers for some time to come. We are grateful to Charles Enoch for summarizing in the Foreword to this book the nature of the discussions during that event. The crisis was inevitable, and we had to have a *ticket to ride* the storm – reminiscent of another Beatles tune.

We begin in Part I with an examination of Systemic Risk by reviewing investor behaviour up to the dawn of the financial crisis in 2007. Richard J. Rosen notes that that period was marked by a rapidly expanding array of structured securities – bonds issued as part of a securitization process. Those securities were very complex and difficult to evaluate even for financially sophisticated investors. Nonetheless, the market grew and over time investors often based decisions on the credit ratings provided by agencies such as Moody's, Standard and Poor's and Fitch. While those agencies have a long track record of evaluating securities, it is probable that the intermediaries involved in issuing structured securities took advantage of overconfidence and (rational) inattention particularly when the agencies continued to give them high ratings. Rosen does not ask whether regulators contributed to the problems that led to the crisis.

Jack Selody then looks squarely into the eyes of systemic risk in Chapter 2 and asks: what constitutes the nucleus of a modern financial system and what makes it vulnerable to failure? He argues that it is the cluster of financial markets and supporting infrastructure that coordinates the activity of financial institutions. Selody maintains that the most significant aspects of the proposed regulatory reforms will not remedy this vulnerability because the principal systemic risk is the fragile liquidity of the core markets as they lack adequate risk-proofing. He believes that the reforms being discussed will raise costs in the regulated sector, push financial activity to the unregulated sector, and thereby create greater system vulnerability over time. A solution to this problem is offered through measures that keep markets liquid during institutional insolvency and by risk-proofing the core infrastructure. There are good reasons to support his hypothesis as evidenced by the progress made in risk-proofing the large-value payment systems and foreign exchange clearing systems.

We now better understand that the absence in several jurisdictions of specialized resolution tools has given a rise to additional costs. Sebastian Schich, in Chapter 3, notes that the result of an inability to close problem banks effectively has been an expansion of government guarantees. The costs associated with such measures have been substantial and seen in many ways particularly in the forms of large and growing contingent fiscal liabilities as well as distortions to competition and incentives. To mitigate such problems risk-based premiums need to be specified, with premium adjustments consistent across borders. Appropriate premiums – be they charged *ex ante* or *ex post* – should ensure a fair distribution of risks and costs, and discourage activities that tend to contribute to systemic risk. Schich concludes his analysis by noting that systemic risk is an externality and surcharges would be appropriate to the extent that they induce financial institutions to internalize more fully this externality.

Rightly so, there was considerable discussion during the April 2010 Symposium on the US. Gillian G. H. Garcia points out in Chapter 4 that 'forbearance in the US for larger institutions appears to be more permanent and is being enshrined in an enlarged safety net'.[3] It is carried out for instance, by merging one troubled large bank into another slightly less-troubled large bank so that the resulting entity is 'far-too-big-to-be-allowed-to-fail'. Hopefully, forbearance will not become a permanent government response under the financial sector reforms that have already been enacted in the UK and that are proposed for the US. Failed institutions avoided prompt corrective action (PCA) restraints by artificially maintaining their well-capitalized status, sometimes with supervisory assistance, almost until they failed. Garcia notes that their supervisors had not deployed their discretionary powers to discipline them.[4]

In Chapter 5, Jean Roy, Rima Turk-Ariss and Yenni Redjah examine the question as to why the Canadian banks performed so well during the global financial crisis. They found in a comparison of Canada and the US that the behaviours of the respective banks were strikingly different. Whereas massive government intervention was needed in the US to bail out the financial system, the Canadian government did not have to inject capital in any banks and none failed. Investors themselves were aware of the difference in risk between the two systems as the Value at Risk of the stocks of major banks in the US was twice as big as those of Canadian banks. They conclude that a more conservative Canadian culture seems to form the basis for the stability of the Canadian financial system.

The global financial crisis has forced a re-examination of risk transmission in the financial sector and how it affects financial stability. Risk management concentrates on the analysis of risk at the level of the individual institution and system-wide. In Chapter 6, Dale F. Gray and Andreas A. Jobst illustrate how contingent claims analysis (CCA) can be applied to improve systemic financial sector risk management. They propose a new framework ('Systemic CCA') developed to estimate the magnitude of contingent liabilities from the financial sector under systemic distress assumptions. This aggregation technique generates an estimate of the joint market-implied contingent liabilities by combining the individual risk-adjusted balance sheets of financial institutions and the dependence between them. The Systemic CCA does not only quantify the magnitude of potential risk transfer to the government but also helps indicate the contribution of individual institutions to contingent liabilities over time depending on their size and interconnectedness.

The political fallout from taxpayer-supported bank bailouts has caused governments to consider the implementation of levies on the financial services industry. John Snape analyses, in Chapter 7, the defensibility of the UK proposal for a tax on the balance sheets of banks. His work explicitly recognizes that both the timing and the context of such a proposal are crucially important. The City of London, though weakened by the financial crisis, is still highly influential, and this presents the government with a difficult policy dilemma. However, revenues from the City's financial services can no longer fund the public services, and the dominant neoliberal theories of taxation are increasingly under pressure from a more political strand of liberal egalitarianism. In these terms, the levy does indeed make sense, but, as stated, timing and context is everything, and all this may quickly change.

PART II: THE SOVEREIGN CRISIS – A GREEK TRAGEDY, AN ICELANDIC MELTDOWN AND THE IRISH SWEEPSTAKES – WHAT IF ANYTHING DO THEY HAVE IN COMMON?

The global financial crisis promoted a debt crisis throughout most of Europe. The first group of countries to undergo a debt crisis included Portugal (with public debt levels of 76.8 per cent of GDP), Ireland (64 per cent), Greece (115.1 per cent), and Spain (53.2 per cent).[5] The total amount of government debt outstanding for those countries was USD1726.9 trillion. With average growth rates for them ranging between 0.7 per cent and 2.6 per cent it will take decades to see debt-to-GDP levels return to pre-crisis levels. Foreign banks were exposed to USD236.2 billion of public and private debt in Greece with nearly one-third of that debt held by French banks. A Greek collapse became a major contagion (the spreading of a very harmful disease or practice) concern that spread across Europe and beyond.

There has always been a direct link between banks and the risk exposure of governments. Governments seek to limit their risks through prudential regulation and limits on coverage of insured deposits in member institutions. At the same time, banks hold substantial sums of sovereign debt; when governments run into financial difficulty so can the banks. That problem was seen clearly in France when Credit Agricole reported huge losses in its international business due to a continuing problem in a Greek bank subsidiary.[6]

The Greek authorities might be correct in their determination not to restructure its debt. This is so because a restructuring would imply a default – something that EU members would not allow to happen due to the undermining effects on the euro. However, we use different titles of The Beatles' songs to try to explain how to cope with the current scenario: *If you've got trouble* and *In spite of all the danger* Greece cannot *Carry that weight*, they have to embark in *Fixing a hole* and *Getting better*, they are experiencing problems *Here, there and everywhere*. Therefore, a possible option is a debt re-profiling (a voluntarily exchange offer prior to default). In other words, the main difference between a debt re-profiling and a debt restructuring is the timing when the exchange offer is performed. A debt re-profiling can help ease part of the Greek pressure of the internal devaluation by reducing their debt servicing burden. Greece should take advantage of the liquidity that has been provided by the European Monetary Union (EMU) and IMF to do an orderly debt re-profiling which will not trigger the credit default swaps linked to the Greek bonds.

The link between the financial crisis and the sovereign debt problem is examined in the next three chapters. In Chapter 8, Arnór Sighvatsson and Gunnar Gunnarsson focus on Iceland's situation noting that the entire financial system failed. In so doing it contributed to a collapse of Iceland's currency, which depreciated by 60 per cent from 1 September 2008 until capital controls were instituted on 28 November 2008. Although the scale of the twin crisis was without precedent they note that the build-up of unsustainable macroeconomic imbalances and misalignments in asset prices followed a typical pre-crisis pattern described in the literature. Lax risk management and low perceived risks based on optimism about the future prospects of the booming economy made the financial institutions and the private sector far too willing to assume imprudent risks. Financial institutions overextended themselves not only domestically but particularly abroad. The large scale of the cross-border and cross-currency operations of the banks became problematic as their principal lender of last resort, the Central Bank of Iceland, could only provide them with liquidity in domestic currency and that made them particularly vulnerable to a run on their foreign liabilities.

In ancient Greece, tragedian Euripides during his stage plays at the peak of a tragic moment used a '*Deus ex Machina*' (Act of God) as a means to solve the plot. The question is whether there is such an Act of God for what is unfolding for the Greek economy to sustain the country through the rough waters that it is currently experiencing. In Chapter 9, Ioannis

Kokkoris, Rodrigo Olivares-Caminal and Kiriakos Papadakis discuss the difficulties of membership in the EMU, with a particular focus on Greece and the implications of an internal devaluation. They also discuss how debt re-profiling can help to support the mechanisms of fiscal rehabilitation and external financing at the sovereign and corporate level.

The Greek case is further explored in Chapter 10. Lee C. Buchheit and Mitu Gulati draw on the lessons learned from sovereign debt restructurings of the modern era, and underscore that it can easily be understood that a sovereign debt crisis can be a painful experience for both the debtor and its creditors. Indeed, a mismanaged sovereign debt crisis can be a catastrophically painful experience. The authors suggest that success could be found in structuring a transaction that would be an exchange offer – new bonds of the Hellenic Republic would be offered for the Republic's existing bonds. The terms of the new bonds would determine the nature and extent of the debt relief that the transaction would provide to Greece. Exchange offers have been the norm for sovereign debt restructuring of middle-income countries since the 'Brady Plan' implemented in 1990. The terms of the 'new' Greek instruments would be a function of the nature and extent of the debt relief the transaction is designed to achieve. At one end of the spectrum there might be a simple 're-profiling' of existing bonds (or some discrete portion of them such as bonds maturing over the next three to five years) involving a deferral of the maturity date of each affected bond. At the other end of the spectrum there could be a transaction designed to achieve a significant net present value (NPV) reduction in the stock of debt.

Ireland has recently been faced with a sovereign debt crisis. Although the Irish distress started slightly before the Greek tragedy it was quickly overshadowed by the magnitude of the latter and underestimated by the rapid response of their authorities in adopting a series of austerity measures to tackle a very delicate situation. The crisis was the result of an expansion of credit resulting from a real estate bubble which was burst by a credit crunch. Apparently, Ireland has run out of its four-leafed shamrocks and the crisis that was temporarily put on the back-burner regained notoriety on the cover of the specialized press due in part from mounting pressure from bondholders fearing for their return and the €7 billion rescue plan put in place in 2009 to help the Allied Irish Bank and Bank of Ireland and the recent nationalization of Anglo Irish Bank in the amount of €34 billion. The Chilean government also put the entire Irish funds industry on a watch-list out of concern for Irish sovereign debt.[7] For those of us old enough to remember the world-famous Irish Sweepstakes that helped finance the building of Irish hospitals in the 1930s and later, we might very well be seeing some form of a comeback – but this time as a way to finance budget deficits. Is this a return of the Irish sweepstakes but without the horses?

PART III: ADDRESSING THE PROBLEM OF 'TOO-BIG-TO-FAIL'

We, along with many others for that matter, have noted that national governments were required to intervene in many ways, given the depth of the financial crisis. For example, in the US, price declines in the residential housing markets contributed to heavy losses at Fannie Mae and Freddie Mac – something in excess of USD225 billion. Interestingly, both of them were created as government-initiated agencies; but when the crisis hit they exhausted their capital from guaranteeing loans on single-family homes and the market looked to the government to backstop the agencies.[8] The lesson from that experience is clear as markets gladly accept the profits from such entities but will look to the authorities if failure is imminent. Contrary to that Beatles song '. . . *when I am home everything seems alright* . . .'. – clearly that has not been the case as Fannie and Freddie have contributed to the hangover being experienced by US taxpayers especially those that do not own homes or now have negative equity positions.

In Part III, we focus on the issue of 'too-big-to-fail' (TBTF) through the work of some leading experts. The recent crisis has caused policymakers to become much attuned to the issue of TBTF and its various derivations – 'too-big-to-save', 'too-big-to-close', etc. – subjects that were previously debated mainly by economists. Beginning in early 2008, an evaporation of liquidity began to have serious consequences for many large banks and non-bank financial institutions and the lack of lending spread and severely damaged major manufacturers such as General Motors and Chrysler. Starting with Bear Stearns unravelling in March 2008, a succession of large and complex financial institutions experienced funding crises that led to either their failure, conservatorship, or forced acquisition; sometimes by or through a government. But, the most severe blow came from the bankruptcy on 15 September 2008 of the USD600 billion investment bank Lehman Brothers, a firm regarded by the authorities not as TBTF but instead 'too-big-to-bail out'. That event was soon followed by the collapse and acquisition by the Federal Reserve Board of American International Group (AIG). The line from a Beatles' tune – '. . . *with a little help from my friends* . . .' – seemed to be getting lots of play on Wall Street!

Geoffrey Wood with Ali Kabiri note in Chapter 11 that competition authorities, and many economists for that matter, usually apply a definition of competition which is frequently misleading in practice and always mistaken in principle. When that is understood it becomes clear that the approach taken to financial regulation is misconceived. Wood examines an alternative approach which may lead to a financial system which is stable, efficient, and innovative. His chapter draws out an interesting comparison between banks and grocery stores – both are quite necessary to function in modern-day life. Wood's argument is that focus on the stability of the individual firm is misguided. Rather, policymakers should be more concerned about the stability of the industry. This is, however, merely reinforcing an existing and well-supported argument. The key point of his chapter is that industry stability matters for banking, and firm stability does not.

A technique is proposed in Chapter 12 as a way to wind down the operations of large complex financial institutions (LCFIs) when they become insolvent. The proposal is that those firms produce 'living wills'. George G. Kaufman notes that those kinds of documents will achieve an orderly resolution of LCFIs whose resolution might otherwise be disruptive with higher private and societal costs than necessary. The idea is 'to focus advance attention of both a firm's management and its regulators on problems that may arise in the unwinding of the firm when insolvency threatens including: accurately inventorying all assets and liabilities, identifying all counterparties, and giving full recognition to the complexity of organization structures across both separately charted subsidiaries and different cross-border and structural jurisdictions'.[9] Such information should reduce the likelihood of pitfalls and make winding down more efficient and lessen the need for policymakers to consider the firm TBTF with all the inefficiencies associated, including the likely use of taxpayer funds.[10] Knowing how to unwind an LCFI may well make regulators more willing to do so.

Arthur E. Wilmarth Jr., in Chapter 13, points out that TBTF remains 'the great unresolved problem of bank supervision', and that the current financial crisis has proven, once again, that TBTF institutions 'present formidable risks to the federal safety net and are largely insulated from both market discipline and supervisory intervention'. This is because TBTF institutions 'pursue riskier and opaque activities and . . . increase their leverage, through capital arbitrage, if necessary, as they grow in size and complexity'.[11] Wilmarth proposes five reforms designed to prevent excessive risk taking by LCFIs and to shrink TBTF subsidies in the US financial system so as to strengthen current statutory restrictions on the growth of LCFIs. Those steps would strip away many of the safety net subsidies that are exploited by LCFIs and would subject them to the same type of market discipline that the capital markets have applied to commercial and industrial conglomerates over the past 30 years. Financial conglomerates,

Wilmarth maintains, have never demonstrated that they can provide beneficial services to their customers and attractive returns to their investors without relying on safety net subsidies and massive taxpayer-funded bailouts. It is long past time for LCFIs to prove – based on a true market test – that their claimed superiority is a reality and not a myth.

The German experience with TBTF is examined by Jens-Hinrich Binder in Chapter 14. He notes that Germany is proceeding with an overhaul of its bank insolvency regime.[12] The key policy objective is to avoid the need for further bailouts of systemically important institutions; be it on the grounds of their size or because of their interconnectedness with other market participants. Binder discusses the constraints on the German approach and whether this very policy objective can realistically be achieved. The chapter also identifies the treatment of close-out and netting arrangements as a major obstacle to the successful procedural treatment of LCFI insolvency. The author observes that while Anglo-Saxon banks are perceived to be the villains of the piece, German banks are in reality the Achilles' heel of the European banking system as they are undercapitalized.[13] A related issue, of course, is that the European banks have been heavily involved in financing sovereign deficits.

Ioannis Kokkoris, in Chapter 15, comments that different types of laws affect the conditions or environment of competition between EU member states. The notion of competition law as a national interest corresponds with the growth of competition law systems in many liberal and democratic sovereign states. The provision of state aid is a contentious issue during a financial crisis as states will be inclined to maintain the viability of the financial sector by providing state aid to the banking industry. State aid, he concludes, must be addressed to meet the challenges of a competitive economy.

PART IV: CROSS BORDER – DID ANYONE MENTION BURDEN-SHARING?

Robert R. Bliss and George G. Kaufman examine, in Chapter 16, the issue of failing LCFIs, noting that they may not be efficiently resolved by either existing domestic bankruptcy or bank insolvency resolution regimes. While some are banks and others have bank-like characteristics, their size, complexity, interconnectedness, international stature, and the scope of the potential externalities suggest that such closures could generate severe problems. Accordingly, such solutions might require a hybrid approach drawing on the most suitable elements of both existing regimes. In the second part of their chapter, they look at the problems that arise in resolving holding companies and, in particular, those companies that operate across countries. Some suggestions are offered for partially mitigating these problems through marginal changes in existing national insolvency laws and corporate structures. Their approach may be more feasible than achieving a broader coordinated change of laws governing LCFI insolvencies in different jurisdictions.

Rosa M. Lastra and Rodrigo Olivares-Caminal note that consolidated supervision has become a premise for global banking as LCFIs increasingly expand the range of their services offered in several countries. The authors note in Chapter 17 that the financial crisis has shown consolidated supervision not to be enough; it needs to be aligned with a more effective resolution process. Although efforts are underway, with both the IMF and the Basel Committee on Banking Supervision Cross-Border Bank Resolution Group working to develop a cross-border resolution framework,[14] the lack of an effective consolidated resolution framework poses a challenge to the future of global banking and finance. Soon, they hope, policymakers will focus on risk-proofing their financial system safety nets and put in effective treaty-like mechanisms to share the burden when cross-border banks fail.

In Chapter 18, Larry D. Wall, María J. Nieto and David G. Mayes note that the European Union has been facilitating the growth of cross-border banking groups with considerable success. But, the job is not yet done as bank supervision remains the responsibility of national supervisors. The authors propose an alternative that would retain the most important advantages of full centralization of chartering and supervision only for those cross-border groups that are systemically important to the EU. All other banks would retain national chartering and supervision. Their chapter explores the idea of an EU-level supervisor that could supervise all systemically important cross-border banking groups without requiring an opt-in by the bank's home country. In this respect, the European supervisory system would work somewhat like that in the US which has long operated under a dual bank chartering system that allows banks to choose between charters issued by the federal government and charters issued by the state government.

PART V: PRUDENTIAL REGULATION – NO AMOUNT OF BANK CAPITAL IS ENOUGH IF IT IS NOT USED WISELY!

The head of the European Central Bank noted recently that central banks have had to undertake a number of measures without 'ever forgetting their medium and long-term goals of price stability and, at times, they have had to ask what will happen in the next week; in the next day; or even in the next few hours'.[15] During the months and years ahead Jean-Claude Trichet suggests that the challenge will be to manage the 'excesses and imbalances accumulated over the previous decades by households, firms and financial institutions – notably the expansion of debt, the build-up of risk and the increase in leverage'.[16]

Since the road to improved bank capital ratios appears to run through Basel, George A. Walker outlines the many twists and turns that led to the proposals of the Committee on Banking Supervision. He notes in Chapter 19 that banks were strongly criticized for holding low capital and liquidity levels immediately before the crisis. That, of course, prevented them from absorbing subsequent losses as the crisis unfolded. Central banks and finance ministries were then forced to inject substantial amounts of market liquidity and bank capital to re-stabilize the markets. He examines the main papers issued by the Basel Committee following the crisis. Some conclusions are drawn with regard to the effectiveness of the emerging new capital and liquidity reserve framework. Walker does not see the end of the road is actually in sight. Instead, it is a new process of adjustments and validation. Basel II and III represent significant advances on Basel I. All of this must simply be incorporated into a larger new macro- and micro-prudential oversight and control framework.

In Chapter 20, Imad Moosa, takes a step back to explore where we are now with the new Basel III requirements. First of all, he observes that the full implementation of Basel II would not have reduced the impact of the financial crisis – far from it given the wholesale lack of attention needed to manage liquidity risk. Notwithstanding the introduction of a number of measures to improve the stability of banks, the Basel III framework is still seen as wanting on a number of fronts that can equally destabilize the financial system; namely, the lack of consideration to regulatory arbitrage, the continued reliance on internal models, and the different treatment of bank and non-bank activities. Overall, the chapter questions whether international standards are the appropriate route to stability emphasizing the need for a more domestic focus as the US has sought to do.

PART VI: COUNTRY CASE STUDIES – THERE IS NO 'COOKIE-CUTTER' APPROACH THAT CAN BE OFFERED

The 2010 Banking Law Symposium provided an opportunity to review policies, practices and indeed success in some countries. It would be very difficult and beyond the scope of this book to produce a complete assessment of each system around the world – that task is being left to future historians. But, some important lessons have been learned regarding cooperation and coordination. The need to better manage systemic risk and the problem surrounding the increase in moral hazard that emerged during the crisis is an issue of paramount importance.

In Chapter 21, Dalvinder Singh places the US reforms introduced with the implementation of the *Dodd-Frank Act 2010* in a historical context and he analyses the resistance to architectural reform in the US. The new Act like many of the predecessors for regulatory reform has been built on the existing institutional framework with micro regulatory reform. Notwithstanding this, the new legislation certainly brings better oversight over banks and non-bank systemic risk, given the reluctance to co-operate between bank and non-bank supervisors.

John Raymond LaBrosse and James F. McCollum examine in detail the safety net arrangements in Canada in Chapter 22. They conclude that the system has many features that work extremely well. Its success in managing through the financial crisis has also been assisted by the healthy state of the Canadian banking system at the beginning of the Great Recession. While high marks can be given to the Canadians, they should not rest on their laurels. Two important gaps in the financial safety net have been identified. The first concerns a means to integrate the prospective national securities regulator into the safety net and the second deals with a need to develop a policy to locate responsibility for financial system stability within the safety net. The fact that Canada uses a continuous improvement process to update its banking legislation every five or ten years should soon lead to proposals that will be watched intensively by many other countries.

In Chapter 23 Ganiyu Ogunleye looks at how the crisis unfolded in Nigeria. Since Nigeria's economy is largely crude-oil dependent it is vulnerable to external shocks and fiscal policy tends to be pro-cyclical. Ogunleye notes that a resilient financial safety-net requires macro-economic stability; mutually reinforcing monetary and fiscal policies; effective regulation; effective depositor/investor protection and sound governance of banking institutions. To what extent has Nigeria attained these imperatives? Perhaps, the jury is still out. But, given Nigeria's vulnerability to external shocks, maintaining macro-economic stability has been a daunting challenge to policymakers. Islamic finance has been experiencing tremendous growth and Islamic assets have reached $750 billion.

The financial crisis felt in Malaysia is reviewed by Khairuddin Hj Arshad in Chapter 24. He notes that the nature of the Islamic bank–customer relationship appears to have made a significant difference.

Indeed, the expansion of global Islamic finance demonstrates its viability and resilience. Those developments have drawn significant interest from global regulators in the role and relevance of Islamic finance-based Shariah principles.

In the final chapter John F. McEldowney notes that financial risk and its assessment is at the centre of various global reform strategies aimed at addressing shortcomings in the regulation and reform of financial institutions. In reference to the UK, McEldowney notes that the tripartite system of financial regulation to achieve financial stability has come under intense criticism and public scrutiny. He proposes that a precautionary principle is required in any future regulatory strategy and that risk management requires transparency and effective accountability if it is to gain public confidence and address the needs of investors. Adopting a precautionary principle is important but even it cannot guarantee that no bank will ever fail which suggests that the response of legislators should be more strategic and systemic in defining the public interest and managing risk. Setting the correct regulatory balance between adequate loans to ensure market growth, financial stability and systemic risk assessment is likely to be a major challenge that is best addressed by the application of the precautionary principle.

Throughout the crisis, governments have been called upon to play an increasingly active role in backstopping banks, LCFIs, insurance companies, financial systems and industries that found their roots in capitalism. In our view five distinct areas of attention have emerged. First, the matter of 'too-big, too-complicated, too-complex, etc. to-fail' has received considerable attention. Second, financial system safety nets have been found to be in need of some attention and possibly major restructuring. Third, despite decades of attention on setting capital rules at an international level, more focus is required on risk management and supervisory practices. Fourth, for decades governments have been under-pricing guarantees they have provided to the banking sector and more appropriate arrangements need to be developed. Finally, the global financial crisis has put a number of sovereigns at risk (of downgrades or even default).

CONCLUDING REMARKS: GOING FORWARD – *HELP!* OR *'HERE COMES THE SUN'*

At this point we might be thinking of another old Beatles tune – *Help!* '. . . *help me if you can I'm feeling down* . . .' Maybe not as we are beginning to see more signs of hope which might suggest an alternative Beatles song forecasting sunnier days ahead. For the first time since the trauma of the

Lehman Brothers failure data compiled by the BIS indicates that cross-border lending by banks is returning. In a recent report it commented that 'global banks boosted lending outside their national borders by USD700 billion, or 2.1 per cent, to USD33 400 billion in the first quarter of 2010'.[17] 'The balance sheet repair of the global banking system continues apace', said Huw van Steenis, a banking analyst at Morgan Stanley. He noted that 'the dominant story of the first half of the year was the credit recovery in northern Europe and the US'. Does this mean that the process of de-globalization that we have witnessed is coming to an end?

Another question that is before economists is whether the US economy is about to enter a period of very sluggish growth or a double dip recession. If it is the latter the Chairman of the Federal Reserve Board of Governors has indicated that the monetary authorities will use every tool at their disposal to prevent it – QE2 has set sail, but it is not a *Yellow Submarine*! The Obama Administration has added that it will propose a major infrastructure spending initiative to bring down the high rate of unemployment.

Bank capital levels are improving through concerted efforts of bank supervisors to re-establish control and banks have been forced to undergo stress tests so that supervisors can better understand the impact of less than favourable scenarios. At the same time, there are persistent worries about German and French banks particularly regarding their capital levels and sovereign debt exposures.[18] However, there are hopeful signs in the sphere of banking as profits of US banks appear to be returning to pre-crisis levels. The TBTF problem might now be less of a concern as some of the largest banks are emerging as smaller versions of their former selves. This is being done by shedding unprofitable business lines and/or certain divisions like proprietary trading have been moved out of regulated entities or given a home in an offshore jurisdiction.

In the sovereign area: Icelanders are returning to their boats and probably finding fishing to be a much less stressful activity than trying to compete as an international financial centre; Greece has not yet collapsed owing to support provided by its euro-zone partners along with assistance from the IMF; blanket deposit guarantees are in many jurisdictions set to be reduced; and General Motors has returned to the equity markets. Unless the demand for credit improves there is a danger that banks will again run up their risk curves and start lending in search of yield.

Much was learned about TBTF during the crisis but actually more was learned about 'too big to close'. Indeed, 2008 will be recalled as an important year in the twenty-first century as it saw the acquisition of Bear Stearns by JP Morgan facilitated by lending by the Federal Reserve Bank of New York; the bankruptcy of Lehman Brothers – a firm 'too-big-to-bail' out; the determination of two government sponsored entities

– Fannie Mae and Freddie Mac – as being 'too-big-to-be-allowed-to-fail' into conservatorship by the Federal Housing Finance Agency; the acquisition by the Federal Reserve Board of AIG which was determined 'too-big-and-too-interconnected-to-be-allowed-to-be-closed', and the absorption of Merrill Lynch into the Bank of America. In 2009 and 2010 the attention turned to the sovereign arena, particularly to the Greek tragedy, the potential spill-over to Ireland, Portugal, Spain and the risks that it entail to the euro-zone, then to the implications of the US Federal Reserve 'throwing dollars from a helicopter' through QE2 and the currency wars that were fought in the lead-up to the Korea G20 Summit.

In the next few years discussions will continue on issues such as cross-border coordination, harmonization, burden sharing, failure resolution, the interactions between monetary policy and regulatory reforms, the need for better macro-prudential tools, crisis management and the use of government guarantees. There is indeed a full agenda that awaits us. Economic activity is expected to improve in many G20 countries and it is hopeful that the Great Recession will not be followed by the Great Disappointment or else we will not be '. . . *sleeping like a log*' for a while yet, like the refrain from that old Beatles song. Instead, maybe *All You Need is Love*.

John Raymond LaBrosse
Rodrigo Olivares-Caminal
Dalvinder Singh
5 November 2010

NOTES

* The reference to the Beatles songs throughout the introduction is for illustrative purposes only and these are all well known. All tracks credited to Lennon and McCartney except for *In spite of all the danger* to Harrison/McCartney and *Here comes the sun* to Harrison.

1. A truly excellent account of 21 tales of the new recession was published by *Vanity Fair* and included in a book entitled *The Great Hangover*, edited by Grayon Carter, Harper Perennial, 2010.
2. Please see http://www.youtube.com/watch?v=26o22Y33h9s
3. Please see Garcia, G.H., *The Troubled Asset Relief Program: Has Forbearance As Far As the Eye Can See Saved the US Economy?* (Chapter 4 in this volume).
4. Garcia, G.H., 'Failing Prompt Corrective Action', *Journal of Banking Regulation*, 2010, V.11, pp. 171–190.
5. *The Globe and Mail*, 1 May 2010, Business section, p. 7.
6. Please see 'Greek Woes Hit Credit Agricole,' http://ftalphaville.ft.com/thecut/2010/08/27/327681/greek-woes-hit-cr
7. Brown, John Murray, 'Chile meeting on Ireland funds awaited', *Financial Times*, 15 November 2010.

8. Please see http://link.ft.com/r/VKY5JJ/C5NYI1/Y88YJ/BMN10H/GKJLMZ/KI/t?a1=2010&a2=8&a3=27
9. Kaufman, G.G., *Living Wills: Putting the Caboose before the Engine and Designing a Better Engine* (Chapter 12 in this volume).
10. Taxpayer support of the banking system in Europe through the financial crisis appears to have cost something close to 17 per cent of GDP. Please see Michel Barnier, found at http://europa.eu/rapid/pressReleasesAction.do?reference=SPEECH/10/470&format=HTML&aged=0&language=EN&guiLanguage=en
11. Ibid.
12. Federal Ministry of Finance, Discussion draft: Law on the restructuring and orderly resolution of credit institutions, on the creation of a Restructuring Fund, and on the prolongation of the limitation period for directors' and officers' liability.
13. Please see Plender, John, 'German banking weaknesses come to light', *Financial Times*, 7 September 2010.
14. The IMF is working on a proposed framework (principles) for cross-border resolution of financial crises. This proposed framework is subject to consideration of the Board (a resolution is expected soon). Also see Bank for International Settlements, Report and Recommendations of the Cross-Border Bank Resolution Group, March 2010 available at http://www.bis.org/publ/bcbs169.pdf?noframes=1.
15. Please see http://www.bis.org/review/r100901a.pdf at p. 1.
16. Ibid.
17. http://www.ft.com/cms/s/0/9442c552-b91c-11df-99be-00144feabdc0.html?ftcamp=crm/email/201096/nbe/EuropeBusiness/product
18. *The Economist*, '*Still in a Spin*', 15 April 2010.

Acknowledgements

This book would not have been possible without the effort and support of a number of people and organizations. The editors would like to thank Jean Pierre Sabourin of the Malaysia Deposit Insurance Corporation, Professor Julio Faundez of the Warwick Law School, Rebecca Probert, Director of the Warwick Legal Research Institute, Anthony Neuberger and Mark Salmon from the Warwick Business School for their personal and financial support of the Banking Law Symposium on Managing Systemic Risk held at the University of Warwick on 7–9 April 2010.

Most of the chapters were drawn from papers delivered at the Banking Law Symposium. We are grateful and thank all of the speakers, presenters and discussants for their contributions and participation. The moderators did a super job and the attendees at the Symposium are thanked for their observations and questions that helped to improve the focus of all of our work. Charles Enoch did an outstanding job in summarizing the Symposium, which we have included as the Foreword to this book. We very much appreciated the assistance of Andrew Jerijian in preparing the chapters.

We appreciate the help of Rose Le-Breton Bagley and Jennifer Wilson of University of Warwick, School of Law, who co-ordinated and provided the essential administrative support to the Symposium. We also acknowledge the efforts of Ben Booth, our commissioning editor, from Edward Elgar Publishing.

Ray LaBrosse would like to thank his mother, Frances, his wife, Gail, as well as Kendra, Scott, and Conrad for their patience. He also thanks Dale Christensen and Ken Paterson for their friendship over so many years.

Rodrigo Olivares-Caminal would like to thank Teresa and Felipe for their love and support; and, my co-organizers and Rosa M. Lastra for their friendship.

Dalvinder Singh would like to thank Sarbjit, Amaryn and Arvind for their love and support.

PART I

Systemic risk

1. Investor behaviour in the period before the 2007–08 financial crisis[1]

Richard J. Rosen

1.1. INTRODUCTION

The period leading up to the financial crisis that began in 2007 was marked by a rapidly expanding array of securities, especially what are known as structured securities. Structured securities, which include bonds issued as part of the securitization process, often are very complex in structure and it is difficult to understand the underlying elements. They can be very difficult to evaluate, even by the financially sophisticated investors that they are marketed to. This chapter explores why investors may have flocked to these securities in the pre-crisis period.

In the wake of the financial crisis, the US passed the *Emergency Economic Stabilization Act of 2008*. That act gave the Treasury Secretary the authority, through the Troubled Asset Relief Program, to purchase troubled assets from banks. The troubled assets that many legislators had in mind were largely structured products such as mortgage-backed securities (MBS) backed by subprime mortgages or collateralized debt obligations (CDO) backed by subprime MBS. Possibly because of the difficulty of pricing these structured securities, the Treasury turned away from asset purchases as the primary means of combating the crisis. The complexity that made valuation difficult during the crisis also was present in the pre-crisis period, yet structured securities markets had been booming, with new products and increased volume in the early part of this century.

In many countries, including the US, only financially sophisticated investors can purchase structured securities. The thought behind restricting the purchasers of these securities is to ensure that all investors have the ability to understand what they are buying. In retrospect, the restriction seems not to have been sufficient. Financially sophisticated investors were willing to purchase extremely difficult to understand (and value) securities. Why? One factor might have been that these securities had done very well in the pre-crisis period. The strong performance of structured finance in general gave three incentives for investors to purchase structured securities such as securitized bonds. First, behavioural finance has identified a number of circumstances where overconfidence affected investor decision-making.[2] The high returns on structured securities in the run-up to the crisis may have led investors to believe the securities were better than they actually were. Second, the credit ratings on these securities had proved reliable in the (recent) past.[3] It may have been rational for busy investors to rely on the recent track record of the securities and the rating agencies rather than to carefully examine each security they planned to purchase. Finally, many of these investors were investing for others (such as mutual fund managers acting on behalf of their fund investors), and this gave them an incentive to reach for yield and to follow the herd.[4]

The factors that attracted investors to structured securities also could explain some of the evolution of the securitization market. The structure of these securities became more complex over time. This is consistent with the intermediaries involved in issuing structured securities taking advantage of overconfidence and (rational) inattention, since overconfident investors are likely to believe they can evaluate the more complicated securities and inattentive investors are unlikely to notice as securities become gradually more complicated as long as credit rating agencies continue to give them strong ratings.

The remainder of the chapter is organized as follows. The next section gives some background on structured securities. In Section 1.3, I discuss why investors would buy securities that do not have a positive expected return. Finally, Section 1.4 offers some concluding comments.

1.2. BACKGROUND

Much of the evolution of financial markets and institutions in recent years resulted in the movement of financing away from traditional bank lending.[5] Many of the new alternatives for borrowers and investors came, directly or indirectly, from what is sometimes called the shadow banking system (SBS).[6] The SBS is the term used for financial institutions that provide alternatives to traditional bank financing.[7] These firms can intermediate between borrowers and lenders, much as banks do. However, they offer a more complex array of products than just simple loans and they are often subject to less intensive regulation.

As part of the move from bank financing to the SBS, one way that financial markets changed dramatically from the mid-1980s through the onset of the financial crisis in 2007 was the rise of structured finance. Structured securities are types of indirect investments. The payments on a structured security can depend on changes in the value of underlying assets, indices, interest rates or cash flows. The bonds issued as parts of securitizations and credit default swaps are two types of structured products. When necessary to give examples, I focus on securitization in this chapter. Securitization is the issuance of bonds backed by the payments on a pool of assets. It allows banks and other lenders to originate assets without the need to hold them on their balance sheets for an extended period of time. The lenders can sell their loans to intermediaries sponsored by commercial and investment banks.[8] For legal reasons, the intermediaries placed the loans they purchased into so-called special purpose vehicles (SPV: sometimes these are called special purpose entities) which were legally separate from the sponsoring institution. A SPV would issue bonds to pay for the loans it purchased. It would then use the payments on the loans to repay the bondholders.

The initial securitizations involved pools of home mortgages, with the bonds issued called MBS. MBS were soon followed by so-called asset-backed securities (ABS), which were bonds backed by the payments on pools of loans such as automobile and credit card loans. In the last 20 years, the types of assets that were part of securitizations expanded to include large corporate loans and mortgages as well as more obscure assets (there was a securitization backed by the royalties on recordings by David Bowie). There have also been securitizations that are backed by the payments on pools of securitized bonds from different deals (collateralized debt obligations). The ability of lenders to easily sell loans into securitizations made the 'originate-to-distribute' (OTD) business model possible. Instead of making a loan and holding it on its balance sheet until maturity, a lender could make (originate) a loan, then immediately sell it. The ability of lenders to use the OTD model is frequently cited as one of the factors that contributed to the financial crisis.

The SBS facilitated innovations such as the advances in securitization, but many of the innovations shifted the responsibility for screening and monitoring borrowers. Traditionally, much intermediated finance was done by banks.[9] A bank would make a loan which would be financed with a combination of equity capital and deposits. The bank, because it kept the loan on its balance sheet, would have an incentive to screen potential borrowers to make sure they were creditworthy and to monitor the loan to maximize the chance it got repaid. Many of the new products facilitated by the SBS shifted some of this responsibility from banks to investors. This introduced two possible problems. First, investors were at least one step further removed from the actual lending decisions, making their ability to screen and monitor more difficult. Second, many of the investors in securities made available by the SBS were in fact agents for other investors, leading to potential incentive problems. I discuss how these two potential problems, especially following a long period of stability and growth in the financial system, can make a crisis more likely.

The evolution of the financial industry and the rise of the SBS may have been motivated by efforts of industry players to capture revenue, but it drastically changed how firms profited from financial intermediation. As the lending process moved away from bank loans to either market-based alternatives such as commercial paper or intermediation-based alternatives such as securitization, revenues for banks moved from interest-based to fee-based. This only accelerated once commercial and investment banks could merge. The move to fee-based earnings reduced the incentives for banks to worry about the long run, and in particular, to worry about the risk of the loans or securities they were selling. This risk was shifted to the buyers. As long as there was someone to buy them, the banks had an incentive to sell them. This leaves the issue of what motivated the purchasers.

1.3. WHY WOULD INVESTORS BUY 'BAD' SECURITIES?

Structured finance was quite popular with both issuers and investors in the period leading up to the financial crisis (for example, Figure 1.1). But as the expansion of securitization went on, there is evidence that newly issued securities were being backed by weaker assets. For example, when housing prices started to fall in 2006 and 2007, it was the most recent vintage of securities (those issued closest to the crisis) that did the worst.[10] Why then did investors flock into these markets until sometime in 2006? One possibility is that the investors were right *ex ante*, but the crisis was just extremely bad luck. This hypothesis cannot be rejected, but given what is known today about the quality of some of the assets in structured securities, bad luck does not seem to be a compete explanation.

In the remainder of this section, I discuss some reasons why investors may have purchased securities that, at least in retrospect, seem to be bad investments. The first set of reasons can explain why 'rational' investors can believe that markets leave money on the table by letting one security have a higher yield than another security with equivalent risk. The last reason can explain why investors may purchase a security that they believe has a worse risk-return trade-off than alternative investments. In the background of these arguments is the role of the credit rating agencies.

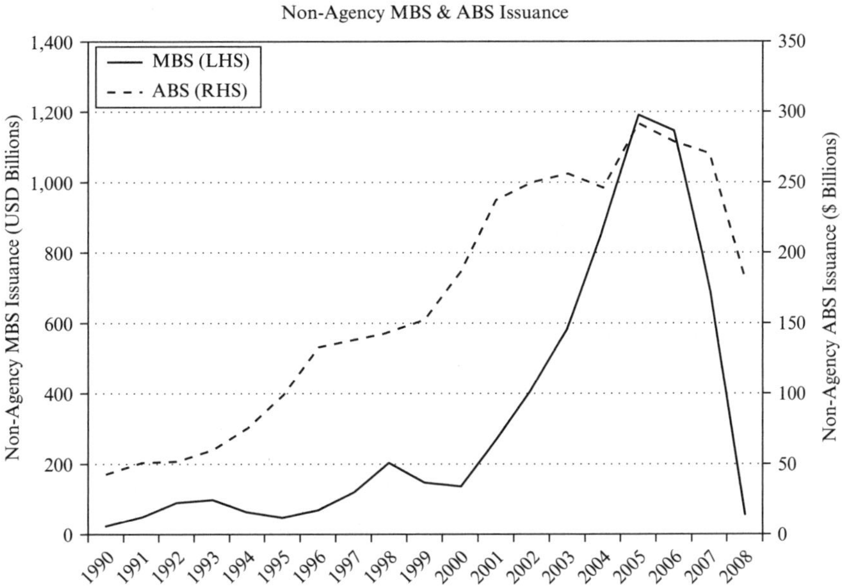

Note: Non-agency MBS are MBS not issued or guaranteed by Ginnie Mae, Fannie Mae, or Freddie Mac; and ABS are bonds issued in securitizations that are not backed by residential mortgages.

Source: Inside Mortgage Finance.

Figure 1.1. Issuance of securitized bonds, 1990–2008

1.3.1. Overconfidence and Inattention

Many structured securities are quite complex. The payments from a pool of underlying assets can be divided into multiple tranches, and the assets themselves can be bonds issued as parts of other securitizations. When making decisions about which securities to purchase (and at what price), investors have access to several tools to help them. They can model returns themselves or they can use third-party evaluations, including those offered by the dealer selling a security. Still, for many of the complex securities, there is no consensus valuation, or even valuation method.[11] This excess of material and lack of consensus on valuation complicates the decision of whether to buy a security at a given price.[12]

Given the complexity of structured securities, how should an investor, who may want to hold hundreds of different securities, evaluate each security? The literature on behavioural finance offers a number of psychology-based reasons why investors may not act as pure profit maximizers. Prior work suggests that investors tend to be overly optimistic or overconfident (I use overconfidence to cover both over-optimism and overconfidence).[13] That is, some investors tend to overestimate their performance or overestimate the precision of their beliefs. There is also evidence of confirmation bias, the tendency to interpret evidence in a way that is consistent with prior beliefs. Confirmation bias leads individuals to put more weight on evidence that confirms their prior beliefs than on evidence that contradicts the beliefs. These aspects of investor behaviour may have played a role in the evolution of structured finance and in setting the conditions for the financial crisis that started in 2007.

In addition to any biases, there is reason to believe that busy investors may take shortcuts, collecting and evaluating only information that they think will have a material effect on the profitability of an investment. Several studies have explored whether so-called rational inattention can be used to explain why individuals do not process all available information.[14] A form of rational inattention, especially when combined with over-optimism and overconfidence, may have helped set the stage for the financial crisis.

How should an investor make the decision to purchase a structured security? One way is to carefully analyse the prospectus and to make projections about future asset prices and default rates. This is extremely time consuming, and as noted above, there may be no consensus valuation method. An alternative is to spend less time on analysis, but instead to rely on some other party's valuation. For example, the investor could base investment decisions on the credit ratings provided by the credit rating agencies including Moody's Investor Service, Standard and Poor's and Fitch Ratings. These credit rating agencies have a long track record of evaluating securities. There is reason to believe that investors relied more on ratings over time, at least prior to the recent financial crisis, perhaps because of the rating agencies' reputations.[15] The track records of the rating agencies may have led investors to pay less attention to the complicated details of each deal and instead to use the ratings assigned by the credit rating agencies as a starting point (and possible ending place) for any analysis. In essence, the credit rating of a security may serve as an anchor around which the investor can interpret any additional evidence.[16]

Consider a busy investor trying to decide whether to invest in a subprime MBS in 2004. The investor may want the extra yield offered by the MBS, but not be certain of how to value the security. She may look into the details of subprime mortgage defaults, which were relatively stable and low for over five years prior to 2004, and evaluate prepayment risk. The implied losses on the MBS bonds based on outside assessments of mortgage default and prepayment rates at that point would imply that the subprime MBS bond yields provide adequate compensation for the risk. This is a reasonable amount of work, and still suggests that the MBS are a good buy. Given the anchor provided by the credit rating, her analysis may be enough to overcome any belief that there rarely is money left on the table by the market.[17] This may happen even if the investor is aware of the debate surrounding the accuracy of credit ratings.

The point at which an investor stops her analysis may depend on how she rates her ability to price securities relative to others in the market. The more confident she is, the more willing she might be to believe that the market is mispricing the security. This may mean that more confident investors stop their analysis earlier than their less confident brethren. An overconfident investor can believe that a high yield on the security is money left on the table. If she considers herself better at analysis than the average investor, she may believe she can estimate default risk better than others. This means that for the securities she chooses to purchase, the overconfident investor incorrectly believes the high yields exist because other investors wrongly, in the mind of the overconfident investor, overestimate default risk. Also, if an overconfident investor believes she can make more precise estimates of the possible return paths of a security than other investors, she can place a lower price on true risk than other investors (since true risk is greater than her perception of risk). Thus, overconfidence can sway an investor toward structured securities because of their high yield relative to their credit rating. Enough overconfident investors can drive yields below a level commensurate with their risk, even if the yield stays high compared to alternative (traditional) securities.

Rational inattention may explain why an investor would shift from doing her own analysis of a particular type of security to relying on a credit rating. The investor has access to two public signals: the payments on the security and the credit rating. During the 2000–2006 period, most structured securities based on pools of mortgages or other assets had very low defaults.[18] Thus, these securities were performing at least as well as their credit rating implied. After doing a detailed analysis once (or more) and finding the credit rating provided a floor for the risk, the investor may decide that the credit rating is reliable enough to allow her to purchase the securities without doing a full analysis. A busy investor allocates her time toward decisions where she believes it is best used. When the securities are performing and there is no external signal to suggest an increase in the expected default rate in the underlying assets, she can choose to be inattentive to the detailed information and rely instead on the credit rating because her initial analysis suggests the information from the rating is a good enough signal to allow her to avoid costly information acquisition.[19]

This is especially true for very safe securities, which rarely provide negative signals to investors. There is evidence that investors in AAA securitization were less informed about the quality of the securities than investors in lower-rated securities.[20]

An investor may not bother to do a detailed analysis even for new securities as long as they seem to her to be close in structure to securities she is already comfortable with since the cost of the analysis may not be worth the expected improvement in valuation. Confirmation bias would likely push the investor toward believing that a reliance on credit rating was a good decision, reducing her perceived need to do a detailed analysis of new securities. Similarly, confirmation bias also suggests that even some noise in the signals, such as the early news about the housing bubble, may not be enough to shake an investor's belief that things are going well. Thus, it may not be until well after there are risk signs that an investor starts to pay careful attention to the details about a particular class of securities. An investor more confident about her ability to evaluate securities is likely to need a bigger change in securities or signals to prompt careful attention.

The above argument suggests that investors may react to a strong track record for a particular type and rating of structured security (or any other investment) by spending less time investigating the details of the investment and, if they are overconfident, becoming more certain that they can analyse the securities better than other investors. These possibilities give issuers an opening to slightly change the structure of the securities they issue so as to increase risk but maintain the same credit rating. This is important because issuers have a strong incentive to add risk because they get fees for arranging securitization deals, and to arrange deals, the issuer needs underlying assets.[21] It is easier to get assets if the issuer can broaden the quality range that the SPV will buy.

The evolution of deals suggests that over time SPV pools got riskier and this led to riskier securitized bonds. Take, for example, subprime MBS. One measure of risk of a subprime mortgage is whether the mortgage was written with full documentation of income, assets, and employment as opposed to those written without full documentation (so-called low-doc or no-doc mortgages). Not surprisingly, low-doc loans were more likely to default than full-doc loans. Consistent with a move toward riskier securities, the share of low-doc loans in subprime security pools increased from 2000–2006 (no-doc loans made up less than one per cent of all subprime loans in pools during the period). In general, there is evidence that 'the quality of [subprime] loans deteriorated for six consecutive years before the crisis and that securitizers were, to some extent, aware of it'.[22] The fact that subprime lending and the share of private-label MBS (which was mostly subprime MBS) both increased during this period, especially from

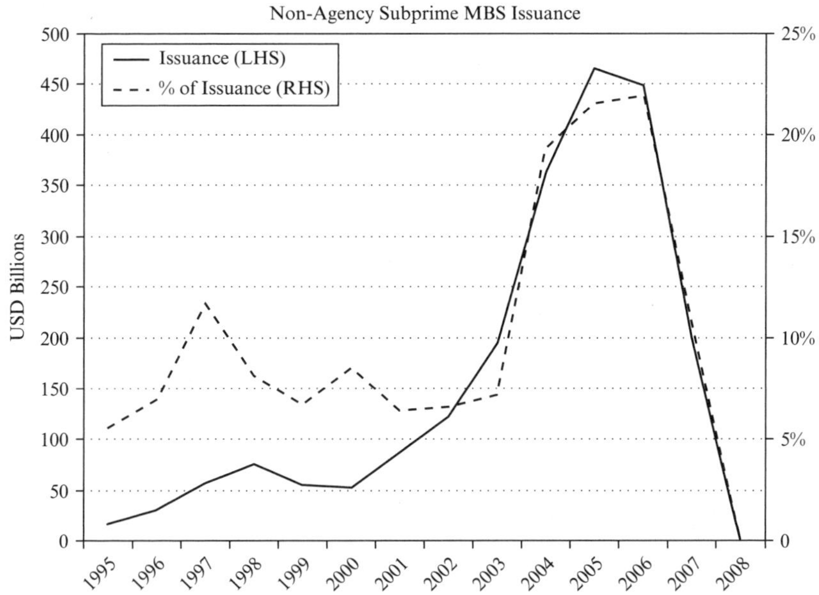

Note: Percent issuance is dollar value of subprime MBS divided by dollar value of all MBS.

Source: Inside Mortgage Finance.

Figure 1.2. Subprime MBS issuance, 1995–2008

2002–2005 (as shown in Figures 1.1 and 1.2), is a sign that investors did not stop purchasing subprime MBS as they got riskier. Thus, the evolution of subprime MBS is consistent with overconfidence, confirmation bias, and rational inattention given the anchor of credit ratings.[23]

One can tell similar stories for the structured finance market as a whole. The new securities that were introduced as the market evolved were often somewhat riskier innovations on prior securities. For example, subprime MBS were similar to prime MBS but slightly riskier because subprime mortgage default rates were historically higher and more variable than prime mortgage default rates. Collateralized loan obligations (CLOs) looked like other ABS such as those based on pools of automobile loans in the sense that both were based on the payments on pools of loans. But, because CLOs included a small number of large loans that required monitoring rather than a large number of small loans which were not monitored unless payments were missed, there were bigger moral hazard problems than in other ABS. Securities like collateralized debt obligations based on pools of MBS and ABS securities were yet more complicated. Investors may have been lulled into a false sense of security by the high yields offered, the strong performance of structured securities in general, and the credit ratings. Thus, overconfident and inattentive investors could have been led into riskier securities without requiring compensating yield increases. That is, the fact that a structured security offered a higher yield than an equivalently-rated corporate bond may have attracted investors, but the excess yield may not have been enough to compensate for the additional, but somewhat hidden, extra risk.[24]

One feature running through this entire argument is the role of credit ratings. The argument relies on the premise that a credit rating did not reflect the true risk of a security, and that this problem was magnified for later vintages of structured securities. There are many who think that credit rating agencies, by working with or for issuers, abetted an increase in risk for structured securities that was not apparent to many investors.[25]

To sum up, overconfidence and inattention may have contributed to the expansion of the SBS and to the severity of the financial crisis. Whatever their motivations for purchase, early investors did well. The strong performance of the economy as a whole, and housing in particular, during the 2001–2006 period meant that very few structured securities defaulted. This strong performance reinforced the opinions of investors and may have led them to rely more on credit ratings (that is, become less attentive). Given the issues with credit rating agencies, this all meant there was room for issuers to produce riskier securities at a given credit rating, something they did.

1.3.2. Other People's Money

Another reason for the evolution of the structured security market may be that many purchasers used other people's money. Section 1.2 discusses the differences between direct and intermediated finance. But within intermediated finance, there are differences in the number of steps between savers and borrowers. In traditional bank financing, a saver deposits with a bank, which then makes loans. However, the process for structured securities and other investments can be much more complicated. The chain from a saver to the ultimate borrower can be long.[26] These long chains can increase agency problems.

Consider the simple case of an individual investing in a bond mutual fund (see Figure 1.3). The mutual fund manager, acting as an agent for the individual, uses the investment to purchase securities, including perhaps structured securities. The structured securities are put together by an issuer who buys the underlying assets from lenders such as banks.

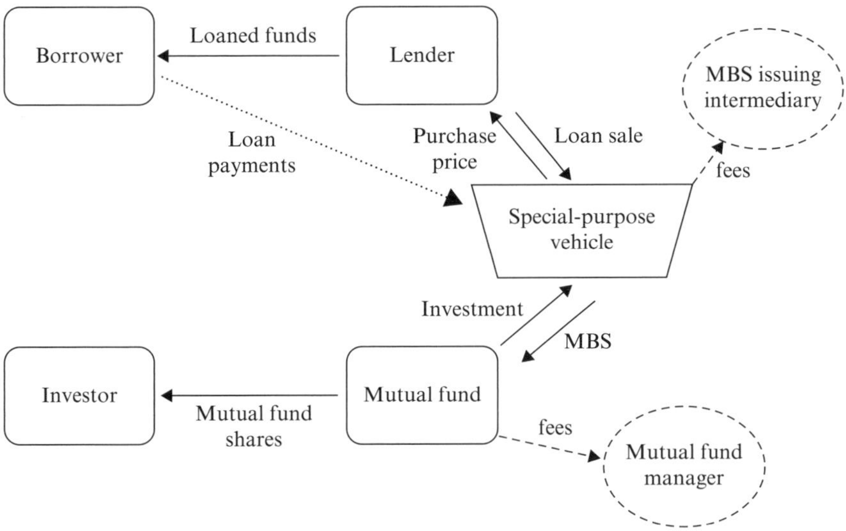

Figure 1.3. Intermediation chain for the purchase of securities through a mutual fund

The banks lend to the borrowers. How should the mutual fund manager choose what to invest in? The fund manager is likely aware that investors tend to put more money into funds that appear to outperform their peers.[27] The fund flows may not be predictive of future returns, and there is some thought that these investors are 'dumb money'.[28] In order to increase her compensation, the fund manager needs to attract investors. This gives her an incentive to report high returns both relative to her peers and overall.[29] Structured securities offer a good way to do this. Thus, even if a fund manager believes that the yields on structured securities are insufficient to compensate for their risk, she may still (rationally) invest in them.

A fund manager's choice of whether to invest in structured securities will depend on the risk of the securities and the fund manager's discount rate, but it can also depend on what other fund managers do. There is evidence of return persistence among mutual funds that perform worse than their peers.[30] To avoid being categorized as a poor performer, a fund manager would want to avoid having her fund perform poorly when other similar funds were performing well. This gives her an incentive to follow the herd.[31] So, if enough fund managers start investing in structured securities to get new investors, other managers will have an incentive to follow them.

Combining the incentives to chase yield to attract new customers and the incentives to herd with overconfidence only reinforces the attractiveness of structured securities. It also gives issuers more reason to be innovative. Securities with high yields where risk is concentrated are likely to be attractive to those investing money for others. High yields are popular with the ultimate investors, and concentrated risk means it is unlikely the agent investing for others will look bad (although when things get bad, they can be very bad). These characteristics are consistent with the evolution of structured finance and the SBS.[32]

1.4. CONCLUDING COMMENTS

The financial crisis that started in 2007 exposed a number of flaws in the US financial system. Many of these flaws were associated with structured securities such as those where the bonds were issued as part of securitizations. The expansion of securitization included many new, intrinsically riskier securities. I explore how natural tendencies of investors may have allowed issuers of securitized bonds (and other structured securities) to increase the risk of these securities without investors focusing on it.

Paradoxically, the good news of the years up to 2006 may have led to the bad news that started in 2007. The strong performance of structured securities fed into the natural overconfidence of some investors. The performance reinforced the decisions of these investors to buy structured securities. It also may have led investors to rely more on credit ratings, since the high credit ratings many bonds received seemed to be confirmed by their performance. Busy investors may have become more willing to trust the ratings since that would allow them to focus their scarce attention elsewhere. The strong performance in the early part of the 2000s also put pressure on investors that were using other people's money to show high returns. This could have led these investors to reach for the high yields offered by structured securities even if they thought that the high yield was insufficient to compensate for the risk of the securities.

A mix of overconfidence, inattention, and desire for high yields on the part of investors gives intermediaries an incentive to create securities that had high yields but a lot of possibly hidden risk. Beyond that, since many investors were relying on credit ratings, it would be more valuable to the intermediaries if they could issue securities that had more risk for a given level of credit rating. It appears now that the intermediaries were able to do this.

As the initial problems associated with the financial crisis have abated, there have been a series of proposals to reform the financial system to minimize the chances of a future crisis. One takeaway from this chapter should be that any proposal needs to factor in the investor-intermediary risk cycle that can originate when investors are overconfident, busy, and investing other people's money and intermediaries are set up to take advantage of investors' tendencies. Among the ways to mitigate the impact of overconfidence and limited attention would be credit rating agency reform aimed towards making credit ratings more accurate by reducing agency problems at the rating agencies. More accurate ratings would reduce the costs for investors of being inattentive to the details of debt securities. Of course, believing that ratings accuracy has increased may lead more investors to rely on ratings rather than their own research, so the impact of ratings agency reform may be limited. Some reform ideas include reducing the role of the SBS. While this would be useful, it may be difficult to accomplish in the long run. Among the reasons for the rise of the SBS were innovations that increased efficiency and arbitraged around regulatory restrictions. The incentives to increase efficiency and evade regulation will remain.

Finally, the argument that the investor-intermediary risk cycle combined with shifts in screening and monitoring caused by the movement from banks to SBS made a financial crisis more likely does not absolve other agents from blame. In this chapter I do not focus on whether regulators contributed to the problems that led to the recent crisis. Sub-optimal actions by regulators (and other parties) could have exacerbated the problems caused by a shift to the SBS. In addition, the highly levered structure of financial intermediaries combined with the maturity mismatch of their balance sheets may have contributed to magnifying the effect of the shock to underlying assets.[33]

NOTES

1. I would like to thank Crystal Cun for research assistance and the participants at presentations at the Federal Reserve Bank of Chicago, the Warwick Law School Symposium on Managing Systemic Risk, and the FUNCAS conference 'Crisis y Regulación Financiera' for comments. These views in this chapter are those of the author and may not represent the views of the Federal Reserve Bank of Chicago or the Federal Reserve System. Please address correspondence to Richard Rosen, Federal Reserve Bank of Chicago, phone 312-322-6368, fax 312-294-6262, and email rrosen@frbchi.org
2. See, e.g., Malmendier, Ulrike and Geoffrey Tate (2005), 'CEO Overconfidence and Corporate Investment,' *The Journal of Finance*, **60(6)**, 2661–2700.
3. See, e.g., Moody's, (2006), 'Default & Loss Rates of Structured Finance Securities: 1993–2005,' April 2006.
4. See, e.g., Scharfstein, David S. and Stein, Jeremy C. (1990), 'Herd Behavior and Investment,' *American Economic Review*, **80(3)**, 465–79.
5. See, e.g., Adrian, Tobias, and Hyun Song Shin (2009), 'Money, Liquidity, and Monetary Policy,' *American Economic Review Papers and Proceedings*, **99(2)**, 600–605.
6. The SBS is a slightly more expansive definition of non-bank alternatives than, for example, the securitized banking sector referred to by Gorton, Gary and Andrew

Metrick (2009), 'Securitized Banking and the Run on Repo,' working paper, and the market-based financial intermediation in Shleifer, Andrei and Robert Vishny (2009), 'Unstable Banking,' working paper.

7. The types of firms that are included as part of the SBS include investment banks, hedge funds, mono-line insurance companies, the government-sponsored entities (GSEs), and a number of specialized entities that are set up to issue derivative financial securities. Banks can be part of the SBS to the extent that they participate in financing different from traditional lending.
8. See, e.g., Rosen, Richard J. (2007), 'The Role of Securitization in Mortgage Lending,' *Chicago Fed Letter*, Federal Reserve Bank of Chicago, November 2007, for a fuller description of the securitization process.
9. I am using the term 'banks' to refer to all kinds of depository institutions.
10. See, e.g., Demyanyk, Yuliya and Otto Van Hemert (2008), 'Understanding the subprime mortgage crisis,' *The Review of Financial Studies*, December 2008.
11. See, e.g., Prince, Jeffrey T. (2006), 'A General Review of CDO Valuation Methods,' *The Journal of Structured Finance*, **12(2)**, 14–21.
12. 'The only entity that really understood the true value and risk in a mortgage-backed security or a CDO was the mortgage broker who originated the loans that made up the underlying assets,' explains Niket Patankar, CEO of hedge fund advisory company Adventity. 'And that person was long gone from the picture by the time they were sold as part of a CDO.' From 'Navigating subprime securities,' Katie Benner, *Fortune Magazine*, August 2007.
13. There are a number of studies of overconfidence in financial markets (e.g., Barber, Brad M. and Terrance Odean (2001), 'Boys will be boys: Gender, overconfidence, and common stock investment,' *Quarterly Journal of Economics*, **116**, 261–293, on stock trading and Malmendier, Ulrike and Geoffrey Tate (2005), 'CEO Overconfidence and Corporate Investment,' *The Journal of Finance*, **60(6)**, 2661–2700, on managerial decision making). See Malmendier, Ulrike and Geoffrey Tate, 2008, 'Who Makes Acquisitions? CEO Overconfidence and the Market's Reaction,' *Journal of Financial Economics*, July 2008, **89(1)**, 20–43 for a review of some of the psychology literature on overconfidence and Rabin, M. and Schrag, J. (1999), 'First Impressions Matter: a Model of Confirmatory Bias', *Quarterly Journal of Economics*, **114(1)**, 37–8 for a discussion of confirmation bias.
14. See, e.g., Sims, Christopher A. (2003), 'Implications of rational inattention,' *Journal of Monetary Economics*, **50(3)**, 665–690. There is also empirical evidence of inattention (whether rational or not) in financial markets (e.g., DellaVigna, Stefano and Joshua M. Pollet (2009), 'Investor Inattention and Friday Earnings Announcements,' *Journal of Finance*, **64**, 709–749, on earnings announcements and Barber, Brad M. and Terrance Odean 2008, 'All that Glitters: The Effect of Attention and News on the Buying Behavior of Individual and Institutional Investors,' *Review of Financial Studies*, **22**, 785–818, on news about stocks).
15. See, e.g., Covitz, Daniel M. and Paul Harrison (2003), 'Testing Conflicts of Interest at Bond Ratings Agencies with Market Anticipation: Evidence that Reputation Incentives Dominate,' working paper.
16. Anchoring refers to a bias in how individuals assess probabilities. People tend to anchor on certain pieces of information, effectively ignoring or underweighting other data (see, e.g., Tversky, Amos and Daniel Kahneman (1974), 'Judgment under Uncertainty: Heuristics and Biases,' *Science*, New Series, **185(4157)**, 1124–1131).
17. Investors who dug deeply enough to believe that the yield spreads for some of the MBS and ABS were insufficient to cover the risks of the structured securities would not have purchased them. Clearly, the growth in structured securities markets suggests that there were relatively few investors like this (or that these investors were agents for others as discussed in the section on other people's money).
18. Each year from 2003–2005, the rate of default on both investment grade and high-yield structured securities was lower than in the prior year (Moody's (2006), 'Default & Loss

Rates of Structured Finance Securities: 1993–2005,' April 2006). By 2005, the default rate was at an all-time low.

19. Brunnermeier, Markus K. and Martin Oehmke (2009), 'Complexity in Financial Markets,' working paper. These authors argue that there can be information overload with complex securities, implying there is a limit to the ability of an investor to analyse information. When this happens, how information is released is crucial, perhaps more than how much information is released. The credit rating can serve as an anchor, as I argue, for investors' analysing the overload of information.
20. See, e.g., Adelino, Manuel (2009), 'Do Investors Rely Only on Ratings? The Case of Mortgage-Backed Securities,' working paper.
21. There is evidence that firms try to take advantage of investor overconfidence and inattention (e.g., DellaVigna, Stefano and Joshua M. Pollet (2009), 'Investor Inattention and Friday Earnings Announcements,' *Journal of Finance*, **64**, 709–749; Daniel, K., D. Hirshleifer and A. Subrahmanyam (1998), 'Investor psychology and security market under- and overreactions,' *Journal of Finance,* **53(6)**, 1839–1885).
22. See n. 10. Note that this view, while held by many, is not universal. See Bhardwaj, Geetesh and Rajdeep Sengupta (2009), 'Where's the Smoking Gun? A Study of Underwriting Standards for US Subprime Mortgages,' Federal Reserve Bank of St. Louis Working Paper 2008-036B.
23. In addition, some investors may have understood what was happening, but overconfidently believed they could sell the overpriced subprime MBS to others. In theory, such beliefs can support a deviation of prices from fundamentals (Scheinkman, J.A. and W. Xiong (2003), 'Overconfidence and Speculative Bubbles,' *Journal of Political Economy*, **111(6)**, 1183–1219).
24. Of course, the risk differences were not that hidden. The historical default rate on structured securities of a particular rating was much higher than the historical default rate on corporate bonds of the same rating as data published by the ratings agencies showed.
25. Kane, Edward J. (2008), 'Who Should Bear Responsibility for Mistakes Made in Assigning Credit Ratings to Securitized Debt?' working paper; Mason, Joseph R. and Josh Rosner (2007), 'Where Did the Risk Go? How Misapplied Bond Ratings Cause Mortgage Backed Securities and Collateralized Debt Obligation Market Disruptions,' working paper; Partnoy, Frank (2006), 'How and Why Credit Rating Agencies are Not Like Other Gatekeepers,' *Financial Gatekeepers: Can They Protect Investors?*, Yasuyuki Fuchita, Robert E. Litan (eds) (2006), Brookings Institution Press and the Nomura Institute of Capital Markets Research. An alternative view of why credit ratings may not have fully reflected the risk of structured securities is that the models used by credit rating agencies were not sophisticated enough and relied on data from an unusually benign period.

26 Shin, Hyun Song (2009), 'Financial Intermediation and the Post-Crisis Financial System,' working paper, for some examples.

27 See, e.g., Sirri, Erik R. and Peter Tufano (1998), 'Costly Search and Mutual Fund Flows,' *Journal of Finance*, **53**, 1589–1622.

28 Frazzini, Andrea and Owen A. Lamont (2008), 'Dumb Money: Mutual Fund Flows and the Cross-Section of Stock Returns,' *Journal of Financial Economics*, **88(2)**, 299–322.

29 Mutual fund flows tend to be negative correlated across categories of fund (Goetzmann, W., R. Ibbotson and L. Peng (2001), 'A new historical database for the NYSE 1815 to 1925: Performance and predictability,' *Journal of Financial Markets*, **4(1)**, 1–32).

30 Hendricks, D., J.S. Patel and R.J. Zeckhauser (1993), 'Hot Hands in Mutual Funds: The Persistence of Performance, 1974–87,' *Journal of Finance*, **48**, 93–130.

31 See, e.g., 4, on herd behaviour.

32 As a side note, for the overall argument here to hold, it is not necessary that all investors were overconfident, inattentive, or agents for others. There may have been investors that made decisions about whether to purchase structured securities based on a purely profit maximizing basis. However, the rapid increases in the sale of these securities and

the losses investors took on them suggest that the profit-maximizing investors may not have been setting the prices for the securities. Why did these investors not short the securities to benefit from any mispricing caused by overconfident and inattentive investors? One possible reason is that it may not be optimal for investors with limited capital to try to bet against non-profit-maximizing investors (see, e.g., DeLong, J.B., A.M. Shleifer, L.H. Summers and R.J. Waldman (1990), 'Noise Trader Risk in Financial Markets', *Journal of Political Economy*, **98**, 703–738).

33 Diamond, Douglas W. and Raghuram G. Rajan (2009), 'The Credit Crisis: Conjectures About Causes and Remedies,' working paper.

2. The nature of systemic risk

Jack Selody[1]

2.1. INTRODUCTION

The fragility of the world financial system after the 2007 meltdown of the US subprime securities market was surprising. Policymakers had been working diligently in the years prior to the shock to strengthen the robustness of the infrastructure connecting major elements of the system. Many national large value payment systems had been risk proofed.[2] The Continuous Linked Settlement (CLS) bank had recently launched, which risk proofed large value foreign exchange transactions in major currencies.[3] Bank deposit insurance was widespread and deposit-taking institutions were heavily regulated.[4] Based on previous crisis experience this risk proofing should have made the world financial system robust even to large shocks and prevented it from going into crisis. Indeed, the newly risk-proofed elements held up well during the crisis.

The episode reminds us that modern financial systems are complex and not well understood. Not surprisingly, the crisis triggered an impetus for regulatory reform that ranges from proposals to strengthen existing controls to calls for a paradigm shift. At issue is how best to protect against systemic risk. Achieving this objective requires a good understanding of the nature of that risk.

In this chapter I look beyond the details of the recent crisis to ask: what constitutes the nucleus of a modern financial system and what makes it vulnerable to failure? I argue that the nucleus is the cluster of financial markets and supporting infrastructure that coordinates the activity of financial institutions. The principal systemic risk is the fragile liquidity of these core markets resulting from inadequate risk proofing of key infrastructure. The most significant of the proposed regulatory reforms will not remedy this vulnerability. Specifically, those reforms aimed at preventing individual institutions from becoming insolvent. The reforms will raise costs in the regulated sector, push financial activity to the unregulated sector, and thereby create greater system vulnerability over time. A better way to mitigate systemic risk would be to keep markets liquid during institutional insolvency by risk proofing core infrastructure. Risk proofing large-value payment systems and foreign exchange clearing systems was a good start but more can be done. Counterparty risk can be mutualized in interbank markets. Contract-fulfilment enforcement can be improved where large contingent payouts are promised in the future. Collateral safeguarding, valuation, and discounting methods can be strengthened. Financial products can undergo greater standardization so they are better suited to trading in markets where information is poor. Trading platforms can be modernized to provide greater transparency and efficiency. And, central banks can provide liquidity directly to core financial markets in the event of a systemic shock.

2.2. WHAT IS SYSTEMIC RISK?

Systemic risk is the probability that the financial system will fail to function as needed to support economic activity in the aggregate.[5] The definition is necessarily vague because a modern financial system is complex and what is essential to its aggregate function can be difficult to discern. Moreover, what is essential can change over time as the system evolves, and so what constitutes systemic risk changes over time as well.[6]

Early discussions of systemic risk focused on how a justified fear of insolvency in one bank could become an unjustifiable fear that other, otherwise solvent, banks would fail. The result would be a run on all banks and system failure. Bordo, in summarizing this view, focused on how unresolved conflicts of interest within a bank (that is, agency problems) and asset prices dropping beyond the bounds of expectation (that is, unmanaged uncertainty) could cause insolvency.[7] Containing these problems is the domain of prudential regulators and supervisors. Some of these regulators and supervisors might argue that systemic risk is when these problems occur in systemically important banks, and so systemic risk is best mitigated by special regulations on key banks to prevent their failure; thereby nipping the problem in the bud.

Mitigating systemic risk by imposing supplementary prudential regulation on systemically important banks may work well in a static bank-dominated financial system, but it is unlikely to be effective in a dynamic system where financial innovation is prevalent. There are a number of reasons for this. First, it would leave an unresolved tension between bank business objectives and regulatory objectives. Some banks would want to pursue innovative business models to profit from financial innovation whereas regulators would be reluctant to let market forces weed out large, complex, or interconnected banks with unprofitable business models. The result would be banks working to circumvent the intent of regulation, that is, regulatory arbitrage. Second, it would do little to mitigate systemic risk originating in the unregulated shadow banking sector. This sector would grow in importance if regulators were to clamp down on innovation in the regulated sector. Third, the resulting implicit guarantee for systemically important banks would represent a moral hazard. Systemically important banks might then take on additional risk in the knowledge that they would obtain extraordinary support in the event of bad outcomes.

More recent (mostly post-crisis) discussions of systemic risk emphasize the additional risk generated by the numerous and complex links between financial institutions.[8] Modern financial institutions are increasingly linked by contingent claims, mark-to-market asset valuations, and lending margins that vary with market conditions. These links are not the contractual obligations predominant in traditional thinking, but rather are correlations in solvency valuations from common exposures to market prices that result from the positive feedback loop between leverage and market values. To capture these new links, new measures of systemic risk are being developed that focus on the additional risk to an institution from being exposed to system volatility. Not surprisingly, this work is still in its infancy as risk analysts were not cognizant of this source of systemic risk until the recent crisis demonstrated how market volatility can have a common effect on financial institutions that is important in aggregate. To many, the best way to mitigate this new manifestation of systemic risk is to impose higher regulatory capital and liquidity requirements on individual financial institutions to better reflect the totality of their risk exposure in the system, and to vary these requirements with the cyclicality of that risk.

Mitigating systemic risk by raising regulatory capital and liquidity requirements to better reflect the risk that individual institutions assume from being linked to the system is unlikely to eliminate system instability for a number of reasons. First, as with all solutions targeted specifically to the regulated sector, it imposes additional costs on regulated institutions which will push intermediation to the unregulated sector and lead to greater system instability over time. Second, it relies on the unrealistic assumption that in setting capital requirements regulators can know more about the details of the risk exposures of an institution than do risk managers in the institution. Third, it does not recognize that there can be a trade-off between system stability and institution stability. Specifically, it would discourage outcomes where greater system stability could be achieved with added risk for some institutions.

An alternative view sometimes heard in current discussions is that systemic risk is the probability that the links in the system themselves might fail, not the probability that an institution might fail because it is linked. The difference is one of emphasis, but nevertheless is important when it comes to differentiating between solutions. These connecting links are mechanisms (i.e., markets and infrastructure) that coordinate the activity of institutions. Systemic risk represents a breakdown in these mechanisms. The failure of a market to generate prices close to fundamental value is an example of such a breakdown. Having inter-bank lending freeze because counterparty risk becomes immeasurable is another example. These coordination breakdowns pose a systemic risk because they disrupt liquidity throughout the system, which distorts asset prices and gives the appearance that institutions are insolvent. Although the breakdown in coordination is often triggered by a legitimate threat to the insolvency of a single institution, it does not correspond to the system itself being insolvent.[9] At the system level, the problem is one of illiquidity, not insolvency, because without a disruption to liquidity there would be no knock-on effects and therefore no widespread threat of insolvency in the system. In this view, mitigating systemic risk requires the risk proofing of key elements of infrastructure to ensure that system liquidity is resilient to the insolvency of one or more of the key institutions in the system. This risk mitigation strategy avoids the pitfalls of other strategies in that it does not differentiate between the regulated and unregulated sectors since infrastructure and markets are common to both, and it does not generally put regulators in tension with bankers (except where an institution has a vested interest in maintaining system reliance on proprietary infrastructure).

But why is systemic risk so hard to pin down? The basic problem is that the two components of credit risk – insolvency risk and illiquidity risk – are confounded in that one rarely occurs without the other. Another problem is that contingent claims can make coordination mechanisms difficult to understand. A third problem is that systemic risk outcomes are infrequent and episodic, which makes empirical identification of underlying causes difficult. A fourth problem is that there is no dominant, generally accepted theory of financial behaviour to guide research. And finally, there can be disagreement about what to look for when determining the cause of a crisis – infrastructure fragilities or capricious financial behaviour.

Despite different perspectives on the nature of systemic risk, there is widespread agreement that systemic risk is related to the interactions or links between key participants in the financial system. An obvious sign of a breakdown in these links is a widespread failure to execute financial transactions that would have taken place had the financial system been liquid. This suggests that greater understanding of the nature of systemic risk can be gleaned by looking at why financial transactions fail, and what might be done to prevent failure.

2.3. HOW DO SYSTEMIC EVENTS HAPPEN?

It may be somewhat surprising that systemic events are often triggered by seemingly innocuous shocks that should have been easily absorbed by the financial system. For example, the recent crisis was triggered by an estimated USD500 billion of losses in subprime mortgages, a much smaller number than the stock market losses after the burst of the technology bubble in 2000 and smaller than the USD600 to USD800 billion lost in the 1990 S&L meltdown, neither of which triggered a crisis.[10] One explanation for this seeming incongruity is that participants in the financial system sometimes behave in ways that generate a widespread build-up of imbalances that even a relatively small shock can reveal as unsustainable. An alternative explanation is that a relatively small shock that hits a part of the financial system that is especially fragile or incapable of adjustment can lead to cascading failures owing to the interconnected nature of the system. In either case, the result is a widespread failure to trade.

The simplest way to picture a systemic event is to imagine the financial system in a state where leverage is at its upper feasible limit – it is therefore short of liquidity-generating capacity – and so all system participants are exposed to a high degree of liquidity risk. If a system in such a state experiences a shock that increases the desire and need to be liquid by simultaneously creating widespread uncertainty and a need to rebalance portfolios, then the system will be pushed beyond the point where it can provide sufficient liquidity endogenously. In theory, the price of liquid assets could temporarily spike relative to the price of illiquid assets to equilibrate demand and supply for liquidity, but in practice transactions at these prices may not be perceived as being feasible because the resulting deviation of price from fundamental value is large and transitory. In such a situation, market makers are likely to pull back from market making owing to the high degree of uncertainty about future prices, along with an inability to fund inventory, and so system participants may be unable to find counterparties even if they are willing to trade. The only way to counteract such a shock is to inject liquidity into the system from a new source, either from the central bank or from reserves held for such a purpose by key institutions within the system.[11]

This simple example highlights the basic mechanism of a systemic event: a shock that exposes a key fragility in the financial system, creating uncertainty about the viability of other parts in the system, thereby cascading into a generalized lack of confidence in the health of the system, causing liquidity to dry up. The precondition for system failure is a vulnerability resulting from fragile behaviour or fragile infrastructure.

At a basic level there are a limited number of ways that markets can freeze and trading can stop.[12]

1. It may not be possible to determine the gains from trade; for example, because a shock exposes information asymmetries that raise doubts about the represented value of a product.
2. It may not be possible to execute trades; for example, because a critical piece of financial system infrastructure has not been properly risk proofed and so fails.
3. It may be too risky to deal with the counterparty to the trade; for example, because a shock causes uncertainty about the solvency of available counterparties.
4. It may be that there is too much uncertainty about the implicit contingencies associated with the trade; for example, because the financial institution that implicitly guarantees to reverse the trade in the event of a crisis may not be able to fulfil the guarantee.
5. It may be that no one is willing to take the other side of a trade; for example, because the system is riskier than previously thought but all participants have exhausted their capacity for risk taking.

The ways in which financial activity can freeze provides a schema for grouping potential fragilities in financial systems and their associated mitigation remedies.

2.4. REMEDIES FOR MITIGATING POTENTIAL SYSTEMIC FRAGILITIES

Systemic fragilities can result in elevated levels of risk that threaten the stability of a financial system. In general, prudential supervisors are responsible for monitoring and constraining the behaviours of key financial participants within an institution or market to ensure risk mitigation practices are appropriate. Supervisors focus on market failures such as conflicts of interest or incomplete contracts that can mute incentives to mitigate risk. The basic thrust of prudential regulation is to align incentives between risk managers and stakeholders, such as shareholders or investors, so that risk is properly mitigated. Solvency protection is basically a private good in that the benefits of proper risk mitigation accrue to stakeholders and not to the general public.

Central banks, as liquidity lenders of last resort, provide liquidity to the system in the event that illiquidity risk threatens the stability of the system. Central banks also have an interest in risk-proofing financial system infrastructure essential to liquidity creation to minimize the need for their service and the credit risk that accompanies it. Central banks provide essential liquidity in response to large systemic shocks where coordination between private participants breaks down and system liquidity dries up. Systemic liquidity protection is provided as a public service since system liquidity is a social good that does not have value to individuals except to facilitate exchange, that is, to support society. The benefits of a liquid financial system accrue to the public at large since the financial system underpins economic activity in aggregate.

2.4.1. Minimizing Confusion About Gains From Trade

Confusion about the gains from trade can result from limited, distorted or asymmetric information about the quality of assets up for sale. These information frictions put institutions at risk of buying assets that are riskier than realized. If widespread, this under-appreciation of risk can threaten the solvency of institutions. And, to the extent that institutions are interconnected, the system can be put at risk. Ensuring information is of sufficient quality so as not to pose a threat to the soundness of the individual elements of the system is the domain of prudential regulators and supervisors.[13]

Encouraging transparency is the leading method by which regulators and supervisors counter information imperfections. For example, the Basel Committee on Banking Supervision has stated that '[t]ransparency in this area [i.e., credit risk in banking institutions] is particularly important since weak credit risk management practices and poor credit quality continue to be a dominant cause of bank failures and banking crises worldwide.'[14]

2.4.2. Robust Trading Infrastructure

Trading infrastructure is critical to the system's ability to generate liquidity endogenously. A breakdown in this infrastructure can result in illiquid markets with effects that cascade through the system. Central banks are particularly concerned with ensuring that critical market infrastructure is properly risk proofed because they are the liquidity lender of last resort to the financial system and therefore on the hook should a breakdown occur.

Risk-proofed infrastructure held up well in the recent crisis. For example, the Committee on the Global Financial System recently reported that 'the wide-spread use of Continuous Linked Settlement (CLS) has helped to mitigate settlement risk. Indeed, it is likely that confidence in the ability of CLS to mitigate this risk was one of the reasons foreign exchange markets continued to function even at the height of the crisis and picked up activity from other markets that had ceased to function.'[15] On the other hand, interbank markets did not have risk-proofed infrastructure, and many of these markets froze because participants withdrew from the market owing to unacceptable counterparty risk.[16] This has led to suggestions that some markets would benefit from having a Central Clearing Party (CCP) to mutualize trading risk. Extending central bank lender of last resort privileges to those CCPs critical to the system would enhance system stability. Also, simplifying infrastructure, as suggested by Haldane,[17] would reduce systemic risk by lessening the unintended consequences of complex financial connections.

2.4.3. Stronger Counterparties

Counterparty risk reflects the potential for the counterparty to a trade to become insolvent before the obligations of the transaction are fulfilled. In a crisis where asset prices are distorted by illiquid markets, solvent institutions can appear to be insolvent. The primary mechanism for mitigating insolvency risk is capital, and prudential regulators set minimum capital standards to manage insolvency as a matter of course. The appearance of insolvency owing to variations in liquidity is cyclical, and this cyclicality has motivated proposals to consider countercyclical capital surcharges as a mechanism for counteracting behaviour that does not see you through the cycle.[18] Similarly, capital surcharges related to the size or connectedness of a financial institution have been suggested as a mechanism for mitigating systemic risk related to network externalities.[19]

Before the crisis, how financial institutions mitigated liquidity risk was largely unregulated. However, as institutions become more reliant on capital markets for funding, the share of liquid assets in total assets has been declining. These institutions seem to be acting as if funding markets will always be open and available to provide liquidity should the need arise, which has not always been the case. As a result, there are calls for regulators to impose formal liquidity standards on financial institutions.[20] An alternative would be to improve the resilience of core funding markets to validate the implicit assumption core funding markets will always be open.[21]

2.4.4. Recognizing Contingent Claims

A contingent claim is an obligation that becomes due in one future state of the world, but not in others. The value of this claim depends on the probability that the future state will materialize, which is unknown.

Current accounting rules and conventions have difficulty in dealing with conditional future values, which leads to asset and liability valuations that are not always fully understood, adequately reported, or properly valued. Many proposals to mitigate the risks coming from contingent claims would require financial institutions to hold contingent capital, that is, to enter into agreements or to issue instruments that would trigger an injection of capital if it fell below a predetermined threshold. Longer term initiatives focus on improving accounting practices so that contingent values are more accurately understood, reported, and valued.

2.4.5. Improving Risk Management Practices

Trade in risky financial products can dry up if financial system participants are unwilling to take on additional risk at a reasonable price. This can happen if all participants suddenly and simultaneously become aware that they have been managing risk badly and now have more risk than they can reasonably handle. This is especially likely if risk managers are not aware of the theoretical shortcuts in the models they use, nor aware of the difficulties in finding a sensible calibration of model parameters.[22] Improved risk management education is a precondition for better risk management practice. Regulators pay attention to the quality of risk management education as part of their oversight of the risk management practices of financial system participants.[23]

Through-the-cycle leverage margining and collateral haircuts can also be used to bring discipline to risk management practices. 'Terms and conditions on secured lending transactions, as well as the changes to the eligible pool of collateral securities and the applicable haircuts on them, affect the access to credit and risk-taking behaviour of leveraged market participants. . . . [The GGFS Study Group chaired by Longworth] recommends a series of policy options, including some for consideration, directed at margining practices to dampen the build-up of leverage in good times and soften the systemic impact of the subsequent deleveraging.'[24]

2.4.6. Moral Hazard

One legacy of the recent crisis will be the moral hazard that official intervention generated. Without doubt, those financial system participants who believe they are critical to the stability of the system now perceive less of an incentive to avoid systemic risk, given the aggressiveness of official intervention in response to the crisis. If left unchecked, this belief will lead to behaviours that increase systemic risk. What might be done to reduce moral hazard going forward?[25]

First, regulators could create offsetting incentives that discourage systemic risk taking by implementing a supplementary capital charge specific to systemic risk. However, a side effect of this charge would be to push more intermediation activity into financial markets since bank-based intermediation would become more expensive. Thus, this change should be augmented by measures to better risk-proof core financial markets.

Second, regulators could set liquidity standards that encourage financial institutions to maintain sufficient liquidity to deal with idiosyncratic and small systemic shocks, and to have policies for sound liquidity management practices.

Third, supervisors could ensure that there are meaningful consequences to financial institution stakeholders when risk mitigation strategies fail. Clear and transparent resolution mechanisms and 'living wills' are initiatives that help in this regard.

Fourth, supervisors could require the use of contingent capital that could be called into play in the event of a large idiosyncratic or systemic shock, thereby largely eliminating the need for official intervention to maintain the solvency of key institutions.

Fifth, central banks could support the implementation of risk-proofed liquidity-generating infrastructure for core markets, such as a central counterparty for repo trades that would make funding liquidity more resilient to shocks. The central bank could also contract to provide the central counterparty with secured liquidity loans in the event of large systemic shocks.

Sixth, central banks could monitor the liquidity of the system – especially the liquidity of core financial institutions and markets – against rigorous standards to verify that the system would be likely to remain resilient to shocks going forward.

These measures would make the financial system more resilient to shocks, and thus increase the credibility of official commitments not to intervene as a normal course. Increasing the resilience of financial markets reduces the probability of systemic failure when one or more financial institutions fail. Similarly, increasing the resilience of financial institutions reduces the probability of systemic failure when financial markets freeze or otherwise cease to function effectively. And, ensuring that the critical infrastructure of the system – such as large-value payment systems and the core liquidity-generating markets at the centre of the financial system – is properly risk proofed will reinforce statements that the goal of crisis intervention is to support the stability of the system, and not to bail out individual system participants, thereby reducing moral hazard.

2.5. LOOKING FORWARD

The lesson I take from the crisis is that what we saw was a classic systemic liquidity crunch, but manifested in core funding markets. The system failure was fragile market infrastructure. The proximate cause was risk management and regulatory practice that did not keep pace with the complexities and hidden risks of the new financial instruments made possible by the information revolution. The trigger was the apparent insolvency of a few relatively unimportant financial institutions, as is typically the case. What did I see that supports this conclusion?

One striking observation is that the crisis spread from the unregulated sector to the regulated sector. It also spread from funding markets to institutions. This suggests that the fundamental cause was not a preference for excess risk in regulated institutions – although in all likelihood these institutions did not fully understand their risk exposures. But, since the excess risk was a mistake not a preference, it means that institutions will learn how to manage risk better. This suggests that a wholesale overhaul of financial institution regulation is not required, nor will it prevent future crises.

Another striking observation is that the newly risk-proofed infrastructure held up well during the crisis. This is unusual in that past crises have often been characterized by disruptions to payment systems and foreign exchange markets. It suggests that risk-proofing more critical infrastructure will help prevent, or at least contain, future crises.

A third observation is that financial intermediation had been moving to financial markets and to the unregulated shadow banking sector before the crisis. The move was made possible by financial innovation and was driven by a search for efficiencies. These trends are likely to re-establish themselves as financial innovation will continue to make market-based intermediation more economical. It will be important to ensure that financial market infrastructure is robust and can bear the weight of the added load. It will also be important not to overburden the regulated sector with costs from regulation, thereby providing an additional, but inappropriate, incentive for intermediation to move to the unregulated sector.

A fourth observation is that the nature of systemic risk was not fully understood. Overstating the point somewhat, there was a view that strong regulation and good supervision of banks would be sufficient to prevent a systemic crisis because markets were largely self-regulating. The importance of strong market infrastructure was not fully appreciated.

This leads me to predict that future financial crises will not be eliminated by stricter capital requirements and more complex regulation on regulated financial institutions. This approach will be counterproductive in the long run as it will simply reinforce the trend toward market-based or unregulated intermediation. Rather, reform should be aimed at strengthening financial infrastructure for the critical components of the financial system, such as core funding markets. Public authorities should act on the lesson that markets are not self-regulating and ensure that the 'rules of the game' are clear, fair, and enforced. Restrictions on behaviour should maintain a balance between costs imposed on regulated institutions and costs imposed on non-regulated market participants. Markets should be regulated to prevent coordination failures such as those that cause inefficiencies in price discovery, not to correct the incentive misalignments common to the agency problems in financial institutions. And, policymakers and risk practitioners need new tools to analyse and control systemic risk – in particular, tools that operate in real time. Better regulation is always helpful, but by itself it will not prevent the next systemic crisis.

NOTES

1. The views, opinions, and interpretations contained in this chapter are attributable to me alone.
2. These risk-proofed systems settle in real time, have mutualized counterparty risk, and have ready access to central bank liquidity if needed. The UK clearing banks moved to such a Real Time Gross Settlement (RTGS) system in 1996.
3. CLS Bank was launched in 2002 and designed to eliminate Herstatt risk – the risk that a counterparty fails mid-transaction (i.e., after the first leg of the transaction is completed in one time zone but before the second leg is completed in a different time zone).
4. Haldane, A. and P. Alessandri (2009), 'Banking on the state', *BIS Review* 139 report that deposit insurance was first introduced in the US in 1934 but did not catch on internationally until the 1960s. By 2009, almost 100 countries had deposit insurance.
5. For example, Kaufman, George G., and Kenneth E. Scott (2003), 'What is systemic risk, and do bank regulators retard or contribute to it?', *Independent Review* 7 (3): 371–91 define systemic risk as the 'probability of breakdowns in an entire system, as opposed to breakdowns in individual parts or components'.
6. Indeed, De Bandt, Olivier, and Phillip Hartman (2002), 'Systemic Risk in Banking: A Survey' in *Financial Crises, Contagion and Lender of Last Resort: A Reader*, Charles Goodhart and Gerhard Illing (eds) Oxford University Press, pp. 249–298 pointed out that 'searching for an ultimate definition of systemic risk may be futile due to ever changing financial markets and institutions [illegible]'
7. Bordo, M.D. (2002), 'The Lender of Last Resort: Alternative Views and Historical Experience' in *Financial Crises, Contagion and Lender of Last Resort: A Reader*, Charles Goodhart and Gerhard Illing (eds), Oxford University Press, pp. 109–126.
8. See, for example, Haldane, A. (2009), 'Rethinking the Financial Network'. Speech delivered at the Financial Student Association, Amsterdam, April and Gauthier, C., A. Lehar and M. Souissi (2010), 'Macroprudential regulation and systemic capital requirements', mimeo, Bank of Canada. Linking systemic risk to dependencies between institutions is gaining greater prominence as methods for systemic-stress testing grow in sophistication.
9. System insolvency relates to the probability that all gains from financial trading will evaporate, which seems highly unlikely. System illiquidity relates to the probability that system participants cannot acquire sufficient means of payment (i.e., fiat money) to settle obligations, or, in a market context, that participants cannot sell assets at prices

close to their fundamental value. There is no obvious reason for the probability of these events to be small.

10. These numbers are taken from Hellwig, M. (2008), 'Systemic Risk in the Financial Sector: An Analysis of the Subprime-Mortgage Financial Crisis', Max-Planck Institute for Research on Collective Goods, Preprints, 2008/43, November 2008, who also makes this point.
11. There are many other ways to generate systemic events. For example, liquidity spirals as in Brunnermeier, M. K. and L. H. Pedersen (2009), 'Market Liquidity and Funding Liquidity'. *Review of Financial Studies* 22 (6): 2201–38; contagion as in Frank, A. and D. Gale (2000), 'Financial Contagion'. *Journal of Political Economy* 108: 1–33; bank runs as in Diamond (2007), 'Banks, Runs and Liquidity Creation', Working Paper, University of Chicago GSB, January 2007, revised August 2007; or a run on repo markets as in Gorton, G. B. and A. Metrick (2009), 'Securitised Banking and the Run on Repo'. NBER Working Paper No. 15223.
12. This reference to markets is not limited to organized or wholesale market places such as exchanges or government bond auctions where financial institutions go to trade products among themselves. It also includes storefront or retail market places where not only banks or brokerage houses but also financial institutions interact with individuals and non-financial institutions. The reference to markets is generic and includes all manners by which the trading of financial products is organized.
13. For example, part of the mandate of OSFI (the Office of the Superintendent of Financial Institutions in Canada) is to '[s]upervise institutions and pension plans to determine whether they are in sound financial condition and meeting minimum plan funding requirements respectively, and are complying with their governing law and supervisory requirements'.
14. Basel Committee on Banking Supervision (2000), 'Best Practices for Credit Risk Disclosure', Basel, September.
15. Committee on the Global Financial System (2010), 'The role of margin requirements and haircuts in procyclicality', CGFS publication No 36. BIS, Basel, March.
16. See, for example, Heider, F., M. Hoerova, and C. Holthausen (2009), 'Liquidity Hoarding and Interbank Market Spreads, The Role of Counterparty Risk', Working Paper Series No 1126, December, European Central Bank.
17. Haldane, A. (2009), 'Rethinking the Financial Network', Speech delivered at the Financial Student Association, Amsterdam, April.
18. Bank of England (2009), 'The role of macroprudential policy', A Discussion Paper, November.
19. Gauthier, C., A. Lehar and M. Souissi (2010), 'Macroprudential regulation and systemic capital requirements', mimeo, Bank of Canada.
20. See, for example, Northcott and Zelmer (2009), 'Liquidity Standards in a Macroprudential Context', Financial System Review, Bank of Canada, December.
21. Fontaine, Selody, and Wilkins (2009), 'Improving the Resilience of Core Funding Markets', Financial System Review, Bank of Canada, December.
22. Milne (2009), 'The Complexities of Financial Risk Management and Systemic Risk', Bank of Canada Review, Summer.
23. See, for example, Basel Committee on Banking Supervision (2000), 'Principles for the Management of Credit Risk', Basel, September 2000. Also note that part of the mandate of OSFI, the supervisor of federally regulated financial institutions in Canada, is to '[a]dvance and administer a regulatory framework that promotes the adoption of policies and procedures designed to control and manage risk.'
24. Abstract from Committee on the Global Financial System (2010), 'The functioning and resilience of cross-border funding markets', CGFS Papers no 37. Report submitted by a joint CGFS/MC Study Group, March, BIS, Basel.
25. This question is addressed in Longworth (2010), 'Bank of Canada Liquidity Facilities: Past, Present, and Future', Remarks at the C. D. Howe Institute, Bank of Canada, 17 February 2010.

3. The government as guarantor of last resort: benefits, costs and the case for premium charges[1]

Sebastian Schich

3.1. INTRODUCTION

At the core of the policy apparatus for responding to financial crises is the financial system safety net. That safety net has traditionally been defined as comprising three major elements (or functions) – a lender-of-last-resort, deposit insurance, combined with a regulatory and supervisory framework.[2] The array of these three functions is performed by several institutions, typically involving the finance ministry, the central bank, a supervisory agency and a deposit insurance agency. The funding of the safety net is provided in a variety of ways by governments, central banks and fees from regulated firms.

Banks will fail and due to the particular nature of their liabilities special resolution regimes are often necessary. In several cases resolution of a problem bank is undertaken by deposit protection agencies under special legislative authorities. Where such regimes exist, it has been shown that involvement of the deposit insurer tends to damp the negative (moral hazard) effect that deposit insurance has on banks' risk taking.[3] Thus, subsuming special bank failure resolution regimes under the deposit insurance function could be justified on the grounds of institutional considerations. In any case, bank failure resolution issues are not part of the focus of the present chapter, although it is noted here that the recent crisis has highlighted once again that the lack of the availability of special resolution tools that allow authorities to wind down failing institutions in a rapid and orderly fashion gives rise to additional costs in a systemic crisis.

Governments have a choice in the kind of support that they can provide to deposit-taking institutions. The primary rationale for governments in adopting an explicit guarantee is to promote stability in the financial sector. Experience shows that depositor and creditor confidence can

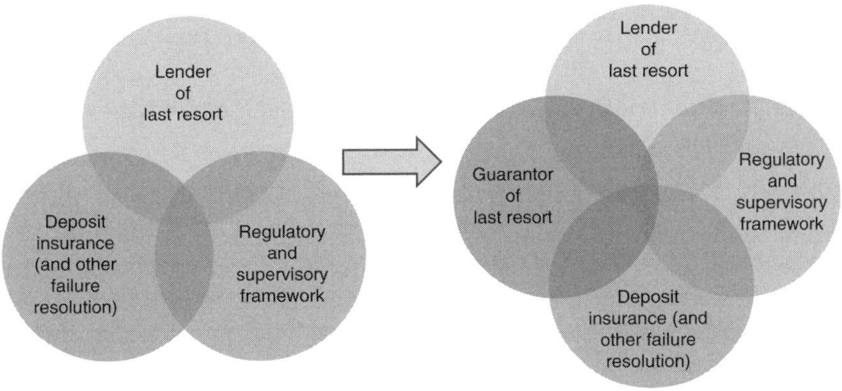

Figure 3.1. From traditional to new definition of the financial safety net

erode quickly and this may have a severe effect even on relatively healthy institutions. To maintain confidence, depositors and creditors require immediate and widespread government assurance of the safety and availability of their deposits and claims.[4] In a financial crisis governments may raise coverage levels to very high levels and may even adopt explicit blanket guarantees in the belief that such measures will provide the authorities with the time and opportunity to restructure problem banks, thereby avoiding the need to deal with closure decisions. This chapter focuses on measures that were taken by many governments to transform implicit guarantees covering bank deposits into explicit and sometimes blanket guarantees thereby effectively enlarging the financial system safety net – the creation of an explicit guarantor of last resort (Figure 3.1). A distinguishing feature of the response to the recent crisis, this chapter argues, has been an enlargement of the safety net and those steps have resulted in costs in the forms of distortions to competition and incentives (an increase in moral hazard).

There is considerable doubt as to whether the enlargement of the safety net can ever be fully transitioned to a more limited scope. Certainly, the development of a credible and effective resolution regime to close problem banks is a helpful step forward. The key point of this chapter is that while explicit guarantees have been provided, the beneficiary institutions have yet to be charged adequate premiums in exchange.

This chapter begins with an overview of policy actions directly targeting several parts of the balance sheets of banks taken in response to the accelerated flight-to-safety occurring after mid- 2008 (Section 3.2). It then looks at the costs and benefits of guarantees in Section 3.3 and examines premium setting issues in Section 3.4, before concluding (Section 3.5).

3.2. POLICY ACTIONS TARGETING DIRECTLY PARTS OF BANKS' BALANCE SHEETS

3.2.1. Central Banks Have Effectively Guaranteed Parts of Banks' Balance Sheets

Central banks, in their role of lender-of-last-resort, typically feature prominently in crisis response efforts, through various tools for supplying central bank money to financial institutions (and markets). This crisis has been no exception in that regard. Central banks injected liquidity over and beyond what would be needed by the banking system under normal circumstances; the injection was accomplished by adding to regular allotments ad hoc fine-tuning operations and supplementary longer-term refinancing operations. In the process, central banks broadened the range of eligible collateral to include some securities with more significant credit risks, and they also directly purchased asset-backed securities. As a result of the various actions, the balance sheets of several major central banks expanded considerably compared to pre-crisis sizes. For example, assets of the European Central Bank at end-2009 exceeded 150 per cent of pre-crisis levels, while those of the US Federal Reserve and the Bank of England tripled over that period (compared to mid-2007 and measured in per cent of the respective regions' GDP).

Moreover, and more importantly, in the context of the focus of this chapter, a number of central banks announced their willingness to lend as needed, thus allaying any concerns about funding liquidity. To the extent that these promises were credible, by making such promises, central banks have in effect become 'guarantors' of some parts of banks' balance sheets.

3.2.2. Government-provided Guarantees Have Targeted Banks' Liabilities and Some Assets

In addition to central bank actions, governments have directly targeted other parts of financial institutions' balance sheets (as shown in the form of a stylized balance sheet in Figure 3.2). Among the most common measures, explicit retail deposit insurance has been introduced where it had not existed and in many cases where it had existed its coverage was significantly expanded (column right in the middle). Also, government-supported guarantees have been extended, among other things, to other types of bank liabilities such as unsecured bond issues (second most-right column). Governments in a few countries, including the Netherlands, the US and the UK, have also adopted measures for guaranteeing (or removing) assets held on bank balance sheets.

Policy measures focusing directly on bank balance sheets

	Assets		Liabilities and capital		
	Guarantee of assets	Purchase of assets	Introduce or expand retails deposit insurance	Guarantee wholesale debt	Inject capital
Australia			◆	◆	
Canada				◇	
France	(◆)			◆	◆
Germany	◆	◆	◆	◆	◆
Italy				◇	◆
Japan		◆			◆
Netherlands	(◆)		◆	◆	◆
Spain		◆	◆	◆	◆
Switzerland		◆	◆		(◆)
United Kingdom	◆		◆	◆	◆
United States	(◆)	◆	◆	◆	◆

Notes:
◆ Policy measure taken.
(◆) Standalone actions.
◇ Announced, but not in use.
Canada and the United Kingdom have offered specific asset purchase facilities that are not restricted to banks (which is why they are not accounted for in the table above, which lists actions directly targeting banks).

Source: Author's estimates based in parts on Panetta, F., T. Faeh, G. Grande, C. Ho, M. King, A. Levy, F.M. Signoretti, M. Taboga, and A. Zaghini (2009), 'An Assessment of Financial Sector Rescue Programmes', BIS Paper No. 48, July (available at http://www.bis.org/publ/bppdf/bispap48.htm) and Schich, S. (2009), 'Expanded Guarantees for Banks: Benefits, Costs and Exit Issues', OECD Financial Market Trends Vol. 2009/2, November 2009 (available at http://www.oecd.org/dataoecd/53/48/44260489.pdf).

Figure 3.2. Overview of policy measures taken in selected OECD countries

The total amount of pledged public support was massive, accounting in 'advanced' G-20 countries to more than 17 per cent of these countries' GDP, with guarantees alone amounting to the equivalent of 11 per cent, according to estimates by the IMF. Much of this pledged support was not used, however. Focusing on support actually used, guarantees again dominate the total headline support provided to banking sectors in many G-20 countries (Figure 3.3). This figure even underestimates the role of guarantees as part of support measures put in place, as it does not account for government-supported changes in retail deposit insurance arrangements.

As regards deposit insurance arrangements, coverage ceilings per bank and per person insured were raised in many jurisdictions. For example, these ceilings were raised in all but eight of the 33 jurisdictions participating in the OECD's *Committee on Financial Markets.* Most remarkable, in the case of nine of the 33 participating jurisdictions, blanket guarantees were extended. These cases are shown here by the fine black bars that go all the way across to the ceiling of Figure 3.4.[5]

3.3. COSTS AND BENEFITS OF GUARANTEES

3.3.1. Benefits of Expanded Government-provided Guarantees

There is widespread agreement among policymakers that the expansion of guarantees has been helpful. For example, discussions at the OECD's Committee on Financial Markets meeting in April 2009 concluded that the various guarantees for banks, especially of their liabilities, together with other policy measures, have succeeded in preventing the feared seizing-up of the financial system.[6]

Compared to other policy measures, upfront fiscal costs associated with guarantees were limited. Unlike bank capital injections or asset purchases, guarantees do not require the immediate outlay of cash and, if the guarantees expire without having been triggered, cash may never be needed. Actually, it turned out that this situation essentially describes the recent experience with guarantees: Payments under the guarantees were rarely triggered and, as a general rule, even substantial additional fee income was generated by the government, especially from newly introduced guarantees, which in most cases consisted of guarantees on wholesale liabilities and assets (see Table 3.1 for the example of the US).

3.3.2. Costs of Expanded Government-provided Guarantees

But even if guarantees do not generate significant upfront fiscal costs, they create large contingent fiscal liabilities, along with other potential costs such as distortions to competition and incentives.

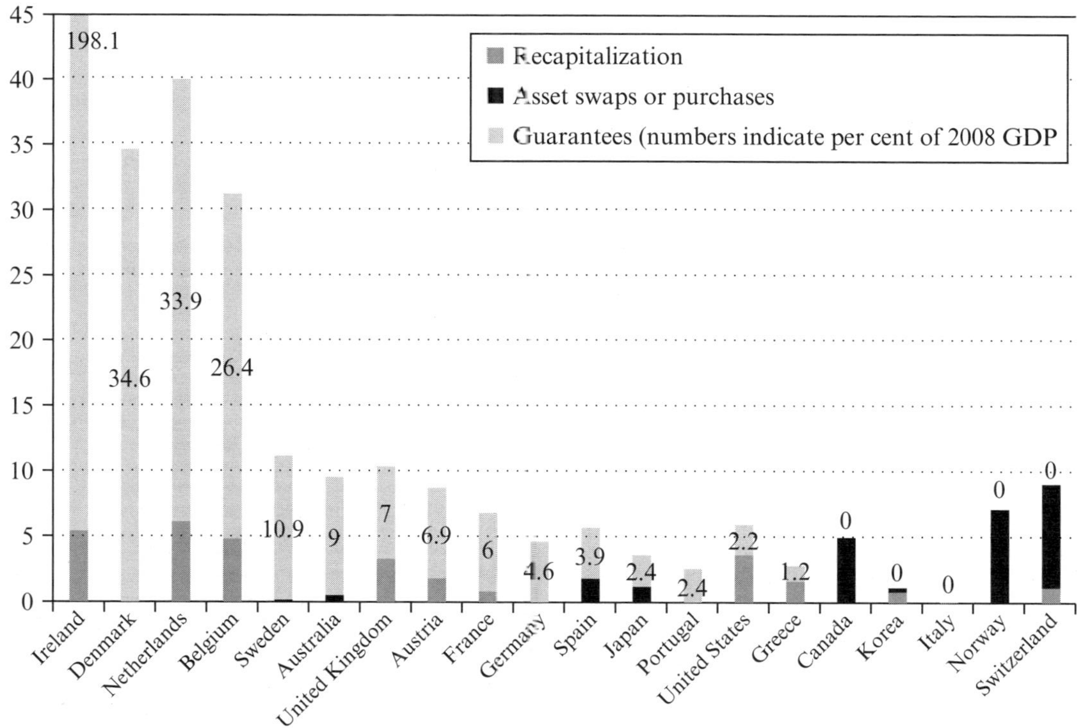

Note: As of August 2009. Excluding deposit insurance provided by deposit insurance agencies. Announced amounts in the cases of Denmark and Ireland. In Switzerland, the Swiss National Bank bought the equivalent of USD 40 billion (initially announced were USD 60 billion) of assets from UBS, or the equivalent of 8 per cent of the country's GDP. In Italy, recapitalization amounts to 0.1 per cent and guarantees used to 0 per cent of 2008 GDP.

Source: IMF (2010), 'Exiting from Crisis Intervention Policies', Prepared by the Fiscal Affairs, Monetary and Capital Markets, and Research Departments, Approved by Olivier J. Blanchard, Carlo Cottarelli, and José Viñals, 4 February, except for Switzerland.

Figure 3.3. Financial sector support (actual use in per cent of 2008 GDP)

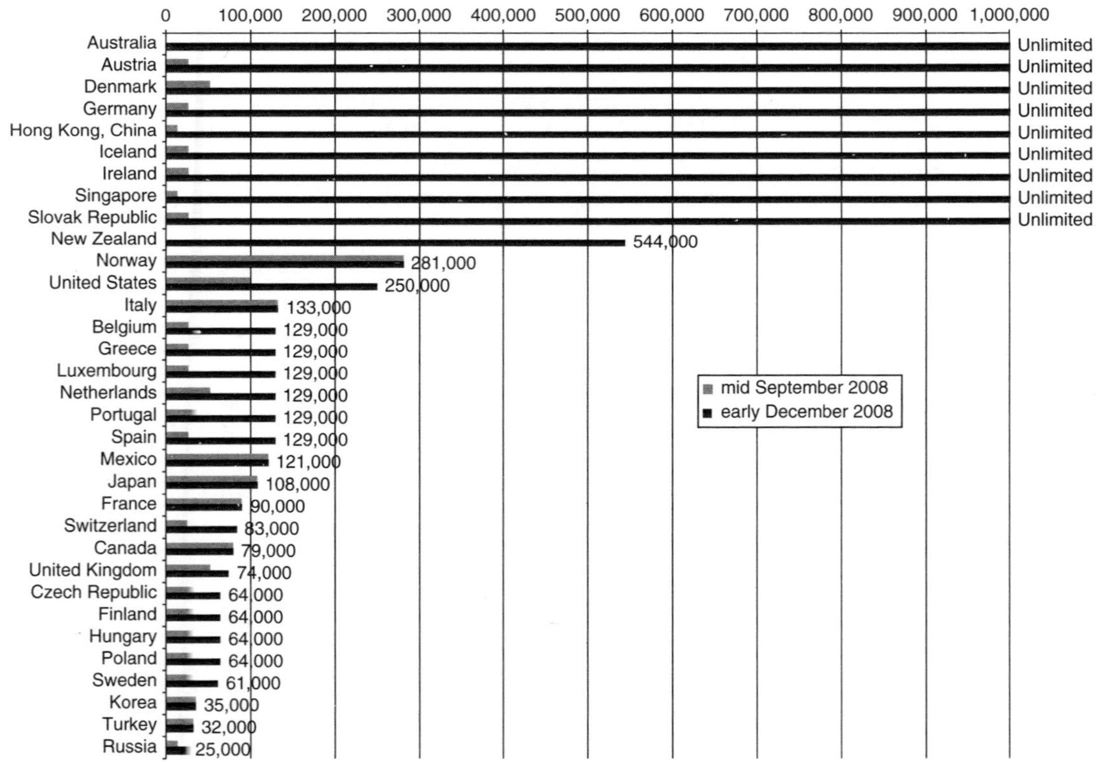

Source: Schich, S. (2009), 'Challenges Associated with the Expansion of Deposit Insurance Coverage during Fall 2008', Economics, The Open Access, Open-Assessment Journal, Vol. 3, 2009–20, 25 May, http://www.economics-ejournal.org/economics/journalarticles/2009–20.

Figure 3.4. Change in deposit insurance coverage (coverage ceilings before and after Fall 2008)

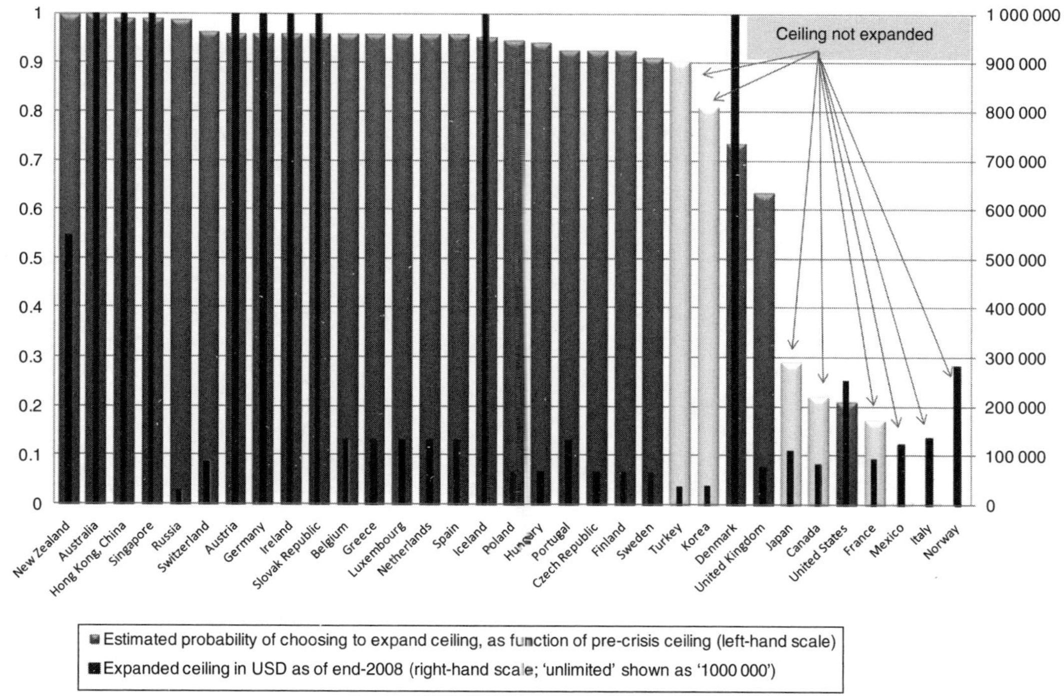

Note: Deposit insurance limits as of December 2008, in USD, indicated by thin bars (for data source see Figure 3.4). Authors' estimates of probabilities of extension of deposit insurance coverage levels ('Yes' or 'No') based on simple probit regression on pre-crisis ceiling levels, indicated by thick bars. Dark thick bars indicate 'Yes' (that is, coverage limits were subsequently expanded) and light thick bars 'No' (that is, coverage limits remained unchanged).

Figure 3.5. *Expanded deposit insurance coverage and likelihood of choice to expand (expanded ceiling and likelihood of increase as function of pre-crisis level)*

Table 3.1. Fees earned and losses incurred under selected guarantee programmes in the US

Agency	Programme	Authority	Who was protected?	What was guaranteed?	Sum guaranteed	Fees earned	Losses
Treasury	Asset Guarantee Program (AGP)	*Emergency Economic Stabilisation Act of 2008* (EESA)	Citigroup (programme terminated) (Bank of America – never used)	Specified asset classes of Citigroup	Up to USD 5 billion	USD 3.8 billion	0
Treasury	Temporary Guarantee Program for Money Market Funds	*Gold Reserve Act of 1934*, as amended EESA, § 131	Money market fund investors	Investors' holdings in participating funds as of 19 September 2008	0, as of Oct 2009 (USD 3.22 trillion peak commitment)	USD 1.2 billion	0
Federal Reserve Board	Asset Guarantee Program (AGP)	*Federal Reserve Act of 1913*, § 13(3)	Citigroup (Bank of America – never used)	Specified assets of Citigroup	Undetermined, non-recourse loans to be made available	USD 57 million	0
Federal Deposit Insurance Corporation (FDIC)	Temporary Liquidity Guarantee Program (TLGP) – including Debt Guarantee Program (DGP)	*Federal Deposit Insurance Act of 1991*	Holders of debt issued by banks	Debt issued by banks and other financial institutions	USD 307 billion principal, plus interest	USD 10.4 billion[1]	0[2]

FDIC	Asset Guarantee Program (AGP)	*Federal Deposit Insurance Act of 1991*	Citigroup (Bank of America – never used)	Specified assets of Citigroup	Up to USD 10 billion	USD 2.7 billion	0

Notes:

1 Fees earned are the total of fees assessed and surcharges.

2 According to the Federal Deposit Insurance Corporation, as of 22 October 2009, there has been one failure of a Temporary Liquidity Guarantee Program-participating institution, an affiliate of which had issued guaranteed debt. While the FDIC anticipated up to a $2 million loss on that issuance, no losses had been paid out at that point in time with respect to that program.[7]

Source: Congressional Oversight Panel (2009) and FDIC.

- There has been a significant widening of sovereign bond spreads in many EU area countries versus German Bunds since autumn 2008, especially since the beginning of 2010. It appears that country-specific fiscal (and external) positions and, in particular the outlook for them, have contributed to the observed widening of sovereign bond and CDS spreads.[8] This development may reflect, at least to some extent, that the expansion of safety nets has resulted in a part of banking sector risk being transformed into sovereign risk. The significance of such a relationship was suggested earlier, for example, by the experience of Ireland. The announcement by the government of its comprehensive guarantee for the liabilities of six domestic banks (covering about EUR 400 billion or about twice the country's annual GDP) on 30 September 2008 was immediately followed by a jump in the CDS on the government bonds from 27 to 60 basis points, while those on bank bonds fell significantly.
- The guarantees will have an influence on competition between entities and instruments benefiting from the guarantees and those that do not. For example, as regards fixed-income bonds, the issuance of bonds backed by guarantees from some highly-rated governments has also had profound effects on the demand for and pricing of investment alternatives, including in particular relatively close substitutes for those guaranteed bonds, such as bonds issued by some lower-rated sovereigns (such as Greece and Ireland) or supra-nationals (such as e.g. the EIB) or other financial intermediaries. Also, within the banking sector, the support measures were geared towards systemically important banks, which tend to be, almost by definition, rather large banks (typically those considered as 'too-large-to-fail' or 'too-large-to-close'). The latter tend to rely more heavily on funding through bond issuance than small banks do and, thus, benefit disproportionately from the availability of government-provided bond guarantees. Furthermore, given that the extent and costs of additional insurance coverage provided under temporarily expanded government support for deposit insurance arrangements and other types of government-supported guarantees have differed across borders, the playing field between internationally competing large banks from different countries might be affected. In particular, there is a risk that some policymakers put in place extensive support measures that are available at low costs to domestic institutions, thus providing them with a competitive advantage as compared to their international peers. Finally, differences in the costs charged for, and the quality of, the government-supported guarantees will have an influence on

competition between beneficiary institutions (an issue that will be discussed further below).

- Last, but certainly not least, like any insurance contract, the provision of such coverage for banks gives rise to moral hazard. Moral hazard is not just a conceptual notion but a real issue that should not be ignored, even in the midst of a crisis. Authorities should not lose sight of the fundamental policy goal of supporting efficiently operating financial markets. In this context, to allow market discipline to play a role and to limit moral hazard, measures need to be taken that either help avoid the perception on the part of potential beneficiaries of guarantees that similar ones will always be available or, if such an option is unavailable, an appropriate premium needs to be charged (an issue that will be discussed in Section 3.4).

3.3.3. Premium Setting Approaches in Practice

Ideally, to limit the various types of distortions discussed above, risk-based premiums need to be specified. Moreover, premium adjustments for the government-provided guarantees would have to be *consistent* across borders, which is particularly difficult to achieve. Efforts to harmonize premium setting approaches across borders have been significant, especially in the European Union. That said, policy decisions had to be taken with short delays. And indeed, the results as regards international consistency of practices have been mixed in actual practice, with the track record differing depending on the specific type of guarantee. In this regard, three types of guarantees are distinguished.

- First, asset loss guarantees have involved *risk-based* charges as a general rule. They have addressed problems at individual (and potentially systemic important) institutions and, despite efforts to use similar broad structures for different institutions (at least on the national level), details such as loss repartition structures and participation in upside risks have actually differed from one instance to another.
- Second, in the case of retail deposit insurance, typically *no extra fees were levied* for the extra government-supported insurance provided (including cases where unlimited retail deposit coverage was announced). There are, nonetheless, exceptions. They include Australia,[9] where a fee is charged for the coverage of retail deposits beyond AUD 1 million per depositor and per bank. This fee is determined in a similar way to the fee charged for government-provided

insurance for wholesale debt. Also, extra government-supported insurance was provided, the expansions of coverage levels were little co-ordinated across borders. Several announcements of coverage increases made explicit reference to other countries' actions, explaining their own efforts as attempts to ensure a level-playing field for domestic banks.

- Third, the pricing of guarantees of bank bonds has tended to be risk-based. In this context, an effort has been made to harmonize fee structures across borders, making fees for the government support depend closely on the respective issuer's credit default swap price or credit rating history. Typically, the fees were specified as a function of some risk measure of the issuer, for example, the issuer's current credit rating in the case of Australia or its record of historical credit default swap premiums in the case of European countries. In the EU, costs for the bank bond guarantee schemes have converged towards a flat fee of 50 basis points plus the issuer's median five year CDS spread between 1 January 2007 and 31 August 2008 for issues with more than one year maturity. The reference period was different in the UK, however, as it started on 2 July 2007 and ended on 1 July 2008. As for the US, fees were charged as a function of the maturity of the instrument to be issued. Despite these differences in the fee-setting structures across borders, the actual fees charged have nonetheless tended to be similar on average. In Europe, a deliberate effort was undertaken to harmonize fee structures, with the same function being used in many countries to map from the banks' CDS history (which was used as a proxy measure of the entities' riskiness) to the guarantee fee charged. The question is, however, whether such harmonization is desirable to avoid competitive distortions?

3.3.4. Should Fee Structures be Identical Across Borders?

A common fee structure across countries as defined above – that is one that differentiates premiums only as a function of the estimated risk profile of the bank but ignores the credit quality of the guarantor itself – is not necessarily the best approach under all circumstances, however. Actually, it would ensure a level playing field for internationally competing banks if – and only if – the quality of the sovereign guarantee were the same across countries. In practice, however, sovereign credit ratings differ between countries and a sovereign guarantee is worth more the better is the credit rating of the sovereign in question. And it turns out that the total costs, that is the sum of guarantee fees and issuance spreads, has been lower for some weak banks from strong countries than for some strong banks from weak countries.[10]

Thus, the aim of co-ordinated policies should not be to achieve similarity of fees across borders, but to achieve consistency of fees. Adjusting fees for the risk profile of banks has long been recognized to be of key importance to avoid distortions, given that differential premiums can reduce cross-subsidization among institutions enjoying the guarantee. But a focus on the risk profile of the bank alone in fee setting does not rule out that additional distortions are created by the fact that the quality of the guarantee provided depends on the identity (and, hence, credit quality) of the sovereign. Thus, for example, co-ordinated policies could aim at undoing all or parts of the advantage enjoyed by issuers with 'strong' sovereigns; in fact, higher-rated sovereigns would need to be allowed (or even encouraged) to charge higher fees for their guarantees – for a given bank risk profile – so as to level the playing field between banks with similar risk profiles in different countries.

Another complication arises because the quality of a sovereign guarantee is not constant over time. It might actually vary – among other things – as a result of the expansion of the national safety net and the actual and contingent liabilities created in this context. An interesting observation in this context is as follows: '. . . there is one key difference between the situation today and that in the Middle Ages. Then, the biggest risk to the banks was from the sovereign. Today, perhaps the biggest risk to the sovereign comes from the banks. Causality has reversed.'[11]

This idea is illustrated in Figure 3.6. That figure shows the changes in the CDS of the Top-3 banks on the vertical axis and the changes of the CDS of their respective governments on the horizontal axis. It shows that there are indeed some cases in which the CDS of banks have improved while the CDS of their respective home governments have deteriorated since the peak of the crisis. These cases are contained in the bottom-right quadrant. While these observations cannot be taken as evidence of causality, a more important point to retain from this figure is that sovereign credit ratings are neither identical nor constant over time. The quality of government-provided guarantees differs depending on the government in question and the point in time when it is assessed; guarantees from 'strong' sovereigns are more valuable than those from 'weak' sovereigns, especially when the latter are considered to be (further) 'weakening'.

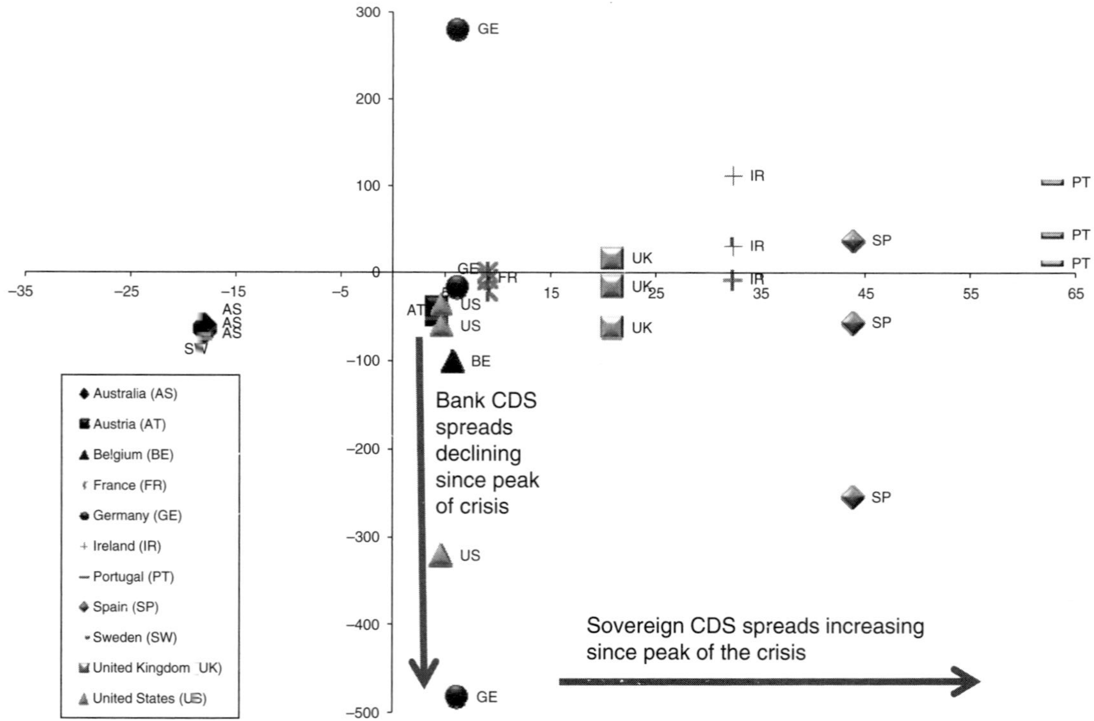

Notes: Average CDS spreads during (six weeks in) February and March 2010 minus average CDS premiums during (six weeks in) October and November 2008 for Top-3 banks by total assets in each country and the respective sovereign.

Source: Author's calculations based on data from *Thomson Reuters Datastream.*

Figure 3.6. Changes in CDS spreads for bank and sovereign from same country (Spring 2010 compared to Fall 2008)

3.4. PREMIUM SETTING ISSUES

3.4.1. Regulation does not Eliminate the Risk of a Systemic Crisis

The financial sector provides intermediation services that involve risk-taking, and the sector is regulated to ensure that risk-taking does not become excessive. Yet, regulation cannot and should not even attempt to completely eliminate the possibility that risk positions are built up and that the materialization of risks results in a financial crisis. Such an effort would require eliminating all significant risk-taking on the part of financial institutions, which would hence deprive them of their core function. As a result, there would be significant adverse implications for real economic activity. What regulation and other policy measures (such as e.g. taxation) should achieve, however, is that the rewards for the provision of financial services to support real economic activity reflect the true extent of the risks involved, including that of the failure of the (financial) system. As has been discussed in the previous sections, the recent financial crisis adds to the lists of examples where systemic failures have triggered the government provision of the financial safety net. What is particularly notable is that financial safety nets in many countries were, in effect, expanded to include the government-provided guarantor-of-last-resort function. This function, which had been present in implicit form prior to the crisis, has become part in more explicit form of the financial safety net. While this addition to the safety net has been helpful in avoiding extremely negative outcomes, it has been provided in an ad hoc fashion and has come with significant additional costs. So far, adequate premiums have not been charged in exchange.

3.4.2. The Guarantor-of-last-resort Function De Facto has Become Part of the Safety Net in a Systemic Crisis

As the crisis has abated, several of the guarantee programmes have expired. But it is questionable whether the guarantor-of-last-resort function can ever be fully withdrawn. Actually, as pointed out before,[12] once a government has ventured down the road of providing extensive guarantees in one specific systemic crisis, it may foster the expectation that similar guarantees will always be made available in similar situations for those institutions that are considered to be systemically important because of their size, interconnectedness or nature of services provided.

In theory, one straightforward way to address this issue is to let one or several systemically important institutions fail in a crisis situation, so as to set a precedent. In practice, that option does not seem to be (yet) available.

One reason is that many governments do not have the tools available to wind down failing institutions in a rapid and orderly fashion. In some countries, such tools had been available, but the scope of the existing arrangements and their funding turned out to be inadequate to effectively deal with the size of the shock recently observed.[13] Thus, in those situations, the choices available narrow to either one of two options. Either let a potentially systemically important institution fail and bear the associated costs or, alternatively, provide public support to keep the institution open.

The first choice tends to be unattractive in practice because of the high costs associated with it. In part, costs are so high because the public and market participants do not expect authorities to make that choice, and act on those beliefs. Disappointing these expectations maybe, they create additional costs. The example of Lehman Brothers, which was denied support on the same conditions as previously granted to Bear Stearns, is a reminder of the potential costs that could arise when such expectations are first created through one bail-out, but then not fulfilled when the triggering event occurs in yet another case. To what extent current efforts to strengthen resolution mechanisms for such situations will be successful is still uncertain at the current juncture. Thus, in practice, the choice for policymakers may narrow even further to just the second choice, thus confirming the prior suspicion of the public and market participants that systemically important institutions are indeed 'too-big-to-fail'.

In short, there is a clear time-inconsistency problem in a systemic crisis. *Ex ante*, policymakers (including regulators) would like to commit to not providing a guarantor-of-last-resort function. Such course of action would not encourage banks to underestimate the costs of extreme negative outcomes. However, this strategy is not optimal *ex post*, and hence systemically important banks can expect the government to renege on that commitment, making it not credible to begin with.

Thus, unless effective and credible resolution mechanisms are available under all circumstances, the guarantor-of-last-resort function may de facto have become part of the financial safety net (at least in situations of severe systemic crises). And some commentators would argue that resolution of a crisis of such a large magnitude might have required the addition of that guarantor role. For example, according to some commentators, while the government has acted as an insurer of last resort in this crisis, this function has been adopted in a rather ad hoc fashion and needs to be further formalized.[14] One specific recommendation in this context is that public authorities issue tradeable options on public insurance provision. While the potential moral hazard issues of such a solution still would need to be carefully addressed, it could be argued that it would not generate any additional moral hazard risk to the extent that the guarantee provided formalizes an implicit guarantee that is perceived to be available. As argued before, the government has already revealed itself as a guarantor of last resort for banks; thus beneficiary institutions need to pay an appropriate premium in exchange. The question is how?

3.4.3. Current Regulatory Proposals Consist of Effectively Imposing Surcharges on Banking Activities

The introduction of any new function raises a host of other issues, including the appropriatedness of the design of the other safety net elements. The safety net is a combination of institutions and rules and there is a certain internal logic and consistency in the structure as traditionally defined. The new structure is not yet well defined, however, and the addition of a new function raises a number of issues. For example, where there is overlap between different safety net functions (as illustrated in Figure 3.1), design aspects of the other elements may also need to be adjusted. Indeed, in response to the recent financial crisis, many aspects of the current regulatory and supervisory framework are being subjected to fundamental reviews with a view to enhancing the stability of the financial system over the long term and reducing the likelihood of any costs associated with systemic financial crises. These efforts need to take into account the observation that the guarantor-of-last-resort function has now become part of the safety net in a more explicit form.

Proposals to reduce the costs of systemic crises attempt to do so either by mitigating the risks of systemic crises or reducing the costs of resolving them, and most of them fall into one or more of the following categories:

- Strengthen self-insurance (e.g. requiring larger and better-quality capital and liquidity buffers; requiring or encouraging use of contingent convertible capital or private capital insurance; tradeable public insurance options).
- Limit risk-taking (e.g. specifying the range of permissible activities or limiting the extent of certain activities; setting leverage ratios; encouraging specific corporate structures that avoid cross-subsidization).
- Charging specific systemic risk levies to fund future crisis resolution and to discourage behaviour that might contribute to this risk (by specifying levies in a way that the institutions contributing to that risk more fully internalize the associated costs).
- Strengthen and complement existing failure resolution mechanisms (e.g. deposit insurance arrangements including failure resolution mechanisms; setting up separate resolution fund for systemic crises).

These different policy proposals and approaches may appear quite diverse; but they may be more unified than is being suggested. Effectively, many of these proposals consist of imposing surcharges on banking activities. They could thus be interpreted as premiums levied in exchange for the guarantor-of-last-resort function.

The different proposals reflect the attempts on the part of authorities to reduce the likelihood of such a situation arising again as well as to limit the costs associated with it. They are part of a wide spectrum of reforms, including those with a micro-prudential and system-wide perspective. These reforms are complemented by additional reforms such as the introduction of system-wide oversight arrangements, strengthened transparency and disclosure, and improvements to market infrastructures. These various measures are to a large extent related to each other and they are complementary; they therefore need to be considered jointly. That said, some proposals are more closely related to charging a form of 'premium' in exchange for the publicly provided guarantor-of-last-resort function than others. Perhaps the idea of charging a systemic risk levy is conceptionally closest to the idea of charging a premium for the guarantor-of-last-resort function.

3.4.4. Systemic Risk Levies as the Quid-Pro-Quo for the Guarantor-of-last-resort Function?

The recent financial crisis has implied the addition of the guarantor-of-last-resort function to the financial safety net, but it is clear that existing tools in many jurisdictions were inadequate to finance resolution of a severe systemic crisis. As mentioned before, regulatory measures will never eliminate all risk of systemic financial instability and there will always be a perception that public authorities will step in as the guarantor-of-last-resort. While the upfront costs associated with that function may be much more limited than in the case of other support measures, the provision of that function comes at a cost that in many cases has to be met by revenue-raising measures. These measures can either be integral to general revenue raising or dedicated to a separate systemic risk resolution fund. They can be applied in advance (*ex ante*) or after a crisis has occurred (*ex post*). And they can be designed either to share the burden widely among taxpayers or to target it more specifically to the financial sector. Whatever the specific solutions, some mechanism for funding the new function is needed.

If the levies are paid by those banks that have benefited from government insurance during the crisis, these taxes can be considered to be a form of *ex post* premium paid for that insurance.[15] The financial crisis responsibility fee proposed in the US could be interpreted as an example of such a type of levy. It is explicitly meant to help ensure a fair burden-sharing between financial institutions (which have enjoyed large profits before the crisis as well as government-provided support during this crisis) on the one hand and the taxpayers on the other.

A key problem with collecting funds after the crisis has happened, however, is that the burden of payment falls on the survivors, a group that will typically include sound and well-managed banks, rather than on the entities that most likely precipitated the crisis. *Ex post* funding measures that do not distinguish entities that most likely precipitated the crisis from those that did not are problematic, as such measures tend to penalize soundly managed banks that survived the crisis. For example, relying just on variables such as profits or balance sheet size as tax bases does not allow one to distinguish between banks that contributed to the crisis and those that did not. On the contrary, taxing current profits or balance sheet growth might penalize those sound and well-managed banks that have survived the crisis without major casualties and are now, as a result especially of their cautious policies adopted before the crisis, in a better position than their less cautious competitors to expand their profit and market shares.

To the extent that the proceeds of the specific levies are used for funding a reserve to be available for interventions in future (systemic) crises, they can be conceived of as *ex ante* premiums for future crisis resolution. The frameworks recently announced in Germany and implemented in Sweden may be examples.[16] The purpose of the adopted and proposed strategies involving *ex ante* funds is to finance measures needed in order to counteract the effect of systemic disturbance to the financial system, and these strategies are parts of a wider effort by governments to improve financial system regulation and supervision as well as financial crisis management by defining a framework for early intervention, resolution and insolvency.

All taxes are distortive of economic activity to some extent. In general, governments should (and do) seek to ensure that taxation measures are neutral, in the sense that taxation should not unnecessarily distort financial market decisions. However, there is a case for taxation measures to depart from neutrality in the case of clearly identified market failures. Systemic risk is a negative externality and a systemic risk tax could be levied on financial firms, which (because of their size, interconnectedness or nature of business) are potential sources of instability for the financial system. To the extent that this risk is not already fully internalized through regulation, a systemic risk levy could induce institutions to do so and, thus, could reduce systemic risk (see e.g. Weder di Mauro, B. (2010), *Taxing Systemic Risk: Proposal for a Systemic Risk Charge and a Systemic Risk Fund*, January 2010, available online at http: //www. international-macro. economics. Uni-Mainz.de/Is/ger/Deteier/Taxing Systemic Risk VZ.pdf), while at the same time raising revenues. How to assess that risk and how to reflect it in the tax is not straightforward, even though there is agreement that some key criteria are helpful in identifying the systemic importance of institutions (size, substitutability, and interconnectedness).[17]

Ex ante financed resolution funds are similar, to some extent, to existing deposit insurance schemes and they could potentially serve to fill a gap left unaddressed by such schemes in systemic crises. That gap arises because deposit insurance schemes are typically not designed to absorb shocks of the magnitude experienced recently.[18] Actual funding levels of most schemes are not such that they can deal with a situation of widespread failures of banks and/or the failures of one or more of the largest banks.

As in the case of existing deposit insurance arrangements, the issue of moral hazard still needs to be carefully considered, in particular, as the creation of any new form of a 'stability fund' might be seen as transforming what still might be perceived by some as an exceptional (insurance) response into an entitlement. The sheer existence of such a fund, if large enough to instil confidence and hence reduce the risk of small shocks spreading to become systemic issues, might also give rise to a false sense of security, thus increasing risk.[19] To address this risk, the parameters of the arrangements need to be designed in such a way that they reduce *ex ante* moral hazard risk, including by appropriately setting premiums and strengthening resolution powers. The focus of the arrangement needs to be on resolution rather than bail-out. If the frameworks are properly designed, the loss of ambiguity that comes from not making it clear whether the government will offer the guarantor-of-last-resort function or not could be more than offset by the improved resolution authority that the new arrangement creates.

3.5. CONCLUDING REMARKS

A key aspect of the policy response to this systemic crisis consisted of making available, in rather explicit form, the government-supported guarantor-of-last-resort function. While that function has always been there implicitly, it has now become a more or less explicit part of the financial safety net. Appropriate premiums – be they charged *ex post* for this crisis or *ex ante* for another crisis – have yet to be charged in exchange, however.

Appropriate 'premiums' to be paid by financial institutions in exchange for the availability of that function to them could consist of higher required capital or liquidity buffers or other surcharges on activities such as specific systemic risk levies; these surcharges should ensure a fairer distribution of risks and costs. Systemic risk is an externality, and the surcharges would be appropriate to the extent that they induce financial institutions to internalize more fully this externality. There is a case for charging institutions more the greater their systemic impact. If the surcharges do succeed in making financial institutions internalize the potential costs of a systemic crisis more fully, systemic risk will be reduced, and the guarantor-of-last-resort function can be expected to be invoked more rarely.

Finally, the provision of the guarantor-of-last-resort function raises another issue that needs to be addressed, namely, the potential for cross-border distortions to competition to arise when the quality of the guarantor differs. Under those circumstances, the fees charged for the provision of this function need to be adjusted in line with the quality of the sovereign for a given risk of the beneficiary bank to avoid situations in which lower quality institutions pay lower fees to borrow simply because of the higher quality of their sovereign guarantee provider.

NOTES

1. Parts of this chapter have been presented by the author to the OECD's Committee on Financial Markets in October 2010 and subsequently been included in an OECD publication (Schich, Sebastian and Kim, Byoung-Hwan, 'Systemic Financial Crises: How to Fund Resolution', *OECD Journal: Financial Markets Trend*, Vol. 2010, Issue 2 (December 2010)). The chapter has benefited from comments by John Raymond LaBrosse and Stephen Lumpkin, although the author remains solely responsible for any errors. The views expressed in this chapter do not necessarily reflect those of the OECD or any of its member countries.
2. Financial Stability Forum Working Group on Deposit Insurance, Bank for International Settlements, Basel, Switzerland, September 2001.
3. Beck, Thorsten and Luc Laeven (2006), 'Resolution of Failed Banks by Deposit Insurers – Cross-country evidence', World Bank Discussion Paper, March, available at http://siteresources.worldbank.org/DEC/Resources/Resolution_of_Failed_Banks_by_Deposit_Insurer.pdf .
4. See e.g. Financial Stability Forum Working Group on Deposit Insurance, June 2000.
5. As an aside, Figure 3.5 illustrates that the lower was the pre-crisis deposit guarantees, as measured in USD equivalents, the higher the likelihood of public authorities adopting the particular policy measure of raising that ceiling. In particular, the figure shows the estimated probabilities from a simple probit regression of the changes in retail deposit insurance ceilings during this crisis (that is, a 0/1 variable) on the levels of pre-crisis ceilings. It shows that the estimated probability is equal to one in the case of New Zealand and Australia, which did not have explicit deposit protection prior to the crisis. By contrast, in the cases of Norway, Italy, and Mexico, which tended to have rather high ceilings prior to the crisis, that probability is estimated to be equal to or close to zero.
6. Schich, S. (2009), 'Expanded Guarantees for Banks: Benefits, Costs and Exit Issues', OECD Financial Market Trends Vol. 2009/2, November 2009 (available at http://www.oecd.org/dataoecd/53/48/44260489.pdf).
7. Congressional Oversight Panel, NOVEMBER OVERSIGHT REPORT: Guarantees and Contingent Payments in TARP and Related Programs, 6 November 2009, and updates for the TLGP based on FDIC, Monthly Reports Related to the Temporary Liquidity Guarantee Program, March 2010.
8. Schuhknecht, Ludger, Jürgen von Hagen, and Guido Wolswijk (2010), 'Government

Bond Risk Premiums in the EU Revisited – The Impact of the Financial Crisis', ECB Working Paper No 1152, February.

9. Another example is Malaysia.
10. Levy and Schich (2010), 'The Design of Government Guarantees for Bank Bonds: Lessons from the Recent Financial Crisis', *OECD Financial Market Trends*, vol. 2010, issue 1.
11. Alessandri and Haldane (2009), 'Banking on the State', Bank of England, November.
12. Schich, S. (2009), 'Challenges Associated with the Expansion of Deposit Insurance Coverage during Fall 2008', Economics, The Open Access, Open-Assessment Journal, Vol. 3, 2009–20, 25 May, http://www.economics-ejournal.org/economics/journalarticles/2009–20.
13. Current regulatory changes in several jurisdictions will result in a widening of that scope.
14. See Caballero, R. and P. Kurlat (2009), 'The "Surprising" Origins and Nature of Financial Crises: A Macroeconomic Policy Proposal', Paper prepared for and presented at the Jackson Hole Symposium on Financial Stability and Macroeconomic Policy, 20 to 22 August.
15. A general problem with introducing any new taxes or extending existing taxes on any particular sector is the question of the real incidence of taxation. Although financial sector firms may be the immediate payers of the tax, it is uncertain whether this will ultimately be borne by the shareholders of the companies in that sector (as perhaps intended) or their customers.
16. For more details see Schich, S. and B.-H. Kim, (2010), 'Funding Systemic Crisis Resolution', *OECD Financial Market Trends*, Vol. 2010/2.
17. A set of principles to guide international work on a systemic risk tax has been suggested by HM Treasury (2010), Budget 2010 Documents, *Chapter 3: Reforming Financial Services*, 24 March; available at http://www.hm-treasury.gov.uk/budget2010_documents.htm, drawing on HM Treasury (2009), *Risk, Reward and Responsibility: the Financial Sector and Society*, December.
18. Thorat, U. (2010), 'Funding of deposit insurance systems', Keynote address by Mrs Usha Thorat, Deputy Governor of the Reserve Bank of India, at the International Conference organized by the Deposit Insurance and Credit Guarantee Corporation (DICGC) with the 8th Asia Regional Committee Meeting, Goa, 18 January.
19. HM Treasury (2009). See note 17.

4. The Troubled Asset Relief Program: has forbearance as far as the eye can see saved the US economy?[1]

Gillian G.H. Garcia

4.1. INTRODUCTION

As work began on this chapter, the Republicans had just won the 'Kennedy seat' in Massachusetts – a most democratic of states. How could this have happened? Health care reform; 'the economy, stupid!' including unemployment, the deficit, and the housing markets; wars; the cold weather; bankers' bonuses; Wall Street punishing Main Street; and disgust with politicians and regulators in Washington. Distrust of the Troubled Asset Relief Program (TARP) and its companion programs that were used to contain the financial crisis epitomize the reasons for 'the winter of our discontent.'[2]

There are two contrasting approaches to dealing with a financial crisis. The first is to expand the financial safety net so that it allows the authorities to forbear from taking punitive action against failing institutions. Under forbearance the regulators relax, or do not enforce, the existing safety-and-soundness rules. In particular, they relax capital requirements to allow weakened banks to continue operating, probably with subsidies, until they earn their way out of trouble. Forbearance was used to nurse the US's weakened major banks during the 1980s Latin American debt crisis. Congress enacted forbearance through phoney capital at the beginning of the 1980s S&L crisis, and the thrift regulators then, and more recently, practiced it to the extreme in their oversight of the banking system by not enforcing the existing laws and regulations.[3]

One problem with enlarging the safety net and conducting forbearance is that they do not discourage their recipients from taking excessive risks again in the future. Instead forbearance encourages risk taking – moral hazard.[4] A second problem is that the assistance that is given preferentially to weak banks makes it harder for their stronger competitors to succeed, with the result that the industry as a whole and the country are weakened. Third, creditors and counterparties in their actions do not take into account the risks that they create but whose costs they do not bear. As a result, banks use the wrong set of prices that do not reflect the risks they are taking when they choose their optimal strategies; they take on too much risk and the economy is destabilized. Fourth, forbearance can be costly and impose heavy losses on taxpayers – as Carmen Reinhart and Kenneth Rogoff point out, fiscal distress typically follows financial crisis.[5]

At the end of the 1980s, scandals over extraordinarily large losses incurred by thrifts that had been granted forbearance convinced the US Congress to adopt the second, alternative approach that requires insolvent banks and thrifts to be put into receivership promptly and be resolved by the Federal Deposit Insurance Corporation (FDIC) at least cost to the insurance fund. When the number of failed thrifts proved to be too large for the FDIC to handle at the end of the 1980s, they were sent to the temporary, specially created, Resolution Trust Corporation (RTC). Providing the RTC with only a temporary charter forced it to dispose of the assets it acquired from failed thrifts promptly, and not to try to retain them until their markets had fully recovered. Insolvent non-depository institutions, such as investment banks and insurance companies – even large ones like Drexel-Burnham-Lambert, went to the courts for resolution. The rationale is that dealing with insolvencies promptly allows the markets to: (1) reach the bottom without delay; (2) identify market-clearing prices to end uncertainty; and so (3) clear the decks for a speedy recovery. Accepting this rationale, Congress tried to inhibit forbearance in the prompt-corrective-action and least-cost provisions of the *1991 FDIC Improvement Act* (FDICIA).

More recently, the academic community has criticized Japan's handling of its problems and has argued that its exercise of forbearance and its reluctance to address its banks' problems led to two decades of no, or low, growth. But TARP and its companion programs show that the US has embraced forbearance as its response to the current crisis. And forbearance is currently not just for depository institutions but for nonbank financial institutions, auto manufacturers, and the housing markets. There is a double standard in forbearance for banks, however: for smaller banks and thrifts it is only temporary; FDIC receivership eventually catches up with small insolvent institutions.[6] There were, however, just too many large failing institutions in this crisis to close. So forbearance for larger institutions appears to be more permanent and is being enshrined in an enlarged safety net. It is carried out, for instance, by merging one large troubled bank into another slightly less troubled large bank so that the resulting entity is 'far too big to be allowed to fail.' Forbearance may become a permanent government response under financial sector reforms that have already been enacted in the UK and are proposed for the US. Initiated because of the multitude of large troubled institutions, forbearance may now become standard practice even if there is only one, isolated large problem bank.

The chapter begins with background on the recent crisis and the US government's responses prior to its panicked appeal to Congress for fiscal resources in the fall of 2008. We then analyse TARP and its implementation by the Bush and Obama administrations before we ask whether the program has succeeded so far in achieving the objectives expressed in its legislation. The final section offers some conclusions.[7]

4.2. THE FINANCIAL CRISIS BEFORE TARP

As explained elsewhere, the US mortgage markets began to experience problems in 2006 with sharply increasing foreclosure rates and signs of stress among subprime lenders.[8] The problems began to accelerate early in 2007 when HSBC wrote off USD10.6 billion in subprime loans in February. As the year progressed, subprime lenders increasingly filed for bankruptcy and two Bear-Stearns hedge funds collapsed during the summer. At the same time, the Federal Reserve remained confident that problems in the subprime markets could be contained without adversely affecting the rest of the economy. At first, the Fed underestimated the seriousness of the deterioration in the housing and finance markets and in the real economy. Chairman Bernanke, for example, told Congress on 28 March 2007 '[A]t this juncture . . . the impact on the broader economy and the financial markets of the problems in the subprime markets seems likely to be contained. But the housing slump could be worse than expected.'[9] Similarly, he said on 17 May 2007, 'The Fed does not foresee a broader economic impact from the growing number of mortgage defaults.'[10] Bernanke still did not appreciate the seriousness of events even by 18 July 2007 when he testified that the economy's growth would be moderate, but slowed by decreased construction activity.[11] The administration also projected confidence when President Bush opined on 9 August 2007, '[T]he fundamentals of our economy are strong . . . there is enough liquidity in the system to enable the markets to correct.'

Yet the financial markets were already experiencing problems and Jim 'Cramer's rant' famously complained in August 2007 that the Fed was ignoring the market's distress.[12] The Federal Home Loan Banks (FHLBs) were already providing lender of next-to-last resort loans to the banking system in 2006.[13] The Fed, however, waited until after the European Central Bank (ECB) had pumped liquidity into its banking system in

August 2007, to offer similar accommodation to the US markets. The Fed soon reversed course and reacted strongly by using all of the tools in its kit-book. By the end of 2008 it had reduced the federal funds rate effectively to zero, had increased its overnight discount window lending to banks, and had exhausted its other existing tools for providing liquidity. It turned to using its emergency powers in Section 13.3 of the *Federal Reserve Act* to creatively invent new tools to auction its credit, lengthen the term of its loans to 90 days, increase its securities lending to primary dealers, rescue large complex ailing financial institutions, lend beyond banks, and finally to purchase assets (agency mortgage-backed securities and debt, and long-term government bonds) in large quantities for its own balance sheet.

As a result, the Fed's balance sheet ballooned from USD800 billion in 2007 to USD2.3 trillion in 2010. By these actions Chairman Bernanke was honouring his earlier pledge to Milton Friedman and Anna Schwartz, 'I would like to say to Milton and Anna: Regarding the Great Depression. You're right, we did it. We're very sorry. But thanks to you, we won't do it again.'[14]

In the meantime, the administration refrained from action until late in 2008. It insisted that the problem was illiquidity, not insolvency, and left it to the Fed to provide liquidity.[15] In many of these expansions of its authority, the Fed essentially took on a responsibility that should have fallen to the fiscal authorities.[16] Why did the Fed feel compelled to do this? Why did the administration not act sooner to confront the crisis?

4.3. THE POLITICAL SYSTEM IN THE US

It is clear that democracies are vulnerable to adverse shocks during elections, especially when one results in a change in government. In the US, the collapse of the banking system in the Great Depression, the S&L debacle in the late 1980s, and the 2008 crisis all occurred at a time when the administration was about to change. When a President knows that he will not be re-elected, because he is facing a political landslide or because he is currently limited to two terms in office, his incentives to take decisive action diminish and likely favour letting the opposing party deal with the problem later. In addition, the incoming administration may not take appropriate action promptly because it is new to the job of governing and in any case has to wait from early November, when elected, to late January to assume office (Roosevelt had to wait until March to take over from Herbert Hoover). In addition, the heads and senior staff of departments are political appointees, who have to wait – sometimes for months – for confirmation by the Senate.

Even when finally in position, the administration frequently faces a hostile Congress, whose majority frequently belongs to the opposing party. This situation will deter the President from requesting an emergency allotment of funds, beyond the subventions that have already been painfully negotiated in the annual budget. The situation is exacerbated when the country's electorate is sharply divided and the politicians are bitterly at loggerheads, as is the case in the US today and throughout the recent crisis.

These circumstances no doubt played a part – along with an ideological predilection for minimal government interference in the financial markets – in explaining the Bush administration's refraining from actions to counter the country's financial problems before they climaxed after Lehman Brothers failed in September 2008. When asked why the administration appeared to have no contingency plan during the crisis, a Federal Reserve official responded 'We were the contingency plan.' Treasury Secretary Paulson reports that Barney Frank quipped in October 2008 when Paulson asked what the administration would do if Congress rejected its request for TARP funds, 'Then you'll go back to Uncle Ben.'[17] As a result, the government was unprepared to deal with the fallout from Lehman's bankruptcy and went to Congress for TARP funds – apparently in panic.

4.4. TARP – THE CRISIS RESPONSE BY TWO ADMINISTRATIONS

For much of 2007 both the Federal Reserve and the Bush administration believed that the fallout from excesses in the subprime markets could be contained without imposing major costs on the national economy. By March 2008, however, the Federal Reserve had come to think differently and took extraordinary actions when it rescued Bear Stearns and provided emergency liquidity to the markets. Later in the year, Lehman Brothers itself, and the markets in the US and abroad, seemed to have expected that Lehman would not be allowed to fail. But the Federal Reserve did not rescue it and Lehman filed for bankruptcy on 15 September. Then the asset-backed securities markets froze, the remaining investment banks were threatened with ruin, money market mutual funds experienced runs, the inter-bank markets collapsed as banks feared that their potential counterparties would default, the stock market crashed, and the economy stalled.

Finally, by mid-September 2008, the Bush administration had to act.[18] It placed two Government Sponsored Entities (GSEs, Fannie Mae and Freddie Mac) into conservatorship, announced a program for the Treasury to purchase agency mortgage-backed securities (MBS), and arranged for the FRB of New York to establish a credit facility for the GSEs. But these actions were not enough to stem the panic in the markets. Two days after the Lehman filing, the government rescued AIG (American International Group) and it guaranteed money market mutual funds on 19 September. The panic continued so that Bernanke and Paulson told Congressional leaders that another Great Depression would follow unless they provided funds for the administration to combat the threat. This, of course, scared everybody. On 20 September, Paulson presented the Senate Banking Committee with a 3-page sketch of its proposal for the Troubled Asset Relief Program (TARP). Advised that the proposal was too nebulous to be enacted, it grew to 110 pages before it was rejected by the House on 29 September. The proposal – to spend USD700 billion to purchase bad assets from ailing banks – was then modified to allow the Treasury to use TARP funds to inject capital into qualified (to be determined by the Treasury) financial institutions.[19] President Bush signed into law the modified plan, contained in the 451-page *Emergency Economic Stabilization Act* (EESA), on 1 October 2008.[20]

4.5. TARP AND ITS IMPLEMENTATION

The EESA was enacted '[T]o provide authority for the Federal Government to purchase and insure certain types of troubled assets for the purposes of providing stability to and preventing disruption in the economy . . .' Thus TARP was initially intended to purchase banks' illiquid assets and thus relieve market pressures. Like earlier bad-bank proposals this one was deferred after being sharply criticized for exposing the government to potentially heavy losses from opportunistic counterparties. Instead TARP funds were initially focused on purchasing preferred stock in the nation's nine largest banks.[21] It was then extended to other 'qualified' banks and it also allocated funds to aid the asset, auto and housing markets. TARP programs were initially supposed to end in December 2009, but Treasury Secretary Geithner extended the program until 3 September 2010.

As the Special Inspector General for the Troubled Asset Relief Program (SIGTARP) points out,[22] TARP encompassed 13 programs that allocated USD350.7 billion to banks and other financial institutions; USD51.4 billion to the asset markets; USD84.8 billion to the auto industry; and USD50 billion for homeowner assistance. (See Figure 4.1.) All 13 programs have been implemented and five have already been terminated.

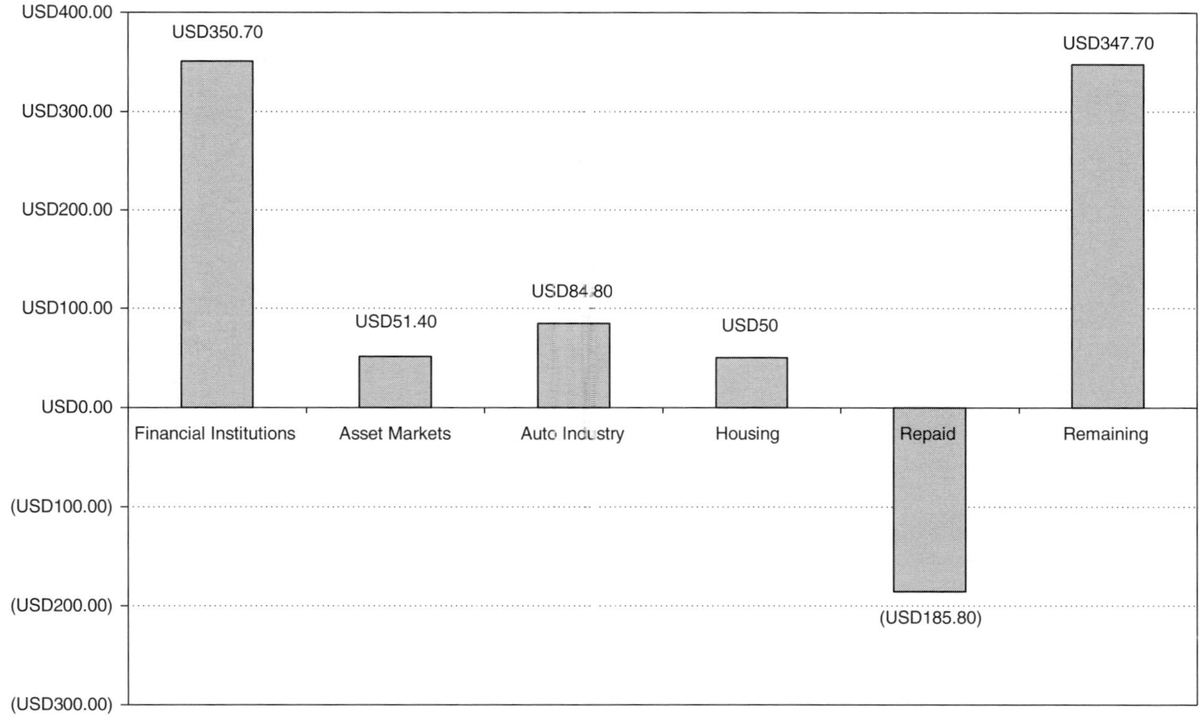

Source: Author's analysis of SIGTARP (2010).

Figure 4.1. TARP Commitments, Repayments and Available Funds, March 2010

4.5.1. Aid to Banks and Other Financial Institutions

The Capital Purchase Program (CPP) was the largest of the six programs designed to assist financial institutions by having Treasury purchase preferred stock or subordinated debentures in qualifying financial institutions to 'stabilize and strengthen the US financial system by increasing the capital of an array of healthy, viable institutions, enabling them to lend to consumers and business(es).'[23] The CPP began on 14 October 2009, when the Treasury invested USD125 billion in the nation's nine largest banks.[24] Regulators conducted an evaluation exercise to determine candidate banks' viability in early 2009 (Board of Governors). By the time the program closed in December 2009, SIGTARP points out that 707 financial institutions (insured banks,[25] their holding companies, thrifts, their holding companies, and insurance companies that owned or bought thrifts) had received USD204.9 billion in TARP funds. By 31 March 2010, USD135.8 billion had been repaid as recipients sought to avoid the accompanying restrictions (particularly those on salaries and bonuses) that they regarded as unduly onerous.

Three of the financial-institution programs went to aid individual institutions. The Systemically Significant Failing Institutions (SSFI) program allocated USD69.8 billion to AIG, which had received USD47.5 billion and had repaid none by the end of March 2010. The Targeted Investment Program (TIP) dedicated USD40 billion to purchasing preferred stock in Citigroup and Bank of America Corporation. The two banks repaid the Treasury and the program is now closed, and Treasury is in the process of selling the warrants it received for its investments. Under the Asset Guarantee Program (AGP), the Treasury, the FDIC and the Federal Reserve approved guarantees on USD301 billion of illiquid mortgage assets held by Citigroup. TARP allocated USD5 billion for this program, but no outlays were made. When the guarantee ended on 29 December 2009, the government retained USD5.2 billion (USD4 billion of which went to the Treasury) in preferred securities as compensation. The remaining two programs – the USD1 billion Community Development Capital Initiative (CDCI) and the USD30 billion Small Business Lending Fund (SBLF) – are still in operation but have been slow to gain traction.[26]

TARP did not adopt two of the Reconstruction Finance Corporation's important safeguarding principles. First, it did not require banks to write down their bad assets before selling preferred stock to the government. Second, although some aided mega institutions made management changes, the government does not appear to have systematically evaluated the managements of assisted banks nor required management changes. Shareholdings were diluted, but creditors and managements were protected; consequently it is questionable whether the penalties imposed on assisted institutions were sufficient to deter risk-taking in the future. The public could be forgiven for perceiving these programs as forbearance and bailout for their recipients.

4.5.2. Support for the Asset Markets

Of TARP's three asset-market programs, the Federal Reserve's Term Asset-Backed Loan Facility (TALF) for increasing credit available for consumers and small-businesses, which was backed by USD20 billion in TARP funds, was the most important.[27] The TALF for non-mortgage Asset-Backed Securities (ABS) and legacy Commercial Mortgage-Backed Securities (CMBS) terminated at the end of March 2010 with an end date for newly issued CMBS being 30 June 2010.

TARP was initially recommended as a program to bolster financial institutions' balance sheets by purchasing their troubled ABS and loans so to free up their capital such that they could expand credit available to support the US economy. It was not until the Public–Private Investment Program (PPIP) was announced on 23 March 2009, however, that it was used for this purpose. Treasury, the FDIC and the Federal Reserve, explained that this asset-purchase program was designed to serve three basic principles, to: (1) maximize the impact of each taxpayer dollar; (2) share risk and profits with private-sector participants; and (3) create a mechanism to determine market prices competitively for the troubled assets held by banks. The PPIP aimed to restart the frozen credit markets by having public–private investment funds (PPIFs) purchase; legacy assets, including existing residential and commercial real-estate related loans and securities from financial institutions. PPIFs were to be joint ventures that combined capital from private equity investors with public equity and debt from TARP. The program was designed to be long-term, lasting eight years or longer. PPIP had two components – a legacy loans program and a legacy securities program, but only the securities program has gone into continuing operation.[28] It utilized equity and debt financing provided by Treasury through TARP to facilitate purchases of CMBS and Residential Mortgage-Backed Securities (RMBS) from financial institutions. It was designed to 'restart the market for legacy securities, allowing banks and other financial institutions to free up capital and stimulate the extension of new credit.' By the end of March 2010, the Treasury had committed $30.4 billion in TARP funds for this program.

In the third asset-market program, Unlocking Credit for Small Businesses (UCSB), announced in March 2009, Treasury said that it would purchase up to USD15 billion (later raised to USD30 billion) in securities backed by

Small Business Administration (SBA) loans to encourage banks to lend to small businesses. By the end of 2009, however, the program's details had not been announced and no funds had been disbursed. In March 2010, Treasury reduced its commitment to USD1 billion and outsourced the program's operations to a private firm.

4.5.3. Automotive Industry Financing Program (AIFP)

Sales of automobiles plummeted leaving US car companies struggling to survive. TARP was originally aimed to aid financial institutions, so that the automotive industry programs had to be justified as aiming to 'prevent significant disruption of the American automotive industry, which would pose a systemic risk to financial market stability and have a negative effect on the economy of the US.'

AIFP made emergency loans to Chrysler, Chrysler Financial, and General Motors (GM), and purchased senior preferred stock from its financial arm (GMAC). As of 31 March 2010, Treasury had committed USD84.3 billion in AIFP investments, of which only USD3.6 billion had been repaid. In return, Treasury received a 9.9 per cent equity stake in New Chrysler and a 61 per cent stake in New GM. The second auto program was the Auto Supplier Support Program (ASSP) to provide government-backed financing to stabilize the automotive supply base and restore credit flows to the industry. (Because of worries that the auto manufacturers would be unable to pay, suppliers had been unable to borrow from banks using their receivables as collateral.) Treasury's original commitment under this program was USD5.0 billion, which had been reduced to USD3.5 billion by year end 2009 – USD1.0 billion for Chrysler and USD2.5 billion for GM. The debts were assumed by New GM and New Chrysler after the companies emerged from bankruptcy. By the end of March 2010, ASSP recipients had repaid all USD413 million of disbursed funds, plus interest and the program terminated in April 2010. The third auto program, the Auto Warranty Commitment Program (AWCP), was designed to bolster consumer confidence in automobile warranties on Chrysler- and GM-built vehicles. The program committed USD0.6 billion, was terminated in July 2009, and the outlays have been repaid.

4.5.4. Aid for the Housing Industry

SIGTARP reported that there were nearly 2.8 million foreclosures initiated in the US in 2009 and that more were expected in 2010.[29] Both administrations implemented programs to avoid foreclosures and the more recent Making Home Affordable (MHA) program, which was introduced by the Obama administration on 18 February 2009, has received TARP funds. The MHA program was designed to offer 'assistance to millions of homeowners making a good-faith effort to pay their mortgages' and 'to protect families and communities from the destructive impact of the housing crisis'. $50 billion in TARP funds have been primarily dedicated to the Home Affordable Modification Program (HAMP), which together with parallel programs funded by Freddie Mac and Fannie Mae, offer assistance to lenders to induce them to reduce homeowners' monthly mortgage payments.

By the end of 2009, according to the Congressional Oversight Panel, HAMP had disappointingly helped few homeowners,[30] so its scope was substantially expanded in 2010 to include foreclosure alternatives (short sales and deeds in lieu of foreclosure) for homeowners who could not complete a HAMP modification, forbearance for unemployed homeowners, modifications for second liens, and incentives for lenders to write down the mortgage principal for homeowners who were underwater. As a result, Treasury now expects to use the full $50 billion allocated to the MHA.

4.5.5. TARP's Implementation

Commitments under the 13 TARP programs are shown in Figure 4.2, which illustrates that the recipients of the most significant part of the funding were financial institutions, particularly Bank of America, Citigroup and AIG. Substantial aid was also given to the auto industry and is planned for foreclosure avoidance under the MHA during 2010.

The Reconstruction Finance Corporation (RFC) laid down principles for investing in troubled banks during the Great Depression. TARP did not follow the RFC's wise admonition to write down each bank's bad assets before investing. Treasury immediately invested $125 billion in the nine largest banks in October 2008 and purchased preferred stock in other large banks soon after. The Federal Reserve and the other regulators conducted the Supervisory Capital Assessment Program (SCAP) for the 19 largest banks in April 2009 and announced the results on 6 May.[31] SCAP estimated each bank's likely losses going forward under two economic scenarios; told the bank (and the public) what capital the bank needed to raise privately. It announced that, if private capital were not forthcoming, the government would need USD75 billion. SCAP was successful as an exercise to increase the public's confidence in banks. But SCAP did not require banks to write down their bad assets. Instead, Treasury planned programs to purchase these assets, possibly at inflated prices to ease the burden on the banks from the ensuing write-downs. Banks were unwilling to sell their troubled assets at market prices, because this would have

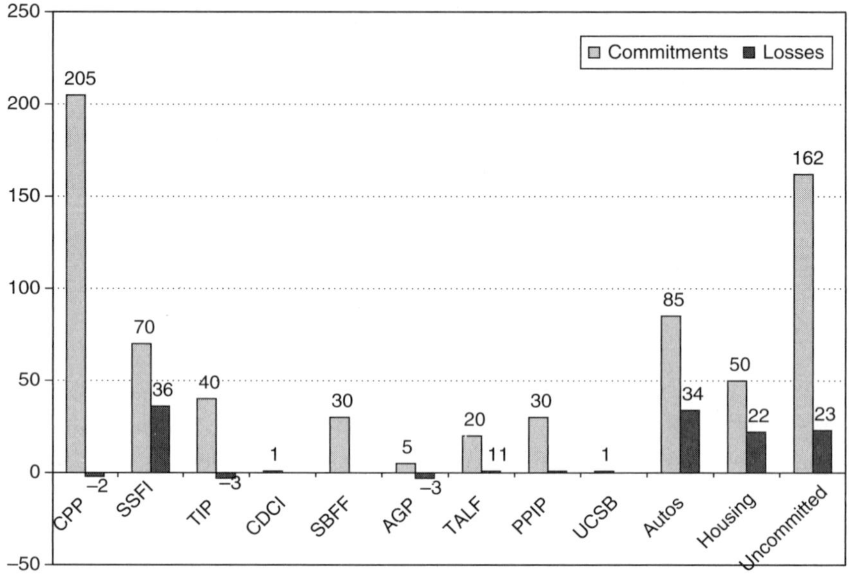

Note: Negative losses indicate that the government received a positive return on its investment. Uncommitted funds do not here include funds that have been repaid.

Source: Author's analysis of data from SIGTARP and the Congressional Budget Office.[32]

Figure 4.2. TARP Commitments and Estimated Losses in USDbillions (31 March 2010)

required them to recognize large losses. Thus the PPIP would have to offer the highest possible price to induce banks to sell. PPIP can be criticized for raising purchase prices for assets by heavily subsidizing the acquirers in non-recourse loans and by the 3:1 ratio of government to private capital.[33]

There was an episode of government rescues – notably of Chrysler Corporation and New York City – in the late 1970s and early 1980s. As a result the Government Accountability Office (GAO) published a set of principles for rescues, which were restated in Congressional Testimony in December 2008 and December 2009.[34] According to the testimony of Williams-Brown and Clower,[35] three fundamental principles provide a framework for considering and administering government support in order to protect the public interest:

> First the problems confronting the industry or institution need to be clearly defined and those that require an immediate financial response differentiated from those that are likely to require more time to resolve. Second, the

> government needs to determine whether the national interest will best be served through some type of government intervention or whether market forces and established legal procedures, such as bankruptcy reorganization, should be allowed to take their course. If the federal government decides that federal financial assistance is warranted, it must set clear objectives and goals for this assistance. Third, given the significant financial risk the federal government may assume on behalf of taxpayers, the structure created to administer any assistance must have appropriate mechanisms to protect them from excessive or unnecessary risk. These mechanisms include concessions by all parties, control over management, compensation for risk, and a strong independent board or other entity managing or overseeing the assistance.

With respect to the first principle, it is not clear that the administration clearly defined the problems, especially those confronting AIG and the auto companies; nor was it able to differentiate between problems needing an immediate financial response from longer-term deficiencies. In addition, it is not clear whether the government analysed the need to intervene rather than let market forces take their course, or if it panicked.

Regarding the second principle, GAO notes that the administration developed four guiding principles to govern its investments in AIG and the auto companies: (1) not to own equity stakes in companies on a long-term basis and to exit from them as soon as possible; (2) not to interfere in the day-to-day management decisions of the company in which it invested; (3) to ensure a strong board of directors; and (4) to exercise only limited voting rights.[36] The administration here assumed that not owning equity stakes, not exercising hands-on management, and not exercising full voting rights is always in the national interest. It might have made a different determination if it had considered each aid grant separately.

Third, attempts to obtain concessions from all parties have been sporadic and unconvincing.[37] Creditors have been protected. The Treasury needs to explain to the public its efforts to restrict dividends and lobbying expenses and to monitor the performance benchmarks that it says it has set. Its efforts to contain executive compensation are better known but do not appear to have enjoyed noticeable success.

4.6. HAS TARP SUCCEEDED?

One way to inquire whether the TARP programs have succeeded is to examine whether they have achieved their stated goals – a task made more difficult by the fact, as the Congressional Oversight Panel has pointed out, that TARP objectives were poorly articulated.[38] Section 2 of the *Emergency Economic Stabilization Act* reads, '[T]he purposes of this Act are –

(1) to immediately provide authority and facilities that the Secretary of the Treasury can use to restore liquidity and stability to the financial system of the United States; and
(2) to ensure that such authority and such facilities are used in a manner that –
(A) protects home values, college funds, retirement accounts, and life savings;
(B) preserves homeownership and promotes jobs and economic growth;
(C) maximizes overall returns to the taxpayers of the United States; and
(D) provides public accountability for the exercise of such authority.'

Indicators in Table 4.1 suggest that by early 2010, the financial markets were more stable and more liquid than they were during the crisis, and the complacency that existed in the financial markets in the period leading up to the crisis has not returned. Evaluating whether the goals for the rest of the economy have been achieved is more difficult. It is widely recognized that the US economy was experiencing an unsustainable boom before the crisis hit. Consequently, we should not expect nor want it to return to pre-crisis levels that were facilitated only by large budget deficits and heavy borrowing from abroad. The table reports levels for a number of indicators at peak before, at nadir during, and recently after the crisis. TARP did not specify what levels it aimed to reach for these indicators and it is left to the reader to determine where sustainable levels have been reached and where weaknesses remain.

4.6.1. Liquidity in the Financial System

Data show that quantitative easing significantly increased Federal Reserve assets and encouraged banks to hold unprecedentedly large amounts of excess reserves, which peaked in February 2010, but fell modestly in the subsequent three months. Monetary growth was strong during the crisis; reached its highest quarterly growth rate in the fourth quarter of 2008, but had decreased substantially at the end of the first quarter of 2010. It seems that TARP together with the Fed's programs has improved liquidity in many, but not all markets. It is not clear, however, whether the markets will remain liquid in the absence of support from the Federal Reserve.

Table 4.1. Progress Toward Achieving TARP's Stated Goals

Indicator	Cyclical Peak		Cyclical Trough		Latest		Source
	Date	Value	Date	Value	Date	Value	
Liquidity							
Fed assets	9/07	USD874 b	4/14/10	USD2432 b	4/28/10	USD2370 b	Fed H.4.1
Bank reserves	3/8/06	USD412 b	2/10/10	USD1246 b	5/ 5/10	USD1030 b	Fed H.4.1
M1 growth	2006	0.2%	2008Q4	29.1%	2010Q1	3.7%	FR Bank of St. Louis
M2 growth	2006	5.3%	2008Q4	14.2%	2010Q1	0.25%	FR Bank of St. Louis
Fed. Funds Rate	2006	5.25%	2008	0–0.25%	5/12/10	0–0.25%	Fed H.15
Credit Availability							
Bank Lending Change	2007Q3	USD236.5 b	2009Q3	–USD210.5 b	2009Q4	–USD127.7 b	FDIC: Quarterly Banking Profile
ABS Issued	2006	USD754 b	2008Q4	USD3.46 b	2010Q1	USD32.3 b	SIFMA
Libor-OIS spread	2006	10bp	10/08	364bp	5/6/10	13.4bp	COP, Bloomberg
TED spread	2006	30bp	10/10/08	465bp	5/12/10	20.2bp	COP, Bloomberg
Non-financial C.P.	2007/7	200 000	2010:1	58 852	10/4	121 691	Fed: commercial paper outstanding
Financial C.P.	08/12	850 000	2009/7	498 452	10/4	556 262	Fed: commercial paper outstanding
Asset-backed C.P.	2007/2	1200	2010/1	390	10/3	400	Fed: commercial paper outstanding
Stability							
No. Bank Failures	2005–6	0	7/09	24	4/10	23	FDIC
Volatility Index	1/2/07	9.89	11/20/08	80.86	5/11/10	28.32	CBOE daily closing VIX index

Table 4.1 (continued)

Indicator	Cyclical Peak		Cyclical Trough		Latest		Source
	Date	Value	Date	Value	Date	Value	
Home Ownership							
House Price Index	4/06	226.7	5/09	152.1			S&P's Case-Shiller 10-city index
Home Ownership	2005Q1	69.1%	2010Q1	67.1%	2010Q1	67.1%	Department of Commerce
Life Savings							
Household fin assets	2007Q1	USD50 759	2009Q1	USD40 208	2009Q4	USD45 115	Fed: Flow of Funds Accounts
Stock Market	10/9/07	1565	3/6/09	667	5/11/10	1156	S&P 500
Jobs							
Employment	11/07	137.9m	10/09	129.6m	4/10	130.2m	Bureau of Labour Statistics: s.a.
Unemployment	5/07	4.4%	10/09	10.1%	4/10	9.9%	Bureau of Labour Statistics: s.a.
Underemployment	10/00	6.8%	10/09	17.4%	4/10	17.1%	BLS U-6: s.a.
Job Growth	4/06	600m	1/09	–800m	4/10	290m	BLS change in employment s.a.

Economic growth							
Real GDP growth	2006Q1	5.4%	2009Q1	–6.4%	2010Q1	3.2%	Bureau of Economic Analysis
Activity Index	1/06	0.75	1/09	–3.75	3/10	–0.07	Federal Reserve Bank Chicago
Industrial Production	12/07	112.4	6/09	95.7	3/10	101.6	Federal Reserve Index: G.17 s.a.
Sales of autos, '000	1/06	1462	2/09	762	3/10	980	Department of Commerce

Source: Author's analysis of government and private data.

4.6.2. Stability

There have been no more failures of large financial institutions, but 140 smaller banks failed in 2009, and many more failed in 2010. Chicago Board of Options Exchange data showed that its volatility index (VIX) – a measure of concerns over solvency – rose from a low of 10 in 2007 to 81 in late 2008, but had fallen to 28 in May 2010.[39] The evidence suggests that TARP has improved stability, but the new crisis in the euro area threatens to spill over to other parts of the world, including the United States.

4.6.3. Credit Availability

Both financial and non-financial commercial paper was issued abundantly immediately before the crisis, but fell sharply during the crisis. The declines continued late into the crisis and showed only modest rates of recovery by April 2010. Issuance of asset-backed commercial paper reacted most sharply to the crisis and had not recovered by April 2010. Risk-free short-term interest rates remain near zero – and may remain there for the foreseeable future. While FDIC data show that bank lending was still declining at the end of 2009, the quarterly Loan Officers' Survey for 2010 revealed that for the first time for nine quarters loan officers were no longer tightening credit.[40] The Libor-OIS and TED spreads had risen sharply by October 2008, but fell back almost to pre-crisis levels in 2010 until the Greek debt crisis raised them again.[41]

4.6.4. Homeownership

Homeownership peaked at 69.1 per cent of the households in 2005, fell to 67.1 per cent in the 1Q 2010. Both Federal Housing Finance Agency, and Standard and Poor's Case-Shiller national house price indices show that house prices peaked in mid-2006, declined through 2009, but began to stabilize in 2010.[42] Although prices have stopped falling nationally by May 2010, there was little evidence of price increases in major US cities. These observations, together with the forecasts of further foreclosures to come, suggest that the housing market remains an area of vulnerability. The Congressional Oversight Panel concluded early in 2010 that TARP has not yet succeeded in protecting home values or containing foreclosures.[43] But completely protecting home values is a task beyond TARP's resources. House prices probably need to fall further to make home-ownership affordable without liar loans and other devices to allow homeowners to obtain mortgages they cannot afford.

4.6.5. Life Savings

The Federal Reserve's Flow of Funds Accounts show that household financial assets fell sharply during the crisis – from USD50.7 trillion in 1Q 2007 to USD40.2 trillion two years later. They had recovered to USD45.1 trillion by the end of 2009. Many households held substantial parts of their life savings in the stock market. The S&P 500 peaked in September 2007, fell by more than 57 per cent by March 2009, but had risen 73 per cent from its nadir by 10 May 2010, so that the S&P 500 then stood at almost three quarters of its peak value.

4.6.6. Unemployment

The job situation is a crucial component of economic recovery. Civilian employment peaked in November 2007 and fell by 8.3 million during the crisis and had only just begun to recover by April 2010. The rates of unemployment and underemployment reached cyclical lows in 2007, then rose to peak at 10.1 per cent and 17.4 per cent, respectively, in October 2009. These rates had declined only marginally by April 2010, when employers had ceased to lay off workers and had begun to hire again. But employment remains a serious issue and probably is a large factor in the reasoning of the National Bureau of Economic Research (NBER), which has not yet declared an end to the Great Recession.

4.6.7. Economic Growth

The economy had, however, begun to grow again in late 2009 and real GDP growth continued into early 2010. The Federal Reserve Bank of Chicago's Activity Index reached its nadir in January of 2009 and by March 2010 the index was still marginally negative. The Fed's index of industrial production peaked at the end of 2007, fell substantially to a low in June 2009, but had recovered to 90 per cent of its peak value by March 2010. As shown in Figure 4.3, auto sales were strong in 2007, fell to a low in February 2009, received a temporary boost from the (non-TARP) cash for clunkers program the following July and August and then fell back again.

4.6.8. Protecting Taxpayers

By March 2010, USD162 billion remained uncommitted from the original USD698.8 billion in TARP funds, while USD185.8 billion had been repaid (or TARP's exposure had been reduced). Consequently, as TARP is a revolving fund, USD347.8 billion remained available to the Treasury to spend on

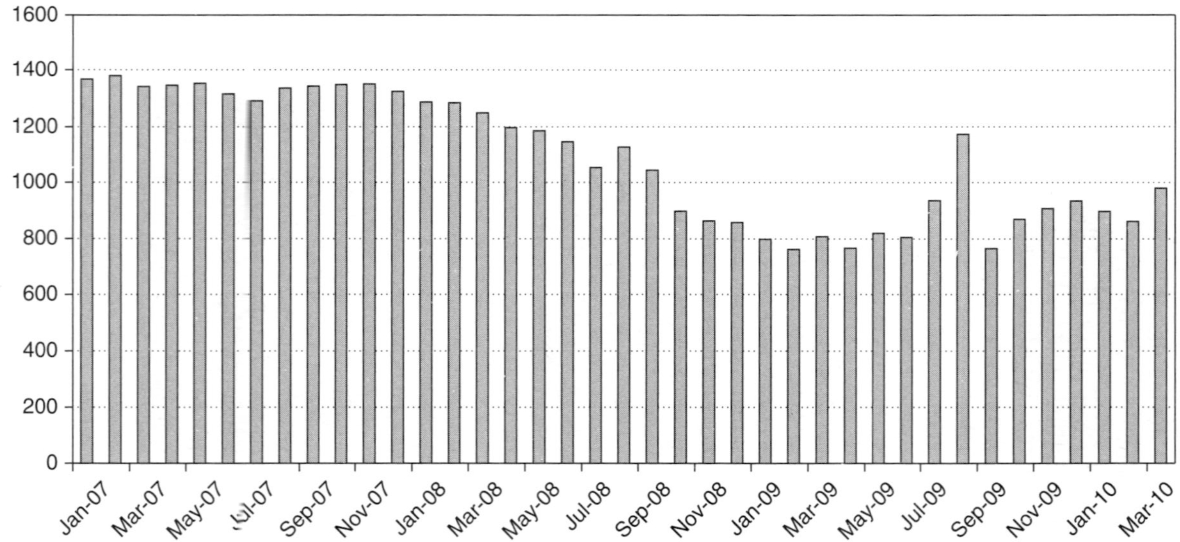

Source: Author's analysis of Department of Commerce data.

Figure 4.3. *Cash for Clunkers Gave a Temporary Boost to Sales of Autos and Light Trucks in thousands*

expanded or additional programs before the program expires.[44] TARP's aim of maximizing returns to taxpayers can be interpreted as minimizing losses and achieving positive returns from interest, dividends and warrants. It is too early to offer more than an indication of progress toward achieving this objective, but the Office of Management and the Budget (OMB) estimated early in 2010 that some programs had shown positive returns but that overall TARP would incur USD127 billion in losses. CBO's February loss estimates are slightly lower at USD109 billion and, as is shown in Figure 4.2, arise mainly from the programs for AIG, autos, and housing.

4.6.9. Accountability

The government is concerned that the USD700 billion be spent wisely. To try to ensure this, Congress created the TARP Congressional Oversight Panel (COP), the Interagency Office of Financial Stability (OFS),[45] and the special inspector general for TARP (SIGTARP). EESA also required the GAO to report to it on TARP performance at least every 60 days. By mid-May 2010, COP had issued 20 reports, just over one a month starting in December 2008. SIGTARP has issued six quarterly reports and three other reports starting in February 2009. GAO had issued 15 reports. The OFS website lists TARP 154 reports. There are so many reviews that they risk being overlooked. This surfeit of information may suffer from the same problem as stock market prospectuses and mortgage documentation that buries what is important in a mass of detail.[46]

4.7. CONCLUSIONS

It is astonishing that the authorities were so unprepared for the crisis of 2008. As the Congressional Review Panel (Congressional Oversight Panel, December Oversight Report – Taking Stock: What has the Troubled Asset Relief Program Achieved? 9 December 2009, p. 15) in its anniversary assessment of TARP explained, 'If policymakers hoped that Lehman's demise would end the cycle of bailouts, their strategy failed. Instead, the efforts to save the financial sector became more extensive and more frantic in the following days.'

Opinions on the program range from rejection to enthusiastic acceptance. President Bush (Statement by the President of the US on the Administration's Plan to Assist the Automakers on 19 December 2008, Roosevelt Room 9:01 A.M. EST) expressed resignation when initiating one of TARP's loan programs he said 'The actions I'm announcing today represent a step that we wish were not necessary. But given the situation, it is the most effective and responsible way to address this challenge facing our nation.' Treasury Secretary Paulson was also unenthusiastic:[47]

> I came to Washington as an advocate of free markets, and I remain one. The interventions we took I would have found abhorrent at any other time. I make no apology for them, however. As first responders to an unprecedented crisis that threatened the destruction of the modern financial system, we had little choice. We were forced to use the often inadequate tools we had on hand.

In contrast 16 months later a *Washington Post* editorial was strongly approving 'Yet today it is clear that TARP not only has been successful, but, in a real sense, it was also a great deal for taxpayers.' But that editorial comment was written on 1 April 2010! April fool?

By May 2010, it does appear that TARP and the other stabilization programs have stopped the panic and turned the economy around. By then the economy was growing again, the stock market had recovered significantly from its low 14 months before, many companies were profitable again; if only because they had cut their expenses as they hunkered down (cut back) to meet decreased demand.

Yet stabilization could, should, have been done better. Small failed banks will still be resolved by the FDIC; other small firms will still be left to bankruptcy laws and, where necessary, the courts to resolve. 'Too-big-to-fail' has been recognized to be a problem since Continental Illinois was rescued in 1984, however, and it still has not been resolved. Rather it, together with 'too-interconnected-to-let-fail-suddenly' appears to be becoming national policy embodied in the law in the UK and awaiting passage by the US Congress. And in the crisis forbearance and rescue were extended to non-bank financial firms – investment banks and insurance companies, Fannie Mae and Freddie Mac, and even to the manufacturing companies GM and Chrysler.

There needs to be a national debate and decision whether giving special treatment to systemically important financial institutions should become national policy not just for banks, but also for other financial firms and non-financial companies. Even if a firm is judged to be too systemically important to be allowed to fail the nation needs to decide whether instead of TARP's capital purchases, it would have been better, despite the US disdain for nationalization, for the government to take full, rather than the partial ownership that was adopted and was accompanied by a 'hands off' approach to the management of the troubled companies.[48]

The government did not clearly state the broader objectives of TARP and the other rescue programs; consequently a taxpayer is sometimes left with the impression that the government's main objective for its programs was to restore the country and its markets to their situation before the crisis. But economists, the press and perhaps the politicians, recognize that that situation was not sustainable. The country's consumers and government had borrowed recklessly, housing prices had risen far out of alignment with incomes and rents, McMansions blotted the landscape, shopping had become a national pastime – 'retail therapy,' the financial markets – particularly the asset-backed securities markets – were opaque, and in places morally, if not legally, corrupt. TARP did not, and possibly could not, fix these problems. They remain to be addressed.

Sadly little has been done yet elsewhere to solve the country's problems. Instead moral hazard has increased, as creditors, and to a lesser extent owners, have been sheltered from the storm. The 'too-big-to fail/systemically-important' problem has grown more pressing, as regulators have merged dying banks into other marginally healthy banks.[49] It may legitimately be argued that finding ways to resolve large financial institutions that span country borders will need international agreement, and none has yet been forthcoming, so that problem remains. Rather, the remedy that has been internationally adopted is forbearance and rescue, not receivership. It appears that henceforth owners may, or may not, be penalized, but creditors of large interconnected firms will be protected. Problems in the securities and derivatives markets remain largely unaddressed. Freddie and Fannie are still in limbo in conservatorship.

An issue remains about how the administration will use the remaining almost $350 billion of uncommitted and repaid TARP funds going forward. Treasury has already used a substantial amount of funds to support the auto industry, its owners, creditors, workers, and suppliers – who were not originally intended to be TARP recipients. The administration wants to do more to help homeowners facing foreclosure. It may use more TARP funds to support Freddie, Fannie, housing sales and real estate prices, especially after the Federal Reserve ceased buying agency paper at the end of March 2010. The danger is that TARP could become a slush fund for bestowing forbearance for troubled entities as political favours when the Congressional mid-term elections approach in November 2010. Transparency is no more the answer to potential bailout malfeasance/incompetence/forbearance than it is in the securities markets. I will keep my fingers crossed that the US will muddle through to a better, honestly reformed future.

NOTES

1. The paper this chapter is based on was presented at the Warwick University Law School Symposium on Managing Systemic Risk, on 9 April 2010. The author is

indebted to George Blackford, Andrew Campbell, Vijay Deshpande, John Raymond LaBrosse, David Mayes, Heidi Mandanis Schooner, Dalvinder Singh and Larry Wall for their comments and to symposium participants for discussing the issues. The author remains responsible for any errors.

2. 'Now is the winter of our discontent made glorious summer by this sun of York.' Shakespeare, Richard the Third Act 1, scene 1, 1–4.
3. See Garcia, Gillian G.H. 'Failing Prompt Corrective Action,' *Journal of Banking Regulation*, Vol. 11, No. 3, June 2010, pp. 171–190.
4. Citibank is a case in point. It received forbearance in the debt crisis in the 1980s, survived major problems in the early 1990s with forbearance and a capital infusion from a Middle Eastern investor. In the recent crisis it, together with AIG, were the largest US recipients of government aid.
5. See Reinhart, Carmen M., and Kenneth S. Rogoff (2009), *This Time is Different: Eight Centuries of Financial Folly*, Princeton, New Jersey: Princeton University Press.
6. See Garcia op. cit. in endnote 3.
7. A companion paper, 'The US Financial Safety Net: Before and After Bear Stearns,' places TARP on the broader context of the currently much expanded US safety net. That paper contains five appendices; (1) a chronology of events. (2) a description of TARP programs; (3) a positioning of TARP's housing programs in to the broader, historical, context of US assistance to support the housing industry; (4) the crisis responses by the FHLBs, the FDIC, and the National Credit Union Association (NCUA); and (5) the actions and programs of the Federal Reserve as it moved decisively to quell the crisis.
8. See Gillian Garcia (2010), 'The US Financial Safety Net: Before and After Bear Stearns.' Unpublished paper presented at the annual meetings of the International Economics and Business Association and the Western Economics Association International, in Portland in July 2010.
9. See Bernanke, *The Economic Outlook*, before the Joint Economic Committee, US Congress, 28 March 2007, accessed 25 February 2010 at http://www.federalreserve.gov/newsevents/testimony/bernanke20070328a.htm.
10. See Bernanke, *The Subprime Mortgage Market*, at the Federal Reserve Bank of Chicago's 43rd Annual Conference on Bank Structure and Competition, May 2007, accessed 25 February 2010 at http://www.federalreserve.gov/newsevents/speech/2007speech.htm.
11. See Bernanke's Semi-annual Monetary Policy Report to the Congress, before the Committee on Financial Services, US House of Representatives, 18 July 2008, accessed 25 February 2010 at http://www.federalreserve.gov/newsevents/testimony/bernanke20070718a.htm.
12. Jim Cramer, famous for excited commentary about market events on his programs on cable news, became especially incensed in 'Cramer's Rant,' *CNBC* on 3 August 2007, accessed 3 March 2010 at www.cnbc.com.
13. See Ashcraft, Adam, Morten L. Bech, and W. Scott Frame (2009), 'The Federal Home Loan Bank System: the Lender of Next-to-Last Resort?' Federal Reserve Bank of Atlanta, Working Paper, 2009-4 (Feb).
14. See Ben Bernanke's Remarks: On Milton Friedman's Ninetieth Birthday at the Conference to Honor Milton Friedman, University of Chicago, Chicago, Illinois, 8 November 2002, accessed 6 February 2010 at http://www.federalreserve.gov/BOARDDOCS/SPEECHES/2002/20021108/default.htm.
15. The author heard a senior Treasury official maintain this position still in September 2008 at an AEI conference, just as the crisis was about to reach its peak.
16. See David Wessel, *In Fed We Trust: Ben Bernanke's War on the Great Panic* (New York, Crown Business, 2009).
17. See Paulson, Henry M., Jr. (2010), *On the Brink: Inside the Race to Stop the Collapse of the Global Financial System*, New York: Business Plus, Hachette Book Group, p. 309.
18. Information in this paragraph is taken from the Crisis Chronology, an appendix in Garcia, op. cit.

19. See the Treasury Press Release, *Treasury Announces TARP Capital Purchase Program Description* on 14 October 2008, accessed 25 May 2010, at http://www.ustreas.gov/press/releases/hp1207.htm.
20. See United States Congress (2008), Emergency Economic Stabilization Act, *Public Law 110-343*, accessed 14 May 2010 at http://thomas.loc.gov/cgi-bin/query/z?c110:H.R.1424.enr.
21. Heidi Schooner argues in 'A Lashing for the Banks: New Federal Ownership Plan for Large Banks May Herald More Punishing Regulation,' *Legal Times*, vol. xxxi, no. 42, 20 October 2008, that the legislative definition of troubled assets was stretched to cover bank equity by adding to the definition 'any other financial instrument' that the Treasury, after consulting with the Federal Reserve and informing Congress, determined was necessary to promote financial stability. An exchange between Representatives Barney Frank and Jim Moran established the legislative intent for this interpretation. Treasury decided which banks were 'qualified.'
22. See Special Inspector General Troubled Asset Relief Program Quarterly Report to Congress, 20 April 2010, accessed 14 May 2010 at http://www.sigtarp.gov/reports/congress/ 2010/April2010_Quarterly_Report_to_Congress.pdf.
23. See SIGTARP cited in footnote 23 at page 36.
24. See Paulson, op. cit.
25. The US use of insured banks is imprecise. The banks' small deposits are insured, not the banks themselves.
26. Under the CDCI, $1 billion was to be used to purchase preferred stock in community development institutions in order to help small businesses. However, by the end of March 2010 Treasury had not begun investing in the program, whose application deadline was extended to 30 April 2010. Under the SBLF Treasury intended to redirect $30 billion of TARP funds to stimulate small-business lending, but it had not done so by the end of March 2010.
27. Through 31March 2010, the Federal Reserve Bank of New York had facilitated 23 TALF subscriptions for a total of $70 billion in TALF loans, consisting of 13 subscriptions for non-mortgage-backed ABSs totalling $58 billion in TALF loans, and 10 CMBS subscriptions resulting in $12 billion in TALF loans. See Federal Reserve Bank of New York (2009), *Term Asset-Backed Securities Loan Facility: Terms and Conditions* (online at www.newyorkfed.org/markets/talf_terms.html).
28. PPIP's Legacy Loans Program was intended to utilize equity provided by Treasury and debt guarantees provided by the FDIC to facilitate purchases of legacy mortgage loans held by banks. FDIC launched a pilot Legacy Loans Program on 31 July 2009, with assets from the Franklin Bank receivership. No TARP funds were used in the sale and Treasury budgeted no funding for the program going forward, and the program was abandoned.
29. See SIGTARP op. cit.
30. See the Congressional Oversight Panel, *Troubled Asset Relief Program: One Year Later, Actions are Needed to Address Remaining Transparency, and Accountability Challenges*, 8 October 2009.
31. See Board of Governors of the Federal Reserve, *The Supervisory Capital Assessment Program: Design and Implementation*, 29 April 2009, accessed 6 February 2010 at http://www.federalreserve.gov/newsevents/press/bcreg/bcreg20090424a1.pdf.
32. See SIGTARP 2010 at page 40 and the Congressional Budget Office, *Report on the Troubled Asset Relief Program*, March 2010 (Washington, D.C., Congressional Budget Office), accessed 14 May 2010 at http://www.cbo.gov/ftpdocs/112xx/doc11227/03-17-TARP.pdf.
33. The Program is described in the Treasury press release http://www.ustreas.gov/press/releases/tg65.htm, and by SIGTARP (2010).
34. See Government Accountability Office, *Troubled Asset Relief Program: One Year Later, Actions are Needed to Address Remaining Transparency, and Accountability Challenges*, at 8 October 2009, p. 80 (online at www.gao.gov/new.items/d1016.pdf.

35. See Government Accountability Office, 'Troubled Asset Relief Program: The US Government Role as Shareholder in AIG, Citigroup, Chrysler, and General Motors and Preliminary Views on its Investment Management Activities,' Statement of Williams Brown, Orice, and A. Nicole Clowers before the Subcommittee on Domestic Policy, Committee on Oversight and Government Reform, House of Representatives, GAO-1 – 325T, 16 December 2009, accessed 19 May 2010 at http://www.gao.gov/new.items/d10325t.pdf.
36. See the Government Accountability Office, *Troubled Asset Relief Program: One Year Later, Actions are Needed to Address Remaining Transparency, and Accountability Challenges*, 8 October 2009, accessed 12 May 2010 at www.gao.gov/new.items/d1016.pdf.
37. The Treasury required TARP recipients to accept limits on executive compensation, while GM and Chrysler had to use their 'best efforts' to reduce workers' compensation to what workers at foreign automakers receive.
38. See Congressional Oversight Panel 2010, op. cit.
39. It rose above 40 during the Greek/Euro crisis in May 2010.
40. See Gruenberg, Martin J., Statement 'On the Condition of Small Business and Commercial Real Estate Lending In Local Markets,' before the Committee on Financial Services and the Committee on Small Business, US House of Representatives, 26 February 2010, accessed 27 February 2010 at www.fdic.gov.
41. Banks are less willing to lend when the Libor-OIS and TED interest rate spreads rise, as in the fall of 2008. Conversely they are more willing to lend when the spreads fall, as they did until the fiscal crisis in Europe.
42. The composite 10-city S&P Case-Shiller index has declined 33.5 per cent.
43. See Congressional Oversight Panel, *Evaluating Progress of TARP's Foreclosure Mitigation Program*, 4 March 2010.
44. An amendment to the financial reform bill before the Senate in May 2010, however, seeks to require Treasury to use repaid funds to reduce the federal budget deficit.
45. See United States Treasury Department, *Citizens' Report on the Troubled Asset Relief Program (TARP)*, 2 March 2010, accessed 4 March 2010 at http://financialstability.gov/about/oversight.html.
46. The two-inch-thick prospectuses written on tissue paper that issuers in the markets release and the oversight agencies' 198 reports obscure more than they reveal. Who has time to read them? The press has not!
47. Paulson, op. cit., pp. 427–8.
48. Nationalization might be worth considering in a bridge bank run by technocrats for the benefit of the country, rather than by politicians using it to provide a piggy-bank for political favors.
49. See Bernanke, Ben S., 'Reducing Systemic Risk,' Speech at the FRB of Kansas City's Annual Economic Symposium, Jackson Hole, Wyoming, 22 August 2008, accessed 1 February 2010 at http://www.federalreserve.gov/newsevents/speech/bernanke20080822a.htm.

5. Why is the Canadian banking system so remarkably stable? A comparative analysis with the US

Jean Roy, Rima Turk-Ariss and Yenni Redjah

During 2009, the US experienced a major financial crisis that spread to several major European countries. Government had to bail out the banking system with unprecedented financial measures. At the same time, Canada showed its banking system had great resilience and stability. This remarkable performance was noted by several international organizations such as Moody's and the World Economic Forum. The contrasting behaviour of the two banking systems is indeed quite surprising given their common Anglo-Saxon heritage and the high level of integration of their economies. This situation raises the question of finding the causes explaining the differences in the behaviour of the two banking systems during the crisis.

Thus, our objective is to review the possible explanations for the better performance of the Canadian banking system relative to its American counterpart during the latest period of financial turmoil. Hopefully, this exercise can identify lessons that can be helpful in preventing systemic risk and fostering financial stability.

The chapter proceeds as follows. First, it will document the striking differences of behaviour of the two banking systems both from a public and a private point of view. Secondly, it will explore to what extent the higher level of market concentration in Canada can provide an explanation. Finally, it will look at regulation and the financial behaviour of both banks and borrowers as potential explanatory factors.

5.1. CANADA AND THE US: A CONTRAST IN FINANCIAL STABILITY

The financial crisis has had very different impacts on markets in Canada and the US. Indeed, in the US it is estimated that the government intervened in 711 banks and injected some USD250 billion of capital in them. Nonetheless, more than 300 banks failed since January 2008.[1] In Canada, by contrast, the government did not have to intervene in any bank, no public funds in the form of capital were injected into the banks and none failed. This being said, it must be stated that the Canadian government did put in place an asset repurchase programme whereby it repurchased some CAD70 billion of already government-insured mortgages. This was, however, meant to fulfil liquidity needs of the banks rather than to address an individual problem. Indeed, the assets repurchased were of a high quality and it is expected that the Canadian government will earn a CAD1 billion profit on the transaction when it resells those assets. In contrast, the TARP (Troubled Assets Relief Program) in the US had an initial budget of some USD700 billion and was to relieve banks of their bad assets, although eventually the money was used in a variety of ways to support the troubled banks. These few statistics illustrate clearly, we believe, the contrasting behaviour of the two banking systems during the crisis.

Complementing this *ex post* information on the actions of the two governments, it is interesting to analyse how financial markets were evaluating the risks of the two banking systems in real time as events were unfolding. For this purpose, we used the standard measure of market risk called Value-at-Risk (VAR). Simply said, VAR identifies a threshold point such that the probability of hitting a realized value less than the VAR over a given horizon (usually a day) has a given probability stated as one minus a target confidence level. For example, a VAR of −3 per cent on a one-day horizon at a confidence level of 99 per cent means the probability of realizing a rate of return of less than 3 per cent during the next day is equal to 1 per cent.

Thus, we computed the VAR for two portfolios of banks, the first one consisting of the six biggest Canadian banks and the second one consisting of the twelve largest US banks. The VAR was computed using three months of historical volatility and a 99 per cent confidence level. Figure 5.1 shows the evolution of the VAR of the two portfolios over the period 2004–09. As can be seen, initially the VAR of the two portfolios had similar values above −2 per cent and ended the crisis also with similar values above −4 per cent. However, during the crisis itself, the VAR for the portfolio of US banks dropped below −14 per cent, whereas the VAR for the portfolio of Canadian banks never fell below −7 per cent, less than half the value of its American counterpart. This is evidence that investors themselves perceived, as events were unfolding, that there was a substantial difference in risk between the two banking systems.

Thus, both the analysis of government interventions and market reactions to the banking system show that the Canadian system

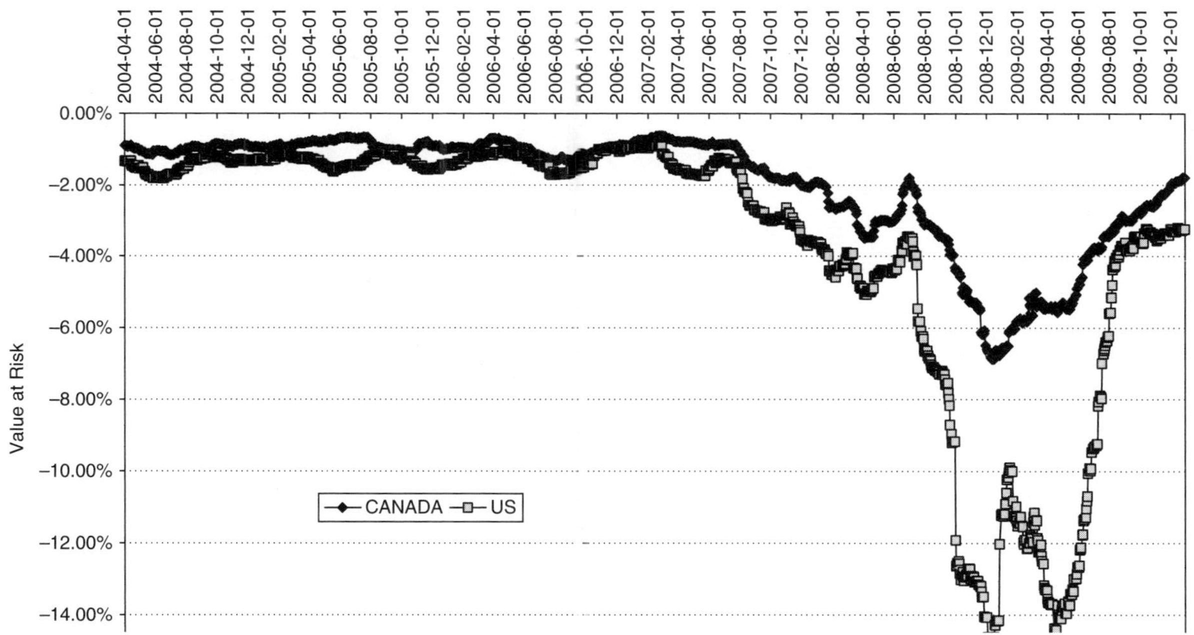

Figure 5.1. *Value-at-Risk at 99 per cent confidence level using three months historical volatility for portfolios of major banks over 2004–2009*

was very resilient and maintained its stability whereas the American system experienced a more pronounced financial crisis. This contrast in behaviour is somewhat surprising and suggests a need for further examination.

5.2. MARKET CONCENTRATION AND THE LEVEL OF COMPETITION

The traditional view, also called the Structure-Conduct-Performance paradigm, is that market concentration leads to less competitive behaviour allowing firms to enjoy higher rates of return while restricting output and taking lower risks. The British economist, Sir John Hicks, summarized this view in a now famous phrase: 'The best of monopoly profits is a quiet life'.[2] According to that theory, when firms possess some market power they have a choice to capitalize on this advantage by either increasing their rate of return or reducing their level of risk, or a combination of the two. Because reducing the level of risk is a less visible benefit and because it may suit better managers with undiversified human capital, it is expected that firms will choose to take a smaller part of their advantage in profitability and a greater part of their advantage in risk reduction. Indeed, it is natural to ask whether this theory would apply to the Canadian case, because its banking sector is quite concentrated with its five biggest banks controlling around 75 per cent of the asset market. In that spirit, the economist Paul Krugman labelled the Canadian banking system as 'boring', alluding to its low level of risk taking and its 'quiet' nature.

Modern economic theory has, however, cast serious doubts on this simple view. Thus, there are now two competing hypotheses relative to the relationship between the level of competition in banking and financial stability. Under the first hypothesis, less competitive banking systems are more stable because market power allows banks to have greater profits, take less risk, and accumulate more capital. Under the second hypothesis, less competitive banking systems are more unstable because the higher rates they charge to their borrowers increases credit risk, and exacerbates moral hazard and adverse selection problems.

Until now, economic theory has not been able to favour clearly one hypothesis over the other. Several recent papers[3] have concluded to the ambiguous results of economic theory relative to the link between the level of competition and financial stability.

In such a situation, empirical research can be used to try to clarify the matter and several researchers have taken that approach. Table 5.1 summarizes the evidence found. They show ambiguous results about the

Table 5.1. Empirical evidence on the link between market concentration, competition and financial stability

Authors	**Effect of concentration**	**Effect of competition**
Berger, Klapper, Turk-Ariss (2009)[1]		Negative
Jimenez, Lopez, Saurina (2007)[2]		Negative
Shaeck, Cihak, Wolfe (2009)[3]	Negative	Positive
Boyd, DeNicolo, Jalal (2009)[4]		Positive
Beck, Demirgüç-Kunt, Levine (2006)[5]	Positive	Positive
All together	Mixed	Mixed

Notes:

1 Berger A.N., Klapper L.F. and Turk-Ariss R., 'Bank Competition and Financial Stability', *Journal of Financial Services Research*, 2009, 35,99–118.
2 Jimenez G., Lopez J.A. and Saurina J., 'How Does Competition Impact Bank Risk-Taking?', Federal Reserve Bank of San Francisco, Working Paper 2007–23.
3 Shaeck K., Cihak M. and Wolfe S., 'Are More Competitive Banking Systems More Stable', *Journal of Money, Credit and Banking*, Vol 41, No 4, June 2009, pp. 711–734.
4 Boyd J.H., De Nicolo G. and Jalal A., 'Bank Competition, Risk and Asset Allocations', International Monetary Fund, Working Paper 09–143.
5 Beck T., Demirgüç-Kunt A. and Levine R., 'Bank concentration, competition and crises: First results', *Journal of Banking and Finance*, 30, 1581–1603, 2006.

relationship between either market concentration or competition and financial stability. Moreover, research leads to the observation that the relationship between market concentration and competition is rather complex. Concentrated markets may behave competitively, if regulation provides for an open market and fosters contestability.

In such a case, it is interesting to try to identify which of the two banking systems behaves more competitively. To measure the level of competition, two indicators are available: the H-statistic as determined by Panzar and Rosse[4] and the Lerner index.[5]

The H-statistic of Panzar and Rosse is the sum of the elasticities of total revenue with respect to the bank's input prices. The range of values for the H-statistic has the following interpretations: $H = 1$ indicates perfect competition, $0 < H < 1$ indicates monopolistic competition, $H<=0$ indicates monopoly or collusive oligopoly.

Table 5.2 presents the values obtained by several researchers for the H-statistic for the Canadian and the US banking systems. As can be seen, the most recent studies tend to show that the Canadian banking system would be less competitive.

As for the Lerner index, it is the proportion by which price exceeds marginal cost. Formally, Lerner index = (Price-marginal cost)/Price. In a

Table 5.2. Measures of the H-statistic for the banking systems of Canada and the US

Authors	Canada	US
Allen, Engert (2007)[1]	0.35	na
Bikker, Spierdijk, Finnie (2007)[2]	0.30	0.48
Claessens, Laeven (2003)[3]	0.67	0.41
Bikker, Haaf (2002)[4]	0.62	0.56

Notes:

1 Allen J. and Engert W., 'Efficiency and Competition in Canadian Banking', *Bank of Canada Review*, Summer 2007, pp.33–45.

2 Bikker J.A., Spierdijk L. and Finnie P., 'The Impact of Market Structure, Contestability and Institutional Environment on Banking Competition', Tjalling C. Koopmans Research Institute, Discussion Paper 07-29, p. 30.

3 Claessens S. and Laeven L., 'What Drives Bank Competition? Some International Evidence', World Bank Policy Research Working paper 3113, August 2003, p. 33.

4 Bikker J.A., Haaf K., 'Competition, concentration and their relationship: An empirical analysis of the banking industry', *Journal of Banking and Finance* 26 (2002) pp. 2191–2214.

perfectly competitive market, price would be equal to marginal cost and the Lerner index would be zero. So, the greater the Lerner index the less competitive is the market. Table 5.3 shows the values of the Lerner index obtained for several of the biggest Canadian and American banks. The Lerner index is on average at 15 per cent for Canada and at 23.7 per cent for the US, indicating that the latter would be less competitive.

Overall, the two indicators provide opposing signals as to which of the two banking systems would be more competitive and, as such, economic analysis sheds very little light on the issue. Neither theory nor empirical research tells us the direction of the relationship between competition and stability and moreover we do not know clearly which of the two systems is more competitive. In this context, the level of competition has to be abandoned as the explanation for the greater stability of the Canadian banking system and explanations are to be found elsewhere.

5.3. REGULATION AND FINANCIAL CULTURE

In this section, we consider regulation and financial culture as explanatory factors of the stability of the Canadian banking system. First, the rankings of Canada with regard to governance and freedom given respectively by the World Bank and the Heritage Foundation are presented. Secondly,

Table 5.3. Measures of the Lerner index for the major banks of Canada and the US

Canada	Lerner	US	Lerner
Royal Bank of Canada RBC	0.171	JP Morgan Chase & Co.	0.189
Scotia Bank	0.187	Bank of America, National Association	0.286
CIBC	0.110	Citibank NA	0.203
Toronto Dominion Bank	0.135	Wells Fargo & Company	0.241
		US Bancorp	0.311
Bank of Montreal	0.165	HSBC Bank USA, National Association	0.190
Desjardins Group	0.113		
National Bank of Canada	0.173	SunTrust Banks, Inc.	0.232
		PNC Financial Services Group Inc	0.228
		Capital One Financial Corporation	0.197
		State Street Corporation	0.195
		BB&T Corporation	0.249
		CIT Group, Inc	0.237
		HSBC Bank USA	0.279
		Regions Financial Corporation	0.219
		Golden State Bancorp Inc	0.168
		Countrywide Bank FSB	0.362
Average	0.151	Average	0.237

the regulatory framework, the banking system and the characteristics of borrowers are examined.

5.3.1. Governance and Financial Freedom

As an introduction to this section, it is interesting to see how two international organizations rank Canada and the US with regard to governance and freedom. In that regard, Table 5.4 presents the aggregate governance indicators determined by the World Bank. It shows that Canada has a stronger position overall compared to the US.

Table 5.5 shows the Heritage Foundation Indices of freedom.[6] It can be noted that Investment Freedom and Financial Freedom have lower values for Canada, consistent with the perception that regulation is stronger in Canada.

Table 5.4. World Bank Aggregate Governance Indicators[7]

Country	Canada	United States	Difference
Period	1998–2008	1998–2008	1998–2008
Voice & Accountability	95.9	88.9	6.9
Political Stability – No Violence	85.8	64	21.8
Government Effectiveness	96.3	92.2	4
Regulatory Quality	93.9	93.1	0.8
Rule of Law	95.2	92.4	2.8
Control of Corruption	94.6	92	2.6

Table 5.5. Heritage Foundation Indices of Freedom[8]

Country	Canada	United States	Difference
Year	1998–2010	1998–2010	1998–2010
Overall Score	75.1	78.7	−3.6
Business Freedom	89.5	87.7	1.8
Trade Freedom	82.5	82.1	0.4
Fiscal Freedom	63.9	66.1	−2.2
Government Spending	47.6	62.5	−14.8
Monetary Freedom	84.1	84.3	−0.2
Investment Freedom	55.8	72.7	−16.9
Financial Freedom	72.3	81.5	−9.2
Property Rights	90.0	89.6	0.4
Freedom From Corruption	88.5	75.2	13.3
Labor Freedom	82.5	82.7	−0.2

5.3.2. The Architecture of Public Institutions for Regulation and Supervision

In Canada, the major public institutions for financial regulation and supervision consist of the Department of Finance, the Bank of Canada, the Office of the Superintendent of Financial Institutions, the Canada Deposit Insurance Corporation, the Financial Consumer Agency of Canada and the Canada Housing and Mortgage Corporation. Overall, this simple architecture is based on the principle of one function-one institution and this avoids conflicts of interests within an institution that would have multiple objectives. To be sure, the structure also avoids conflicts between institutions that would pursue similar objectives. Thus, this framework can achieve both effectiveness and efficiency.

The most important piece of legislation governing the financial sector is

Table 5.6. The relative importance of the banking system in the Canadian and American economies (Data in billion $ as of 31 December 2008)

	Canada	% GDP	US	% GDP
GDP	1602		14265	
Number of banks	46		7022	
Total assets	2988	186.50 %	12311	86.30 %
Deposits	1917	119.70 %	8954	62.80 %
Loans	1630	101.70 %	7874	55.20 %
Securitization	249	15.50 %	6911	48.40 %

the *Bank Act*. That Act has an important clause that forces government to review the law regularly, as often as every five years. This clause has helped the Canadian government revise the law in a continuous and steady fashion. A stream of changes has taken place over the years, adjusting the law to the evolving environment without provoking shocks that could have disrupted the stability of the financial system.

5.3.3. The Banking System

The most striking point when comparing the financial systems of the US and Canada is that the latter has a much more bank-based system as the figures in Table 5.6 illustrate.

In relative terms, assets, deposits and loans are roughly twice as big in Canada, whereas securitization is three times smaller than in the US.

That being said, the differences between the two banking systems are not only quantitative but also qualitative. Several of these differences may explain the difference in stability evident during the last financial crisis.

First, Canadian and American banks have held different types of assets, especially with respect to mortgages. Basically, Canadian banks do not originate nor hold subprime mortgages. Moreover, all mortgages with a Loan to Value (LTV) ratio over 80 per cent must be insured by the Canada Housing and Mortgage Corporation (CHMC) or by a 90 per cent CHMC-backed private insurer. In contrast, mortgages in the US are fully insured up to 80 per cent LTV by the Federal Housing Administration and the remaining is insured by the private sector.

Secondly, Canadian banks enjoy a high source of depository funding. The five biggest Canadian banks all have ratios of deposits to assets ranging between 65 per cent and 71 per cent. Moreover, a high fraction of these deposits are so-called 'core deposits', that is deposits of less than CAD100 000, that are held mainly for transaction purposes such that they are not sensitive to interest rates and to the banks those balances provide for very stable funding. Therefore, their strong deposit base has shielded Canadian banks from the volatility of wholesale market funding.

Finally, Canadian banks were generally very well capitalized as the Canadian regulator imposes a safety margin of 3 per cent over and above the 4 per cent required for tier I capital mandated by the Basel II Accord and a 2 per cent safety margin over the 8 per cent requirement for total capital.

5.3.4. The Behaviour of Borrowers

It is also evident that Canadian households behave in a more prudent and conservative fashion than their American counterparts. It is acknowledged that Canadian households do not face the same incentives to borrow. Indeed, interest paid on mortgages is not deductible against income tax in Canada in the way that it is in the United States.

Consequently, in 2008 homeowners' equity as a share of the total value of real estate was around 70 per cent in Canada but only 45 per cent in the US. Similarly, household debt was around 120 per cent of disposable income in Canada, while it was close to 190 per cent in the US. Not surprisingly, mortgage delinquencies (90 days+) in 2007 were around 0.30 per cent in Canada and close to 1.60 per cent in the US.

5.3.5. The Overall Picture

Overall, the stability of the Canadian banking system seems to be explained by several interacting factors, namely an effective regulatory regime, a traditional banking system holding fairly safe loans, especially prime mortgages adequately government insured when needed, financed mainly through stable deposits and relatively conservative borrowers having, on average, a solid equity position in their homes.

5.4. CONCLUSION

During the financial crisis, the Canadian and American banking systems behaved in a strikingly different fashion. Whereas massive government intervention was needed in the US to bail out the financial system, the Canadian government did not have to inject capital in any banks and none failed. Investors themselves were aware of the difference in risk of the two systems as the VAR of the stocks of major banks in the US were twice as big as those of Canadian banks. The purpose of this chapter was to explore the reasons that explain such a puzzling contrast in stability.

The first natural path is to examine whether the traditional Structure-Conduct-Performance paradigm may be a source of explanation. Admittedly, the Canadian banking system is more concentrated than the American one. It is then tempting to conclude that it is less competitive. Thus, Canadian banks could take less risk, be more profitable and accumulate more capital, altogether making them more stable.

However, theory and empirical research challenge all these relationships. A concentrated system can be competitive if it is contestable. On the other hand, the relationship between competitiveness and stability is not clear whether in theory or in practice. Finally, the H-statistic and the Lerner index give opposing signals as to which of the two countries has the more competitive banking system. Clearly, this path of investigation does not provide any clear conclusions and one is led to consider a different perspective.

The stability of the Canadian banking system is explained, we believe, by its prudent regulation and effective supervision. More generally, that a conservative financial culture prevails in the behaviour of private participants is also an important factor. Indeed, Canadian banks do not participate in any way in the subprime market for mortgages and securitization of even prime mortgages remains rather limited. Moreover, Canadian banks enjoy a strong and stable deposit base for their funding and maintain capital positions well in excess of the Basel II Accord requirements. Households themselves have a strong equity position in their homes, have lower debt loads than their American counterparts and consequently have much lower delinquency rates. The interacting prudent behaviour of regulators, banks and households thus characterizes the Canadian financial culture. This conservative culture seems to form the basis for the stability of the Canadian financial system.

NOTES

1. The information has been obtained from www.fdic.gov (as of 28 October 2010).
2. Hicks, J.R. (1935), 'The Theory of Monopoly', *Econometrica*, Vol. 3 No. 1, pp. 8.
3. Allen, F. and D. Gal (2004), 'Competition and Financial Stability', *Journal of Money, Credit and Banking*, 36 No. 3, pp. 453–480; Boyd, J.H. and G. DeNicolo (2005), 'The Theory of Bank Risk Taking and Competition Revisited', *Journal of Finance*, LX, No 3, pp. 1329–1343; Beck T. (2008), 'Bank Competition and Financial Stability: Friends or Foes?', The World Bank, Policy Research Working Paper 4656, June 2008, p. 32.
4. Panzar, J.C. and J.N. Rosse (1987), 'Testing for Monopoly Equilibrium', *Journal of Industrial Economics*, 35, pp. 443–456.

5. Lerner, A.P. (1934), 'The Concept of Monopoly and the Measurement of Monopoly Power', *The Review of Economic Studies*, 1 (3), pp. 157–175.
6. According to the Heritage Foundation, economic freedom is the fundamental right of every human to control his or her own labor and property. In an economically free society, individuals are free to work, produce, consume, and invest in any way they please, with that freedom both protected by the state and unconstrained by the state. In economically free societies, governments allow labor, capital and goods to move freely, and refrain from coercion or constraint of liberty beyond the extent necessary to protect and maintain liberty itself. The economic freedom index is construed based on the measurement of ten different components of economic freedom (i.e. Business Freedom, Trade Freedom, Fiscal Freedom, Government Spending, Monetary Freedom, Investment Freedom, Financial Freedom, Property Rights, Freedom from Corruption and Labor Freedom) and assigning a grade in each using a scale from 0 to 100. The ten component scores are then averaged to give an overall economic freedom score for each country. For further enlargement on the topic and a detailed explanation of the methodology used, please see http://www.heritage.org/index/
7. See http://info.worldbank.org/governance/wgi/index.asp
8. See http://www.heritage.org/index/

6. Systemic contingent claim analysis – a model approach to systemic risk

Dale F. Gray and Andreas A. Jobst[1]

6.1. INTRODUCTION

Since 2008 unprecedented and sweeping crisis interventions have arrested a market panic, effectively stabilized the global financial system, and helped shore up investor confidence. In spite of this positive development, the encouraging picture has been tainted by mounting concerns surrounding the fiscal positions of sovereigns that have borrowed excessively to stabilize their financial systems and the related potential for contagion across the most vulnerable countries. Support measures provided to large financial institutions have resulted in considerable risk transfer to the government, which has intensified concerns about overall long-term fiscal sustainability as a swift recovery of the financial sector remains uncertain.[2] Moreover, the unresolved moral hazard problem of large complex financial institutions (LCFIs) that are deemed 'too-important' or 'too-networked' to fail, continues to imply large contingent liabilities for the public sector. Such contingent liabilities may imperil fiscal sustainability as they increase the susceptibility of public finances to the potential impact of systemic distress in the financial sector.

Given the elusive nature of systemic financial risk[3] from these contingent liabilities, policy-makers recognize the need for a multi-faceted approach comprising complementary measures in areas of regulatory policies, supervisory scope, and resolution arrangements as part of a sustainable solution towards a more resilient financial sector. Current policy efforts are aimed at establishing a regulatory framework that helps mitigate systemic risk from linkages between institutions and the extent to which they amplify incentive conflicts and coordination failure in various segments of financial markets. Some measures under discussion include more stringent prudential standards,[4] such as limits on leverage and higher capital requirements as a way to limit the scale and scope of banking activities, a broader adoption of contingent capital initiatives, designing 'living wills', strengthening resolution processes for LCFIs, possibly in combination with the establishment of a specialized macro-prudential supervisor of systemically important firms. The most recent proposals for financial sector reform also foresee surcharges in the form of taxes or levies on 'too-big-to-fail' (TBTF) firms directly related to their contribution to systemic risk as a result of their sources and term structure of funding, their leverage and their relationship with other financial firms.[5]

Against this background, we propose the systemic contingent claims analysis ('Systemic CCA') framework to estimate the magnitude of contingent liabilities from the financial sector under systemic distress assumptions. This aggregation technique generates an estimate of the joint market-implied contingent liabilities by combining the individual risk-adjusted balance sheets of financial institutions and the dependence between them. The Systemic CCA does not only quantify the magnitude of potential risk transfer to the government but also helps indicate the contribution of individual institutions to contingent liabilities over time depending on their size and interconnectedness.

Section 6.2 describes the benefits of applying CCA and extends its concept to the measurement of government contingent liabilities. It then takes a closer look at the dependence between financial institutions and describes a framework to analyse government and financial sector risk linkages. Subsequently, estimation results of the Systemic CCA framework for a large G-7 economy are presented. The chapter concludes by providing some caveats on systemic risk measurement and offers suggestions on new directions in managing financial sector and sovereign risk.

6.2. CONTINGENT CLAIMS ANALYSIS (CCA)

CCA is a generalization of the option pricing theory (OPT) pioneered by Black and Scholes[6] as well as Merton.[7] When applied to the analysis and measurement of credit risk, it is commonly called the Merton Model.[8]

In its basic concept, CCA assumes that owners of corporate equity in leveraged firms hold a call option on the firm value after outstanding liabilities have been paid off. They also have the option to default if their firm's asset value ('reference asset') falls below the present value of the notional amount of outstanding debt ('strike price') owed to bondholders at maturity. So, corporate bondholders effectively write a European put option to equity owners, who hold a residual claim on the firm's asset value in non-default states of the world. Bondholders receive a put option premium in the form of a credit spread above the risk-free rate in return for holding risky corporate debt (and bearing the potential loss) due to the limited liability of equity owners. The value of the put option is determined by the duration of debt claim, the leverage of the firm, and asset-price volatility.

CCA determines the risk-adjusted balance sheet of firms, based on three principles. They are: (i) the values of liabilities (equity and debt) are derived from assets; (ii) liabilities have different priority (i.e. senior and junior claims); and (iii) assets follow a stochastic process. Assets (such as the present value of income flows and proceeds from asset sales) are stochastic and over a horizon period may be above or below promised payments on debt which constitute a default barrier. Uncertain changes in future asset value, relative to the default barrier, determine the default risk which occurs when assets decline below the barrier. When there is a chance of default, the repayment of debt is considered 'risky', to the extent that it is not guaranteed in the event of default. If all or some of the principal is protected, the discounted value of the economic cost from insuring against default can be quantified as the expected loss borne by a third-party guarantor, such as the government.[9]

The concept of a risk-adjusted balance sheet is instrumental in understanding default risk. More specifically, the total market value of firm assets, A, at any time, t, is equal to the sum of its equity market value, E, and its risky debt, D, maturing at time T.[10] The asset value follows a random, continuous process and may fall below the value of outstanding liabilities, which constitute the bankruptcy level ('default threshold' or 'distress barrier') B.[11] B is defined as the present value of promised payments on debt discounted at the risk-free rate. These uncertain changes in future asset value, relative to promised payments on debt, is the driver of default risk. Indeed, default happens when assets are insufficient to meet the amount of debt owed to creditors at maturity.

When there is a chance of default, the repayment of debt is considered 'risky', to the extent that it is not guaranteed in the event of default. The value of risky debt is equal to default-free debt minus the present value of expected loss due to default. These expected losses associated with outstanding liabilities can be valued as an implicit put option

$$P_E(t) = Be^{-r(T-t)}\Phi(-d_2) - A(t)\Phi(-d_1),$$

which is calculated based on the default threshold B as strike price on the asset value A subject to the duration of debt claim, the leverage of the firm, and asset return volatility σ_A, which determine $d_1 = [\ln(A(t)/B) + (r + \sigma_A^2/2)(T-t)](\sigma_A\sqrt{T-t})^{-1}$ and $d_2 = d_1 - \sigma_A\sqrt{T-t}$, given the cumulative probability $\Phi(.)$ of the standard normal density function.[12] The market value of assets cannot be observed directly but it can be model implied.[13] From the observed prices and volatilities of market-traded equity, one can estimate the implied values and volatilities of the underlying assets. Also, in some cases asset and asset volatility can be estimated directly and can be used to calibrate risk-adjusted balance sheet models.[14] Once the asset value and asset volatility are known, together with the default barrier, time horizon (denoted as remaining maturity $T - t$), and discount rate r, the value of the implicit put option can be calculated at each point in time.

6.3. MEASURING EXPECTED LOSSES AND CONTINGENT LIABILITIES

The implicit put option calculated for each financial institution from equity market information using CCA can be combined with information from credit default swap (CDS) markets to estimate the government's contingent liabilities. If guarantees do not affect equity prices in a major way (especially when firms are in distress), implicit guarantees reduce default risk, so that the price of insuring against default, which is expressed as CDS spreads for contracts at different maturity tenors, captures only the expected loss *retained* by the financial institution – and borne by unsecured senior creditors. Hence, the scope of market-implied guarantees affecting firm valuation can be defined as difference between the total expected loss (i.e., the value of a put option derived from the firm's equity price) and the value of an implicit put option derived from the firm's CDS spread s_{CDS} (in basis points).

The implicit put option derived from the firm's CDS spread can be written as

$$P_{CDS}(t) = (1 - \exp(-(s_{CDS}/10{,}000) \times T))Be^{-rT}$$

and reflects expected losses associated with default net of any financial guarantees.[15] Thus, we can determine the fraction

$$\alpha(t) = 1 - P_{CDS}(t)/P_E(t)$$

of expected losses covered by implicit guarantees that depress the CDS spread below the level that would otherwise be warranted for the actual default risk implied by equity prices.[16] In the next section we estimate these contingent liabilities over time and determine their significance on aggregate within an entire financial system in order to gauge the magnitude of systemic risk.

6.4. THE SYSTEMIC CCA METHOD

The Systemic CCA framework[17] combines CCA-derived risk-adjusted balance sheets of individual financial institutions and the dependence between them in order to quantify systemic financial sector risk jointly posed by these institutions. Based on individual estimates of contingent liabilities from explicit and implicit guarantees, this aggregation technique utilizes a novel application of extreme value theory (EVT)[18] in order to generate a multivariate limiting distribution that formally captures the potential of joint extreme realizations of contingent liabilities.

A suitable assessment of systemic risk stemming from multiple institutions warrants measuring joint default risk in the financial sector, which entails a non-trivial aggregation problem. Since the simple summation of implicit put options of sample institutions would presuppose a coincidence of individual defaults, the correct estimation of aggregate risk requires knowledge about the dependence structure of individual balance sheets and associated contingent claims. However, since traditional (pair-wise) correlation measures are ill-suited for systemic risk analysis when extreme events occur jointly (and in a non-linear fashion), one way forward is to view the financial sector as a portfolio of individual contingent claims (with individual risk parameters). This method of measuring 'tail dependence' is better suited to analysing extreme linkages of multiple (rather than only two) entities.

As an integral part of this approach, the multivariate distribution is generated from the separate analysis of the relative magnitude of individual contingent liabilities and their linear and non-linear dependence. The marginal distributions of individual default risk are assumed to be 'fat-tailed' (and fall within the domain of the Generalized Extreme Value Distribution (GEV)),[19] which identifies asymptotic tail behaviour of normalized extremes.[20] The dependence function is non-parametric and optimizes the coincidence of multiple series of cross-classified random variables similar to a Chi-statistic.

By accounting for the dependence structure of individual balance sheets and associated contingent claims, this approach can be used to quantify the contribution of specific institutions to the dynamics of systemic risk (at different levels of statistical confidence),[21] how this systemic risk affects contingent liabilities, and how policy measures may influence the size and allocation of this systemic risk over time.

Since this approach also considers the time-variation of point estimates due to a periodic updating, it is more comprehensive than alternative measurement approaches to systemic risk, such as CoVaR,[22] CoRisk,[23] and Systemic Expected Shortfall (SES),[24] as well as extensions thereof, such as the Distress Insurance Premium (DIP).[25] Neither approach applies multivariate density estimation like Systemic CCA, which allows the determination of the marginal contribution of an individual institution to concurrent changes of both the severity of systemic risk and the dependence structure across any combination of sample institutions for *any* level of statistical confidence. In contrast, CoVaR, CoRisk and SES examine incremental effects that cover only a fraction of available data that could be usefully integrated to assess the system-wide sensitivity of contingent liabilities to individual default risk of banks (and the associated cost to governments upon realization states of distress).

6.5. CASE STUDY: EXPECTED LOSSES AND CONTINGENT LIABILITIES IN A LARGE G-7 ECONOMY

This section highlights some of the most salient results from applying the Systemic CCA methodology to the financial sector of a large G-7 economy, based on market and balance sheet information of 36 large commercial banks, investment banks, insurance companies, and special purpose financial institutions using daily data between 1 January 2007 and end-January 2010.[26] The following charts (see Figures 6.1–6.4) illustrate – in broad strokes – the analytical progression from the summation of individual contingent liabilities derived from implicit put option values to their multivariate distribution. Based on these results, we also present the individual contributions of sample institutions to the change of joint contingent liabilities (see Figure 6.5) and propose one possibility of how risk metric of systemic risk can inform the calculation of an institution-specific fair value charge.

6.5.1. Individual Contingent Claims

We first inspect the estimation results of fraction of expected losses, which might become contingent liabilities to the public sector in cases of individual distress, by plotting the changes of the median and the interquartile range of the alpha-values (as defined above) for all sample institutions over time (see Figure 6.1). We observe a secular increase of implied financial sector support as a result of a widening gap between default risk implied by equity and CDS put option values. Sudden declines in alpha-values around April 2008, October 2008, and May 2009 are attributable to a greater alignment of changes in market capitalization and the market price of default risk as explicit or implicit financial sector support have

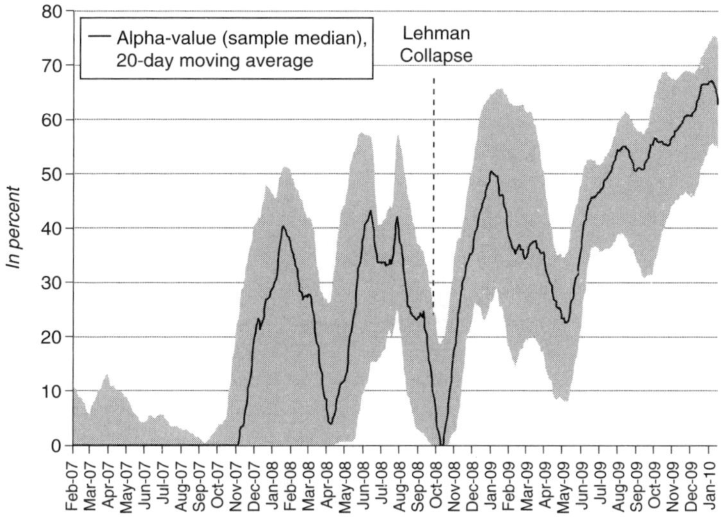

Note: Sample period: 01/03/2007–01/29/2010 (743 obs.) of individual alpha-values of 27 sample banks and other financial institutions, excluding insurance companies and government-sponsored housing agencies. The grey shaded area shows the inter-quartile range (IQR) between the 25th and the 75th percentile of the entire sample of alpha-values.

Figure 6.1. Large G-7 Economy: Financial Sector – Time Pattern of Alpha-Value

little or no impact on slowing the rise of CDS spreads amid falling equity prices of distressed firms.[27]

Figure 6.2 shows that total expected losses (area) and contingent liabilities (line) are highest between the periods just after the collapse of Lehman Brothers in September 2008 and end-July 2009. The analysis suggests that markets expected that – on average – more than 50 percent of total expected losses could have been transferred to the government in the event of default. The sum of individual contingent liabilities peaks at about 1.0 percent of GDP at the end of March 2009, averaging 0.5 percent of GDP over the entire sample period.

While the summation of expected losses and contingent liabilities represents a correct measure of aggregate systemic risk, it does not reflect the concurrent realization of individual distress. Thus, it is critical to take into account the inter-temporal changes in the dependence structure between this 'portfolio' of risk-adjusted balance sheets of sample institutions and their dependence for the estimation of systemic risk arising from the joint default probability. After controlling for the dependence structure between the risk-adjusted balance sheets of sample institutions using the

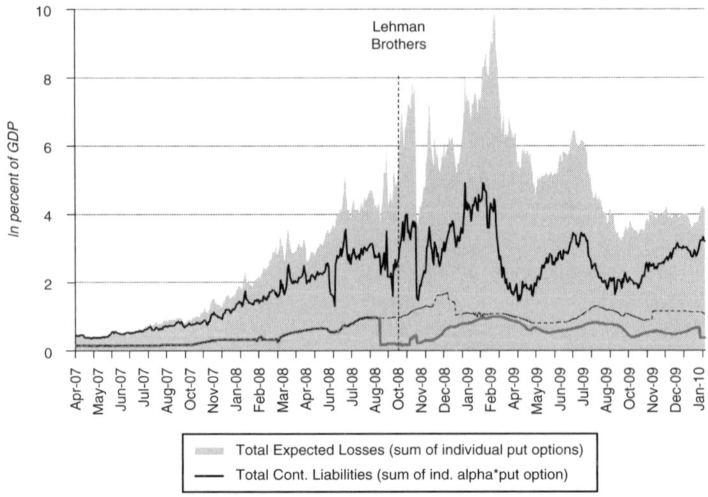

Note: Sample period: 01/03/2007–01/29/2010 (743 obs.) of individual put option values (i.e., expected losses) conditional on the endogenous alpha-value of implicit guarantees of 36 sample banks, insurance companies, and other financial institutions, estimated over a window of 60 working days (with daily updating). There are two 50th percentile lines in this figure. The thicker dotted line shows results for the case where government-sponsored financing agencies were de facto nationalized (which warrants their exclusion from the sample on 8 September 2008). The second, thinner line shows the case where these government-sponsored financing agencies are left in the sample. Note that daily equity prices were still available after the exclusion date but it can be argued these data may be much less informative. The sudden drop of both expected losses and contingent liabilities in October 2008 is due to the exclusion of Lehman Brothers from the sample.

Figure 6.2. Large G-7 Economy: Financial Sector – Total Contingent Liabilities and Multivariate Density of Contingent Liabilities ('Systemic CCA')

Systemic CCA methodology, the median value of joint contingent liabilities drops significantly.

6.5.2. Systemic Risk from Expected Losses

After the collapse of Lehman Brothers, the extreme tail risk in the system increased sharply. The point estimates of the 95th percentile expected shortfall jumped to more than 20 percent of GDP (see Figure 6.3), with the shaded areas indicating the confidence bands at one and two standard deviations around the point estimates. In other words, during this period of exceptional systemic distress, market prices of sample institutions

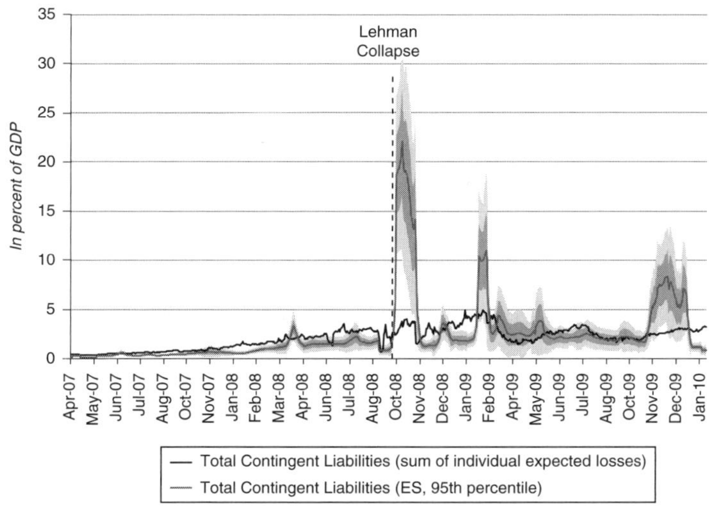

Note: Sample period: 01/03/2007–01/29/2010 (743 obs.) of individual put option values (i.e., expected losses) of 36 banks, insurance companies, and other financial institutions, estimated over a window of 60 working days (with daily updating). The dark line shows the expected shortfall (ES) for the entire sample at a 95th percentile threshold within a confidence band of one and two standard deviations (grey areas).

Figure 6.3. Large G-7 Economy: Financial Sector – Average Daily Expected Shortfall (ES) [95th Percentile] based on Multivariate Density of Expected Losses

implied joint expected losses of 20 percent of GDP with a probability of five percent over a one-year time horizon. The magnitude of such tail risk, however, dropped to under 2 percent of GDP during the remainder of 2008 before rising again in January, May and November the next year.

6.5.3. Systemic Risk from Contingent Liabilities

The systemic risk from contingent liabilities was considerable during the credit crisis and differed from the evolution of systemic risk from expected losses. After controlling for the market perception (via CDS prices) about the residual risk retained in the financial sector, the time pattern of joint contingent liabilities shows spikes as early as April 2008, indicating already high potential government exposure to joint financial sector distress in the wake of the Bear Stearns bailout. The potential tail risk transferred to the government exceeds 9 percent of GDP in April and almost reached 20 percent of GDP in October 2008 (see Figure 6.4). The red line shows the

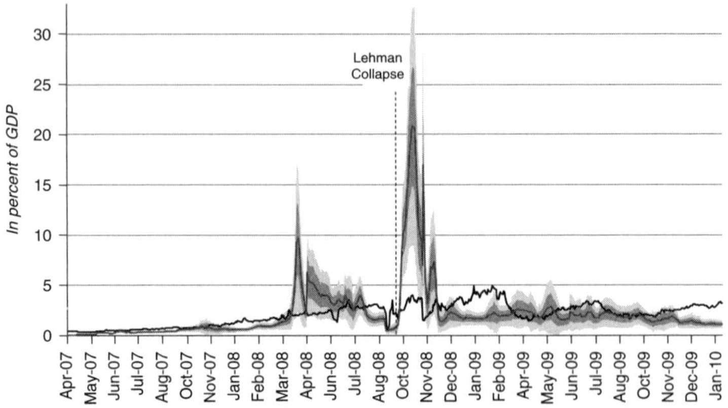

Note: Sample period: 01/03/2007–01/29/2010 (743 obs.) of individual put option values (i.e., expected losses) conditional on the endogenous alpha-value of implicit guarantees of 36 banks, insurance companies, and other financial institutions, estimated over a window of 60 working days (with daily updating). The dark line shows the expected shortfall (ES) for the entire sample at a 95th percentile threshold within a confidence band of one and two standard deviations (grey areas).

Figure 6.4. Large G-7 Economy: Financial Sector – Average Daily Expected Shortfall (ES) [95th Percentile] based on Multivariate Density of Contingent Liabilities ('Systemic CCA')

95th percentile expected shortfall within a confidence band of one and two standard deviations (grey areas).

The spike in April 2008 is absent in the earlier chart showing expected losses (see Figure 6.3), which underscores the distinction of expected losses and contingent liabilities for the purpose of systemic risk measurement purposes. The bailout of Bear Stearns led to expectations of public support and induced highly correlated expectations of government support across numerous institutions, while residual risk outside anticipated public sector support was considered less susceptible to co-movements in asset prices.

6.5.4. Contributions to Systemic Risk from Contingent Liabilities

Failed and bailed-out firms were the large contributors to systemic risk-from joint contingent liabilities, especially prior to the collapse of Lehman Brothers. An examination of the percentage share of systemic risk in different periods (see Table 6.1 and Figure 6.5) suggests that pre-crisis (up to 14 September 2008), the nine financial institutions that either failed (6) or were rescued (3) later on were the biggest contributors at 69.5 percent.

Table 6.1. Large G-7 Economy: Financial Sector – Average Individual Contribution to Systemic Risk from Contingent Liabilities (In percent, average expected shortfall at the 95th percentile)

	Contribution to Systemic Risk from Contingent Liabilities (*in percent*)			
Sample group	*Pre-Crisis*: July 1, 2007– Sept. 14, 2008	*Crisis Period 1*: Sept. 15– Dec. 31, 2008	*Crisis Period 2*: Jan. 1– May 8, 2009	*Crisis Period 3*: May 11– Dec. 31, 2009
Banks	15.6	36.1	34.6	37.7
Insurance companies	13.9	9.8	14.1	23.7
Other, non-bank financial institutions	3.0	31.8	32.2	21.0
Failed or bailed-out financial institutions	69.5	22.3	19.1	17.6

	Total Sample Period (April 1, 2007–Jan. 29, 2010)			
Relative Measure (in percent)	Banks	Insurance companies	Other, non-bank financial institutions	Failed or bailed-out financial institutions
Contribution to Systemic Risk	27.2	15.8	14.7	43.1
Share of Total Liabilities	37.2	16.3	2.8	43.7
Share of Total Contingent Liabilities	7.6	4.9	0.9	86.7

Note: Each group's percentage share in the first table aggregates groupwise each constituent institution's time-varying contribution to the expected shortfall at the 95th percentile of the multivariate density of total contingent liabilities during different time periods. The share of failed or bailed-out financial institutions declines over time as they drop out of the original sample of 36 institutions. The second table compares the groupwise contribution to systemic risk from joint contingent liabilities to other relative measures, such as the share of total contingent liabilities (i.e., the sum of individual equity put option values multiplied by the corresponding alpha-values) and the share of total reported liabilities.

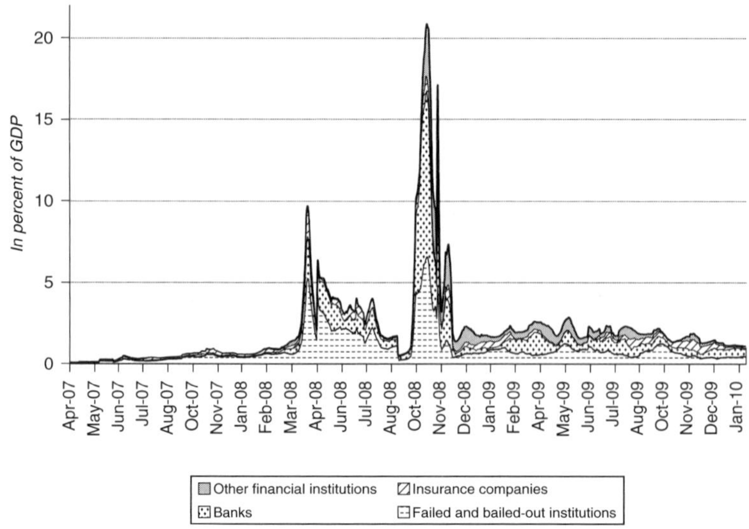

Note: Sample period: 01/03/2007–01/29/2010 (743 obs.) of individual put option values (i.e., expected losses) conditional on the endogenous alpha-value of 36 banks, insurance companies, and other financial institutions, estimated over a window of 60 working days (with daily updating). The chart shows the groupwise contribution to expected shortfall (ES) at a 95th percentile threshold.

Figure 6.5. Large G-7 Economy: Financial Sector – Decomposition of Average Daily Expected Shortfall (ES) [95th Percentile] based on Multivariate Density of Contingent Liabilities ('Systemic CCA')

As the six failed institutions gradually drop out of the sample after 15 September 2008, large banks increase their share to about one-third of total systemic risk. Interestingly, the contribution of insurance companies remains low during the height of the credit crisis before rising to nearly 24 percent during the second half of 2009.

Based on these findings the identification of the individual contribution to systemic risk seems non-trivial and yields results that differ significantly from naïve solutions. For instance, ignoring the dependence structure of risk-adjusted balance sheets and individual tail risk by simply summing up group-wise contingent liabilities would overstate the contribution of failed/rescued financial institutions while understating the contribution of all other, individually more resilient financial institutions, including insurance companies. That being said, using the share of reported total liabilities of each group in the financial sector seems more consistent with the groupwise contributions to systemic risk derived from the Systemic

CCA approach, especially for failed/rescued financial institutions and insurance companies.

6.5.5. Calculating a Systemic Risk Surcharge for Contingent Liabilities

A fair value price for guarantees or risk surcharges for systemic risk can be calculated from models that quantify the magnitude of risk transfer from the financial sector to the sovereign balance sheet, such as the Systemic CCA model.[28] The amount of estimated market-implied contingent liabilities can deliver a fair value price of a possible systemic risk surcharge. To illustrate this, we combine estimated joint contingent liabilities together with the sum of individual default barriers for all sample firms to inform a subjective default probability. More specifically, the fair value (in basis points) of a risk-based surcharge that would compensate for contingent liabilities at a confidence level of $1 - a$ can be written as

$$-\frac{1}{T}\ln\left(1-\frac{\sum_t^T \text{Joint Contingent Liabilities}_m}{\sum_t^T\sum_j^m B_j e^{-r(T-t)}}\right)\times 10000,$$

where B represents the aggregate default barrier of all m-institutions in the sample, r is the risk-free rate, with the joint contingent liabilities derived as an average point estimate of the multivariate distribution of fraction $\alpha(t)$ of expected losses $P_E(t)$ (equity put option).

Based on the results obtained from the contingent claims analysis (CCA), a reasonable average systemic surcharge for systemically important financial institutions would be about 50 basis points per year (T-t=1). A reasonable average systemic surcharge for the financial institutions sample during the pre-crisis period would have been 39 basis points per year, based on observations between July 2007 and September 2008 (before the Lehman collapse). Under greater statistical confidence (95 percent), this value would have reached 60 (and 317) basis points shortly before (after) the collapse of Lehman Brothers if most tail events were also priced into the systemic risk charge (see Table 6.2).[29]

The idea of large financial institutions to pay a risk-based levy to reflect the systemic risk implications of their activities has considerable appeal but is not without risks. A systemic risk surcharge would secure stability of the financial system (if it dissuaded incentives to perpetuate moral hazard from a too-big-to-fail status) while limiting future burdens on taxpayers. At the same time, the institutionalization of systemic importance could

Table 6.2. Large G-7 Economy: Financial Sector – Estimated Fair Value Surcharge for Systemic Risk based on Total Contingent Liabilities (average values of point estimates at the 50th and 95th percentiles)

Period	50th percentile		95th percentile	
	USD billion	annual fee (*basis points*)	USD billion	annual fee (*basis points*)
Total: April 1, 2007–Jan. 29, 2010	74	**49**	214	142
Pre-Crisis: July 1, 2007–Sept. 14, 2008	59	39	91	60
Crisis Period 1: Sept. 15–Dec. 31, 2008	43	28	479	317
Crisis Period 2: Jan. 1–May 8, 2009	119	76	359	232
Crisis Period 3: May 11–Dec. 31, 2009	88	58	227	150

aggravate the underlying problem of moral hazard by breeding a sense of entitlement to government support.[30]

6.6. CONCLUSION

This chapter presented a new modelling framework ('Systemic CCA'), which can help the measurement, analysis and management of systemic risk by estimating the joint expected losses and associated contingent liabilities of financial institutions. An example of Systemic CCA applied to a large G-7 economy showed useful insights about the dynamics of systemic risk from market-implied contingent liabilities and the contribution of individual institutions. In particular, the magnitude of potential risk transfer to the government indicates sustained financial sector stresses.

However, assessing the magnitude of systemic risk is not a straightforward exercise and requires a significant departure from conventional statistics. In particular, there is danger of underestimating practical problems of applying systemic risk management approaches to a real-life situation as complex modeling risks losing transparency, with conclusions being highly dependent on the assumptions used. Thus, recognizing the impact of parameter sensitivity and estimation risk on systemic risk models warrant the use of multiple approaches to enhance robustness. In this regard, our approach offers a tractable approach to the management of systemic financial sector risk.

Going forward, the Systemic CCA framework could inform more accurate representation of the impact of systemic risk on financial stability (and economic growth, if modeled in the context of inter-linkages between the financial sector, households, and the government). In particular, this framework can be used to analyse potential (non-linear) destabilizing feedback processes between the financial sector and the sovereign balance sheet.

NOTES

1. The authors would like to thank Laura Kodres, Chris Towe, Robert C. Merton, Robert Engle, Michael Gordy, Zvi Bodie, Mikhail Oet, Christoph Memmel, and Andrea Maechler for useful comments and suggestions. We are also grateful for helpful feedback received from participants at several seminar presentations to national authorities in the context of the IMF's Financial Sector Assessment Program (FSAP) consultations with the United States (2010), Germany (2011), and the United Kingdom (2011) as well as Article IV consultations with Switzerland (2009), Sweden (2010) and Israel (2010). The views expressed in this chapter are those of the authors and do not necessarily represent those of the IMF or IMF policy.
2. See Gray, D. F., and A. A. Jobst, 2010, 'Risk Transmission between Sovereigns and Banks in Europe', *Global Financial Stability Report*, Chapter 1, October (Washington: International Monetary Fund), pp. 12 and 40–44.
3. Systemic financial risk is the risk that a shock will trigger a loss of economic value or confidence in, and attendant increases in uncertainty about, a substantial portion of the financial system. While this definition restricts systemic risk to the financial sector for measurement purposes, it does not preclude the possibility of a financial sector shock from triggering a significant decline in real activity. In fact, it is highly likely that externalities of a financial shock also induce significant adverse real effects, such as substantial reductions in both economic output and employment. See also González-Hermosillo, B., C. Capuano, D. Gray, H. Hesse, A. Jobst, P. Mills, M. Segoviano, and T. Sun, 2009, 'Methods to identify systemic financial risks', *Vox* (April 23), available at: http://www.voxeu.org/index.php?q=node/3495.
4. This approach involves reducing the size and business activities of large financial institutions and providing incentives for downsizing via capital and liquidity requirements in order to lessen potentially systemic linkages.
5. However, such surcharges entail important policy considerations as they could create an additional burden on the financial sector at a time when capital is scarce and credit supply is so much needed to sustain a recovery. Thus, a careful calibration and possible implementation is essential to ensure that the availability of adequate credit to support the ongoing recovery is not impeded.
6. Black F. and M. Scholes, 1973, 'The Pricing of Options and Corporate Liabilities', *Journal of Political Economy*, Vol. 81, No. 3, pp. 637–54.
7. Merton, R. C., 1973, 'Theory of Rational Option Pricing', *Bell Journal of Economics and Management Science*, Vol.4 (Spring), pp. 141–83.
8. *The Merton approach assumes that the firm's debt consists of a zero-coupon bond B* with a notional value F and a maturity term of T periods. The firm's outstanding liabilities constitute the bankruptcy level, whose standard normal density defines the 'distance to default' relative to the firm value. This capital-structure-based evaluation of contingent claims on firm performance under the risk neutral measure implies that a firm defaults

if its asset value is insufficient to meet the amount of debt owed to bondholders at maturity. Conversely, if the 'distance to default' is positive, and the asset value of the firm exceeds the bankruptcy level, the call option held by equity holders on firm value has intrinsic value (in addition to its time value until the maturity of debt). Initially developed for valuation of corporate firms, CCA has been adapted to financial institutions and sovereigns.

9. Merton, R. C., 1977, 'An Analytic Derivation of the Cost of Loan Guarantees and Deposit Insurance: An Application of Modern Option Pricing Theory', *Journal of Banking and Finance*, Vol. 1, pp. 3–11.
10. We identify contingent liabilities based on the standard Black-Scholes-Merton (BSM) framework of capital structure-based option pricing theory (OPT). See Merton, R. C., 1974, 'On the Pricing of Corporate Debt: The Risk Structure of Interest Rates', *Journal of Finance*, Vol. 29 (May), pp. 449–70.
11. Moody's *KMV CreditEdge* defines this barrier equal to total short-term debt plus one-half of long-term debt.
12. The asset and asset volatility are valued after the dividend payouts. For more information on the implementation of this approach see Gray, D. F., A. A. Jobst, and S. Malone, 2010, 'Quantifying Systemic Risk and Reconceptualizing the Role of Finance for Economic Growth', *Journal of Investment Management*, Vol. 8, No. 2, pp. 90–110. Note that the above option pricing method does not incorporate skewness, kurtosis, and stochastic volatility. However, the classical Merton model can be refined without altering the analytical form by means of the closed-form Gram-Charlier model in Backus, D. K., S. Foresi, and L. Wu, 2004, 'Accounting for Biases in Black-Scholes', Working Paper, New York University, Goldman Sachs Group, and Baruch College, which is constructed using the same diffusion process for asset prices.
13. An implied value refers to an estimate derived from other observed data. Techniques for using implied values are widely practiced in options pricing and financial engineering applications.
14. In this chapter, we estimate implied asset values using equity option prices without any assumptions on the underlying diffusion process. We derive the risk-neutral probability distribution of the underlying asset price at the maturity date of the options by adapting the Breeden and Litzenberger method (Breeden, D. and R. Litzenberger, 1978, 'Prices of State-Contingent Claims Implicit inOption Prices', *Journal of Business*, Vol. 51, pp. 621–65), together with a semi-parametric specification of the Black-Scholes option pricing formula according to Aït-Sahalia, Y. and A. W. Lo, 1998, 'Non-parametric Estimation of State-Price Densities Implicit in Financial Asset Prices', *Journal of Finance*, Vol. 53, pp. 499–547.
15. Note that this is a simplified expression from the more detailed exposition offered in Gray, D. F. and A. A. Jobst, 2009, 'New Directions in Financial Sector and Sovereign Risk Management', *Journal of Investment Management*, Vol. 8, No.1, pp. 23–38.
16. While this definition of market-implied contingent liabilities provides a useful indication of possible sovereign risk transfer, the estimation of the alpha-value depends on a variety of assumptions that influence the assessment of the likelihood of government support, especially at times of extreme stress during the credit crisis. The extent to which the put option values differ from the ones implied by CDS spreads might reflect distortions stemming from the modeling choice (and the breakdown of efficient asset pricing in situations of illiquidity), changes in market conditions, and the capital structure impact of crisis interventions, such as equity dilution in the wake of capital injections by the government, beyond the influence of explicit or implicit guarantees. For a more detailed discussion of certain qualifications that need to be attributed to the estimated magnitude of contingent liabilities, see Gray, D. F. and A. A. Jobst, forthcoming, 'Systemic Contingent Claims Analysis (Systemic CCA) – Estimating Potential Losses and Implicit Government Guarantees to the Financial Sector', IMF Working Paper (Washington: International Monetary Fund).
17. Gray, D. F. and A. A. Jobst, 2010, 'Using the CCA Framework to Estimate Potential

Losses and Implicit Government Guarantees to the US Financial Sector', United States: Publication of Financial Sector Assessment Program Documentation – Technical Note on Stress Testing, Country Report No. 10/244 (July 30) (Washington: International Monetary Fund), pp. 58–83.

18. EVT is a useful statistical concept to study the tail behavior of heavily skewed data, which specifies residual risk at high percentile levels through a generalized parametric estimation of order statistics.
19. The choice of the empirical distribution function of the underlying data to model the marginal distributions avoids problems associated with using specific parameters that may or may not fit these distributions well. See Gray, D. F. and A. A. Jobst, 2009, 'Higher Moments and Multivariate Dependence of Implied Volatilities from Equity Options as Measures of Systemic Risk', *Global Financial Stability Report*, Chapter 3, April (Washington: International Monetary Fund), pp. 128–31.
20. Coles, S. G., J. Heffernan, and J. A. Tawn, 1999, 'Dependence Measures for Extreme Value Analyses', Extremes, Vol. 2, pp. 339–65; Jobst, A. A., 2007, 'Operational Risk – The Sting is Still in the Tail But the Poison Depends on the Dose', *Journal of Operational Risk*, Vol. 2, No. 2 (Summer), pp. 1–56; Poon, S.-H., M. Rockinger and J. Tawn, 2003, 'Extreme Value Dependence in Financial Markets: Diagnostics, Models, and Financial Implications', *The Review of Financial Studies*, Vol. 17, No. 2, pp. 581–610.
21. The contribution to systemic (joint tail risk) is derived as the partial derivative of the multivariate density relative to changes in the relative weight of the univariate marginal distribution of each bank at the specified percentile.
22. CoVaR quantifies how financial difficulties of one institution can increase the tail risk of others. CoVaR for a certain institution is defined as the VaR of the whole sector conditional on a particular institution being in distress. See Adrian, T. and M. K. Brunnermeier, 2008, 'CoVaR', Staff Reports 348, Federal Reserve Bank of New York.
23. Chan-Lau, J., 2010, 'Regulatory Capital Charges for Too-Connected-To-Fail Institutions: A Practical Proposal', IMF Working Paper 10/98 (Washington: International Monetary Fund).
24. The Marginal Expected Shortfall (MES) specifies historical expected losses, conditional on having breached some high systemic risk threshold. Adjusting MES by the degree of firm-specific leverage and capitalization yields the Systemic Expected Shortfall (SES). See Acharya,V. V., L. Pedersen, T. Philippon, and M. Richardson, 2009, 'Regulating Systemic Risk', in: Acharya, V. V. and M. Richardson (eds), *Restoring Financial Stability: How to Repair a Failed System*, New York: Wiley.
25. The systemic risk measure is defined as the insurance cost to protect against distressed losses in a banking system, is a summary indicator of market-perceived risk that reflects expected default risk of individual banks and the correlation of defaults approximated by equity returns. Huang, X., H. Zhou, and H. Zhu, 2010, 'Assessing the Systemic Risk of a Heterogeneous Portfolio of Banks during the Recent Financial Crisis', Working Paper (26 January), 22nd Australasian Finance and Banking Conference 2009 (available at http://ssrn.com/abstract=1459946).
26. For the individual CCA, we apply an enhanced version of the Merton framework. Key inputs used were the daily implied asset values derived from equity option data (over the sample time period with a time-to-maturity of three months), the default barrier estimated for each firm based on quarterly financial accounts (from Moody's *KMV CreditEdge*), the risk-free rate of interest (r = 3.0 percent), a one-year time horizon $T = 1$, and one-year credit default swap (CDS) spreads on senior debt (from *MarkIt*). The default barrier is set equal to total short-term debt plus one-half of long-term debt, consistent with the approach taken by Moody's *KMV CreditEdge*. Outputs were the expected losses (i.e., the implicit put option value over a one-year horizon) and the associated contingent liabilities from each bank (i.e., alpha-value times the implicit put option derived from equity).
27. This means that potential contingent liabilities to the financial sector have not disappeared but are persistent (outside the current specification of the alpha-value).

28. Recently, several governments announced plans to impose a financial transactions tax (possibly in combination with a systemic risk fee).
29. After considering the time-variation of contingent liabilities (and their distributional behavior), it would be possible to devise a counter-cyclical surcharge by combining estimates at different percentile levels of statistical confidence.
30. There is also the question of whether such fees should be charged ex post or ex ante, and whether proceeds would go to special funds or to general government revenue.

7. Tax and the city: the UK's proposals for a bank levy

John Snape[1]

7.1. INTRODUCTION

The issue of whether there exists some public interest, beyond the 'natural' operation of the markets, is the central ideological question in a world where the future shape of neoliberal society is gravely in doubt. Nowhere, perhaps, has this proposition been more vividly illustrated than in the debate about how governments, whether acting together or unilaterally, should legislate for the reform of financial markets. Questions have centred, to a large extent, on the vexed issue of whether a special levy should be imposed on banks, one which would reflect the systemic risks that the financial services sector presents to the developed economies of the world.[2] Imposing such a levy is not, of course, the only possibility for the greater regulation of the banks, as the various contributions to this volume demonstrate. Discussion of the merits of a bank levy has weaved itself inextricably around the other, related yet distinct, questions, which have long preoccupied analysis of the deliberations of both the European Commission and the Basel Committee on Banking Supervision.[3] Preeminent among these, of course, is the issue of how to strengthen banks' 'buffers' of capital and liquidity, each of which gives rise to problems themselves shaped and prioritized by the feasibility of a bank levy. Regardless of the shape a bank levy might ultimately take, the nature and quality of the arguments, both for and against it, are of crucial importance for the future of the society in which we live.

The purpose of this chapter is to analyse the progress of legislative proposals for a bank levy, as they unfolded in the UK between August 2009 and July 2010. Since the UK has taken the initiative in the area, and since, as things have transpired, it will become the first country after Sweden to introduce such a levy, the UK's experience is of particular relevance. The temporal parameters of the study are marked out by two events, the earlier of which turned out to be very significant, while the implications of the later one are yet to be judged. The event in August 2009 was Lord Turner's expression of the idea that a worldwide tax on banking transactions – a 'Tobin tax' – should become the subject of widespread debate.[4] July 2010 saw the publication, under the auspices of Mark Hoban, the Financial Secretary, of HM Treasury's consultation document on the design, not of a worldwide Tobin tax, but of a unilateral UK levy on the balance sheets of banks above a certain size.[5] Merely reviewing these events is enough to illustrate their significance. The UK's bank levy proposal affords a rare example of the rise of an idea that has been shaped by individual identifiable contributions.[6]

The scaling back of policy aspirations over this 12-month period illustrates the dilemmas to which a levy on banks gives rise, whether imposed unilaterally or co-ordinated internationally. Banks, and bankers, are already subject to a range of UK levies, a number of which have been introduced, or strengthened, with the financial services sector specifically in mind. The UK's bank levy proposal would add a further burden of taxation on banks themselves. As announced by George Osborne, the UK Chancellor, in June 2010, the levy will charge the more risky elements of banks' balance sheets.[7] It will, from 1 January 2011:

> . . . apply to the balance sheets of UK banks and building societies, and to the UK operations of banks from abroad. There will be deductions for tier 1 capital and insured retail deposits, and a lower rate for longer maturity funding. Smaller banks with liabilities below a certain level will not be liable for the levy.[8]

In this chapter, I ask whether, in its ideological context, and on its own terms, the imposition of the bank levy (initially, at 0.04 per cent of liabilities) is defensible. Policy decisions on the dilemmas presented by difficult circumstances need to be taken in anticipation of, and in response to, fast-moving events. Context, as might be said, is everything. The often bewildering nature of events has been compounded in these 12 months by the uncertainties surrounding the UK's change of administration, on 11 May 2010. Lord Turner's idea had eventually been taken up by Gordon Brown, the Labour Prime Minister, at the November 2009 G-20 summit. Originally leaning towards a Tobin tax, Mr Brown subsequently endorsed a worldwide balance sheet levy. So, what started as an ambitious plan in the hands of the former Labour Prime Minister, Gordon Brown, has become a more modest, but still significant, proposal in the hands of the Coalition administration of his successor, David Cameron.

To try to capture the significance of this 12-month period, the discussion has been cast in two interrelated parts. First, I want to ask what precisely has changed, in ideological terms, to make a levy on banks possible. Secondly, I would like to assess how well, given that context, the proposals for the levy have been fashioned over the period concerned.

These are worthwhile questions, since, whether or not the proposed bank levy becomes a reality, the climate of ideas in its early history will become ever more difficult to recover. Besides, during the period covered by the chapter, the debate has been political, rather than technical, a fact that has drawn attention to the essentially public law nature of the bank levy proposal.[9]

7.2. SCOPING A BANK LEVY

The most striking feature of media deliberations on the bank levy proposal is the dominant presence of the City of London. 'The City' – that is, the domestic and overseas banks with a presence in Cheapside, Moorgate and Canary Wharf – tends to engage in these debates through two representative bodies: the Corporation of London, and, more especially, the British Bankers' Association (BBA). Following the financial crisis of 2007–08, the City's position has certainly been weakened, since the perceived cause of the crisis (greed)[10] and concern at its aftermath (continued excessive bonuses)[11] were themselves of such a nature as to call into question its disinterested judgment on matters of public policy. Yet there is still reason to believe that the City has exerted considerable influence in shaping the public interest in relation to the bank levy. This is not, it seems to me, through a crude economic coercion, nor is it merely because, as one satirical magazine has suggested,[12] there are close historical links between the Conservative members of the Coalition administration and the BBA. The City's influence is much more subtle, yet also more tangible, than either of these somewhat mechanistic explanations would suggest. It is exerted, rather, by addressing Her Majesty's Government (HMG) directly, constantly confronting it with the unknowable consequences of the latter's policy decisions and forever reminding it of the profundity of the truth that the City's interest is that of the economy as a whole. Moreover, the arguments enlisted to this purpose tend to be good, or at least highly plausible, given the economic and ideological context in which they are at work.

When engaging in public debate on taxation policy, the City's characteristic mode of operation is to play in the ministerial consciousness upon what Murphy and Nagel characterize as a distinctive characteristic of taxation policy, namely, the 'large empirical uncertainties about the economic consequences of [the] different choices' entailed by it.[13] So the City consistently argues that HMG's next big tax policy decision – in this case the bank levy – is the watershed, the one which, if found contrary to their interest, will cause banks to leave the jurisdiction. Whether or not this is ever correct, no-one beforehand knows for sure. True, certain effects of proposed taxation measures can be modelled with some accuracy, but the interplay of those projections with other economic factors, or, indeed, with factors that, though generated by economic inequality or self-interest, are of a more overtly conflictual, or political kind, is absolutely unpredictable,[14] at least in the terms that, say, Taleb would regard as viable.[15] In its relations with the City, therefore, HMG is forced to assess the unknown outcomes of decisions of profound ideological significance. So it is with a levy on the banks. Although the potential effect of taxation measures adverse to the City is extremely difficult to predict, the economic benefit that the City confers on the UK seems too great for an administration working within a neoliberal world view to jeopardize.

Is it simply, then, with the bank levy, a matter of 'who blinks first'?[16] Well, possibly not. The uncertainties just marked out would be intolerable, but for the presence of two factors that seem to have reconfigured the terms of the bank levy debate, at least for the time being. One factor is the demise of a particular view of the City's role in the public finances. The other, which embodies a dominant ideological assumption about the realistic ends of tax policy, is the emergence of new political conclusions being drawn from the crisis. The combination of these factors may, for now, have made it easier for HMG to launch the proposed levy against the City. So, before considering a number of its detailed aspects, I would like to show how these two factors, one rather specific, the other somewhat general, might shape a realistic criticism of the proposal.

7.2.1. The Bank Levy and the End of Labour's Taxation Consensus

One factor is that the City is perceived to have failed to deliver on the general benefits it once promised. Worse, it has presented the UK taxpayer with a crisis, the fiscal cost of which the IMF has estimated at just over 6 per cent of GDP.[17] Of course, the perception of the City's role may change, and it is *just* possible that the long-term significance of the crisis has been overstated. The City is still, as already stressed, very influential. Yet something has altered, and it is both a function of the crisis itself and of May's change of administration.

During the years of the Labour administration, the City's political significance was long different from that of Wall Street, since its prosperity was the basis of a political settlement under which the huge financial services sector that it represents would generate profits, the taxation of which would help to pay for the public services, in a political climate averse to an increased burden of taxation overall.[18] Until, in autumn 2009, when Alistair Darling, the then Chancellor, emphasized that responsibility for reducing the public finance deficit caused by interventions after 2007–08 should fall on the 'broad-shouldered', the essence of Labour tax policy had for many been summed up in Peter Mandelson's worrying aphorism, that 'We [HMG] are intensely relaxed about people getting filthy rich as long as they pay their taxes'.[19] Such a view was highly contingent on there being a 'benign' economy. There were redistributive tax measures, certainly, but tax fairness seemed mainly to be expressed in a plethora of economically-inspired anti-avoidance provisions. Not until just before the crisis broke, in September 2007, were the inequalities produced by this credo becoming a matter for widespread concern. When it did break, the basis of the settlement between HMG and the City came to be seen as ever more problematic. 'The contribution of financial services to public services [wrote John Kay, in November 2009] has been not only removed but reversed'.[20] The reality was what added ever more piquancy to Mr Brown's historic claims that he had achieved 'an end to boom and bust' since, had he done so, this plan might have worked.

7.2.2. The Bank Levy and the Role of Taxation in Neoliberal Societies

The other, more general, factor that seems to have reconfigured the bank levy debate is an ongoing tension between the dominant neoliberal discourse and an increasingly insistent discourse of a kind of Keynesian 'egalitarian liberalism'.[21] With neoliberalism, economics has pole position; with egalitarian liberalism, a greater prominence is given to political choices.

What Labour tax policy seemed simply to assume, until almost the very end, was that the role of tax was limited, the possibilities for serious political debate on taxation policy being commensurately so. Questions surrounding the kind of bank levy currently under consideration tend to perpetuate this assumption, although they do not explicitly reference neoliberalism as such. Indeed, Manfred Steger and Ravi Roy point out that, while politicians have tended not specifically to use the term, their language nonetheless betrays adherence to its tenets.[22] Martin Wolf mistrusts neoliberalism as a 'nonsense' word,[23] but Steger and Roy are surely right to argue that it has come to denote a distinctive economistic ideology, whose limited aspirations to social justice contrast with those of twentieth-century egalitarian liberalism.[24] The tension between these two liberal strands has become increasingly apparent, and it bears on the bank levy debate in at least two contrasting ways.

On the one hand, we find the dominant justification for the levy to be, not a political conception of fairness, but an economic one. Since this is so, the case for the bank levy is that the crisis has highlighted certain 'externalities', caused by the tendency of bankers to take unnecessary risks in the conduct of their business.[25] This hegemony assumes, in line with European Enlightenment ideas, that the market is a 'natural' phenomenon,[26] and that taxation is an intervention to 'correct' those areas in which the market fails. Even unfairness in taxation is a market failure, on this matrix. Yet, as John Plender has emphasized, a financial sector in which certain banks are 'too-big-to-fail' (TBTF) is in no sense a component of a natural market,[27] since it undervalues the risk of carrying on business unsuccessfully. Moreover, this economism instantiates an approach to tax policy that is technocratic rather than political,[28] and that regards taxation as the intervention of last resort only: '[g]ood economics [as one of Mr Darling's aides was quoted as saying in 2009] are good politics . . .'.[29] The idea that taxation is disincentivizing was illustrated by the opposition of ardent neoliberals (the Canadian government) to the proposal by a lapsing one (Gordon Brown) for the worldwide bank levy.[30] This died, as the *Financial Times* correspondent put it, at the G-20 meeting in Busan, in the early hours of 5 June 2010.[31]

However, as a consequence of the crisis, we find a rival discourse to have some place in justifying the bank levy. So far, it has been found less in academic writing than in popular support for the Tobin tax idea.[32] Here, the roles of politics and economics are reversed.[33] Commentators from this position, possibly mistrusting the bank levy as a neoliberal irrelevance, have tended to concentrate their fire on breaking up the banks. This would, so the argument runs, strike at the roots of the problem of banks being TBTF, and therefore bypass the need for the less radical solution of a bank levy. In Plender's words, unless banks are disaggregated:

> [w]e are left with a financial system in which over-leveraged banking behemoths operate as an off-balance sheet adjunct of the public sector, while nurturing many profit centres that are increasingly oligopolistic.[34]

It is not just a matter of breaking up the banks, though. Even before the crisis, John Kay was arguing that the idea of 'market failure' is misconceived, based as it is on an imperfect understanding of how markets operate.[35] Since this is so, there are no automatic technical answers such as market failure seems to provide. Politics must take over. Moreover, it is argued, the only reason that economic inequalities were politically possible in the boom years was that the banks employed irresponsible lending policies, which is why Colin Crouch has called the pre-crisis neoliberalism 'a regime of privatised Keynesianism'.[36] By extension to this argument, a bank levy would be justifiable as a means of redressing the balance, and ensuring that the banks made an appropriate contribution in the bad times. Something like this was the approach taken by Mr Osborne, in his appearance before the House of Commons Treasury Select Committee on 15 July 2010. Linking the levy's introduction to the projected increase in the standard rate of value added tax, from 4 January 2011,[37] Mr Osborne told the Committee that:

> Asking the general population to accept a VAT rise, asking them to accept that there were going to be changes to welfare eligibility and the like, doing these things is a difficult thing for any government to do but I thought it would be totally inappropriate not to ask the banking sector to make a contribution as well.[38]

This is obviously a frank recognition of the more 'political' of the rival discourses. Appropriately so, since it comes from the mouth of the Minister responsible for the measure.

What I have attempted in this part of the chapter is a 'map' of the parameters of a realistic critique of the levy proposal. The levy, in short, is rendered possible by a shift away from an economistic view of tax policy, and the overlaying of this technocratic tendency with a more politically-inspired liberal egalitarian approach.

7.3. SUCCESSFULLY SHAPING THE LEVY'S POLICY GOALS

The very existence of the media debate on the bank levy, and the prominence within it of the City of London, draws attention to two inter-related features of tax policy. One is that taxation is a public policy area in which governments have unusually wide competences.[39] The other is that governments are therefore often tempted to unrealistic taxation policy initiatives, the penalty of which is failure.[40] It would thus be impossible to overstate the importance of rational public debate on tax law proposals. So, when Angela Knight, chief executive of the BBA, said (of the UK's 2009 bank payroll tax),[41] that '[i]t's good politics, yes, but it doesn't make any sense',[42] she was merely repeating a well-known misconception. Good politics is, by definition, amenable to rational analysis, since it manifests public reason in action. Bad politics is not so amenable, at least in this political society.

With these points in mind, three questions seem especially relevant. They are elaborated from Martin Loughlin's suggested approach to the study of public law in general, and, as such, need to be considered, of course, in the light of the ideological and economic factors that I have just analysed.[43] First, are the justifications for the levy comprehensible, in the terms that they are actually offered? Secondly, if so, are the explanations consistent with those offered for other policy measures in the same, or similar, areas? Thirdly, do the various justifications for the levy themselves harbour internal contradictions, when viewed in the light of earlier explanations? Critical, contextual, examination of these issues suggests that, though the justifications are untidy, the levy does just now stand up fairly well to rational scrutiny.

7.3.1. The Intelligibility of the Levy's Justifications

George Osborne's announcement of the UK's unilateral imposition of a bank levy was accompanied by promises from the German and French governments to introduce similar taxes. The terms Mr Osborne used were in part shaped by the justifications already suggested by the IMF in its report on the subject,[44] and in part by the political realities discussed above:

> In putting the nation's finances in order, we must remember that this was a crisis that started in the banking sector. The failures of the banks imposed a huge cost on the rest of society, so I believe that it is fair and right that in future banks should make a more appropriate contribution, reflecting the many risks that they generate.[45]

Similar language, offering an additional justification, appeared in the consultation document: 'the Levy is intended to encourage banks to move away from riskier funding—problems with risky funding lead to serious liquidity problems that played a key role in the financial crisis'.[46] True, the Chancellor is saying, this is a technical matter, but it is a political one too: the technical arguments have to be assessed in the context of a huge peacetime deficit of GBP149 billion. Except for its unilateral nature, the reasoning coheres closely with that of Alistair Darling, when suggesting a worldwide tax; and, crucially, it avoids any reference to the earmarking of the funds raised by the levy.

It is important to appreciate the premises here, in the light of the various elements analysed in the previous part. For a commentator, it is not really a case of deciding whether the bank levy is a 'political gesture', since, as public law, tax legislation is by its very nature political legislation.[47] The question is, instead, how well the intellectual case for the levy has been made out, given the dominant ideological framework, economic circumstances, and the relationship between HMG and the City. Neither, however, is it simply a matter of deploying economistic criteria out of context. Politics has a considerable role to play, not least because, as the IMF says, '[u]nderstanding of the proper roles of corrective taxation and regulation in this context is . . . quite limited'.[48] Thus, although some of the justifications for the levy appear similar to those invoked, say, for green taxes, they cannot simply be transposed from that context to the externalities created by a risky banking system. Instead, since politics – as Lord Butler said – is 'the Art of the Possible',[49] the technical arguments must make due allowance for the political juncture discussed above.

Basing the levy on banks' balance sheets means that it should capture 'risk considerations' more accurately than would a tax with a different base.[50] By focusing, too, on the riskier liabilities, rather than on 'risk-weighted assets', the levy closely follows the IMF's recommendation for ensuring, so far as possible, that it complements, rather than competes with,[51] the Basel Committee's capital 'buffer' requirements. Moreover, there is a close relationship between the justifications for the levy as stated by the Labour administration and by Mr Osborne. For Alistair Darling, a levy on banks was also 'a charge . . . for the systemic dangers they pose to the wider economy'.[52] More surprising, perhaps, is the echo of Mr Brown's 'implicit economic and social contract between our financial institutions and the society they serve',[53] and in Mr Osborne's 'new settlement between our banks and the rest of society'.[54] That said, there is a distinction between these justifications, on the one hand, and the one which was originally offered for a Tobin tax, on the other. The latter, which the IMF categorizes as a Financial Transactions Tax (FTT),[55] would, it is argued, actually shrink the financial services sector by weeding out 'socially useless' activities.[56] Moreover, in charging total liabilities less deposits and capital, the bank levy will be similar to the now abandoned US Financial Crisis Responsibility Fee. This, again, is different from a Tobin tax, which would have been charged on individual financial transactions. The merit of the former over the latter is that it is much more targeted. There is considerable evidence to suggest that a Tobin tax, that 'roving solution ever in search of a problem',[57] would have in fact impacted on anyone except the banks.[58] Finally, unlike a Tobin tax, the main purpose of which would have been to generate cash, the bank levy should, as well as generating public revenue, provide a 'marginal' incentive for banks 'to move to safer funding mechanisms'.[59]

The fact that levy proceeds will not be earmarked for a particular purpose in part illustrates the political nature of the levy's justification, but it also demonstrates that the levy is in this respect a 'thin' implementation of the IMF's recommendations. If the IMF's recommendations had been 'thickly' adopted, the levy would have formed part of a mechanism for a Financial Stability Contribution (FSC), a mechanism for the specific purpose of funding, not the subsidization of failing banks, but the costs of their orderly dissolution.[60] The UK levy, unlike the one being adopted in Germany and that outlined in EU proposals,[61] does not allocate the proceeds in this way. Instead, the levy proceeds are to go to general revenues. The argument in favour of this is a limited fairness issue, not fairness in global terms (a Tobin tax, incidentally, would have been designed in part to raise money for worthwhile causes), but fairness in ensuring that the risks of the City are not borne by society at large. This, too, is an approach that was favoured by Alistair Darling, although Gordon Brown was on record as wanting to use the proceeds from a worldwide tax to 'help tackle poverty in developing nations'.[62]

Whilst there is some tension about whether the levy is intended to be primarily regulatory or distributive, the justifications, at this juncture, seem to cohere rather well. In his evidence to the Treasury Committee, Mr Osborne emphasized that:

> we made it clear that we are targeting a revenue sum rather than a particular rate because we think that is an appropriate contribution that balances fairness with the competitiveness of the UK banking sector.[63]

On this basis, the levy had been designed to raise GBP2.5 billion per annum. It remains to be seen whether, as suggested by Mr Osborne himself,[64] there is still scope for following up one of the other possibilities examined in the IMF report, a Financial Activities Tax (FAT),[65] or the possibility highlighted in late July 2010, of an excess profits tax[66] specifically directed at the City.

7.3.2. The Levy's Consistency with Other Regulatory Measures

If, as I have suggested, the justifications for the levy are reasonably coherent, then that quality will be greatly enhanced by the consistency of its justifications with those of the surrounding regulatory regimes. The ideological context within which the levy is being crafted, with its strong presumption in favour of markets, is such as immediately to throw suspicion on the motives for its enactment. In a neoliberal society, taxes are bad in principle, so their justifications must, as we have seen, be compelling ones. They will be all the more compelling if, as a regulatory instrument, a bank levy matches the justifications for banking regulation and taxation in general.

Recently, the political justifications for the levy have shifted from a focus on the past to the future. Previously, there was a significant emphasis on the need for the banks to 'repay' taxpayers for the public rescue of the financial services sector in 2009, a key feature of the bank payroll tax. Now, the reasons for the levy's imposition are a rather more forward-looking combination of ensuring a significant financial contribution from the banking sector, and weakening the incentive for banks to allow the taking of unjustifiable risks by their employees. Both objectives are consistent with related measures, such as the EU's recent attempt to restrict the levels of bankers' bonuses, by making 'upfront bonuses' performance-related, and requiring bonuses beyond certain levels to be deferred.[67] However, it is worth drawing attention to one other element, not captured by requiring the financial sector to contribute, nor by the need to reduce risk, but with which the levy may yet prove inconsistent. This is the potential effect of the levy on the urgent need to recapitalize the banks.[68]

The EU's bonus measures should have that same effect, since the relevant directive requires banks to give priority to recapitalization over bankers' pay.[69] The problem with a bank levy, however, is that it could, in principle, have precisely the opposite effect. This point was made by Jim Flaherty, the Canadian finance minister, as a reason for deferring Gordon Brown's global bank levy. 'A tax [he said, in late April 2010][70] would deplete banks of capital and make them more, not less, vulnerable to crises'.[71] This was why, according to an official at HM Treasury in December 2009, a windfall tax on banks had been ruled out at an early stage: 'We've just spent taxpayers' money trying to make the banks stronger: it doesn't make much sense to take it back again now'.[72] So the question of whether a unilateral UK bank levy will militate against the somewhat tightened capital rules of Basel III[73] remains a concern. It might be premature to say so, but Kevin Cummings' guarded and judicious criticism (see [2011] BTR 24) that the levy could possibly be held to conflict, too, with the 'EU Treaty fundamental freedoms or . . . the Capital Requirements Directive' seems a little unrealistic just now, given the strong justifications for the levy and its equivalents elsewhere in Europe.[74] A related worry, of course, is whether the corporation tax bias in favour of debt finance should be addressed for similar reasons of consistency.

Mention of corporation tax is a reminder that the essence of the bank levy is quite different, since it is a charge on the levels of risk with which a bank has been capitalized, not on its profits. There is a good reason for this choice of tax base, quite irrespective of the drawbacks of a Tobin tax, or of the desire to ensure that banks are capitalized appropriately. This is the fact that, as a result of trading losses incurred during the 2007–08 crisis, some banks are carrying huge corporation tax losses, which, when carried forward under loss relief provisions,[75] will mean that they will not be liable to pay corporation tax for many years. In 2008, for example, Royal Bank of Scotland was reported to be carrying losses of GBP24.1 billion, all of which should be available to set against any profits generated in many subsequent years.[76] A tax such as the bank levy, which uses liabilities rather than profits as its base, is not subject to the same structural weakness as corporation tax. More than that, though, the levy avoids the necessity of introducing, as the Conservatives were originally proposing, restrictions on the loss carry-forward provisions.[77] This would have been manifestly unsatisfactory for a number of reasons, however viscerally appealing it may at first have seemed. One reason is that it would weaken banks' balance sheets by reducing 'the value of their deferred tax assets, which reflect their ability to carry-losses forward',[78] while another is that restricting loss reliefs would retard their progress towards profitability, by choking off their ability to pay their debts.[79] So, while a bank levy may not at first seem consistent with the carry-forward of losses, or, for that matter, with the Coalition's proposed staged reduction in corporation tax generally, it is a 'least worst' reconciliation with the other regulatory objectives. There is, moreover, the objection that restricting loss carry-forward within the corporation tax code, unlike the introduction of a particular levy for a particular sector (something sanctioned by the history of green taxes), would be 'a radical shift in policy'.[80]

7.3.3. Apparent Self-Contradictions in the Levy's Justifications

My final group of questions centres on the success with which HMG has maintained certain policy positions on the bank levy that do not contradict its earlier ones. Of all foci for the weaknesses of public policy justifications, none perhaps is more powerful than the commentator's ability to draw attention to some position, some statement or other, that manifestly contradicts an earlier one in the same, or a related, field. That said, detecting such apparent self-contradictions requires some care, given that, as has been emphasized throughout this discussion, time works changes in how heavily certain factors weigh in the legislator's mind. In this story of the bank levy, one might reasonably expect the UK's change of administration, in May 2010, to have wrought some specific shifts in this respect. And so it has. However, although I have identified three areas of possible internal self-contradiction, I have found, somewhat to my surprise, that they can mostly be satisfactorily explained.

One example of an apparent self-contradiction, which actually coheres on closer inspection, is HMG's structuring the proposed levy as a tax on balance sheet liabilities, rather than as a Tobin tax. When the Conservatives were in opposition, they had consistently opposed the structuring of any levy on the banks in the way that Tobin had suggested. This approach may itself have been symptomatic of a wider plan to marginalize any ideas associated with Lord Turner, the legitimacy of whose supervisory jurisdiction in relation to the banks (as Financial Services Authority chair), the Conservatives regarded as having been eviscerated by the events of 2007–08. Conservative attitudes to the Tobin tax may also, in fairness, have been informed by its long-understood technical problems.[81]

These problems only became apparent to Gordon Brown when it was too late to reconcile differing approaches. By the time that, in association with President Sarkozy,[82] he was advocating an FTT, Mr Brown was already contradicting his earlier statement that a Tobin tax 'had big problems attached to it'.[83] Though no poor, crippled, Philip Snowden,[84] out of his depth in political economy, Mr Brown was certainly by then 'making a hash of his special subject'.[85] The danger, from the Conservatives' perspective, remains that, since Tobin taxes (as a sub-category of FTTs), remain on the IMF's menu of financial instruments for further use,[86] the Conservatives will fall into the same trap as Mr Brown. Unless something changes, some factor emerges that renders the criticisms referred to above less powerful, the Conservatives need to resist reverting to this idea as a basis for future policy. The fact that pressure groups continue to espouse the Tobin tax should, so far as the Conservatives are concerned, be entirely irrelevant, given their earlier policy position. More than this, given the ideological constraints within which the discourse is developing, it is clearly of the first importance that HMG is not seen to be promoting a policy which would undermine efficiency in global markets.

If the Conservatives are safe from charges of self-contradiction on the levy's structure, the same argument is less sustainable in relation to the use of the levy proceeds. Here, however, events have so chiselled at the arguments that the impression of evolving justifications has effaced what would otherwise seem to be inconsistencies of reasoning. Early in 2010, George Osborne was reported as favouring a 'worldwide insurance levy on financial institutions', the purpose of which would be 'to protect the taxpayer from the costs of a future crisis'.[87] It was left to John Kay, in his *Financial Times* column, to point out, in an argument that swiftly gained widespread acceptance, that an insurance fund would 'aggravate the underlying problem of moral hazard' and institutionalize state funding of the banks.[88] The force of his argument derived not merely from the evident difficulties thus presented for neoliberal ideology market ideas, but also, as the Greek debt crisis swiftly demonstrated, from the idea that, in extreme circumstances, there was not even taxpayer capacity in a particular state to underwrite a financial crisis.[89] The preference, both of Germany and of the European Commission, for the much more narrowly-justified hypothecation discussed above, in the form of a bank resolution regime,[90] illustrates the scaling back of this idea in response to unfolding complex events.

Overall, therefore, the Coalition's plans for a bank levy survive the charge of internal self-contradiction in two important areas: the structure of the levy, and the destination of the proceeds. One further area in which it may yet prove exceedingly difficult to reconcile historically divergent positions, however, is that of the Conservatives' willingness, from a very early stage, to impose a unilateral UK bank levy if necessary.[91] Gordon Brown and Alistair Darling, true to their historic conception of the importance of the City to the economy, never wavered from the contention that such a levy had to be imposed multilaterally among the G-20 nations, or not at all. To them, this seemed the only approach which could meet City objections, by restraining the arbitrage possibilities created by a globalized neoliberal society. The Coalition view has, however, been a consistently different one. This is not simply because, from March 2010, its future Conservative members have been prepared to follow a unilateral approach (for whatever reasons), but also because, as the Coalition's most distinguished Liberal-Democrat member tellingly put it: 'Britain is in a uniquely exposed position because banking has such a high share of the economy'.[92] Clearly, both viewpoints cannot be correct all of the time. Equally clearly, though, one or other argument might be correct some of the time, since times change. The neoliberal ideas discussed above need only to be brought to mind to sense the perceived economic dangers to the UK. What may be the salvation of the Coalition's approach, unilateral but 'co-ordinated' with Germany and France, is a coalescence of two factors, the existence of which neither Mr Darling nor Mr Brown, in thrall to convictions born of happier times, seems to have acknowledged. First, as I have already explained, the financial services sector cannot now be relied on to fund the public services from taxes such as corporation tax, which take profits as their tax base. The Deputy Prime Minister, Nick Clegg, underlined this point rather forcibly during the General Election campaign, by describing tax revenues from the City as having 'fallen off a cliff'.[93] In these circumstances, as John Plender has pointed out, it is difficult now to see what the 'comparative advantage' of the City might be.[94] Secondly, although there are signs that Labour taxation measures directed primarily against the City (namely, the 50p income tax top rate, the bank payroll tax, the GBP30000 annual fee for 'non-doms' to retain the remittance basis,[95] and the increase in capital gains tax), have had some effect, and although they may yet prove to affect future location decisions, they have not yet led to an 'exodus' of banks from London.

In combination, these three areas of apparent self-contradiction seem to me, for the time being at least, to be reconcilable. As I indicated, this is not simply because some common strands can be found in their internal logic, though they can. It is, too, because circumstances change, and they will do so again. None of these points undermines the truth that, in principle, the national interests of the states of a globalized world are best served by mutual co-operation. But great virtuosity is required of ministers seeking to maintain the integrity of these positions in the face of changing events. The political danger is that, if HMG acts differently in the face of City protests, public opinion may itself reconcile the apparent contradictions in terms such as those of John Plender, on the international failure to address the TBTF problem, namely, that '[t]he lobbying power of the banks will continue to be deployed to dilute the whole regulatory agenda'.[96]

7.4. CONCLUSIONS

A harsh truth of debating the way in which we should live is the extent to which we are prisoners of ideas and of ways of living for which we are not individually responsible. We are not free to devise approaches to public policy, somewhat in a Rawlsian vein, independent of the dominant ideas that, in Isaiah Berlin's words, have the capacity both to liberate us and to enslave us.[97] No part of public policy making is more intricate, or more fundamental, than taxation policy, and everyone has more or less good ideas on both the means to, and the ends of, that most intractable area of legislative endeavours.

The proposal for the UK's bank levy is a forceful illustration of the validity of these points, since the period chronicled by this chapter has seen the rise and fall of an ambitious idea. What was originally proposed as a global tax on financial transactions will become a UK tax on banks' balance sheets. During that period, every part of the original idea has been subjected to the most careful interrogation. The banks will not now be taxed as heavily as once thought. Such is the E66 and flow of political realities – HMG has not been the first to blink. It does not follow, however, that the values of neoliberal society are an absolute bar to the expression in tax systems of more political values, ones not necessarily consonant with that most economistic of ideologies. If introduced, the levy will mark a minor advance for a more political notion of fairness in tax policy, and something of a setback for a primarily economistic one. It plausibly embodies an idea of the public interest which is distinct from the interest of a vociferous industry. At the same time, the proposal is broadly consistent with other tax and regulatory measures. What may be its undoing is its unilateral nature, but circumstances are different now from the time when globalization arguments held absolute sway. Other times, different combinations of circumstances, may yet make the proposal less (or indeed more) plausible. For the present, events have created an ideological climate in which a bank levy is thinkable, and HMG's response has been, at least so far, one of a range of prudent possibilities. To that extent, it is defensible. What the bank levy might demonstrate is a realization that, for neoliberal society to survive, there may be no prudential alternative but to temper the economistic analyses of neoliberalism with politics.

NOTES

1. If the first four words of the title are felicitous, then I willingly acknowledge the quicksilver wit of Nick Murza; if not, then the blame is mine. Either way, I cannot claim any originality for it. Nick originally suggested the title ('Tax and the City') to me in summer 2008, but – disappointingly – it was subsequently used as the title for an article in the *Daily Telegraph*. The text is intended to reflect relevant developments in the public domain as at 30 July 2010.
2. Plender, John (27–28 June 2009), 'How fading political will has let banks off the hook', *Financial Times*, p. 11.
3. Plender, John (15 July 2009), 'Banks let off the hook as flawed model is preserved', *Financial Times*, p. 32.
4. 'Adair Turner roundtable: How to tame global finance', *Prospect*, September 2009, pp. 34–41. Lord Turner was (and is) chair of the Financial Services Authority.
5. HM Treasury, *Bank levy: a consultation*, July 2010 (available from http://www.hm-treasury.gov.uk/consult_bank_levy.htm, accessed 25 July 2010).
6. The story is told in various places: in certain 'milestone' policy documents (one being the consultation document already mentioned); in newspaper reports, primarily the *Financial Times*; in journals, especially *Prospect*, the *Economist* and, latterly, specialist publications such as the *Tax Journal*; and, obviously, in reports of parliamentary proceedings.
7. Barker, A., B. Masters, and T. Braithwaite (22 June 2010), 'Levy aims to make City play fair', *Financial Times*, p. 2; Helen Buchanan, 'Bank levy and more bonus scrutiny', *Tax Journal*, 12 July 2010, p. 11.
8. Hansard HC, vol. 512, 22 June 2010, col. 176 ('Financial Statement').
9. See Loughlin, Martin (2003), *The Idea of Public Law*, Oxford: Oxford University Press, p. 134.
10. See n. 2 above.
11. Eaglesham, Jean (8 December 2009), 'Well-off become target as Labour seeks core vote', *Financial Times*, p. 3.
12. Anon, (30 April 2010), 'Banking on Tories', *Private Eye*, No. 1261, p. 10.
13. Murphy and Nagel (2002), *The Myth of Ownership: Taxes and Justice*, New York: Oxford University Press, p. 4.
14. Pimlott and Cohen, 'Economic decline worse than expected', *Financial Times*, 25–26 July 2009, p. 2.
15. See, e.g., Taleb, Nassim N. (2007), *Fooled by Randomness: The Hidden Role of Chance in Life and in the Markets*, 2nd ed., London: Penguin, ch. 13.
16. A conversation with Mark Cook suggested the appositeness of this expression here.
17. Staff of the International Monetary Fund, *A Fair and Substantial Contribution by the Financial Sector: Final Report for the G-20*, June 2010, p. 7 (available from http://www.imf.org/external/np/g20/pdf/062710b.pdf, accessed 27 July 2010) (hereafter, 'IMF').
18. Peston, Robert (2005), *Brown's Britain*, London: Short Books, esp. chs 5 and 8; Lee, Simon (2007), *Best for Britain? The Politics and Legacy of Gordon Brown*, Oxford: Oneworld, pp. 90–93.
19. Quoted in Parker, George (8 December 2009), 'A fiscal focus', *Financial Times*, p. 13. On the inequalities, see, e.g., Thomas F. Crossley and Cormac O'Dea, *The Wealth and Saving of UK Families on the Eve of the Crisis* (London: Institute for Fiscal Studies, 2010), esp. pp. 1–3.
20. Kay, John (1 July 2009), 'Britain has sunk itself deep into a fiscal black hole', *Financial Times*, p. 13.
21. See Steger, Manfred B. and Ravi K. Roy (2010), *Neoliberalism: A Very Short Introduction*, Oxford: Oxford University Press, p. 9.
22. *Ibid.*, p. x.
23. Wolf, Martin (2005), *Why Globalization Works*, New Haven and London: Yale University Press, pp. 13, 321n.

24. See n. 21 at pp. 5–6, 11.
25. IMF, see n. 17 at, p. 12.
26. See n. 17 at, ch. 2.
27. Plender, John (24 February 2010), 'Just targeting symptoms of the crisis is too neat', *Financial Times*, p. 32; Andrew G. Haldane and Piergiorgio Alessandri, 'Banking on the state', BIS Review 139/2009 (available from http://www.bis.org/review/r091111e.pdf, accessed 27 July 2010).
28. Confirmed by early impressions of the Mirrlees review (see, Adam *et al.* (2010), *Dimensions of Tax Design: The Mirrlees Review*, Oxford: Oxford University Press).
29. See n. 19 above.
30. Dickson, Julie (9 April 2010), 'Protecting banks is best done by market discipline', *Financial Times*, p. 13 ('embedded contingent capital' as an alternative to a levy).
31. Giles, C., Parker, G. and Hall, B. (7 June 2010), 'Osborne to press on with bank tax regardless of G20 hostility', *Financial Times*, p. 1.
32. See, e.g., http://robinhoodtax.org.uk (accessed 27 July 2010).
33. See, e.g., http://robinhoodtax.org.uk (accessed 27 July 2010).
34. See n. 27 above.
35. Kay, John (August 2007), 'The failure of market failure', *Prospect Magazine*, Issue 137, pp. 36–42.
36. Crouch, C. (2008), 'What Will Follow the Demise of Privatised Keynesianism?', 79 *Political Quarterly*, 476–487.
37. HM Treasury, *Budget 2010* (House of Commons Papers, Session 2010–2011, 61) (London: TSO, 2010), p. 51.
38. House of Commons Treasury Committee, *1st Report. June 2010 Budget* (House of Commons Papers, Session 2010–2011, 350) (London: TSO, 2010), p. 39.
39. Using the term in the sense deployed by Loughlin, n. 9 at p. 84.
40. The Australian government's proposal for a Resource Super Profit Tax on the mining industry, which claimed the political career of Kevin Rudd, offers a recent dramatic example.
41. *Finance Act 2010*, s. 22, and sched. 1.
42. Murphy, Megan and Vanessa Houlder (8 December 2009), 'Bankers warn of exodus over windfall tax', *Financial Times*, p. 3.
43. Elaborated from Loughlin, Martin (1992), *Public Law and Political Theory*, Oxford: Clarendon Press, p. 36.
44. IMF, n. 17 at p. 17.
45. Hansard HC, vol. 512, 22 June 2010, col. 175 ('Financial Statement').
46. HM Treasury, n. 5 at p. 5.
47. Loughlin, n. 9 above.
48. IMF, n. 17 at p. 10.
49. Butler, R.A. (1971), *The Art of the Possible: The Memoirs of Lord Butler*, Harmondsworth: Penguin, ix.
50. IMF, n. 17 at p. 17.
51. *Ibid.*
52. Parker and Giles (20–21 March 2010), 'Darling to use Budget to back banks tax', *Financial Times*, p. 1.
53. Brown, Gordon (9 November 2009), 'How we can restore trust in financial institutions', *Financial Times*, p. 15.
54. Quoted in Eaglesham, Jean (17 June 2010), 'Vision focuses on fairness and firmness', *Financial Times*, p. 3.
55. IMF, n. 17 at pp. 19–21.
56. Turner, n. 4 at p. 36.
57. Editorial (2 January 2010), 'No triumphant return of the state', *Financial Times*, p. 10.
58. Houlder, Vanessa and Chris Giles (13–14 February 2010), '"Robin Hood tax" seen as a stealth tax', *Financial Times*; Tim Harford (20–21 February 2010), 'If that's the Robin Hood tax, I'm the sheriff of Nottingham', *FT Magazine*, p. 13.

59. Barker, Masters and Braithwaite, n. 7 above.
60. IMF, n. 17 at p. 25.
61. Harrison, J. (2010), 'The banking levy is dead . . . long live the banking levy', *Tax Journal*, p. 7; European Commission, *Bank Resolution Funds*, 26 May 2010, COM(2010) 254 final (available from http://ec.europa.eu/internal_market/bank/docs/crisis-management/funds/com2010_254_en.pdf, accessed 28 July 2010).
62. See n. 49 above.
63. HC Treasury Committee, n. 37 above, p. 38.
64. Parker, G., A. Barker, and P. Jenkins (24 June 2010), 'Osborne to explore further levy on banks', *Financial Times*, p. 4; Taylor, D. (2010), 'Budget analysis – banks', *Tax Journal*, p. 17; See n. 7 above.
65. IMF, see n. 17 at pp. 21–24, 66–70.
66. *Ibid.*
67. Tait and Masters (1 July 2010), 'EU bank bonus rules sow confusion', *Financial Times*, p. 1; *Proposal for a Directive . . . for the Supervisory Review of Remuneration Policies*, SEC (2009) 974 final, SEC (2009) 975 final (available from: http://ec.europa.eu/prelex/detail_dossier_real.cfm?CL=en&DosId=198446, accessed 28 July 2010).
68. Editorial (29 June 2010), 'Shock therapy is the best cure for banks', *Financial Times*, p. 10.
69. See n. 63 above.
70. Masters, Brooke (4 May 2010), 'Basel chief warns global tax "premature"', *Financial Times*, p. 6.
71. Beattie and Braithwaite (24–25 April 2010), 'Nations struggle to find consensus on bank taxes', *Financial Times*, p. 5.
72. Quoted in Parker, G., C. Giles, and N. Timmins (7 December 2009), 'Darling lines up assault on bonuses', *Financial Times*, p. 1.
73. Masters, Brooke (27 July 2010), 'Basel breakthrough in drive to tighten rules on global banking', *Financial Times*, p. 1.
74. IMF, see n. 17 at pp. 63–64.
75. *Corporation Tax Act 2010*, s. 45.
76. Arnold, Martin (7 December 2009), 'Two sides of Osborne plan to limit loss relief for banks', *Financial Times*, p. 3.
77. *Ibid.*
78. *Ibid.*
79. *Ibid.*
80. *Ibid.* It is not, however, inconceivable (see Taylor, see n. 64 above).
81. Anon (29 January 2005), 'Tobin or not Tobin?', *Economist*, p. 70.
82. Brown and Sarkozy (9 December 2009), 'For Global Finance, Global Regulation', *Wall Street Journal* (available from http://online.wsj.com, accessed 23 July 2010).
83. Quoted in Pimlott, Daniel (9 November 2009), 'Return of a cause célèbre to the world stage', *Financial Times*, p. 2.
84. Chancellor in 1924 and from 1929–1931.
85. Editorial (10 November 2009), 'Brown lets off a damp tax squib', *Financial Times*, p. 14 (also Anon (14 November 2009), 'Desperate measures', *Economist*, p. 68).
86. FTTs 'should not be lightly dismissed – the administrative and practical difficulties are not as great as some have claimed' (IMF, see n. 17 at p. 19).
87. Parker, G., J. Eaglesham, and F. Guerrera (16–17 January 2010), 'Osborne to push for global bank levy', *Financial Times*, p. 1.
88. Kay, John (3 February 2010), 'Why "too big to fail" insurance will not fix finance', *Financial Times*, p. 15.
89. Plender, John (30 June 2010), 'Fragile state of banks means recovery is still precarious', *Financial Times*, p. 32.
90. i.e. not a bank *rescue* regime (expressed by one IMF official, in his blog, thus: 'I come to bury Caesar, not to bail him out'). (See http://blog-imfdirect.imf.org/2010/04/25/fair-and-substantial%E2%80%94taxing-the-financial-sector/, accessed 28 July 2010.)

91. Parker, G., P. Jenkins, and J. Pickard (22 March 2010), 'Tory levy risks City jobs, says Darling', *Financial Times*, p. 3.
92. Vince Cable, quoted, *ibid.*
93. Barker, Alex (12 January 2010), 'Clegg would target "bias towards City"', *Financial Times*, p. 2.
94. See n. 2 above.
95. See, e.g., Lee, Natalie (ed.) (2009), *Revenue Law – Principles and Practice*, 27th edn, Haywards Heath: Bloomsbury, p. 444.
96. See n. 85 above. Buchanan (see n. 7 above) says this lobbying power is likely to be feverishly deployed throughout summer 2010.
97. Berlin, Isaiah (1978), 'Does Political Theory Still Exist?', in Henry Hardy (ed.), *Concepts and Categories: Philosophical Essays*, London: Hogarth Press, pp. 143–172, at 159.

PART II

Sovereign debt

8. Iceland's financial disaster and its fiscal impact

Arnór Sighvatsson and Gunnar Gunnarsson

8.1. INTRODUCTION

In October 2008, Iceland experienced a financial calamity of unprecedented scale. The sustainability of government finances immediately came into question. Overnight, after the implosion of all of its major banks, with massive losses to foreign creditors, Iceland became ostracized from international capital markets for an extended period of time. The sudden stop of international capital flows lead to the collapse of Iceland's currency, which depreciated by 60 per cent from 1 September 2008 until capital controls were instated on 28 November 2008. Although the scale of the twin crisis was without precedence (see Figure 8.1), the build-up of unsustainable macroeconomic imbalances and misalignments in asset prices followed a typical pre-crisis pattern described in the literature.[1] Lax risk management and low perceived risks based on optimism about the future prospects of the booming economy made the financial institutions and the private sector far too willing to assume imprudent risks. Financial institutions overextended themselves, not only domestically but particularly abroad. The large scale of the banks' cross-border and cross-currency operations while their principal lender of last resort (LOLR), the Central Bank of Iceland (CBI), could by and large provide them with liquidity only in domestic currency made them particularly vulnerable to a run on their foreign liabilities.[2]

In a few years, the three major banks had become among the largest in the world relative to the home country economy. More specifically, they grew to more than ten times Iceland's GDP. Not only were the banks that failed exceptionally large relative to their source of support, but the combined share of the failed banks relative to the domestic banking system was also unusually large. The three major banks that collapsed in October 2008 represented about 90 per cent of Iceland's banking system in terms of total assets. Most of the remaining financial institutions, including the largest savings bank and the wholesale arm of the savings bank group,

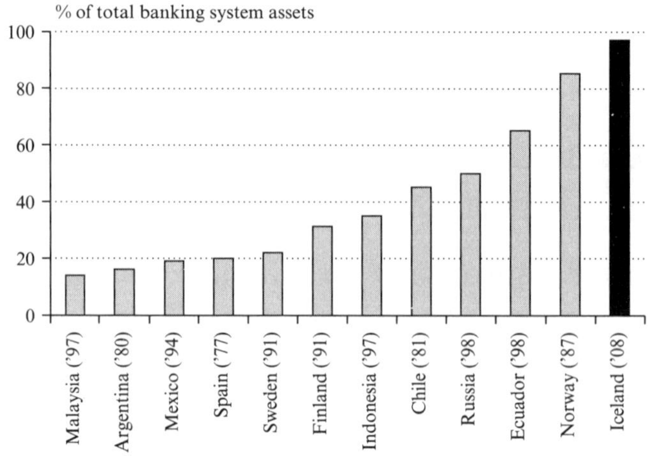

Note: The year in parentheses represents the onset of the crisis in the country concerned.

Source: Caprio, Klingebiel, Laeven and Noguera (2005), Central Bank of Iceland.

Figure 8.1. Share of banking system in insolvency in various previous crises

were either taken over by the Icelandic Financial Supervisory Authority (FME) in March 2009 or have since received significant Government support. Hence, by and large, Iceland's entire financial system failed.

There had been ample signs of imbalances in the Icelandic economy for years: an unprecedented current account deficit, rapid credit growth, persistent inflation, and a housing bubble. High growth in activity was to a great extent based on soaring asset prices and low perceived risks by the banks, households and businesses which increasingly relied on external funding. It was acknowledged by the CBI that overextended balance sheets would come under great pressure should global financial conditions change for the worse. Risk premia on the debt of Iceland's banks had been elevated since early 2006, when their aggressive strategy of international expansion first ran into difficulties. Nevertheless, in 2007, most Icelanders and many external observers took the view that Iceland was fundamentally a strong economy. It was an economy increasingly characterized by free markets after a decade of privatization, high employment, low public debt, a fully funded pension system and – despite some criticism – broadly prudent fiscal policies. Like the Asian miracle countries of the 1990s, Iceland was in many ways regarded as a model of economic reform. The concluding statement of the IMF mission that visited Iceland in June

2007 proclaimed, 'The medium-term prospects for the Icelandic economy remain enviable.'[3]

The sovereign, still highly rated only a few months previously, was suddenly teetering on the brink of non-investment grade ratings, and indeed fell below investment grade in the assessment of one rating agency, as the general Government debt outlook shifted from one of the brightest in Europe to one of the darkest. How could this happen?

Although Iceland is a very small economy, it has all the institutional features of a modern market economy and, as a member of the European Economic Area (EEA), it is formally subject to the same regulatory framework as other European countries. The Icelandic cross-border banks could obtain licences to operate branches in all EEA countries on the basis of the European 'Passport'. Hence the Icelandic experience should not be regarded merely as that of a curious outlier. In our view, it might carry important lessons that are relevant to the international community at large and Europe in particular. The EU/EEA banking framework is designed to promote cross-border expansion of European banks within the EEA, but it is flawed in that supervision, deposit insurance, and LOLR remained national in scope. Cross-border banking comes with cross-currency liquidity risk that can take two forms: currency mismatches and maturity mismatches between foreign currency assets and liabilities. In the EU/EEA framework, cross-border banks from small countries outside the euro area can be at great risk of a run on their foreign liabilities, given the limited ability of the domestic central bank to serve as LOLR in foreign currency, as it is limited by the size of its reserves and the willingness of other central banks to help.[4] This proved to be the Achilles heel of Icelandic banks, although there were many other factors that contributed to their demise. There is no European supervisor, and the resolution mechanism to deal with cross-border banking crises is inadequate. During the height of the turmoil, there was a lack of information sharing and co-operation as UK authorities froze and ring-fenced assets to protect the interests of UK depositors. What prompted this was an obvious flaw in the design of the deposit insurance system within the EU/EEA framework. The crisis has shown that the idea of having a bank's home country bear the responsibility of deposits in the bank's foreign branches is flawed, especially when the deposits are in foreign currency, since the insurance principle of pooling is violated. European deposit insurance is needed for European cross-border banks. The lesson learnt from Icelandic cross-border banking expansion is that there needs to be a European supervision and resolution mechanism to deal with cross-border banking crises because, if national authorities cannot limit their size, as domestic banks can quickly grow beyond governments' and central banks' ability to assist them in periods of distress, putting sovereign fiscal sustainability and financial stability within the EEA at risk. The Icelandic banks were private companies. They were not rescued. Yet their demise resulted in an enormous transfer of private sector liabilities to the government sector. If this happened to a larger economy, and one characterized by somewhat less favourable initial conditions than Iceland enjoyed, the aftermath would be a significant global problem.

The crisis has been very costly to the public sector. That cost will unavoidably be borne by the taxpayers. It poses an inherently difficult challenge to disentangle the part of the overall loss that stems from the inevitable correction of economic imbalances, on the one hand, and the part that is the direct effect of the financial crisis, on the other hand. In our efforts, we estimated the overall cost of the fiscal impact to taxpayers rather than limiting ourselves to the direct cost of recapitalizing the banking system. We estimate the first-year gross cost to taxpayers at 57 per cent of GDP. The recurring gross cost, indicating the fiscal adjustment needed, is 11 per cent of GDP, and it reflects costs incurred during the bust period of the cycle that would not have been incurred in the absence of the crisis.[5] It can reasonably be argued that the net cost to taxpayers should reflect the fact that benefits accrued to taxpayers from banking activity during the boom period and should therefore be subtracted from losses from the banking collapse. In part, then, tax rate hikes in the bust period are therefore a reversal of tax rate cuts in the boom period. Taking that into account and the likely recouping of bank recapitalization outlays through reprivatisation, we estimate first-year net cost at 30½ per cent of GDP and recurring net cost at 5½ per cent of GDP.

8.2. PRE-CRISIS FISCAL POSITION OF THE GENERAL GOVERNMENT

In some sense Iceland was lucky. When the disaster struck, Iceland's fiscal position was quite strong, owing to mainly two factors. First, as a result of its privatization programme, in 1998–2005 the Government had sold assets worth ISK 211 billion at average 2009 prices, approximately 15 per cent of 2009 GDP. The proceeds of privatization had been allocated partly towards reducing government debt and government-funded pension liabilities, contributing to lower interest outlays and building up a substantial cushion of deposits in the Central Bank of Iceland (CBI). Second, during the boom years the central government was run with a substantial surplus, as revenues repeatedly exceeded projections. As a result of these two factors, central government net debt declined from roughly ⅓ of GDP in the mid-nineties to a narrow positive position in the years before the crisis. Without this relatively strong fiscal position, Iceland would be facing even more difficult problems than it does today. A caveat is appropriate, however, because to some degree it was the strong fiscal position that enabled the financial institutions to increase their leverage as they did, since creditors and the rating agencies alike looked to the Government for implicit or perceived bailout guarantees because of its strong position even if the Government remained vague on this issue for moral hazard reasons. Nevertheless, after assuming enormous liabilities associated with the collapse of banks, the Government has been forced to tighten its fiscal stance significantly in the middle of a severe recession, in order to restore medium-term the sustainability of public finances and regain confidence of international creditors.[6] Without the extra cushion of revenue from earlier privatization and low debt, this would have required even more pro-cyclical policies.

8.3. THE BUILD-UP OF RISK

The cost of a financial crisis to taxpayers and creditors will be determined to a large extent by a number of inter-related factors such as: (1) the size of the financial sector; (2) the level of bank risk accumulated on the balance sheet of financial institutions during the preceding expansion; (3) the size of macroeconomic imbalances during the period leading up to the crisis; and (4) the commitment of public money in an effort to prevent or contain the crisis. The indirect costs resulting from the accumulation of risk on private sector balance sheets during the expansion and the subsequent amplifying interaction between the financial sector and the real economy during the crisis are substantial. Consequently, to understand fully how a financial disaster affects public finances, we must look at the pre-crisis period.

Starting with the authorities' preference for growth policies in the early days of the pre-crisis boom period, a massive expansion of credit was ultimately initiated. This was partly fuelled by the announced hike of the maximum loan-to-value ratio for residential mortgages and the combined ample supply of credit in international markets. Asset prices soared and real disposable income increased at a record pace (see Figures 8.2–8.5). On the back of expanding economic activity and higher collateral values the financial accelerator amplified the effects of favourable financial conditions on the real economy. The credit accelerator had an even greater effect through the risk-taking channel, as creditor balance sheets offered them opportunities to take risks and thus have an effect on the real economy and monetary policy transmission.[7]

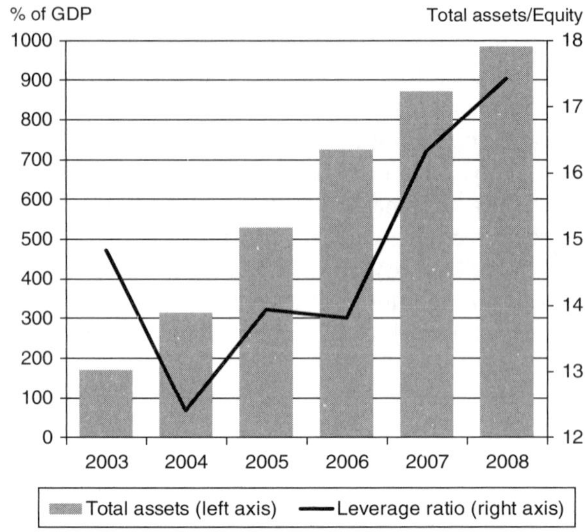

Note: Consolidated accounts of three largest commercial banks. 2008 data is end-June.

Source: Central Bank of Iceland.

Figure 8.2. Banks' balance sheet expansion and leverage

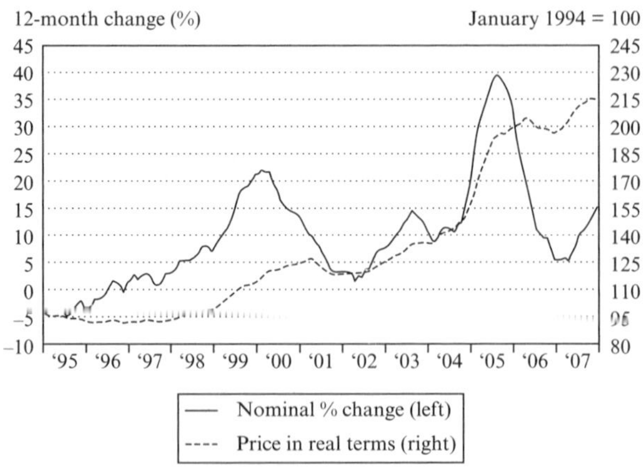

Source: Icelandic Property Registry, Statistics Iceland.

Figure 8.3. Housing market prices in Greater Reykjavik

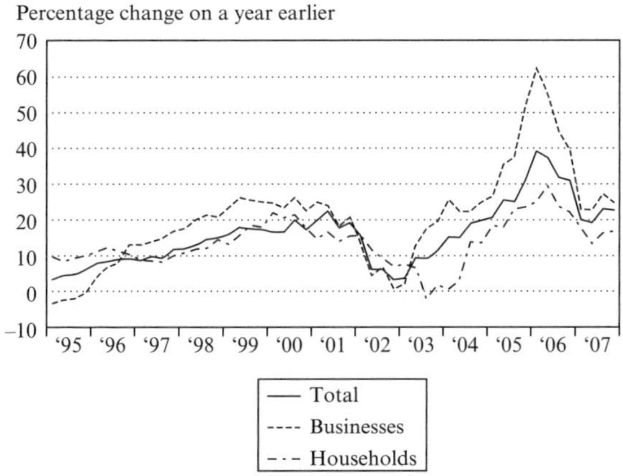

Source: Central Bank of Iceland.

Figure 8.4. Credit system lending growth

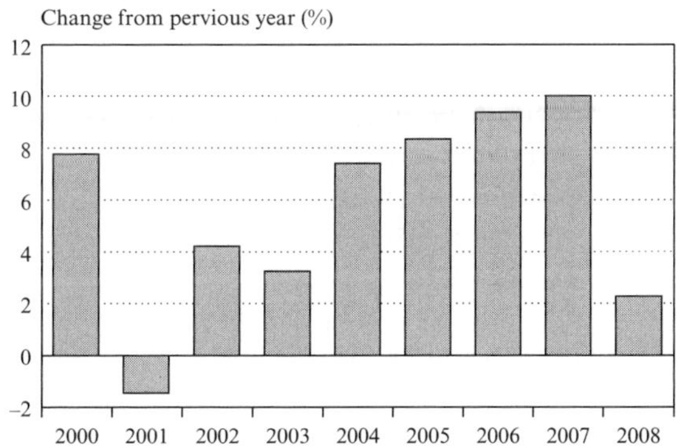

Source: Statistics Iceland.

Figure 8.5. Real disposable income growth 2000–2008

As imbalances grew during the 2004–2007 expansion the CBI stepped on the monetary brakes to a great extent, in order to induce a soft landing. However, as a significant part of credit to the non-financial private sector, intermediated via the Icelandic banks, was denominated in foreign currency, at interest rates determined in the money markets of the respective currencies, the transmission of monetary restraint was weakened during the expansion. As domestic interest rates rose, it encouraged massive

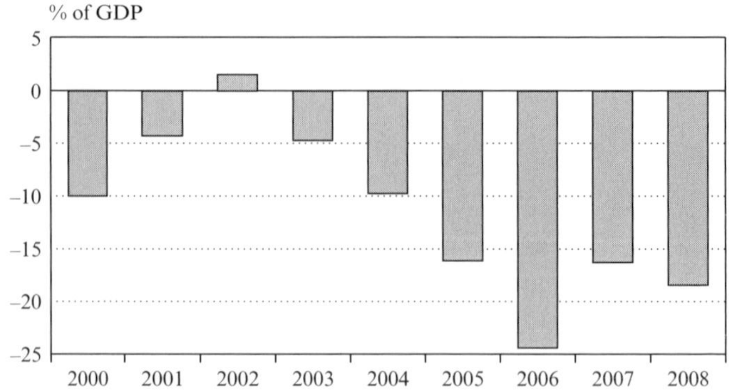

Source: Central Bank of Iceland.

Figure 8.6. Current account balance 2000–2008

short-term capital inflows of a speculative nature and growing foreign currency exposure in sectors without natural hedging. The more the Icelandic economy became out of sync with the rest of the world, the more carry traders seeking higher yields expanded their ISK positions in periods when the risk of ISK depreciation was considered low or moderate.

By their counter-cyclical design, automatic fiscal stabilizers, amplified by positive balance sheet effects, generated record fiscal surpluses. On the other hand, discretionary fiscal policy was pro-cyclical, as tax rates were lowered substantially, raising disposable income, thus leaving discretionary counter-cyclical policy measures to the CBI.

Although the ferocity of the collapse and its high fiscal costs caught many observers unawares, financial sector problems and a hard landing for the Icelandic economy should not have come as a surprise, and indeed, a recession had been forecast by the CBI for years.[8] Moreover, all of the well-known alarm bells for potential financial sector instability were sounding loud and clear. Over the period 2003–2007, domestic credit expanded by 451 per cent. Credit to non-residents grew 46 times over, although starting from a low level. There was a clear sign of a bubble in the real estate market. Some argued, of course, that the increase was driven mostly by fundamentals, as income was expanding almost as rapidly. The problem with that argument is that there was a credit-driven bubble in incomes, as was evidenced by an unsustainable and unprecedented double-digit current account deficit from 2004 until the financial crisis hit in 2008 (see Figure 8.6). All of the above, together with lax risk management and the willingness to assume imprudent risk, such as the growing foreign exchange exposure among households and businesses with limited foreign currency income, would be sufficient to raise questions about the long-term health of Icelandic banks. Despite apparently healthy short-term indicators, such as the banks' profitability, capital adequacy CAD ratios[9] and even, in most cases, liquidity ratios, questions were rightly raised about the quality of their assets and hence the stability of their liabilities.

It was widely recognised that the economy was seriously overheated. The private sector's accumulation of debt meant that, given the sector's intertemporal budget constraint, a spending adjustment was imminent, as was most evident in the enormous current account deficit. In real terms, the króna was clearly overvalued. Either the nominal exchange rate would have to depreciate, or credit supply would have to tighten substantially. While the latter could be seen as an attempt to escape a disorderly depreciation of the króna in order to protect households' and businesses' balance sheets, both options were bound to result in a sharp contraction in economic activity. About a year before the crisis struck, credit conditions became significantly tighter, as investors became less willing to take greater risk and falling returns on assets prompted a cycle of deleveraging. Stock markets began to decline, as did house prices. A drop in house prices and the resulting loss of household wealth most often results in a credit squeeze. So, even in the absence of a financial crisis, households and businesses would have needed to adjust their spending plans drastically, with commensurate impact on the real economy.

Domestic macroeconomic imbalances were not what precipitated the collapse of the Icelandic banks, however, although indirectly they were an important contributing factor. The Achilles' heel of the Icelandic banks was their funding, which in turn was a function of their rapid growth, made possible by a combination of the high credit ratings they inherited from their State-owned predecessors and the global liquidity glut. Wholesale capital markets were open to the banks at a relatively low premia until early 2006. As rapid expansion at home and abroad raised questions about asset quality, it gradually dawned on global creditors that neither the Government nor the CBI might be in a position to rescue the banks in case of severe distress, even if they were deemed to be solvent.

Credit default swap (CDS) spreads on the banks started to rise in late 2005 (see Figure 8.7). At first, this development was dismissed by the banks as a sign of market imperfections in the market for credit default insurance, but by 2006 it became clear that the situation was turning into a serious refunding problem. As a result of actions taken by the banks themselves, as well as global factors, the credit squeeze abated from late 2006 but then returned with a vengeance in 2008. The banks responded to their initial funding problems by looking for new markets. In 2006,

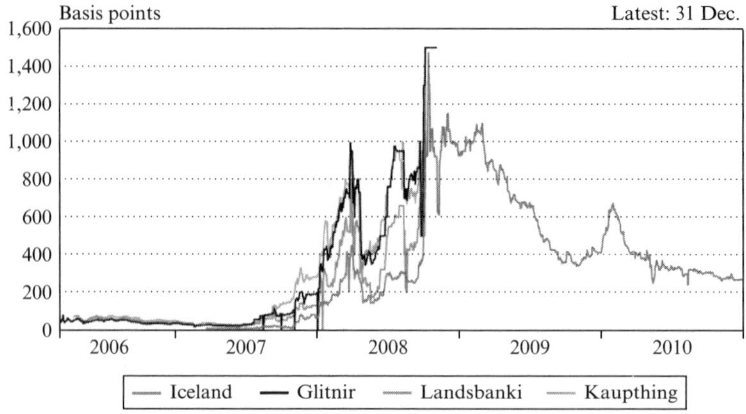

Source: Bloomberg.

Figure 8.7. CDS spreads for Iceland and the three major cross-border banks

they embarked upon a funding strategy that later turned out very costly for Iceland's taxpayers. Landsbanki in particular was quite successful in attracting deposits over the Internet through its UK and Dutch branches, the so-called Icesave accounts. Collateralized debt obligations (CDOs) issued in the US also became a major source of funding. A large part of them contained Icelandic bank bonds, as well as sub-prime loans and other toxic assets. This funding established a direct link between the US sub-prime crisis and the Icelandic banks' access to foreign funds.[10] The banks faced an increasingly unfavourable maturity structure on their funding. Hence, once the international crisis reached its peak in September 2008, the Icelandic banks were extremely vulnerable on their funding side, and the fact that their balance sheets had outgrown Iceland's GDP by a factor of ten made it far too costly to rescue them. Even in the absence of expensive rescue operations, the cost of the banking collapse is enormous.

There should be no doubt that the credit expansion intermediated by the banks substantially boosted real economic activity in the boom period and that the credit crunch following the collapse of the banking system has also amplified the contraction, as households and businesses that relied on external financing during the boom are forced to deleverage. Trying to disentangle the effect of the normal correction of imbalances from the particular amplification effect of the financial system break-down poses an inherently difficult challenge. In the next section we examine in detail the costs of the financial crisis to taxpayers, so as to give an idea of the magnitude of the fiscal impact of the banking failure.

8.4. THE COST OF THE CRASH TO TAXPAYERS

In this section, we attempt to dissect the various components of the cost of the banking system meltdown to public finances. This should be regarded as a preliminary assessment, as the situation is still evolving. It represents the estimated short- to medium-term direct and indirect costs of the crisis. The long-term impact is more difficult to assess. Some long-term benefits may even accrue, or a country may embark upon a low growth track, as Argentina did in the early twentieth century, resulting in cumulative losses many times its GDP. Neither of these scenarios is predictable, as they are dependent on the political development; thus they are not explored here.

Collateralised lending will probably prove to be the single most costly factor of the banking failure. Indirectly, the scale of the cost to public finances is affected by the fact that the banks had a large share of their operations in multiple foreign currencies, while their LOLR, the CBI, could only provide near-unlimited liquidity in domestic currency. Once global sources of foreign exchange liquidity dried up in 2008, the banks tried to gain access to foreign exchange liquidity through two main channels: the domestic interbank market and, ultimately, the Central Bank of Iceland; and (via their subsidiaries in Luxembourg) the European Central Bank (ECB). With the CBI unable to provide foreign exchange liquidity via its main refinancing operations, the foreign exchange liquidity squeeze quickly translated into a shortage of ISK liquidity, as the banks scrambled to buy foreign currency on the interbank foreign exchange market by selling ISK borrowed in the money market. Hence demand for collateralised loans through the Central Bank's regular refinancing operations as well as overnight loans escalated sharply in 2008 (see Figure 8.8). The banks' sudden demand for short-term CBI credit led to a sharp deterioration of the quality of collateral they could provide, inciting abuse of the rules on collateral. The banks became increasingly creative in their efforts to access liquid funds from the CBI and the ECB. They issued debt (so-called love letters) that other financial institutions, mainly the saving banks, could use as collateral against CBI loans, lending the funds to the issuing banks. This abuse of the rules on collateral and the growing exposure of the CBI balance sheet in the event of a systemic crisis prompted both the CBI and the ECB to tighten their collateral policy in the spring and summer of 2008. By contributing to the sharp ISK depreciation, the banks' behaviour also caused extensive damage to the asset side of their

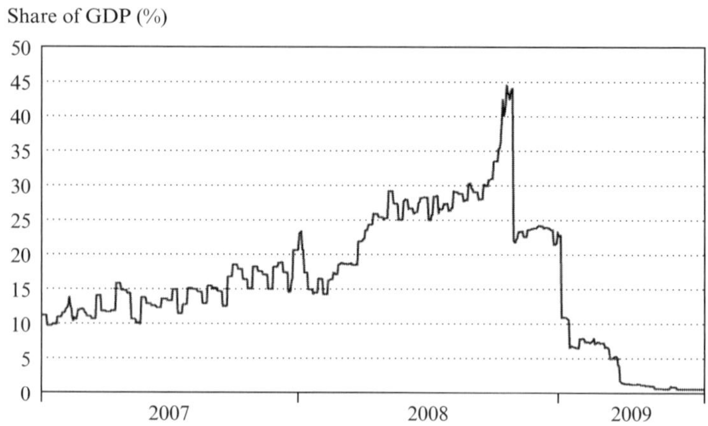

Source: Statistics Iceland, Central Bank of Iceland.

Figure 8.8. CBI lending against collateral to the banking sector before and after the crash

balance sheets, reducing the expected rate of asset recovery. The loss from surety notes is estimated at ISK 295 billion, plus an additional ISK 35 billion of losses due to loans against securities. This loss would have left the Central Bank with negative equity. To recapitalise the Central Bank, the Treasury issued a debt instrument in the amount of ISK 270 billion, in exchange for notes issued by domestic financial institutions. The Treasury took over most of the surety notes. The Treasury's net loss from surety notes is estimated at ISK 220 billion, and the loss from loans against securities at ISK 35 billion. The Central Bank absorbed the rest of the loss by reducing its equity capital by ISK 75 billion. The total loss from collateralised lending is estimated at ISK 330 billion, equivalent to more than a fifth of GDP.[11]

The cost of recapitalising the banks is a function of the size of the new banks, on the one hand, and their ownership structure, on the other hand. For various reasons, a clear good bank/bad bank split was not deemed feasible. Rather, domestic deposits and assets were taken into the new banks, leaving foreign assets and liabilities in the old (failed) banks. This also made the balance sheets of the new banks larger than they would have been if a pure good bank/bad bank strategy had been followed as a great deal of impaired assets were left on the banks' balance sheets. A tedious evaluation process ensued, together with negotiations with creditors on an instrument of compensation, to compensate creditors for assets in excess of liabilities (deposits) transferred to the new banks. On the other hand, soon after the crash, it became public policy to try to involve creditors in efforts to recapitalise the new banks. As it turned out the Government will almost fully recapitalize only one of the banks. The remaining two banks have primarily been recapitalized by the old banks' creditors, indirectly via asset holding companies owned by the estates of two of the failed banks, Kaupthing and Glitnir. This significantly reduces the immediate cost to the Government, as well as the likelihood of litigation by creditors over the evaluation process, as the process gives them a share in potential upside risk to the evaluation. Conversely, it will also limit the State's gain from potential asset recoveries. To a large extent, those gains will accrue to creditors, who are mainly foreign parties. The equity contribution of the Treasury to the new banks amounts to ISK 135 billion, about 9 per cent of GDP. The Treasury's holdings in New Landsbanki will be 81 per cent, as opposed to only 13 per cent in Arion Bank (based on the old Kaupthing) and 5 per cent in Íslandsbanki (based on the old Glitnir). In addition, the Treasury provides subordinated loans to the latter two banks. The total financing contributed by the Treasury to the new banks' recapitalization is therefore ISK 184 billion. An additional ISK 22.5 billion will be injected into the saving banks. Altogether, the Treasury will have to inject capital equivalent to 14 per cent of GDP into the banking system. The Government followed the principle of saving the banking intermediation function of the financial system by starting up new banks rather than attempting to rescue the old banks. No money was transferred to shareholders or the creditors of the old banks. Hence we assume that the Government will recoup its recapitalization outlays to the new banks with marginal net fiscal impact with an upside risk.

The cost of compensating foreign depositors in foreign branches is still subject to considerable uncertainty. The gross claim on the Depositors' and Investors' Guarantee Fund (DIGF) amounts to GBP 2350 million from the UK, plus EUR 1329 million from the Netherlands. This amounts to 42 per cent of Iceland's GDP. There is significant uncertainty concerning asset recovery ratios, which would reduce the cost of compensating depositors in the UK and Dutch branches of Landsbanki. Landsbanki's assets are estimated to cover 86 per cent of deposit claims. However, since the payout will not begin until this year at the earliest and will probably last beyond 2020, Iceland pays significant interest on the gross amount during this period. The Central Bank estimated the net present value of the claim according to terms of the agreement reached in 2009 between the Icelandic, British and the Dutch governments at ISK 220 billion, or 14 per cent of GDP. That agreement was rejected in a national referendum. The governments resumed negotiations, and a more favourable deal is now on the table, but the new agreement is still being debated and has not been passed into law by Parliament. The net present value of the claim is now estimated at ISK 47 billion, or 3 per cent of GDP.

Before the crash, banking had become the largest sector of Iceland's economy, contributing directly about 9 per cent to the country's GDP. Corporate tax revenues from financial enterprises plus capital gains tax on dividends and profit from the sale of banking shares amounted to 2.8 per cent of GDP in 2007, at the height of financial activities, out of total tax revenue amounting to 34.9 per cent of GDP in 2007. After the near-total collapse of the financial sector, the vast majority of those tax revenues have vanished. Rebuilding the financial sector as a major pillar of the economy seems neither feasible nor desirable in the near future. Hence, the loss of revenue from banking sector operations has to be regarded as largely permanent. The central government thus lost up to 8 per cent of its revenue, with the gross loss estimated at about 2 per cent of GDP in the bust period. While it is somewhat misleading to make a comparison with the height of the banking boom, but such a comparison demonstrates the size of the fiscal impact. The net permanent loss is somewhat lower, since a large part of the pre-crisis revenue was not permanent revenue but rather a part of the bubble. The pre-crisis bubble component of tax revenues from financial enterprises in the boom period is estimated[12] at 1½ per cent of GDP, leaving the net loss at ½ per cent of GDP.

Confidence is a precious commodity whose value is only fully appreciated when lost. Loss of confidence adds substantially to the cost of financing the fiscal deficit that results from the crisis. As a result of limited confidence in Iceland's ability to repay its debt, its access to global credit markets closed immediately following the collapse of the banks. Even now, foreign credit is apparently available only at punitive terms. CDS spreads have recently come down to around 300 basis points, after rising above 1000 basis points. Over the medium term, the shock to confidence is cushioned by the Stand-By Agreement with the IMF and related bilateral loan agreements. On average, the terms on those loans are 275 basis points over the London Interbank Offered Rate (LIBOR). By contrast, in 2006 the Treasury was able to issue a EUR 1 billion bond at 1 basis point below the five-year swap rate at the time. Capital controls have also shielded Government finances from the full cost of lost confidence. Demand from pension funds and other domestic investors that are prevented from investing abroad by the controls has probably significantly reduced the cost to the public sector from the loss of confidence. Due to this loss of confidence, the Central Bank will need to hold excess reserves in order to secure the refinancing of debt falling due over the next couple of years – via global capital markets – and facilitate the gradual removal of capital controls. These are borrowed reserves and will cost significant interest differentials, as reserve assets will have to remain fairly liquid and low-risk. The extra interest expense in the wake of the crisis can be categorized as stemming from two sources. First, there is the interest expense on all new interest-bearing debt excluding new debt to raise reserves. Second, there are interest differentials from holding excess reserves to stabilize the currency. Concerning the first category, we estimate the extra interest expense per year on new debt at 3.4 per cent of GDP, while the estimated interest differential from holding excess reserves amounts to 1 per cent of GDP. That is 4.4 per cent of GDP in total, an estimated 2 percentage points of which represents the premium interest paid due to loss of confidence. With gross general Government debt at 102 per cent of GDP, gross interest-bearing Icesave claims at 42 per cent of GDP and gross debt of the CBI at 14 per cent of GDP the consolidated interest-bearing debt is 158 per cent of GDP; thus every 100 bp increase in the interest rate translates to an interest payment amounting to 1.58 per cent of GDP. Without the IMF programme and the capital controls, the Government's costs would be at least 1.7 per cent of GDP higher, but most likely significantly higher based on CDS spreads. There is great uncertainty surrounding this figure because there really were no funds available in the wake of the crisis and the authorities would have been forced to follow a different strategy.

Turning now to the more indirect and uncertain costs of the financial disaster, the balance sheet effects on automatic fiscal stabilizers contributed substantially to boosting income to the Government during the banking bubble, as was the case in many OECD countries.[13] The damage done to private sector balance sheets as result of the financial crisis is extensive and has amplified the contraction. The process of repair will likely be protracted. When estimating the size of automatic fiscal stabilizers, one must keep in mind that they are not constant but change continually over time. Estimating the structural balance can therefore be difficult and, to a large extent, a matter of judgement, especially, in a very small open economy. In standard structural balance estimation methodology, the elasticity of tax revenues with regard to the output gap is used to measure the cyclical component of tax revenues. The deviation of elasticity from historic average values during the last boom can serve as a partial measure of balance sheet effects. If the change in elasticity is not adjusted for, the cyclical component of revenues will be underestimated, leading to overestimation of the structural balance during expansions and underestimation during recessions. The elasticity of total tax revenue had been relatively stable previous to the banking-driven boom, but rose markedly in the period 2003–08, from an average of 2.88 to 3.83.[14] Attributing the change in elasticity to balance sheet effects leads to the conclusion that the balance sheet effects amplified the automatic fiscal stabilizers by a factor equivalent to 4 per cent of GDP

Source: Central Bank of Iceland.

Figure 8.9. Effective exchange rate of the króna

during the contraction.[15] How much of this is attributable to the financial crisis in addition to permanent loss of tax revenue from the financial sector itself is hard to estimate, but we estimate it to be one-quarter.[16] The gross fiscal impact of going from positive balance sheet effects to negative in the bust period is therefore estimated at 3 per cent of GDP. As the positive and negative balance sheet effects will most likely cancel each other out in the long run, even though the negative effects will last longer, we assume the net cost to be slightly negative when looking strictly at the boom-bust cycle. That, however, will really only be determined after the fact.

Another cost factor whose permanence is highly uncertain is the loss on pre-crisis foreign-denominated debt caused by the ISK depreciation. Financial crises have typically been followed by a protracted period of below equilibrium real exchange rates. It was Iceland's good fortune that the Government's foreign debt was relatively low before the crisis. At year-end 2007, the Government had outstanding foreign-denominated debt in the amount of 13.4 per cent of GDP, mainly denominated in Euros. By 1 September 2008, the Icelandic króna had already depreciated by nearly 33 per cent against the Euro from the beginning of the year (see Figure 8.9). A sizable depreciation of the króna had been imminent even in the absence of the banking collapse. Although views differ on the long-term equilibrium real exchange rate of the Icelandic króna it can be argued that the króna was close to or below its equilibrium level in mid-2008.[17] The ensuing sudden stop of capital inflows that commenced in September led to a very significant overshooting of the króna, even if we assume that the equilibrium rate is significantly below the end-2007 level. The sudden stop caused a further 46 per cent depreciation increasing outstanding foreign debt by 6 per cent of GDP in ISK terms. This is the gross fiscal impact, which consists of interest expense effect and the balance sheet effect. The interest expense effect we have already covered, but the balance sheet effect, especially as it relates to the net fiscal impact estimate, is more difficult to pin down. Predicting currency exchange rates is notoriously difficult and, at this point in time, we cannot with confidence forecast how fast the overshooting of the real exchange rate will correct itself. But we assume that it will and that the net fiscal impact will be marginal with a downside risk.

Although this is not included in our overall estimate of the fiscal impact, it should be mentioned that Government-guaranteed debt also increased considerably during the crises, as nearly all of it is either denominated in foreign currency or indexed to the consumer price index (CPI). The Government guarantees the debt of utility companies and the Housing Financing Fund (HFF). Guaranteed debt amounted to 58 per cent of GDP before the crisis but increased to 71 per cent of GDP afterwards. The guaranteed debt is different from direct Government debt in that the debt of the utilities and the HFF are backed by collateral as well as the future stream of revenue to these companies that can be used to service the debt, leaving only the potential shortfall to be covered by the Government.

For many decades, Iceland's labour market has been characterised by full employment (and significant labour shortages over extended periods) making the labour market participation rate among the highest in the world. The distribution of labour income has been fairly equitable. In addition to frugal benefit schemes, at least in Nordic comparison, this has implied relatively modest social transfers. The financial crisis may trigger a long-lasting increase in social contributions. Unemployment rose from 1 per cent below NAIRU of 3 per cent to 9 per cent after the crash, raising unemployment sharply. Some of the adjustment in unemployment benefits is simply an inevitable cyclical adjustment. A sharp deterioration of household balance sheets also significantly increases the need for social transfers. It is estimated that the gross fiscal impact will amount to some 2 per cent of GDP. A significant part of the increase might be quite persistent leaving the net impact at 1 per cent of GDP.

A strong point of the Icelandic economy has been its fully funded pension system.[18] It still is, but being fully funded also implies that pension funds incurred losses as a result of the crash losses that, to some extent, must be borne by the State. The pension funds operated by the State and the municipalities are rights-based. The claims against them do not depend on the pension funds' asset returns, as in the case of private sector funds. The respective governments *de facto* guarantee these pension rights. Hence negative asset returns increase the Government's debt to the pension funds. The Icelandic pension system's net assets available to pay out pensions amounted to 129 per cent of GDP at year-end 2007. Two years later, after having recovered somewhat from the level when negative returns were at their worst, net assets amounted to 119 per cent of GDP. It should be noted that the favourable impact of the depreciation of the króna on the ISK value of pension funds' foreign assets is substantial, but as the pension funds lost their means to hedge their foreign currency exposure, they may incur further losses if the króna appreciates. Claims against the public pension funds are indexed to wages, but in the case of most private sector funds they are largely dependent on asset returns. Adjusting for wage developments, net assets relative to claims have depreciated by 3.8 per cent which leaves the Government's share of incurred losses at 1.3 per cent of GDP. If we view the potential increase in pension insurance premiums that would maintain pre-boom pension rights in the same way as a tax increase, the estimated cost to taxpayers rises considerably.

To summarise, the gross fiscal impact in the bust period, the above-listed direct and indirect costs of Iceland's financial disaster, add up to 57 per cent of the country's GDP. This bottom-up assessment of the cost is fairly consistent with recent forecasts, which, it should be noted, assume very significant fiscal adjustment. The gross general government debt position is forecast to rise from 30 per cent of GDP at year-end 2007 to 105 per cent of GDP[19] at year-end 2010, an increase of 75 per cent of GDP,[20] including the estimated net present value of the DIGF guarantee of the debt to the Dutch and British governments, the gross liability of which amounts to 42 per cent of Iceland's GDP (see Figure 8.10). As there are substantial assets to be acquired or recovered against new debt (e.g. excess reserves), net debt will rise less than gross debt. The *net* debt position of the general government, where only monetary assets that are liquid are deducted from the gross debt position, will rise from 11 per cent of GDP to 90 per cent of GDP for the same period, 21 percentage points more than the gross fiscal impact of 57 per cent, which means that the vast majority of the fiscal impact is directly caused by the financial crisis. The net fiscal impact when adjusted for the gains from the financial boom and imbalances in the pre-crisis boom period is somewhat lower, at 30½ per cent of GDP. The net fiscal impact gives the net cost of the financial system´s boom-bust cycle. The gross fiscal impact is the shock to the balance sheet if no fiscal adjustments are implemented. Adjustments will be made to the fiscal impact, however, as the Government plans to consolidate in the order of 10 per cent of GDP in the 2009–12 period to counter the deterioration of the income statement in order to bring the primary structural balance back to surplus.

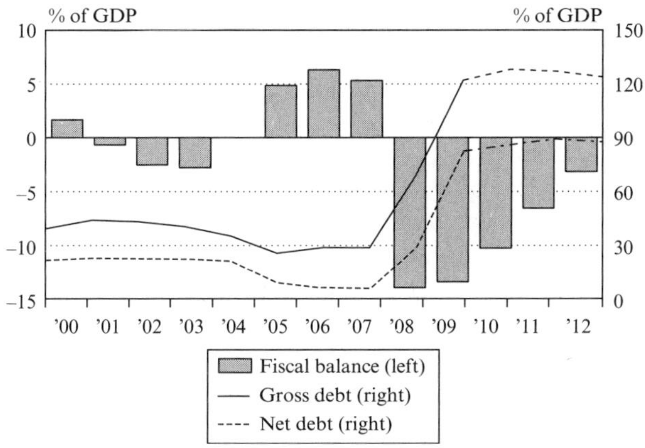

Note: 1. Central Bank baseline forecast 2009–2012.

Sources: Ministry of Finance, Statistics Iceland, Central Bank of Iceland.

Figure 8.10. Public sector finances 2000–2012[1]

Table 8.1. Fiscal impact of the financial crisis

Item	**Percent of GDP**	
	Gross fiscal impact	**Net fiscal impact**
Collateralised lending	22	22
Bank recapitalisation	14	0
Compensation to foreign depositors	3	3
Permanent tax revenue loss from banking	2	½
Balance sheet effect	3	1
Interest expense	4	3
Loss on pre-crisis FX debt	6	0
Increase in social contribution	2	1
Loss of pension funds	1	0
Total	**57**	**30½**

8.5. CONCLUSION

Iceland's financial disaster has been a very expensive lesson for Iceland itself, and indeed for the whole of Europe and the world. It is important that these lessons not be forgotten as soon as the economy recovers.

So, what have we learnt? First, although EU directives are intended to promote cross-border activity and competition in financial services, governments would be well advised to make every effort to limit the scale of cross-border banking relative to the size of their foreign currency LOLR so as to keep their banks from becoming too large. Second, small countries with 'peculiar currencies of their own' are particularly vulnerable in this respect. Significant maturity mismatches in foreign currency coupled with rollover risks can build up and lead to a run on foreign liabilities if the LOLR is not credible. The Icelandic banking saga clearly demonstrates that a banking crisis can become very costly when the banks operate in a multi-currency environment and have outgrown domestic country and currency support. The interaction between the financial sector, the real economy, and the currency fuelled the economy during the boom, undermined confidence during the subsequent period of growing distress, which culminated in the collapse of the banks, and amplified the contraction that followed, exacerbating the loss of Government revenue and the damage to banks' balance sheets and those of households and firms. A key lesson is that small countries with independent currencies should either make a special effort to limit the size and riskiness of their financial sector or join a monetary union. Perhaps a EMU membership would not have prevented the collapse of the banking system, but it would have reduced the cost of lost collateral, as it would be shared by the entire euro system. This would be little consolation to Iceland's partners, however. Third, if Europe wants to reap the benefits of cross-border financial services competition, it must also have pan-European supervision similar to that proposed in the Turner review (2009), as well as a deposit insurance, crisis management, and resolution mechanism. Fourth, even when banks are private companies, their demise can instantly shift large amount of private sector debt to the public sector balance sheet. Countries that fail to contain their financial systems must compensate for it by taxing such activities or by running more prudent fiscal policies than would otherwise be required. They should aim for very low public debt or even build substantial contingency reserves while building into the system proper incentives that internalize the cost of risky behaviour of banks engaged in international operations.

ACKNOWLEDGEMENTS

The authors would like to thank the editors of this collection and also Asgeir Danielsson, Markus Moller, Thorvardur Tjorvi Olafsson, Thorarinn G. Petursson and Thorsteinn Thorgeirsson from the Central

Bank of Iceland for constructive and helpful comments. Views expressed are ours and do not necessarily reflect those of the Central Bank of Iceland.

NOTES

1. See, for example Allen *et al.* (2007), Barro *et al.* (2008), Chang *et al.* (2001), Classens *et al.* (2008), Englund (1999), IMF WEO (1998), Lall *et al.* (2008), Mishkin (1992, 1996), Moe *et al.* (2004), Radelet *et al.* (1998) and Sachs *et al.* (1996).
2. See Buiter and Sibert (2008).
3. Iceland – 2007 Article IV Consultation Concluding Statement, June 11, 2007.
4. See Gudmundsson and Thorgeirsson (2010) for more detail.
5. Reinhart and Rogoff (2009) report fiscal deficit reversals (page 231). The reversals show the change in central government deficit from a year before the crisis to the peak deficit following. At the top of the list are Sweden (1991) with a 15.4 per cent of GDP reversal and Finland (1991) with 11.8 per cent. In Iceland´s case the reversal was 16.9 per cent of GDP from 2007 to 2008.
6. See Hemming *et al.* (2003) for a discussion on fiscal vulnerabilities and financial crisis.
7. For more detail on the financial and credit accelerators see for example Dalsgaard *et al.* (2002) and Adrian and Shin (2008).
8. See for example various issues of *Monetary Bulletin* in 2006–2008, where CBI forecasts are published.
9. The CAD ratio is a bank‘s capital base divided by its risk-weighted assets. The regulatory minimum is 8 per cent. For further information see the Basel II definitions.
10. See, for example, Milleker (2007)
11. At year-end 2009, the Central Bank bought back the assets in question to be sold into a subsidiary of the CBI, Central Bank of Iceland holding company (ESÍ), which will divest them when market conditions permit.
12. It is difficult to estimate accurately the bubble component of asset prices, but we benefit from hindsight. Our approach is that of looking at the difference of the price-dividend ratio before and after the onset of the credit expansion as a proxy to the bubble component. We base this partly on Campbell and Shiller's (Campbell, John Y. and Robert J. Shiller (1998), 'Valution Rations and the Long-Run Stock Market Outlook', *Journal of Portfolio Management*, 24, 11–26), present value model, which links variations in stock prices to changes in expected dividends and discount factors.
13. See, for example, Jourmard and André (2008).
14. If estimated according to conventional methodology, the parameters are 1.92 and 2.55. The Icelandic experience from cyclical adjustment is that the output gap alone does not fully capture the cyclical component because tax revenue are also very dependent on the real exchange rate in a very small open economy. When the real exchange rate is strong, excise duties are high and vice versa. To capture this, the standard elasticity must be higher by a factor of 1.5 to obtain a plausible structural balance, which is done in this case.
15. Out of a net income surplus of 5.4 per cent of GDP in 2007, two percentage points may be accredited to balance sheet effects, with an output gap estimated at 4.7 per cent.
16. Wealth effects stemmed mostly from higher stock and house prices. 75 per cent of the wealth effect comes from the appreciation of homes and non-financial stocks according to tax returns. See Schneider and Tornell (2004).
17. See, for example, Sighvatsson (2001) and Tchaidze (2007).
18. While the private pension scheme is considered fully funded, the civil service pension scheme was estimated in 2008 to be only 60 per cent funded.
19. The net liability of Government guarantees is included in gross Government debt figures if it is more likely than not that the guarantee will have to be paid. Here the

net Icesave liability is included in the gross debt figure, as it is still only a Government guarantee and not an outright debt. Gross Government debt excluding Icesave is 102 per cent of GDP. Gross Icesave depositors' claims amount to 42 per cent of GDP; thus the interest-bearing stock of debt is 144 per cent of GDP.

20. Reinhart and Rogoff (2009) report a historical average of 86 per cent of cumulative increase in real public debt in the three years following past banking crises (page 323). Finland (1991) and Colombia (1998) top the list with a nearly 175 per cent increase in public debt. In the case of Iceland, which started from a low level, the increase in real public debt was 198 per cent between year-end 2007 to year-end 2010.

9. The Greek tragedy: is there a *Deus ex Machina*?[1]

Ioannis Kokkoris, Rodrigo Olivares-Caminal and Kiriakos Papadakis[2]

9.1. INTRODUCTION

The purpose of this chapter is twofold: firstly, to discuss the difficulties that being a member of the European Monetary Union (EMU) entail, with particular focus on Greece and on the implications of an internal devaluation. Secondly, how debt re-profiling can help to support the mechanisms of fiscal rehabilitation and external financing at the sovereign and corporate level. Among other issues, we clarify the situation confronting the Greek authorities and provide a description of the different mechanisms to restructure/re-profile sovereign debt.

9.2. THE GLOBAL FINANCIAL CRISIS AND ITS IMPACT ON SOVEREIGN DEBT

The global financial crisis of 2007 has resulted in an overall increase of sovereign debt levels. Fiscal balances (as a ratio of gross domestic product (GDP)) have deteriorated. This deterioration is mainly because of falling revenues resulting from decreased real and financial activity. According to IMF's data[3] in 2010 advanced countries will average a budget deficit of (−8.3 per cent) while emerging economies one of (−3.3 per cent). In advanced economies public debt to GDP ratio will reach in 2010 the level of 97 per cent (rising from below 75 per cent in 2006) while in emerging economies will be 37 per cent (almost equal to 2006 level). This is the result of a shift in risk allocation in advanced economies. In other words, the turmoil of the markets has calmed down by pouring government financial aid which in turn resulted in a considerable increase in the amount of sovereign debt. Although financial markets seem to be at ease, sovereign debt markets remain fragile.

Research by Reinhart and Rogoff shows that a debt to GDP ratio beyond the range of 60 per cent to 90 per cent for developed countries may become counterproductive for the economy (i.e. further government spending may not lead to growth) and a debt spiral may be created in cases where GDP growth falls below the weighted average interest paid on the bonds.[4]

On 16 February 2010, the Ecofin Council approved the Hellenic Stability and Growth Programme (SGP). The aim of the SGP is to bring the fiscal deficit of Greece to less than 3 per cent by 2012 and reduce the government consolidated debt as a percentage of GDP from 2012 onwards. In order to safeguard this deficit-reduction target, the government adopted additional measures aiming at reducing costs and enhancing revenues. The Greek government's short- and medium-term fiscal and reform strategy measures include budget, tax, social security, and public administration reform, as well as institutional changes to enhance the credibility and sustainability of policies.[5] These measures will be supported with a EUR 110 billion package provided by EU Member States (EUR 80 billion) and the IMF (EUR 30 billion). The programme will be monitored through 12 quarterly reviews.

Following the most recent restatement of Greek data by Eurostat, Greece recorded a budget deficit of (−13.6 per cent) and a debt/GDP ratio of 115 per cent in 2009. The profile of deficit reduction is more modest in the revised SGP than it was in the SGP published in February, reflecting the upward revision of the estimated deficit numbers and a downward revision to the growth projections. In the revised SGP, the Greek government is projecting a budget deficit of (−4.9 per cent) of GDP in 2013 with an outstanding debt/GDP ratio of 149 per cent. The restatement of the data together with the effect that the global financial crisis has had on the economy led the rating agencies to downgrade Greece to Ba1 (Moody's) with stable watch, BB+ (S&P) and BBB− (Fitch) with negative watch. Figure 9.1 illustrates the history of Greek ratings.[6]

9.3. THE GLOBAL RECESSION AND INTERNAL DEVALUATION PROCESSES FOR PEGGED FX REGIMES

The theory of an optimum currency area ('OCA') was pioneered by Nobel laureate Robert Mundell. The main rationale behind the theory is that an OCA is a geographical region in which economic efficiency would be maximized by sharing a single currency. It describes the optimal characteristics for the merger of currencies or the creation of a new currency.

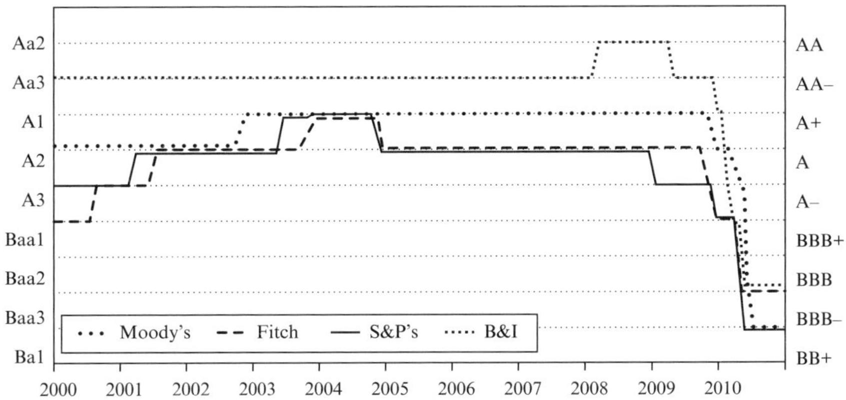

Figure 9.1. Historical evolution of Greece's sovereign debt ratings

The four often more cited criteria for a successful currency union are: (1) labour mobility across the region; (2) capital mobility and price and wage flexibility across the region which will produce an efficient allocation of resources; (3) similar business cycles (when one country experiences a boom or recession, other countries in the area are likely to follow) which allows for a common central bank to promote growth in downturns and to contain inflation in boom periods; and (4) a risk-sharing system such as an automatic fiscal transfer mechanism to redistribute money to areas/sectors which have been adversely affected.

By being part of the EMU there are two main constraints that the member countries are facing. Firstly, member states lose the ability to have an independent monetary policy (ability to print money). Secondly, a member state has no control in setting a benchmark interest rate which drives the cost of money in the domestic economy. These two issues are interlinked monetary policies, both of which have been delegated to the European Central Bank (ECB).

Figure 9.2 shows the evolution of ECB's benchmark interest rate ('main refinancing rate').[7] In order to reduce the cost of money and stimulate the EMU economies, the ECB reduced the rate from 4.25 per cent in July 2008 to 1.00 per cent since May 2009.

Currently, it seems that the PIIGS (Portugal, Italy, Ireland, Greece and Spain) are at a different point in the business cycle from the core countries of EMU like Germany and France. Given the existing growth trends, the markets seem to have already priced in a 25bps–50bps increase in the ECB refinancing rate throughout the first half of 2011. What this will imply for PIIGS economies where the unemployment rate is already in double

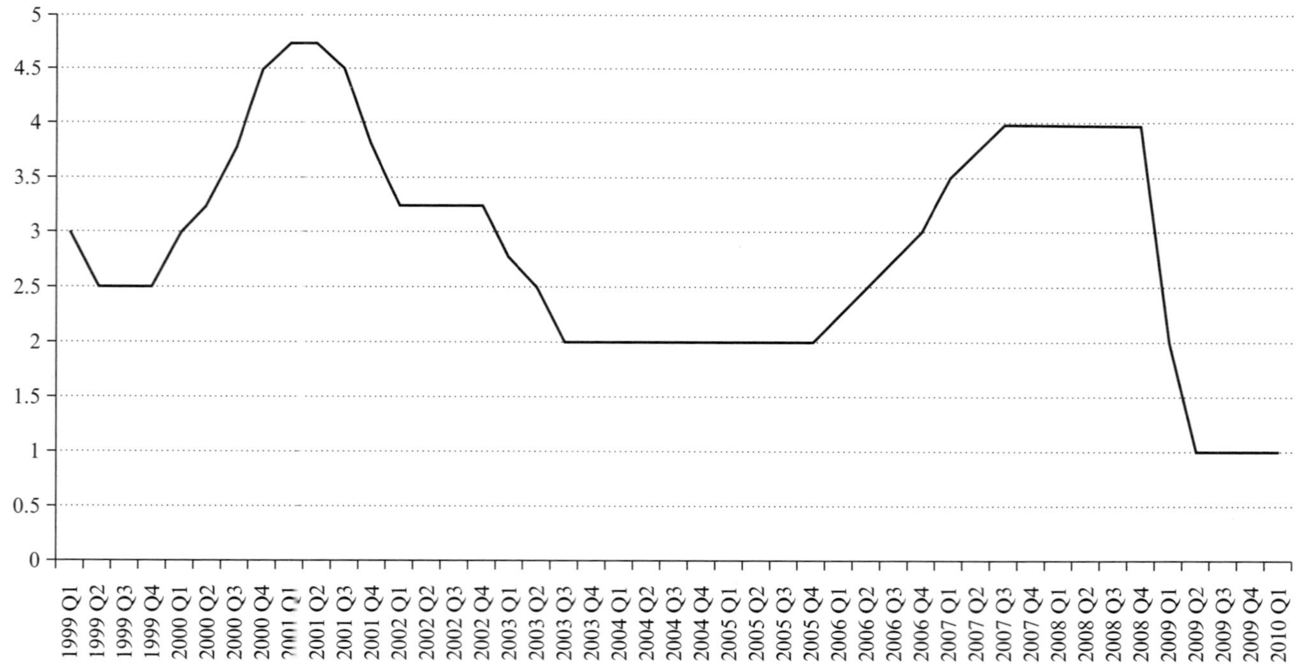

Figure 9.2. *Evolution of ECB's benchmark interest rate*

digits in some cases (Spain almost 20 per cent, Greece at 13 per cent and climbing higher) remains to be seen. Those member states are adopting measures to reduce their deficits and decrease their debt to GDP ratios.

The combination of servicing debt with high interest rates and austerity measures to reduce budget deficits and thus control sovereign debt, can be a 'toxic' combination which raises many questions.

On 2 May 2010, Greece officially received the support of the EMU and the IMF by activating the fourth pillar (IV) of an OCA: a risk sharing system. A credit line of almost EUR110 billion will be available for the next three years consisting of EUR80 billion provided by the EMU and EUR30 billion from the IMF. This eases the current liquidity concerns since refinancing of short-end debt will be achieved at lower interest rates than what would be the case if the government had to access the capital markets. However, austerity measures of equal to EUR30 billion equal to almost 13 per cent of Greek GDP have to be implemented as a condition of the arrangement.

There are two additional elements that should also be taken into account: (1) Greece lose the ability to have an independent monetary policy in order to buy its way out by means of printing money, devaluating the currency and external inflation; and (2) interest rates may soon increase because of inflationary concerns in France and Germany. Bearing these two additional issues, internal devaluation (adjustment of internal salaries and prices) is the only viable solution. This forces to ask the question: what could be the repercussions of an internal devaluation? In this sense, we can use Latvia as an interesting case study because although it has its own currency it maintains a pegged exchange rate with the Euro, having several similarities with Greece who effectively has its currency fixed by being a member of EMU. In the period from 2008 to 2009, Latvia has seen a historical decline of GDP of more than 25 per cent. This makes Latvia's loss bigger than that of the US during the Great Depression of 1929–1933. By implementing an internal devaluation, all the adjustment is made through downward pressure on prices and wages. With Latvia's unemployment rate reaching 22 per cent this adjustment has been very painful.

Argentina in a similar case in 1999–2001, suffered a deep recession (above 20 per cent reduction in GDP) as it tried unsuccessfully to adjust its economy under a fixed exchange rate regime where its currency was pegged to the US dollar. With rising interest rates to finance budgetary deficits – which resulted in a rising public debt burden – this proved impossible and in December 2001 the country defaulted on its external obligations leading also to abandonment of the pegged exchange rate.

The biggest challenge that Greece is now facing is how to effectively implement the tough measures required in order to comply with IMF/EU requirements and more importantly to sustain these measures through the delicate situation of its economy. People can argue about the correct approach to implement the measures but not whether they should be implemented. Nobody will be willing to provide a bail-out without something in exchange. Therefore, now politicians have to deal with angry voters feeling the pinch in their pockets while trying to get Greece out of this delicate situation. Experience in other countries has showed that it is not easy. Using Argentina again as an example, there have been five presidents over a one month period and serious protests that led to fatalities (as in the case of Greece).

9.4. GREEK DRAMA OR TRAGEDY?

The current discussions in relation to the Greek crisis and its outstanding billions of debt seems to focus on two possible scenarios dubbed in this article the Greek Tragedy and the Greek Drama.

The Greek Tragedy, as the title indicates, implies a tragedy, i.e. pulling out of the euro-zone. By pulling out of the euro-zone, Greece will regain its monetary policy which is now in the hands of the ECB and regain an ability to use monetary policy as a means to print money to ease the burden of repaying debts. This will come – hand-in-hand – with inflation, devaluation and the need of a new currency (e.g. Roccos, just to assign an imaginary name to the new currency) or the re-issuance of an old currency (e.g. Drachmas). This tragic scenario will allow Greece to default on its debt without receiving pressure from other EMU members, forcing a restructuring with a substantial haircut, which can trigger a bank run and a *de facto* nationalization of the domestic banks. This will imply a steep discount on Greek indebtedness and chaos for two or three years (probably more).

The Greek Drama – assuming that a 'drama' is less negative than a 'tragedy' – is the scenario where Greece remains within the euro-zone. As an EU member, Greece cannot devaluate its currency to recover faster[8] and gain international competitiveness. Therefore, although there will be no formal devaluation and no new currency, there still are some very difficult times ahead. The measures already adopted to achieve internal devaluation are very unpopular and affect Greek citizens dearly. Similar measures adopted in other countries in the 1980s, 1990s and early 2000s have ended with social unrest, unemployment rates above 20 per cent and an increase in poverty. In some of these cases the adopted measures proved ineffective. Although this will help re-align Greek interests with those of other EMU members, Greek citizens need some additional assistance to ease the burden of the measures.

Despite the implementation of a three-year financial aid package of EUR110 billion (from the EU and IMF) there is no reason to believe that investors will invest in Greek bonds without receiving in exchange a high interest rate. The speculative risk associated with Greek finances increases after 2013, with a rise in the debt/GDP ratio from 115 per cent to 149 per cent. Whether the EU and/or the IMF intends to roll over the EUR110 billion facility beyond the three years remains unclear though investors soon will start taking for granted that a roll-over will take place. In addition, existing Greek bondholders have become subordinated to the EU and IMF financial aid package which further complicates their risk analysis given that they have not been convinced that this aid package will actually work.

The word credit comes from Latin '*creditus*' which means to believe and trust, something that certainly the Greek bonds lack. In other words, Greece has obtained fresh liquidity (more debt) to pay existing debts at high interest rates. Any new debt incurred by Greece (e.g. new bond issuances) with the exception of concessional or emergency lending provided by multilateral agencies will carry higher interest rates. This is precisely what happened in the 1980s and was dubbed 'a debt trap', giving rise to the Brady Plan.[9]

Finally, given this lack of credibility (which is amplified from the prospective losses that European banks will face if Greece restructures its debt), the European interbank market (the market where banks lend each other) seems to have been affected. This has already led to higher Euribor rates[10] implying higher costs for banks and thus higher charges from banks to non-financial costumers (thus monetary tightening is happening without ECB increasing its benchmark rate). A lack of confidence leads to higher financing costs and thus, further obstacles for new investment and consumption, depriving economies even further from much-needed growth.

9.5. MECHANISMS OF SOVEREIGN DEBT RE-PROFILING

The legal literature on sovereign debt has understood that a sovereign state cannot be declared insolvent. Despite the fact that sometimes it is said in a figurative way that a country is insolvent or bankrupt because it is unable to pay its debts as they become due, technically speaking, a country cannot reach this situation. First and foremost, a sovereign state always has the possibility of taxing its citizens, to dispose of its resources (e.g. natural resources or even part of its territory as it had happened in the past with Alaska or the state of Louisiana in the US), or even in extreme circumstances it can recourse to the expropriation of assets of its own citizens. Therefore, the legal literature has mainly focused on the restructuring aspects of sovereign debt.

Sovereign debt restructuring comprises multilateral, bilateral and private debt instruments. The first two have their own set of policies and rules on how to perform such a restructuring. However, the latter is devoid of a structured or institutional approach. Therefore, we will focus on private sovereign debt restructuring.

Broadly speaking, sovereign debt restructuring is understood as the mechanism used by a state to prevent or resolve debt issues and to achieve a sustainable level of debt. It basically has two aspects: procedural and substantial. While the procedural aspect focuses on the ways in which the restructuring should be performed (i.e., its architecture), the substantial aspect is the actual restructuring of debt, which is normally characterized by rescheduling amortization schedules as well as writing off the debt principal.[11] It is worthy to note that since sovereigns cannot technically go bankrupt, the only available mechanism is an exchange offer that can be enhanced by different techniques. So far, in the sovereign debt restructuring episodes of the 1990s, the issue of major concern has been the holdout creditors. In view of this situation, the international community has come up with a statutory approach proposing the establishment of an international bankruptcy-type regime based on the US Chapter 11, which was referred as a 'Sovereign Debt Restructuring Mechanism' (SDRM). The market response was the use of contractual features: (1) exit consent or exit amendments;[12] and (2) the use of collective action clauses (CACs).[13]

While there is widespread interest in a revamped sovereign debt restructuring process for private claims, there is disagreement over what the actual process should be.[14] The financial community is confronted with court-supervised workouts in a bankruptcy-type proceeding or a purely voluntary bond workout.[15] The question is: when sovereign debt restructuring, re-profiling, and write-off becomes necessary and unavoidable, what will be the appropriate regime that will provide orderly restructuring while safeguarding the balance of rights both of creditors and the debtor?

In other words, the current debate is between the establishment of an international bankruptcy regime and the use of voluntary and contractual arrangements such as exchange offers, CACs, and other devices. The IMF believes that the scope for some voluntary mechanisms used in the past has been greatly diminished, particularly due to the shift from syndicated bank loans to bonds in sovereign borrowing. This shift has led to a wider dispersion of creditors and debtors, a larger variety of debt contracts, and it has also been associated with the growing spread and integration of the capital markets and innovations in sourcing foreign capital.[16]

Debts documented in syndicated loans were – in comparison – easy to restructure because they were renegotiated within the framework of the London Club.[17] On the other hand, bonds are more difficult to restructure since they are held by different types of creditors encompassing different interests (a so-called multilegitimacy problem). The interests of investment banks in keeping the debt performing due to accounting issues is not the same as that of a retail investor that has invested all his lifetime savings or the interest of a vulture fund that is trying to obtain a substantial gain. This becomes much more complicated particularly if there are many outstanding series which could be subject to different applicable laws, and where holders are scattered throughout the world.[18] Transactions are governed by the law chosen by the parties. In the case of a bond issuance it is the issuer who decides which will be the applicable law.[19] The applicable law is relevant when a sovereign is under distress because the debtor's alternatives would be different depending on the applicable law.

In the specific case of Greece, Buchheit and Gulati have noted that:[20]

(1) 90 per cent of the total Greek debt is governed by Greek law (the remaining 10 per cent is governed by English law).
(2) Most of the bonds subject to Greek law do not contain provisions permitting the holders to amend the terms of the bonds after issuance (other than to correct obvious errors or technical matters). In other words, they do not contain CACs (bonds subject to foreign law do include CACs).
(3) Bonds subject to Greek law do not include a negative pledge clause.
(4) Greece's negative pledge clauses pertain only to foreign law bonds issued prior to 2004 and would only be triggered by the creation of a lien to secure a non Euro-denominated Greek debt.
(5) A cross-acceleration, cross-default and moratorium event of default clauses in these bonds are triggered by a default on an external Indebtedness (i.e. a payment default on a Greek Euro-denominated bond, or the acceleration of such an instrument, would not have cross-default consequences across much of the outstanding debt).

The method and techniques currently used for restructuring sovereign debt have several similarities with corporate debt restructuring. The most significant difference is that both parties in the corporate context – debtor and creditor – know that upon failure of the debt restructuring process there is a last resort (i.e. bankruptcy). It is true that sovereign states cannot be subject to a judicial bankruptcy process but they can and do become insolvent in the sense of being unable to pay their debts as they become due (Wood, 2003).[21] Although a regime based on US Chapter 11 has been considered in relation to the situation of sovereigns (i.e. SDRM), the lack of fear of being wound up through a liquidation process – something which is not and would not be available for sovereign states – alters the whole rationale in sovereign debt restructuring. Neither the government of a sovereign can be replaced nor can the sovereign be closed down and sold to the highest bidder.[22] Since the bankruptcy option does not exist in the sovereign context, some debtors and creditors have become more aggressive in their techniques and negotiations.

Recent restructurings by Belize, Grenada and the Seychelles clearly establish that restructuring is possible within the given parameter and limitations by the tactical and often complementary use of collective decision-making provisions and exchange offers. Collective decision-making provisions are contractual terms that allow the bond to be restructured on the basis of a favourable vote of the majority of the bondholders. Exchange offers are voluntary processes where holders of an outstanding bond are offered to exchange their bonds for newly issued bonds, usually with less attractive financial terms. The terms of the bonds in each of these cases had determined the restructuring technique that was to be adopted, that is exchange offers and amendments to the contractual terms.

Another available option is a debt re-profiling. A debt re-profiling is a voluntary exchange offer prior to default. In other words, the main difference between a debt re-profiling and a debt restructuring is the timing when the exchange offer is performed. A debt re-profiling can help ease part of the Greek pressure of an internal devaluation by reducing the debt-servicing burden. Jamaica provided an excellent example, where interest costs and principal repayments exceeded the country's revenues. Through a voluntary domestic debt exchange offer performed in early 2010 without a default, Jamaica reduced some of its servicing debt burden. Therefore, following this example, Greece should take advantage of the liquidity that has been provided by the EMU and IMF to do an orderly debt re-profiling (voluntary exchange offer) which will not trigger the credit default swaps (CDSs) linked to the Greek bonds.

9.6. IMPLICATIONS OF DEBT RESTRUCTURING OR DEFAULT: SOME FINAL CONSIDERATIONS

Given the debt maturity profile as illustrated in Figure 9.3[23] and the rationale of a self-fulfilling prophecy, which the markets have the power to enforce by speeding up a process that would have anyhow materialized

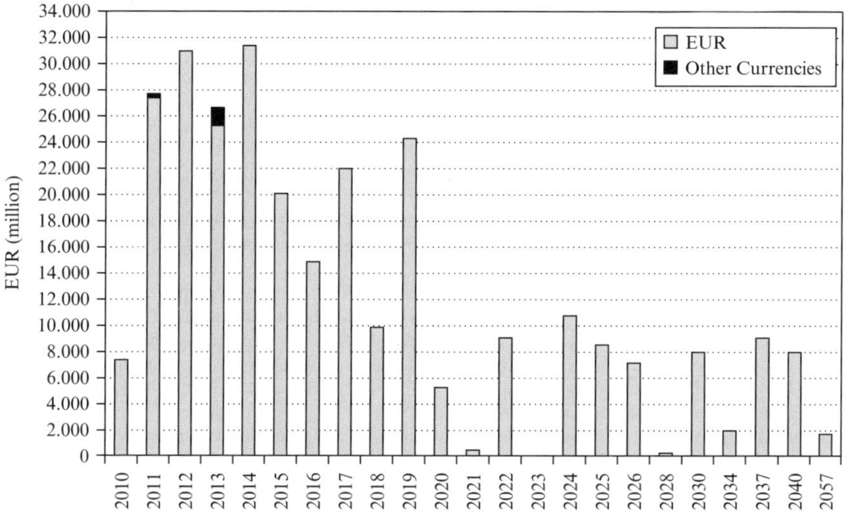

Figure 9.3. Debt maturity profile

in the future, Greece seems almost certain to need the help of a debt re-profiling mechanism.

To be more specific, Greece is currently obliged to borrow (if attempted in the international capital markets) at very high interest rates and short maturity periods, a debt re-profiling (i.e. an exchange offer to extend maturity and include with it a reduction of the interest rate coupon) should be urgently considered, so as to avoid the worst case scenario of a default.

Note that in 2001 Argentina defaulted on USD81.8 billion of sovereign debt after months of turmoil which included a closing of the country's banking system. The end result was that Argentina abandoned its exchange rate regime and GDP fell by 10.9 per cent that year. In addition, Argentina has been locked out of the international capital markets ever since.[24] In a similar scenario, in 2003, Uruguay managed to re-profile its external debt being able to re-access the capital markets in just a month receiving very positive credit ratings.

In ancient Greece, tragedian Euripides during his stage plays at the peak of a tragic moment used a '*Deus ex Machina*' (Act of God) as a means to solve the plot. The question is whether there is such an Act of God for what is unfolding for the Greek economy to sustain the country through the rough waters that it is currently experiencing. It may be the case that what Greece needs is to rise from its ashes as the phoenix does, as there may not be a '*Deus ex Machina*' able to guide Greece through these waters.

NOTES

1. A previous version of this article has been published in *International Corporate Rescue*, Volume 7, Issue 4, 2010.
2. The opinions expressed herein are personal and do not necessarily reflect those of the institutions that the authors represent.
3. International Monetary Fund (IMF): 'World Economic Outlook' (April 2010).
4. See Carmen M. Reinhart, Kenneth S. Rogoff, and Miguel A. Savastano, 'Debt Intolerance', Brookings Papers on Economic Activity (2003) and Carmen M. Reinhart, Kenneth S. Rogoff, *This Time is Different: Eight Centuries of Financial Folly*, Princeton University Press (2009).
5. See Ministry of Finance of Greece, http://www.minfin.gr/portal/en/resource/contentObject/contentTypes/genericContentResourceObject,fileResourceObject,arrayOfFileResourceTypeObject/topicNames/stabilityGrowthProgram/pageNumber/1/resourceRepresentationTemplate/contentObjectListAlternativeTemplate#fragment-6.
6. Data obtained from www.pdma.gr.
7. Data obtained from www.ecb.int.
8. Although the Euro has already fallen relative to a basket of currencies, Greece's main trading partners are Euro countries.
9. The Brady Plan was articulated in 1989 by US Treasury Secretary Nicholas F. Brady to address the debt crisis that occurred in the developing countries (at that time LDC – *less developed countries*) during the 1980s as the result of continuous money pouring by banks to keep the loans performing. By injecting fresh money to restructure principal and keep interests performing, debtors entered a debt trap that was not able to escape until the Brady plan was put into place. Although the Brady plan evolved on a case by case basis, its main features were: (1) adjustment programmes; (2) menus of debt restructuring options assuring the collection of the credit and that the new debt would be traded in order to diversify risks; and (3) new money. According to EMTA's Debt Trading Volume Surveys, the Brady bond market share in the year 2000 was approximately 25 per cent of total trading (USD 712 billion). See Emerging Markets Trading Association, The Brady Plan, available at http://www.emta.org/emarkets/brady.html. For an enlargement on the Baker and Brady Plans see Lex Rieffel, *Restructuring Sovereign Debt: The Case for Ad-hoc Machinery*, Brookings Institution Press, 2003, pages 149–177; and Ross P. Buckley, 'Emerging Markets Debt: An Analysis of the Secondary Market', Kluwer, 1999.
10. For instance both three and six month commercial paper rates have increased and these are the main rates used for retail loans.
11. See Rodrigo Olivares-Caminal, *Legal Aspects of Sovereign Debt Restructuring*, Sweet & Maxwell, 2009.
12. Exit consent is the technique by which holders of bonds in default who decide to accept an exchange offer, at the moment of accepting said offer grant their consent to amend certain terms of the bonds that are being exchanged. By using the exit consent technique, the exchange offer is conditioned to a minimum threshold of creditors' acceptance and the amendments to the terms are performed once the required majority has been obtained. By means of these amendments, the defaulted bonds subject to the exchange offer become less attractive (in legal and financial terms), forcing a greater number of bondholders to accept the exchange offer. Otherwise, if holdout bondholders do not accept the exchange offer, they will be holding an impaired bond not featuring some of the original contractual enhancements.
13. CACs are clauses whereby, if they are included in the prospectuses of the bonds, the interaction of the bondholders is required. There are four different types of CACs. These are: (1) collective representation clauses; (2) majority action clauses; (3) sharing clauses; and (4) acceleration clauses. Within CACs, majority action clauses are the type of clauses that have been strongly pursued by the official sector and many academics, and they were effectively incorporated in bond issuances. Majority action clauses

enable the amendment of any of the terms and conditions of the bonds, including the payment terms, if the required majority therein established is obtained. So far, the required threshold to amend the terms of the bonds containing majority action clauses has been 75 per cent in aggregate principal amount of the outstanding bonds (e.g. Egypt, Lebanon, Mexico, Qatar, Uruguay, etc). Brazil has been the only case where 85 per cent has been required.

14. Alinna Arora and Rodrigo Olivares-Caminal, "Rethinking the Sovereign Debt Restructuring Approach", *Law and Business Review of the Americas*, 2003.
15. Lee Buchheit and Mitu Gulati, 'Sovereign Bonds and the Collective Will', *Emory Law Journal, 2002.*
16. See UNCTAD, 'Trade and Development Report 2001'.
17. The London Club is an informal group of commercial banks that join together to negotiate the terms of their claims against a sovereign debtor.
18. For example, in the recent Argentine 2001–2002 debt crisis, there were 152 series of bonds governed by eight different laws. It was estimated that at the moment of the default there were over 700 000 creditors around the globe, mainly in Italy (15.6 per cent), Switzerland (10.3 per cent), US (9.1 per cent), Germany (5.1 per cent), Japan (3.1 per cent), United Kingdom (1.1 per cent), the Netherlands (1 per cent) and Luxembourg (0.8 per cent). See the report prepared by the Secretariat of Finance of the Argentine Ministry of Economy titled 'Lineamientos de la Reestructuración de Deuda Soberana' dated 22 September 2003, pages 23–24.
19. Rodrigo Olivares-Caminal, 'The Use of Corporate Debt Restructuring Techniques in the Context of Sovereign Debt', *International Corporate Rescue,* Volume 2, Issue 5, Kluwer Law International, 2005.
20. This analysis is based on the authors' analysis of some series of Greek bonds. See Lee Buchheit and Mitu Gulati, 'How to Restructure Greek Debt' (7 May 2010), available at SSRN: http://ssrn.com/abstract=1603304.
21. Philip Wood, 'Pari Passu Clauses: What Do they Mean?' *Journal of International Banking and Financial Law* (2003).
22. Lex Rieffel, "Restructuring Sovereign Debt: The Case for Ad-hoc Machinery", Brookings, Washington, DC (2003).
23. Data obtained from www.pdma.gr (data as of 19 May 2010).
24. Currently after almost 10 years it tries to resolve a discussion with residual holders of almost USD20 billion of bonds.

10. Restructuring a nation's debt[1]

Lee C. Buchheit and Mitu Gulati

The EUR110 billion EU/IMF bailout package announced in the first week of May 2010 was intended by its framers to permit Greece to pay its maturing debt, in full and on time, by drawing on official sector funds. If it works, a restructuring of Greece's massive debt stock will be avoided, at least for a time. But if that Plan A doesn't work, or if Plan A only succeeds in pushing the need for a debt restructuring down the road a way, what might Plan B look like?

Greece's total debt at the end-April 2010 was approximately EUR319 billion. Of that figure, the vast majority – approximately EUR294 billion – was in the form of bonds, with another EUR8.6 billion issued as Treasury bills. Virtually all of this debt stock was denominated in Euros. Small amounts (in aggregate, less than 2 per cent of the total) are outstanding in US dollars, Japanese yen and Swiss francs. Information about the holders of Greek bonds is anecdotal. From press reports it appears that French and German banks have the heaviest exposures, but mutual funds, pension funds, insurance companies, hedge funds and other categories of investors also own Greek bonds. Significantly, the extent of retail ownership appears to be small.

A large amount of Greek bonds have been discounted by European commercial banks with the European Central Bank (ECB). On 3 May 2010, the ECB announced that those bonds would continue to be eligible for discounting, notwithstanding the downgrading of Greek bonds that occurred the prior week.

10.1. LEGAL ASPECTS OF THE DEBT STOCK

From the legal standpoint, the salient feature of Greece's bond debt is that approximately 90 per cent of the total is governed by Greek law. Only about EUR25 billion of the bond debt was issued under the law of another jurisdiction, and most of that under English law.

In terms of collective action clauses, it does not appear from our survey of Greek bond documentation that the instruments issued under local law contain provisions permitting the holders to amend the terms of the bonds after they are issued (other than to correct obvious errors or technical matters).

Before 2004, Greek bonds issued under English law contained collective action clauses (CACs) that appear to permit holders of 66 per cent of an issue to modify payment terms in a manner that would bind all other holders. After 2004, Greece altered this clause in its English law bonds. This new version of the CAC permits amendments to payment terms of a bond, as well as certain other key features of the instrument, with the consent of holders of 75 per cent or more of an issue.

Most of the Greek bonds we have examined in the survey incorporate a standard set of events of default (variations can be found in a few bonds). These include:

- failure to pay interest (with a 30-day grace period);
- other covenant defaults (with a 30-day grace period after written notice to the issuer);
- 'External Indebtedness' (above a *de minimis* threshold) is accelerated, or a payment is missed under such External Indebtedness and continues beyond the specified grace period;
- a general moratorium is declared on External Indebtedness; and
- any government order or decree that prevents Greece from performing its obligations under the bonds.

Before 2004 (when Greece adopted a new form of CAC), individual bondholders could accelerate their bonds following a default. Bonds issued after that time incorporate a requirement that holders of 25 per cent of the bonds vote in favour of an acceleration. (Individual rights of acceleration are now rarely found in emerging market sovereign bonds.)

Greece would enjoy some distinct advantages in the restructuring of its debt, as well as a few disadvantages, in comparison with other countries that have been forced to undergo the process.

10.1.1. Advantages

Greece's debt is overwhelming in the form of bonds, a characteristic shared by countries like Argentina (2001–05), Ecuador (2000) and Uruguay (2003). So Greece will be able to avoid the complexities and inter-creditor rivalries that can be occasioned by a diverse creditor universe. Iraq (2005–08), for example, faced a commercial creditor class composed of banks, suppliers, construction companies, various kinds of trade creditors and even individuals. In the end, Iraq had to settle more than 13 000 individual claims dating back to the Saddam era.

Greece's debt records are fresh and up-to-date. When sovereign debts have been in default for prolonged periods before they are restructured (for example, Liberia (2009) – more than 25 years in arrears; Iraq (2005–08) – more than 15 years in arrears), the task is much harder.

Greece enjoys considerable financial support from multilateral and bilateral sources. This opens up the possibility of the country being able to 'credit enhance' any new Greek debt instrument that might be issued as part of a debt restructuring. Greece is therefore in a position similar to the countries that issued collateralized Brady Bonds starting in 1990.

The fact that so few Greek bonds seem to have fallen into the hands of retail (non-institutional) investors may also be a blessing. Those countries (for example, Argentina (2001–05)), that have had to deal with thousands of retail bondholders in a debt restructuring have found this a messy and thankless task.

By far, however, the greatest advantage that Greece would enjoy in a restructuring of its debt derives from the fact that so much of the debt stock is expressly governed by Greek law (90 per cent or more, if our figures are correct). This raises the possibility, discussed in more detail below, that the restructuring could be facilitated in some way by a change to Greek law.

Several other countries have restructured local law-governed debts. Russia restructured Russian law-governed instruments known as GKOs and OFZs in 1998 in parallel with the restructuring of its English law commercial bank debt. Uruguay restructured its local law bonds (on the same terms as its foreign law bonds) in 2003. In each of these cases, however, the local law bonds were also denominated in local currency and formed only part of the overall stock of the debt being restructured. While the Euro is certainly now the local currency of Greece, it is a good deal more besides that. No other debtor country in modern history has been in a position significantly to affect the outcome of a sovereign debt restructuring by changing some feature of the law by which the vast majority of the instruments are governed.

10.1.2. Disadvantages

Several features of the Greek situation may complicate any restructuring of its debt. For example, a significant percentage (perhaps more than 30 per cent) of the bonds are believed to be owned by Greek institutional holders. A restructuring that dramatically impairs the value of that paper could, therefore, place further strains on the Greek domestic financial sector.

Jamaica, which restructured its local currency debt in 2010, had to walk very gingerly in designing its transaction because so much (perhaps as much as 75 per cent) of the affected paper was held by Jamaican financial institutions.

European banks are the largest holders of Greek bonds. So the stability of those institutions will be very much on the minds of Greece's multilateral and bilateral supporters should a debt restructuring prove unavoidable. The sovereign debts that triggered the global debt crisis of the 1980s were nearly all owed to international commercial banks. When the debt crisis broke in 1982, the official sector overseers of the restructuring process therefore had to keep one eye on the debtor countries and the other on the stability of the banking systems in the industrialized creditor countries. It remained an uncomfortable position for nearly seven years until the banks had time to build up the loan loss reserves that permitted them to accept losses in Brady Bond exchanges without alarming regulators, stockholders or their own creditors.

In contrast, sovereign debt crises of the last ten years or so have affected mostly non-bank creditors – hedge funds, pension funds, other institutional holders of emerging market sovereign debt, sometimes even individuals. Those crises did not threaten the stability of the banking sectors in creditor countries. A restructuring of Greek debt will, in this respect, rekindle fretful memories of the global debt crisis of the 1980s in the minds of official sector observers.

Greece's debt is denominated in Euros, a currency shared by other members of the European Union. When Mexico or the Philippines restructured debts denominated in US dollars in the 1980s, no one – for that reason alone – lost confidence in the US dollar. This same assurance cannot be given about the restructuring of Euro-denominated debts owed by an EU member state.

10.2. HOW MIGHT IT BE DONE?

Which brings us to the main event. If one were to attempt to learn the lessons of the 50 or 60 sovereign debt restructurings of the modern era, what would they teach about how a Greek debt restructuring should be managed in order to achieve a prompt, orderly and fair outcome?

There is one lesson from this history that is inescapable. A sovereign debt crisis can be a painful experience for both the debtor and its creditors; a mismanaged sovereign debt crisis can be a catastrophically painful experience.

The most likely structure for such a transaction would be an exchange offer – new bonds of the Hellenic Republic would be offered in exchange for the Republic's existing bonds. The terms of the new bonds would determine the nature and extent of the debt relief that the transaction would provide to Greece. Exchange offers have been the norm for sovereign debt restructurings of middle income countries since the first Brady Bond transactions in 1990.

10.2.1. Eligible Debt

The debt eligible to participate in such an exchange would presumably be all outstanding Greek bonds, excluding perhaps the Treasury bills. Short-term Treasury bills have been excluded from a number of recent sovereign debt restructurings in order to keep that market sweet for the government's emergency financing needs.

An interesting question will be whether some way can be found to exclude from the restructuring process the bonds in retail hands, or at least to moderate the terms of any restructuring of those bonds. This will depend on two things. First, the total amount of bonds in the hands of natural persons would have to be relatively small. Institutional holders may recognize the public relations benefit of not having widows and orphans complaining on the evening news, but only up to a point.

If the exclusion of retail holders appreciably increases the severity of the financial sacrifice that must be borne by institutional creditors, these sympathies will quickly fade. Second, some mechanism must be found that will permit the government to identify which bonds are in retail hands when the restructuring is announced. Otherwise, bonds will tend to migrate temporarily into the hands of individuals until the restructuring storm passes over.

10.2.2. New Instruments

The terms of the new instrument or instruments that would be offered in such an exchange will be a function of the nature and extent of the debt relief the transaction is designed to achieve. At the soft end of the spectrum might be a simple 're-profiling' of existing bonds (or some discrete portion of them such as bonds maturing over the next three to five years) involving a deferral of the maturity date of each affected bond. In 2003, Uruguay stretched out the maturity date of each of its bonds by five years, while leaving the coupons untouched.

At the sharper end of the spectrum would be a transaction designed to achieve a significant net present value (NPV) reduction in the stock of debt. If Brady Bonds were chosen as the model for the transaction, this might entail allowing holders to elect to exchange their existing credits for either a Par Bond (a new bond exchanged at par for existing instruments, having a long maturity and a low coupon), or a Discount Bond (a new bond exchanged for existing instruments at a discount from the face amount of those instruments, but typically carrying a higher coupon and perhaps a shorter maturity than the Par Bond). The precise financial terms of the Par Bond and the Discount Bond would be calibrated to achieve an equivalent NPV reduction.

Some version of a collective action clause appears in most of Greece's foreign law-governed bonds. There is no reason not to use these clauses to minimize the number of non-participating creditors. It would work as follows: each tender of an existing bond containing a CAC would contain a power of attorney from the owner of that bond in favour of the government (or its exchange agent) to vote that bond at a bondholders' meeting (or in a written action by bondholders) in favour of a resolution that, if approved by the requisite supermajority of holders of that instrument, would either cause the totality of that bond to be tendered in the exchange or cause the payment terms of the bond to be amended so as to match the terms of one of the new instruments being offered in the exchange. Such a resolution, if approved by the requisite supermajority of holders (66 per cent or 75 per cent in Greek bonds governed by English law) would automatically bind all holders.

As part of the restructuring process, Greece would have to consult with significant holders of its paper, or with committees or other ad hoc groups representing those holders. Such consultations would be necessary to garner widespread support for the restructuring. In addition, the IMF's so-called 'Lending Into Arrears' policy requires a member country facing a debt restructuring to make "a good faith effort to reach a collaborative agreement with its creditors".

10.2.3. Credit Enhancement

If Greece's multilateral and bilateral supporters were prepared to allow some portion of their emergency financing to be used for this purpose, Greece might be able to enhance the attractiveness of the new bonds it would offer in the exchange. In the typical Brady Bond context, for example, the issuing countries borrowed money from the IMF and the World Bank and used those funds to purchase US Government zero coupon obligations that were then pledged to secure the principal payment due on the Brady Bonds at maturity. In many cases, a pool of cash equal to 12 to 24 months of interest accruals on the Brady Bonds was also set aside and pledged as partial security for the interest due on the Brady Bonds.

So the Brady Bonds represented US Government risk for principal due at maturity, and issuing country risk for interest during the life of the bond (apart from any amount pledged as rolling interest collateral).

Credit enhancement need not take the form of collateral security. Indeed, over time, the market grew less fond of Brady Bonds and most countries retired their Brady Bonds early. Obtaining a partial guarantee of the new instruments from a creditworthy party is another option. (The Seychelles obtained a partial guarantee from the African Development Bank of the new debt instrument issued by the Seychelles in connection with its debt restructuring in 2010.) Another alternative would be to offer holders of the new instruments a continuing 'put' of those instruments to a creditworthy party, presumably at some discount from face value. This would assure an institutional holder of the paper that the instrument will always have a minimum floor value, no matter what happens to the trading price in the secondary market.

10.2.4. The Tactical Implications of Local Law Bonds

International investors are often leery of buying debt securities of emerging market sovereign issuers that are governed by the law of the issuing state. Why? Because investors fear that the sovereign might someday be tempted to change its own law in a way that would impair the value or the enforceability of those securities. Such changes in local law would normally be respected by American and English courts if the debt instruments are expressly – or otherwise found to be – governed by that local law.

International capital market borrowings by industrialized countries sometimes follow a different model. Many of these countries have found that foreign investors are prepared to purchase local law-governed debt securities of the sovereign. These investment decisions are presumably based on a belief that industrialized countries are less likely than some of their emerging market brethren to risk eroding future investor confidence by opportunistically changing their own law in order to reduce government debt service burdens.

No country in Greece's position would lightly consider a change of local law as an easy method of dealing with a sovereign debt crisis. The following factors, among others, counsel extreme caution before embarking on such a remedy.

If done once, future investors will fear that it could be done again. The debtor country may therefore be compelled in future borrowings (in which international investor participation is sought) to specify a foreign law as the governing law of its debt instruments.

A dramatic change in local law by one country might allow a worm of doubt to slip into the heads of capital market investors in other similarly-situated countries, driving up borrowing costs around the board.

The official sector supporters of the debtor country will presumably baulk at any action of this kind that could unleash the forces of contagion and instability upon other countries whose debt stocks also contain predominantly local law-governed instruments.

The more dramatic or confiscatory the effect of the change of law, the higher the likelihood that it would be subject to a successful legal challenge. We shall discuss some of the elements of the challenges below.

One legislative measure that might be perceived as balanced in these circumstances, however, would be to enact what amounts to a statutory collective action clause. It could operate in this way: local law would be changed to say that if the overall exchange offer is supported by a supermajority of affected debt holders (say, 75 per cent, to use the conventional CAC threshold), then the terms of any untendered local law bonds would automatically be amended so that their payment terms (maturity profile and interest rate) match those of one of the new instruments being issued in the exchange.

Such a law, let's call it a Mopping-Up Law, would thus operate in the manner of a contractual CAC in a syndicated debt instrument. Once the supermajority of creditors is persuaded to support an amendment to the payment terms of the instrument, their decision automatically binds any dissident minority. Viewed another way, the Mopping-Up Law would merely replicate at the level of the sovereign borrower the same protection enjoyed by corporate borrowers in many countries, including Greece. For example, we understand that in corporate reorganization proceedings under Greek bankruptcy law, if a plan of reorganization is accepted by two thirds of the affected creditors (including at least 40 per cent of 'privileged claims' such as secured or senior claims), it will – with court approval – bind all creditors.

A Mopping-Up Law would achieve a similar result but at the level of a sovereign borrower in need of a debt reorganization. Facilitating a sovereign debt restructuring through some form of Mopping-Up Law would be consistent with the fundamental principle that a sovereign debtor bears the burden of persuading its creditors that a debt restructuring is essential, that the terms of the restructuring are proportional to the debtor's needs, and that the sovereign is implementing economic policies designed to restore financial health. The only question is whether the sovereign must persuade every last debt holder of these elements, or just a specified supermajority of affected creditors. The trend in recent years, as evidenced by the rapidity with which CACs have been introduced into New York-law sovereign bonds, is in favour of the supermajority threshold.

Even the relatively mild step of facilitating a debt restructuring through the passage of a Mopping-Up Law of some kind, however, could draw a legal challenge. In the case of Greece, such a challenge could come from three possible sources. The first is Article 17 of the Greek Constitution. That Article declares that no one shall be deprived of property 'except for public benefit' and conditional upon payment of full compensation corresponding to the value of the expropriated property.

The question, it seems to us (non-Greek lawyers that we are), is whether a mandatory alteration of the payment terms of a local law Greek bond in the context of a generalized debt restructuring could be said to impair the value of that bond; an instrument that, in the absence of a successful restructuring, would have in any event been highly impaired in value. Also of possible relevance may be Article 106 of the Greek Constitution which gives the State broad powers to 'consolidate social peace and protect the general interest'.

A second source of possible legal concern might lie in the European Convention on Human Rights and its Protocols. Article 1 of Protocol No. 1 protects the right to the 'peaceful enjoyment of possessions'. This right may be restricted only in the public interest and only through measures that do not impose an individual and excessive burden on the private party. That said, Article 15 of the Convention permits measures, otherwise inconsistent with the Convention, to deal with a 'public emergency threatening the life of the nation'.

Finally, foreign holders of local law-governed Greek bonds subject to the Mopping-Up Law might look to Greece's Bilateral Investment Treaties (BITs) for redress. BITs protect against expropriation without compensation, as well as unfair and inequitable treatment. It appears that Greece has signed more than 40 BITs with bilateral partners.

Assuming some version of a Mopping-Up Law could survive any legal challenge, however, it could have significant tactical implications for a Greek debt restructuring. More than 90 per cent of Greek bonds are governed by local law. If, to use our example, holders of 75 per cent of all eligible bonds (local law and foreign law) were to support a restructuring, our version of a Mopping-Up Law should operate to ensure that more than 90 per cent of the debt stock will be covered by the restructuring. The Mopping-Up Law would not affect holders of foreign law bonds. Participation by those holders would need to be encouraged by moral suasion and the use of contractual collective action clauses in the relevant bonds.

10.2.5. How Long Would a Restructuring Take?

Our guess? If done efficiently, five to six months; less if necessary. One month or so would be needed for preparation; one to two months for creditor consultations; one month during which the exchange offer would be in the market and road shows would take place; another four to six weeks to convene bondholder meetings for those bonds containing CACs, and two to four weeks to prepare for a closing. If done efficiently.

10.2.6. Some Additional Considerations

Two additional things have happened that could affect both the timing and the nature of any restructuring of Greek debt. One week after promising a EUR110 billion bailout package designed specifically for Greece, the European Union and the IMF announced another EUR750 billion stabilization mechanism that would provide financing – with strings and conditions, naturally – to other EU members that encounter difficulty in the refinancing of their debts. The details of how the mechanism will work have not yet been released.

Of perhaps even greater significance for a possible restructuring of Greek debt, however, was the decision taken by the ECB a few days later to commence buying the debt securities of countries like Greece and Portugal. To date (19 May 2010), the ECB has purchased more than EUR16.5 billion of such instruments. If this programme continues, it will make the ECB, in its own name and not just as the custodian of collateral posted by commercial banks coming to its discount window, the single largest holder of Greek bonds. This, if a restructuring becomes unavoidable, is both good news and bad news. Good, in the sense that the ECB will have a powerful voice and vote in such a restructuring, making it more likely that collective action thresholds (contractual or statutory) will be met. Unfortunate news, in the sense that an official EU institution may have to book significant losses on its investments as part of the restructuring.

10.3. CONCLUSION

No one knows whether the ECB will go gentle into the good night of a debt restructuring should one become unavoidable, or whether it may at the time try to claim for itself the status of a 'preferred creditor' similar to the IMF. But if, when the time comes, the Greek debt stock carries a large layer of *soi-disant*[2] senior creditors, the restructuring terms imposed on the others must be that much more severe.

NOTES

1. This chapter was previously published under the same title in the *International Financial Law Review*, June 2010, pages 46–49.
2. From the French, so-called or self-styled.

PART III

Addressing the problem of 'too-big-to-fail'

11. Firm stability and system stability: the regulatory delusion[1]

Geoffrey Wood with Ali Kabiri

11.1. INTRODUCTION

When the regulators examine the grocery business in the UK they are invariably concerned with competition. Is one firm or another too dominant? Is it treating customers appropriately? How is it treating its suppliers and its small competitors? In short, is the industry competitive is always, in one form or another, the question that is being asked. Concern is often prompted by the (entirely inappropriate) test of market share. A question that is never asked is how robust a particular individual firm is.

This is distinctly odd to anyone familiar with regulation in the financial sector. In the UK, a question that is always in regulators' minds is how stable a particular firm is. Why is that not asked of firms in the grocery sector? Banking services are important, but so, after all, is the supply of food. Yet the regulators never worry about what would happen if, to take a wildly implausible example, Tesco were to fail overnight.

Why is that question not asked? The answer is surely in two parts. First, and very important for the failing firm's suppliers and employees, there is for such firms a well-established and well-tested insolvency regime. That regime has for many years worked well in the sense of enabling orderly winding up or selling on of insolvent businesses, and has done so within a time period which in most cases has no doubt been irritating but seldom literally intolerable. Second, there is no fear that a vacuum would be left by such insolvency. To continue with our example, if Tesco were to fail, far from there being a dearth of groceries, within hours Sainsbury, Morrison, and so forth would be fighting vigorously over this new market opportunity.

Accordingly, then, the analogy of the grocery business with the banking business would imply that, if we have a suitable bankruptcy code and easy entry and exit for banking, regulators need no longer concern themselves with individual firms. For the 'effective' industry would no longer be the total of the firms currently in it, but rather the total of actual members plus potential entrants.

The aim of this chapter is to consider whether that is an appropriate way to think about banking, or if banking can be changed so that it becomes the appropriate way. Doing so would both improve market discipline and make life easier for regulators.

To address this, two matters particularly need to be considered. These are first barriers to entry, and second the insolvency code. They are considered in that order.

11.2. BARRIERS TO ENTRY

What are these barriers? The term originated in the industrial economics literature of the immediate post-Second World War period.

Many industrial economists of that period were concerned to explain data apparently inconsistent with the competitive model, and resorted to monopoly as an explanation. The particular phenomenon that troubled many was the persistence of higher rates of return in some industries than in others. Why, they asked, did new entry not eliminate this?[2] The answer given was that there were barriers to entry. But there was no unanimous definition of these barriers. The three best known are those of Bain, Stigler and Ferguson.

Bain wrote that the existence of such barriers was demonstrated, and their size measured, by '. . . the extent to which established firms can elevate their selling prices above the minimal average costs of production and distribution . . . without inducing potential entrants to enter the industry'.[3] Ferguson defines barriers as '. . . factors that make entry unprofitable while permitting established firms to set prices above *marginal* cost, and to persistently earn monopoly return' [emphasis not added].[4] For Stigler, barriers were '. . . a cost of production (at some or every rate of output) which must be borne by a firm which seeks to enter an industry but is not borne by firms already in the industry'.[5]

These definitions differ in their implications. For Bain and Ferguson, economies of scale could be a barrier, while for Stigler they could not be so long as the same production technology was available to all. And there are other differences. But what they have in common is that different possibilities may face insiders and outsiders. And that is exactly why they miss something important in the present discussion. Consider the availability of licences to operate as a taxi driver. In London these are in perfectly elastic supply with regard to the price at which they are sold, for the only requirement is to pass a test.[6] But suppose there were a restricted supply of such licences, and in the first instance they had to be bought from the local authority at a market-determined price, although they could subsequently be traded. In this case outsiders and insiders would all face the same costs, and bidding for the licences would eliminate monopoly profits, but there would still be a barrier to entry, created in this case by the restriction on the supply of licences.

Because they neglect such legally imposed entry barriers these commonly used approaches to the study of barriers to entry are not helpful in the study of a regulated industry. And indeed, in the particular case of banking, they suffer from two crucial weaknesses. The first is that identified by the taxi licence example. Lott has pointed out that if licences are not tradable then the possibility for monopoly profit exists.[7] For example, financial sector regulators may impose unpriced entry condition, such as the requirement that senior management be 'fit and proper' for their posts. This may be relevant for the consumer protection aspect of regulation, but only indirectly for the stability aspect. Discussion of it is therefore deferred for the moment.

The other matter the industrial economics notions of barriers completely neglect is speed of entry. If our concern is with a stable industry supply curve (recognizing that only perfectly competitive industries have supply curves but making use of the concept nonetheless by use of the assumption that the demand curve is stable), then what matters is that if a firm in the industry gets into difficulties and fails, a new entrant can speedily take over its business and take its place. For that, it must be possible for the new firm to enter rapidly, and, equally important, for the failed firm to leave rapidly. These are taken in turn.

11.3. RAPID ENTRY

Why can new firms not enter banking rapidly? Why, if bank A fails, cannot bank B come in overnight and start trading? The reasons are several, and to an extent involve the bankruptcy code. But before discussing that code, we must consider the matters of familiarity, the clearing house, and the regulator.

It is plain that people prefer to deal with familiar names. A well-known demonstration of this is the notorious difficulty with which foreign banks enter a country and start business there. Numerous studies have attested to this, noting in particular the years of low, possibly negative, profits that must be faced, particularly through the number of 'lemon customers' these firms acquire in their initial years.[8]

This can be circumvented, but the only obviously successful way is to take over an existing firm, and gradually gain acceptance of the new name and business practices through slow development of the previously well-known company. A notable example of this in the UK was the takeover in November 2004 by Santander of the Abbey Bank. The latter was initially branded jointly with Santander, and only after some years was the Abbey name dropped. This was possible because while Abbey was certainly not doing particularly well at the time of the takeover, it certainly had not failed, so a leisurely approach could be followed. A subsequent consequence of the establishment of Santander's name in Britain was that when later (in 2009) Santander took over a failed bank, it could start using its own name immediately when running the business.

It also appears to be possible for firms with a reputation in one area to transfer that reputation to another. Sainsbury's was a well-established grocer when it moved into banking. Tesco is following the same route, as is John Lewis on a much smaller scale – at least at the moment. But even that route can face a difficulty. There must be no possibility of exclusion from the clearing house by its existing users. This has implications for the ownership of the clearing house. Having it owned solely by its users presents tremendous opportunities for delay. A preferable ownership structure would be a free-standing regulated monopoly, regulation being of the same model as that used for the UK's regulated utilities. Ownership by the state might seem attractive at first glance, but apart from all the inefficiency that such ownership usually brings there must be no question of political influence over entry to the clearing house. Even the fear of it could deter potential entrants – entrants such as Santander might well fear implicit protectionism. The regulated monopoly would have (as part of its monopoly right) the duty not to 'unreasonably exclude' new entrants. Tests of unreasonableness could be laid down in advance, but no doubt these would have to be examined in the courts.

And finally in this section comes the regulator. If it is easy to exit banking, then the gatekeeper role of the regulator is much simplified. Regulators need not greatly concern themselves with the competence of the potential new management. What would mainly matter would be the honesty of that management. For if they were fraudulent, this would be very troublesome, at the least, for their customers, and issues of compensation could arise, thus inviting *ad hoc* political support for hard cases – and such support of course rewards becoming a hard case.

All these changes would be close to pointless, however, if struggling firms did not leave the industry, but were – if they really got into difficulties – supported by the taxpayer through his agent, the government. Recent practice has been to support such firms. Can that be stopped? To answer that it is useful to look at a particularly well-documented example of support for a failing bank.

11.4. THE SUPPORT OF NORTHERN ROCK

When at the end of 2008 Northern Rock got into difficulties, the Authorities (the term for the collective of the Bank of England, the FSA, and the Treasury) did not follow the traditional, well-tested and shown to be robust, nineteenth-century approach.[9] They could have considered whether the troubled institution was of sufficient importance that its failure would have damaged the reputation of London, as they did in the case of Barings in 1890, and if it failed that test it would have been allowed to sink or swim (and liquidity provided to the rest of the banking sector as needed to calm any subsequent panic).

Northern Rock was not allowed to sink or swim. There was a determined attempt to keep the institution going, or to find a rescuer for it. This can certainly not be justified by the size or reputation of Northern Rock. It was not a particularly large institution, and even its greatest admirer would not claim that it was a bank of international renown similar to that of Barings in 1890, one whose failure even if orderly might fundamentally damage the reputation of London. Why, then, did the Authorities act as they did?

A range of factors probably influenced the decision. First and most obviously is that the problem came as a shock, and one to previously untested regulatory and money market regimes. Then there are some factors about which it is possible at this time only to speculate, although more data may become available in the future when archives are opened (if written records of discussions were kept).

Gordon Brown had just become Prime Minister. Opinion polls suggested that there had been a subsequent sharp leap in the popularity of the ruling Labour government, and there was much speculation that an election would be called. Closing a bank (or nationalizing it) would probably have done little good for the government's prospects of victory. A second consideration is that such action might not have reflected well, at least in the popular press, on the 'Tripartite Arrangements'[10] for financial stability, and these arrangements had been put in place when Gordon Brown was Chancellor of the Exchequer. Third, Northern Rock was headquartered in an area where unemployment was above the national average. The political background was not favourable for the sink or swim option.

There were, however, also good economic reasons why the traditional course was not followed. There was, first, a technical aspect of the Bank's money market operations, and then, more fundamentally, the nature of interbank linkages. These latter made it extremely difficult to subject a commercial bank to a normal corporate insolvency procedure. And finally, the nature of retail bank deposits in the twenty-first century differed from that in the nineteenth, and in a way which made even orderly closures of a bank difficult both politically and economically.

The nature and extent of interbank linkages create a problem with the 'sink or swim' option in the following way. When Northern Rock got into difficulties there was no separate legal framework for handling bank insolvency; it would have been subject to the normal law of corporate insolvency. Its transactions, its assets, and its liabilities would be frozen. A court-appointed liquidator would try, avoiding a 'fire sale', to dispose of the assets at the best possible price, taking quite possibly some time to do so in order to minimize the loss for creditors. This would of course cause problems for a modern banking system, as it could leave many transactions uncompleted for months or even years.[11]

Northern Rock's failure highlighted the absence in the UK of any regime for handling bank insolvency, such as was available in some other countries. Such a regime would provide a mechanism for maintaining critical banking services and ensuring an orderly resolution of bank assets and liabilities.

Finally on the reasons for the Authorities' actions, when 'sink or swim' was the course of action, retail depositors differed in two ways from their modern-day counterparts. They were more prosperous than the average citizen, and they did not rely to the same extent on bank transactions for day to day living – banking services were not as crucial to functioning in nineteenth-century society as they are now. In Britain today the politicians, who make the ultimate decision over bank closure, could not tolerate bank customers, especially poor ones, losing both money and access to banking services. Indeed, aside from any questions of protecting savings, loss of access to banking services would impede economic efficiency in many ways, by for example forcing reliance on cash and unwarrantedly destroying credit ratings.

Britain does have a deposit protection insurance scheme supposedly intended to deal with these things, but despite changes since Northern Rock it remains significantly defective. There are no practical arrangements for ensuring that guaranteed depositors are paid out in any reasonably short time frame; they could and very likely would have to wait months for the money that is due to them.

11.5. FREEDOM TO EXIT

11.5.1. What Can be Done to Replace the Need to Preserve Firms by Easily Allowed and Readily Tolerated Freedom to Exit?

Much has already been done in the UK. It is now possible to take a bank away from its shareholders and management while it is still solvent, and keep it running so that all who transact with it can continue doing so. The bank can then be sold on, in an orderly way, in whole or in parts, to buyers who will keep it running and restore it to financial health. The proceeds from the sale are used to settle the bank's debts, and anything left goes to the shareholders.[12]

Such a facility, which has existed for some years in the US, was proposed in the UK by the Treasury Select Committee of the House of Commons, and the proposal was implemented in the *Banking Act 2009*. The procedure has, indeed, already been successfully used to carry out the closure of the Dunfermline Building Society in 2009.

11.5.2. Does Anything Else Need to be Done?

The answer to that question is in two parts. First, if banks are to be capable of being closed while still solvent, their capital must be monitored, and not just by their management – for in distress there would be, at the least, a desire to be optimistic. Such monitoring would, however, increase rather than reduce freedom of exit; for the regulators would surely be aware of the opprobrium they would incur if they exercised forbearance which turned out to be unjustified. But some banks would be – by virtue of their size or their complexity or interdependencies with the rest of the system – hard to handle in such a manner without extensive advance planning. Here the concept of the 'living will' comes in.

Regulators should prepare for failure. They should do that because it is almost certain that something will go wrong at some time, and because the consequence of lack of preparedness when Northern Rock got into difficulties was a nearly disastrous bank run. This preparation should have two parts. The regulators should regularly plan what they are going to do in the event of a big bank needing help, and, because each bank will be somewhat different, there should be a plan for every bank, and these plans should be regularly updated. These plans, one for each bank, would be based on each bank's 'living will'.

11.6. THE 'LIVING WILL'

The Governor of the Bank of England has recently urged that banks be required to draw up 'living wills'. The Treasury Select Committee of the House of Commons has also recommended the idea. What are these wills? Why are they desirable?

The term 'living will' comes from a development in English law relating to individuals and their well-being. When an individual dies, if he or she leaves a will which is legal then whatever property left on death is disposed of according to the testator's wishes, subject to taxes and any challenges from parties who think they were entitled to a bequest (or a bigger bequest). A 'living will' does very much the same thing, but for an individual who although incapacitated is not dead. The 'will' appoints 'attorneys', who can take decisions for the individual who can no longer do so, either according to instructions given in the 'living will' or if discretion has been given then according to what they think best for the individual. These decisions can appertain either to medical treatment (including its withdrawal or withholding) or to financial matters, or both.

The idea is then that banks draw up an analogous document. Why has this idea taken hold, and what would the document do?

11.7. EARLIER PROBLEMS

To continue with the analogy, when a company is declared bankrupt it has its affairs wound up under the bankruptcy code. This is analogous to the will of a person, except that every company has the same will; the order in which creditors are paid off, and the proportions if apportioning is necessary, are prescribed in law. This normally works well, giving a degree of certainty to commercial transactions by letting people know the risks they are exposed to if things go wrong with a company with which they are dealing. Changes were made to it over the years, but there was no questioning of whether it was an appropriate procedure for all kinds of company.

Then, in 2007, the banking system got into difficulties. In Britain this showed first in the struggles of Northern Rock. This bank was eventually nationalized. But no one desired nationalization to be the only feasible response in dealing with a nearly insolvent bank. As described above, a special insolvency regime for banks was quickly put in place, and that regime has already been used successfully. Why then is there call for a 'living will' for banks? Given that banks can now have orderly funerals promptly conducted under this new legislation, why should they bother with 'living wills'?

The existing legislation applies in principle to all commercial banks and building societies. It does not, however, cover investment banks even in principle, and while it does in principle cover large, complex, international banks, there are, and surely correctly, doubts about whether it could be applied to them.

There are doubts about the applicability of the current prompt closure procedure to investment banks simply because these banks are not deposit-taking institutions, but rather institutions which arrange deals and act as counterparties in complex transactions. A very important aspect of the latter is shown by their role in structured products such as the fairly widely sold 'guaranteed equity return' funds. These guarantee a minimum return from a portfolio in return for there being a cap on returns from the portfolio. The closure of Lehman's (in September 2008) cast a good number of these products into jeopardy. Orderly closure along the lines of prompt corrective action would not help much here, nor would it help with, for example, holdings of credit default swaps.

Due to the fact that international banks have assets and liabilities in many countries, they can – if they face an emergency capital shortage – call on many countries. This could mean that no country felt responsible. And large banks could, quite simply, be beyond the capacity of the liquidators to understand and wind down in a reasonable period of time. These are the problems 'living wills' are designed to deal with.

11.8. WHAT THE WILLS WOULD DO

Essentially, they would tell an outsider how the bank worked. Of particular importance, they would clearly assign different assets and liabilities to different subdivisions of the bank. They would provide an accessible list of counterparties, and their associated transactions. They would clearly describe provisioning and write-off procedures that had been adopted in particular cases and were adopted as general rules. In short, just as a person's 'living will' lays out what should be done when he or she can no longer do it for themselves, so would a bank's living will provide all the information needed for someone to intervene when it was in trouble and to run it down (or otherwise dispose of it) in a prompt and orderly manner. The 'will' would need updating from time to time, but frequency of updating should depend not primarily on the passage of time but on the frequency of occurrence of material changes to the bank's structure or portfolio.[13]

These 'living wills' would thus be important in two ways. First, they would ensure that when some institution, however large or complex, got into difficulties, it could be handled without major and harmful spillover effects. That in itself is a good argument for 'living wills'.

Second, and associated with that, these wills would make future crises less likely. For they would ensure that no bank was ever again 'too-big-to-fail'. The 'brooding presence' (to quote Lee Bucheit[14]) of the risk of failure would once again make bankers act in a prudent way. Further, ensuring that no bank ever again was 'too-big-to-fail' would make market discipline effective, and the so far fruitless search for effective methods of regulatory discipline otiose.

11.9. CONSUMER PROTECTION?

When transacting in financial products consumers generally receive protection additional to that which they receive when buying other types of good. The case for their doing so has been questioned. Benston, for example, argues strongly against it.[15] It is unnecessary to enter that argument here. But it is worthwhile to consider, if we take for granted that consumers require additional protection in this area, how this protection should be provided if the arguments above on the role of the regulator insofar as stability goes are accepted.

The new model regulator would be concerned not with the stability of individual firms but with the stability of the industry, and would aim to achieve this by ensuring easy entry and exit in banking. The latter would conflict with consumer protection. For however readily new entrants replace departing firms, it is hard to imagine that the process would be entirely free of inconvenience for the consumers directly involved. There would thus be a conflict if one regulator were charged both with consumer protection and the protection of system stability. The first responsibility would lead to seeking the protection of existing firms, while the latter would be concerned to ensure a speedy exit at the first sign of trouble. This tension would be exacerbated by inevitable political pressures. Consumers are regularly and frequently complaining, either directly to the regulator or through their political representatives, that one financial institution or another has treated them badly. They seldom write in to complain that an institution is endangering financial stability. Resources and attention would therefore be focused on only one aspect of the regulator's duties.

The case for what has become known as the 'twin peaks approach', that is to say separating maintenance of stability from consumer protection, is on the arguments immediately above already a strong one. Recognizing that stability-focused regulators should be concerned with the industry not the firm strengthens the case.

11.10. A DIGRESSION IN THE HISTORY OF ECONOMIC THOUGHT

At the start of this chapter it was observed that because economics has tended to focus on a particular notion of competition the arguments put forward here have not been as widely applied to financial regulation as they should have been.

The most common definition of competition used, implicitly or explicitly, by economists, is that of atomistic competition. In this view there is competition in a market when there is a large number of firms, each producing at the least cost point of its long run average cost curve, and with, even temporarily, no pricing power. This is a notion particularly convenient in a general equilibrium model. But it is not the only notion of competition.

Baumol, along with several co-authors, has developed the notion of contestable markets. His key points are that a 'perfectly contestable market' is 'characterised by optimal behaviour yet applies to the full range of industrial structures . . .'.[16] That, and particularly important, '. . . oligopolistic structure and behaviour are freed entirely from their previous dependence on the conjectural variations of incumbents, and, instead, are generally determined . . . by the pressure of potential competition to which Bain directed our attention so tellingly'.[17] And third, that there is not a '. . . rough continuum, in terms of industrial performance, ranging from unregulated pure monopoly as the pessimal arrangement to perfect competition as the ideal . . .'.[18] He cites Bain[19] as his most notable predecessor, but also notes the arguments of Fama and Laffer[20] that even two firms can be enough to guarantee optimality.

In fact the idea that the threat of entry affects behaviour extends much further back in the history of economics. A notable example is the use that Alfred Marshall made of the 'trees of the forest' analogy, to explain how firms died and were replaced, or even crowded out before death, by thriving new enterprises.

> . . . but here we may read a lesson from the young trees of the forest as they struggle upwards through the benumbing shade of their older rivals. Many succumb on the way and few survive: those few become stronger every year, they get a larger share of the light and air with every increase of their height, and at last in their turn they tower above their neighbours and seem as though they would grow on forever . . .. but they do not. One tree will last longer in full vigour and attain a greater size than another: but sooner or later age tells on them all. Though the taller ones have better access to light and air than their rivals, they gradually lose vitality: and one after another they give their place to others.[21]

The above passage on the 'trees in the forest' which, in the first five editions, had gone on '. . . as with the growth of trees, so it is with the growth of businesses' was changed in the Sixth Edition (1910) to read 'as with the growth of trees, so it was with the growth of businesses as a general rule before the great recent development of vast joint-stock companies'.[22] But Marshall still believed that his hypothesis of the life cycle held '. . . in many industries and trades'.[23] He also added the qualification that, while the joint-stock firm might grow in size, it would not obtain increased internal economies as it grew.

A further change was made in the Eighth Edition of 1920; if conditions in an industry were such that new firms could quickly master the economies of scale, then it would be likely that the established firms would be '*supplanted quickly by still younger firms with yet newer methods.*'[24]

Schumpeter's 'perennial gale of creative destruction'[25] surely invites invocation at this point, perhaps even to suggesting that the gale can help thin out the forest and allow new enterprises to emerge.

In short, the idea of competition that emerged not from the formal Walrasian analysis but from the less formal Marshallian and Austrian approaches is helpful in guiding regulatory policy. The formal approach, in contrast, despite its numerous uses, has tended to encourage regulators, or at least many of the economists who advise them, to look in the wrong direction.

11.11. CONCLUSIONS

There is much concern among regulators to ensure the stability of banks. Liquidity requirements and capital requirements are to be raised, and regulation is, we are told, to be tightened (whatever that means) and made more intrusive. The argument of this paper is that focus on the stability of the individual firm is misguided. Rather, focus should be on the stability of the industry. Key to that is not the stability of individual members of the industry, but rather free entry to and exit from the industry. Promoting that should be concern of regulation.

This also implies that regulators concerned with banking stability should not also have the responsibility of consumer protection. This is, however, merely reinforcing an existing and well-supported argument. The key point of this chapter is that industry stability matters for banking, and firm stability does not.

NOTES

1. We are indebted to Rae Balbach, Charles Goodhart, and Martin Ricketts for most helpful comments.
2. Bain, J.S. (1956), *Barriers to New Competition*, Harvard University Press, p. 252. In fact the observation is not in general inconsistent with competition. The theory predicts the equalization of marginal returns, but what is generally observed is accounting, that is to say average, returns. Average returns equal marginal only if all factors of production are in perfectly elastic supply.
3. It should be remarked that this is not a definition like the others; it gives the consequences of a barrier, rather than saying what the barrier is.
4. Ferguson, J.M. (1974), *Advertising and Competition: Theory, Measurement, Fact*, Cambridge, Ballinger, p. 10.
5. Stigler, G. (1968), *Barriers to entry, economies of scale and firm size: The Organisation of Industry*, RD Irwin, p. 67.

6. As it takes different people different amounts of time to learn to pass the test, the existence of the test allows rents on ability to be earned.
7. Lott, J.R. (1987), 'Licensing and Non-Transferable Rents', *American Economic Review*, 77(3), pp. 453–455.
8. Hoggarth, G., A. Milne, and G. Wood (1998), 'Alternative Routes to Banking Stability', *Bank of England Financial Stability Review*, pp. 55–68, Autumn, Issue 5.
9. Detailed description and analysis of the Northern Rock episode can be found in Milne, A., and G. Wood (2009), 'Shattered on the Rock? British financial stability from 1866 to 2007', *Journal of Banking Regulation*, 10(2).
10. See Milne and Wood, n. 9.
11. In an insolvency REPO borrowing (financing through an initial sale of a security and its later repurchase at a slightly higher price) is closed out, in a similar way to OTC derivative transactions, but unsecured borrowing, such as Northern Rock relied on because it lacked eligible collateral for REPO finance, must be left finally to be resolved through the insolvency procedure.
12. For banks for which that can be done, the choice of capital ratio could be left to the management of the institutions concerned; they would simply be told that if it went below some fairly arbitrary number they would be expropriated.
13. This of course reminds us that however well designed rules are, use of judgement is inescapable.
14. 'The sanction that capitalism imposes on imprudence, incompetence, sometimes just bad luck, is failure. It is the brooding presence of that sanction that keeps managers on their toes, that keeps them acting in a prudent way.' (Lee Bucheit (Cleary Gottlieb Steen & Hamilton LLP) to the House of Lords Economic Affairs Committee, 2009).
15. Benston, G.J. (2004), Henry Thornton Lecture, City University, London.
16. Baumol, W. (1982), 'Contestable markets: An uprising in the theory of industrial structure', *American Economic Review*, 72(1), pp. 1–15.
17. See n. 16, at p. 2.
18. See n. 16, at p. 2.
19. Bain, J.S. (1956), *Barriers to New Competition*, Harvard University Press.
20. Fama, E. and A. Laffer (1972), 'The number of firms and competition', *American Economic Review*, 62(4), pp. 670–674.
21. Marshall, A. (1890), *Principles of Economics*, 1st edn, London, Macmillan, pp. 315–316.
22. Marshall, A. (1910), *Principles of Economics*: 6th edn, London, Macmillan, p. 316.
23. See n. 22, at p. 316.
24. Marshall, A. (1920), *Principles of Economics*: 8th edn, London, Macmillan, pp. 286–287.
25. Schumpeter, J.A. (1942), *Capitalism, Socialism and Democracy*, New York, Harper Bros, pp. 82–85.

12. 'Living wills': putting the caboose before the engine and designing a better engine

George G. Kaufman[1]

'Living wills' have recently been recommended by many analysts as an important part of any reform program to attempt to prevent or at least minimize the impact of future financial meltdowns. Such wills are included in many of the legislative proposals currently being considered in the US Congress, as well as in other countries and by the Bank for International Settlements (BIS) and the International Monetary Fund (IMF).

12.1. 'LIVING WILLS'

'Living wills' are plans or strategies to be developed by specified large complex financial institutions (LCFIs) including banks for winding down their operation if and when they become insolvent with minimum disruptions both to themselves and to the economy.[2] Thus, 'living wills' are an attempt to achieve orderly resolutions of firms whose closure might otherwise be disruptive with higher private and societal costs than necessary. Their purpose is to focus advance attention of both a firm's management and its regulators on problems that may arise in the unwinding of the firm when insolvency threatens including:

- Accurately inventorying all assets and liabilities,
- Identifying all counterparties, and
- Giving full recognition to the complexity of organization structures across both separately charted subsidiaries and different cross-border and structural jurisdictions.

Such information should reduce the likelihood of pitfalls and make winding down more efficient when it is required and lessen the need for policy makers to consider the firm 'too-big-to-fail' (TBTF) with all the inefficiencies associated therewith, including likely use of taxpayer funds. Knowing how to unwind an LCFI will make regulators more willing to do so.

Preparation of meaningful wills, however, requires full advance knowledge of the 'rules of the game' established for resolving insolvencies. Different rules are likely to solicit different plans or strategies by the institution. It makes a difference in developing the plans whether, for example, in resolution uninsured depositors have equal or preferred status to unsecured creditors, netting of derivative contracts is permitted, or master derivative contracts are subject to stays or not. In terms of a sports analogy, it matters to the coach of a US football team in designing a strategy whether the football field is 100 yards or 80 yards or 120 yards long and whether there are 8 or 11 or 15 players on the team. Different rules solicit different strategies. In addition, not only must the rules of the game be known in advance to all players, but the rules cannot be changed without sufficient advance notice to rewrite all contracts by mutual agreement.

It follows that it is useful if not necessary to develop regimes for resolving insolvent LCFIs before developing the 'living wills'. To be of maximum use, 'living wills' should be subject to realistic scenario simulations or 'war games' by both the firm and its identified regulators to observe the unwinding process and end results under varying conditions. It should be noted that the relationship of the regime and the will is endogenous. The outcome of the wills for a given resolution regime may not achieve the results desired by the regulators. If so, regulators may modify the resolution regime, which will likely, in turn, force a change in the 'living will'. This process is likely to be iterative until the optimal resolution regime that produces a doable unwinding process is developed. If the LCFI operates across jurisdictions, the acceptance of a plan by the home country regulators should require the acceptance of the plan by regulators in each jurisdiction in which the institution operates.

The development of an optimal resolution regime for LCFIs that minimizes, if not eliminates, the need for TBTF bailouts is probably the most important challenge for financial reform. A good insolvency regime that minimizes the need for TBTF, reduces moral hazard externalities, reduces the number and severity of LCFI failures, and, in turn, increases economic efficiency and welfare.

12.2. BANKS REQUIRE SPECIAL RESOLUTION REGIMES

Banks (depository institutions) have long been widely perceived to be 'special' for a large number of reasons, including:

- Banks are among the broadest of financial institutions and some are individually large relative to GDP,
- Bank deposits (debt) are held by a large proportion of the population, including households of limited financial means and expertise, and in a wide range of denominations, including very small amounts,
- Bank deposits collectively comprise the largest share of the country's money supply and are the primary medium of exchange,
- Bank deposits represent a significant portion of the public's most liquid assets,
- Banks have a large proportion of their liabilities in very short-term debt that is shorter on average than their assets and that can easily be withdrawn (through a run on the bank),
- Banks are major providers of credit to households, business firms, and governments,
- Banks are central to the operation of the payments system,
- Banks are closely interconnected with each other through interbank deposits, loans, and derivative transactions,
- Dealer banks are interconnected with other LCFIs,
- Bank assets are widely perceived to be less transparent than assets of most non-bank firms,
- Banks have complex organizational structure,
- Ownership and location of bank assets can be transferred quickly and at low cost, and
- Individual bank size and market concentration has increased greatly through time.

Failures of banks that may interrupt the continuous provision of their critical activities are likely to have serious adverse effects on the economy of the affected banks' market areas and frequently beyond. The larger the bank, the stronger and wider the potential adverse externalities. Thus, banks are perceived to require special resolution regimes that minimize such costs. More recently, a number of nonbank financial institutions, such as investment banks (broker-dealers), insurance companies, and finance companies, have grown rapidly and are now also perceived to be special. They:

- Offer bank-like products,
- Rely on short-term funding of risky and/or longer-term assets,
- Are closely interconnected with each other and with banks through derivative contracts, particularly if dealers,
- Have complex organizational structures,
- Operate across structural and geographic jurisdictions, and
- Have grown rapidly in size and market share.

Thus, similar to the failure of banks, the failure of LCFIs beyond banks is now also believed to cause serious adverse externalities. But in the US these institutions are currently subject to resolution regimes that do not necessarily recognize this problem, so that failure is likely to interrupt their more critical operations. Similar to banks, the fear of this happening at larger nonbank institutions has led to regulators fearing closing these firms when they become insolvent. Like large banks, these institutions are now likely to be treated and viewed as TBTF by their regulators.

12.3. 'TOO-BIG-TO-FAIL'

In the US, TBTF applied primarily to banks and other depository institutions that were subject to a different insolvency resolution regime than nonbank firms, which were generally subject to the *Federal Bankruptcy Act*. At least in the US, however, TBTF does not really mean what it says. Since the mid-1980s through to the current financial crisis, insolvent banks failed.[3] With rare exception, the bank charter was revoked and shareholders' interest eliminated, except for any residual value after resolution. What TBTF meant was that a bank was 'too big to permit losses to some or all de-jure uninsured depositors, other unsecured creditors, and counter-parties'. That is, the bank and its shareholders may be dead, but its creditors are still alive. Pro-rata sharing in the insolvent bank's losses by all or certain uninsured depositors, unsecured creditors, and derivative counterparties were believed to cause substantial disruptive spill-over effects on third parties and destabilize financial markets. Failure losses not allocated to these protected parties are allocated instead for banks first to the FDIC deposit insurance fund and for nonbank LCFIs any special fund that may be created if and when TBTF is extended to them and, only if these funds are exhausted, then to taxpayers. But protection of these parties against loss encourages excessive risk-taking moral hazard behavior.

The objective of TBTF should be an orderly resolution (market stability) without abandoning market discipline. Most, if not all, uninsured claimants should share in any losses. The major ongoing policy debates center on who are the creditors to be protected and who, if not them, will bear their losses. Some parties favor imposing this loss on a pool of funds established through premiums, preferably paid in advance, by large and/or complex firms in the designated industry while others prefer to have all the losses paid directly by the de-jure uninsured parties of the insolvent institution(s).

12.4. CURRENT US INSOLVENCY RESOLUTION REGIMES

The resolution regimes for different types of financial institutions in the US vary widely.[4] Banks and other insured depository institutions are subject to the *Federal Deposit Insurance Act* (FDIA) as amended by the *FDIC Improvement Act* (FDICIA) of 1991. General corporations (including parent bank holding companies) are subject to Chapters 7 and 9 of the Federal Bankruptcy Code. State and local governments are subject to Chapter 9 of the Federal Bankruptcy Code. Broker-dealers are subject to Chapter 7 (liquidation) of the Federal Bankruptcy Code. Insurance companies come under state bankruptcy regimes. This suggests that LCFIs that are likely to have one or more bank, insurance, finance, dealer-broker and/or nonfinancial subsidiaries are subject to a large number of different resolution regimes. Moreover, if these institutions operate across geographic jurisdictions, as almost all of them do, they encounter additional differences in resolution regimes.

The current process serves to make resolutions of LCFIs in practice very time consuming, uncertain, and expensive. The structural complexity of LCFIs is shown in Table 12.1 and of Lehman Brothers, when it filed for bankruptcy, in Table 12.2. In 2007, Citigroup, for example, operated 101 banks, 35 insurance companies, nearly 1300 mutual and pension fund subsidiaries, nearly 600 other subsidiaries, and over 1000 nonfinancial subsidiaries across numerous countries. Lehman Brothers in 2007 shortly before its demise operated 433 subsidiaries in 20 countries, only one-half of which were in the United States. US financial regulators have complained that this complex structure does not permit orderly resolutions. In particular, Chapter 11 resolutions, which focus on reorganization and rehabilitation, are said to have the following disadvantages when it comes to LCFIs:

- Failure by creditors rather than regulators is too slow and clumsy,
- Numerous ex-ante appeals are permitted that could delay the process,
- Control by court, not by regulators (who have no standing),
- Consideration only of creditors, not externalities (public interest),
- Equal treatment of all creditors in a given class (no flexibility to subdivide),
- Need to find financing for ongoing firm (debtor-in-possession),
- Generally no change of management is mandated, at least in the beginning of the reorganization (rehabilitation) process, and
- Insufficient flexibility to tailor solution to problem.

Table 12.1. Breakdown by industry of subsidiaries of Large Complex Financial Institutions (Yearend 2007)

LCFIs	Banks	Insurance Companies	Mutual & Pension Funds/ nominees/ trusts/ trustees	Other financial subsidiaries	Non-financial subsidiaries
ABN AMRO Holding NV	50	7	129	204	280
Bank of America Corporation	32	24	396	282	673
Barclays Plc	49	21	309	239	385
BNP Paribas	88	74	102	433	473
Citi	101	35	706	584	1009
Credit Suisse Group	31	4	91	63	101
Deutsche Bank AG	54	9	458	526	907
Goldman Sachs Group, Inc	7	4	48	151	161
HSBC Holdings Plc	85	37	246	381	485
JP Morgan Chase & Co	38	17	229	145	375
Lehman Brothers Holdings Inc	9	3	84	210	127
Merrill Lynch & Co. Inc.	16	9	85	89	68
Morgan Stanley	19	22	225	170	616
The Royal Bank of Scotland Group Plc	31	29	168	450	484
Societe Generale	81	13	93	270	387
UBS AG	29	2	121	66	199
Total By Industry	720	310	3490	4263	6729
% by industry	5%	2%	22%	27%	43%

Source: Herring.

In its white paper outlining the Administration's recommendations for financial reform, the US Department of the Treasury argued:

> The federal government's responses to the impending bankruptcy of BearStearns, Lehman Brothers, and AIG were complicated by the lack of a statutory framework for avoiding the disorderly failure of nonbank financial firms, including affiliates of banks or other insured depository institutions. In the absence of such a framework, the government's only avenue to avoid the disorderly failures of Bear Stearns and AIG was the use of the Federal Reserve's lending authority. And this mechanism was insufficient to

Table 12.2. Corporate structure of Lehman Brothers Holdings Inc (Yearend 2007)

Country	Number of majority-owned subsidiaries
USA	238
United Kingdom	120
Cayman Islands	18
Australia	9
Luxembourg	6
Ireland	5
Netherlands	5
Bermuda	4
France	4
Hong Kong	4
Japan	4
Korea (Republic of)	4
Germany	3
Singapore	2
Thailand	2
Argentina	1
Canada	1
Switzerland	1
India	1
Mauritius	1
Total	433
Number of countries	20

Source: Herring.

prevent the bankruptcy of Lehman Brothers, an event which served to demonstrate how disruptive the disorderly failure of a nonbank financial firm can be to the financial system and the economy.[5]

What do the regulators want? It appears that they would prefer a regime that would allow them to help shape the resolution process and outcome for TBTF institutions. This would include their ability to, among other things:

- Determine the timing of closure (failure, receivership, insolvency, bankruptcy),
- Choose the form of rehabilitation (reorganization) or liquidation – sell, merge, recapitalize, conservatorship, liquidate, pre-packaged resolution,

- Wipe out shareholder value (except for residual value),
- Allocate losses or protection across and within creditor classes to achieve orderly resolution,
- Maintain critical services uninterrupted,
- Determine the timing of access to designated funds for depositors, creditors, and loan customers,
- Select management while in resolution (reorganization/bridge) process,
- Claw back inappropriate recent fund transfers,
- Coordinate with other affected (cross-border) jurisdictions,
- Cover losses not allocated to uninsured depositor/creditors by an industry fund paid by LCFIs,
- Not be second guessed by courts.

But there is considerable disagreement on how to achieve these objectives. One group, particularly the regulators, favor using the bank resolution regime in the FDI Act. Others basically favor using modifications of Chapter 11 of the Federal Bankruptcy Code. This difference in approach is vividly demonstrated in two recent conflicting statements by Ben Bernanke, Chairman of the Federal Reserve System, and Paul Singer, a hedge fund manager. Bernanke argued:

> A prototype for such a framework already exists – namely, the rules set forth in the *Federal Deposit Insurance Corporation Improvement Act of 1991* for dealing with a failing bank . . . The resolution agency should not be allowed to protect shareholders and other capital providers and it should have clear authority to impose losses on debt holders, override contracts, and replace management and directors as appropriate.[6]

Singer argued:

> We already have an incredibly robust time-tested 'authority' to handle failing companies – the US bankruptcy code. With decades of case law and precedent, it is sufficiently flexible to handle almost any type of insolvent company . . . Congress should legislate specific fixes to the existing bankruptcy code.[7]

12.5. BANK AND CORPORATE RESOLUTION REGIMES

The bank and corporate resolution regimes differ substantially. The salient features of each are described below.

- Bank
  - Administrative

  - Effectively liquidation, charter revoked, and management terminated
  - If it is a large bank, a new temporary bridge bank may be chartered
  - No ex-ante appeals
  - Creditors other than FDIC have no standing
  - Objective – minimize cost only to FDIC fund, *except*
    - Systemic risk exception for externalities (prevent financial instability)
  - FDIC limited discretion to modify creditor priority (flexibility)
  - Bridge bank capitalized/guaranteed by FDIC, not private DIP
  - Bridge bank management selected by FDIC
  - Limited stays
  - Considerable opacity in deposit and asset dispositions and
  - Considerable regulatory discretion if systemic risk exception is invoked.

- Corporate
  - Judicial
  - Rehabilitation (Chapter 11) or Liquidation (Chapter 7)
  - Creditors have standing
  - Transparent
  - Widespread automatic stays
  - Management generally maintained in Chapter 11 at least temporarily
  - Requires private DIP financing
  - Court approval of major actions
  - Absolute credit priority subject to negotiation among creditors.

Each regime has its advantages and disadvantages. Listed below are the more important advantages and disadvantages of Chapters 7 and 11 of the Federal Bankruptcy Code followed by the same for the bank resolution regime in the FDI Act.

- Chapters 7 and 11 Bankruptcy Resolution
  Advantages
  - Long history – well-established principles (case law and precedents)
  - Choice of rehabilitation (Chapter 11) or liquidation (Chapter 7)
  - In Chapter 11, maintain existing business relationships
  - If Chapter 11, no loss of competitor
  - Legal standing for all direct stakeholders
  - Impartial bankruptcy court (judicial review)

- Stays – maintain funding
- Right of ex-ante appeal by parties with legal standing
- Pro-rata losses according to creditor legal priority and negotiation
- Transparency
- Pre-packaged resolutions possible
- Renegotiate many contracts
- Strategic sale of assets
- Difficult to bailout uninsured creditors
- Minimum moral hazard.

Disadvantages
- Old (existing) management generally remains in control, at least initially
- Venue shopping
- Stays – block creditor access to funds
- Delay in initiating bankruptcy filing petition in court
- Resolution need not consider externalities/public interest
- Usually lengthy process
- Holdouts possible by junior claimants
- High legal costs
- Need to obtain DIP financing
- Difficult to bailout uninsured creditors.

- FDIA Insolvency Resolution
  Advantages
  - Quick initiation (declaration) of insolvency and receivership at pre-specified capital ratio (including positive values) in PCA framework by regulators
  - Quick termination of bank and old management
  - For large banks, transfer most deposits, assets, and services to new bridge bank to wind down orderly. (*Transfer price should be recovery value*)
  - No need for DIP financing; bridge bank funded or guaranteed by FDIC
  - Usually terminate old management
  - If bridge bank, new management appointed by FDIC
  - Pre-insolvency intervention under PCA to attempt to prevent insolvency
  - Greater legal certainty re depositor/creditor legal priority (no negotiation)
  - Pro-rata losses for uninsured deposits and other unsecured creditors, *except*

- If protection is consistent with LCR or
- Systemic risk exemption, permitting partial or total protection ('bailouts') of uninsured creditors/depositors by creditor subclass (concern about externalities)
- Insured depositors paid quickly
- Advance dividends to uninsured/unprotected depositors/creditors if it is not the major creditor based on estimated recovery values
- Renegotiate many contracts
- Low legal costs.

Disadvantages
- FDIC not impartial uninvolved party
- Resolution least cost only to FDIC (LCR)
- Less concern about uninsured general creditors
- No ex-ante appeals
- Limited judicial review
- No rehabilitation (loss of business relationships)
- Eliminates competitor
- Lack of transparency
- No legal standing of any interested parties other than FDIC
- Need for quick determination of what to transfer to bridge bank
- Excessive regulator flexibility and power[8]
- Inefficient, fire sale losses on overly hasty sales of assets
- Bridge bank unfair competition
- FDIC assumes bridge bank losses
- TBTF protection too easy and results in moral hazard.

12.6. AN OPTIMAL RESOLUTION REGIME FOR LCFIS

The broad differences in the two regimes suggest that one may be able to develop a more appropriate resolution scheme that is more likely to achieve the objectives of an efficient resolution of insolvent LCFIs in terms of achieving an orderly resolution without sacrificing market discipline, by selecting and combining parts of the bank and corporate regimes.[9] A listing of important objectives for LCFIs (including large banks) should include:

- Stable and efficient financial sector in both short and long term
- Impartial and experienced administrator
- Fairness for all parties according to their contract

- Maximizing value of assets/firm to all stakeholders according to their contract priority
- Transparency
- Predictability
- Rapid closure of insolvent institutions by regulators according to existing powers/authority in FDIA
- Standing for all directly interested parties:
  - Depositors, creditors, loan customers, other private stakeholders of institution at insolvency
  - Regulators for public interest
- To be subject to ex-ante appeal by parties with standing, except for closure
- Minimize moral hazard
- Consider adverse externalities from treatment of depositors/creditors
- Maintain critical services
- Minimize cost to taxpayers
- Be free from political influences
- Allow PCA/pre-packaging.

Using the two regimes as 'Chinese menus,' I pick and choose those components that in sum appear most likely to achieve the above objectives for resolving LCFIs efficiently. The result, not surprisingly, is basically a hybrid or modified Chapter 11, in which the regulators have legal standing and, using powers similar to those under PCA, can act quickly to put a troubled institution in receivership or liquidation. The main elements of the 'optimal' resolution regime are:

- Structure – legal court of experts or masters (judicial)
- Choice of Chapter 11 rehabilitation (not terminate charter nor eliminate a competitor) and Chapter 7 liquidation
- Initiation of filing for bankruptcy/insolvency/receivership by regulators using PCA triggers for minimum capital or all factors now included in the FDIA
- Legal standing – regulators for public; private direct stakeholders
- Oversight – court
- Final authority – court
- Insolvency prevention – regulators using PCA provisions
- Externality (systemic risk) exemption – Regulators as provided in FDICIA with more limited flexibility for protection by creditor class
- If reorganize/rehabilitate, no need for bridge institutions
- Losses – pro-rata by non-depositor creditors class with negotiation.

If externality exemption invoked, additional loss charged to pool paid by LCFIs (*Questions of what LCFIs and ex-ante or ex-post premiums*)

- Management during rehabilitation – new management recommended by regulators and approved by court; old management generally terminated
- Stays – too be determined
- DIP – by government or private
- Payment of uninsured claims – advance dividends on estimated recovery values for class
- Clawback – non-normal course of business recent cross-jurisdiction payments.

12.7. CONCLUSION

'Living wills' have been widely proposed recently as a means for increasing the efficiency of the resolution process for insolvent LCFIs, including financial firms beyond banks, and thus avoiding the need for inefficient TBTF bailouts by regulators. This chapter argues that drafting 'living wills' that will be meaningful for this purpose requires prior knowledge of the resolution regime in place or expected to be in place at the time of the resolution. Different resolution regimes will solicit different resolution or unwinding strategies by the institutions. The preference for alternative resolutions regimes may, however, be affected by the desirability of the unwinding strategy that they bring forth. Nevertheless, the first step in this iterative process should be the development of the characteristics of an optimal resolution regime for LCFIs in terms of achieving an orderly resolution consistent with market stability without sacrificing market discipline by protecting uninsured creditors and counterparties. Such a regime is constructed in the approach articulated above. The engine is thereby put in front of the caboose.

The chapter examines the pros and cons of the two major alternate resolution regimes in the US. Banks are resolved by the provisions of the administratively-based FDI Act. Most other corporations are resolved by the provisions of the judicially-based *Federal Bankruptcy Act*. The chapter concludes that the goals of efficient resolution of LCFIs may best be achieved by taking the appropriate elements of both regimes to construct a hybrid or modified Chapter 11-type process. This encloses the current bank resolution process, that is driven by the regulators, within a judicial framework borrowed from Chapter 11 of the *Federal Bankruptcy Act*. Using this as a starting point, first round 'living wills' consistent with this regime may be developed jointly by the LCFIs and their regulators to examine their feasibility and desirability.

NOTES

1. The original paper was prepared for presentation at the 'Symposium on Managing Systemic Risk' sponsored by the University of Warwick Law School, Coventry, UK, 7–9 April 2010. I am grateful to Robert Bliss (Wake Forest University) and the other participants in the symposium for helpful comments and suggestions. Some of the ideas in this chapter build on earlier papers co-authored with Bliss, particularly Bliss and Kaufman, 2010. Robert Bliss and George Kaufman, 'Resolving Large Complex Financial Institutions Within and Across Jurisdictions', in Richard J. Herring (ed.), *Cross-Border Issues in Resolving Systematically Important Financial Institutions*, The Wharton Financial Institutions Center, 2010.
2. See Herring, Richard (2009), 'Wind-down Plans as an Alternative to Bailouts', in Scott, K., G. Shultz and J. Taylor (eds), *Ending Government Bailouts*, Stanford: Stanford University Press, pp. 125–126; Grundfest, Joseph (2009), 'Wind-down Plans, Incomplete Contracting, and Renegotiation Risk', in Scott, K., G. Shultz and J. Taylor (eds), *Ending Government Bailouts*, Stanford: Stanford University Press, pp. 163–176; Avgouleas, et al. (February 2010), 'Living Wills as a Catalyst for Action', DSF Policy Paper No. 4, Amsterdam, Duisenberg School of Finance; and Huertas, Thomas F. (12 February 2010), 'Living Wills: How Can the Concept Be Implemented', Conference on Cross-Border Issues in Resolving Systemically Important Financial Institutions, Wharton School, University of Pennsylvania.
3. A history of TBTF for banks appears in Kaufman, G., 'Too Big To Fail in U.S. Banking: Quo Vadis?' in Benton Gup, ed., *Too Big To Fail*, Westport, CT: Praeger, 2009, pp. 153–167.
4. An analysis of the differences between the bank and corporate insolvency resolution regimes appears in Bliss, R. R. and Kaufman, G. G. 'U.S. Corporate and Bank Insolvency Regimes: A Comparison and Evaluation', *Virginia Law and Business Review*, Spring 2007, pp.143–177.
5. US Treasury (2009), p. 76.
6. Bernanke, Ben (20 March 2010), 'Speech', Washington, D.C.: Board of Governors of the Federal Reserve System, p. 3.
7. Singer, Paul (23 March 2010), 'The Dodd Bill and U.S. Competitiveness', *Wall Street Journal*, p. A21.
8. Government Accountability Office (GAO), *Federal Deposit Insurance Act:* Regulators' Use of Systemic Risk Exception Raises Moral Hazard Concerns and Opportunities Exist To Clarify the Provision (GAO-10-100), Washington, D.C., April 2010.
9. Another proposal for an optimum Chapter 11-type bankruptcy code for LCFIs appears in Jackson, Thomas H. (2009), 'Chapter 11: A Proposal for the Use of Bankruptcy to Resolve Financial Institutions', in Scott, K., G. Shultz and J. Taylor (eds), *Ending Government Bailouts*, Stanford: Stanford University Press, pp. 217–251.

13. Finding a solution to the 'too-big-to-fail' problem

Arthur E. Wilmarth, Jr.

13.1. INTRODUCTION

The financial crisis – widely viewed as the worst since the Great Depression[1] – has inflicted tremendous damage on financial markets and economies around the world.[2] It has revealed fundamental weaknesses in the financial regulatory systems of the US, the UK, and other European nations, making regulatory reforms an urgent priority. Publicly-funded bailouts of 'too-big-to-fail' (TBTF) financial institutions have provided indisputable proof that (i) TBTF institutions benefit from large explicit and implicit public subsidies, and (ii) those subsidies undermine market discipline and distort economic incentives for large, complex financial institutions (LCFIs).[3] Accordingly, a primary objective of regulatory reforms must be to eliminate (or at least greatly reduce) TBTF subsidies, thereby forcing LCFIs to internalize the risks and costs of their activities.

This chapter proposes five reforms designed to prevent excessive risk-taking by LCFIs and to shrink TBTF subsidies in the US financial system.[4] The proposed reforms would (1) strengthen current statutory restrictions on the growth of LCFIs, (2) create a special resolution process to manage the orderly liquidation or restructuring of systemically important financial institutions (SIFIs), (3) establish a consolidated supervisory regime and enhanced capital requirements for SIFIs, (4) create a special insurance fund for SIFIs in order to cover the costs of resolving failed SIFIs, and (5) rigorously insulate banks that are owned by LCFIs from the activities and risks of their nonbank affiliates.

13.2. REFORMING FINANCIAL REGULATION TO SHRINK TBTF SUBSIDIES

The enormous competitive advantages enjoyed by TBTF institutions must be eliminated (or at least significantly reduced) in order to restore a level playing field for smaller financial institutions and to encourage the voluntary breakup of inefficient and risky financial conglomerates.[5] The financial crisis has proven that large universal banks operate based on a dangerous business model that is riddled with conflicts of interest and prone to speculative risk-taking.[6]

Taking the above into account, US and European governments should adopt reforms that will (i) greatly reduce the scope of governmental safety nets and thereby significantly diminish the subsidies currently provided to LCFIs, and (ii) facilitate the orderly failure and liquidation of LCFIs under governmental supervision, with consequential losses to managers, shareholders and creditors of LCFIs. I believe that five key reforms are needed to accomplish those objectives: (1) strengthening current statutory restrictions in the US on the growth of LCFIs, (2) creating a special resolution process to manage the orderly liquidation or restructuring of SIFIs, (3) establishing a consolidated supervisory regime and enhanced capital requirements for SIFIs, (4) creating a special insurance fund for SIFIs, in order to cover the costs of resolving failed SIFIs, and (5) rigorously insulating banks that are insured by the Federal Deposit Insurance Corporation (FDIC) and owned by LCFIs from the activities and risks of their nonbank affiliates. The following sections provide an overview of my proposed reforms.

13.2.1. Statutory Limits on the Growth of LCFIs Should Be Strengthened

The *Riegle-Neal Interstate Banking and Branching Act of 1994* (Riegle-Neal) imposes nationwide and state-wide deposit concentration limits (deposit caps) on interstate expansion by large banking organizations.

Under Riegle-Neal, a bank holding company (BHC) may not acquire a bank in another state, and a bank may not merge with another bank across state lines, if the resulting banking organization (together with all affiliated FDIC-insured depository institutions) would hold (i) ten percent or more of the total deposits of all depository institutions in the US, or (ii) 30 percent or more of the total deposits of all depository institutions in any state.[7]

Unfortunately, the effectiveness of Riegle-Neal's nationwide and statewide deposit caps is undermined by three major loopholes. First, the Riegle-Neal deposit caps do not apply to intrastate bank acquisitions or intrastate bank mergers. Second, the deposit caps do not apply to acquisitions of, or mergers with, thrift institutions and industrial banks, because those institutions are not treated as 'banks' under the Riegle-Neal Act.[8] Third, the deposit caps do not apply to acquisitions of, or mergers with, banks that are 'in default or in danger of default' (the failing bank exception).[9]

The emergency acquisitions of Countrywide, Merrill Lynch (Merrill), Washington Mutual (Wamu) and Wachovia in 2008 demonstrated the significance of Riegle-Neal's loopholes and the necessity of closing them. In reliance on the 'non-bank' loophole, the FRB allowed Bank of America (BofA) to acquire Countrywide and Merrill even though (i) both firms controlled FDIC-insured depository institutions (a thrift, in the case of Countrywide, and a thrift and industrial bank, in the case of Merrill), and (ii) both transactions allowed BofA to exceed the ten percent nationwide deposit cap.[10] Similarly, after the FDIC seized control of Wamu as a failed depository institution, the giant thrift was sold to JP Morgan Chase (Chase) even though the transaction enabled Chase to breach the ten percent nationwide deposit cap.[11] Finally, although the FRB determined that Wells Fargo's acquisition of Wachovia gave Wells Fargo control of just under ten percent of nationwide deposits, the FRB could probably have approved the acquisition in any case by designating Wachovia as a bank 'in danger of default.'[12]

Those acquisitions enabled BofA, Chase and Wells Fargo to surpass the ten percent nationwide deposit cap.[13] To prevent further breaches of the Riegle-Neal concentration limits, Congress should extend the nationwide and state-wide deposit caps to cover all intrastate and interstate transactions involving any type of FDIC-insured institution, including thrifts and industrial banks. In addition, Congress should significantly narrow the failing bank exception by requiring federal regulators to make a 'systemic risk determination' (SRD) in order to approve any transaction involving a failing FDIC-insured depository institution that would exceed the nationwide or state-wide deposit caps.

Congress should establish the following procedural requirements for an SRD. First, the FRB and FDIC should determine jointly, with the concurrence of the Treasury Secretary, that the proposed transaction is necessary to avoid a substantial threat of severe injury to the banking system, the financial markets or the national economy. Second, each SRD should be audited by the Government Accountability Office (GAO) to determine whether regulators satisfied the criteria for an SRD. Third, each SRD should be reviewed in a joint hearing held by the House and Senate committees with oversight of the financial markets. The foregoing procedure for approving and reviewing an SRD (the 'SRD Procedure') would ensure much greater public transparency of, and scrutiny for, (i) any federal agency order that invokes the failing bank exception to the Riegle-Neal deposit caps, and (ii) regulatory decisions of similar importance, as described below.

The Obama Administration has announced its support for a proposal by former FRB Chairman Paul Volcker to prohibit mergers and acquisitions that would allow a single financial institution to acquire control of more than ten percent of total bank liabilities other than insured deposits (the 'Volcker liabilities cap'). The Volcker liabilities cap would supplement the existing Riegle-Neal deposit caps and would be subject to the same exemption for acquisitions of banks 'in default or in danger of default'.[14] If enacted, the Volcker liabilities cap would present a significant barrier to further acquisitions of banks by BofA, Chase, and Citigroup.[15] The Volcker liabilities cap would have the greatest impact on Citigroup, because Citigroup currently is not close to exceeding the Riegle-Neal nationwide deposit cap. In contrast, the Riegle-Neal nationwide deposit cap already blocks the three major rivals of Citigroup (BofA, Chase and Wells Fargo) from making further interstate acquisitions of banks.[16]

The Volcker liabilities cap has been criticized as vague and unworkable.[17] It remains to be seen whether the proposal can be clarified in a manner that would give it a utility and ease of application comparable to the Riegle-Neal deposit caps. If it is appropriately clarified, the Volcker liabilities cap should be adopted as a supplemental method of restricting the growth of very large BHCs (e.g., Citigroup, Goldman Sachs (Goldman), and Morgan Stanley) that rely mainly on the capital markets, rather than deposits, for their funding.[18] For the reasons stated above with regard to the Riegle-Neal deposit caps, the Volcker liabilities cap should apply to all interstate and intrastate acquisitions of FDIC-insured depository institutions (including thrifts and industrial banks), and regulators should not be able to invoke the 'failing bank' exception unless they comply with the SRD Procedure.

13.2.2. A Special Resolution Regime Should Be Established for Systemically Important Financial Institutions

During the financial crisis – as shown by the FRB's assistance for Chase's acquisition of Bear Sterns (Bear), the traumatic bankruptcy of Lehman Brothers (Lehman), and the federal government's massive bailout of American International Group (AIG) – federal regulators confronted a 'Hobson's choice of bailout or disorderly bankruptcy' when they decided how to respond to a SIFI's potential failure.[19] A statutory resolution process for SIFIs, similar to the existing resolution regime for FDIC-insured depository institutions, would be a highly beneficial 'third way, between bankruptcy and bailout that would either euthanize SIFIs peacefully or resuscitate them under new management.'[20] The special resolution regime for SIFIs should include three essential elements.

First, Congress should establish a Financial Stability Oversight Council (FSOC) with voting members that include the leaders of the federal financial regulatory agencies and with additional non-voting members that represent state regulators of state-chartered banks, insurance companies and securities firms.[21] By a two-thirds vote, the FSOC should be authorized to determine that a BHC or a nonbank financial company should be designated as a SIFI and should be subject to the special resolution regime for SIFIs. The criteria for identifying a financial firm as a SIFI should be based on factors relevant to systemic risk, including the firm's size and the risk of contagion from the firm's failure due to (i) the firm's interconnectedness or correlations of risk exposures with other important financial institutions or financial markets or (ii) the firm's role as a key participant within one or more important sectors of the financial markets.[22]

Some commentators have opposed any public identification of SIFIs, due to concerns that firms designated as SIFIs would be treated as TBTF by the financial markets and would create additional moral hazard.[23] However, moral hazard already exists in abundance because the financial markets are currently treating major LCFIs as TBTF. During the current crisis federal regulators publicly identified and supported the 19 largest BHCs, as well as Bear and AIG, as TBTF institutions.[24] As a result of this massive and explicit governmental support, credit rating agencies (CRAs) depositors, and bondholders are currently giving highly preferential treatment to LCFIs that are viewed as TBTF.[25]

Accordingly, it is no longer credible for federal regulators to pretend that they can retreat to their former policy of 'constructive ambiguity' by asserting their willingness to allow major LCFIs to collapse into disorderly bankruptcies similar to the Lehman debacle.[26] Any such assertion would not be believed by the public or the financial markets.[27] An effective way to impose discipline on SIFIs, and to reduce the federal subsidies they receive, would be to designate them publicly as SIFIs and to impose stringent regulatory requirements that would force them to internalize the potential costs of their TBTF status.

Second, the FDIC should have the authority to initiate a new special resolution regime for a failing SIFI by making a concurrently with the FRB and the Treasury Secretary. The SRD should follow the SRD Procedure (as described above) and should require a finding that the SIFI either (i) has fallen below a specified minimum capital threshold or (ii) is facing a near-term risk of insolvency or bankruptcy due to a lack of adequate liquidity or a threatened acceleration of outstanding creditor claims. In addition, the SRD should include a finding that the systemic resolution process is needed to prevent the SIFI's imminent failure from posing a risk of serious harm to the banking system, the financial markets or the national economy. The resolution process for a failed SIFI should be administered by the FDIC, given its experience in resolving large bank failures.[28]

Third, the resolution process for SIFIs should incorporate the following principles: (A) stockholders must lose their entire investment if the SIFI is unable to pay all valid creditor claims, (B) senior managers must be dismissed, together with other employees who were responsible for the SIFI's failure, and (C) unsecured creditors must be required to accept meaningful 'haircuts,' either in the form of a significant reduction in the amount of their debt claims or an exchange of a substantial amount of their debt claims for equity interests in a successor institution. In other words, the resolution process for a SIFI should resemble, to the maximum extent feasible, the outcome of a Chapter 11 bankruptcy proceeding.[29] The FDIC should be required to prepare a SRD, and to comply with the SRD Procedure, if it decides either that (A) it must depart from any of the foregoing principles, or (B) it must advance funds to support the SIFI's resolution without a reasonable assurance of repayment from the proceeds of the resolution. Any net proceeds realized by the FDIC from a SIFI's resolution (over and above the FDIC's expenses in carrying out the resolution) should be added to the Systemic Risk Insurance Fund (SRIF), described below.

13.2.3. SIFIs Should Be Subject to Consolidated Supervision by the FRB and Enhanced Prudential Requirements

Congress should designate the FRB as the consolidated supervisor for SIFIs, subject to the oversight of the FSOC. Given the FRB's experience as the regulator of BHCs and as the 'umbrella supervisor' for financial holding companies (FHCs), it is the logical choice as the consolidated supervisor for SIFIs.[30]

As consolidated supervisor, the FRB should have power to examine, and require reports from, SIFIs and their subsidiaries and affiliates. The FRB should also have authority to take enforcement actions (including cease-and-desist orders, civil money penalty orders, and orders removing directors and officers) against SIFIs and their subsidiaries and affiliates. The FRB's authority in these matters should be direct. The FRB should not be required (as it is under current law) to rely primarily on actions taken by regulators of functionally regulated subsidiaries (for example, banks, securities broker-dealers and insurance companies).[31]

If a functional regulator (for example, the Office of the Comptroller of Currency (OCC) or the Securities and Exchange Commission (SEC)) believes that actions by the FRB as systemic risk regulator are creating an unwarranted conflict with the functional regulator's supervision of a functionally regulated subsidiary, the functional regulator should have the right to appeal to the FSOC. By a two-thirds vote, the FSOC could require the FRB to rescind or modify any regulatory action with regard to a functionally regulated subsidiary of a SIFI that the FSOC determined was not necessary or appropriate to prevent a serious threat to the stability of the SIFI or any of the SIFI's FDIC-insured subsidiaries.

The FRB should also have authority, with the concurrence of the FDIC, to establish systemic risk capital requirements (SRCRs) for SIFIs. The FDIC should be given a concurrent role in establishing SRCRs in view of its role as administrator of the SRIF. The FDIC's responsibilities for administering the SRIF would encourage the FDIC to apply strict discipline against SIFIs in order to protect the SRIF's solvency. Accordingly, the FDIC's tendency toward supervisory stringency would serve as a desirable counterweight against the FRB's tendency toward supervisory forbearance (which arises out of the FRB's concern with preserving the stability of the financial markets).[32] If the FRB and the FDIC disagreed over the appropriate level of SRCRs, the FSOC could resolve the disagreement and specify SRCRs by a vote of at least a majority of its voting members other than the representatives of the FRB and FDIC.

SRCRs should include a leverage capital requirement, which would be calculated based on the total (unweighted) assets of each SIFI. A leverage requirement is a useful tool for limiting excessive risk-taking by financial institutions, and it is an essential supplement to risk-based capital requirements. In 2007, European banks and US investment banks operated with very high asset-to-equity ratios (usually above 30:1) because they were subject only to risk-based capital rules and did not have to satisfy a leverage capital requirement. By contrast, asset-to-equity ratios for US commercial banks were typically below 25:1 because those banks had to comply with a leverage requirement as well as risk-based capital rules. To provide an additional margin for safety, the minimum leverage capital requirement for SIFIs should be increased to a level well above the current requirement of five percent for well-capitalized institutions.[33]

In addition to a leverage requirement, SRCRs should incorporate risk-based components, including rules that emphasize 'the importance of common equity' as well as the need to 'reduce pro-cyclical tendencies by establishing special capital buffers that would be built up in boom times and drawn down as conditions deteriorate.'[34] The marginal rates for risk-based SRCRs should become progressively higher as a SIFI poses greater systemic risk due to (a) increases in its size, complexity or interconnectedness with other LCFIs, (b) hazards created by an aggressive compensation structure for managers or for key employees who work in high-risk areas (for example, proprietary trading), and/or (c) weaknesses in the SIFI's liquidity.[35] In addition, SRCRs should take full account of all risk exposures of a SIFI, whether those exposures are held on the SIFI's balance sheet or are linked to off balance sheet (OBS) entities.[36]

One intriguing proposal would require each SIFI to issue 'contingent capital' as one component of its SRCR. This contingent capital would be issued in the form of convertible subordinated debt. That debt would convert automatically into common stock upon the occurrence of a designated event of financial stress, such as (i) a decline in the SIFI's capital below a specified level that would 'trigger' an automatic conversion, or (ii) the initiation by the FRB and the FDIC of the special resolution process for a SIFI. One advantage of contingent capital is that the SIFI's common equity would be increased (due to the mandatory conversion of subordinated debt) at a time when the SIFI would face significant financial stress and probably could not sell stock in the market. Additionally, mandatory conversion would encourage holders of convertible subordinated debt to exercise greater discipline over the SIFI's management, since those holders would risk losing their entire investment if mandatory conversion occurred.[37]

The biggest problem with the contingent capital proposal is that outside investors would be reluctant to purchase convertible subordinated debt unless the terms of the debt included a relatively high interest rate or other investor friendly features (for example, a voluntary conversion option on favorable terms) that would offset the risk of forfeiture due to a mandatory conversion event. SIFIs and outside investors therefore might not be able to agree on an interest rate and other terms for contingent capital that would be acceptable to both sides.[38]

As I have suggested previously, contingent capital would be a particularly attractive option for compensating senior managers and other key employees. Managers and key employees should be required to accept convertible subordinated debentures in payment of a significant portion (e.g., one-third) of their annual compensation. Managers and key employees should not be allowed to make voluntary conversions of their subordinated debentures into common stock until the expiration of a minimum holding period (for example, three years) after the termination date of their employment. Such a minimum post-employment holding period would discourage managers and key employees from taking excessive risks to boost the value of the conversion option during the term of their employment. At the same time, managers and key employees would know that their debentures are subject to mandatory conversion into common stock upon the occurrence of a designated event of financial stress. Thus, requiring managers and key employees to hold a significant portion of contingent capital would give them positive incentives to avoid excessive risk-taking and to manage their SIFI prudently in accordance with the interests of creditors as well as shareholders. Such a requirement would also force managers and key employees to share a significant portion of the loss if their SIFI was threatened with failure.[39]

13.2.4. SIFIs Should Pay Risk-based Premiums to Establish a Systemic Risk Insurance Fund Administered by the FDIC

To accomplish a further reduction in TBTF subsidies, Congress should require SIFIs to pay risk-based insurance premiums to establish the SRIF.[40] The FDIC should be required to impose risk-based SRIF premiums in order to establish, within a period not to exceed five years, a SRIF that would provide reasonable protection to taxpayers against the cost of a future systemic financial crisis. Those risk-based premiums should be determined by the FDIC based on (i) the estimated probability of failure of each SIFI, and (ii) the loss that the FDIC would expect to incur in resolving the failure of that SIFI.

Federal regulators provided USD290 billion of capital assistance to the 19 largest BHCs (each with assets of more than USD100 billion) and to AIG during the current crisis.[41] It therefore appears that (i) USD300 billion (appropriately adjusted for inflation) would be the minimum acceptable size for the SRIF, and (ii) SRIF premiums should be paid by all BHCs with assets of more than USD100 billion (also adjusted for inflation) and by all other designated nonbank SIFIs. As with SRCRs, the marginal rates for SRIF premiums should become progressively higher as SIFIs pose greater systemic risk, adopt riskier compensation structures and/or maintain inadequate liquidity.[42] In addition, the FDIC should impose additional assessments on SIFIs in order to replenish the SRIF within three years after the SRIF incurs any loss due to the failure of a SIFI.

For at least four reasons, it is essential to establish a pre-funded SRIF. First, it is unlikely that most SIFIs would have adequate financial resources to pay large SRIF premiums after one or more of their peers failed during a financial crisis. LCFIs are frequently exposed to highly correlated risk exposures during a serious financial disruption, because they followed similar high-risk business strategies ('herding') during the credit boom that led to the crisis.[43] Many LCFIs are therefore likely to suffer severe losses and to face a substantial risk of failure during a major disturbance in the financial markets.[44] Consequently, a post-funded SRIF (i) would probably not be able in the short term to collect enough premiums from surviving SIFIs to cover the costs of resolving one or more failed SIFIs, and (ii) would therefore have to borrow large sums from the federal government to cover short-term resolution costs. Even if the SRIF ultimately repaid the borrowed funds by imposing ex post assessments on surviving SIFIs, the public and the financial markets would understandably conclude that the federal government provided bridge loans to bail out creditors of the failed SIFIs.[45] Accordingly, a post-funded SRIF would not be successful in eliminating many of the implicit subsidies (and associated moral hazard) that the US Government's past TBTF rescues have created.

Second, in a post-funded system, the most reckless SIFIs (which would be the most likely to fail) would effectively shift the potential costs of their risk-taking to the most prudent SIFIs, because the latter would be more likely to survive and bear the ex post costs of resolving failed SIFIs. Thus, a post-funded SRIF is undesirable because 'firms that fail never pay and the costs are borne by surviving firms.'[46]

Third, a pre-funded SRIF would create beneficial incentives that would encourage each SIFI to monitor other SIFIs and to alert regulators to excessive risk-taking by those institutions. Every SIFI would know that the failure of another SIFI would deplete the SRIF and would also trigger future assessments that it and other surviving SIFIs would have to pay. Thus, each SIFI would have good reason to complain to regulators if it became aware of unsound practices or conditions at another SIFI.

Fourth, a pre-funded SRIF would reduce the TBTF subsidy for SIFIs by forcing them to internalize more of the 'negative externality' (i.e., the potential public bailout cost) of their activities.[47] A pre-funded SRIF would provide a reserve fund, paid for by SIFIs that would protect governments and taxpayers from having to incur the expense of underwriting future bailouts of failed SIFIs.

To further reduce the potential TBTF subsidy for SIFIs, the SRIF should be strictly separated from the existing Deposit Insurance Fund ('DIF'), which protects depositors of FDIC-insured banks. To ensure this separation, Congress should repeal the 'systemic-risk exception' that is currently included in the *Federal Deposit Insurance Act* ('FDI Act').[48] The FDIC relied on that exception when it joined with the Treasury Department and the FRB in providing more than USD400 billion of asset guarantees to Citigroup and BofA.[49] The DIF should no longer be available as a potential source of protection for shareholders and creditors of SIFIs. Instead, the SRIF should be designated as the exclusive source of future funding for resolutions of failed SIFIs. Thus, the systemic-risk exception for the DIF should be repealed, and the FDIC should be required to apply the least-cost test in resolving all future bank failures.[50] Repeal of the systemic-risk exception would ensure that the DIF is no longer viewed as a potential bailout fund for TBTF banking organizations.

13.2.5. Banks Controlled by Financial Holding Companies Should Operate as 'Narrow Banks' so that They Cannot Transfer Their Federal Safety Net Subsidies to Their Nonbank Affiliates

In January 2010, President Obama announced his support for the 'Volcker rule' proposed by former FRB Chairman Paul Volcker. The Volcker rule would prohibit FDIC-member banks and companies controlling such banks from owning or controlling hedge funds or private equity funds or from engaging in proprietary trading (that is, buying and selling securities, derivatives and other tradable assets for their own account). Trading in the capital markets by banks and their holding companies would be limited to 'market making' activities conducted on behalf of clients.[51] The primary purpose of the Volcker rule is to prevent government safety nets from 'protecting and supporting essentially proprietary and speculative activities.'[52] As this chapter went to press, it was uncertain whether Congress would adopt the Volcker rule. One of the most frequently-stated critiques of the rule was the difficulty in distinguishing between permissible market-making for clients and prohibited proprietary trading for a bank's own account.[53]

In my view, the most feasible way to accomplish the basic purpose of the Volcker rule – namely, to prevent SIFIs from using the federal safety net to subsidize their speculative activities in the capital markets – would be to create a two-tiered structure of bank regulation and deposit insurance. As described below, the first tier of 'traditional' banking organizations would provide a relatively broad range of banking-related services, but those organizations would not be allowed to engage, or affiliate with firms engaged, in securities underwriting or dealing, insurance underwriting or derivatives dealing. In contrast, the second tier of 'narrow banks' could affiliate with 'non-traditional' firms engaged in capital markets activities, except for private equity investments. However, 'narrow banks' would be prohibited from making any extensions of credit or other transfers of funds to their nonbank affiliates, except for lawful dividends paid to their parent holding companies. The 'narrow bank' approach provides the most practicable method for ensuring that banks cannot transfer their safety net subsidies to affiliated companies engaged in speculative activities in the capital markets, and it is therefore consistent with the spirit of the Volcker rule.[54]

13.2.6. The First Tier of Traditional Banking Organizations

Under my proposal, the first tier of regulated banking firms would be 'traditional' banking organizations that limit their activities (including the activities of all holding company affiliates) to lines of business that meet the 'closely related to banking' test under Section 4(c)(8) of the *Bank Holding Company Act* (BHC Act).[55] For example, this first tier of traditional banks could take deposits, make loans, offer fiduciary services, and act as agents in selling securities, mutual funds and insurance products underwritten by non-affiliated firms. Additionally, they could underwrite and deal solely in 'bank-eligible' securities that national banks are permitted to underwrite and deal in directly.[56] First-tier banking organizations could also purchase, as end-users, derivatives solely for bona fide hedging transactions that qualify for hedging treatment under Financial Accounting Standard (FAS) Statement No. 133.[57]

Most first-tier banking firms would probably be small and midsized community-oriented banks. Those banks do not have any comparative advantage – and therefore have not shown any substantial interest – in engaging as principal in insurance underwriting, securities underwriting or dealing, derivatives dealing or other capital markets activities. Community banks are well positioned to continue their established business of attracting core deposits, providing relationship loans to consumers as well as small- and medium-sized business firms, and offering wealth management services to local customers through their fiduciary operations.[58]

In order to provide reasonable flexibility for this first tier of traditional banks, Congress should amend Section 4(c)(8) of the BHC Act by permitting the FRB to expand the list of 'closely related' activities that are permissible for holding company affiliates of traditional banks.[59] However, Congress should prohibit first-tier BHCs from engaging as principal in underwriting or dealing in securities, underwriting any type of insurance (except for credit insurance), dealing in over-the-counter (OTC) derivatives or making private equity investments. Furthermore, traditional banks and their holding companies should continue to operate under their current supervisory arrangements, and all of the banks' deposits (up to the current statutory limit of USD250 000) would be covered by deposit insurance.

13.2.7. The Second Tier of Non-traditional Banking Organizations

The second tier of 'non-traditional' banking organizations would be allowed to engage in (i) underwriting and dealing (that is, proprietary trading) in 'bank-ineligible' securities, (ii) underwriting insurance, and (iii) dealing or trading in derivatives. Second-tier organizations would include: (A) Financial holding companies (FHCs) registered under Sections 4(k) and 4(l) of the BHC Act,[60] (B) holding companies owning grandfathered 'nonbank banks', and (C) grandfathered 'unitary thrift' holding companies.[61] In addition, firms controlling industrial banks should be required either to register as FHCs or to divest their ownership of such banks if they cannot comply with the BHC Act's prohibitions against commercial activities.[62] Second-tier holding companies would thus encompass all of the largest banking organizations, most of which are heavily engaged in capital markets activities, together with other financial conglomerates that control FDIC-insured depository institutions.

13.2.7.1. Congress should require a 'narrow bank' structure for second-tier banks

Under my proposal, FDIC-insured depository institutions that are subsidiaries of second-tier holding companies would be required to operate as 'narrow banks.' The purpose of the narrow bank structure would be to prevent a 'non-traditional' second-tier holding company from transferring the bank's deposit insurance subsidy to its nonbank affiliates. As such, narrow banks could offer FDIC-insured deposit accounts, including checking and savings accounts and certificates of deposit. Narrow banks would hold all of their assets in the form of cash and marketable, short-term debt obligations, including qualifying government securities, highly-rated commercial paper and other liquid, short-term debt instruments that are eligible for investment by money market mutual funds ('MMMFs') under the SEC's rules. Narrow banks could not hold any other types of loans or investments, nor could they accept any uninsured deposits. Narrow banks would present a very small risk to the DIF, because (i) each narrow bank's non-cash assets would consist solely of short-term securities that could be 'marked to market' on a daily basis, and the FDIC could therefore readily determine whether a narrow bank was threatened with insolvency, and (ii) the FDIC could promptly convert a narrow bank's assets into cash if the FDIC decided to liquidate the bank and pay off the claims of its insured depositors.[63]

Thus, narrow banks would be able to offer FDIC-insured MMMFs. In order to prevent unfair competition with narrow banks, and to avoid future government bailouts of uninsured MMMFs, MMMFs should be prohibited from representing, either explicitly or implicitly, that they will redeem their shares based on a 'constant net asset value' ('NAV') of USD1 per share.[64] Currently, the MMMF industry (which manages USD3.3 trillion of assets) leads investors to believe that their funds will be available for withdrawal (redemption) based on a 'stable price' of USD1 per share.[65] Not surprisingly, 'the USD1 share price gives investors the false impression that money-market funds are like [FDIC-insured] banks accounts and can't lose money.'[66] However, '[t]hat myth was shattered in 2008' when Lehman's default on its commercial paper caused Reserve Primary Fund (a large MMMF that invested heavily in Lehman's paper) to suffer large losses and to 'break the buck.'[67] The Reserve Primary Fund's inability to redeem its shares based on a NAV of USD1 per share caused an investor panic that precipitated runs on several MMMFs. The Treasury Department responded by establishing the Money Market Fund Guarantee Program (MMFGP), which protected investors in participating MMMFs between October 2008 and September 2009.[68]

Critics of MMMFs maintain that the Treasury's MMFGP has created an expectation of similar government bailouts if MMMFs 'break the buck' in the future.[69] In addition, Paul Volcker has argued that MMMFs weaken banks because of their ability to offer bank-like products without equivalent regulation. MMMFs typically offer accounts with check-writing features, and they provide returns to investors that are higher than bank checking accounts because MMMFs do not have to pay FDIC insurance premiums or to comply with other bank regulations.[70] A Group of Thirty report proposed that MMMFs 'that want to offer bank-like services, such as checking accounts and withdrawals at USD1 a share, should reorganize as a type of bank, with appropriate supervision and government insurance.'[71] In contrast, MMMFs that do not wish to operate as banks 'should not maintain the implicit promise that investors' money is always safe' and should be required to base their redemption price on a floating NAV.[72]

For the above reasons, uninsured MMMFs should be prohibited from representing, explicitly or implicitly, that they will redeem shares based on a stable NAV. If Congress imposed this prohibition on MMMFs and adopted my proposal for a two-tiered structure of bank regulation, many MMMFs would probably reorganize as FDIC-insured narrow banks and would become subsidiaries of second-tier FHCs.[73] As noted above, rules restricting the assets of narrow banks to commercial paper, government securities and other types of marketable, highly-liquid investments would protect the DIF from any significant loss if a narrow bank failed.

13.2.7.2. Four additional rules would prevent narrow banks from transferring safety net subsidies to their affiliates

Four supplemental rules are needed to prevent second-tier holding companies from exploiting their narrow banks' safety net subsidies. First, narrow banks should be prohibited from making any extensions of credit or other transfers of funds to their affiliates, except for the payment of lawful dividends out of profits to their parent holding companies.[74] During times of financial stress, the FRB has repeatedly waived the current restrictions on affiliate transactions mandated by Sections 23A and 23B of the *Federal Reserve Act*.[75] Those waivers allowed bank subsidiaries of FHCs to provide extensive support to affiliated securities broker-dealers and

MMMFs. By granting those waivers, the FRB enabled banks controlled by FHCs to transfer the safety net subsidy provided by low-cost, FDIC-insured deposits to their nonbank affiliates.[76] With respect to second-tier banking organizations, my proposal would replace Sections 23A and 23B with an absolute prohibition on any extensions of credit or other transfers of funds by second-tier banks to their nonbank affiliates. That reform would effectively prevent the FRB from approving any similar transfers of safety net subsidies by narrow banks to their affiliates.

Second, as discussed above, the 'systemic risk' provision currently included in the FDI Act should be repealed. By repealing that provision, Congress would require the FDIC to follow the least costly resolution procedure for every failed bank, and the FDIC could no longer rely on the TBTF policy as a justification for protecting uninsured creditors of a failed bank's parent holding company or other nonbank affiliates of a failed bank.[77]

Insulating the DIF from any possibility of TBTF bailouts would have important benefits. It would make clear to the financial markets that the DIF could only be used to protect depositors of failed banks. Uninsured creditors of FHCs – regardless of their size – would no longer have any reasonable expectation of being protected by the DIF. Shareholders and creditors of FHCs and their nonbank subsidiaries would therefore have stronger incentives to monitor the financial condition of such entities.

Additionally, smaller banks would no longer bear any part of the cost of rescuing uninsured creditors of TBTF banks. Under current law, all FDIC-insured banks must pay a special assessment (allocated in proportion to their total assets) to reimburse the FDIC for the cost of protecting uninsured claimants of a TBTF bank under the 'systemic risk' provision.[78] A FDIC report in 2000 noted the unfairness of expecting smaller banks to help pay for 'systemic risk' bailouts when 'it is virtually inconceivable that they would receive similar treatment if distressed.'[79] The FDIC report suggested that the way to correct this inequity is 'to remove the systemic risk exception from the [FDI Act],'[80] as I have proposed here

Third, second-tier narrow banks should be prohibited from dealing in derivatives or from purchasing derivatives except as end-users for bona fide hedging purposes pursuant to FAS 133.[81] All other derivatives activities of second-tier banking organizations must be conducted through separate nonbank affiliates. This rule would prevent FHCs from continuing to exploit federal safety net subsidies by conducting risky derivatives activities within their FDIC-insured bank subsidiaries.

Fourth, second-tier banks and their affiliates should be prohibited from making private equity investments. To accomplish this reform, Congress must repeal Sections 4(k)(4)(H) and (I) of the BHC Act,[82] which allow

FHCs to make merchant banking investments and insurance company portfolio investments.[83] Private equity investments by second-tier banking organizations should be banned because they involve a high degree of risk and have inflicted significant losses on FHCs in the past.[84] In addition, private equity investments 'could potentially weaken the separation of banking and commerce' by allowing FHCs 'to maintain long-term control over entities that conduct commercial (that is, nonfinancial) businesses.'[85] Such affiliations between banks and commercial firms are undesirable because they are likely to create serious competitive and economic distortions, including the spread of federal safety net benefits to our commercial sector of the economy.[86]

In combination, the four supplemental rules described above would help to ensure that narrow banks cannot transfer their federal safety net subsidies to their nonbank affiliates. Restricting the scope of safety net subsidies is of utmost importance in order to restore a more level playing field between small and large banks, and between banking and nonbanking firms. Safety net subsidies have increasingly distorted our regulatory and economic policies over the past three decades. During that period, nonbanking firms have pursued every available avenue to acquire FDIC-insured depository institutions so that they can secure the funding advantages provided by low-cost, FDIC-insured deposits. At the same time, nonbank affiliates of banks have made every effort to exploit the funding advantages and other safety net benefits conferred by their affiliation with FDIC-insured institutions.[87] The enormous benefits conferred by federal safety net subsidies are conclusively shown by the following facts: (i) no major bank organization has ever voluntarily surrendered its banking charter, and (ii) large nonbanking firms have aggressively pursued strategies to secure control of FDIC-insured depository institutions.[88]

The most practicable way to prevent the spread of federal safety net subsidies, as well as their distorting effects on regulation and economic activity, is to establish strong barriers that prohibit narrow banks from transferring their subsidies to their nonbanking affiliates, including those engaged in speculative capital markets activities.[89] The narrow bank structure and the supplemental rules described above would force financial conglomerates to prove that they can produce superior risk-related returns to investors without relying on governmental subsidies. As I have previously explained elsewhere, economic studies have failed to confirm the existence of favorable economies of scale or scope in financial conglomerates, and those conglomerates have not been able to generate consistently positive returns, even under the current regulatory system that allows them to capture extensive federal subsidies.[90]

In late 2009, a prominent bank analyst suggested that if Congress enacted new rules that imposed severe restrictions on affiliate transactions, and thereby prevented nonbank subsidiaries of FHCs from relying on low-cost deposit funding provided by their affiliated banks, large FHCs would not be economically viable and would be forced to break up voluntarily.[91] It is noteworthy that many of the largest commercial and industrial conglomerates in the US and Europe have been broken up through hostile takeovers and voluntary divestitures during the past three decades because they proved to be 'less efficient and less profitable than companies pursuing more focused business strategies.'[92] It is long past the time for financial conglomerates to be stripped of their safety net subsidies so that they will be subject to the same type of scrutiny and discipline that the capital markets have applied to commercial and industrial conglomerates during the past 30 years. The narrow bank concept provides a workable plan to impose such scrutiny and discipline on FHCs.

13.2.7.3. Responses to critiques of the narrow bank proposal

Critics have raised three major objections to the narrow bank concept. First, critics point out that the asset restrictions imposed on narrow banks would prevent them from acting as intermediaries of funds between depositors and most borrowers. As noted above, many narrow bank proposals would require such banks to invest their deposits in safe, highly marketable assets such as those permitted for MMMFs. Narrow banks would therefore be largely or entirely barred from making commercial loans. As a result, critics warn that a banking system composed exclusively of narrow banks could not provide credit to small and midsized business firms that lack access to the capital markets and depend on banks as their primary source of outside credit.[93]

However, my two-tiered proposal would greatly reduce any disruption of the traditional role of banks in acting as intermediaries between depositors and bank-dependent firms, because my proposal would allow first-tier 'traditional' banks (primarily community-oriented banks) to continue making commercial loans that are funded by deposits. Community banks make most of their commercial loans in the form of longer-term 'relationship' loans to small and midsized firms. Community banks have significant advantages in making such loans, because (i) their main offices are located in the communities where they make most of their commercial loans and their employees are therefore well informed about the character, reputation, and skills of local business owners, (ii) they maintain greater continuity in their branch managers and loan officers, thereby creating stronger relationships with local business owners, and (iii) they typically provide greater flexibility to their loan officers and business customers.[94] Under my proposal, community banks could carry on their deposit-taking and lending activities as first-tier banking organizations without any change from current law, and their primary commercial lending customers would continue to be smaller, bank-dependent firms.

In contrast to community banks, most big banks do not make a substantial number of relationship loans to small firms. Instead, big banks primarily make loans to large and well-established firms. In addition, when big banks do provide credit to smaller firms they primarily do so through automated 'transaction-based' programs that (A) disburse loans in relatively small amounts (usually under USD100 000), (B) use centralized, impersonal approval methods based on credit scoring, and (C) enable loans to be securitized into asset-backed securities sold to investors in the capital markets.[95] Under my proposal, as indicated above, most large banks would operate as subsidiaries of second-tier 'non-traditional' banking organizations. Second-tier holding companies would conduct their business lending programs through nonbank finance subsidiaries that are funded by commercial paper and other debt instruments that are sold to investors in the capital markets. This operational structure should not create a substantial disincentive for the small business lending programs offered by big banks, because major segments of those programs (for example, business credit card loans) are already financed by the capital markets through securitization. Accordingly, my two-tier proposal should not cause a significant reduction in bank loans to bank-dependent firms, as big banks have already moved away from traditional relationship-based lending funded by deposits.

The second major criticism of the narrow bank proposal is that it would lack credibility because federal regulators would retain the inherent authority (whether explicit or implicit) to organize bailouts of major financial firms during periods of severe economic distress. Accordingly, some critics maintain that the narrow bank concept would simply shift the TBTF problem from the insured bank to its nonbank affiliates.[96] However, the force of this objection would be greatly diminished if Congress establishes a new comprehensive regime for regulating SIFIs as described above, including a special resolution process, SRCRs, consolidated supervision, and mandatory payment of SRIF insurance premiums. This proposed systemic-risk supervision regime would ensure that all nonbanking firms that might be considered for TBTF bailouts are designated and regulated as SIFIs. In addition, all SIFIs would be required to pay premiums to fund the SRIF, and a fund separate from the DIF would therefore exist to resolve the failure of major nonbanking firms.

Thus, the narrow bank structure would prevent FDIC-member banks that are controlled by SIFIs from transferring their safety net subsidies to their nonbank affiliates, and the systemic risk supervisory regime would force nonbank SIFIs to internalize the potential risks to financial and economic stability that result from their operations. In combination, both regulatory reforms should greatly reduce any TBTF subsidies that might otherwise be available to large nonbank firms.

The third principal objection to the narrow bank proposal is that it would place US FHCs at a significant disadvantage in competing with foreign universal banks that are not required to comply with similar constraints.[97] Again, there are persuasive rebuttals to this objection. For one thing, government officials in the UK are giving serious consideration to the possible adoption of a narrow banking structure based on a proposal developed by John Kay.[98] If the US and the UK both decided to implement a narrow banking structure (together with other needed systemic risk regulations), their combined leadership in global financial markets would place considerable pressure on other developed countries to adopt similar financial reforms.[99]

Moreover, the financial sector accounts for a large share of the domestic economies of the US and UK, and both economies have suffered severe injuries from two financial crises during the past decade (the dotcom-telecom bust and the subprime lending crisis). Both crises were produced by the same set of LCFIs that continue to dominate the financial systems in both nations. Accordingly, regardless of what other nations may do, the US and the UK have compelling national reasons to make sweeping changes to their financial systems in order to protect their domestic economies from the threat of a similar crisis in the future.[100]

Finally, the view that the US and the UK must refrain from implementing fundamental financial reforms until all other major developed nations have agreed to do so rests upon two deeply flawed assumptions: (i) the US and the UK must allow foreign nations with the weakest systems of financial regulation to dictate the level of supervisory constraints on LCFIs, and (ii) until a comprehensive international agreement on reform is achieved, the US and the UK must continue to provide TBTF bailouts and other safety net subsidies that impose huge costs, create moral hazard and distort economic incentives simply because other nations provide similar benefits to their LCFIs.[101] Both assumptions are unacceptable and must be rejected.

13.3. CONCLUSION

The TBTF policy remains 'the great unresolved problem of bank supervision,' more than a quarter century after the policy was invoked to justify the federal government's rescue of Continental Illinois in 1984.[102] The current financial crisis has proven, once again, that TBTF institutions 'present formidable risks to the federal safety net and are largely insulated from both market discipline and supervisory intervention.'[103] The crisis has also confirmed that TBTF institutions 'pursue riskier and opaque activities and . . . increase their leverage, through capital arbitrage, if necessary, as they grow in size and complexity.'[104] Accordingly, as I observed in 2002, 'fundamentally different approaches for regulating financial conglomerates and containing safety net subsidies are urgently needed.'[105]

To respond to that need, this chapter has outlined a reform program to shrink safety net subsidies, force SIFIs to internalize the risks and costs of their activities, and create a more level playing field between smaller, traditional banks and LCFIs. My five-part program would (i) strengthen existing statutory limits on the growth of LCFIs, (ii) create a special resolution process to manage the orderly liquidation or restructuring of failed SIFIs, (iii) establish a consolidated supervisory regime and special capital requirements for SIFIs, (iv) create a special insurance fund (the SRIF), financed by assessments on SIFIs, in order to protect taxpayers against the costs of resolving failed SIFIs, and (v) mandate a 'narrow bank' structure for FDIC-member banks owned by LCFIs for the purpose of insulating those banks and the DIF from the risks of nonbank affiliates.

In combination, my proposed reforms would strip away many of the safety net subsidies that are currently exploited by LCFIs and would subject them to the same type of market discipline that the capital markets have applied to commercial and industrial conglomerates over the past 30 years. Financial conglomerates have never demonstrated that they can provide beneficial services to their customers and attractive returns to their investors without relying on safety net subsidies and massive taxpayer-funded bailouts. It is long past time for LCFIs to prove – based on a true market test – that their claimed superiority is a reality and not a myth.

NOTES

1. Wilmarth, Jr., Arthur E. (2009), 'The Dark Side of Universal Banking: Financial Conglomerates and the Origins of the Subprime Financial Crisis', *Connecticut Law Review*, 963, 41, p. 966 n. 3.
2. Portions of this chapter are adapted from: Wilmarth, Jr., Arthur E. (2010), 'Reforming Financial Regulation to Address the Too-Big-To-Fail Problem', *Brooklyn Journal of International Law*, 35, pp. 707–83. This chapter includes developments through June 15, 2010. It therefore does not take account of charges made by the *Dodd-Frank Wall Street Reform and Consumer Protection Act*, which was signed into law by President Obama on July 21, 2010.
3. As used in this chapter, the term 'large, complex financial institution' (LCFI) includes major commercial banks, securities firms and insurance companies as well as

'universal banks' (i.e., financial conglomerates that have authority to engage, either directly or through affiliates, in a combination of banking, securities and insurance activities). *See* Wilmarth, *supra* note 1, at 968 n. 15.

4. For a preliminary survey of the causes and consequences of the financial crisis, see Wilmarth, *supra* note 2, pp. 718–47.
5. As I have argued previously, large financial conglomerates have never proven their ability to achieve superior performance without relying on the extensive TBTF subsidies they currently receive. *See* Wilmarth, *supra* note 2, pp. 740–44, 748–49.
6. Saunders, A., Smith, Roy C. and Walter, I. (2009), 'Enhanced Regulation of Large, Complex Financial Institutions' in *Restoring Financial Stability: How to Repair a Failed System*, New York: John Willy & Sons, Inc., pp. 143–47; Wilmarth, *supra* note 1, pp. 970–72, 994–1002, 1024–50; Kay, John (15 Sept. 2009), *Narrow Banking: The Reform of Financial Regulation*, pp. 12–16, 41–44, 86–88.
7. *Riegle-Neal Act*, §§ 101, 102, 108 Stat. 2340, 2345 (codified as amended in 12 U.S.C. §§ 1831u(b)(2), 1842(d)(2)). The Riegle-Neal Act permits a state to waive or relax, by statute, regulation or order, the 30 percent statewide concentration limit with respect to interstate mergers or acquisitions involving banks located in that state. *See* 12 U.S.C. §§ 1831u(b)(2)(D), 1842(d)(2)(D).
8. *See* 'Order Approving the Acquisition of a Savings Association and an Industrial Loan Company (Bank of America Corporation),' *Federal Reserve Bulletin* B13, B14 (Mar. 2009) [hereinafter FRB BofA-Merrill Order] (noting that thrifts and industrial banks '"are not banks" for purposes of the [Riegle-Neal] Act and its nationwide deposit cap').
9. 12 U.S.C. §§ 1831u(e), 1842(d)(5).
10. *See* 'Order Approving the Acquisition of a Savings Association and Other Nonbanking Activities (Bank of America Corporation),' *Federal Reserve Bulletin* C81–C82, C83 n.13 (Aug. 2008); FRB BofA-Merrill Order, *supra* note 8, at B13–B14, B14 n.6.
11. Adler, Joe (10 Dec. 2009), 'Thrift M&A Could Suffer As Frank Slams "Loophole"', *American Banker*, p. 1.
12. *See* 'Statement by the Board of Governors of the Federal Reserve System Regarding the Application and Notices by Wells Fargo & Company to Acquire Wachovia Corporation and Wachovia's Subsidiary Banks and Nonbanking Companies (Wells Fargo & Company)', *Federal Reserve Bulletin* B40, B41–42 (Mar. 2009) (determining that 'the combined organization would not control an amount of deposits that would exceed the nationwide deposit cap on consummation of the proposal'); *id.* at B48.
13. *See* Ackerman, Matt (28 Oct. 2008) 'Big 3 Deposit Share Approaches 33%', *American Banker*, p. 16.
14. Christie, Rebecca and Mattingly, Phil (4 March 2010), 'Volcker Rule' Draft Signals Obama Wants to Ease Market Impact', *Bloomberg.com*.
15. *Id.* (reporting that US banks held $10.4 trillion of liabilities, while Chase, BofA and Citigroup held liabilities of USD1.5 trillion, USD1.3 trillion and USD1 trillion, respectively).
16. *See supra* note 13 and accompanying text; Dobbs, Kevin (25 Nov. 2008), 'Even After Infusion, Citi Seen Needing Fix', *American Banker*, p. 1.
17. Hopkins, Cheyenne (25 Jan. 2010), 'Obama to Banks: Big Is Bad', *American Banker*, p. 22.
18. *See* Landy, Heather (30 Dec. 2009), 'Review/Preview: Goldman and Morgan Stanley Ditch Banking Script, So Far', *American Banker*, p. 1; *supra* note 16 and accompanying text.
19. FRB Governor Tarullo, Daniel K. (26 Feb. 2010), 'Financial Regulatory Reform', Speech at the US Monetary Policy Forum [hereinafter *Tarullo Regulatory Reform Speech*].
20. Blinder, Alan (Feb. 2010), 'Time for Financial Reform, Plan C', *The Economists' Voice*, Vol. 7, Issue 1, Article 5 p. 2. *See also* Senate Report No. 111-176, p. 4 (2010).
21. *See* Senate Report No. 111-176, p. 47.
22. *See*, e.g., Acharya, Viral V., Pedersen, Lasse, Philippon,Thomas and Richardson,

Matthew, 'Regulating Systemic Risk', in Viral V. Acharya and Matthew Richardson (eds), *Restoring Financial Stability: How to Repair a Failed System*, New York: John Wiley & Sons, Inc., 2009, pp. 283, 283–92.
23. *See* Manickavasagam, Malini and Ferullo, Mike (23 Mar. 2009), 'Regulatory Reform: Witnesses Warn Against Identifying Institutions as Systemically Significant', *Securities Regulation Law Report* (BNA), 41, p. 502.
24. *See* Sorkin, Andrew R. (2009), *Too Big To Fail: The Inside Story of How Wall Street and Washington Fought to Save the Financial System from Crisis – and Themselves*, New York: Viking, pp. 373–407, 513–34; Wilmarth, *supra* note 2, pp. 736–47.
25. *See* Allen Berger et al. (2008), 'How Do Large Banking Organizations Manage Their Capital Ratios?', *Journal of Financial Services Research*, 34, pp. 123, 138–39, 145; Wilmarth, *supra* note 2, pp. 742–43.
26. Thomson, James B. (2009), 'On Systemically Important Financial Institutions and Progressive Systemic Mitigation' (Fed. Reserve of Clev. Policy Discussion Paper No. 27), pp. 8–9.
27. In March 2010, Treasury assistant secretary Herbert Allison received a hostile reception when he claimed at a hearing before the Congressional Oversight Panel (COP) that '[t]here is no "too big to fail" guarantee on the part of the U.S. government.' Members of the COP responded to Mr. Allison's claim with derision and disbelief. COP member Damon Silvers declared, 'I do not understand why it is that the United States government cannot admit what everyone in the world knows.' Cheyenne Hopkins (5 Mar. 2010), 'Pandit Sees a New Citigroup, But Others Aren't Convinced', *American Banker*, p. 1.
28. *See* Morrison, Edward R. (2009), *Is the Bankruptcy Code an Adequate Mechanism for Resolving the Distress of Systemically Important Institutions?* 10–16 (Columbia Law & Economics Working Paper No. 362).
29. *See* Wilmarth, *supra* note 2, p. 757.
30. *See* Schooner, Heidi Mandanis (1998), 'Regulating Risk Not Function', *University of Cincinnati Law Review*, 66, pp. 441, 478–86.
31. Under current law, the FRB is required to rely 'to the fullest extent possible' on reports provided and examinations conducted by primary regulators of functionally regulated subsidiaries of BHCs and FHCs. The FRB has only limited authority to require reports from, to conduct examinations of, or to take enforcement actions against, functionally regulated subsidiaries of BHCs and FHCs. *See* 12 U.S.C. §§ 1844(c), 1844(e), 1844(g), 1848a; Carnell, Richard S., Macey, Jonathan R. and Miller, Geoffrey P. (2009), *The Law of Banking and Financial Institutions*, New York: Aspen Publishers, 4th Edn, pp. 457–60.
32. Tarullo, Daniel K. (2008), *Banking on Basel: The Future of International Financial Regulation*, 99–130 (Washington, DC: Peterson Institute for Int'l Economics).
33. For sources supporting the imposition of a leverage capital requirement, and noting the disparity between the asset-to-equity ratios at US commercial banks and the significantly higher (and more risky) ratios at US investment banks and European banks in 2007, see Blundell-Wignall, Adrian and Atkinson, Paul (2008), 'The Sub-prime Crisis: Causal Distortions and Regulatory Reform', in Paul Bloxham and Christopher Kent (eds), *Lessons from the Financial Turmoil of 2007 and 2008: Proceedings of Conference on 14–15 July 2008*, pp. 93–96.
34. *Tarullo Regulatory Reform Speech*, *supra* note 19.
35. For one approach to calculating SRCRs, see Acharya et al., 'Regulating Systemic Risk', *supra* note 22, at pp. 289–93.
36. *See* Wilmarth, *supra* note 2, pp. 731–33.
37. For discussion of proposals for a contingent capital requirement, see, e.g., Culp, Christopher L. (Fall 2009), 'Contingent Capital vs. Contingent Reverse Convertibles for Banks and Insurance Companies', *Journal of Applied Corporate Finance*, pp. 17, 23–27.
38. *See* Culp, *supra* note 37, p. 27.

39. Wilmarth, *supra* note 2, p. 7612. For another recent proposal that calls for managers and key employees to be receive part of their compensation in debt securities in order to encourage them to avoid excessive risk-taking, see Bebchuk, Lucian and Spamann, Holger (2010), 'Regulating Bankers', Pay', *Georgetown Law Journal*, 98, pp. 247, 283–86.
40. The following discussion of my proposal to establish a SRIF, funded by risk-based premiums paid by SIFIs, is adapted from Wilmarth, *supra* note 2, pp. 761–64.
41. *See* Wilmarth, *supra* note 2, pp. 737–38.
42. Acharya et al., 'Regulating Systemic Risk', *supra* note 22, at pp. 293–94.
43. A recent study concluded that market returns of the 100 largest banks, securities firms, insurers and hedge funds became 'highly interconnected,' and their risk exposures became 'highly interrelated,' during the current financial crisis as well as during (i) the dotcom-telecom bust of 2000–2002 and (ii) the crisis surrounding Russia's debt default and the threatened failure of Long-Term Capital Management, a major hedge fund, in 1998. Monica Billio et al. (2010), *Measuring Systemic Risk in the Finance and Insurance Sectors* (MIT Sloan Sch. Mgmt. Working Paper 4774-10), pp. 16–17, 40–47.
44. *See* Yap, Rodney and Pearson, Dave (11 May 2010), 'Subprime Mortgage-Related Losses Exceed USD1.77 Trillion', *Bloomberg News*.
45. Statement by FDIC Chairman Sheila C. Bair on 'The Causes and Current State of the Financial Crisis' before the Financial Crisis Inquiry Commission (14 Jan. 2010).
46. *Id.*
47. Acharya et al., 'Regulating Systemic Risk,' *supra* note 22, at 293–95.
48. 12 U.S.C. § 1823(c)(4)(G) (2006) (allowing the FDIC, with the concurrence of the Treasury Secretary and the FRB, to disregard the least-cost requirement for bank resolutions if the failure of a bank 'would have serious adverse effects on economic conditions or financial stability'). *See also* Carnell, Macey and Miller, *supra* note 31, pp. 731–32 (discussing 'systemic-risk exception').
49. Those asset guarantees protected shareholders and creditors of Citigroup and BofA and both companies' nonbank subsidiaries, as well as uninsured depositors and other creditors of both companies' subsidiary banks. *See* Press Release, Joint Statement by Treasury, Federal Reserve and the FDIC on Citigroup (23 Nov. 2008); Statement by FDIC Chairman Sheila C. Bair on 'Bank of America Acquisition of Merrill Lynch' before the House Committee on Oversight and Government Reform and the Subcommittee on Domestic Policy (11 Dec. 2009).
50. The least-cost test requires the FDIC to 'meet the obligation of the [FDIC] to provide insurance coverage for the insured deposits' in a failed bank by using the approach that is 'least costly to the [DIF].' 12 U.S.C. § 1823(c)(4)(A)(i), (ii) (2006).
51. *See* Cheryl Bolen et al., 'Regulatory Reform: White House Seeks Tough Limits on Size, Trading Activities of Large Financial Firms', 94 *Banking Rep.* (BNA) 127 (26 Jan. 2010).
52. Dennis, Brady (3 Feb. 2010), 'Volcker Urges Senators to Adopt Obama's Rules on Banking', *Washington Post*, at A11 (quoting testimony by Mr Volcker). *See also* Senate Report No. 111-176, at 8–9, 90–92 (2010).
53. Wilmarth, *supra* note 2, at n. 223 and accompanying text. *See* Carnell, Macey and Miller, *supra* note 31, pp. 130, 528–29.
54. The following discussion of my proposal for a two-tiered structure of bank regulation and deposit insurance is adapted from Wilmarth, *supra* note 2, pp. 764–79. I am indebted to Robert Litan for a number of the concepts incorporated in my two-tiered proposal. *See generally* Litan, Robert E. (1987), *What Should Banks Do?*, Washington, DC: Brookings Institution, 1987, pp. 164–89.
55. *See* 12 U.S.C. § 1843(c)(8) (2006); Carnell, Macey and Miller, *supra* note 35, at 442–44.
56. *See* Wilmarth, Jr., Arthur E. (2002), 'The Transformation of the U.S. Financial Services Industry, 1975–2000: Competition Consolidation, and Increased Risks,' *University of Illinois Law Review* 2002, pp. 225, 225–26 n. 30; Carnell, Macey and Miller, *supra* note 31, pp. 132–34.

57. *See* Wilmarth, *supra* note 2, p. 766 (discussing FAS 133).
58. For a discussion of the business strategies typically followed by community banks, see, e.g., Wilmarth, *supra* note 56, at 268–72.
59. Unfortunately, the *Gramm-Leach-Bliley Act* (GLBA) prohibits the FRB from approving any new 'closely related' activities for bank holding companies under Section 4(c)(8) of the BHC Act. *See* Carnell, Macey and Miller, *supra* note 31, p. 444. Congress should revise Section 4(c)(8) by authorizing the FRB to approve a limited range of new activities that are 'closely related' to the traditional banking functions of accepting deposits, extending credit, discounting negotiable instruments and providing fiduciary services. *See* Wilmarth, *supra* note 2, p. 767 n. 229.
60. 12 U.S.C. § 1843(k), (l) (2006). *See* Carnell, Macey and Miller, *supra* note 35, pp. 467–68.
61. *See* Carnell, Macey and Miller, *supra* note 35, pp. 468–70.
62. For a discussion of my reasons for proposing that commercial firms should be prohibited from owning industrial banks, see generally Wilmarth, Jr., Arthur E. (2007), 'Wal-Mart and the Separation of Banking and Commerce', *Connecticut Law Review*, 39, pp. 1543–44, 1554–1620.
63. *See* Wilmarth, *supra* note 2, p. 768.
64. *Cf.* Maxey, Daisy (2 Feb. 2010), 'Money Funds Exhale After New SEC Rules, But Should They', *Wall Street Journal*, at C9.
65. Reilly, David (3 Feb. 2010), 'Goldman Sachs Wimps Out in Buck-Breaking Brawl', *Bloomberg.com*.
66. *Id. See also* Kay, *supra* note 6, p. 65.
67. Reilly, *supra* note 65.
68. Reilly, *supra* note 65; Manickavasagam, Malini (22 Sept. 2009), 'Mutual Funds: Citing Stability, Treasury Allows Expiration of Money Market Fund Guarantee Program', 93 *Banking Report* (BNA) 508.
69. Quinn, Jane Bryant (29 July 2009), 'Money Funds Are Ripe for "Radical Surgery"', *Bloomberg.com*. *See also* Reilly, *supra* n. 65.
70. Quinn, *supra* note 69.
71. Quinn, *supra* note 69. *See* Group of Thirty (2009), *Financial Reform: A Framework for Financial Stability* 29.
72. Quinn, *supra* note 69; *See* Group of Thirty, *supra* note 71, at 29. *See also* Reilly, *supra* note 65; Kay, *supra* note 6, p. 65.
73. *See* Quinn, *supra* note 69 (describing strong opposition by Paul Schott Stevens, chairman of the Investment Company Institute (the trade association representing the mutual fund industry), against any rule requiring uninsured MMMFs to quote floating NAVs, because '[i]nvestors seeking guaranteed safety and soundness would migrate back to banks' and '[t]he remaining funds would become less attractive because of their fluctuating price').
74. Wilmarth, *supra* note 2, p. 771.
75. 12 U.S.C. §§ 371c, 371c-1 (2006).
76. Wilmarth, *supra* note 56, pp. 456–57, 472–73.
77. *See supra* notes 48–52 and accompanying text.
78. 12 U.S.C. § 1823(c)(4)(G)(ii) (2006).
79. Federal Deposit Ins. Corp., Options Paper, Aug. 2000, p. 33.
80. *Id.*
81. *See* Wilmarth, *supra* note 2, p. 766 (discussing FAS 133).
82. 12 U.S.C. § 1843(k)(4)(H), (I) (2006).
83. *See* Carnell, Macey and Miller, *supra* note 31, pp. 483–85 (explaining that 'through the merchant banking and insurance company investment provisions, [GLBA] allows significant nonfinancial affiliations' with banks).
84. *See* Wilmarth, *supra* note 56, pp. 330–32, 375–78.
85. Wilmarth, *supra* note 62, pp. 1581–82.
86. For further discussion of this argument, see *id.*, pp. 1588–1613.

87. *Id.* at 1569–70, 1584–93.
88. *Id.*, at 1590–93.
89. *See* Kay, *supra* note 6, pp. 57–59.
90. Wilmarth, *supra* note 2, pp. 740–44, 748–49.
91. Kaper, Stacy (2 Dec. 2009), 'Big Banks Face Most Pain Under House Bill', *American Banker*, p. 1 (quoting Ms. Petrou).
92. Wilmarth, *supra* note 56, p. 284. *See also* Wilmarth, *supra* note 2, p. 776.
93. *See*, e.g., Wallace, Neil (1996), 'Narrow Banking Meets the Diamond-Dybvig Model', *Quarterly Review*, 20, p. 3.
94. Wilmarth, *supra* note 56, pp. 261–66. *See also* Allen N. Berger et al. (2005), 'Does Function Follow Organizational Form? Evidence from the Lending Practices of Large and Small Banks,' *Journal of Financial Economics*, 76, pp. 237, 239–46, 254–62, 266.
95. Wilmarth, *supra* note 56, at pp. 264–66.
96. *See* Wilmarth, *supra* note 2, at p. 778.
97. *See* Kay, *supra* note 6, pp. 71–74; Wilmarth, *supra* note 2, at p. 778.
98. *See* Kay, *supra* note 6, pp. 51–69.
99. Kay, *supra* note 6, p. 74; Wilmarth, *supra* note 2, pp. 778–79. *See also* Tarullo, *supra* note 32, pp. 45–54 (describing how the US and UK reached agreement on risk-based bank capital rules and then pressured other developed nations to agree to the Basel international capital accord).
100. *See* e.g., Hoenig, Thomas M., President, Federal Reserve Bank of Kansas City (6 Aug. 2009), 'Leverage and Debt: The Impact of Today's Choices on Tomorrow', Speech at 2009 Annual Meeting of Kansas Bankers Association, pp. 4–10; Kay, *supra* note 6, at 14–17, 20–24, 28–31, 39–47, 57–58, 66–75, 86–87.
101. *See* e.g., Hoenig August 6, 2009 Speech, *supra* note 100, at pp. 4–10; Kay, *supra* note 6, at 42–46, 57–59, 66–75.
102. Wilmarth, *supra* note 56, p. 475. *See also id.* pp. 300–01, 314–15.
103. *Id.* at p. 476.
104. *Id.*
105. *Id.*

14. 'Too-big-to-fail' – can alternative resolution regimes really remedy systemic risk in large financial institutions' insolvency?

Jens-Hinrich Binder*

14.1. INTRODUCTION

Substantial fiscal costs have been incurred in the bailouts of financial institutions, deemed systemically important. In view of the moral hazard inevitably triggered by such operations among bank owners and bank creditors, improved resolution procedures for large, complex financial institutions (LCFIs) are clearly needed on the legislative agenda at both the national and international levels. International standard-setting bodies such as the Basel Committee,[1] the then Financial Stability Forum (now the Financial Stability Board),[2] the European Union[3] as well as national governments have announced initiatives to improve existing systems. With the passage of the *Banking Act 2009*, the UK has taken the lead and implemented a complete overhaul of its previous arrangements.[4] Germany, to give another example, has just followed with a reformed bank insolvency regime that came into force in January 2011.[5] Evidently, the key policy objective common to all such initiatives is to avoid the need for further bailouts of systemically important institutions, be it on the grounds of their size – i.e. motivated by 'too-big-to-fail' (TBTF) considerations – or their respective interconnectedness with other market participants is expected to trigger a domino effect upon formal closure and liquidation.

This chapter discusses the prospects and constraints on such concepts. While a detailed analysis of the vast range of technical problems associated with alternative resolution regimes is outside its scope, the chapter develops an assessment of such plans and the likelihood of their success. The question is central in the search for solutions to the TBTF problem more generally: If the answer is negative, that is, if *procedural* options, by their very nature, have to be ruled out as solutions in insolvency cases of LCFIs, remedies may only be found in *prudential* concepts, if at all.[6] Following a short analysis of the policy issues behind the trend towards resolution regimes tailored to the needs of LCFI insolvency, the key requirements to be fulfilled by such regimes will be assessed in more detail.

14.2. THE BACKGROUND

14.2.1. Fiscal Cost a Trigger of Insolvency Reform

Around the globe, emergency subsidies to the financial sector have been the method of choice to address the global financial crisis and its impact on the real economy.[7] The one notable exception where public financial assistance was denied – Lehman Brothers in September 2008 – clearly indicated that in environments of heightened instability, the outright liquidation of a large, complex institution is not really an option, in view of its impact on global financial stability. Subsidies have taken numerous forms, including emergency liquidity assistance, the purchase of equity capital by government agencies or emergency funds set up ad hoc, the purchase of distressed assets, guarantees for obligations in the inter-bank market, and even the outright nationalization of insolvent institutions by government agencies. The fiscal costs incurred by such interventions have been enormous and may rise further. To cite but one example, in 2009 the German Stabilization Fund, which is in charge of providing direct financial assistance to banking institutions under the emergency legislation enacted throughout the crisis,[8] experienced an annual deficit of EUR4.26 billion[9] mainly attributable to the Fund's losses in the case of the HypoRealEstate banking group, acquired by the Fund in October 2010.[10]

In addition to fiscal cost, deep entanglement of government institutions with the banking sector continues to be the consequence of public emergency intervention in many jurisdictions. Many national governments have built up significant shareholdings, as crisis resolution has been making use of corporate law instruments, e.g. the acquisition of shares, and the exercise of shareholder rights, rather than submitting the relevant institutions to formal resolution procedures. Established procedures for the resolution of insolvent institutions have not been applied, if not ignored altogether. Hence, in addition to the fiscal fallout of such policies, most, if not all programmes are struggling to resolve the inevitable moral hazard problem arising out of the support granted to the industry as a whole.

14.2.2. Systemic Risk – A Working Definition

Alternative resolution procedures of the sort discussed in this chapter are, or rather should be, designed to prevent the systemic implications that would arise in a way that avoids moral hazard to bank owners, management and creditors. The meaning of systemic risk, its causes and manifestations, is therefore crucial for the understanding of such procedures; indeed, the capacity to contain systemic implications is the very standard by which they have to be measured. Even prior to the financial crisis of 2008–10, the concept of systemic risk and its constitutive elements in connection with the insolvency of major participants in the financial markets had been addressed extensively by both academics and through the development of international standards.[11]

Two such findings are of particular importance: first, empirical research has helped to qualify the classic assumption that depositor runs on insolvent banks may give rise to systemic runs into currency and thus threaten financial stability regardless of the macroeconomic situation. In fact, it would appear that depositors, facing a classic prisoners' dilemma, may indeed initiate a run on a bank they perceive to be at risk of failure. But this does *not* automatically result in widespread distrust in the stability of savings across the market, in particular not where credible safety nets are in place.[12] To be sure, empirical studies to that effect have so far been conducted only in the US, but their findings are consistent with observations made in other jurisdictions.[13] Under normal conditions, incidents of insolvency of even medium-sized financial institutions do not warrant an exemption from the usual market mechanisms that will penalize inefficient producers by loss or failure.

Secondly, even in an otherwise stable market, contagious effects of an individual firm's insolvency may arise from that firm's participation in the inter-bank market, and especially in payment and securities settlement systems. As systemic risk in that context can occur even in the case of small- or medium-sized firms, all procedural rules in the applicable regime, be they located in general insolvency law or in special insolvency procedures for banks or financial institutions more generally, need to make provision for the protection of such systems. This, again, does not require *per se* insolvent institutions to be kept operational at all costs, but can be effectively addressed through appropriate amendments in the relevant provisions applicable to procedural safeguards in the opening of formal insolvency procedures and the legal framework for the realization of the assets at the dissolution stage.

In view of these findings, and given the drastic illustration provided especially by the Lehman Brothers failure in 2008, it is certainly not necessary to elaborate in great detail on what constitutes systemic risk, its causes and implications in this chapter. While a clear-cut definition and methodical devices to measure systemic risk still remain to be developed,[14] it is sufficient to define, for the present purposes, systemic risk as a multi-faceted phenomenon, which is connected with: (1) the size of the institution involved, (2) the complexity of its organization and business structure, (3) the degree of interconnectedness of the relevant institution with other market participants, in particular through payment systems, the inter-bank money market, and financial derivatives contracts, and (4) the overall market conditions: In sound and stable financial markets, only a failure of a very large institution may be considered too big for the institution to be submitted to orderly resolution procedures, whereas in the midst of a financial crisis, even smaller incidents, of the size of, say, Northern Rock, may cause policymakers to intervene by way of open financial assistance.

14.3. THE AGENDA

14.3.1. Requirements for Bank Insolvency Procedures Generally

Based on the analysis above, a number of structural principles can be identified that should be satisfied by *any* procedural regime applicable to banks and other financial institutions. Different considerations apply under normal market conditions on the one hand and in circumstances where the application of the usual procedures could lead to consequences that may compromise systemic stability on the other hand. Although the chapter focuses on the latter, it is nonetheless appropriate to examine the key principles applicable to the resolution of financial institution insolvencies, where financial support for expensive reorganizations usually will be neither available nor necessary to resolve the individual case and prevent systemic implications.

In the event of a small- or medium-sized insolvency, it is crucial that such problems are identified, and responded to, promptly, decisively, comprehensively and in a way that is proportional to the circumstances.[15] Corrective action will usually be authorized under the relevant statutory framework for banking regulation. Such measures will be adopted by the responsible supervisory authority, and thus be governed by administrative law, not by the general laws of insolvency.[16] From a functional perspective, external supervisory action taken at this stage, in addition to its *administrative* character, bears a *semi-corporate* nature. At this stage, the supervisory authority assumes functions that are exercised exclusively by directors and managers in non-financial companies. Their mandate includes the obligation to monitor the firm's financial performance, to respond to identified problems and to keep the firm in operation. If, and to the extent that, a supervisory authority intervenes and prescribes specific measures to be adopted within the firm,[17] it acts in a capacity similar to that of a non-executive director who can influence fundamental business decisions, but is not involved in the actual management.[18]

Speed, effectiveness, and comprehensiveness are also the governing principles for the next stage, where isolated efforts for corrective action are no longer appropriate in view of the relevant firm's deteriorated financial position. This stage will be invoked in cases where the relevant institution has already become insolvent or is likely to become insolvent shortly (imminent insolvency). That could mean that the bank is unable to pay its debts as they fall due *and* are actually called in for payment or to be expected to be so called in within a foreshortened period of time (illiquidity, or cash-flow insolvency). At this stage, corrective measures adopted purely on an inter-partes approach – i.e., imposed and enforced by the supervisory authority vis-à-vis the relevant institution – are no longer commensurate to the severity of the institution's financial position. This is so because any such measure bears the risk that, if it fails to reach its objective, the financial interests of third parties – notably the firm's creditors – will suffer the loss of all or part of the economic value of their claims against the firm.

General insolvency law usually mandates the assumption of control over distressed firms by some sort of insolvency official as soon as a trigger event – frequently defined by reference to either the balance-sheet test, or the cash-flow test, or both – has occurred.[19] Not infrequently, duty is also imposed on the responsible management to petition for the initiation of insolvency procedures in those circumstances, failure to comply with which will result in personal liability.[20] To the extent that such mechanisms do not apply to financial institutions – e.g., because they are subject to a specialized insolvency regime – the applicable law must ensure that equivalent safeguards are in place in order to prevent further losses throughout the reorganization procedure. For example, legislation may provide for some sort of a moratorium, which will usually encompass both a ban on all payments and a stay of proceedings and enforcements against it. Moratoria of that sort usually parallel similar mechanisms under general insolvency legislation, which frequently provides for a freeze of assets upon the petition for the opening of insolvency proceedings and prior to the insolvency court's decision if, and to what end, such proceedings are to be initiated.[21]

Unlike the insolvency of a non-financial firm, however, a moratorium respecting a financial institution, while beneficial as an effective mechanism against the risk of a customer run, the default on payments to other market participants will immediately trigger the complete breakdown of the institution's relationships with those actors. The result is usually an accelerated loss of value of financial contracts. Close-out and/or netting provisions frequently used in standard master agreements for derivatives contracts and clearing try to protect the respective counterparties precisely against the fallout of forced interruptions in their contractual relationships against insolvent institutions. Those features have long been recognized as insolvency-proof by international standards and as a legitimate tool for the reduction of systemic risk in LCFI insolvency.[22] As a result, any moratorium or similar measure will usually trigger the right of counterparties to close-out pending contracts and claim their respective net position against the failing institution. This will abruptly end that institution's trading activities, but also cause substantial havoc in the derivatives markets if the relevant institution's market share is large. Hence, a moratorium in the context of the insolvency of a financial institution can hardly ever serve as a restructuring tool. Rather, it is often confined to a purely conservatory function as part of the preparation of ensuing liquidation procedures.[23] If at all feasible, restructuring efforts must therefore be implemented within a very short timeframe, preferably outside normal trading hours.[24] This latter requirement also helps to mitigate the impact of any transfer of rights and obligations on the payment and securities settlement systems in which the delinquent firm participates.

Once financial problems within an institution have matured to a stage where restructuring is no longer feasible, liquidation is usually the only realistic option absent extraordinary measures, such as open bank assistance. 'Liquidation' in this context means the collection and unwinding of the institution's assets and distribution of the proceeds to its creditors, regardless of the form this may take (and including, e.g. a sale of parts of the business to competitors, a transfer of insured deposits to another institution under the assistance of the relevant deposit insurance system, etc . . .). Unlike the earlier stages discussed above, speed is less important. In fact, a timeframe that respects the duration of performing long-term contracts with third parties (e.g. borrowers) and thus protects rather than terminates an earning asset, may prove more advantageous than outright and accelerated unwinding of all contractual relationships.[25]

14.3.2. The (not so) Special Case: Structural Principles for Crisis Management in Circumstances of Systemic Distress

Compared to the substantive requirements for bank insolvency regimes generally, insolvency management in circumstances where an individual failure may have systemic implications is less different than may be expected. This is certainly true for the restructuring of insolvent institutions, whose closure appears to be inopportune in view of its size or the significance of its operations in payment and/or securities settlement systems. Just as any other insolvent financial institution, an institution that is considered TBTF or 'too-connected-to-fail' realistically has to be restructured within an extremely short time. In order to minimize the systemic impact, no formal action involving adjustments in the relevant firm's contractual obligations to third parties should be taken within normal trading hours.

The size and complexity of large international financial institutions and their trading activities will create significant obstacles to restructurings. This is because any restructuring efforts, regardless of their nature – e.g., through an assisted merger or by way of a recapitalization that may be facilitated by temporary financial support from a government agency – will be difficult to plan and execute within the time available. Also, the size of a bank's positions in inter-bank markets, especially in the markets for financial derivatives, will make it difficult to compensate counterparty losses in a way that avoids a domino effect. Another problem might be a breakdown in global derivatives markets and given the complexity of pending legal relationships it might be difficult to assess, let alone disentangle, in a reliable way. This explains why – even prior to the present crisis – the support of emergency financial assistance to LCFI has come to be accepted as probably inevitable in times of financial distress,[26] notwithstanding the controversy over the justification of TBTF exemptions to insolvency liquidation more generally.[27] At least, it indicates that, if successful restructurings of LCFI are to be achieved at all, a strong and capable actor (not necessarily the government or its agencies) must be present to provide temporary financial support to the transaction, and thus to mitigate counter-party risk in systemically important contracts.

As discussed before, however, *if* market economies resort to open bank assistance in order to avoid or to mitigate systemic risk, a key concern must be to maintain or substitute the incentive structure associated with the application of the general or specialized insolvency regimes to the extent possible.[28] Preferably, a combination of temporary financial support *and* formal resolution approaches should be implemented. Such alternative regimes, involving, for example, bridge bank mechanisms[29] or the outright transfer of assets and liabilities to a private sector acquirer through purchase-and-assumptions transactions of the sort known under US banking laws for some time,[30] will almost certainly require significant financial support in the short run. But they will, at least, reduce the adverse incentives inevitably associated with the traditional concept of implicit TBTF exemptions in bank insolvency regimes, associated with ad hoc emergency support granted out of public funds in times of systemic distress.

14.4. ALTERNATIVE RESOLUTION PROCEDURES – THE GERMAN REFORMS

The reform of bank insolvency management in Germany provides a good illustration of the technical options available for LCFI insolvency and addresses the structural problems discussed above. Essentially, the reform provides for a two-stage model to be implemented as a substitute for ordinary liquidation procedures under the general statutory framework for banking and insolvency law[31] if an institution is considered too important for outright closure, in view of the systemic impact that would be triggered by a moratorium on payments. The first stage presents a legal framework for autonomous, but court-supervised restructuring efforts to be implemented at the initiative of the relevant institution. The second stage process provides for a transfer of all or part of the insolvent institution's assets and liabilities to a third party acquirer, be it a competitor institution or a bridge bank to be established on the initiative of the supervisory authority.

14.4.1. 'Stage 1': Semi-autonomous Restructuring Efforts with or without Third-party Effects

The first stage relies on the concept of reorganization measures implemented by the relevant institution itself, albeit under the control of the supervisory authority. In this context, the reform provides for two alternatives, to be selected according to the urgency of the relevant case. A special rehabilitation procedure (the 'Sanierungsverfahren') will be available if a credit institution appears to be in need of reorganization. This approach is taken if such a reorganization can be realized through internal measures without an effect on creditors and other third parties. The procedure is initiated by the relevant institution itself by lodging an application with the supervisory authority, presenting a 'rehabilitation plan', and nominating a 'rehabilitation adviser', who will execute the plan within the institution.[32] The supervisory authority will then assess the plan and, if it is approved, apply to a court of appeals,[33] which will then decide on the execution of the plan and appoint the rehabilitation adviser.[34] If, however, internal measures do not appear to be promising, the relevant institution may instead apply for the commencement of a 'reorganization procedure', which is designed to include a modification of third-party rights and entitlements. Similar to the 'rehabilitation procedure', the reorganization will be based on a formal plan (the 'reorganization plan') to be developed by a 'reorganization adviser', similar to an insolvency administrator under general insolvency law appointed by the court.[35] The adviser will also be responsible for the execution of the plan, which has to be authorized by the court. In this process, creditors are grouped together as they would be under general insolvency law. In particular, the plan may provide for a debt-to-equity swap. Both creditors and existing shareholders will have a right to vote on the plan, with cram-down provisions in place to prevent obstruction.[36] In fact, the entire procedure has been modelled after the 'Insolvenzplanverfahren', the equivalent of US-style Chapter 11 bankruptcy procedures, provided under general German insolvency law.[37] It is thus an attempt to adapt an ordinary, court-supervised restructuring regime to the technical needs of bank insolvencies.

However, whether this mechanism is really suitable for application to a systemically important institution – let alone an institution that forms part of a large, complex banking group – appears open to doubt. Given the sheer complexity of the business operations in such circumstances, there is little reason to be overly optimistic. Importantly, the procedure is public and thus prone to adverse market reactions and, possibly, creditor runs. Even though an outright closure may be avoided, the drafting, and dispute settlement inevitably associated with the proposed regime will most probably require an amount of time for negotiations. Not surprisingly, for a larger institution active in volatile markets, this approach may simply not be available. In short, this regime will most likely be subject to much the same difficulties as any formalized procedure with creditor participation.[38]

In our view, too little attention has been paid to the problems created by close-out netting provisions and cross-default arrangements in financial derivatives contracts. If an institution is subjected to formal reorganization this very decision is likely to be treated as a trigger event for the termination of pending derivatives contracts. This may not only result in the total disruption of a significant part of an institution's commercial relationships with other market participants, but also in massive losses to the institution itself and, potentially, in similar disruptive effects on the relevant counterparties as well.[39] In short, the application of this mechanism is rather likely to trigger precisely the sort of consequences that would be brought about by the application of ordinary resolution regimes. While the new law seeks to prevent this by suspending the termination of contracts in response to an institution's application for the commencement of such proceedings by one business day,[40] it remains at least doubtful if that clause will be recognized by the jurisdictions governing the usual master agreements. And even *if* that was the case, a mere suspension of close-out and netting provisions arguably fails to resolve the implications that may arise out of the losses incurred by the relevant counterparties as a result of a subsequent failure of the restructuring efforts.[41]

14.4.2. 'Stage 2': Transfer Order to be Imposed by Supervisory Authority

If either a 'rehabilitation plan' or a 'reorganization plan' fails to achieve its objectives, or if a reorganization procedure appears inappropriate in view of the size of the financial problems, the second stage of the reformed framework will then become relevant. That stage involves the transfer ('Übertragungsanordnung') of all or parts of the insolvent institution's assets and liabilities to another body corporate, which may be a competitor or indeed a government agency. Alternatively, a spin-off of part of the institution's assets and liabilities may be accomplished. In either case, the process is initiated with an order by the Supervisory Authority. The acquirer of the 'good bank' will then continue trading, but the remaining 'bad bank' will be wound up in insolvency proceedings under general insolvency law.[42] This procedure bears no resemblance to existing concepts of general insolvency legislation, but is clearly influenced by the UK *Banking Act 2009*. Under that Act, the Bank of England, as part of its 'stabilization powers' to be used to address systemic risk, may order the transfer of systemically relevant assets and liabilities to a third party or a 'bridge bank' established by the Bank of England. That process facilitates a restructuring (with or without public financial assistance) while the relevant institution's business is kept open as a going concern.[43] Such transactions can be implemented virtually over a weekend and thus minimizes the impact of the failure on customers, the payments and settlement system and any systemically relevant financial contracts with other market participants. This occurs while maintaining the usual consequences of insolvency liquidation on the legal positions of existing management and shareholders. Unlike conventional, court-supervised restructuring procedures, this regime seeks to accommodate the needs of a bank failure by avoiding not just the outright closure. It also interferes with negotiations between creditors and shareholders.[44] In its essence, the model differentiates between the corporate entity and its systemically relevant business. The former, of course, is subjected to ordinary insolvency proceedings, while the latter is being transferred to an entity which will carry on servicing the relevant contracts.

In principle, rather similar characteristics are present in the reformed German procedure. Just like the UK model, the principal objective is to resolve insolvencies while avoiding the disruptive impact of a closure on customers and markets. While it is too early to present a definite assessment of the practicality and effectiveness of the new regime, the new procedural framework certainly brings German law in line with the approach followed by a growing number of important financial jurisdictions.[45] In this regard, the existence of the proposed Bank Restructuring Fund helps to provide financial assistance to be funded exclusively by the market participants themselves.[46] It may also be a valuable addition to the existence of a bridge bank mechanism as such, since any successful restructuring of a LCFI as a going concern will require substantial temporary funding, at least until a private sector purchaser can be found.

With regard to the safeguards for systemically important financial contracts, however, the new regime compares less favourably. Under the new law, contractual relationships to which the relevant institution is a party may not be terminated on the occasion of a transfer order or a spin-off under the regime.[47] If the counterparties to such contracts nonetheless exercise a right to terminate the contract, the supervisory authority may transfer the contract back to the original bank, so that the counterparty will receive effectively nothing.[48] Thus, counterparties may still have sufficient incentives to terminate their respective positions. And, if the law governing the respective contract fails to recognize the prohibition under German banking law, it may still be able to do so. The result would be a breakdown in the relevant institution's contractual relationships in the inter-bank market and, possibly, a significant loss in its own financial position. Outside the institution, the execution of termination rights could trigger severe repercussions in the markets more generally.[49] Following this approach, the reformed German model clearly falls still short of the growing international consensus in some important areas. A short-term suspension of derivatives contracts, coupled with the transfer of rights and obligations under systemically important financial contracts to a solvent acquirer, has come to be recognized as a workable solution to the problems created by close-out netting provisions in the management of LCFI insolvency.[50]

That said it should be noted that there are some important considerations. Bridge bank solutions in general and technical instruments to protect, and transfer, the rights and obligations of insolvent counterparties to financial derivatives contracts subject to commonplace master agreements have not been really tested particularly in the case of a truly large insolvent financial institution, or group of institutions, with a significant stake in global derivatives markets. Even *if* the acquisition of the relevant contractual positions by a solvent third party could be financed, e.g. by a vehicle such as the German Restructuring Fund for Credit Institutions or by a national deposit insurer, it remains difficult to predict whether a limited period of, say, a weekend or a few business days provides sufficient time for the preparation and execution of that sort of transaction given the size and complexity of the relevant institution's positions.

14.5. CONCLUSION

The recent German reform, as well as the British changes implemented in 2009, certainly do present a number of interesting formulations. This is particularly the case for more conventional procedures, but this also extends to alternative ones to avoid the closure of systemically relevant banks. This is done by transferring the relevant business to new providers, with or without public financial support. Bridge banks, in particular, are becoming increasingly popular and may play an important role in reducing both the systemic impact and the fiscal cost of individual failures.

However, there is reason to believe that neither of the three aspects of systemic risk – *size and complexity*, the *degree of interconnectedness*, and *market conditions* – can be expected to be remedied through improved resolution procedures alone. To note, the *size* of the firm may prevent the implementation of a successful restructuring plan simply because the financial basis for the on-going operation of relevant business lines. This is because the provision of payments and bank accounts may not be available, particularly in situations where customer confidence has already deteriorated. Perhaps even more importantly, the technicalities of standard market contracts, in particular close-out netting and cross-default, cast doubts on the suitability even of alternative resolution procedures, such as transfer orders, in cases of LCFIs. For similar reasons, *complexity* and *interconnectedness* probably will create severe obstacles to all procedural solutions with creditor and shareholder participation. If a restructuring relies on mutual agreement among stakeholders, the restructuring process simply will take far more time to implement than what could be available. This is particularly relevant when markets are already in turmoil. And, even without creditor participation, the drafting process, as well as the financial support required to safeguard the operation, may simply be too difficult to accomplish within the necessary short timeframe.

In summary, a rather cautious conclusion seems warranted. Alternative procedures can provide some help in expanding the supervisory toolbox. This is particularly the case when medium-sized insolvencies occur in distressed markets, where similar results would not be feasible by using more traditional formal insolvency procedures and/or market-driven rescue operations. At the very essence of the problem, however, particularly for large, potentially international banking institutions and banking groups, the prospects seem far less bright. The sheer complexity of the business and the contractual relationships to third parties may well render impossible a formalized procedure which involves elements of creditors and shareholder participation. Probably the most fundamental problem common to the different models, though, is their vulnerability to the systemic repercussions associated with any form of formalized insolvency procedure. This is particularly the case with respect to the still unresolved issue of preventing the execution of close-out netting and cross-default provisions in standard market agreements.

NOTES

* For most valuable comments and discussions, the author would like to thank organizers and participants of the Symposium on 'Managing Systemic Risk' at the University of Warwick law school in April 2010, as well as participants of staff seminars with Deutsche Bundesbank economists and lawyers in Frankfurt in November 2008 and the Federal Ministry of Finance in Berlin in January 2010, of a workshop at the European Business School Departments of Law and Economics and Finance, Accounting and Real Estate in October 2009, and of the European Master in Law & Economics (EMLE) Midterm Meeting at the University of Hamburg in February 2009.

1. Basel Committee on Banking Supervision (March 2010), 'Report and recommendations of the Cross-border Bank Resolution Group', www.bis.org/publ/bcbs169.pdf, accessed 30 July 2010.
2. Financial Stability Forum (April 2008), 'Report of the Financial Stability Forum on Enhancing Market and Institutional Resilience', pp. 49–52, www.fsforum.org/publications/r_0804.pdf; *id.*, 'Follow Up on Implementation' (October 2008), www.fsforum.org/press/pr_081009f.pdf, pp. 26–7.
3. 'On the recent public consultation regarding a proposed EU framework for Cross-Border Crisis Management in the Banking Sector', http://ec.europa.eu/internal_market/consultations/2009/banking_crisis_management_en.htm.
4. Walker, George A. (2009), 'Bank crisis resolution: The Banking Act 2009', *Financial Crisis Management and Bank Resolution* (LaBrosse, J. R., R. Olivares-Caminal, and D. Singh, eds), pp. 187–202.
5. Law on the restructuring and orderly resolution of credit institutions, on the creation of a Restructuring Fund, and on the prolongation of the limitation period for directors' and officers' liability [Gesetz zur Restrukturierung und geordneten Abwicklung von Kreditinstituten, zur Errichtung eines Restrukturierungsfonds für Kreditinstitute und zur Verlängerung der Verjährungsfrist der aktienrechtlichen Organhaftung (Restrukturierungsgesetz)], 9 December 2010, BGBl. I at 1900. The Law passed the first chamber of parliament on 28 October 2010.
6. Claessens, S., R. J. Herring, and D. Schoenmaker (2010), 'A Safer World Financial System: Improving The Resolution Of Systemic Institutions', *Geneva Reports on the World Economy*, 12.
7. Panetta, F. et al. (2009), 'An assessment of financial sector rescue programmes', *BIS Papers*, 48, www.bis.org/publ/bppdf/bispap48.pdf.
8. The *Finanzmarktstabilisierungsfonds* (hereafter: 'the Stabilization Fund') was established under an emergency Act, entitled *Finanzmarktstabilisierungsgesetz* (Act on the Implementation of Measures for the Stabilization of Financial Markets, hereafter: 'the Stabilization Act'), as a vehicle to provide financial assistance in October 2008 [Gesetz zur Umsetzung eines Maßnahmenpakets zur Stabilisierung des Finanzmarktes (Finanzmarktstabilisierungsgesetz) – FMStG of 17 October 2008, BGBl. I 1982].

9. 'Bundesanstalt für Finanzmarktstabilisierung' (21 May 2010), www.soffin.de/de/presse/pressemitteilungen/2010/20100521_pressenotiz_soffin.html.
10. *See*, for further information on this case and other engagements, the Fund's website at www.soffin.de.
11. De Bandt, O. and P. Hartmann (November 2000), 'Systemic Risk: A Survey', *European Central Bank Working Paper* 135, www.ecb.int/pub/pdf/scpwps/ecbwp035.pdf.
12. Diamond, D. M. and P. H. Dybvig (1983), 'Bank Runs, Deposit Insurance, and Liquidity', 91 *J. Pol. Econ.* 401.
13. Binder, J. (2005) *Bankeninsolvenzen im Spannungsfeld zwischen Bankaufsichts- und Insolvenzrecht*, p. 116.
14. Huang, X., H. Zhou, and H. Zhu, 'A Framework for Assessing the Systemic Risk of Major Financial Institutions', *Bank for International Settlements Working Paper*, 281 (April 2009), www.bis.org/publ/work281.pdf.
15. Basel Committee on Banking Supervision (March 2002), 'Supervisory Guidance on Dealing with Weak Banks, Report of the Task Force on Dealing with Weak Banks', www.bis.org/publ/bcbs88.pdf, pp. 14, 68; Asser, T. M. C. (2001), *Legal Aspects of Regulatory Treatment of Banks in Distress*, pp. 67–8.
16. Asser, T. (2001), *Legal Aspects of Regulatory Treatment of Banks in Distress*, pp. 72–6.
17. *Ibid.*, pp. 59–61, 78–88.
18. Binder, J. (2005), *Bankeninsolvenzen im Spannungsfeld zwischen Bankaufsichts- und Insolvenzrecht*, p. 290.
19. World Bank (2001), *Principles and Guidelines for Effective Insolvency and Creditor Rights Systems*, p. 99, www.worldbank.org/ifa/ipg_eng.pdf.
20. Germany: § 15a Insolvenzordnung [Insolvency Act].
21. World Bank (2001), *Principles and Guidelines for Effective Insolvency and Creditor Rights Systems*, p. 94, www.worldbank.org/ifa/ipg_eng.pdf.
22. Basel Committee on Banking Supervision, *Report and Recommendations of the Cross-Border Bank Resolution Group*, op. cit. (n. 1), pp. 105–14; Bliss, R. R. and G. G. Kaufman (2006), 'Derivatives and systemic risk: Netting, collateral, and closeout', 2 *J. Fin. Stability* 55.
23. Asser, T. (2001), *Legal Aspects of Regulatory Treatment of Banks in Distress*, p. 95.
24. Binder, J. (2005), *Bankeninsolvenzen im Spannungsfeld zwischen Bankaufsichts- und Insolvenzrecht*, pp. 543–4, 564 and Hadjiemmanuil, Christos (2004), *Bank Resolution Policy and the Organization of Bank Insolvency Proceedings: Critical Dilemmas*, in: Who Pays for Bank Insolvency? 272 Mayes, D. G. and A. Liuksila (2003), *Who Pays for Bank Insolvency*, Basingstoke: Palgrave, p. 296.
25. Murton, A. J. (1989), 'Bank Intermediation, Bank Runs, and Deposit Insurance', *FDIC Banking Rev.*, pp. 397, 399.
26. OECD (1997), *Regulatory Reform in the Financial Services Industry*, pp. 27, 37–8.
27. Goodhart, C. and G. Illing (2002), 'Myths about the Lender of Last Resort', *Financial Crises, Contagion, and the Lender of Last Resort*, pp. 227, 241 and G. G. Kaufman (1990), 'Are Some Banks Too Large to Fail?', 8 *Contemp. Pol'y Issues*, 1.
28. Asser, T. (2001), *Legal Aspects of Regulatory Treatment of Banks in Distress*, pp. 92–3.
29. Asser, T. (2001), *Legal Aspects of Regulatory Treatment of Banks in Distress*, pp. 144–7; LaBrosse, J. R. (2009), 'International Experience and Policy Issues in the Growing Use of Bridge Banks', *Financial Crisis Management and Bank Resolution* (LaBrosse, J. R., R. Olivares-Caminal, and D. Singh, eds), p. 217.
30. 12 U.S.C. 1823(c)(2).
31. Under the reformed regime, credit institutions licensed and supervised by the German authorities will continue to be subject to general insolvency law, albeit with significant modifications throughout the initial stadium of formal insolvency resolution, which are beyond the scope of the present chapter.
32. Law on the Reorganization of Credit Institutions (Gesetz zur Reorganisation von Kreditinstituten – Kreditinstitute-Reorganisationsgesetz), § 2(1)–(2).
33. *Ibid.*, § 2(3).

34. *Ibid.*, § 3.
35. *Ibid.*, § 7, 4.
36. *Ibid.*, §§ 9, 12, 13–17, 19–23.
37. Insolvenzordnung, §§ 217–69.
38. Ayotte and Skeel, op. cit. (n. 26).
39. International Swap Dealers Association (1992), *Master Agreement*, § 5(a)(vii).
40. Law on the Reorganization of Credit Institutions (Gesetz zur Reorganisation von Kreditinstituten – Kreditinstitute-Reorganisationsgesetz), § 13.
41. *Cf.*, in this context, the critical assessment of the proposed provision presented by the International Swap Dealers' Association in the consultation process (letter of 19 July 2010, available at www.isda.org/speeches/pdf/Germany_ISDAComments_RestructuringAct_Jul10.pdf), pp. 4–6.
42. Reformed Banking Law (Kreditwesengesetz), *supra* (n. 5), §§ 48a–s.
43. *Banking Act* (2009) c. 1, ss. 10 (transfer to private purchaser), 11 (transfer to bridge bank), 7 (general conditions required), 8 (specific conditions for transfers to private sector purchaser and bridge bank).
44. *Supra*, note 4 and accompanying text.
45. LaBrosse, J. R. (2009), 'International Experience and Policy Issues in the Growing Use of Bridge Banks', *Financial Crisis Management and Bank Resolution* (LaBrosse, J. R., R. Olivares-Caminal, and D. Singh, eds), p. 217.
46. Law on the Establishment of a Restructuring Fund for Credit Institutions ("Gesetz zur Errichtung eines Restrukturierungsfonds für Kreditinstitute – Restrukturierungsfondsgesetz") (*supra*, n. 5).
47. *Reformed Banking Act* (Kreditwesengesetz), *supra* (n. 5), § 48g(6).
48. *Ibid.*, § 48j.
49. ISDA, loc. cit. (n. 41) (criticizing the proposed concept as unreliable and impractical).
50. Basel Committee on Banking Supervision, *Report and recommendations of the Cross-border Bank Resolution Group*, op. cit. (n. 1), pp. 115–19.

15. To divest or not to divest: that is the question . . .

Ioannis Kokkoris

> In Europe the provision of subsidies and other forms of aid by the State still forms an accepted part, indeed often a central part, of economic policy, even in those countries most attached to the model of the free market. Yet the very existence of State Aid poses obvious problems for the single market for which the European Union is striving. The EC law of State Aid therefore raises issues of the greatest social, economic and political importance as well as a great variety of difficult and fascinating legal problems. Seldom have the rules of Community law on State Aid been invoked more frequently than at present. Seldom has the definition of a State Aid presented more difficulty.[1]

15.1. INTRODUCTION

Different types of laws affect the conditions or environment of competition within and between member states. 'Competition law', therefore, potentially has a very wide scope, encompassing all laws that determine the conditions of competition.[2] If a member state adopts a system of competition law, that system can be characterized as a national interest in the sense that the State believes that competition and its regulation serve values and interests deemed important for domestic and international reasons. The notion of competition law as a national interest corresponds with the growth of competition law systems in many liberal, democratic sovereign states. Competition law has become part of the capitalist ethos in many democratic societies, and serves as a national interest in a number of ways.

This chapter will present a brief account of State Aid legislation in the EU. Then it shall discuss some controversial specific issues related to the enforcement of State Aid legislation. Finally the chapter focuses on the impact that the recent financial crisis had on the enforcement of State Aid legislation.

15.2. STATE AID LEGISLATION

The purpose for which aid is granted will be considered for the purpose of applying the derogations provided for under Article 107(2) and (3) TFEU (Treaty for the Functioning of the European Union).[3] Article 107(1) aims at the prevention of State Aid affecting competition,[4] while Article 107(2) and (3) allows for specific policy objectives being considered for the approval of an aid measure. In *Italy v. Commission* the European Court of Justice (ECJ) developed its effects-based approach, arguing that 'Article 107 does not distinguish between the measures of state intervention concerned by reference to their causes or aims but define them in relation to their effects'.[5]

Under the Treaty, the EU Commission ('the Commission') is given the competence to determine whether or not the notified aid measure constitutes State Aid in the sense of Article 107(1). This assumes that Member States should be able to assess what constitutes State Aid under the TFEU. Article 107 identifies the criteria whose cumulative fulfilment entails the existence of an aid.[6] According to the text of Article 107, any aid granted by a member state or through State resources which distorts or threatens to distort competition by favouring certain undertakings or the production of certain goods is incompatible with the common market. Article 107 also outlines the acceptable forms of aid.[7]

Thus, Article 107(1) prohibits any aid that distorts or threatens to distort competition in the common market. State Aid may lead to distortion of competition by favouring certain firms or the production of certain goods. Therefore, State Aid control guarantees a level playing field for all firms operating within the internal market. 'EU Member State', for the purposes of Article 107(1), encompasses central government and all public authorities. The aid provided by a public or private body, designated or established by the State, falls under Article 107(1) as aid from state resources. The Court has actually made clear that the attribution to the State of a measure adopted by the public entity cannot be presumed, but has to be inferred from a set of indicators arising from the particular circumstances of the case.[8] In *Stardust Marine*, the Court came up with a list of factors:

- the degree to which the requirements of the public authorities or any guidelines issued have influenced the decision taken;
- the degree of integration of the public entity into the structures of the public administration;
- the nature of the undertaking's activities and their actual exercise in the market under normal market conditions;

- the legal status of the undertaking; and/or
- any other indicators showing the likelihood or not of state involvement.

In order for aid to fall into the remit of Article 107(1), it needs to be 'granted by the State or through state resources'. If the aid, in order to fall within Article 107(1), needs to be granted by the member state, then the first question is whether the measure can be imputed to the State. The second issue to be decided is whether the aid derives in fact from state resources. In the *Sloman Neptun* case,[9] the wording of Article 107(1) was said to be aimed at 'bringing within the definition of aid not only aid granted directly by the State, but also aid granted by public or private bodies designated or established by the State'.[10] In the *Preussen Elektra* case,[11] the Court clarified that 'only advantages granted directly or indirectly through state resources are to be considered aid within the meaning of Article 107(1). The distinction made between aid granted by a member state and aid granted through state resources does not signify that all advantages granted by a state, whether financed through state resources or not, constitute aid'. In order to be authorized, the aid needs to be necessary for the project to be carried out. If an undertaking has the potential to pursue an activity without public funds (i.e. if its own financial means and resources are sufficient for the objective set to be attained), then clearly the aid is not necessary. Transparency is a key word in the weighing process. The Commission should always be in a position to estimate with a degree of certainty the intensity of the aid. The member states have, therefore, a duty to provide the Commission with all information and data required so that the costs may be reasonably quantified.

Article 107(2) and (3) provide for a set of mandatory and discretionary exemptions respectively, whose correct application is entrusted to the Commission. The general principle of incompatibility under Article 107(1) calls for a restrictive interpretation of the derogatory provisions. The burden of proof lies therefore with the member state, to show that the proposed aid meets the conditions for its approval.[12] According to Article 107(2), aid satisfying the conditions is automatically compatible with the common market, not bestowing any discretion to the Commission. The automatic exemption from the general ban on State Aid does not, nevertheless, exonerate the member state from its duty to notify the Commission. Article 107(2)(a) exempts 'aid having a social character, granted to individual consumers, provided that such aid is granted without discrimination related to the origin of the products concerned'. An example of this type of social aid is aid in the form of discounted air fares for island residents.[13] Article 107(2)(b) renders compatible with the common market aid to make good the damage caused by natural disasters or exceptional circumstances. The aid is meant 'to make good the damage', to neutralize the damage and the loss of profit suffered and not to over-compensate the recipients.[14]

While under Article 107(2) the aid, as a matter of law and provided that the conditions set are met, 'shall be compatible with the Common Market' under Article 107(3) the aid 'can be declared compatible', the Commission enjoying a wide measure of discretion as to its approval or not. Under the first section of Article 107(3)(b) the execution of an important project of common European interest may entail the grant of aid. In this case, the aid will be granted to promote the project. 'An important project of common European interest' is a broad concept which could extend to projects benefiting also non-EU countries or initiated by non-EU countries. The derogation may still apply to projects carried out in a single member state, not necessarily supported by several Member States, but which can still be deemed to be of common interest.

A further category of potentially compatible aid under this subparagraph concerns aid to remedy a serious disturbance in the economy of a member state. the 'serious disturbance' must affect the whole of the economy of a member state or at least several sectors rather than merely a region or a sector, in which case the regional or sectoral exemptions respectively may come into play. Consequently, the most appropriate remedial instrument under these circumstances would be a scheme of aid. Individual aid to solely one company could, arguably, be justified if the latter's collapse was likely to induce a negative domino effect across the whole of a Member State's economy or across several sectors. In such an extreme case, aid could be authorized to both the firm in difficulty and those affected by its situation.[15] The rationale behind this derogation being strictly the absorption of the shocks caused by the serious economic turmoil, the aid released must by no means place the undertakings receiving it in a stronger position to the position they used to hold before the occurrence of the disturbance.

The Commission's significant discretion under Article 107(3)(c) does not constitute a departure from the principle that the derogations to the general prohibition are to be interpreted narrowly. The Commission has developed its doctrine of compensatory justification.[16] The primary concern being the contribution to the attainment of a Community objective as opposed to a purely national one. The aid will be justified provided that there is 'a contribution by the beneficiary over and above the normal play of market forces for the achievement of a Community objective'.[17] Article 107(3)(c) provides for the facilitation of the development of certain economic areas, where such aid does not adversely affect trading conditions to an extent contrary to the common interest. As the General Court has ruled, a greater distortion of competition can be accepted for the most disadvantaged regions covered by Article 107(3)(a)than for those covered by Article 107(3)(c).[18] The exemption in Article 107(3)(c) is wider in scope than Article 107(3)(a). In addition, the sectoral aid provided for under Article 107(3)(c), facilitates the development of certain economic activities in cases where such aid does not adversely affect trading conditions to an extent contrary to the common interest. This sectoral aid is the most common ground alleged by the Member States for the justification of State Aid in a number of industries. The wide scope of this derogation led to the adoption of numerous guidelines which set the framework for the application of specialized sectoral rules or horizontal rules with a wider scope.

The Commission may, under Article 107(3)(a), authorize aid to promote the economic development of areas where the standard of living is abnormally low or where there is serious underemployment. The exemption under this subparagraph is therefore concerned with regional aid. The Guidelines on national regional aid for 2007–2013,[19] a corollary principally of the enlargement of the Union, are a reflection of Europe's social model in the context of State Aid policy. The promotion of economic development in the meaning of the derogation of Article 107(3)(a) is unlikely to be achieved through ad hoc regional aid to financially troubled undertakings.[20] Where, individual aid to a single firm or aid confined to one area of activity is notified, the burden of proof lies with the Member States to demonstrate that the project is regionally beneficial and does not unduly distort competition.

National regional aid, addressed also in Article 107(3), consists of: (1) aid for investment granted to large companies, or exceptionally; (2) operating aid targeted at specific disadvantaged regions; and (3) increased levels of investment aid to small- and medium-sized enterprises (SMEs) located within the disadvantaged regions over and above what is allowed in other areas.[21]

Articles 108 and 109 provide the procedural framework for the application of the State Aid rules. Member States must notify their plans to grant or alter aid, waiting for the Commission's final decision before actually implementing their measures. The investigation for existing aid is regulated by Article 108(1) and for new aid by Article 108(3). The formal investigation prescribed under Article 108(2), which is initiated in cases of doubt as regards the compatibility of the aid, is the same for both categories of aid. When new aid is planned to be introduced, the Commission is supposed to be informed of any plans to grant or alter aid in sufficient time to enable it to submit its comments. The member state concerned shall not put its proposed measures into effect until the Commission has reached a final decision. If the Commission concludes that the aid is not compatible, then it shall start an investigation procedure under Article 107. The fact that the member state has to wait for clearance before implementation provides the Commission with important powers in preventing State Aid that can harm competition in the market.

Article 108(1) provides that the Commission shall, in cooperation with Member States, keep under constant review all systems of aid existing in those states. There are four categories of existing aid:

(1) aid put into effect before the entry into force of the Treaty of Rome;[22]
(2) aid authorized by the Commission or the Council, aid deemed to have been authorized following the two months the Commission has to adopt a decision;[23]
(3) aid awarded to the beneficiary 10 years before any action taken by the Commission; and
(4) aid which was not deemed to be aid when put into effect.

Article 109 empowers the Council to make any appropriate regulations for the application of Articles 107 and 108, and in particular to determine the conditions in which Article 108(3) shall apply and the categories of aid exempted from this procedure. In 1999, pursuant to Article 109, the procedural regulation 659/1999 was adopted.[24] The Regulation states that the Council may make any appropriate regulations for the application of Articles 107 and 108 and may in particular determine the conditions in which Article 108(3) shall apply and the categories of aid exempted from this procedure.

The EU Treaty, and secondary legislation, does not define State Aid. Therefore, it is not always clear what measure constitutes 'State Aid' under the EU Treaty. What is crucial is the assessment of the recipient's position compared with his competitors before and after the grant of the aid. If the recipient has improved its competitive position as a result of the aid, the determination of aid will be easy. In the Commission and Court decisions, as a rule, all four following criteria have to be met so that the State measure is considered to be 'State Aid' under the Treaty.

15.3. STATE AID SPECIFICS

The provisions on State Aid ensure that state interventions do not harm the unimpeded function of the internal market and the competitiveness of the Community, and facilitate the structural adaptation of the economy of Member States. A measure will be regarded as State Aid if it gives the firm an economic or financial advantage it would not otherwise have enjoyed[25] under 'normal market conditions'.[26] The Commission adopted and has renewed its Community Guidelines on State Aid.[27] As early as 1961, the ECJ stated that 'the concept of aid is . . . wider than that of a subsidy because it embraces not only positive benefits, such as subsidies themselves, but also interventions which are normally included in the budget of an undertaking and which, without therefore being subsidies in the strict meaning of the word, are similar in character and have the same effect'.[28] As Farantouris argues, the Commission Guidelines signal progress towards legal certainty and the effective application of EC competition policy on State Aid at three levels: (1) they ensure that rescue aids are limited to reversible, temporary, and short-term economic support, restricted to the period of time necessary to apply a full restructuring plan; (2) they focus on EC control of large undertakings that exercise commercial activities in more than one member state and, therefore, on State Aid that affects more the conditions of competition and intra-Community trade; and (3) they support the principle of beneficiary, according to which beneficiaries of the aid are expected to make a real and significant contribution to the restructuring plan from their own resources.

With regard to restructuring aids, the Guidelines require the substantial contribution of the beneficiary to restructuring. The beneficiary's contribution aims at demonstrating that markets (owners, creditors, etc.) believe in the possibility of the return to viability within a plausible time frame and ensuring that restructuring is limited to the minimum required to restore viability, while limiting distortion of competition. The general principle for restructuring aid is to allow the grant of restructuring aid only in circumstances in which it can be demonstrated that it does not run against the Community interest.[29] As Farantouris argues, this will only be possible if strict criteria are met (net effect of redundancies resulting from the firm's going out of business, combined with the effects on its suppliers, would exacerbate employment problems), and if it is certain that any distortions of competition will be offset by the benefits flowing from the firm's survival.[30,31] Given that these conditions apply cumulatively, if the Commission holds that one of them is not fulfilled, the aid will normally be considered incompatible with the common market.[32]

While the rules for State Aid control are the responsibility of the Commission, enforcement of the rules is mostly the responsibility of the Member States. Before opening the 'formal investigation procedure', information is channelled through the aid-granting member state by the notification process, or in some cases it may be initiated by a third-party complaint. Typically, the authorization of aid is contingent upon the fulfilment of a number of Commission conditions, the majority of which have been codified in the rescue and restructuring aid Guidelines.[33] The Guidelines reflect a shift towards closer scrutiny of the distortion created by the granting of aid for rescue and restructuring operations. The 'one time–last time' principle is elevated and further clarified so as to avoid repeated rescue and restructuring to keep companies artificially alive.[34] We should emphasize that rescue grants preserve their transitional character, to provide a company in difficulty the opportunity to elaborate on a rescue or restructuring scheme. Thus rescue grants aim at keeping a company in business for a limited period, during which its future can be assessed.[35]

The Commission Decision in the *Northern Rock* case[36] is an example of rescue aid to the banking sector. Northern Rock PLC, based in Newcastle-upon-Tyne, is the UK's fifth-largest UK mortgage bank with a balance-sheet total of GBP 101 billion (EUR 150 billion) as of 31 December 2006. Northern Rock's core activity is residential mortgage lending, which represents more than 90 per cent of all outstanding loans made by the bank. The Bank of England granted emergency liquidity assistance to Northern Rock against sufficient collateral and a punitive interest rate was charged. The difficulties of Northern Rock were further aggravated by a bank-run, which started after the news on the Bank of England granting support to Northern Rock was made public. In order to stop the bank run and to avoid contagious effects leading to a wider banking crisis, the UK Treasury announced guarantee arrangements for all existing accounts in Northern Rock on 17 September 2007. On 26 November 2007, following contacts between the UK authorities and the Commission, the UK communicated the details of the measures taken. The Commission concluded that the emergency liquidity assistance provided by the Bank of England on 14 September 2007, which was secured by sufficient collateral and was interest-bearing, did not constitute State Aid.[37] However, the guarantee on deposits granted by the Treasury on 17 September 2007, as well as the measures granted on 9 October 2007, which provided further liquidity and guarantees to Northern Rock and were secured by a Treasury indemnity, did constitute State Aid.

In March 2008, the UK notified a restructuring plan for Northern Rock. This plan provided for a reduction in Northern Rock's lending operations and in the size of its balance sheet. Northern Rock started to reduce its market presence in accordance with that plan in March 2008. The UK authorities submitted a revised restructuring plan in March 2009. The main change introduced is the split of Northern Rock into two entities, a relatively small 'good' bank (with an opening balance sheet of around 20 per cent of Northern Rock's balance sheet pre-crisis) which would continue commercial activities (i.e. mortgage lending and deposit taking), and a 'bad' bank holding the majority of the risky mortgage loans made by Northern Rock in the past.

As this case indicates rescue aid aims at temporary assistance to keep an ailing firm afloat for the time needed to work out a restructuring and/or a liquidation plan. Therefore, the aid should be accompanied, on notification, by an undertaking given by the member state concerned. Pursuant to this undertaking, the member state needs to communicate to the Commission no later than six months after the rescue aid measure has been authorized,[38] a restructuring plan or a liquidation plan or proof that the loan has been reimbursed in full and/or that the guarantee has been terminated.[39] Thus, in the *Guascor* case, the Commission held that the eighteen-month loan guarantee granted by the Spanish government did not fulfil the above condition.[40]

If rescue aid is granted to a firm that has already received restructuring aid, it can be considered that the beneficiary's difficulties are of a recurrent nature and that repeated state interventions give rise to distortions of competition that are contrary to the common interest.[41] Repeated state interventions are not to be permitted, except when, for example, restructuring aid follows the granting of rescue aid as part of a single restructuring operation. Furthermore, aid for the purchase of the assets cannot be authorized, since it constitutes aid for initial investment.[42] The Commission has confirmed the principle above in many instances of repeated state interventions.[43]

EU State Aid control has thus a potential to significantly constrain the level of subsidies in the Member States. Control of State Aid ex ante can allow opportunity costs of State Aid to be considered and re-direct State Aid to activities where more positive outcomes can be expected. The provision of rescue or in difficulty may be justified by social or regional policy considerations, by the need to take into account the beneficial role of SMEs to the economy or, exceptionally, by the desirability of maintaining a competitive market structure when the demise of firms could lead to a monopoly or to a tight oligopolistic situation.

While the Commission has the competence to adopt detailed State Aid rules, the enforcement of the rules and procedures depends to a large extent on Member States. Article 108(3) has a direct effect and gives national judges the power to suspend and provisionally recover aid granted illegally before its approval by the Commission. Private litigation in front of national courts could therefore provide increased discipline in the field of State Aid.

Hence the effects of State Aid on the home country has to be assessed to determine if net effects are positive and if these net effects are sufficient to outweigh the negative effects on trade and competition on the European market. If not, such aid has an adverse effect on the EU as a whole and is incompatible with the EU market – this is the basic idea of a balancing test of the effects of State Aid.[44]

State Aid measures can sometimes be effective tools for achieving objectives of common interest (services of general economic interest, social and regional cohesion, employment, research and development, sustainable development, promotion of cultural diversity) and for correcting 'market failures'. For various reasons (e.g. externalities, market power, co-ordination problems between market operators), markets sometimes do not function efficiently from an economic point of view. Member States may then intervene by granting State Aid. State Aid may therefore be compatible with the TFEU, provided that it fulfils clearly-defined objectives of common interest and does not distort competition to an extent contrary to the common interest.[45]

The State Aid rules, laid down in Articles 107–109 TFEU, aim to ensure that competition in the common market is not distorted. The State Aid law aspires to safeguard a smooth symbiotic relationship between public and private forces active in the market, targeting in particular potentially obscure and indirect ways of state interventionism. Article 107(1) applies to aid measures notified to the Commission prior to their implementation, but also aid measures implemented in disregard of the 'non-implementation' obligation enshrined in Article 108(3). The threat of an effect upon trade is sufficient to activate the deterrence mechanisms of Article 107(1).[46] We should note that an aid measure will only distort competition if it is selective and assists a particular sector of the economy or a specific undertaking. Aid measures can be restricted to certain companies or types of company,[47] they can be less intense as sectoral measures,[48] they can be directed to certain industries[49] or only to certain business sectors.[50] The criteria of distortion of competition and effect on inter-state trade, despite being separate under Article 107(1), have often been treated by the Commission as complementary.

The EC regulation of public undertakings and EC State Aid law are increasingly important parts of EC competition law. The case law at national and European levels is growing in both number and importance. The reasons for this increasing focus on public intervention in the economy are numerous and varied but they primarily relate to the impact of such intervention on the completion of the internal market and the current liberalization and privatization processes. As the following section illustrates, the role of State Aid in periods of crises is essential in the sustainment of the economy during such periods.

15.4. STATE AID IN FINANCIAL CRISES[51]

In the context of the recent financial crisis, the EU Commission initially used Article 107(3)(c) TFEU[52] as a legal basis for allowing national aid measures in favour of banks and applied the specific legal basis for crisis aid measures contained in Article 107(3)(b) TFEU on the basis of 'aid to remedy a serious disturbance in the economy of a Member State'.

In the light of the above the Commission has adopted four Banking Communications concerning state support measures in favour of banks in times of crisis.[53] The first three Communications set out the requirements for certain aid measures and determine the necessity and the extent of the required restructuring for certain banks. The fourth Communication (the Restructuring Communication) then sets out the details of the necessary follow-up measures of banks that took recourse to State Aid to overcome the crisis.

Within a mere couple of weeks from the outbreak of the crisis, it became obvious that existing State Aid rules were not suitable for dealing effectively with the problems facing financial markets. The Commission, therefore, proceeded to adopt the following new measures:

- The application of State Aid rules to measures taken in relation to financial institutions in the context of the current global financial crisis.
- The recapitalization of financial institutions in the current financial crisis:
  - limitation of aid to the minimum necessary
  - safeguards against undue distortions of competition.
- The treatment of impaired assets in the Community banking sector.
- Temporary framework for State Aid measures to support access to finance in the current financial and economic crisis (and its amendments).
- The return to viability and the assessment of restructuring measures in the financial sector in the current crisis under the State Aid rules.

On 13 October 2008, turning to each of the above crisis measures in detail, the EU Commission published a Communication on the application of State Aid rules to measures taken in relation to financial institutions.[54] According to this Communication, support schemes introduced by the Member States, such as guarantees to cover their liabilities or recapitalization schemes, can be approved by the Commission in an accelerated procedure. In order to proceed in such a way, they must fulfil conditions which guarantee that they are well-targeted and proportionate to the objective of stabilizing financial markets and contain certain safeguards against unnecessary negative effects on competition.

The Commission emphasizes the exceptional character of this exemption and that it cannot be used as a matter of principle in other sectors. Such use can risk that they have an immediate impact on the economy of the member state as a whole and that the measures can be applied only as long as the crisis situation persists. Therefore, reviews carried out at least every six months as well as reporting to the Commission are prescribed for the Member States.

National schemes of aid must be limited in time. This means that their duration should not go beyond the minimum necessary and Member States are obliged to carry out reviews every six months, assessing the justification and the potential need for adjustment. In addition, aid must be limited to the strict minimum, and a significant contribution from the beneficiaries and/or the sector should be ensured. In order to avoid an undue distortion of competition, Member States must include a combination of behavioural constraints or appropriate provisions enforcing behavioural constraints ensuring that the beneficiary does not engage in aggressive expansion.

The Commission expects Member States to inform it of their intentions and notify their measures as early as possible and in any event before the implementation of the measures in question. Such notifications could be dealt with, if necessary, very promptly (24 hours).

In December 2008, the Commission adopted a Communication on the recapitalization of financial institutions in the current crisis.[55] The common objectives of the Communication are the restoration of the financial stability of the banks, ensuring the lending to the real economy and avoiding the systemic risk of possible insolvencies.

State measures must be therefore proportional and temporary and they have to distinguish between fundamentally sound and less performing banks. The Commission pointed out that it will pay particular attention to the risk profile of the beneficiaries and that it will need a basis for a differentiation of remuneration rates for different banks such as compliance with regulatory solvency requirements and prospective capital adequacy, pre-crisis spreads and ratings.[56]

The Communication refers to the safeguards against possible abuses and distortions of competition mentioned in the Banking Communication. High remunerations require less safeguards. However, safeguards may be necessary to prevent aggressive commercial expansion financed by State Aid and mergers and acquisitions should be organized on the basis of a competitive tendering process. The Banking Communication includes possible measures in return for the provision of State Aid in order to ensure that the competitiveness of the market does not deteriorate due to the aid.

According to the Banking Communication:[57]

- In order to avoid an undue distortion of competition, Member States must include a combination of behavioural constraints or appropriate provisions enforcing behavioural constraints ensuring that the beneficiary does not engage in aggressive expansion.
- Another instrument for avoiding distortions of competition is adjustment measures for the sector as a whole and/or by the restructuring or liquidation of individual beneficiaries.

State Aid offered to banks proved to be an important tool in coping with the crisis, but it could not avoid structural reform of individual banks. In addition to restructuring measures, cleaning-up impaired assets was necessary for many banks. In order to provide guidance to the State interventions for financial institutions to clean their balance sheets of 'toxic assets', the Commission adopted on 25 February 2009 a Communication on the treatment of impaired assets in the EU banking sector.[58]

The Communication offers specific guidance on the application of State Aid rules to asset relief. Asset relief can be a measure to safeguard financial stability and underpin the supply of credit to the real economy, as it would directly address the uncertainty regarding the quality of bank sheets and revive confidence in the sector. Not only immediate objectives of safeguarding financial stability should be pursued, but also long-term considerations such as behavioural safeguards and restructuring should be included in a government intervention. In order to give incentives for banks to participate in asset relief with public policy objectives, an enrolment window limited to six months from the launch of the scheme by the government should be introduced. Participation to the scheme may be mandatory or voluntary. In the latter situation, additional incentives may be provided to the banks so as to facilitate take-up. However, the principles of transparency and disclosure, fair valuation and burden sharing must be respected. Behavioural constraints should always condition the access to asset relief.[59]

The Restructuring Communication complements the previous guidance on the assessment of State Aid for banks concerning guarantees, recapitalization and the treatment of impaired assets. These Communications have explained in particular under which conditions banks are required to submit a restructuring plan. This Communication[60] adopted on 14 August 2009 outlines how the competition rules will be applied to support financial stability, as the return of banks to viability is the best guarantee for stability and for their sustained ability to lend to the economy. Restoring long-term viability of financial institutions is the central issue of this Communication. The Restructuring Communication complements the existing criteria and explains how the Commission will assess the compatibility of restructuring aid to financial institutions under Article 104(3)(b). The restructuring plans submitted by Member States should be comprehensive, detailed and based on coherent concepts and must include a comparison with alternative options. When a bank cannot be restored to viability, the restructuring plan will indicate how to wind it up in an orderly fashion. It also includes possible divestments in return for the provision of State Aid in order to ensure that the competitiveness of the market does not deteriorate due to the aid.

State Aid prolongs past distortions of competition that are created by excessive risk-taking and unsustainable business models. In addition, it deteriorates the competitiveness of the market by artificially supporting the market power of beneficiaries (moral hazard for the beneficiaries), by weakening the incentives for non-beneficiaries to compete, invest and innovate and by shifting an unfair share of the burden of structural adjustment to other Member States. In addition, the provision of aid leads to entry barriers and undermines incentives for cross-border activities.

State Aid to rescue and restructure distressed banks may harm the position of banks that have remained fundamentally sound, with possible negative effects for financial stability. National interventions in the current crisis will, by their very nature, tend to focus on the national markets risking a possible fragmentation of the European single market. Thus, restructuring aid should lead to the restoration of viability of the undertaking in the longer term without State Aid and needs to be accompanied, to the extent possible, by adequate burden sharing and by measures to minimize distortions of competition.

According to the Restructuring Communication:

- Banks benefiting from State Aid may be required to divest subsidiaries or branches, portfolios of customers or business units (par. 35) or to limit their expansion in certain business or geographical areas (par. 36).
- State Aid cannot be used to fund anti-competitive behaviour such as acquisition of competing business (par. 40) or offering other terms which cannot be matched by competitors which do not receive aid (par. 44).

The measures to limit the distortions that arise from the provision of State Aid depend on the nature of the distortion of competition, measures in respect of liabilities and/or in respect of assets. The nature and form of such measures will depend on two criteria, the amount of the aid and the conditions and circumstances under which it was granted and, second, the characteristics of the market or markets on which the beneficiary bank will operate. We need tailor-made measures to ensure that effective competition is preserved and we should take into account that divestments may generate adverse consequences and may not be necessary in order to achieve the desired outcomes. In certain cases, limitation of organic growth may be preferred to divestments.

Typical compensatory measures include divestment, closure of capacity or withdrawal from certain markets or activities (banks may be required to divest subsidiaries or branches, portfolios of customers or business units). In addition recipients of State Aid may be required to get rid of loss-making assets, disengage from marginal activities and focus on core business and customers make companies stronger. Such restructuring intensifies competition and in the longer term enables companies to offer better products and to enter new markets.

The first actions taken by the Commission targeted the State Aid rules in relation to financial institutions. The impact of the economic crisis was also felt in the private sector, a serious downturn affecting the wider economy and hitting households, business and jobs. Banks became much more risk-averse than in the previous years and this lead to a credit squeeze, which threatened to affect healthy companies. Therefore, a framework setting up the rules for state interventions in this sector became necessary. In December 2008, the Commission adopted a Communication setting up an EU Framework for State Aid measures to support access to finance in the current financial and economic crisis[61] which allowed Member States to grant aid under existing instruments for all sectors of the economy through higher limits on grants, credit guarantees, risk capital and loans.

During, and as a result of this crisis financial institutions found themselves in distressful situations. It was expected that member state measures would raise concerns and would have to be assessed by the Commission. It shall be interesting to see the results of this assessment.

One of the most important State Aid cases is the Lloyds Banking Group ('LBG') case, where the Commission approved a package of financial support measures to the banking industry in the UK.[62] The UK notified a restructuring plan for LBG on 16 July 2009, in respect of the recapitalization measures that bank had received six months earlier. LBG's need for State Aid was largely due to the acquisition of HBOS and the latter's difficulties. Prior to its takeover, HBOS was on the brink of collapse because of its high-risk lending practices and excessive use of leverage. The takeover offer was conditional upon the receipt of the large government aid necessary to rescue HBOS. In January 2009, LBG received a State recapitalization of GBP 17 billion which resulted in the UK government having an equity ownership in LBG of 43.5 per cent. The aid allowed Lloyds TSB to acquire HBOS and significantly increase its market shares. In addition, the acquisition eliminated a challenger, in markets which were already concentrated.

In order to ensure that LBG re-emerges as a stable, profitable bank measures will concentrate on reducing the balance sheet of LBG, reducing the risk profile of the business, reducing the funding gap of the bank. In addition, these measures will result in the disposal or run-down of non-core businesses and activities in the corporate, wholesale, personal and small business segments. LBG shall not acquire any financial institutions and shall not make any other acquisitions whose purpose is to expand LBG's activities outside of its business model.

LBG is required to conduct a tendering procedure for the sale of the assets that it must divest as result of the Commission's assessment ('Divestment Business'). It will also undertake an asset reduction programme to achieve a GBP 181 billion reduction in a specified pool of assets by 31 December 2014. LBG plans to dispose of a retail banking business (its branches, staff, customers, customer accounts and support infrastructure) include the following:

- The TSB brand;[63]
- Mortgage and savings of the Cheltenham and Gloucester (C&G) branches network;
- Lloyds TSB Scotland retail branches and its banking licence;
- Supplementary branches in England and Wales, selected to provide broad geographical coverage for a potential acquirer (around 600 branches in total); and
- Intelligent Finance, a direct bank with current account, mortgage and savings customers.

These branches must be branches located in England and Wales, and must in combination with the rest of the Divestment Business amount to at least a 4–6 per cent share of the Personal Current Account (PCA) market. The coverage of the supplementary branches shall be such that the Divestment Business has a reach of at least 43 per cent of the geographic area where LBG operates. In addition, the branches must be such that the average gross ground floor area of all branches in the Divestment Business is at least 220 square metres. The firm that would buy the divested assets should have a market share in the PCA market of no more than 14 per cent in the UK. In addition the buying firm must be independent of LBG, and must satisfy all the necessary conditions imposed by competition authorities. Finally, the buyer must satisfy the Financial Services Authority (FSA) as to: (1) the adequacy of its financial resources (both in respect of liquidity and capital); (2) the competency and experience of the leadership to drive the business forward; and (3) ensure the long-term viability, success and sustainability. In addition the buying firm must make sure that it has adequate risk and control standards in place, and will ensure high quality of service.[64]

The Commission went into such detail as regards the description of the divestment package and the buyer, in order to ensure that the divested entity will provide an appropriate means of increasing competition on the concentrated UK retail banking market. With the TSB brand, the Lloyds TSB Scotland branches, the C&G branches, supplementary branches assuring proportional geographical coverage and Intelligent Finance, the carved-out entity will constitute a sufficiently attractive target for some competitors wishing to enter the UK market.

15.5. CONCLUSION

During, and as a result of this crisis financial institutions found themselves in distressed situations. It was expected that member state measures would raise concerns and would have to be assessed by the Commission. It shall be interesting to see the results of this assessment. An initial indication is illustrated by the fact that as of December 2009, from a total of 81 member state measures, 75 have been approved with no objections and only 6 have been approved conditionally. There are still some outstanding cases under review, but the Commission (as well as Member States) appears to be pragmatic in their assessment of State Aid measures during the crisis.

The statistics reveal that Member States' notifications have largely been approved unconditionally. As the new rules are vey lenient, the few cases where the Commission has raised concerns relate to measures that were so complex that the devised solutions could not fit well into any set of EU rules and thus the Commission had to initiate the relevant investigations.

The special rules for the financial services sector are quite permissive. The Commission signalled its intention to allow aid for that sector. The Commission has been willing to apply more lenient rules in view of the gravity of the situation in that sector as banks that receive public funds for restructuring may not be required to undertake divestments to the same extent as other undertakings that received aid for the same purpose in the past.

NOTES

1. Biondi, Eeckhout and Flynn (2004), *The Law of State Aid in the European Union*, Oxford: Oxford University Press.
2. Fidler, D. (1992), 'Competition Law and International Relations', *The International and Comparative Law Quarterly*, 41 (3), pp. 563–58.
3. Treaty for the Functioning of the European Union ('Treaty').
4. Fidler, D. (1992), 'Competition Law and International Relations', *The International and Comparative Law Quarterly*, 41 (3), pp. 563–58.
5. Case 173 (1973) *Italy v. Commission*, (1974) ECR 709.
6. *Procedural Regulation 659* (1999) Article 1(a): 'aid shall mean any measure fulfilling all the criteria laid down in Article 92(1) (now 107(1) EC) of the Treaty'.
7. The following shall be compatible with the common market:
   (a) aid having a social character, granted to individual consumers, provided that such aid is granted without discrimination related to the origin of the products concerned;
   (b) aid to make good the damage caused by natural disasters or exceptional occurrences;
   (c) granted to the economy of certain areas of the Federal Republic of Germany affected by the division of Germany, insofar as such aid is required in order to compensate for the economic disadvantages caused by that division.
   The following may be considered to be compatible with the common market:
   (a) aid to promote the economic development of areas where the standard of living is abnormally low or where there is serious underemployment;
   (b) aid to promote the execution of an important project of common European interest or to remedy a serious disturbance in the economy of a member state;
   (c) aid to facilitate the development of certain economic activities or of certain economic areas, where such aid does not adversely affect trading conditions to an extent contrary to the common interest;
   (d) aid to promote culture and heritage conservation where such aid does not affect trading conditions and competition in the Community to an extent that is contrary to the common interest;
   (e) such other categories of aid as may be specified by decision of the Council acting by a qualified majority on a proposal from the Commission.
8. Ibid (*Stardust Marine*).
9. Joined cases C-72/91 and C-73/91, *Sloman Neptun Schiffahrts AG v. Seebetriebstrat Bodo Zeisemer der Sloman Neptun Schiffahrts AG*, (1993) ECR I-10107.
10. Ibid, paras 19 and 21.
11. See Case C-379/98, *Preussen Elektra v. Schleswag*, (2001) ECR I-2099.
12. See Case C-364/90, *Italy v. Commission*, (1993) ECR I-2097.
13. See e.g. the recent Commission approval of social aid for air travel between mainland Portugal and the Autonomous Region of Madeira. Commission Press Release IP/07/1900, 11.12.2007.
14. See Case C-73/03, Judgment of 11.11.2004, *Spain v. Commission* (unpublished).
15. See Quigley and Collins (2003): *EC State Aid Law and Policy*, Hart Publishing, Oxford.
16. See Memorandum No. 2, COM (84) 72 final, Section IV, point 14.
17. Ibid.
18. See T-380/94, *AIUFFASS and AKT v. Commission*, (1996) ECR II-2169, para. 54.
19. 2006/C 54/08.
20. Joined cases T-126/96 and T-127/96, *BFM & EFIM v. Commission*, (1998) ECR II-3437, para. 101.
21. Ibid.
22. The Treaty of Rome came into force in 1957.
23. See Case 120/73, *Gebrüder Lorenz GmbH v. Germany et Land de Rhénanie-Palatinat*, (1973) ECR 1471, paras 4–5.
24. Council Regulation (EC) No 659/1999 of 22 March 1999, laying down detailed rules for the application of article 93 of the EC Treaty, OJ 1999 L 83/1.

25. See Case 61/79, *Amministrazione delle Finanze v. Denkavit Italiana*, (1980) ECR 1205.
26. Case C-39/94, *SFEI v. La Poste*, (1996) ECR I-3547, para. 60.
27. For instance, Commission Guidelines on State Aid for research and development, EE C 45, 17.2.1996, p. 5, and EE C 111, 8.5.2002, p. 3; Commission Guidelines on state guarantees, C 71, 11.3.2000, p. 14; Commission Guidelines on State Aid for environmental protection, EE C 37, 3.2.2001, p. 3; Commission Guidelines on regional State Aid, EE C 74, 10.3.1998, p. 9, as amended, EE C 258, 9.9.2000, p. 5; Commission Guidelines on State Aid in the agricultural sector, EE C 28, 1.2.2000, p. 2, etc. Revised Guidelines were taken into effect in 2004 (EE C 244, 1.10.2004, p. 2).
28. See Case 30/59 (1961), *Steenkolenmijnen v. High Authority*, ECR 3.
29. Commission Decision of 6 Mar. 2002, C 19/2002 (ex EE 133/2000) (*Olympic Airways*), EE C 98, 23.4.2002.
30. Case T-371 & 394/94 (1998), *British Airways, Scandinavian Airlines System Denmark-Norway-Sweden, Koninklijke Luchtvaart Maatschappij, Air UK, Euralair international, TAT European Airlines & British Midland Airways v. Commission*, ECR II-2405, para. 235.
31. In the case of SMEs, and the agricultural sector, the Commission may approve aid only if the beneficiary is qualified as a firm in difficulty and under the conditions provided in the Guidelines. Points 55–59 and Ch. 5 of Commission Guidelines 2004, above, n. 7.
32. Case C-17/99, *France v. Commission*, (2001) ECR I-2481, paras 49–50; Case T-152/99, *HAMSA v. Commission*, (2002) ECR II-3049, para. 79; Case C-278/00, *Greece v. Commission*, (2004) ECR I-3997, paras 100–101; Case T-171/02, *Regione autonoma della Sardegna v. Commission*, (2005) ECR II-213, para. 128; and Case T-17/2003, *Schmitz-Gotha Fahrzeugwerke v. Commission*, Judgment of 6 Apr. 2006, para. 45.
33. Community guidelines on State Aid for rescuing and restructuring firms in difficulty, OJ 244, 01.10.2004, pp. 2–17. Aid for rescuing and restructuring companies is a special category of State Aid that has given rise to some highly controversial competition law cases, most recently the *Northern Rock* case in the banking sector.
34. Commission Guidelines (2004) above, n. 7, points 72 et seq. Cf. Case T-149/95, *Ducros v. Commission*, (1997) ECR II-2031, para. 66; Case T-244/94, *Wirtschaftsvereinigung Stahl v. Commission*, (1997) ECR II-1963, para. 115.
35. See also, Commission Guidelines on State Aid to air transport, EE C 350, 10.12.1994, p. 5.
36. Commission Decision of 4 Dec. 2007 (rescue aid to *Northern Rock*), IP/07/1859.
37. Farantouris, N. (2009), 'EU Competition policy on State Aid for rescuing and restructuring companies' in I. Kokkoris and I. Lianos (eds), *The Challenge of an Optimal Enforcement System*, (Kluwer, 2009).
38. Inter alia, Commission Decision of 9 Apr. 2002, NN 5/2002 (*Bankgesellschaft Berlin AG*), EE C 141, 14.6.2002; Commission Decision of 13 Nov. 2002, C 9/2002 (*Bull*).
39. Commission Guidelines 2004, point 25. Cf. Case C-303/108, *Italy v. Commission (ENI-Lanerossi)*, (1991) ECR I-1433, para. 37; See also, Commission Decision of 2 June 1993, N 232/93 (*Hermann Berstorff Machinenbau GmbH*), EE C 209, 3.8.1993, IP(93)422; Commission Decision of 10 Nov. 1993, N 473/93 (*Muho AG & Deckel AG*), EE C 322, 30.11.1993, IP(93)964; Commission Decision of 19 Aug. 1994, NN 10/93 (*Guascor SA*), IP(94)724; Commission Decision of 24 Jan. 1996, NN 193/95 (*Comptoir des Entrepreneurs*), EE C 70, 8.3.1996, IP(96)80; Commission Decision of 27 Nov. 2002, NN 161/2002 (*British Energy plc*), EE C 39, 18.2.2002; Commission Decision of 11 Dec. 2002, N 634/2002 (*Grundig AG*), NN C 82, 5.4.2003.
40. Commission Decision of 19 Aug. 1994, NN 10/93, (*Guascor SA*), IP(94)724.
41. See Farantouris, N., 'EU Competition policy on State Aid for rescuing and restructuring companies' in I. Kokkoris I. Lianos (eds) *The Challenge of an Optimal Enforcement System*, (Kluwer, 2009).
42. Commission Guidelines 2004, above, n. 7, point 77.
43. Commission Decision of 13 June 1995, N 222/95 and NN 63/94 (*SEAT*), EE C 237, 12.9.1995, IP(95)433; Commission Decision of 13 Nov. 2002, C 9/2002 (*Bull*).

44. T. Besley and P. Seabright, 'The effects and policy implications of State Aids to Industry: an economic analysis' (1999) 14(28) *Economic Policy*, 13–53.
45. Case C-142/107, *Belgium v. Commission*, (1990) ECR I-959, para. 56; Case C-39/94, *Syndicat Français de l'Express International v. Commission*, (1996) ECR I-3547, para. 36.
46. Ibid.
47. See, for instance, Case C-143/99, *Adria Wien Pipeline GmbH and Wietersdorfer & Peggauer Zementwerke GmbH v. Finanzlandesdirektion für Kärnten*, (2001) ECR I-8365.
48. For instance, Aid to sectors exposed to international competition (*Maribel Bis/Ter* scheme in Belgium: OJ L 95/1997).
49. For instance, Aid by France to Textiles, OJ L 334/1997.
50. See e.g. Ireland Corporation Tax 2003/601/EC, L 204/2003.
51. Kokkoris, I. and R. Olivares-Caminal (2010), *Antitrust Policy Amidst Financial Crises*, Cambridge University Press. See also: Marsden, P. and I. Kokkoris (2010), 'The Role of Merger and State Aid Policy', JIEL, Vol. 13, No. 3, September 2010.
52. '*aid to facilitate the development of certain economic activities or of certain economic areas*'.
53. Communication from the Commission on the application of State Aid rules to measures taken in relation to financial institutions in the context of the current global financial crisis, (2008) OJ C270/8 (the 'Banking Communication'); Communication from the Commission – The recapitalisation of financial institutions in the current financial crisis: limitation of aid to the minimum necessary and safeguards against undue distortions of competition, (2009) OJ C10/2 (the 'Recapitalisation Communication'); Communication from the Commission on the treatment of impaired assets in the Community banking sector, (2009) OJ C72/1 (the 'Impaired Asset Communication'); Commission Communication – The return to viability and the assessment of restructuring measures in the financial sector in the current crisis under the State Aid rules, (2009) OJ C195/9 (the 'Restructuring Communication').
54. OJ 2008 C 270/8.
55. OJ C 16, 2009, pp. 2–10, consolidated version OJ C 83, 2009.
56. Kokkoris, I. and R. Olivares-Caminal (2010), *Competition Enforcement Amidst Crises*, Cambridge University Press.
57. Paragraph 27.
58. OJ C 72, 26.03.2009, pp. 1–22.
59. See further, Kokkoris, I. and R. Olivares-Caminal (2010), *Competition Enforcement Amidst Crises*, Cambridge University Press.
60. OJ C 195, 19.08.2009, pp. 9–20.
61. Communication from the Commission – Temporary framework for State Aid measures to support access to finance in the current financial and economic crisis, OJ 2009/C 16/01.
62. State Aid case N 507/2008, 13 October 2008.
63. Lloyds TSB will sell the TSB brand name.
64. See the Commission's decision for a detailed analysis.

PART IV

Cross-border issues

16. Resolving large complex financial institutions within and across jurisdictions[1]

Robert R. Bliss and George G. Kaufman

16.1. INTRODUCTION

The ultimate objective of resolving insolvent firms is to treat stakeholders fairly, according to their legal contract, and to minimize the loss of value of the firm or its assets in order to maximize the value to the stakeholders. But disagreement exists on how this objective may be achieved efficiently and how one may identify the relevant stakeholders, including the general public. As a result, insolvency or bankruptcy resolution regimes for firms differ across jurisdictions both within and across national boundaries, as well as across industries – as in some countries such as the US. In particular, disagreements revolve around the existence, importance and nature of any externalities that spill over from the failure and resolution of the insolvent firm to the welfare of the economy as a whole.

To understand how best to deal with distressed large complex financial institutions (LCFIs), which include large complex banks, we review salient aspects of the current bank resolution and general corporate bankruptcy procedures in the US, considering the institutional incentives in both cases.[2] We need to understand the similarities and differences in these benchmark processes before examining the problems that arise when LCFIs become seriously distressed.

We next discuss the reasons that a special new insolvency regime may be warranted by noting the similarities and differences between smaller banks and LCFIs.[3] We then offer our own set of objectives. Our analysis concludes that a modified, or hybrid, bankruptcy reorganization is preferable to both the current bank resolution process and current Chapter 11 bankruptcy.

The second part of the chapter looks at the problems that arise in resolving holding companies and in particular holding companies that operate across countries. We offer some suggestions for partially mitigating these problems through marginal changes in existing national insolvency laws and corporate structure. These may be more feasible than achieving a broader coordinated change of laws governing LCFI insolvencies in relevant jurisdictions.

16.2. EXISTING ALTERNATIVE US INSOLVENCY REGIMES

The differences in goals and philosophy of bank insolvency and Chapter 11 corporate bankruptcy resolutions – charter termination and liquidation and the need to preserve essential functions on the one hand, and reorganization and the need to preserve going concern value on the other – result in a large number of procedural differences. In a 2007 paper, we explored these in detail. Most importantly, bankruptcy is a judicial process and bank resolution is an administrative process. Other important differences are summarized in Table 16.1.

Countries frequently have special provisions within their bankruptcy regime to deal with bank (depository institution) insolvencies. This follows from a widespread perception that 'banks are special' and should be treated differently when they become distressed. The separation of corporate bankruptcy from bank insolvency resolution in the US through the creation of two entirely separate bodies of insolvency law, is an extreme expression of this impulse to treat insolvent banks differently.

The 'banks are special' perception derives from a number of sources. Some of these apply to individual banks and others to banks in aggregate. The concerns historically included:

- The important role of banks as sources of liquidity for households and firms through the provision of demand deposit accounts;
- The key role of banks in clearing and settlement of payments;
- Banks are financially fragile due to borrowing short and lending long, and thus being subject to runs by depositors;
- The involvement of the government in the provision of deposit guarantees;
- Bank assets are opaque;
- Banks are interconnected through interbank deposits and loans.

Failure of an individual bank would potentially disrupt liquidity provision and payments clearing for its clients, thus adversely disrupting the local economy and, for large banks, possibly beyond to the financial sector and economy as a whole. The minimization of those disruptions is a primary

Table 16.1. Selected Differences between the Corporate and Bank Insolvency Codes

Provision	**Corporate Bankruptcy**	**Bank Receivership**
Objective	Maximize value of firm as 'going concern' or liquidation	Minimize loss to FDIC (least cost resolution)
Exception to Objective	None	Systemic risk exemption, if threat to stability of financial system
Pre-failure intervention	By negotiation (voluntary)	Statutory (prompt corrective action and other statutory grounds) (involuntary)
Initiation (declaration) of insolvency	Major creditors and/or management petition bankruptcy court	Chartering or primary federal regulator
Creditor stays	General (explicit)	Less general, major exception is insured depositors (implicit)
Clawbacks (pre-insolvency transfers)	Permitted, except 'normal course of business' transfers	Only in cases of actual fraud
Receiver/trustee	Appointed by court	FDIC (statutory)
Management of entity during bankruptcy	Court appointed management (trustee; in Chapter 11 usually the existing management initially)	FDIC
Supervisor of receiver/trustee	Bankruptcy court	FDIC
Structure of Process	Judicial	Administrative
Deviation from Priorities	Negotiated among stakeholders	1) Systemic risk exemption 2) If consistent with least cost resolution[1]
Legal standing of creditors	By statute	None
Creditor Representation	Representative process	None
Creditor Approval	Unanimous agreement	None
Timeliness of bankruptcy initiation	Requires default event	Regulators can act pre-emptively
Final word	Bankruptcy court	FDIC (with limited right of judicial review)

Table 16.1. (continued)

Provision	Corporate Bankruptcy	Bank Receivership
Judicial Review and appeal	Ex-ante	Limited, ex-post
Legal Certainty	Weak	Strong
Right of offset	Variable	Strong
Creditor payment form	Liquidation – cash Reorganization – securities of reorganized firm	Cash Receivership certificates
Legal and administrative expenses	High	Low
Shareholder Interests	Weak and subject to negotiation	Terminated, except for residual value
Post insolvency financing	Debtor in possession	n/a

Note: [1] This is the position of the FDIC, but has not been legally tested.

Source: Bliss and Kaufman (2007), 'US Corporate and Bank Insolvency Regimes: A Comparison and Evaluation', *Virginia Law & Business Review*, Vol. 2, No. 1, Spring 2007, 143–177.

goal of the US bank insolvency process. Deposit guarantees through insurance is itself an attempt to deal with the financial fragility problem.

16.2.1. US Bank Insolvency

The US bank insolvency system has evolved to address these issues in a highly efficient manner. Bank insolvency is an administrative process and the administrator has wide powers to unilaterally decide matters relating to the insolvency and its resolution. Creditors and other stake-holders have little standing (legal rights to be involved) to question or appeal decisions made or to negotiate alternative outcomes. The primary purpose of US bank insolvency resolution is to liquidate the bank.[4] When a bank is placed into an administrative receivership, its charter is revoked, and it ceases to be a legally functioning bank. Following closure, the receiver, invariably the Federal Deposit Insurance Corporation (FDIC), generally either immediately sells some or all of the assets and liabilities to another bank in a pre-arranged purchase and assumption transaction, or creates a new temporary bridge bank to keep the closed bank's critical operations functioning while the bank is being liquidated piecemeal in an orderly fashion. Occasionally the bank is literally closed, insured depositors are paid out and the assets, when liquidated, used to reimburse the deposit insurance fund as well as uninsured depositors and other creditors if recoveries are sufficient.

When the bank is placed in receivership, those creditors' claims that are not transferred to an acquiring bank or a bridge bank are given receivership certificates to be liquidated later in order of absolute priority. Bank insolvency law provides a mechanism for early legal intervention in a distressed bank to either forestall closure or ensure closure takes place while the bank is yet (barely) solvent. This pre-insolvency intervention, called prompt corrective action (PCA), represents a very different view of stockholder rights than what exists in corporate law. Bank regulators may seize banks without an explicit default on any of its contractual credit obligations. The law provides for closure if capital requirements are violated and even for judgmental closure if the supervisors believe the bank is likely to fail to meet its obligations in the future. This pre-emptive closure is justified by belief that closing the bank before its net worth turns negative will reduce the adverse externalities of bank failure. Such closure is possible because of the conditional nature of the bank charter, which is granted by the chartering agency and may be revoked if the bank does not operate in a 'safe and sound manner' as determined by law, regulations, and supervisory judgment.[5]

The FDIC conducts bank resolutions under a legal requirement to minimize losses to the deposit insurance fund, known as 'least cost resolution' or, in exceptional circumstances, the receivership may be conducted under a systemic risk exemption (SRE) that allows the FDIC to focus on externalities of the insolvency rather than only on its private costs. Invoking SRE requires a formal approval process involving the FDIC, the Federal Reserve and the Secretary of the Treasury. This process was introduced in the *FDIC Improvement Act* (FDICIA) of 1991. In practice, systemic risk exemptions are rare and the FDIC may itself determine that paying certain depository and non-depository creditors, for instance by including all qualified financial contracts in the assets sold to an acquiring bank, increases the net proceeds of the purchase and assumption transaction, and thus is consistent with least cost resolution. After assuming the insured depositors' claims, the FDIC, as depositor-creditor, shares equally in losses with uninsured depositors. Least cost resolution is achieved when all depositors have been made whole.

16.2.2. Corporate Reorganization

While corporate bankruptcy comes in two forms – liquidation, or Chapter 7, and reorganization, or Chapter 11 – most large corporate bankruptcies are initially filed as Chapter 11 proceedings.[6] The premise underlying Chapter 11 is that the firm has more value to the creditors at large as a live going concern than would be the case were it dead and liquidated.[7] Both Chapters 7 and 11 are designed to solve a collective action problem, maximizing the value of the firm's assets for the collective benefit of all creditors.[8] Bankruptcy can be initiated by petition of its creditors if the firm defaults or voluntarily by management if they anticipate that the firm will not be able to meet its obligations.

Bankruptcy is a judicial process. Creditors, divided into similarly situated classes, and in the case of Chapter 11, the managers are represented by counsel and participate in negotiations to reach a commonly agreed (by vote) liquidation or reorganization plan. The court oversees the process and ensures that the law is followed and contractual rights of creditors are protected. The officers of the court are required to have no financial interests in the case and the court itself is neutral at least in that sense.

Central to bankruptcy is the legal device of staying creditor actions to allow time for the court to gather claims and assets and decide how best to dispose of them. The stay suspends creditors' rights to take actions, such as seizing collateral, which they would have under debtor/creditor law outside of bankruptcy. However, the stay does not change the nature of the creditors' claim. In contrast, bank insolvency does not have a stay and contracts must be either affirmed or rejected upon initiation of the receivership, usually within one business day.

16.3. DIFFERENCES IN BANK RESOLUTION AND BANKRUPTCY PROVISIONS

The statutes governing bankruptcy and bank insolvency resolution in the US differ in many ways, some of which are detailed in Table 16.1. This section examines a number of the salient areas.[9]

16.3.1. Initiation of Bankruptcy

Most non-bank corporations are subject to the Federal Bankruptcy Code.[10] Involuntary bankruptcy may be initiated either by a minimum number of creditors, whose claims are in default, or voluntarily by the firm itself in anticipation of a default or for strategic reasons.[11] In either case, a petition is made to one of a number of regional federal bankruptcy courts. Court approval of the creditors' petition or merely filing a voluntary petition initiates the process.

Unlike corporate bankruptcy law, bank resolution is initiated exogenously by the chartering agency or the institution's primary federal regulatory agency, or the FDIC.[12] The relevant authority can do so if it believes that the bank is not being operated in a safe and sound manner, and that the bank is unlikely to meet its deposit obligations. Perhaps the most significant of the reasons for bank closure, since the passage of FDICIA in 1991, is becoming 'critically undercapitalized' while the bank is still book value solvent, defined as a minimum of 2 per cent equity capital to total assets, and possibly even market value solvent.[13] Thus, the mandatory 'critically undercapitalized' criterion serves as a backstop intended to prevent regulators from delaying closing a bank for other discretionary prudential reasons.

Once legally closed, the bank's charter is revoked by the chartering agency and it is passed on to the FDIC, which serves as receiver or conservator. The bank's managers are ousted and shareholder control rights are terminated, although shareholders maintain a claim on any residual value remaining after creditors' claims are satisfied.

16.3.2. Stays

The ability to temporarily prevent creditors from pursuing their claims (termed 'stays') is central to the corporate bankruptcy process. Stays permit the bankruptcy court to 'call time out' to collect and validate claims, to determine the best way to dispose of assets in an orderly, value-maximizing manner, and to treat all like-priority creditors equally. Stays prevent creditor runs and keep contracts in force – the counter party is bound by the contract; claims on the insolvent firm remain pending; and collateral may usually not be liquidated. This facilitates the coordination of creditor claims.

Certain qualified financial contracts (e.g. derivatives master agreements) are exempt from the stays that apply to most contracts under the corporate bankruptcy code.[14] These derivatives master agreements contain close-out provisions which, when triggered, allow the solvent counter party to immediately terminate the contract (and all transactions under the master agreement), net the values, and pay the net amount due or file a claim if the net amount is owed after liquidating any collateral they hold.[15] However, these rights are not immediately enforceable for banks placed unto receivership or conservatorship. The FDIC has the power to prevent close-out for one business day in the case of receivership and indefinitely in the case of conservatorship or for contracts that are transferred to a bridge bank, for virtually any reason except non-performance (default or failure to meet collateral calls).[16] Thus, while most contracts, with the exception of qualified financial contracts, are automatically stayed by courts in the event of a corporate bankruptcy, the opposite situation results in the event of a bank's insolvency.

16.3.3. Management of the Insolvency Process

Corporate bankruptcies are resolved in special federal bankruptcy courts. The proceedings are judicial in nature with each party being represented by its own lawyers. The court appoints an agent to co-ordinate the process. For a liquidation this agent would be a receiver and for reorganization, a trustee. In Chapter 11 reorganization proceedings, the insolvent corporation's senior management is usually allowed by the court to continue operating the company and has exclusive rights to formulate a reorganization plan during an exclusion period of 120 days. A bankruptcy court may, at its discretion, grant extensions of this period and has routinely done so in the past.[17] Creditors may, however, petition the court to appoint an independent trustee under certain circumstances. All creditors have 'standing' to be represented in the proceedings, although the dynamics of voting may lead to certain minority blocks being effectively frozen out. Each creditor group, and in reorganizations also management and shareholders, must vote to approve the plans proposed by management, a receiver, or a trustee.[18] Decisions undertaken during the course of the proceedings (e.g., releasing collateral to secured creditors, partial payment of claims, paying employees, new post-insolvency – debtor-in-possession (DIP) – borrowing) are taken by the receiver/trustee with the approval of the court (the judge overseeing the case). If the parties cannot agree, the court can 'cram down' the plan that it considers most equitable. Decisions undertaken by the bankruptcy court may be appealed to higher courts, and many decisions are litigated before they finally take effect.[19]

In contrast, bank insolvencies are handled in an administrative proceeding. The bank's charter is revoked and shareholder controlling interests are terminated by the bank's primary regulator, and senior management is removed by the FDIC as receiver or conservator, all without involvement of any court.[20] Following its appointment as receiver or conservator, FDIC is solely in charge. As receiver or conservator, the FDIC collects information from the bank, its depositors, and other creditors, determines the validity of claims and then, within the confines of the law and its own regulations, disposes of the assets and pays off or transfers the liabilities.

16.3.4. Priorities, Collateral and Offsets

Legal priority, security interests, and right of offset, where protected, jointly determine what a creditor is entitled to under the law.[21] Both bankruptcy law and the FDIC Act provide a list of priorities specifying the order in which creditors should be paid out.[22] In both cases, the costs of administering the insolvency come first. These costs can be very substantial in the case of corporate insolvencies. The majority of unsecured corporate creditors are lumped together as general creditors.[23] In Chapter 11 proceedings, creditors are generally paid in securities of the reorganized firm, often in more junior securities.

In 1993, the *Depositor Preference Act* assigned domestic depositors, including the FDIC through its subrogation of the insured depositors' claims, priority over unsecured general creditors.[24] Insured depositors are paid in full by the FDIC, which 'steps into their shoes' and assumes (subrogates) their claims. Uninsured domestic depositors and the FDIC share equally (on a pro rata basis) in any recoveries, up to the par amount of the deposit liabilities. Any excess recoveries are distributed to general creditors, and then to shareholders (including parent company equity interests).[25]

Commercial law provides mechanisms for creditors to establish security interests in the property of the debtor through collateralization of their claims. If the proper legal forms have been followed, bankruptcy courts will enforce these rights. Thus, secured general creditors may enjoy higher recoveries than would unsecured creditors. Banking law discourages collateral arrangements on the part of a bank's depositors. In the US, generally only the Department of the Treasury, state, and municipal governments can secure their deposits with collateral. Non-deposit creditors (including foreign depositors) have greater opportunity to secure their claims through collateralization, repurchase agreements, etc. Federal Reserve lending through the discount window and advances from Federal Home Loan Banks are also fully collateralized.

During Chapter 11 rehabilitation, the bankrupt firm can contract, with the court's permission, for additional DIP financing to allow it to continue operating. This new debt is effectively given priority over the existing, pre-bankruptcy debt.[26] Such borrowing may reduce ultimate payments to existing creditors, if economic firm value continues to be eroded. While there is no private (financial market) DIP financing for banks, pre-closure financing in the form of Federal Reserve discount window lending and post-closure FDIC-provided guarantees serve much the same purpose.[27]

16.3.5. Pre-Insolvency Transfers

The treatment of pre-insolvency transfers is another important area of differences between corporate bankruptcy and bank insolvency. Bankruptcy law is designed to ensure that creditors with equal claims, after taking into account security interests and priority, are in fact treated equally. One issue that arises is the possibility that one creditor may benefit at the advantage of another through transfers made prior to, but in anticipation of filing for bankruptcy.

Under the bankruptcy code, the bankruptcy trustee has the power to 'avoid' certain of these 'preferential transfers'.[28] Pre-petition transfers made within 90 days of bankruptcy filing (one year for transfers to insiders) are presumptively preferential and the trustee may seek to recover, or 'claw back', those assets and return them to the bankruptcy estate. This presumption that pre-petition transfers are avoidable preferential transfers is subject to a 'normal course of business' exception. Routine payments, such as employee wages or regular payments to suppliers or scheduled payments such as retiring debt in accordance with provisions of the indenture (e.g., at maturity or for sinking fund), are considered normal course of business and not preferential transfers and are not subject to clawback.

Bank insolvency law does not contain mechanisms for clawing back preferential transfers.[29] Consequently, deposits that are withdrawn prior to, even if done in anticipation of bank closure (i.e., runs), as happened, for example, in the failure of MCorp in 1989 and Bank of New England in 1991, are not able to be recovered by the FDIC. Similar runs – close out of accounts – at non-bank financial firms may be subject to clawbacks.

16.3.6. Legal Certainty of Claims

The dynamics of the corporate bankruptcy process increases the uncertainties as to both the value and timing of creditor recoveries. The straightforward priorities of payout under bankruptcy law only apply in liquidation. An essential element of corporate reorganization is that creditors participate in a renegotiation of their claims, the outcome of which, while subject to collective approval, may depend as much on bargaining power of the different claimants as on their theoretical priorities in liquidation. Furthermore, security interests may lead to an apparent, if not real, redistribution between theoretically equal-priority creditors. The corporate bankruptcy process, with its use of class voting and the possibility of junior holdouts, may also reduce at least the present value of the aggregate final recovery value. This frequently leads to dynamics where more senior creditors give up part of their legal claim in the hopes of achieving a settlement that yields a larger present value recovery (smaller, more immediate portion of a bigger, or at least more certain, pie). Leaving aside the possibilities that claims will be disallowed for various reasons, the precise distributional outcome of reorganization under bankruptcy is uncertain.

Bank insolvencies generally do not suffer from this problem. Offset and collateral are usually not major issues (particularly, for small and medium banks), and depositor preference is usually adhered to.[30] Absolute priority may be violated in bank insolvencies only under two conditions. Firstly, if the systemic risk exemption is invoked and some general creditors are made whole, while uninsured depositors and the FDIC are not. Secondly, if minimal cost resolution is achieved by transferring some non-insured deposit liabilities – for instance complex financial contracts – to a bridge bank rather than liquidating them, thus protecting those creditors from the credit losses that other creditors may incur. Neither of these two conditions is likely to occur frequently, but both are more likely to occur in large bank failures.

16.3.7. Timeliness

The timeliness of insolvency resolution has two components: the ability to initiate the process before the potential credit losses to debt claimants become large, and the ability to resolve the insolvency and pay the depositors as well as other creditors the recovery values of their claims in an expeditious manner once it is initiated minimizing liquidity losses. Prompt legal closure deprives shareholders and managers of the option to gamble for resurrection at the depositors' and creditors' expense and minimizes credit losses, while prompt resolution mitigates both credit losses, as asset values generally decline after insolvency has been declared, and liquidity losses to depositors and creditors, who have their funds tied up in the insolvent bank.

There is no mechanism for non-bank corporate creditors to preemptively precipitate a bankruptcy proceeding so as to limit their losses except in some instances through runs and acceleration, both of which may also exacerbate the losses. Creditors must await an event of default that permits them a basis for petitioning the court to place the firm into bankruptcy. So long as firms can meet current financial obligations, including through asset liquidations, there is little that creditors can do even if the firm is believed to be insolvent. Managers can and sometimes do file for bankruptcy, usually Chapter 11, in anticipation of an actual default. However, in such a voluntary action the managers may not always be acting solely in the creditor's interests. On the other hand, bank regulators have broad powers to legally close a bank on the basis that it may get into financial trouble (i.e. operating in an unsafe and unsound manner) and a positive requirement to close it before it becomes book-value insolvent.

The FDIC Act recognizes the special character of bank deposit claims, specifically that because of their liquidity they serve as money. Thus, the FDIC Act requires that 'payment of the insured deposits . . . shall be made by the Corporation [FDIC] as soon as possible'[31] and authorizes the FDIC 'to settle all uninsured and unsecured claims with a final settlement payment' based on average past recovery values in order 'to maintain essential liquidity and to prevent financial disruption'.[32] The FDIC also has the authority to make advance dividend payments to claimants based on its estimates of recovery values for the bank being resolved.[33] Like the prompt payment of insured deposits, advanced dividends on uninsured deposits minimize liquidity losses. However, advanced dividends are likely to be less than par value, so that the uninsured claimants may suffer credit losses, at least initially. Thus, because of the prompt payment of insured depositors at par and the potential for accelerated payment of the expected recovery value of uninsured deposits, liquidity issues are potentially separate from the time in receivership.

Except for insured depositors, whose claims are usually settled immediately by transferring the deposits to another bank and are made immediately available, both uninsured depositors and other creditors, once their claims have been approved by the FDIC are given receivership certificates. These are paid in cash as this becomes available through sale of assets, or earlier through the aforementioned advanced dividends. The timing and amount of any dividends are determined by the FDIC and may be spread over several months or years. Liquidation of a bank's assets, once it has been legally closed, is not immediate and asset values may deteriorate as they do in Chapter 11 proceedings.[34]

16.4. WHY ARE LCFIs SPECIAL?

In recent years, large financial institutions that have 'bank-like' characteristics have grown rapidly. LCFIs are important because their failure may have systemic implications for the financial system. That is, their individual failure can lead to knock-on effects that impose serious costs or even failure on other major firms in the markets in which they operate. This impact may be direct, through failure to make good on existing contracts, or it may be indirect by leading to a sharp change in perceived riskiness of similarly situated counterparties, rising risk aversion, and a locking up of segments of the financial market. In either case, the direct costs of the systemic event can be substantial and, if the systemic consequences are not rapidly ameliorated, can lead to serious adverse impact on the macro economy. For this reason, the failure of a LCFI may require actions by regulators to contain the systemic consequences. This will usually mean a rapid and effective initial response to the failure of the individual LCFI in distress. However, LCFIs are large and complex firms and not all parts are systemically important. So it may not be necessary that the entire firm's insolvency process be rapidly concluded, merely that the situation be rapidly contained. This could mean resolving only the systemically important parts quickly.

LCFIs may include large banks, as well as large non-bank financial institutions. LCFIs share some characteristics with small- and medium-sized banks, but these points of similarity are qualitatively different and differ in scale. LCFIs also have important characteristics that are not generally true for most banks, though they are true for the few banks that are LCFIs. Two points of similarity between banks and non-bank LCFIs are connectedness and financial fragility.

16.4.1. Connectedness

More than anything else, it is their connectedness to other large financial complex institutions that makes LCFIs systemically important. Because of the heavy concentration of large financial firms in markets such as derivatives, securitization originations, repurchase agreement financing, prime brokers for hedge funds, etc., the failure of any one will have a greater impact on the financial markets as a whole than would the failure of a smaller, less interconnected financial institution.

16.4.2. Fragility

Financial fragility for LCFIs arises from a combination of the short-term nature of funding, leading to a possibility of runs; a low percentage of cash or cash-like assets, potentially leading to fire-sale losses; and low capital that can be wiped out by relatively small losses. For LCFIs, short-term funding frequently represents a large portion of total funding and is subject to runs if doubts arise about the solvency of the firm and wholesale funding terms change adversely (increased haircuts on repurchase agreements), traditional funding evaporates (commercial paper purchasers decline to roll over their positions, other firms refuse to lend in the interbank markets), and customers withdraw their funds or close out their positions requiring return of their collateral.

Derivatives market practices can produce another source of fragility. The value of large unbalanced positions, such as AIG's portfolio of credit default swaps that it had written, can change quickly. Over-the-counter (OTC) collateral practices, unlike the margining of exchange-traded, central counterparties (CCP)-cleared, derivatives, is not always forward looking. Thus, changes in the value of derivatives can create sudden large losses in the value of positions. While these losses need not be paid immediately, they can produce immediate demands for more collateral to cover the position. The collateral a firm is required to maintain may also depend on the actual or perceived creditworthiness of the firm. When this changes, the resulting demand for collateral can produce a need for immediate liquidity of significant size.[35]

16.5. RESOLUTION REGIME PROPOSALS

As a result of the financial crisis and perceived inadequacy of existing options for resolving insolvent LCFIs, regulators and legislators in the US have passed new resolution procedures that would be applied to LCFIs. Their main aim is to:

1. Control the timing of the initiation of the insolvency process;
2. Replace management of an insolvent LCFI;
3. Control the allocation of realized losses across different creditors;
4. Control the manner and terms of disposition of assets, including the decision of whether to liquidate in the private sector or transfer parts into a bridge institution;
5. Transfer any losses not borne by the creditors of the LCFI to other LCFIs, producing a mutualization of losses and protecting the taxpayer from losses.

These ideas are all based on the model of the US bank insolvency process. As such, they presume an administrative rather than judicial process and a receivership rather than a restructuring. Although not part of the current proposals, regulators may also want to influence the international aspects of the insolvency, including approving the validity of foreign claims and the prioritization of domestic and foreign recoveries.

Two overarching, but somewhat philosophical, questions that should be asked in evaluating such a structure are:

1. Whether moving the insolvency outside of the judicial process is desirable, and
2. Whether a process designed to liquidate the firm, whole or piecemeal, rather than to preserve its going concern value is better.

We will examine the pros and cons of the above components both as to their own merit and as to whether they can be met better with a minimally-modified bankruptcy process rather than effective elimination of the bankruptcy regime.

16.5.1. Insolvency Initiation

Regulatory control of the timing of insolvency harkens to the PCA found in banking law. PCA has the overall objective of placing the bank into regulatory insolvency before it is economically insolvent. This should reduce the problems of the insolvency itself as assets should cover claims. While in practice, PCA almost never succeeds in closing banks while they have positive equity, the principle is sound and may in any case be expected to reduce losses.

Equally, if not more, important, as a practical matter, the threat of regulatory closure has been a powerful tool for motivating distressed firms to pursue solutions outside of insolvency processes. Lastly, PCA is not just an early closure rule, but a series of increasingly onerous restrictions on what a firm may do as it transitions from apparent robust financial health through various degrees of distress to insolvency. By providing a clear menu of consequences for not maintaining adequate capital, PCA provides an advance notice of consequences which may have a salutary effect on management. It also provides a benchmark against which regulator's pre-insolvency actions may later be reviewed.

PCA's weaknesses include its current primary reliance on book value capital measures. However, capital, even if correctly measured, is not a complete measure of risk. Problems of liquidity and unanticipated large and correlated changes in the value of assets have been the proximate causes of failure of firms that were apparently well capitalized shortly before, or even on the day, they failed.

It may be questioned whether regulators should have the sole authority to initiate the LCFI insolvency process. Retaining the ability of creditors in bankruptcy to also initiate the process would provide a supplement and check on regulators, should they wish to forbear. Since pre-insolvency closure is the goal, creditors should be provided the same criteria for petitioning to initiate insolvency as the regulators. It makes little sense to demand creditors exert market discipline while depriving them of a constructive tool for influencing managers.

16.5.2. Appointing Management

In the past, one of the alleged weaknesses of Chapter 11 has been deference to existing pre-insolvency management, effectively granting them initial control of the resolution and setting up a situation where management can hold creditors hostage for as long as they control the process. This exclusionary period has recently been limited, though it may be too early to assess the effects of the new limitations.

The argument for leaving managers in place is that they are most knowledgeable and thus best able to shepherd the firm through the process. But this argument suffers from the perception and perhaps reality that those who produced the problems should not be trusted and rewarded by the chance to solve them, sometimes with considerable personal profit.

Granting the regulators the power to replace management as part of their PCA powers would provide added leverage for regulators to pursue pre-insolvency solutions. The primary interest of the government in seeing that management is replaced when a firm becomes insolvent should be to ensure that incentives of pre-insolvency managers are compatible with sound financial management and that they do not benefit in the insolvency.

Post-insolvency, another group of interested parties comes into play – the creditors – and if the insolvency is proceeding through a bankruptcy process, a new agent, the trustee, is introduced. The trustee is an agent for the court and responsible for the appointment of management. Insofar as both the government and private creditors have similar interests in minimizing the losses in a LCFI insolvency, in a new resolution regime they could co-operate in the recommendation of the trustee, perhaps with the ultimate decision being made by the court, as is done in Chapter 11 reorganizations. Creditor's rights and due process may best be maintained by the government pursuing its objectives through its standing in the process rather than giving it control of the process by granting it the exclusive power to appoint the trustee and management. The creditors are not less able to determine ability of prospective managers than are government agents.

16.5.3. Allocating Losses

The desire of the government to have creditors share in realized losses arises from a desire to maintain market discipline. However, bankruptcy also imposes losses on creditors.[36] Bankruptcy does this according to contractual rights, legal priorities and bargaining among creditor groups. The latter can result in deviations from strict priority, but it is based on a collective agreement principle and it is unclear why an administrative allocation would be superior in protecting legal rights.

Another role of the government in a LCFI insolvency resolution is to look out for systemic externalities and try to mitigate them. Such mitigation might involve guaranteeing some creditors and/or counterparties, and making them partially or totally whole. The justification for doing so is that the firm or some parts of the firm are systemically important and must continue to operate and that this can only be done by guaranteeing their counterparties and transferring the resulting losses to other not-systemically-important creditors, a pool of LCFI, or the government. Any increase in government losses resulting from such carve outs may be transferred to all or parts of the financial industry, who benefit most directly from the rescues.

This argument has considerable validity. However, the decision as to whether or not a particular area or function is systemically important or not is judgmental. As we have argued earlier, one of the characteristics of most large important financial firms is that their creditors include other large important financial firms. The collective nature of bankruptcy decision making could be employed to aid in making the decision as to which, if any, parts of the firm are systemically important. The industry could be represented by trade groups, such as the International Swaps and Derivatives Association. If the industry, which would bear both the direct externalities of an LCFI failure and much of the costs of bailing out all or part of the insolvent firm, were to assert that it was preferable not to grant special protection to the particular part, it is hard to see on what basis the government could assert systemic importance and protect the creditors despite the fact that some market participants may see some action as benefiting them by eliminating one or more competitors.

Derivative counterparties and prime broker customers offer easily identified parties who stand to lose if the related systemically important function was allowed to fail with losses. In other cases, the parties at risk may be more diffuse or lack representative market organizations to speak on their behalf. At the same time, being subject to political considerations, the government's representatives may be unduly risk averse. Thus, the government may possibly make unsubstantiated claims of systemic importance, which would allow it to invoke the systemic risk exemption, and arbitrarily allocated losses in insolvency and impose unnecessary costs on the industry.[37] Any claim of unsubstantiated (by the presumed loss bearers) systemic importance and need for carve out should be decided by the court allowing for the creditors and the government to argue the pros and cons of the case. It is important that the language setting out this procedure define the allowed circumstances narrowly and not give overriding deference to the government in the assertion of facts that will be necessarily hard to establish.

16.5.4. Disposition of Assets

In the reorganization of a complex multinational firm with large numbers of operating divisions it is likely that decisions will have to be made as to how to sell off parts. In a receivership, the entire purpose is to liquidate and sell off the firms, in whole or in part. Once creditors' rights vis-à-vis each other are established and protected, the process for determining the valuation of a disposition (or retention) of assets is critically important as it determines the losses that the creditors will bear.

Bankruptcy provides a collective process for determining the disposition of assets. As a collective process where each group of creditors can participate, the rights of all creditors are protected. The court has the obligation and power to ensure that decisions are made in the collective interest and to maximize the value of the insolvent firm for the benefit of all creditors. The court can block actions by parties seeking to gain advantage over other creditors. Being a judicial process the decisions made are transparent and are subject to review.

An administrative process provides neither transparencies nor explicit protections of creditors' rights. By excluding creditors from participation in the decisions that will determine the amount of recovery they will obtain, an administrative insolvency process places great reliance on the judgment, abilities, and incentives of the administrator. Where the administrator is overwhelmed by the demands of the process or a reasonable desire to expedite the process to reduce possible contagion, they may make choices that may weigh rapidity on the deposition over maximizing recovery. This is particularly true as the administrator does not bear the costs of the decisions they make. Political considerations may also intrude into their objectives. These distortions are likely to be destructive of value and raise the costs of insolvency. The lack of transparency undermines the credibility of the process, particularly where the institution being resolved is extremely complex.

Bankruptcy has been criticized as too slow to address systemically important firms. However, the bank insolvency process is only quick for the initial decisions, and may be too hasty. The disposition of unsold assets, the 'tail' of the process, can stretch out for years. And as we have suggested, rapidity has its downsides. The recent unplanned large bankruptcy of Lehman Brothers has demonstrated that some courts in a single jurisdiction can act quickly to stabilize the situation of a systemically important institution. Pre-packaged bankruptcies of C.I.T., Chrysler and General Motors have been reasonably rapid. Many of them resulted in claims that the process unduly destroyed value by disposing of assets too cheaply, but then too so have some FDIC receiverships, most notably WaMu in 2008.

While both bankruptcy and administrative receivership can act quickly, as a systemic failure would require, and rapidity of decision-making may increase losses, the difference is that a bankruptcy is a collective process with creditor participation.

16.5.5. Mutualization of Losses

Because of the scale of LCFIs and the market stresses that are likely to accompany (or precipitate) their distress, the involvement of outside or government funds is almost inevitable. While the saving (or controlled resolution) of a systemic institution may produce public benefits, having the public bear the costs of intervention may be politically unpopular. Imposing losses on the taxpayers also produce moral hazard. As LCFIs exist in the context of a financial market of similar firms doing more or less similar things, it can be argued that making the market in which these losses occur bear the residual losses of the insolvency (those not borne by pre-insolvency creditors), as is the case with the FDIC insurance fund, might have a salutary effect on how markets function. This might lead the industry to develop market structures that prevent or at least mitigate such events.

While the principle is sound, the problem lies in defining the class of institutions subject to the assessments to reimburse the government for the losses they temporarily incur in the resolution process. Pre-funding requires identifying the class to be taxed ex ante. Had we done so prior to the current crisis it is likely that the large investment banks would have been included, but AIG may have escaped notice. So there is a danger that pre-funding does not cover all firms that eventually generate the losses. Post-funding also requires identifying the relevant group of firms to be assessed and in any case it is probable that the 'guilty' parties have departed. In addition, the availability of on-hand funds signals the possibility of government bail-outs, increasing moral hazard and may increase the likelihood of such bailouts.

Private loss mutualization is an essential component of the rationale for favouring modified bankruptcy over administration. If, through private loss mutualization, the taxpayers are only temporary participants in the process, providing only loans (lender of last resort), and the process is designed to ensure the repayment of the funds they advance, the argument for depriving the creditors (and the financial industry) of their rights through an administrative resolution process is reduced.

16.5.6. Control of International Aspects

There are two components of this problem: the co-ordination of the international components of the pre- and post-insolvency resolution and the allocation of domestic and foreign recoveries. Pre-insolvency consultation among national regulatory authorities takes the form of information sharing to avert insolvency in the first place. International negotiations are essential to constructing a pre-insolvency strategy that avoids the costs and disruptions of any insolvency process or to arrange a pre-packaged solution without precipitating a destructive pre-emptive grab of the assets subsidiaries and branch offices by national authorities.

Post-insolvency allocation of recoveries is, however, best not left to domestic regulators. Ad hoc, politically-driven determination of when to allow payments across borders are not conducive to international cooperation. A better solution is to define in law the rules governing payment of foreign claims in each country with as much clarity as possible and then for the courts to enforce these rules. This will have the twin advantages of creating predictability and providing regulators and politicians political cover from any resulting recriminations. The temptation will be to write these laws to favour domestic over foreign creditors. This is currently the case in US banking law. This attitude is inconsistent with the needs of global financial markets for regulatory and supervisory cooperation and coordination in the resolution of cross-border insolvencies. We discuss these issues at greater length later in this chapter.

16.6. DESIDERATA OF AN IDEAL LCFI INSOLVENCY SYSTEM

It follows from the above arguments that the desirable characteristics of an ideal insolvency system for LCFIs would incorporate elements of both FDIA bank insolvency and Chapter 11 bankruptcy in a modified or hybrid bankruptcy proceeding. Such a system should:

- Incorporate regulatory rights of pre-insolvency intervention (PCA) and pre-insolvency or pre-default closure petitions on a timely basis by both regulators and private creditors;
- Provide an expedited judicial proceeding where both regulators and creditors have standing to petition the court to initiate but not delay insolvency proceedings;
- Give regulators standing to represent the interests of the public;
- Preserve the going concern value of the insolvent firm as a whole as much as possible, but permit a change in management;
- Impose pro-rata losses on all creditors according to their contractual priorities, except where systemic risk considerations clearly require otherwise (an externality exemption). The system should give the government/regulators adequate, but not unlimited, scope to represent the interests of the financial system and the public in reducing the adverse externalities of the failure;

- If any creditors must be made whole, any resulting losses from the action should be mutualized within the finance (LCFI) industry rather than being shifted to remaining creditors of the resolved firm, non-systemic financial firms, or to the tax-payers;
- The system should be predictable and identify who is subject to it known well in advance of its application so that markets can price insolvency risks accordingly;
- Preserve creditors' rights to represent their own interests, and provide reasonable rights of appeal and expeditious review of decisions;
- Decisions should be subject to a review of a neutral court of experts that can weigh arguments, balance claims and ensure that all parties' rights under the law are respected.

It is not obvious whether Chapter 11 rehabilitation or an *Federal Deposit Insurance Act* (FDIA) closing followed by a bridge institution is more desirable. Chapter 11 rehabilitation is more likely to maximize the asset values of an insolvent institution but does not usually introduce new management. In bank resolution a bridge institution results in unfair competition and moral hazard problems from the FDIC (or other agency) guarantee of its liabilities and a competitor is removed from an increasingly concentrated group of LCFIs. The pros and cons of each approach need to be studied further.

16.6.1. Gaining Time

The US bank insolvency process seeks to liquidate the failed bank while keeping its critical functions going in one of two ways – through delay in closure or through the bridge bank. The primary bank regulator controls the timing of bank closure. As long as the bank can continue to meet its ongoing obligations the formal closure can be delayed while the FDIC is arranging the disposition of the bank's assets and liabilities. Once the bank is legally closed, its assets and liabilities sold or passed to a bridge bank. This is effectively equivalent to a 'pre-pac' bankruptcy where the court serves to validate an agreement reached outside of bankruptcy proceeding by the creditors. Delay, however, depends critically on the ability of the bank to continue to make contractually required payments. Banks usually have enough ready funds to meet normal transactions requirements, or can raise them through insured deposits and secured borrowing. But if a funding run does occur, it may become impossible for a LCFI to make the contractually required payments.

When a corporation files for bankruptcy (most) creditors' claims are stayed and the corporation can continue to do business while not making all of its scheduled payments. Stays keep contracts in place but temporarily suspend contractual terms that would take assets out of the bankruptcy estate to the detriment of other creditors. To fund the ongoing operations of the corporation while it is in Chapter 11, US bankruptcy law provides for DIP financing. As an inducement to creditors to extend financing to a firm in such circumstances, priority is given to DIP financing in the event that the reorganization fails and the firm is liquidated. Furthermore, only pre-insolvency debts are subject to reorganization. With these advantages, DIP financing can usually be found sufficient to carry the firm through the time it spends in bankruptcy.

It is in providing DIP financing that the government can make a critical contribution to the resolution of a LCFI. Those entities depend on access to funding and it is unlikely that private institutions would be willing or able to do so, both because of the likely scale of the needed funding and because it is probable that LCFI failures would take place while credit markets are already stressed. Stays and DIP financing are not open to banks as they do not enjoy bankruptcy protection, bank insolvency law does not provide for stays, and it is implausible that a primary regulator could allow a bank to continue to do business while refusing to make required payments.

The method for gaining time for an orderly liquidation in a US bank insolvency is either through a bridge bank, if the bank must be immediately closed to stop a run, or by delaying closure while a purchaser is found so that the purchase (of selected assets) and assumption (of deposits) may be completed in conjunction with closing of the bank. Those assets, liabilities, operations that are transferred into the bridge bank continue to function, while those left behind in the defunct old bank lose all rights except to payment of claims at some point in the future. Creditors left in the old closed bank are not stayed as their contracts cease to exist and are replaced with claims on the receivership for liquidated damages. Creditors of the bridge bank are not likely to run (though they are free to do so) because the bridge bank is a separate institution owned and operated by the FDIC which has a credit line on the US Treasury and is widely understood to be backed by the full faith and credit of the Federal Government. The FDIC does not require that the bridge bank be capitalized, so only operating expenses need be paid.

16.6.2. Avoiding Government Guarantees

A bridge bank is not, however, the same as a Chapter 11 proceeding. As noted, in Chapter 11 the failed firm continues in operation. In bank resolution, the failed bank's charter is revoked and a new bridge bank chartered. In Chapter 11, all functions continue, while in bank insolvency only those contracts and functions transferred into the bridge bank continue. At initiation of a bank's insolvency process, the FDIC must choose what to transfer and what to leave behind in the receivership. However, the FDIC need not transfer the full amount of uninsured deposits and other liabilities. This decision must be made within one business day after closing and cannot be revised. Creditors in Chapter 11 remain creditors of the bankruptcy estate. They may or may not be eventually paid the amount of their claims, but they have no claim on the court or the government. Creditors of a failed bank, whose contracts are transferred into a bridge bank, become creditors of the bridge bank – that is, of the FDIC. Once transferred, there is no legal mechanism by which the FDIC can impose losses on creditors of the bridge bank, although the full value of uninsured deposits need not be transferred to the bridge bank. When the government controls and funds the process, the government effectively guarantees creditors and counter parties against default of the bridge bank.

16.7. CROSS-BORDER ISSUES

Because most LCFIs are multinational institutions, their resolution presents particular challenges not present in smaller institutions or large standalone institutions in a single jurisdiction. There are four main areas of concern.

- Branching across jurisdictions can produce incentives for the home country regulators to act in the interests of domestic rather than foreign (branch country) constituencies and to discriminate between domestic and foreign creditors in insolvency resolution;
- Having legally distinct subsidiaries in different countries means that no single resolution authority will be solely in charge of the proceedings;
- National resolution authorities will have a tendency to distinguish between domestic and foreign creditors, and favour the former;
- In a holding company structure with legally distinct subsidiaries, inter-affiliate transactions can alter the recoveries received by outside creditors.[38]

Bankruptcy and bank insolvency resolution attempt to create an orderly resolution of an insolvent firm by forestalling the destructive and uncoordinated grab for assets by creditors. But the ability of a court or resolution authority's ability to do so is limited by the scope of their legal jurisdiction, which is national. In some instances, as in the US, their jurisdiction may be limited to certain types of institutions, e.g., banks, as well. This means that multiple resolution authorities may become involved in the resolution of a LCFI.

The United Nations Commission on International Trade Law (UNCITRAL) has attempted to deal with similar issues in constructing a model law for countries to adopt, but its efforts explicitly excluded financial institutions. Within the EU, some progress has been made in providing a predictable structure for cross border financial insolvencies. The home country court of the insolvent institution takes the lead and conducts the main proceeding, while the host country courts conduct ancillary proceedings in support of the main proceeding in the home country. This is a sensible arrangement in theory, but is hampered in practice by differences in laws in the different countries.[39] Perhaps more importantly, the reach of this arrangement is limited to the EU and most LCFIs operate both in the EU, the US and elsewhere.

There is a fundamental inconsistency between the economic and legal structures of a LCFI. A solvent LCFI operates across national boundaries, through subsidiaries and branches. It is running this network as an interconnected whole for the benefit of the parent company. However, in insolvency and particularly in a receivership, the subsidiary network is apt to disappear, leaving a collection of more or less standalone companies incorporated in different countries, which necessarily must be resolved in those countries. As has been often noted, LCFIs are international in life and (their dismembered parts) national in death. So long as they are subject to the same jurisdiction, a country's bankruptcy courts can co-ordinate the resolution of a failed holding company and its legally distinct components by bringing the separate proceedings into a single administrative process. But no court can reach into another country to take control of a subsidiary company that is incorporated there. Absent a supranational bankruptcy court, a LCFI failure resolution will necessarily be fragmented.

The effects of fragmented proceeding might be mitigated if countries had similar laws so that perceptions that creditors in one country would be harmed if another country's laws were applied to them were removed. However, as a recent study by the Basel Committee on Bank Regulation (Basel, 2009) concluded, differences in legal philosophy and national politics make such harmonization all but impossible. But even complete harmonization of applicable laws would not suffice to produce perfect cooperation between national courts involved in the same LCFI insolvency. Inevitable differences in the distribution of assets and liabilities across countries means that creditors in some countries will benefit from a ring-fenced approach that addresses their claims first, before turning over any surplus to foreign courts for the benefit of foreign creditors. The US has adopted an explicit ring-fencing (territorial) position for US subsidiaries (and other assets) of foreign-parented holding company insolvencies. It does, however, take a unitary (universal) position with respect to US-chartered parent banks with foreign subsidiary operations.

In the absence of any central coordinating authority, such conflicts of interest among national resolution agents limit the voluntary cooperation that may be expected. It may create incentives for regulators to move foreign assets into their jurisdiction and then to freeze them. When multiple regulators act in this way, it sets up a scramble for assets, destroying any possibility for a pre-insolvency workout, thus precipitating the collapse of weak LCFIs.

Within a holding company structure, inter-affiliate transactions, whether they be asset sales or financing, create a distinction between internal (to the holding company) and external sales, debt and equity may change the payoffs to different participants. Both sides of internal transactions are ultimately controlled by the (common) parent holding company. Moving assets between subsidiaries does not directly change the financial situation of the parent but can have a substantial impact in bankruptcy on both the external creditors and the equity holders of the holding company.

The parent or the parent's regulators might seek to exchange risky assets in one subsidiary for safe assets in another, or move cash by borrowing between subsidiaries. But the problem is larger than these perhaps obvious preferences. The different roles subsidiaries play in the holding company can lead to economic efficiencies for a healthy LCFI, but may disadvantage some outside creditors, and advantage others, in insolvency. For instance, a holding company may be raising funds in one country/subsidiary and lending them to another subsidiary in another country to be invested there where returns are better. Appendix A shows via examples how such inter-affiliate transactions can alter the payoffs of the various parties in liquidation. Since these arrangements can be long term and 'normal business' we refer to them as structural preferences to distinguish them from the single transactions that may take place in anticipation of insolvency.

16.8. RECOMMENDATIONS FOR CROSS-BORDER RESOLUTIONS

To consider how to mitigate the problems presented by the distress and failure of a LCFI, in both its domestic and international dimensions, it is necessary to identify the goals to be achieved. The first goal should be insolvency avoidance. Formal insolvency processes are destructive of value, and for a LCFI disruptive to markets. Failing to prevent insolvency, there are several potential objectives for insolvency resolution in its international dimensions.

16.8.1. Insolvency Avoidance

Avoiding formal insolvency proceedings in the first place has two components: structured early intervention by regulators and creating incentives and avoiding disincentives for pre-insolvency workouts by the firm itself and its counter parties. Extending the concept of prompt corrective action to domestic LCFIs, with a sequence of progressive restrictions based on appropriate measures of financial condition incorporating economic capital, liquidity and risk. In the international context this process should be as consistent across home countries as local laws permit. In its international execution, structured early intervention should be coordinated across home and host country regulators, with regulators in all relevant jurisdictions acting in concert. Such a coordinated process would alert regulators in all jurisdictions to developing problems, lessening the scope for responses that merely shift problems. The credibility of the threat to place the firm into an insolvency resolution regime will be enhanced if regulators everywhere are seen by the institution to be 'on top' of developing problems. However, such coordination may be difficult to achieve. Home country regulators may be reluctant to share information suggesting the parent is in difficulty and host country laws may limit disclosure of detailed subsidiary (and client) information about cross-border institutions. Different national regulators may have different abilities to monitor and act. Regulators who are more able to monitor and thus gain valuable information leading up to a failure, may be unwilling to share information about cross-border institutions with other national regulators as this would reduce their ability to act in the interests of domestic creditors, for instance by requiring the distressed multinational institution to transfer assets into their jurisdiction. National regulators may also be sensitive to perceived directions from regulators in other countries.

As an LCFI becomes more distressed, national regulators should intensify their monitoring and progressively restrict inter-affiliate transfers to prevent pre-insolvency positioning of assets. Requiring authorization from country regulators before material assets are exchanged between a subsidiary under their control and another subsidiary outside their jurisdiction need not prevent self help measures or conduct of normal business. It would also enhance regulators' ability to better monitor the liquidation value of the subsidiary they supervise when the possibility of liquidation becomes significant. Enforcing such prohibitions may be difficult however. International clearing and settlement systems may not be adaptable to preventing unauthorized transfers, so compliance needs to be approached through ex post measures. These might include international agreed fines to be assessed against the parent's bankruptcy estate. Additionally, prior notification that regulators were imposing restrictions might be the basis for imposing automatic claw/give backs (see below). Structured early intervention by regulators can be most effective and help prevent the firm from becoming insolvent, if self-help (e.g., unwinding derivatives positions, raising equity) and market-based solutions (private workouts, asset sales) are also encouraged to supplement and enhance regulatory discipline.

16.8.2. Goals of International LCFI Insolvency Resolution

International insolvency resolution will involve multiple processes, applying different laws to different parts of an essentially dismembered institution. Three alternative goals arise that may be pursued:

- Domestic creditors get the same payouts they would if a branch or subsidiary was in home country;
- Domestic creditors get same payout they would if the parent was in a host country;
- Domestic creditors get the same payout they would if an inter-affiliate transactions were unwound.

The first of these is the ideal embodied in the EU approach to cross-border insolvencies. It is, however, unlikely for most LCFIs, given the ring fence approach adopted by the US and the tendency for national courts to apply national laws and to favour domestic constituents in their application in ancillary proceedings. The second is likewise problematic. In a single jurisdiction holding company insolvency, a court can take control of the parent and all subsidiaries and sort out the internal and external claims and the assets in a manner that is consistent with a single set of laws and procedures and in the interests of all the creditors. Without control of all parts of a LCFI no one court can achieve this. This leaves the third objective.

16.8.3. Undoing Internal Preferences

As noted, a major source of conflict in a cross-border LCFI insolvency resolution is distortions in an LCFI's external creditors' positions that arise from internal transactions (structural preferences). To address this we suggest two remedies:

- Automatic clawbacks of recent inter-affiliate asset transfers;
- Subordinating internal creditors to external creditors.

Clawbacks are common to bankruptcy law in many jurisdictions. They reverse recent transactions that took assets outside the bankruptcy estate prior to filing and which may have been intended to benefit one creditor at the expense of another. To accomplish this, the courts sue the beneficiary to recover the transferred assets.

This principle may be adapted to multi-jurisdiction insolvencies. We propose that material inter-affiliate transfers occurring within a certain period before the insolvency, e.g. 30 or 90 days, be automatically reversed by courts on both ends of the transaction. This couples the idea of 'claw back' with that of a reciprocal 'give back'. Every transfer of assets has an offsetting action that would also be reversed – a liquidated debt would be restored and the payment returned; a security sale would restore the security to the seller and the purchase price to the buyer. Where this is not possible, the party returning the purchase price could be given a senior claim tied to the value of the asset that could not be returned. Automatically unwinding recent pre-insolvency transfers and allowing the parties to then pursue any inter-affiliate claims in the normal manner, would reduce the ability to engage in pre-insolvency asset shifting, which in turn might reduce the incentives for national regulators to grab assets and precluding a more desirable resolution outside insolvency proceedings.

Clawbacks necessarily have exceptions for normal transactions. But, as we have pointed out, even normal inter-affiliate transactions can have adverse consequences for external creditors. To address this problem we suggest that the distinction between internal (to the holding company) and external creditors be recognized and that internal creditors be required (by law or regulation) to be junior to external creditors. This would correct some, but not all, of the distortions discussed in the Appendix, while permitting firms to structure their businesses as they saw fit. Consideration should also be given to regulators discouraging the subordination of external debt by using it to fund internal equity investments. This could be done by giving internal equity a penalty weight in the computation of capital adequacy ratios of subsidiaries holding equity in affiliates.

16.8.4. Failure Rehearsals ('Living Wills')

Smooth functioning of a LCFI insolvency resolution depends on more than adequate laws and agreements. It also depends on information, procedures, systems, and relations between regulators. The development of laws, processes and systems should be iterative, with draft legislation and regulations being subjected to realistic scrutiny before being enacted. The process should include developing draft resolution procedures and then subjecting the laws and procedures to critical, including cross-border analysis and simulations by regulatory staffs working with industry groups to ascertain the feasibility and possible unintended consequences of the proposed laws and procedures. Trust, shared expectations, and working relations need to be developed at all levels before they are actually needed. As with any disaster planning, both realistic exercises, including extreme scenarios, are needed to observe potential outcomes, to work out the kinks in plans and build the necessary interpersonal network.

Failure rehearsals, which are implied in the recently advanced concept of 'living wills', presume there is an initial set of proposed laws and procedures to be implemented.[40] We have earlier provided recommendations as to the structure of such regimes. Failure rehearsals can play an important part in refining legislation and procedures in their planning stages and may also provide evidence to motivate various parties to provide the legal and institutional framework that is needed. Waiting until disaster happened has not worked well. Neither will a completely speculative, untested approach to finding solutions.

16.8.5. Structural Complexity

Finally, we make two recommendations regarding holding company structure. The use of subsidiaries in host countries provides a degree of oversight and control over in-country assets and liabilities that branching does not provide. It also provides greater clarity over how events (and payouts) might play out in the event of one or more LCFI failures. While the operating efficiency benefits of cross-border branching exceeds those of subsidiaries for private purposes, they may not do so for public purposes. For this reason, we believe that international branching should be discouraged.[41] But, the use of subsidiaries often leads to more complex corporate structures. Structural complexity needs to be monitored and where it increases opacity or the likely costs of insolvency resolution without good reason, regulators should suggest or require simplifying corporate structures within the sanctions included in PCA.

16.9. CONCLUSION

This chapter has explored how to enhance the efficiency of resolving insolvencies of LCFIs both domestically, primarily in the US, and across jurisdictions and national boundaries. We conclude that an efficient regime would incorporate parts of both Chapter 11 of the general bankruptcy code and the bank resolution regime codified in the FDIA in a modified bankruptcy proceeding. In particular, from the bank regime, the process would give the regulators standing to represent the public, but with judicial safeguards. It would also incorporate provisions for prompt corrective action to intervene to avoid insolvency and to close the institution in a timely manner if necessary; the ability to transfer some or all of the assets and liabilities to a new bridge institution with new management; an externality (systemic risk) exemption to avoid imposing haircuts on creditors if necessary to protect the financial system against serious instability, and mutualizing in the finance industry losses beyond those imposed on creditors. From the bankruptcy code, we select preservation of the going concern value of the insolvent LCFI and the protection of creditor rights to represent their own interests in the resolution process. In addition, we would extend the right to petition the court to close a troubled institution to both regulators and creditors on the basis of the provision of the PCA guidelines, but not to deny closure. We would also create a neutral court with special masters that would ensure all parties rights under law and need to approve major actions by the administrator and a structure that is predictable and identifies clearly who is and is not covered.

For multi-national LCFIs, we recommend greater and coordinated emphasis on insolvency avoidance, the introduction of clawback provisions for inter-affiliate fund transfers occurring shortly before insolvency, subordination of internal creditors of the organization to external creditors, rigorous testing of resolution regimes jointly by the regulators and the industry before final acceptance, the use of subsidiaries rather than branching for cross-jurisdiction expansion, and simplification of complex corporate organizational structures when cross-border institutions become subject to PCA sanctions.

NOTES

1. This chapter published in *Cross-Border Issues in Resolving Systemically Important Financial Institutions*, ed. R. Herring, Wharton Financial Institutions Center, 2011, is reprinted with permission.
2. While acknowledging that many LCFIs may be systemically important in failure, we wish to avoid the suggestion that 'systemically important financial institutions' conveys that the government must and will intervene in every case. There are also special insolvency resolution regimes for broker-dealers, government-sponsored enterprises (GSEs), and for insurance companies.
3. For ease of exposition, we will use LCFI to designate both bank and non-bank large complex financial institutions.
4. Bank resolution is effectively liquidation. There exist provisions for conservatorship

under US banking law. These are sometimes used for technical reasons to immediately pass a thrift through into receivership. Bridge banks are operated as conservatorships, but bridge banks are not the bank that was closed. The use of bank conservatorship, in the sense of keeping the distressed bank open while it is being legally restructured (cf Chapter 11 of the US bankruptcy code), is extremely rare.

5. The same logic could of course be applied to corporate insolvency, but the balance between the interests of the public and creditors and those of the stockholders and managers are weighed differently.
6. If the reorganization is unsuccessful and the court determines that the firm has no going concern value the proceeding is converted to Chapter 7 liquidation. Most small corporate insolvencies go straight to Chapter 7 liquidations.
7. The FDIC sees the deposit franchise as primary source of going concern value in a bank. This is preserved by finding a solvent bank to assume the deposits.
8. See Jackson, Thomas (2001), *The Logic and Limits of Bankruptcy*, Washington, DC: Beard Books.
9. This section draws greatly on Bliss and Kaufman (2007). A comparison of banking law with that for GSEs appears in Carnell, Richard (2005), 'Handling the Failure of a Government Sponsored Enterprise', 80 *Washington Law Review*, 565ff.
10. 11 USC 109(b).
11. Examples of strategic motives include fixing open-ended tort claims (e.g. asbestos litigation), restructuring labour contracts, and off-loading pension and health plans. Bankruptcy may be also be used to sell a firm free and clear of potential claims arising from pre-sale events.
12. Chartering agencies are the Comptroller of the Currency (OCC) for nationally chartered banks, state bank regulator agencies for state chartered banks and thrift institutions, and the Office of Thrift Supervision (OTS) for federal thrift institutions. Primary Federal regulators are the OCC for nationally chartered banks, the Federal Reserve for state chartered member banks, the FDIC for state chartered non-Federal Reserve member banks, and the OTS for federal thrifts. The FDIC may also appoint itself conservator or receiver. See 12 USC 1821(c)(4).
13. Thus, there are four distinct forms of insolvency: book-value insolvency defined by book values determined according to appropriate accounting standards; regulatory insolvency, also defined in terms of book values but set at a higher threshold; economic insolvency, determined by the market value of assets and present value of liabilities; and liquidity insolvency, when a debtor defaults on a payment that has come due, regardless of the state of the balance sheet.
14. *Id.*
15. The benefits and disadvantages of this exemption to the usual staying of contracts during an insolvency proceeding are discussed in R. Bliss and G. Kaufman (2006), 'Derivatives and Systemic Risk: Netting, Collateral and Closeout', *Journal of Financial Stability*, Vol. 2, No. 1, April, 55–70.
16. An important question concerns the status of in-the-money qualified financial contracts transferred to a bridge or other bank or kept in force in a conservatorship. The FDIC may effectively guarantee the values of these contracts (which will continue to fluctuate in response to changes in value of the underlying sources of risk), thus removing the element of credit risk from these contracts if they are not disavowed (and permitted to close-out) within the stipulated one business day. It is not clear how this would be squared with least cost resolution without requiring that the systemic risk exemption be invoked, a complicated and potentially time-consuming process, since the derivatives counter parties, who are technically subordinated to domestic depositors, would in effect receive full value on their positions.
17. It is not unusual for large Chapter 11 proceedings to remain under management control for several years, e.g., United Airlines remained in bankruptcy for some three years before emerging in February 2006 under new ownership. The *Bankruptcy Abuse Prevention and Consumer Protection Act of 2005* now limits extensions of the exclusion

period to 18 months for filing a management plan and 20 months for approving such a plan.

18. Voting is done by creditor classes. Classes are determined by the court with the intention that all members of a class have similar interests (priority, security interests, etc). Voting within creditor classes is by claim amount and number of creditors. One large creditor cannot freeze out other members of the class, nor can one small creditor 'hold up' the other members of the class.
19. A bankruptcy court typically rules on numerous intermediate matters (for instance, the choice of a trustee or disposition of assets). The parties may then choose to appeal these rulings, during which time the court may stay its own ruling until the appeals are resolved.
20. One exception, however, is that the FDIC Act grants the directors of a bank 30 days following self-appointment of the FDIC as conservator or receiver in which to file an appeal. See 12 USC 1821(c)(7). This right appears to have been rarely exercised and never successfully. No right of appeal exists for a primary regulator-initiated bank closure.
21. 'Priority' refers to the order in which various unsecured creditor classes are paid to be off from the assets of the bankruptcy estate. 'Security interest' refers to liens on property that reduce the assets available to the estate; collateral being a common example. 'Offset' is the process of combining (netting) offsetting multiple contracts between the insolvent firm and a given counterparty to reduce both the assets available to the estate (amounts owed by the counterparty) and unsecured claims against the estate (amounts owed to the same counterparty); bank loans and deposits are an example.
22. See 11 USC 507(a) and 12 USC 1821(d)(11)(A).
23. A number of creditors have subordinated claims. These include subordinated debenture. However, such subordination is contractual rather than statutory. The default priority for creditors under the Bankruptcy Code is 'general creditor'.
24. A number of states had previously provided for depositor preference in their banking legislation, which applied to state-charter banks that were resolved under state laws. See G. Kaufman (1997), 'The New Depositor Preference Act', *Managerial Finance*, 23(11), 56–63. State laws, which govern insurance company insolvencies, frequently grant policy holders priority over other creditors.
25. Nearly all large commercial banks in the US are currently fully owned subsidiaries of bank or financial holding companies.
26. Most DIP financing of ongoing regular business expenses (e.g., wages) is classified as 'administration expenses' and thus enjoys the senior priority that the law awards such costs (in both bank and general corporate insolvencies) over other unsecured creditors. Under such terms, banks are frequently willing to provide working capital to Chapter 11 insolvencies. It is also possible, though rare, for courts to award DIP financing a senior secured status displacing previous secured creditors. Bankruptcy procedures, though they may not always be successful, are designed to ensure that post-filing lending is not employed to obtain preferential recoveries on pre-filing debt.
27. Since distressed bank financing by regulators is fully collateralized, the risk of reduced recoveries by uninsured depositors, and indeed the FDIC itself, is present in such efforts to avoid insolvency. Open bank assistance was intended to keep a bank viable while it is returned to financial health, as DIP financing is intended to allow a non-bank corporation to attempt to return to financial health. In both cases, the danger lies in the possibility that the firm may in fact not be viable and that delays facilitated by these financing mechanisms will further erode value.
28. The legal meaning of the term 'avoid' is the opposite of the common usage of 'averting' or 'preventing' something that has not yet happened. Legal 'avoidance' is the nullification or reversing of something that has already happened.
29. Under 12 USC 1821(d)(17) the FDIC may claw back fraudulent transfers made within five years of closure. This requires court action to recover the assets and demonstrating

the intent to defraud, a much more difficult process than the presumptive provisions that apply under the bankruptcy code.

30. The insolvency resolution of Superior Bank, which failed in 2001, may be a possible exception. The FDIC negotiated with the previous owners of the failed bank to share the part of the proceeds of litigation against the bank's auditors, Ernst and Young, arguing that this would result in a higher total recovery. See Johnson, Christian (2005), 'Justice and the Administrative State: The FDIC and the Superior Bank Failure', *Loyola University Law Review*, 36, 483ff.
31. See 12 USC 1821(f).
32. See 12 USC 1821(d)(4)(B).
33. The FDIC is also empowered to pay advanced dividends to uninsured claimants based on past average recovery values rather than expected recovery values (12 USC 1821(4)(B)(iii)), but has not done so.
34. It is important to remember that delay does not necessarily produce asset value erosion, though egregious examples of loss of value in some FDIC resolutions (e.g., NextBank in 2002) and during Chapter 11 proceedings focuses the attention on that possibility. Rapid liquidation of assets under adverse market conditions or without proper incentives to maximize value can be similarly deleterious to the welfare of creditors.
35. AIG was not required to post collateral on its credit default swap (CDS) exposures so long as it retained a AAA rating. When its rating was reduced, this triggered a demand for collateral that could not be met, leading in turn to the government intervening to support AIG.
36. A problem that we note in passing is that the government is not a single agent when it comes to lending to distressed institutions. It is possible for an institution to have Federal Home Loan Bank loans, loans from various Federal Reserve credit facilities and potential liabilities to the Deposit Insurance Fund. This can lead to conflicts among agencies over objectives and differing sensitivity to losses.
37. The considerable hurdles posed by the systemic risk exemption process for banks in FDICIA, if applied to LCFIs may reduce the probability of unnecessary invocation of systemic risk claims.
38. This applies to both domestic and multi-national holding companies.
39. For example, in the case of BCCI's European insolvency, the Luxembourg court was the lead, while the UK courts took an ancillary role. Most of the European assets of BCCI were in the UK. The UK court applied UK netting law, which differed from Luxembourg law. The Luxembourg court refused to accept most of the creditors' claims that the UK court had certified. The UK court simply held back sufficient assets to cover the creditors' claims as the UK court had decided them, rather than deferring to the Luxembourg court.
40. Living wills constitute a plan for how an insolvency resolution would proceed. Failure rehearsals would be akin to war games to test the plan under simulated realistic conditions.
41. New Zealand is at the forefront of dealing with the problems posed when foreign-parented banks become insolvent. It requires that operations be conducted through subsidiaries, rather than branches. It further requires that the subsidiaries keep sufficient assets in country to cover their liabilities and that then have plans to ensure that their systems can continue to function in the event that the parent becomes insolvent.
42. Notice that this transforms USD9 of senior external debt into USD9 of junior equity.

APPENDIX A THE EFFECTS OF INTER-AFFILIATE FINANCING

Holding companies do not always rely exclusively on external debt and equity provided by the parent to fund their subsidiaries. Inter-affiliate transfers of funds, either in the form of equity or loans, can serve legitimate business purposes by moving funds to where they are most productive. However, such transfers can alter the payouts that external creditors and parent company equity holders receive in the event of a failure. Where subsidiaries are located in different countries this can lead to creditors in one jurisdiction receiving lower payouts than they would have if the internal funds transfers had not occurred, while creditors in another jurisdiction benefit. Perhaps more importantly, inter-affiliate transfers can concentrate the insolvency risk in one or more subsidiaries, so that other subsidiaries and the parent may survive a decline in asset values.

Figures 16.A1 through 16.A3 illustrate how this can happen. In each case the parent raises USD1.50 in external equity and USD0.50 in external debt. It downstreams USD1.00 to each of two subsidiaries. Each subsidiary also raises USD9.00 in external debt. *In toto* the holding company invests USD20.00 in securities.

Figure 16.A1a illustrates the base case where there are no inter-affiliate funds transfers and each subsidiary invests USD10.00 in securities. Following an 8 per cent loss in the value of the securities, Figure 16.A1b, both subsidiaries remain solvent, but the parent is insolvent and the holding company equity holders are whipped out. Holding company bond holders also suffer a loss.

In Figure 16.A2a, instead of investing the USD10.00 it starts with in securities, Subsidiary-A lends it to Subsidiary-B (at the holding company's direction). Subsidiary-B then purchases USD20.00 of securities. In this case, when the securities lose 8 per cent of their value, Figure 16.A2b, Subsidiary-B defaults on both the external and internal debt. However, the payoff to the internal loan, Loan-AB, is sufficient to cover Subsidiary-A's external debt. The equity remaining in Subsidiary-A is sufficient to pay off the parent holding company's external debt and leave the parent stock holders with a positive equity.

Finally, instead of lending $10.00 to Subsidiary-B, Subsidiary-A invests the USD10.00 as equity in Subsidiary-B, Figure 16.A3a.[42] When the USD20.00 security investment by Subsidiary-B suffers the 8 per cent loss, Figure 16.A3b, Subsidiary-B remains solvent. A pro rata division of equity returns insufficient funds to Subsidiary-A to pay off Subsidiary-A's external debt, but leaves positive equity in Subsidiary-B, to be passed up to the parent holding company, pay off the parent holding company external debt and leave a positive surplus to the external stock holders.

In both the second and third panels the parent company equity and debt holders benefit at the expense of one or the other of the subsidiary external debt holders, even though from a firm-wide perspective the total investment in securities and decline in security values is the same as in the base case with no inter-affiliate transfers.

In a transparent and static world one would expect the external debt holders to price the risks arising from the internal inter-affiliate transactions. In a complex and opaque holding company, as most LCFIs are, with dynamic investments and financial structures, it may not always be easy to appreciate and price these effects. Furthermore, recall that this disadvantage only becomes manifest when asset price declines produce a default. During normal times the efficiency gains may make the holding company appear more financially sound. In the body of this chapter we suggest a way of addressing the ex post disadvantage of internal loans without giving up the potential benefits of moving funds to where they are most productive. The transformation of external debt into internal equity is less easily dealt.

Parent HC			
Assets		Liabilities	
Equity-A	USD1.00	Debt-HC	USD0.50
Equity-B	USD1.00	Equity	USD1.50

Sub-A				Sub-B			
Assets		Liabilities		Assets		Liabilities	
Securities	USD10.00	Debt-A	USD9.00	Securities	USD10.00	Debt-B	USD9.00
		Equity-A	USD1.00			Equity-B	USD1.00

Figure 16.A1. *No Inter-Subsidiary Transfers*
Figure 16.A1a. *Securities valued at par*

Parent HC			
Assets		Liabilities	
Equity-A	USD0.20	Debt-HC	USD0.40
Equity-B	USD0.20	Equity	USD -

Sub-A				Sub-B			
Assets		Liabilities		Assets		Liabilities	
Securities	USD9.20	Debt-A	USD9.00	Securities	USD9.20	Debt-B	USD9.00
		Equity-A	USD0.20			Equity-B	USD0.20

Figure 16.A1b. *Securities valued at 92%*

Parent HC			
Assets		Liabilities	
Equity-A	USD1.00	Debt-HC	USD0.50
Equity-B	USD1.00	Equity	USD1.50

Sub-A				Sub-B			
Assets		Liabilities		Assets		Liabilities	
Loan-AB	USD10.00	Debt-A	USD9.00	Securities	USD20.00	Debt-B	USD9.00
						Loan-AB	USD8.00
		Equity-A	USD1.00			Equity-B	USD1.00

Figure 16.A2. Inter-Subsidiary Debt
Figure 16.A2a. Securities valued at par

Parent HC			
Assets		Liabilities	
Equity-A	USD-	Debt-HC	USD0.50
Equity-B	USD0.63	Equity	USD0.18

Sub-A				Sub-B			
Assets		Liabilities		Assets		Liabilities	
Loan-AB	USD9.68	Debt-A	USD9.00	Securities	USD18.40	Debt-B	USD8.72
						Loan-AB	USD9.68
		Equity-A	USD0.68			Equity-B	USD-

Figure 16.A2b. Securities valued at 92%

Parent HC			
Assets		Liabilities	
Equity-A	USD1.00	Debt-HC	USD0.50
Equity-B	USD1.00	Equity	USD1.50

Sub-A				Sub-B			
Assets		Liabilities		Assets		Liabilities	
Equity-AB	USD10.00	Debt-A	USD9.00	Securities	USD20.00	Debt-B	USD9.00
						Equity-AB	USD8.00
		Equity-A	USD1.00			Equity-B	USD1.00

Figure 16.A3. Inter-Subsidiary Equity
Figure 16.A3a. Securities valued at par

		Parent HC					
		Assets		Liabilities			
		Equity-A	USD-	Debt-HC	USD0.50		
		Equity-B	USD0.84	Equity	USD0.35		
Sub-A				Sub-B			
Assets		Liabilities		Assets		Liabilities	
Equity-AB	USD8.55	Debt-A	USD8.55	Securities	USD18.40	Debt-B	USD9.00
						Equity-AB	USD8.55
		Equity-A	USD-			Equity-B	USD0.85

Figure 16.A3b. Securities valued at 92%

17. From consolidated supervision to consolidated resolution

Rosa M. Lastra and Rodrigo Olivares-Caminal

17.1. INTRODUCTION

Consolidated supervision has become a premise for global banking as complex financial institutions increasingly expand the range of their services offered in several countries. However, the financial crisis of 2007–09 has shown that consolidated supervision is not enough; it needs to be aligned with a more effective resolution process. Though efforts are under way at the international level, with both the International Monetary Fund (IMF) and the Basel Committee on Banking Supervision Cross-Border Bank Resolution Group working to develop a cross-border resolution framework,[1] the lack of an effective consolidated resolution framework poses a challenge to the future of global banking and finance.

That form of supervision is based on the assumption that financial groups form a single economic entity. However, with respect to the resolution of a failed multinational bank, or of a complex financial group with different units performing different activities which include various legal entities (i.e. subsidiaries) incorporated in various jurisdictions, the assumption that financial groups form a single economic entity cannot be said to be a legal reality. In a bankruptcy scenario, a financial group is typically split up into its various components or into various legal entities who are subjected to the insolvency laws of the jurisdiction where they have been incorporated. Even foreign branches of multinational banks or companies are some times liquidated and treated as separate units. Consolidated or married in life, single when they pass away, that is the current reality.

In recent decades financial markets and institutions have become global, while regulation, supervision, resolution and insolvency remain largely nationally based, constrained within the domain of domestic jurisdictions. Financial stability, however, is a goal that transcends geographic boundaries. It is essential to find mechanisms and tools to advance in the area of international supervision and resolution.[2]

This chapter first analyses the notion of consolidated supervision in the case of financial conglomerates and complex cross-border financial institutions. Subsequently, it considers the particularly vexing issue of the complications in dealing with different sectoral entities even within domestic law. In other words, (1) the fact that, *lex specialis* typically only applies to banks (though the US and other jurisdictions are considering extending the special regime to systemically significant financial institutions), while other sectors of the financial industry are subject to *lex generalis*; and, (2) the problems with regard to financial conglomerates and complex cross-border financial institutions are exacerbated in the case of bankruptcy since countries are reluctant to apply the principle of unity and universality of bankruptcy. Finally, we conclude that in the absence of international substantive harmonized standards for the resolution of cross-border banks and financial conglomerates, policymakers need to adopt measures to allow for consolidated resolution.

17.2. INTERNATIONAL FINANCIAL CONGLOMERATES AND THE RISE OF COMPLEX CROSS-BORDER FINANCIAL INSTITUTIONS

The understanding of what constitutes an international financial conglomerate or a complex cross-border institution varies according to practices in different jurisdictions. Cross-border establishments take various legal forms which often result in a complex web of branches, subsidiaries and joint ventures. This has resulted in a web of authorities involved in the supervision of financial conglomerates. Branches generally tend to gravitate towards the home jurisdiction, i.e. the jurisdiction of the country in which the parent entity is headquartered. Subsidiaries tend to gravitate towards the host jurisdiction, i.e. the jurisdiction of the country of their incorporation. This is, however, not a neat divide, and the concept of consolidated supervision provides only a partial answer to the logistical problems involved in the network of authorities that have to deal with financial conglomerates and complex cross-border institutions. Colleges of supervisors – also an extension of the 'network' principle based on co-operation – are also only a partial solution in the case of conflicts. The same could be said about the possible establishment of 'resolution colleges'. The need for either a lead authority or a binding system of mediation in case of conflicts ought to be considered further. The problems with regard to financial conglomerates and complex cross-border institutions are exacerbated in the case of bankruptcy since countries are reluctant to apply the principle of unity and universality of bankruptcy.

A financial conglomerate can be organized under three basic structures that permit the combination of banking and non-banking activities. However, it is essential to stress the difference between legal and functional separateness. The former implies separate legal entities with different management, accounting, boards of directors and capital while the latter derives from a regulatory or self-imposed restriction ('Chinese walls') to restrain integrated provision of different financial services.[3] Following UNCITRAL's definition of an enterprise group, which provides that an enterprise group is a group of 'two or more legal entities (group members) that are linked together by some form of control (whether direct or indirect) or ownership';[4] and, based on the arguments mentioned above, it can be said that that a financial conglomerate is an enterprise group providing significant services in at least two different financial sectors, i.e. banking, securities and/or insurance while a complex cross-border financial institution is an enterprise group with a certain degree of complexity operating across borders (usually more than two).

One thing is very clear, legislation addressing the treatment of financial conglomerates or complex cross-border financial institutions is rare although such institutions represent a significant percentage of gross national product.

17.3. NOTION OF CONSOLIDATED SUPERVISION AND HISTORY OF THE CONCEPT[5]

Consolidated supervision is a comprehensive approach to prudential regulation that seeks to assess the strength of a banking or financial group. In order to achieve this 'consolidation', parent bank and parent supervisory authorities monitor the risks incurred by the different entities that compose the group (parent and subsidiaries/affiliates), as well as the adequacy of their capital which is decided on the basis of the totality of their business wherever conducted. This group-wide approach to supervision, whereby all the risks of a banking group are taken into account, wherever they are booked, goes beyond accounting consolidation.[6] The rationale of the concept is that no foreign bank establishment should escape adequate supervision, a logic that is also helpful in a resolution context.

In order to properly understand provisions on consolidated supervision, incorporated in EU Directives based on recommendations of the Basel Committee on Banking Supervision, it is important to refer to its history, which is linked to the history of the Basel Committee.

Throughout its 35 years of existence, the Basel Committee on Banking Supervision (the 'Committee') has conducted work in two main areas: (1)

supervision of cross-border establishments (mainly international branches and subsidiaries) and (2) capital adequacy. The rules for the supervision of branches and subsidiaries of banks were originally formulated in the 1975 Basel Concordat, revised in 1983 and further refined and redefined in 1992, particularly as regards to the key principles of consolidated supervision of international banking groups.

Following the collapse in 1974 of the German bank, Bankhaus I.D. Herstatt and of the US bank, Franklin National Bank, the Committee issued in September 1975 a paper which was subsequently known as the Basel Concordat (the 'Concordat') outlining some principles – in the form of recommended guidelines of best practices – regarding the supervision of banks operating internationally through branches, subsidiaries and joint ventures.[7] The Committee's aim was to prevent foreign banking establishments from escaping adequate supervision. The main features of this 1975 Concordat can be summarized as follows:

1. The solvency of branches (i.e., legally dependent units) is the responsibility of the home or parent country supervisor.
2. The solvency of subsidiaries (i.e., legally independent units) and joint ventures is the responsibility of the host country supervisor or country of incorporation. However, the parent country should take account of the exposures of their domestic banks' foreign subsidiaries and joint ventures because of the parent banks' moral commitments to these foreign establishments.
3. The liquidity of branches, subsidiaries and joint ventures is the responsibility of the host country supervisor. The home country nevertheless should monitor the liquidity of its international banks.

Those general principles for the supervision of international banks were tainted by a domestic approach towards banking regulation since the domestic approach established a division of labour in the supervision of international banks between separate national authorities (a 'who-does-what' approach). The Committee did not design an overarching common framework to be applied to several jurisdictions, but rather provided guidelines as regards the assignment of responsibilities for international branches and subsidiaries among national supervisors. As a result supervision though international by source, continued to remain national in character.

The first breakthrough in the nature of international banking regulation took place with the revision of the Concordat in 1983, following the collapse of the Luxembourg-based Banco Ambrosiano Holdings in 1982. The revised 1983 Concordat was released to the public under the title 'Principles for the supervision of banks' foreign establishment in the form of recommended guidelines of best practices for the reference of supervisors.[8] Banco Ambrosiano's failure had raised concerns about the treatment of banks, holding companies and joint ventures, the tendency of capital standards in the major international banks to be eroded, the supervision of Eurocurrency markets (which had no lender of last resort) and off-shore centres.

The 1983 report acknowledged that '[a]dequate supervision of banks' foreign establishments calls not only for an appropriate allocation of responsibilities between parent and host supervisory authorities but also for contact and cooperation between them'.[9] Accordingly, the revised Concordat emphasized two regulatory principles: the 'dual key' approach, whereby home and host authorities assess the quality of each other's supervision, and the need for consolidated supervision, which refers to the ability of the parent authorities to monitor the risk exposure and capital adequacy of a bank or a banking group on the basis of the totality of their business wherever conducted. Though the formulation of this principle of consolidated supervision contained some loopholes, a first step towards harmonization was nevertheless achieved by stressing the need for further cooperation and shared responsibility between host and home authorities, given the overlapping nature of supervisory responsibilities.

The 1983 paper identified some of the problems caused by having either inadequate host country supervision or inadequate home country supervision. In the first case, if the host country feels unable to carry out adequate supervision, it should inform the home country, which could either choose to supervise the foreign establishment, or prevent the parent bank from continuing to operate such an establishment. Furthermore, when a foreign entity is classified as a bank by the home country, but not by the host, the supervisory responsibility lies with the home authority. Lastly, if the host country has reason to doubt the adequacy of the supervision exercised by the home country, the host country should either discourage or prohibit the operations of that company, or impose conditions on the conduct of its business.

The revised 1983 Concordat elaborated in more precise terms the nature of the risks in the operation of a bank's foreign establishment (branches, subsidiaries and joint ventures) that each supervisory authority was expected to monitor. As regards the supervision of foreign exchange operations, the Committee recommended joint responsibility of home and host authorities. Concerning solvency regulation, the Committee reiterated that although the solvency of branches is the responsibility of the parent authorities, the host authorities can also demand endowment capital for foreign branches. The solvency of subsidiaries is the joint responsibility of both host and home authorities, i.e. host authorities are responsible for those subsidiaries incorporated in their territory, while the home authorities are responsible for them as part of larger banking groups. Solvency of joint ventures is the primary responsibility of the authorities in the country of incorporation, although the Committee cautioned that the parent (home) authorities of the shareholder banks should be involved in cases where dominant shareholdings prevail. The supervision of liquidity remains the primary responsibility of the host country, though in the case of branches, liquidity will also be a concern for the home authorities, too. The 1983 document specifically stated that references to the supervision of liquidity did not relate to the lender of last resort aspects of the role of central banks, but to the control systems and procedures established by banks, which enable them to meet their obligations as they fall due including, as necessary, those of their foreign establishments. In 1990, the Committee issued a 'Supplement' to the 1983 document, which sought to define more clearly how the Concordat was to be implemented in practice. It outlined recommendations on authorization procedures, information flows, bank secrecy constraints and external audits.

Another crisis was required to demonstrate the limitations of some of the principles agreed in 1983. That crisis was provided by the closure of the Bank of Credit and Commerce International (BCCI) in July 1991 and, to a lesser extent, by the events of the Atlanta branch of the Banca Nazionale del Lavoro (BNL). Though the 'dual key' approach of the 1983 Concordat was intended to reverse the tendency for banks to gravitate towards the least-regulated jurisdiction, the BCCI case demonstrated the limitations of that principle alone. The lesson learnt was that for the 'dual key' approach to work, it should be accompanied by the setting up of common rules, agreed by the nations (like the 1988 Basel Agreement on minimum capital requirements), in the same way as the principle of mutual recognition in the EC requires the prior harmonization of banking essentials. Moreover, though the principle of consolidated supervision was established to avoid regulatory vacuums, it contained some exceptions. For instance, the 1983 report stated that '[w]here holding companies are at the head of groups that include separately incorporated banks operating in different countries the authorities responsible for supervising those banks should endeavour to coordinate their supervision of those banks, taking account of the overall structure of the bank in question'.[10] BCCI was an example of that type of structure. It was not subject to consolidated supervision by its home authorities, because its parent entity – BCCI Holdings, a Luxembourg Holding Company – escaped regulation under Luxembourg law as it was not classified as a bank. BCCI's two main subsidiaries were incorporated in Luxembourg and the Cayman Islands, where supervision is weak and bank secrecy strong; BCCI's main shareholders were in Abu Dhabi while the operating headquarters were in London. Host authorities of the countries where BCCI conducted operations, such as the UK, were limited in their supervisory efforts by the fragmentation of regulatory responsibilities. BCCI's set up was clearly aimed at avoiding effective supervision. These type of banks, those that seek to escape regulation, should be most closely monitored. The demise of BCCI clearly illustrated that the principle of consolidated supervision should allow for no exceptions.

In July 1992, the Committee issued new [soft law] 'rules' for the supervision of international banking operations, through a document called 'Minimum Standards for the Supervision of International Banking Groups and their Cross-border Establishments', reformulating some of the principles that the Concordat had enshrined.[11] Given the importance of these standards, their principal features are worth spelling out in full:

1. 'All international banking groups and international banks should be supervised by a home-country authority that capably performs consolidated supervision.'

Such 'capability' should encompass powers to prevent corporate affiliations, which could undermine consolidated financial supervision or otherwise hinder effective supervision, and powers to prevent the bank or banking group from creating foreign banking establishments in particular jurisdictions.

The idea of a single lead 'capable' supervisory body is designed to ensure that banks do not deliberately split management functions among several centres with a view to make supervision more difficult. The BCCI case evidenced the inefficiency of having a 'college' of regulators – from eight countries – and the consequent need to have a single capable regulator in charge.

2. 'The creation of a cross-border banking establishment should receive the prior consent of both the host-country supervisory authority and the bank's, and if different, the banking group's home-country supervisory authority.'

Before granting their consent, the authorities should review the strength of the bank's capital and its risk management procedures, paying special attention to the degree of support that the parent institution is capable of providing. If either authority – home or host – concludes that the allocation of supervisory responsibilities suggested in the Concordat is inappropriate, or if there is a significant change in the bank's or banking group's activities or structure, then that authority should initiate consultations with the other authority to reach an explicit understanding on which of them is in the best position to take primary responsibility either generally, or in specific activities. The practical implication of this standard, whereby host-supervision may supersede home-supervision and home-supervision may supersede host-supervision, is that bilateral consultations between countries take precedence over the Concordat's principles in order to assure adequate supervision.

3. 'Supervisory authorities should possess the right to gather information from the cross-border banking establishments of the banks or banking groups for which they are the home country supervisor.'

This gathering of information can be done through a variety of means, including on-site examinations, to be deemed satisfactory by the recipient of such information.

4. 'If a host-country authority determines that any one of the foregoing minimum standards is not met to its satisfaction, that authority could impose restrictive measures with these minimum standards, including the prohibition of the creation of banking establishments.'

The host authority should judge: (1) whether the bank or banking group is chartered in a jurisdiction from which it can gather information (i.e., whether or not bank secrecy rules can be relaxed, if necessary); (2) whether consent for outward expansion has been given by the appropriate home country authority; and (3) whether the bank or banking group's home authority has the practical capability to perform consolidated supervision.

The 1992 Basel guidelines provided a floor, in effect, minimum standards. The standards were formulated in broad terms to allow flexibility of implementation according to differing legal and structural circumstances across countries. Countries were expected (though not legally compelled) to adopt such standards, but they could also choose to toughen some of the requirements in relation to their jurisdiction. The 1992 guidelines were written to avoid another crisis like the one experienced by BCCI; however, the Committee recognized that the standards do not and cannot anticipate every possible application. The unfolding of international banking rules will generally be limited by this remedial rather than preventive character.

The Basel standards imposed an implicit penalty on weak bank regulatory jurisdictions. In the EC, the principle of mutual recognition (which implies mutual trust) requires the prior harmonization of essential banking rules. Mutual recognition presupposes the equivalence of the objectives of national legislation and the existence of similar public-interest goals, although such goals can be reached by different means (which explains why EC directives are the preferred instruments for the design of a single market in financial services). Likewise, at an international level, the rules to be agreed upon by national regulators should be preceded by an agreement as regards the goals to be pursued, which in turn will generate mutual trust.

17.4. FINANCIAL CONGLOMERATES AND COMPLEX CROSS-BORDER FINANCIAL INSTITUTIONS IN DISTRESS

The legal arrangements with regard to the supervision and crisis management (including insolvency) of financial conglomerates present a number of challenges for regulators, supervisors and policymakers. There is first the cross-sector dimension, by which we mean the different lines of business (banking, securities, insurance) typically involved in a financial conglomerate.

Lex specialis typically only applies to banks (though the US is considering extending the special regime to systemically significant financial institutions), while other sectors of the financial industry are subject to general bankruptcy law.

There is also the cross-jurisdiction dimension, since international financial conglomerates operate in different jurisdictions (e.g. branches that tend to gravitate towards the home jurisdiction and subsidiaries tend to gravitate towards the host jurisdiction).[12]

The problems with regard to financial conglomerates are exacerbated in the case of bankruptcy. This results from the fact that countries are reluctant to apply the principle of unity and universality[13] of bankruptcy when their own interests are at stake. In addition, there is no substantial standard on insolvency that has been agreed at an international level. Territoriality as a manifestation of sovereignty tends to be the reigning principle in bankruptcy. This is, of course, wholly inadequate for institutions that have a global dimension.

International financial conglomerates suffer from all the problems that big institutions suffer at the national level when they are systemically relevant, such as 'too-big-to-fail' (TBTF) or the modern versions of this concept, such as too-complex-to-fail or too-interconnected-to-fail (not to mention 'too-big-to-save' or 'too-important-to-ignore').[14] The risks to financial stability are all too clear. International financial conglomerates can and do pose risks to taxpayers through their implicit or explicit support. Their systemic effect though recognized, has not been tackled yet through the establishment of an adequate legal framework.

The financial crisis has provided ample examples of financial institutions in distress in the US, UK, Iceland, the Netherlands and many other countries particularly in continental Europe, though the crisis has also affected other parts of the world in somewhat different ways (broadening government guarantees has been one of the popular measures). Despite the depth and severity of the crisis, there have been just a few cases of insolvency and some other cases of near-insolvency, which is a clear testimony of the close involvement that governments have had with troubled financial institutions, preventing them from failing via rescue packages, 'bail-outs', state aid, recapitalization, guarantees and insurance of assets, and many other 'protective' measures.

In the US, there are two episodes that we consider particularly relevant from the point of view of insolvency law. Bear Stearns was a case of near-insolvency, while Lehman Brothers was a case of insolvency, where market discipline was applied (to a catastrophic effect). These two cases have changed the public's views on the need and effectiveness of government intervention.

The inadequacy of the legal framework to deal with troubled financial institutions that operate globally is all too clear. It started with some early indicators at the domestic level, mainly in the US and UK. Some of these early indicators included Bear Stearns suspending the redemption from its High Grade Structured Credit Strategies Enhanced Leverage Fund in January 2007 and the subsequent liquidation of two funds investing in mortgage-backed securities in July 2007. However, those events did not get the necessary attention until Northern Rock received emergency liquidity assistance from the Bank of England in September 2007, which led to its subsequent nationalization. This was followed by massive announcements of losses and writedowns by different financial institutions (including inter alia Merrill Lynch, Citigroup, UBS, Credit Suisse, Wachovia, Bank of America, Barclays, Morgan Stanley, etc.). It was the demise of Lehman Brothers in September 2008 that poignantly evidenced the inadequacy of the current system of national regulation and insolvency and international markets. That episode, together with the hastily arranged take-overs of Bear Stearns by JP Morgan in March 2008 and of Merrill Lynch by Bank of America in September 2008, the 'bailout' of Freddie Mac and Fannie Mae, AIG and the rescue package for Citigroup suggested the need to revisit the conventional wisdom about the extent and effectiveness of financial crisis management instruments and of government intervention. This was followed by the nationalization of the Royal Bank of Scotland

and Lloyds in the UK and the rescue of Dexia and Fortis in the EU. The above reproduction of facts is not exhaustive, but merely illustrative to evidence the magnitude of the crises and inadequacy of regulation and resolution mechanisms.

Another interesting case of a banking crisis that resulted in a sovereign debt crisis is that of the banks in Iceland. The collapse of Kaupthing, Glitnir and Landsbanki, three internationally active Icelandic banks brought about a different type of banking crisis, i.e. a banking crisis that developed into a currency crisis and escalated into a sovereign debt default crisis with severe international implications.[15]

The Government of Iceland did not have the capacity to bail out these institutions. This inability of the government to save the troubled banks led to a currency crisis which put Iceland on the brink of a sovereign debt crisis. These banks were both 'too-big-to-fail' and at the same time 'too-big-to-be-saved'.

During the recent global financial crisis, we have seen bail-outs of various troubled financial entities. Although these bail-outs have contributed to restoring confidence in the financial system in the short term, the question is at what price. By reducing bank default risk, sovereign default risk is increased in the long term. Iceland is a small country with only 300000 inhabitants, with a large internationally exposed banking sector and with a limited fiscal capacity. The Central Bank of Iceland could have been an effective lender of last resort if the banks were only exposed in domestic currency, where printing money or taxing its inhabitants would have been two possible solutions but at a dear cost. However, the case of Iceland is a case where private financial institutions were bigger than the country's own economy.

The Icelandic case has severe connotations since Iceland can be used to reassess the whole theoretical notion of countries not being able to become insolvent. Despite the fact that sometimes it is said in a figurative manner that a country is insolvent or bankrupt, technically speaking, a country cannot reach this situation.[16]

As evidenced by the Icelandic case, despite the oversight and/or supervision of central banks or the supervisory authorities, banks – companies performing a business with a particular nature – fail. If companies and banks fail, a financial conglomerate, which is a group of companies, can also fail. The reasons are diverse and can go from bad management to fraud, from economic shocks or financial crisis to excessive risk, just to name a few.

If some organizations are too big, too complex or too interconnected to be allowed to fail, then it naturally suggests that those organizations are safer than others, which results in distorting the market because they will have an *ex ante* competitive advantage. There is no set criterion to consider an organization 'too-big-to-fail'. In this sense, a policy of ambiguity associated with the provision of support for troubled organizations should be maintained because making explicit guarantees will weaken market discipline (increase moral hazard). The knowledge that the authorities will allow an organization (even a big/complex or interconnected one) to fail is an important demonstration of market discipline. Central banks will always have a lender of last resort ('LOLR') function to deploy in exceptional cases. However, it has been argued that in exceptional circumstances governments may have to step in to address systemic crises.[17] In this regard it is important to note that a central objective for the banking system will be to avoid a price anticipation for bail-outs.[18] Also, it is important to stress that central banks and banking regulators should not reduce due diligence by market participants who should monitor and understand the risks associated with their investments.[19]

Hence, policymakers and regulators must foresee the possibility of a distressed financial conglomerate and the risks that it poses to the entire system and be prepared to manage it through efficient means. Even if it does fail, upon a distressed situation it can affect other market players who will take defensive positions producing a shortage of liquidity.

Particularly when dealing with financial conglomerates, the issues of bigger concern are the coordination of creditors and the competent courts resulting from the fragmented framework. In the case of financial conglomerates we will be dealing with different industries (subject matter, convenience of a subsidiary or business line v. convenience of the whole group, etc.) in different jurisdictions (different aim in the regulators or insolvency laws, e.g. general law v. special law; pro-debtor v. pro-creditor; plurality of insolvency v. universality of insolvency, etc.). These pose a certain number of procedural problems: (1) the law of which country shall be applied? (2) which court shall have the jurisdiction to deal with disputes? (3) which law shall be applied, i.e. general insolvency law or specific insolvency law? (4) shall we apply a plurality of insolvency procedures or a universal insolvency? These are only some questions that can become difficult when faced with competing jurisdictions with different agendas (e.g. subsidiary v. the whole group; or, pro-creditor v. pro-debtor). Considering the differences in bankruptcy laws in the member states of the EU, it was noted that large banking institutions and financial conglomerates could be incorporated as *Societas Europeae* (as Nordea proposed) and that a special insolvency regime could apply to them.[20]

The main aim of insolvency laws is to provide an organized debt collection procedure that protects the value of the assets of the distressed entity and the rights of its creditors. These main features aim to avoid maverick litigation or a fire sale. The key features contemplated under insolvency laws is a stay or standstill that will bar creditors from collecting on their claims and would allow the court to envisage the best option to maximize the value of assets (sale as a going concern, restructuring, etc.). Once an entity is placed into insolvency, the interest of creditors will prevail over any other interests.

It is important to stress the difference between a separate entity approach and the universality or enterprise approach in the analysis of a possible consolidated resolution regime. The former relies on the separate legal personality principle of corporate law, where limited liability of shareholders and duties of directors are separate in each company of the group. The latter is based on the economic reality or integration of the different members of the group as a whole. Two examples of legislation that consider a group of companies as a single enterprise are: (1) corporate legislation, like in New Zealand, that allows for substantive consolidation or pooling orders; and (2) public companies, like in Germany, acting as a group are classified as integrated groups, contract groups or de facto groups.

A mechanism should be in place to allow for a voluntarily or court-ordered cross-border consolidation when a group has reached a substantial level of economic, operational and organizational integration through control or ownership that is very difficult, costly and time consuming to disentangle.[21] This will be a step further from coordination, where the assets remain separate. The consolidation of assets will imply the pooling of assets and liabilities of the whole group in a single estate. This should work as an exception to the separate legal personality principle (piercing/lifting the corporate veil) which forms the core element of corporate law and should be the general rule. This will facilitate coordination, transparency, efficiency, reduce costs and unify conflicting issues (e.g. suspect period, etc.).

For example, in the case of a financial conglomerate trading over-the-counter (OTC) securities even being in a distress situation requires firms to keep on trading to unwind their positions. Otherwise, a stay in trading is highly likely to worsen the situation for both creditors and debtor. In the case of a distressed bank, the stay can also produce substantial consequences due to spill-over effects that can spread to the development of systemic problems (e.g. the collapse of Lehman Brothers or the Icelandic banks referred above as well as many other cases experienced in the recent crisis). On the other hand, a stay can work, for example, in an insurance company where the value of the assets does not deteriorate at the same rate that financial assets do. Substantial differences in insolvency laws open the dilemma of *pars condictio creditorum* and *pari passu*[22] v. set-off.[23] In other words, a dilemma between a pro-debtor system where the main aim is the conservation of the value of a bankrupt estate and a pro-creditor system allowing the use (and enforcement) of ex-ante contractual provisions to set-off (payments netting and close-out netting). The use of set-off can be very beneficial in the context of financial conglomerates where companies are operating in the financial markets due to the number of bi-directional transactions generated per day (interbank payments, foreign exchange (FX) positions, risk hedging, etc.) and allow them to keep operating even if one of the parties is a distressed entity as long as they maintain a favourable position. The International Swap and Derivative Association ('ISDA') has successfully carved out an exception from various pro-debtor laws enabling the set-off providing protection for payment systems and derivatives.

Throughout its 35 years of existence, the Basel Committee has addressed various issues concerning the allocation of supervisory responsibilities like home-host, capital regulation and other principles for the effective supervision of international banks. The Basel Committee, however, provides little guidance concerning bank exit policies and the problems involved in the resolution of cross-border banking crises.[24]

Although there is no international treaty on the insolvency of conglomerates, there have been some modest attempts at reaching some commonly agreed-upon international rules (mostly 'soft law') on group insolvencies or cross-border issues. The next section provides a survey on the different international initiatives on group and cross-border insolvencies.

17.5. A SURVEY OF INTERNATIONAL INITIATIVES ON CONGLOMERATES AND CROSS-BORDER INSOLVENCIES[25]

In a financial crisis, it is desirable to have a clear and predictable legal framework in place to govern how a financial conglomerate would be reorganized or liquidated in an orderly fashion so as not to undermine financial stability. There is no such framework yet with regard to cross-border financial institutions. Although incipient work has been done, some tangible progress can be seen in regard to conflict of laws or private international law rules (an example of which is the Directive 2001/24/EC on the reorganization and winding-up of credit institutions). However, thus far, there is no international substantive harmonized standard for banks, even less for financial conglomerates, although the IMF and the Basel Committee Cross-Border Bank Resolution Group are working towards some soft law in this area. The EU Commission commenced a process that should lead to harmonized standards through the publication of a communication on an EU Framework Cross-Border Crisis Management in the Banking Sector on 20 October 2009.[26]

Insolvency laws vary widely across countries. They differ in various ways. Given the intimate link between insolvency law and other areas of commercial law, different legal traditions (civil law, common law) have given rise to different insolvency rules. Some laws are more favourable to creditors, while others are more pro-debtor. The choice between *lex generalis* and *lex specialis* leads to different approaches to bank insolvency.[27]

In the absence of an international insolvency legal regime, the solution to the liquidation of a financial conglomerate with branches and subsidiaries in several countries needs to be based on national legal regimes and on the voluntary co-operation between different national authorities, usually in the format of memorandums of understanding (MoU). This co-operation is often uneasy and the division of responsibilities between home and host country authorities remains a matter of controversy.[28]

As stated by Krimminger, '[m]ost nations currently apply a territorial approach to cross-border insolvencies. This simply is a consequence of the domestic focus of most insolvency laws.'[29] Sovereignty as a supreme power is typically exerted over the territory of the state: the principle of territoriality. Sovereignty, however, has a territorial dimension. The demise of national frontiers in today's global financial markets shows the limitations and inadequacies of this principle (territoriality – sovereignty) to deal with financial conglomerates, international holding structures and cross-border banking and finance. These inadequacies are particularly evident in the case of insolvency.[30]

The principle of 'plurality of bankruptcy' – which typically goes hand-in-hand with the 'separate entity' approach to liquidation – means that bankruptcy proceedings are only effective in the country in which they are initiated and, therefore, there is a plurality of proceedings, as they need to be initiated in every country in which the insolvent bank holds realizable assets or branches. Thus, this principle assigns territorial effect to the adjudication of bankruptcy. Under a separate entity approach a domestic branch of a foreign bank receives a liquidation preference, as local assets are segregated for the benefit of local creditors ('practice of ring fencing'). Ring fencing is contrary to the *pari passu* principle, since some creditors receive more favourable treatment than others.[31] Under the separate entity approach, local branches of a foreign bank are treated as separate entities. This is the approach the US applies to the liquidation of US branches of a foreign bank. US bank insolvency law is territorial for US branches of a foreign bank.[32]

The inconsistency of the US legal approach to the liquidation of multinational banks, depending on whether it is dealing with foreign branches in the US or with US branches of a foreign bank, illustrates the difficulties in reaching a common international platform with regard to the liquidation of multinational banks, which to a certain extent reflects the problems in the case of financial conglomerates.

There are three possible approaches to deal with the problems of cross-border insolvency.[33]

1. Creation of an international authority. However, the idea of an international bankruptcy court appears far-fetched and, even at the EC level, the idea of a single authority appears distant (if not impossible).
2. Establishment of common rules. Rule harmonization and regulatory convergence appear to be the solution. Some rules are procedural and some others are substantive. In the field of insolvency some conflict of laws/private international law/division of labour type of rules have been harmonized, but so far there is no international substantive standard applicable to cross-border insolvency of financial conglomerates.
3. Co-operation and information sharing, through memoranda of understanding (bilateral and multi-lateral agreements) and other mechanisms. However, resolution procedures (in particular if they imply burden sharing) cannot be expected to rely upon 'ex post co-operation'. They need ex ante rules and dispute settlement mechanisms.

UNCITRAL has been active in the drafting of international standards for the harmonization and unification of the law of international trade, with a particular focus on insolvency law under Working Group V. In 2006, the UNCITRAL Working Group V on insolvency started working on the treatment of corporate groups[34] in insolvency, examining both domestic and cross-border issues. Working Group V recently released a commentary and recommendations of part three of the UNCITRAL Legislative Guide on Insolvency Law.[35] The main documents are:[36] (1) A/CN.9/WG.V/WP.92, which addresses the treatment of enterprise groups in the domestic context; and (2) A/CN.9/WG.V/WP.92/Add.1, which addresses the international context. These documents were considered at the thirty-eighth session in New York on 19–23 April 2010. This was a great achievement towards the harmonization of corporate group insolvencies, both at the national and international level. In our view, this effort could substantially contribute to untangle the web and layers of issues involved in dealing with conglomerates and could become the right forum to develop common principles concerning bank insolvency.

In addition to the new developments regarding 'enterprise groups' on the Legislative Guide on Insolvency Law, on 1 July 2009, UNCITRAL adopted a Practice Guide on Cross-Border Insolvency Cooperation.[37] The aim of this guide is to provide information for insolvency practitioners and judges on practical aspects of cooperation and communication in cross-border insolvency cases. This document analyses several cross-border agreements (e.g. written agreements approved by courts or oral arrangement between parties to the proceedings). Building on issues and conflicts that might arise in cross-border insolvency cases, the Practice Guide stresses the importance and encourages the use of cross-border agreements tailored to meet the specific needs of each case and the particular requirements of applicable law.

A recent welcome development is the establishment of a new Basel Working Group – set up in December 2007 – and co-chaired by Michael Krimminger and Eva Hüpkes to study the resolution of cross-border financial institutions. This group, which has been working together with UNCITRAL, could provide a degree of harmonization (legislative convergence) with regard to some key issues such as: the definition of triggers for commencement of proceedings; the role of supervisors; minimum rights and obligations of debtors and creditors; right to set-off; netting, treatment of financial contract; and the protection of the payment system.

In the absence of a formal international insolvency legal regime, countries resort to bilateral voluntary agreements, often in the form of an MoU. Those instruments are non-binding and establish some principles of cooperation in the regulation of cross-border establishments. As of now, there are more than 90 MoUs in place between different countries.[38] Of significant importance is the recent announcement by the Federal Deposit Insurance Corporation (FDIC) and the Bank of England regarding their agreement to expand their cooperation when they act as resolution authorities in resolving troubled deposit-taking financial institutions with activities in the US and the UK.[39] This MoU aims at enhancing the collaboration of these institutions to promote greater coordination in the case of distressed banks in these jurisdictions. Some of the features of this MoU are: (1) close and effective communication about the operations of financial institutions; (2) consultation on developing issues; (3) cooperative contingency planning; (4) supporting appropriate recovery and resolution plans; and (5) the need to work closely together with other authorities in the US and the UK.

The EU insolvency regime consists of one regulation on insolvency proceedings (Council Regulation (EC) No. 1346/2000 of 29 May 2000) and of two directives: a directive on the reorganization and winding-up of credit institutions (Directive 2001/24/EC of 4 April 2001); and a directive concerning the reorganization and winding up of insurance undertakings (Directive 2001/17/EC of 19 March 2001). As stated above, the EU

Commission published a communication on a framework for cross-border bank crisis management on 20 October 2009, which should lead to a revision of Directive 2001/24/EC as well as other EU legislative initiatives.[40]

The EU insolvency regime is binding for all EU member states. As such, the EU regime is the clearest example of binding supranational/regional rules in the field of insolvency law in general and of bank insolvency law in particular. However, the EU rules have been mainly in the form of private international law in character. They introduce the principles of unity and universality of bankruptcy, conferring exclusive jurisdiction to the home member state, but they do not seek to harmonize in a substantive way national legislation concerning insolvency proceedings, which remain different across the member states of the EU.

Under Directive 2001/24/EC, where a credit institution with branches in other member states is wound up or reorganized, the winding-up or reorganization is initiated and carried out under a single procedure by the authorities of the member state where the credit institution has been authorized (known as the home member state). This procedure is governed by the law of the home member state. This approach is consistent with the principle of home member state Supervision pursuant to the EU Banking Directives. The Directive does not aim at harmonizing national legislation, but at ensuring mutual recognition of member states' reorganization measures and winding-up proceedings as well as the necessary cooperation between authorities. Due to the mere coordinating nature of the Directive, member states have different reorganization measures and winding-up proceedings. Consequently, insolvency proceedings for credit institutions differ. Some member states use the same company and insolvency laws for the reorganization and winding-up of credit institutions as for other businesses, while others have special reorganization proceedings for credit institutions.

The Directive covers only the insolvency of branches of credit institutions in other member states, but do not cover subsidiaries of banking groups in other member states.

Directive 2001/24/EC is limited to procedural aspects concerning each legal entity within a cross-border banking group. The limited scope does not take into account synergies within such a group, which may benefit all creditors in case of reorganization. This lack of group-wide approach to winding up and reorganization could lead to the failure of subsidiaries or even the group, which could otherwise have been reorganized and remained solvent in whole or part.[41]

On 16 December 2002 the European Parliament and the Council adopted Directive 2002/87/EC on the supplementary supervision of credit institutions, insurance undertakings and investment firms in a financial conglomerate (the 'Financial Conglomerates Directive').[42] The Financial Conglomerates Directive establishes the rules for prudential supervision of financial conglomerates and financial groups providing services in different industry sectors. The ultimate goal of the directive is to foster the stability of the financial system. In order to achieve this ultimate goal, the aims of the Directive on Financial Conglomerates are: (1) to oversee the capital adequacy of conglomerates; (2) to assess the calculation of the conglomerate's solvency position; and (3) to reduce the regulatory burden and promote efficiency by establishing a single lead regulator for financial conglomerates.

In October 2009, the EU Commission issued a communication to the European Parliament, the Council, the European Economic and Social Committee, the European Court of Justice and the European Central Bank to establish a EU framework for Cross-Border Crisis Management in the Banking Sector. The communication envisages two main objectives in the establishment of a cross-border framework for banking institutions: (1) to ensure that all national supervisors have adequate tools to identify problems in banks at a sufficiently early stage and to intervene to restore the health of the institution or group, or prevent further decline; and (2) allow cross-border banks to fail without serious disruption to vital banking services or contagion to the financial system as a whole.[43]

17.6. 'LIVING WILLS' AND CONSOLIDATED RESOLUTION

Recovery and resolution plans or simply 'living wills' consist of a recovery plan set up (and kept up to date) by the financial institution for a distressed situation. This constitutes an effective resolution tool that together with other tools can contribute to the building of a credible framework for resolution and early intervention for cross-border banking and financial groups as well as tackling the moral hazards in the too big to fail problem and its variants. The concept of living wills builds upon some of the tenets that underpin consolidated supervision. In the UK, the *Financial Services Act* imposes 'living wills' for banks and other systemically significant financial institutions.[44]

The new FSA duty to require firms to produce Recovery and Resolution Plans ('RRPs') or 'living wills' is indeed a very welcome development, one that has also been encouraged by the Financial Stability Board and that is being considered by the IMF to develop guidelines for countries to follow. Living wills or RRPs can facilitate an 'orderly resolution' (as opposed to a chaotic one) and can complement early intervention procedures, as well as a mechanism for ex ante burden sharing. RRPs provide firm specific contingency planning and help ensure that institutions have robust recovery (capital and liquidity) plans to deal with periods of stress without recourse to support from taxpayers' money. Living wills also address the issue of multi-level governance since they can combine the national, the European and the international dimensions. By preparing an institution's own funeral, a living will can help avoid the chaos that would surely ensue in the event of insolvency, given the tangled web of counterparties and derivatives contracts of many banks nowadays. If troubled institutions expect governmental assistance, bank managers will have little incentive to pre-arrange an orderly resolution and market discipline will be distorted. The contingent resolution plan, which has been likened[45] to the plan electric utilities develop in order to disconnect a power plant from the grid without bringing down the grid and with minimal disruption to consumers, would provide the information the authorities need to proceed to carry out an orderly resolution, in particular with regard to how to 'unplug' the bank from the payment, clearing and settlement infrastructures.

Critics of living wills – many predictably from the banking industry – claim that they might result in a return to a world of national markets in order to make things simpler for the authorities. Others claim that such wills may discourage a bank from entering into new lines of business or expand its operations. However, dealing with the 'too-big-to-fail' problem or too-interconnected-to-fail problem by reducing the advantage of being big (or complex) can be construed as an advantage.[46]

Another important development is the introduction of the Special Resolution Regime ('SRR'), a notable feature of the 2009 *Banking Act*. The SRR was a step in the right direction and it worked very well in the management of the Dunfermline Building Society case in 2009. However, the SRR is not designed to deal with non-banks nor with cross-border aspects of banking and finance.

On 2 December 2009, the ECOFIN Council adopted proposals advanced by the European Commission on 23 September 2009 to 'upgrade' the EU bodies of national supervisors that monitor individual banks and insurance companies as well as securities markets into a European System of Financial Supervisors (ESFS) and to establish a European Systemic Risk Board for macro prudential supervision.[47]

Supervision and crisis management are parts of a seamless process; a sound institution can quickly turn into an unstable one, which inevitably will lead – if conditions further deteriorate – to crisis management. Early intervention by the supervisor, resolution of financial institutions leading to a possible reorganization or winding-up of an insolvent one could be partly overlapping stages, going well beyond supervision proper, but clearly a process into which national supervisors have a key role in designing. The European Commission's recently published Communication, 'An EU Framework for Cross-Border Crisis Management in the Banking Sector', makes the link from supervision to crisis management explicit.[48]

17.7. CONCLUDING OBSERVATIONS

Following the collapse of Lehman Brothers, Thomas Huertas (FSA Director of Supervision) famously stated that financial institutions are global when alive, national when dead. This reflects the economic reality of modern business, something that has also been evidenced through the numerous bail-out plans that have been put into place to save institutions on a cross-border basis as a whole due to their size, importance or interconnectedness and not as individual companies (e.g. Bear Stearns,[49] Royal Bank of Scotland Group plc,[50] Lloyds Group plc,[51] Citigroup,[52] Bank of America,[53] etc.). Therefore, it is evident that the legal structure does not always reflect the economic reality.

In this chapter we have argued that despite the success of consolidated supervision, another building block for global banking and finance is required, measures to promote consolidated resolutions are required. The challenges in achieving an effective framework of consolidated resolution are numerous, in particular with regard to financial conglomerates. Yet this is a challenge that the international community must confront. As Einstein famously remarked: '[w]e can't solve problems by using the same kind of thinking we used when we created them.' We must find ways to resolve the problems posed by large cross-border systemically important financial institutions. Though we are still a long way away, it is reassuring that following the mandate of the Group of Twenty, the IMF is looking at solutions to this problem and that initiatives by the EU Commission and the Basel Cross-Border Resolution Group are under way.

NOTES

1. The IMF is working on a proposed framework (principles) for cross-border resolution of financial crises. This proposed framework is subject to consideration of the Board (a resolution is expected soon). Also see Bank for International Settlements, Report and Recommendations of the Cross-Border Bank Resolution Group, March 2010 available at http://www.bis.org/publ/bcbs169.pdf?noframes=1.
2. See generally Rosa M. Lastra (ed.), *Cross Border Bank Insolvency*, Oxford University Press (2011).
3. For an enlargement on this issue see Richard J. Herring and Anthony M. Santomero,

'The Corporate Structure of Financial Conglomerates', *Journal of Financial Services Research*, 1990, p. 481.

4. UNCITRAL Legislative Guide on Insolvency Law, Part Three, A/CN.9/WG.V/WP.92, p. 5.
5. In this part we draw substantially on chapter 3, *Central Banking and Banking Regulation* (1996) by Rosa Lastra, Financial Markets Group, London School of Economics.
6. See <http://www.asbaweb.org/Grupos/libros/fscommand/doc7.pdf> [accessed 31 March 2010].
7. This document was entitled 'Report to the Governors on the Supervision of Banks' Foreign Establishments' and was issued on 26 September 1975. This document is available at http://www.bis.org/publ/bcbs00a.pdf?noframes=1.
8. This document is available at http://www.bis.org/publ/bcbsc312.pdf?noframes=1.
9. See Basel Committee on Banking Supervision, 'Principles for the supervision of banks' foreign establishment', page 1, available at http://www.bis.org/publ/bcbsc312.pdf?noframes=1.
10. See Basel Committee on Banking Supervision, 'Principles for the supervision of banks' foreign establishment', page 3, available at http://www.bis.org/publ/bcbsc312.pdf?noframes=1.
11. This document is available at http://www.bis.org/publ/bcbsc314.pdf?noframes=1.
12. For an enlargement on the cross-jurisdiction dimension, see n. 2 above and Rosa M. Lastra and Rodrigo Olivares-Caminal, 'Cross Border Insolvency: The Case of Financial Conglomerates', in John Raymond LaBrosse, Rodrigo Olivares-Caminal and Dalvinder Singh (eds), *Financial Crisis Management and Bank Resolution*, Informa 2009, pages 269–289.
13. The principle of unity or universality of the assets of the debtor states that there is only one competent court to decide on the insolvency of the distressed entity (unity), and that the insolvency law of the country in which the process has been initiated is effective in all other countries where the distressed entity has assets or branches (universality). All assets and liabilities of the parent entity and its foreign branches are wound up as one legal entity (extra-territorial effect to the adjudication of insolvency). Under this unitary system it is impossible to start separate insolvency proceedings against a domestic branch of a bank that has its head office in another country (US law applies this unitary principle to the liquidation of a US bank with foreign branches). Contrary to the principle of unity or universality is the 'separate entity approach'. The separate entity approach to liquidation, i.e. insolvency proceedings are only effective in the country where they are initiated, promotes a plurality of proceedings (initiated in every country in which the insolvent entity holds realizable assets or branches. Under a separate entity approach a domestic branch of a foreign entity receives a liquidation preference, as local assets are segregated for the benefit of local creditors ('ring fencing'). Ring fencing is contrary to the *pars condictio creditorum* and the *pari passu* principle, since some creditors receive more favourable treatment than others. This is the US approach to the liquidation of US branches of a foreign bank. The different treatment given by the US to national banks with branches abroad and to the branches in US territory of foreign banks provides an additional element of inconsistency.
14. Throughout this chapter we use the concept 'too-big-to-fail' which encompasses its modern versions.
15. In late February 2010 there has been a breakdown in the talks between Iceland and the governments of the UK and the Netherlands to resolve the Icesave originated as a result of the deposit insurance outlays of these two governments on the failed Icelandic internet bank Icesave. In addition, in early March 2010 the Icelandic electorate rejected a referendum on legislation to compensate these governments. Moody's has stated that the failure to reach a new agreement is likely to lead to an extended delay on an IMF programme which put Iceland's Baa3 under downgrade pressure (see Moody's: Iceland's Rating Pressured by Breakdown in Icesave Talks, Global Credit Research – 26 February 2010). Standard & Poor's is maintaining its BBB-/A-3 long- and

short-term foreign currency ratings and its BBB+/A-2 long- and short-term local currency ratings on the Republic of Iceland on CreditWatch, where they were placed with negative implications on 5 January 2010 (see Standard & Poor's, Research Update: Icelanders' Referendum Rejection of Plan to Repay Icesave Debt has no Immediate Impact on Iceland Sovereign Rating).

16. A sovereign state always has the possibility of taxing its citizens, to dispose of its resources (e.g. natural resources or even part of its territory as it had happened in the past with Alaska or Louisiana in the US), or even in extreme circumstances it can recourse to the expropriation of assets from its citizens.
17. See House of Commons Treasury Committee, Too important to fail – too important to ignore, Ninth Report of Session 2009–10, Volume 1, HC 261-I, paragraph 8.
18. Ibid, paragraph 27.
19. Ibid, paragraph 65.
20. Rosa M. Lastra, 'Cross border resolution of banking crises' in Evanoff, D., LaBrosse, J.R. and Kaufman, G. (eds), *International Financial Instability: Global Banking and National Regulation*, Vol. 2, World Scientific Publishing Company Pte Ltd, Singapore, 2007, pp. 311–330.
21. This raises different issues, e.g. whether a solvent company can be part of an insolvency procedure without having complied with the standard to commence an insolvency procedure or the fact that creditors of a solvent (or more solvent) legal entity are pooled together with creditors of an insolvent entity on a *pari passu* basis. This last example is also applicable to the shareholders of the distressed entity.
22. The equal step or standing of the parties.
23. Set-off can be understood as a reduction or elimination of a debt by means of netting the amounts owed by one party with those that are due from the other.
24. In 1992, the Basel Committee published a document on The Insolvency Liquidation of a Multinational Bank. This document is available at http://www.bis.org/publ/bcbs10c.pdf.
25. This part of the paper draws from Rosa M. Lastra and Rodrigo Olivares-Caminal, 'Cross Border Insolvency: The Case of Financial Conglomerates', in John Raymond LaBrosse, Rodrigo Olivares-Caminal and Dalvinder Singh (eds), *Financial Crisis Management and Bank Resolution*, Informa 2009, pp. 269–289.
26. See Commission Communication on an EU Framework for Cross-Border Crisis Management in the Banking Sector, COM (2009)561 final of 20 October 2009, available at: <http://eur-lex.europa.eu/LexUriServ/LexUriServ.do?uri=COM:2009:0561:FIN:EN:PDF>.
27. In this section we draw on Rosa M. Lastra, 'Cross Border Resolution of Banking Crises', in Douglas D. Evanoff, John Raymond LaBrosse, and George G. Kaufman (eds), *International Financial Instability: Global Banking and National Regulation*, Vol. 2, Singapore, World Scientific Publishing Company Pte Ltd, 2007, pp. 311–330.
28. For instance, the issue of foreign ownership of banks makes some host jurisdictions (where foreign ownership is high) reluctant to rely upon home country control. This has relevant implications in many eastern European countries (such as Poland).
29. See Krimminger, M. (2005), 'Deposit Insurance and Bank Insolvency in a Changing World: Synergies and Challenges', in *Current Developments in Monetary and Financial Law*, Vol. 4, International Monetary Fund, Washington, DC.
30. Above note 27.
31. Article 13.1 of UNCITRAL's model law on cross-border insolvency does not permit 'ring-fencing'.
32. See Curtis, 'The Status of Foreign Deposits under the Federal Deposit Preference Law', (2000) 21 *University of Pennsylvania Journal of International Economic Law* No. 2, p. 254, cited in Lastra, 'Cross-Border Bank Insolvency: Legal Implications in the Case of Banks Operating in Different Jurisdictions in Latin America' (2003), *Journal of International Economic Law*, JIEL, Vol. 6, No. 1, pp. 79–110.
33. Above note 27.

34. The term used by UNCITRAL to refer to corporate groups is enterprise groups. According to the draft document on the treatment of enterprise groups in insolvency, the term 'enterprise group' covers different forms of economic organization that can be described as two or more legal entities that are linked together by some form of control or ownership. Control or ownership is understood as the capacity to determine (directly or indirectly) the operational or financial policies of an enterprise. See UNCITRAL, Working Group V (Insolvency Law), document prepared for the thirty-eighth session, New York, 19–23 April 2010, A/CN.9/WG.V/WP.92.
35. This commentary and recommendations are revised versions of the text previously included in documents A/CN.9/WG.V/WP.90 and Addenda 1, revised on the basis of the Report of Working Group V on the work of its thirty-seventh session in November 2009 (A/CN.9/686).
36. These documents are available at http://www.uncitral.org/uncitral/en/commission/working_groups/5Insolvency.html.
37. The text of the Practice Guide on Cross-Border Insolvency Cooperation is available at http://www.uncitral.org/pdf/english/texts/insolven/Practice_Guide_english.pdf.
38. Robert A. Eisenbeis, 'Home Country versus Cross-Border Negative Large Externalities in Large Banking Organization Failures and how to Avoid Them', in Douglas Evanoff, George Kaufman and John R. LaBrosse (eds), *International Financial Instability: Global Banking and National Regulation*, World Scientific, Singapore, 2007.
39. A copy of the memorandum is available at http://www.bankofengland.co.uk/publications/other/financialstability/srrmou.pdf.
40. Above note 26.
41. For a critique of this Directive see generally Gillian Garcia, Rosa M. Lastra and Maria Nieto, 'Bankruptcy and Reorganization Procedures for Cross-border Banks in the EU: Towards an Integrated Approach to the Reform of the EU Safety Net', *Journal of Financial Regulation and Compliance*, Vol. 7, No. 3, 2009.
42. Directive 2002/87/EC amended Council Directives 73/239/EEC, 79/267/EEC, 92/49/EEC, 92/96/EEC, 93/6/EEC and 93/22/EEC, and Directives 98/78/EC and 2000/12/EC of the European Parliament and of the Council.
43. See Communication from the Commission to the European Parliament, the Council, the European Economic and Social Committee, the European Court of Justice and the European Central Bank – An EU Framework for Cross-Border Crisis Management in the Banking Sector {SEC(2009) 1389} {SEC(2009) 1390} {SEC(2009) 1407} COM/2009/0561 final, available at http://eur-lex.europa.eu/LexUriServ/LexUriServ.do?uri=CELEX:52009DC0561:EN:HTML.
44. Section 7 of the *Financial Services Act* introduces section 139B – F in the *Financial Services and Markets Act 2000*.
45. See, for example, the presentation by Thomas Huertas on 'Too big to fail, too complex to contemplate: What to do about systemically important firms' at a London School of Economics conference on 15 September 2009.
46. On living wills see the paper by Charles Goodhart, Emilios Avgouleas and Dirk Schoenmaker, 'Living Wills as a Catalyst for Action', available at SSRN: http://ssrn.com/abstract=1533808.
47. See <http://europa.eu/rapid/pressReleasesAction.do?reference=IP/09/1347&type=HTML>, Commission adopts legislative proposals to strengthen financial supervision in Europe(see MEMO/09/404 and MEMO/09/405), 23 September 2009. Ecofin Council on 2 December 2009 approved the creation of the three new European Supervisory Authorities, which together with the European System Risk Board (for which broad political agreement was reached on 20 October 2009) form the new EU supervisory structure. <http://www.consilium.europa.eu/uedocs/cms_Data/docs/pressdata/en/ecofin/111706.pdf>.
48. See Rosa M. Lastra, Parliamentary Brief, December 2009. See also Statement of the European Shadow Financial Regulatory Committee, Stockholm, of 30 November 2009.

49. JP Morgan purchased Bear Stearns for USD 236 million assisted by the US Federal Reserve which provided a USD 30 billion credit line to ensure the rescue could take place.
50. The UK Government provided a GBP 45.5 billion assistance to rescue the bank. In exchange, the government received 84.4 per cent of the shares.
51. The UK Government provided more than GBP 17 billion in assistance to rescue the bank. In exchange, the government received 41 per cent of the shares.
52. Citigroup received a USD 45 billion investment through TARP. Additional aid was provided by means of: (1) government guarantees to limit losses from a USD 301 billion pool of toxic assets; (2) a USD 5 billion commitment from the Treasury; (3) a USD 10 billion commitment by the FDIC; and (4) a USD 220 billion commitment by the Federal Reserve.
53. Bank of America received USD 45 billion through TARP (including USD 10 billion originally allocated for Merrill Lynch). Additionally, aid was provided by means of: (1) government guarantees to limit losses from a USD 118 billion pool of troubled assets; (2) a USD 7.5 billion commitment from the Treasury; (3) a USD 2.5 billion commitment by the FDIC; and (4) a USD 87.2 billion commitment by the Federal Reserve.

18. Creating an EU-level supervisor for cross-border banking groups: issues raised by the US experience with dual banking*

Larry D. Wall, María J. Nieto and David G. Mayes

18.1. INTRODUCTION AND MOTIVATION

The European Union (EU) has been facilitating the growth of cross-border banking groups with considerable success, but bank supervision remains the responsibility of national supervisors. The difficulties this poses have been vividly highlighted by the problems encountered in the present crisis that have increased moral hazard. The conundrum has long been recognized and various proposals have been offered to address this weakness, ranging from full centralization of prudential supervision,[1] to strengthened cooperation via colleges of supervisors and resolution authorities.[2] An alternative that would retain the most important advantages of full centralization is that of centralization of chartering and supervision only for those cross-border groups that are systemically important to the EU. All other banks would retain national chartering and supervision. In many respects this would be similar to the arrangements in the US where there are federal and state charters.

Decressin and Čihák,[3] also consider a system with both an EU charter and a national charter. However, they leave open the question of the structure of the prudential supervisor including the possibility that EU chartered banks would be supervised by national authorities. A key part of their proposed framework would be freedom of choice for banks between national and European charters. In the authors' view, this would deliver a prudential level playing field (all banks would have the choice) and allow market forces to play a role in determining the optimal mixture of EU-level and national-level prudential frameworks. Hertig, Lee and McCahery,[4] propose that member states will have the option to delegate the supervision of banks that pose EU-wide prudential risks to the European Central Bank (ECB) under an opt-in approach. The opting-in process would require a member state to enter into a binding agreement with the ECB, which would spell out coordination and cooperation in normal times as well as in periods of crisis, and which may also contain member state specific provisions.

In contrast with these prior discussions of two charter types in Europe, this chapter explores the idea of an EU-level supervisor that could supervise all systemically important cross-border banking groups without requiring an opt-in by the bank's home country. In this respect, the European supervisory system would work somewhat like that in the US which has long operated under a dual bank chartering system that allows banks to choose between charters issued by the federal government and charters issued by the state governments. In the US, a bank's choice of charter determines its choice of bank supervisor(s). The American experience suggests that a system with dual charters requires careful consideration of the boundaries between authorities at different levels. This study will focus on three boundaries that would be important to Europe: (1) the criteria for eligibility for the EU charter and the possibility of arbitrage between charters; (2) who would take responsibility for providing the safety net; and (3) the interaction between the dual charter and the national business conduct regulation.

We do not advocate for or against Europe's adoption of US policies on any of the various issues and/or an EU-level supervisor against the background of the US experience. US policies have been tailored to the US political and financial systems as they have evolved through time. What the US experience can do is help to identify the more important issues and demonstrate some of the consequences of some possible solutions.

The rest of the chapter is organized as follows: Section 18.2 briefly reviews the origins of the US dual banking system in contrast with the EU institutional framework for supervision. The regulatory issues raised by the dual charter are analysed in section 18.3, where we explore what could be the criteria for eligibility for an EU charter and the chartering authority; whether some or all banks that qualify for an EU charter be required to convert to an EU charter and under what circumstances could a bank with an EU charter be allowed to convert back to a national charter. The issues raised by the lack of an EU-level safety net are also analysed in this section that explores alternatives that would return control over their fiscal exposure to the member states. Lastly, that section discusses issues associated with pre-emption in the business conduct regulation. We conclude and present policy implications in the last section.

18.2. BACKGROUND

The creation of an EU-level supervisor for cross-border banks has become a somewhat more intellectually attractive solution to the supervision of these banks in the EU in the light of the experiences in the autumn of 2008 and the institutional changes in supervision agreed to by policymakers. The EU-level banking supervisor should have full authority over the banking group as a whole, including the required information and powers to act should any problem be detected, with a mandate to protect the financial stability of each country in which the group operates. Such a system would allow for continued differences in the supervision of groups that are, at most, of systemic importance to their home country while focusing a new EU-level supervisory agency on the cross-border banking groups. The cross-border banks we are referring to are those where at least one host country regards its operations as being of systemic importance – its failure would be a threat to financial stability.[5] However, the creation of such a dual supervisory system at national and EU levels would also raise a number of new issues. Among these issues are a set of concerns relating to the relationship between the two levels of supervisors (agencies), and with investor protection regulators (whether a separated agency or not of the prudential supervisor); how the two levels of supervisors would work with the agencies running the safety net – the deposit insurers and lenders of last resort.[6] Clearly unless the EU-level agency was in charge of systemic concerns for every member state of the EU there is a potential problem of coordination with the national agencies that have that task. Furthermore, given the absence of any noticeable ability to make fiscal transfers and other adjustments, such as investments, that would ease the impact of regional shocks as in the US, the need for treating localized financial instability directly in the EU is much greater than in the present US.[7]

In contrast to proposals that the EU deliberately adopt a dual chartering system, the US dual banking system was an unintended consequence of the creation of the National Banking System in 1863 to help fund the Union effort in the Civil War by increasing demand for government bonds.[8] The federal charter was not created to facilitate interstate banking; the legal changes to facilitate widespread interstate commercial banking were not adopted until the 1980s. Nor was the federal charter created to control safety net subsidies better. The modern US lender of last resort was created by legislation passed in 1913 and the deposit insurance system which was created by legislation passed in 1933. Instead of the federal charter being created to facilitate change, it is much more the case that these important changes to the US commercial bank regulatory and safety net systems were structured to work within a dual chartering system.

The differences in the origin of dual chartering between the EU and the US do not relate to the issues that must be addressed but to the order. Rather than cross-border banking and safety net policies being developed in consideration of the prior existence of dual chartering as in the US, the EU would need to develop its dual chartering and supervisory policies in the light of existing supervisory and safety net structures.[9]

18.3. REGULATORY ISSUES RAISED BY THE EXISTENCE OF A DUAL CHARTER

18.3.1. Who is Subject to EU-level Supervision?

The US regulatory system mixes elements of state and federal supervision. State banks are subject to federal supervision by one of two federal agencies as a condition for being member institutions whose deposits are insured by the Federal Deposit Insurance Corporation (FDIC) while all national banks are subject to supervision by a third agency. There are additional complications in the US supervisory structure but these exist for a variety of historical and political reasons that are not relevant to Europe.[10] For the purpose of our analysis, what is relevant is that the US system: (1) allows banks to change their charters and supervisors at rather low cost subject to the approval of the new supervisor; and (2) the supervisors have used their power in a way that has resulted in almost all of the largest banks selecting a national charter and almost all of the small banks selecting a state charter.

The ability of banks to change their charters at relatively low cost is regarded by most banks as a critical part of the US dual banking system as it encourages the supervisors to use their discretion in ways favourable to each supervisor's clientele of banks. US supervisors' discretion is limited as many aspects of prudential supervision are established by statutes and regulations that are virtually identical for all commercial bank supervisors, such as for the capital adequacy requirements. However, the various supervisors retain some important discretion over the writing of some regulations, such as in the range of financial products that may be offered, and the supervisors also have some discretion over the implementation of the various regulations.

One of the advantages claimed for supervisory competition is that it discourages unnecessarily restrictive regulation. Bankers cite cases where the state supervisors denied banks permission to engage in a new activity which was authorized by the federal supervisors (or vice versa with state supervisors approving the activity). Another advantage is that it puts pressure on supervisors to be efficient. State supervisors and the national bank and thrift supervisors depend on fees collected from their banks to fund their operations.[11] If banks start changing charters that raises the revenue of the supervisor gaining the charter and lowers the revenue of the supervisor losing the charter.

Conversely, opponents of the dual banking system accuse it of promoting competition in laxity. Wilmarth[12] argues that the Office of the Comptroller of Currency (OCC) has tried to get state-chartered banks to adopt a national charter by promoting its ability to pre-empt stricter state business conduct regulation. Appelbaum and Nakashima[13] discuss how the OTS's efforts to increase the agency's revenues by expanding its set of regulatees led to weak prudential supervision.[14] In one particular case, Countrywide, the OTS induced a national bank regulated by the OCC to change to a federal thrift charter.[15]

In theory, national supervisors in the EU could compete for national bank charters under the current legal framework only subject to the requirement of minimum harmonization imposed by the Banking Directive. Under the 'single passport' concept, a bank that is properly authorized in any EU country may branch into any other EU country. In principle, a bank that finds its home country supervisors too strict, could move its charter to a more accommodating country, provided that the change is approved by the bank's new home country. Indeed, in theory the degree of regulatory competition in the EU could be far greater than among states in the US. While banks in the US can change supervisors, virtually all US banks have to comply with federal laws and regulations. In contrast, in the EU, such changes can take two forms. The bank could move its headquarters and main operations to a different member state or it could become a European Company under the European Company Statute.

In practice, moving charters is not so easy in the EU. While banking laws may not prohibit movements, a variety of other considerations such as language, national traditions, taxes, deposit insurance payments and the franchise value greatly raise the cost of transferring charters.

While the US dual banking system was not started with present circumstances in mind, it has continued in part as a way of inducing lower cost supervision. The US system allowing banks to pick their own charter and change charters at minimal costs reflects this goal. An EU dual charter system would start with a different goal, that of better supervising systemically important cross-border groups. This difference in goals suggests that were the EU to adopt a dual charter, it would need to address three chartering questions from the perspective of improved cross-border supervision:

(1) What are the criteria for eligibility for an EU charter?
(2) Will some or all banks that qualify for an EU charter be required to convert to an EU charter? and
(3) Under what circumstances, if any, will a bank with an EU charter be allowed to convert back to a national charter?

The answers to these questions will determine the effectiveness of the EU charter including the extent of competition and possibilities of arbitrage between national and EU-level supervisors.

18.3.1.1. Criteria for eligibility

The criteria for eligibility for an EU charter could be subjective (such as a college of supervisors' assessments of systemic importance)[16] or objective (such as market share, size or presence in several EU countries). A narrow set of criteria would start with the extent to which the bank has cross-border operations either via presence (branch or subsidiary) or operations (interbank, foreign exchange (FX), and/or derivatives markets). Another consideration might include the absolute size or market share of the group as a proxy for its systemic importance to the EU. A third consideration would be the number of the countries in which the group is systemically important as per the decision made by the college of supervisors. The CRD envisages that colleges of home and host country supervisors do need to decide on the systemically important character of both branches and subsidiaries and it provides some guidance in Article 42a(a) in this respect.

18.3.1.2. Must eligible banks convert?

Once the various EU chartering criteria are satisfied, the question arises as to whether conversion to an EU charter would be mandatory and who would be the chartering authority. If the goal of creating an EU-level supervisor is to address the problems of supervising and resolving cross-border groups better, the answer would appear to be that all groups meeting the established criteria would be required to convert to the EU charter. This will leave room for competition at the start as some groups may be able to restructure themselves in a way that allows them to retain national supervisors. Even more competition will arise, if conversion is not mandatory. Regulatory competition, however, would be limited by the EU centralized authority on Competition. Nonetheless, in order to limit the incentive to arbitrage between charters there is an economic rationale for calibrating the EU charter at a level that makes this charter attractive for Europe's major cross-border banks, for example, establishing a Single Special Resolution Regime for the EU chartered banks that reduces the coordination costs among national resolution authorities. Moreover, certain prudential regulations with a marked national character such as countercyclical capital buffers that would apply to EU chartered banks would reflect the geographic composition of the bank's portfolio of exposures and calculate their variable buffer add-on as a weighted average of the add-ons which are being applied in member states to which those banks have an exposure.

18.3.1.3. Converting back

Once cross-border banking groups have taken an EU charter, a further question is whether they would be allowed to convert back to a national charter. The answer to this question may seem obvious if some institutions are required to convert to an EU charter, they obviously would not be given permission to convert back to a national charter. However, consider the case where the group no longer satisfies the criteria for an EU charter. A group may no longer meet the criteria because of a deliberate decision to sell or spin off part of its operations (e.g. banks that received government capital injections have been required by the EU competition authority to divest lines of business and financial affiliates). Or, it may be that the group is shrinking relative to the requirements for an EU charter. Were any of these to happen, should the group be required to retain an EU charter, required to convert to a national charter or given the option to convert back to a national charter? When the groups do not meet the criteria that supervisors established to grant the EU charter (e.g. the bank has been restructured in the aftermath of a crisis), the bank will want to shift to a national charter more suitable for its new structure. If conversion back to a national charter is envisioned, the frequent charter switches should be discouraged by requiring that the group not just fail the minimum criteria for an EU charter but that it must fail the criteria by a substantial margin. Another way to prevent frequent switches would be to require that the bank fail the criteria for more than a certain number of years before being allowed to convert back to a national charter.

18.3.2. Who is Responsible for Providing the Safety Net?

The US did not have an official lender of last resort or national deposit insurance system at the start of the dual banking system.[17] However, commercial-bank clearinghouses in some major cities provided a sort of lender of last resort and accompanied it with some bank supervision from the 1850s through to the creation of the Federal Reserve, according to Gorton and Mullineaux.[18] While clearinghouses were valuable in mitigating the impact of bank panics, they in effect required private institutions to provide a public good in the form of reduced financial instability. After the

Panic of 1907, some major New York banks determined that the private costs of providing this public good exceeded these banks' share of the gains, according to Moen and Tallman.[19] The *Federal Reserve Act of 1913* provided for the new central bank to lend on good collateral to its member banks: the Act required national banks to become members. The Act also allowed state chartered members to become members of the Federal Reserve, but required as a condition of membership that state-chartered member banks (state member banks) submit to Federal Reserve supervision, including on-site examinations.[20]

Deposit protection during the dual banking era initially took the form of state-run deposit insurance systems adopted by eight states in the early 1900s, according to Calomiris (1989). All eight of these state plans were exclusively for banks chartered by that state. All eight of these systems collapsed with the waves of bank failures in the 1920s and early 1930s.[21] Federal deposit insurance started with the creation of the FDIC by the *Banking Act of 1933*. That Act required Federal Reserve member banks (national and state member) to join the FDIC. State non-member banks, that are banks which had not been subject to inspection by federal bank supervisors, were authorized to join the FDIC but only after examination and approval by the FDIC.[22] The *Banking Act of 1935* gave the FDIC the power to terminate a bank's insured status.[23] This was a draconian penalty that, when invoked, would typically result in the bank's closure.

Thus, the pattern in the US is clear. The entity providing lender of last resort or deposit insurance was generally provided with the authority to examine and discipline the banks to which it had contingent financial exposure. The Federal Reserve was created when the clearinghouses became exposed to decisions of trusts that were not part of the clearinghouse. Federal Reserve lending was initially limited to member banks. Individual state deposit insurance systems were limited to banks chartered by that state. The FDIC was given the authority to examine banks before they became members and later given the authority to terminate a bank's deposit insurance.

Both the Federal Reserve and FDIC are exposed to losses at institutions for which they are not the primary federal supervisor; however, both are provided with tools to mitigate their risk exposure. Both agencies have access to the examination reports filed by the other two federal regulatory agencies. The Federal Reserve's exposure to national banks and state non-member banks is tempered by the requirement that its loans be secured by acceptable collateral. The Federal Reserve Banks are authorized to require any information they need to satisfy themselves that the collateral is acceptable.[24] For those institutions where the FDIC is not the primary supervisor, the agency has backup examination authority.[25]

In the EU, while it may be possible to create an EU-level prudential supervisor for cross-border banking groups, responsibility for safety net provision will almost surely remain a national responsibility for the foreseeable future. The primary difficulty in shifting safety net responsibility to the EU is that the EU lacks taxing authority; that power remains lodged in its member states. Buiter[26] argues that the lack of backing by a fiscal authority could be a problem for a central bank as the collateral it takes for its loans may turn out to be worth less than the value of its loans. He notes that while individual member states stand behind their national central bank, no fiscal authority stands behind the ECB. However, the national central banks are the shareholders of the ECB and should they need to subscribe more capital they can call on their respective governments.[27]

While the lack of fiscal support is of debatable importance for the central bank, it represents a clearer concern for deposit insurance agencies. Even agencies that have accumulated an ex ante fund may find the funds are inadequate during peak loss periods, as has happened in the US with the Federal Savings and Loan Insurance Corporation (FSLIC) and may happen with the FDIC during the current global financial crisis. However, contingent funding from member states could be set up pending replenishment of the fund by the industry after the crisis. More difficult would be covering ex ante the sort of bailout financing that has been used in some countries in the present crisis (the divestures required by the EU Competition authority is a good example of bank restructuring aimed at repaying the government fiscal support). Even ex-post they may be on a scale where repayment by the banking industry or by private purchasers of nationalized assets becomes a very drawn-out process if it is not to create a prolonged recession along the way.

Thus, the creation of an EU-level supervisor threatens to create a situation where the member state providers of the safety net do not have direct control over parts of their loss exposure. The potential problems with this are both economic and political. The root of the economic problem is a principal (the voters and taxpayers of a member state) that has no direct control over that of an agent. In practical terms, this means that an EU-level prudential supervisor may assign lower priority to minimizing taxpayer losses of a particular country than would be the case if the supervisor were accountable to the taxpayers of the responsible country through that country's political system. The political problem is the lack of a fully binding ex-ante commitment on the part of the national governments to provide funding as necessary. The voters and taxpayers of a country may refuse to bear the fiscal burden of a large financial crisis over which neither they nor their elected representatives had much control. Such a refusal is more likely to the extent that the EU-level supervisor is perceived to have failed to perform its supervisory duties adequately.

One alternative that would return control over their fiscal exposure to the member states would be to adopt the approach taken by the Federal Reserve and FDIC with regards to banks they do not directly supervise. That is, give the national central bank, supervisor and national deposit insurers the power to: (1) request additional information; (2) undertake their own backup examinations; and (3) where appropriate, to deny the loan or terminate the insurance coverage.[28] The first two powers are consistent with an EU-level prudential supervisor that operationally relies on a network of national supervisors. This is not a perfect solution from the perspective of the national safety net authorities or the EU-level supervisor. The national safety net authorities are still somewhat dependent upon the EU-level supervisor to decide to take action when a cross-border banking group encounters financial problems. However, from the EU supervisor's perspective, alerting national safety net authorities could be problematic. The problem is that the national authorities could take actions (such as starting reorganization and winding-up proceedings or terminate deposit insurance of a distressed subsidiary bank) that could aggravate the banking group's problems at a time when the EU-level supervisor believes it still has a good chance of returning to health. Without such national backup powers, the situation is in many ways analogous to the current situation where the member states are exposed to losses arising from cross-border banks and banking groups over which they have little or no supervisory power.

18.3.3. Business Conduct Regulations

The US has had a long-running dispute over the ability of its states to impose business conduct regulations on federally chartered financial firms. Federal courts have generally held that business conduct regulations on federally chartered depositories (commercial banks and thrifts) is the exclusive province of the federal government, in US terms federal law pre-empts state law.[29] However, state and local governments have periodically sought to enforce their conduct regulations when they perceive federal rules to be too weak or inadequately enforced.[30]

This presents a problem that does not exist in the EU at present. While cross-border banks operating directly or through branches are subject to home country prudential control they are subject to host country conduct of business and consumer protection rules. We explore the experience of the US in order to consider the relative advantages of creating an n+1th conduct of business regime in order to improve the ease of entry into national markets.

One of the rationales for federal banking law pre-empting state banking law is that states might otherwise impose laws that place federally chartered banks at a competitive disadvantage.[31] Another rationale for federal pre-emption is that a change in state laws or their interpretations may impose losses on the federal safety net.[32] A third rationale for pre-emption is that state business conduct regulation may be used to limit competition in that state.[33]

A fourth argument for pre-empting state laws is that of greater operational efficiency. In the absence of pre-emption, national banks would need to tailor their operations in each state to that state's business conduct regulations. Among the possible results could be that application forms, training procedures, and computer systems could all have to be tailored to meet each state's idiosyncratic requirements. With pre-emption, the bank can implement a uniform procedure for delivering services across its entire network.

The opponents of pre-emption tend to favour the approach proposed by the Obama administration under which federal business conduct regulations set minimum standards for federally chartered banks but states should have the option of writing and enforcing tougher standards. The Consumers Union[34] gave a list of state measures intended to 'protect . . . constituents from unfair banking practices and escalating fees' that were rendered less effective and in some cases effectively blocked by federal pre-emption.[35] Another argument that opponents of pre-emption make is that allowing federally chartered institutions to avoid state regulation may undercut states' ability to enforce consumer regulations on state-chartered institutions. In part, this argument arises because the federal chartering authorities are competing to attract existing and potential future state chartered institutions to adopt federal charters. The federal authorities may make a federal charter relatively more attractive by implementing less strict regulations. Indeed, Wilmarth[36] references comments by then Comptroller of the Currency Hawke as touting the OCC's ability to pre-empt state consumer laws as one of the advantages of adopting a national bank charter. Moreover, the competitive advantages of being able to pre-empt state law can be so large that a large fraction of the business shifted to federally chartered banks. For example, Furletti[37] discusses the impact of pre-emption on the US credit card industry and argues that it helped national banks become by far the largest suppliers of credit cards in the US.[38]

The issues associated with pre-emption in the EU are generally similar to those in the US. National authorities might use business conduct regulations to disadvantage EU chartered banks, although that possibility is largely limited by the principle of minimal harmonization, while EU supervisory authorities may use pre-emption to give their banks a competitive advantage. National authorities may establish laws that 'protect consumers from abuses' but their ability to 'limit competition' is itself limited because competition is an EU responsibility. Compliance with different national business conduct regulations would definitely reduce the efficiency of EU chartered banking groups.

The weighting of the various advantages and disadvantages of pre-emption in the EU may differ from that of the US in at least two important ways. First, there are greater differences across the EU in culture and commercial codes than within the US. The US does not have a uniform culture nor do all states have exactly the same commercial code. However, the shared history of the states of the US and state efforts to produce a recommended 'Uniform Commercial Code' have greatly reduced the differences across the states relative to that of the member states of the EU. The cultural and legal differences across the EU are likely to extend to some aspects of some financial products. One implication of this is that investors' expectations of the rules may differ dramatically, implying a greater value to local rules. Second, another implication is that independent of business conduct rules, cross-border banks in the EU will need to tailor their offerings more to local markets than is necessary in the US – probably reducing the efficiency advantages of the EU charter.

On the other hand, the EU is unlike the US in that it has an explicit goal of a single market in financial services and, hence harmonization also holds for business conduct rules and consumer protection. While in theory such harmonization should be the minimum necessary for an efficient and competitive market, greater integration will eventually need further harmonization. Allowing member states to impose differential rules on cross-border groups will hinder movement towards that goal.

18.4. CONCLUSIONS AND POLICY IMPLICATIONS

The idea of having an EU-level prudential supervisor for cross-border banks with systemic impact in the EU in addition to national supervisors for the rest of the system has considerable intellectual attractions. It addresses the issue of having a consistent arrangement for the regulation and supervision of such groups for which the principle of minimum harmonization has proved insufficient. Moreover, if the EU-level supervisor also applies a single set of rules rather than simply trying to ensure that the plethora of national rules and supervisory practices are applied and reconciled if they conflict, this could result in considerable simplification and reduction in compliance costs if it is efficiently provided. Additionally, it will solve the problem of the lack of incentives to share information among the national supervisors of the cross-border banks. However, it has the disadvantage that two levels of supervision can be applied in one member state. We look to the US for evidence on the experience with a dual banking system with two levels of supervision. There, the experience is somewhat mixed as while regulatory competition may encourage supervisors to be efficient in order to attract banks it may also encourage them to be lax or set lower standards. The EU has traditionally used the approach of harmonization to pursue the integration of the financial markets (in any case, the differences in regulation are defined along national lines and do not discriminate between purely national and cross-border banks). Moreover, competition policy in the Single Market is an EU-level competence, limiting the possibility of a race to the bottom. More relevant, however, are the potential conflicts when the safety net has to be invoked. In the US, the safety net is at the federal level even before interstate banking was developed. Solving this analogously for the EU would involve a second EU-level agency unless the EU-level supervisor was also the insurer and resolution authority. This solution would be preferable to coordination problems among agencies that may result in national deposit insurers to be unwilling to pay out or national authorities to fund if they view the problem to be the fault of the EU-level agency.

One aspect of the dual mandate which the EU would be well-advised not to emulate is conduct of business regulations. The EU is harmonizing conduct of business and consumer protection regulations subject to minimum standards with the prevalence of the host country rules. While cross-border banks would be keen to see a single set of rules and providing such rules would no doubt accelerate the process of financial integration, this is not something that is key to financial stability. Moreover, competition policy is already centralized in the EU and it is proving to be a powerful restructuring tool.

NOTES

* The authors thank the participants in the Symposium on Managing Systemic Risk organized by the University of Warwick, 7–9 April 2010 for their useful comments. The views expressed in this chapter are those of the authors and do not necessarily represent the views of the Banco de España, the Federal Reserve Bank of Atlanta or the Federal Reserve System.

1. A Prati, and G J Schinasi, (1999), 'Financial Stability in European Economic and

Monetary Union', *Princeton Studies in International Economics* 86, International Economics Section, Department of Economics, Princeton University.

2. D Mayes, M J Nieto and L D Wall, (2008), 'Multiple safety net regulators and agency problems in the EU: Is Prompt Corrective Action partly the solution?' *Journal of Financial Stability*, (September), pp. 165–304.
3. J Decressin, and M Čihák, (2007), *The Case for a European Banking Charter* (July). IMF Working Papers 07/173 pp. 1–34. Available at SSRN: http://ssrn.com/abstract=1007922 (accessed on 8 March 2010).
4. G Hertig, R Lee and J A., McCahery, (2009). *Empowering the ECB to Supervise Banks: A Choice-Based Approach* (August). TILEC Discussion Paper No. DP 2009-001; Amsterdam Center for Law & Economics Working Paper No. 2009-01; ECGI – Finance Working Paper No. 262/2009. Available at SSRN: http://ssrn.com/abstract=1327824 (accessed on 8 March 2010).
5. We intentionally avoid having to define what is 'systemic' for the purpose of this chapter.
6. We deal here with the more tractable proposition of banks that are headquartered and operating in the EU/EEA. If banks are headquartered further afield or have major activities elsewhere, the problem will remain difficult to handle without a supranational agency in charge and better alignment of international bank insolvency legislation.
7. The degree of self-insurance, such as through holding wealth outside the member state, is also lower in Europe than in the US.
8. See C W Calmoris, (1989), 'Deposit Insurance: Lessons from the Record', *Economic Perspectives*, Federal Reserve Bank of Chicago, (May/June), 10–30 for a brief discussion of some of the changes due to the *National Banking Act*. The Act imposed a 10 per cent federal tax on state-chartered bank notes (currency) to eliminate competition from state-chartered banks. This ended state bank issuance of notes but state-chartered banks were able to survive by switching to deposit-based banking.
9. See C M Kahn and J A C Santos, (2005), 'Allocating bank regulatory powers: Lender of last resort, deposit insurance and supervision', *European Economic Review*, (November), vol. 49(8), pages 2107–2136, analyse the consequences of the allocation of lender of last resort and supervisory functions in the euro area for the degree of forbearance in closing distressed banks and for the level of diligence in bank supervision. D C Hardy and M J Nieto (forthcoming), in 'Cross-border coordination of prudential supervision and deposit guarantees', *Journal of Financial Stability*, study the optimal design of supervision and bank crisis resolution in a multi-country setting, with an integrated banking market, such as the EU, where policymakers have either similar or asymmetric preferences regarding profitability and stability of the banking sector.
10. Commercial Banks may choose between a national (federal) charter with supervision by the Office of the Comptroller of the Currency (OCC) or a state charter. State-chartered banks may choose between supervision by the Federal Reserve and the FDIC. Additionally, the holding company of all groups owning a commercial bank is supervised by the Federal Reserve. Any holding company owning a thrift (savings bank) but not a commercial bank is supervised by the Office of Thrift Supervision (OTS). The *Dodd-Frank Wall Street Reform and Consumer Protection Act* will abolish the OTS and distribute its supervision of thrifts to the FDIC and OCC, and its supervision of thrift holding companies to the Federal Reserve. This complication of multiple federal supervisors and distinctions among financial institutions that are all regarded as being banks in the EU would not need to be repeated in a European equivalent of the US system.
11. The FDIC and Federal Reserve do not charge fees but depend on other sources of income.
12. A E Wilmarth, (2004), 'The OCC's Preemption Rules Exceed the Agency's Authority and Present a Serious Threat to the Dual Banking System and Consumer Protection', *Annual Review of Banking and Financial Law*, Vol. 23, pp. 225–364. Available at SSRN: http://ssrn.com/abstract=577863 (accessed on 8 March 2010).

13. B Appelbaum and E Nakashima (2008), 'Banking Regulator Played Advocate Over Enforcer: Agency Let Lenders Grow Out of Control, Then Fail', *Washington Post*, (23 November), http://www.washingtonpost.com/wp-dyn/content/article/2008/11/22/AR2008112202213_pf.html (accessed on 8 March 2010).
14. Ibid.
15. Ibid., quote a former Countrywide executive as saying 'The general attitude was they (the OTS) were going to be more lenient.'
16. The Capital Requirement Directive (CRD) establishes that prudential supervisors of host and home countries decide jointly on the designation of branches and subsidiaries as being systemically important in the host country. The consolidating supervisor shall take account of the potential impact on the stability of the financial system in the member states.
17. Calomiris (1989) notes that three states' insurance programmes predating the *National Banking Act* continued in operation until 1865 or 1866.
18. G Gorton and D Mullineaux, (1987), 'The Joint Production of Confidence: Endogenous Regulation and 19th Century Commercial-Bank Clearinghouses', *Journal of Money, Credit, and Banking*, 19 (November), 457–68.
19. J R Moen and E W Tallman New York and the Politics of Central Banks, 1781 to the *Federal Reserve Act* (December 2003), FRB of Atlanta Working Paper No. 2003-42. SSRN: http://ssrn.com/abstract=498742 (accessed on 8 March 2010).
20. The all or nothing bargain offered to state-chartered banks also included other benefits and costs for joining the Federal Reserve. The sets of benefits and costs unique to Federal Reserve membership have been reduced over time so that the primary remaining benefit and cost is that of Federal Reserve supervision for state member banks.
21. Calomiris (1989) argues that flaws in the structures of these programmes were important factors in their collapse. In particular, he pointed to the fact that the eight state programmes provided their member banks with weak incentives to monitor each other.
22. FDIC (1984), Chapter 3.
23. FDIC (1984), Chapter 6.
24. 12 Code of Federal Regulation 201, http://ecfr.gpoaccess.gov/cgi/t/text/text-idx?c=ecfr&sid=de1a245501fa2479f877eb5242fbcf65&rgn=div5&view=text&node=12:2.0.1.1.2&idno=12#12:2.0.1.1.2.0.1.3
25. J F Coburn and J P O'Keefe (2003), 'Risk Assessment: Results of an International Survey of Deposit Insurers', *FDIC Banking Review* (vol. 15, no. 1), http://www.fdic.gov/bank/analytical/banking/2003apr/article2.html (accessed on 8 March 2010).
26. W Buiter (2008), 'Can Central Banks Go Broke?' Centre for Economic Policy Research Policy Insight No. 24 (May), http://www.cepr.org/pubs/PolicyInsights/PolicyInsight24.pdf (accessed on 8 March 2010).
27. In practice this problem is rather unlikely as the lender of last resort function is disaggregated in the Eurosystem and even with credit easing operations of the ECB it is relatively unlikely that it would need recapitalizing given its conservative collateral policy but it is inherent in crises that problems that have not been thought likely do occur.
28. The deposit insurer would need to give advance notice of its intention to terminate deposit insurance, as is the case for terminations by the FDIC.
29. This section focuses on regulations specific to the financial sector. State laws applicable to the conduct of business in general, such as their commercial codes, apply to all banks, regardless of whether it has a federal or state charter.
30. The Obama administration's regulatory reform proposals include provisions that would allow states to impose and enforce laws that are tougher than federal standards. However, while the recently adopted *Dodd-Frank Wall Street Reform and Consumer Protection Act* expands state power to enforce business conduct regulation, the changes do not go nearly as far as the administration's proposal.
31. An early test case of federal law, *Tiffany v. National Bank of Missouri*, arose when the state of Missouri imposed a lower loan rate ceiling on banks not chartered by the state of Missouri. If allowed to stand, this law could have put national banks at a

substantial competitive disadvantage. The US Supreme Court held that federal law was not intended to allow states to put national banks at such a competitive disadvantage. *Tiffany v. National Bank of Missouri*, 85 US 18 Wall. 409409 (1873), <http://supreme.justia.com/us/85/409/case.html>.

32. The Supreme Court of the State of California ruled that the enforcement of certain loan terms was 'unconscionable' under California law in certain circumstances according to Mason, et al. (J R Mason, R B Kulick and H J Singer, 'The Economic Impact of Eliminating Preemption of State Consumer Protection Laws', *University of Pennsylvania Journal of Business Law*, Vol. 12, No. 3, Spring 2010. The effect of this decision and similar changes in the laws of other states would have been to impose significant losses on federally chartered savings and loans according to Mason, et al. (2010). In order to prevent this decision from having an adverse impact on federally chartered thrifts, the Federal Home Loan Bank Board pre-empted the state laws. The US Supreme Court upheld the pre-emption in *Fidelity Fed. S. & L. v. De la Cuesta*, 458 US 141 (1982).
33. For example, Mason, et al. (2010) note a Massachusetts law that allowed a non-Massachusetts bank to set up an ATM in Massachusetts only if that Massachusetts banks could set up an ATM in that state. However, even where the laws are clearly intended to benefit consumers, their anticompetitive impact may actually be adverse to consumers. As an example, Mason, et al. (2010) point to municipal ordinances in San Francisco and Santa Monica that banned banks from charging ATM fees to customers of other banks. Such regulations reduce the charges to consumers when they are able to access an ATM owned by another bank. However, these laws also have the effect of limiting consumers' access to ATMs, both by encouraging banks to limit ATMs to their own customers and by discouraging banks from placing ATMs in new locations.
34. Consumers Union (1998), 'OCC's Aggressive Preemption of States' Consumer Banking Protections,' http://www.consumersunion.org/finance/9171rptdc798.htm (accessed on 8 March 2010).
35. This list of state measures highlights a key philosophical difference between most advocates of pre-emption and most of its opponents. Opponents of pre-emption tend to view strict government regulation as necessary to protect consumers from making mistakes. In contrast, advocates of pre-emption tend to view competition as providing the best combination of services and prices to consumers in the long-run.
36. Wilmarth (2004), see note 12.
37. M J Furletti (2004), 'The Debate Over the *National Bank Act* and the Preemption of State Efforts to Regulate Credit Cards', *Temple Law Review*, Vol. 77 Federal Reserve Bank of Philadelphia Payment Cards Center Discussion Paper No. 04-02. Available at SSRN: http://ssrn.com/abstract=572581 (accessed on 8 March 2010).
38. Albeit, in part this is because of the way it allowed national banks to avoid state usury laws at a time when these ceilings had a binding impact on credit card rates. In this case pre-emption may be regarded as a desirable policy that increased the availability of credit cards to consumers or as undesirable policy that allowed consumers to be 'exploited' by excessive credit card rates.

PART V

Prudential regulation

19. Capital and liquidity reform – a new global agenda

George A. Walker

A new framework for capital and liquidity regulation has been agreed to by the Basel Committee on Banking Supervision. Banks were strongly criticized for holding low capital and liquidity levels immediately before the crisis which prevented them from absorbing subsequent losses as the crisis unfolded. Central banks and finance ministries were then forced to inject substantial amounts of market liquidity and then bank guarantees and capital to stabilize the markets.

The Basel Committee on Banking Supervision has been examining the lessons to be drawn from the crisis and revising its capital adequacy framework over the last two years and was able to agree a core new framework in September 2010. It has also extended this to include a basic liquidity framework for the first time. This was a significant achievement especially on the second anniversary (to the week) of the collapse of Lehman Brothers in September 2008. Work continues in other areas including requiring banks to draw up resolution and recovery plans (referred to as 'living wills' in the UK or 'funeral plans' in the US). Special bank resolution regimes have been adopted in many countries, such as under the *Banking Act* of 2009 in the UK, and larger macro-prudential oversight regimes are being established to monitor sector- and systems-wide risks and exposures. Governance and compensation arrangements have been strengthened with a number of new codes of practice or guidelines issued in connection with executive remuneration and with the threat of further levies or tax penalties in the event that an appropriately moderate approach is not followed on compensation and dividend payments. The European Union has also been considering other more dramatic, but probably equally counterproductive, proposals such as imposing activity or transaction taxes. Capital and liquidity reform will constitute the key component within whatever larger new post-crisis regulatory framework is constructed.

This chapter examines the main papers issued by the Basel Committee following the crisis. The specific recommendations on credit risk capital and market risk amendment are assessed. The Committee's parallel work on developing global liquidity standards is also considered. Other post-crisis initiatives including on compensation, governance and cross-border bank resolution are also outlined. Final conclusions are drawn with regard to the effectiveness of the emerging new capital and liquidity reserve framework and the Basel Committee's larger reform agenda.

19.1. THE FINANCIAL CRISIS

The Committee had reformulated its more general approach to the financial crisis by December 2009[1] which was further clarified during 2010.[2] The primary objective of its reform programme was to increase the resilience of the banking sector and to promote more sustainable growth in the short and longer term. The key objective of the Committee's reform agenda was to promote financial stability in support of the real economy. A number of characteristics of the pre-crisis financial system were identified. There had been excessive leverage in the banking and financial system and insufficient high-quality capital to absorb loss. Excessive credit growth had accumulated on the basis of weak underwriting standards and under-pricing of liquidity and credit risk. Insufficient liquidity reserves had been maintained and an overly aggressive policy of maturity transformation followed. There had been inadequate risk governance and weak incentives to manage risks to reflect more prudent longer-term objectives especially through poorly designed compensation packages. Banks had inadequate cushions to limit the inherent pro-cyclicality within financial markets and market participants. There was a failure to monitor systemic risks and interconnection between financial institutions which aggravated 'too-big-to-fail' conditions.

The banking sector was vulnerable to shocks whatever their source with the depth and severity of the crisis being amplified by excessive leverage, inadequate liquidity and capital and poor incentives for risk taking. Confidence had specifically collapsed in the solvency and liquidity of many banking institutions following the collapse of Lehman Brothers. This weakness was allowed to be transmitted to the rest of the financial system and real economy leading to a significant contraction in liquidity and credit.

The Committee did not attribute direct fault to the banking sector. Weaknesses within the larger financial system are nevertheless acknowledged and the inability of the banking system to absorb shocks in the event of an internal or external shock. Reference is specifically made to the loss in confidence in banks in the middle of the crisis. The Committee nevertheless repeatedly refers to the deficiencies within the larger financial system, not simply the banking sector, including leverage, reserves and incentives.

The Committee's reform agenda would deal with the weaknesses identified. This would be based on ensuring that capital requirements reflect all material risks and that a sufficiently high-quality capital is maintained to absorb losses. Regulatory, supervisory and risk management frameworks would be strengthened with a credible leverage ratio built into pillar 1 to support risk-based reserves. Provisioning adjustments and counter-cyclical capita buffers are to be promoted to increase the ability of banks to absorb shocks and minimum global liquidity standards should be introduced. Systemically important institutions would be better regulated and supervised and forced to internalize the risks they create. Risk governance and management need to be strengthened especially through the pillar 2 review process and market discipline under pillar 3 improved. The Committee would also strengthen arrangements for the management of cross-border bank resolution. These objectives were developed through a series of over 20 documents issued by the Committee over the last two years.

The Basel Committee issued a number of statements throughout the crisis through addresses given by key personnel on necessary reforms.[3]

The Committee had announced its original initial strategy in November 2008 to address fundamental weaknesses following the recent financial crisis in global markets.[4] This was based on eight objectives concerning the strengthening of the risk capture of the Basel II framework (especially for trading book and off-balance sheet exposures), enhancing the quality of tier 1 capital, building additional shock absorbers into the capital framework during stress and to limit pro-cyclicality, a leverage review through possible supplemental risks with gross measures in prudential and risk management frameworks, strengthening cross-border liquidity supervision, strengthening risk management and governance practices under Basel II, strengthening counter party credit risk capital, risk management and disclosure at banks and promoting globally co-ordinated supervisory follow-up exercises to ensure implementation of supervisory and industry sound principles.[5] The Committee would attempt to ensure that the reviews were conducted as part of a larger process that balanced the objective of maintaining an innovative competitive banking sector in good times against the need to enhance resilience in future periods of financial and economic stress. The primary objective would be based on strengthening capital buffers and containing leverage on- and off-balance sheet activities. This would be supported by stronger risk management and governance practices to limit risk concentrations.

The Committee has since specifically been reviewing the operation of its Basel II framework in light of the crisis and the development of parallel global principles for liquidity risk management and supervision. An outline agreement on the main capital reforms to be adopted following the crisis was eventually approved by the Governors and Heads of Supervision in July 2010.[6] Some criticisms were made in the financial press and media that the standards had been over-diluted following industry lobbying. In carrying out this work, the Committee has attempted to implement the reform requests issued by the G20 and FSB, although in a balanced and informed manner that targeted the flaws revealed by the crisis and strengthened banks and the banking system going forward.

19.2. CAPITAL ADEQUACY AMENDMENT

The Basel Committee has issued a number of specific measures designed at strengthening global capital adequacy requirements in light of the lessons learned from the financial crisis. Rather than respond in an immediate and ill-considered manner, the Committee has examined the separate issues that have arisen and consulted with relevant national regulatory and market interests as well as international organizations including the IMF and the EU Commission.

19.2.1. Capital Reform

The Basel Committee accepted in March 2009 that the level of bank capital had to be strengthened to raise resilience to future episodes of economic and financial stress. This would be achieved by a combination of measures including the introduction of standards to promote the build-up of capital buffers that could be drawn down in periods of stress, strengthening the quality of bank capital, improving the risk coverage of the capital framework and introducing a non-risk based supplementary measure. The regulatory minimum 8 per cent level would be reviewed in 2010 taking into account all relevant factors. The objective was to ensure that the global capital framework enhanced confidence and set down the foundation for a more resilient banking system. The Committee accepted that current reactions in the marketplace had been highly pro-cyclical although global minimum requirements would not be substantially increased during the current economic and financial stress conditions.

19.2.2. Strengthening Banking Resilience

The Basel Committee issued a formal consultation package to strengthen global capital and liquidity standards following its meeting on 8–9

December 2009.[7] The mandate was approved by the Governors and Heads of Supervision of the Reform Committee at their meeting on 7 September 2009 with the programme also being adopted by the Financial Stability Board (FSB) and the G20 at the Pittsburgh Summit. The objective was to secure more resilience within banks and a sounder banking and financial system through the capital and liquidity amendments proposed. The capital base of banks would be increased to improve the quality, consistency and transparency of their capital positions. This would allow them to absorb losses more effectively on a going concern (solvent) and on a 'gone' concern (closure) basis.

Tier 1 capital will principally be made up of common shares and retained earnings with comparable levels being held through non-joint stock companies. Capital deductions and prudential filters have been harmonized. Any other tier 1 items must be subordinated, have fully discretionary non-cumulative dividends or coupons and not have a maturity date nor incentive to redeem. Hybrid instruments with redemption incentives (such as 'step-up clauses') are to be phased out. Specific tier 1 levels will be calibrated following an impact assessment with tier 2 instruments being harmonized and tier 3 capital phased out. The Committee would strengthen the risk coverage of the capital framework with further improvements on counter-party credit risk exposure on derivatives, repurchase agreements and securities financing activities in addition to the earlier changes announced in connection with trading book and securitization.

A leverage ratio would be introduced as a supplementary requirement under Basel II to limit model risk and measurement error and avoid the build-up of excessive leverage within the system. Further measures would be brought in to promote the build-up of capital buffers on a counter-cyclical basis to assist to dampen rather than amplify economic and financial shocks. A minimum global liquidity standard would be introduced with a 30-day liquidity coverage ratio requirement and a longer-term structural liquidity ratio. Further specific capital, liquidity and other supervisory amendments are also being considered to reduce the external effects of systemically important institutions. The Committee would undertake a comprehensive impact assessment to allow for a sequenced introduction of the new measures to avoid damaging bank lending activity in the short term. This would be carried out during the first half of 2010 with more specific calibrations being announced by end-2010. Implementation is intended by end-2012.

The oversight body of the Basel Committee, the Group of Central Bank Governors and Heads of Supervision, welcomed the progress secured in implementing the Group's September 2009 agreements into a package of measures to strengthen capital and liquidity in international financial markets. Chairman Jean-Claude Trichet stressed the need to deliver timely completion to achieve a more resilient banking system that can support economic growth over the long-term. The Committee had developed a series of micro-prudential reforms to strengthen the level and quality of international capital and liquidity standards as well as include macro-prudential mechanisms to deal with pro-cyclicality and systemic risk. Further progress would be taken forward in the areas of provisioning, counter-cyclical capital buffers, systemic banking institutions, contingent capital and liquidity. This follows the Committee's papers produced on 17 December 2009. It is expected that the new measures will be completed by end-2010 and implemented by end-2012.

19.2.3. Capital and Liquidity Reform

The Group of Governors and Heads of Supervision secured final agreement on the overall design of the capital and liquidity reform package for internationally active banks on 26 July 2010.[8] The agreement increases the quality, quantity and international consistency of capital, strengthens liquidity standards, discourages excessive leverage and risk-taking and reduces pro-cyclicality with a series of amendments being made to the definition of capital, treatment of counter-party credit risk, leverage ratio and global liquidity standards and with the Committee finalizing regulatory buffers before the end of 2010. Calibration and transition arrangements would be agreed in September 2010. This was considered to be a landmark achievement in the strengthening of banking sector resilience in light of the key lessons of the recent crisis. The Governors and Heads of Supervision had considered the comments received during the consultation period with the results being published in August 2010.

The agreements included amendments to permitted capital deductions with regard to minority interests, investments in other financial institutions and variations between International Financial Reporting Standards (IFRS) and Generally Accepted Accounting Principles (GAAP) treatments. A cap was to be imposed on the deduction of significant investments in the common shares of unconsolidated financial institutions, mortgage servicing rights and deferred tax assets. Counter-party risk was to be adjusted with the bond equivalent approach to the calculation of the credit value adjustment (CVA) being amended to deal with hedging, risk capture, effective maturity and double counting. A simple, transparent, non-risk based leverage ratio would be imposed with a general minimum 3 per cent tier 1 ratio including off-balance sheet (OBS) and derivatives items subject to a 10 per cent convergence factor and netting. Supervisory monitoring would begin 1 January 2011 with the final measures imposed by 1 January 2018. The Committee had proposed a global liquidity coverage ratio (LCR) and net stable funding ratio (NSFR) although further amendment was required to the calibration of the NSFR. Different figures would be imposed on different sets of assets. The Committee was considering capital adjustments, contingent capital and possible capital surcharges for systemically important institutions. The package also includes further measures with regard to provisions, cyclicality and regulatory buffers.

The agreements reached in July 2010 to secure a substantial strengthening of capital requirements were endorsed by the Group of Governors and Heads of Supervision in September 2010.[9] They were then presented to the G20 Leaders at the Seoul Summit in November 2010 with separate standards on global liquidity. Minimum common equity would be increased from 2 per cent to 4.1 per cent with banks holding an additional conversion buffer to 2.5 per cent to withstand future periods of stress with a new total 7 per cent common equity rule. The new requirements will be phased in between 1 January 2013 and 1 January 2015 to prevent any possible damage to the recovery. Tier 1 capital would be increased from the current 4 per cent to 6 per cent by 2015. The use of the conservation buffer should limit the payment of excess discretionary bonuses and high dividends during periods of capital stress. An additional counter-cyclical buffer between 0–2.5 per cent of common equity or other fully loss absorbing capital would be implemented depending on national election and circumstances.

A separate non-risk based leverage ratio is to be introduced as a backstop to support the risk-based requirements. It had been agreed in July to test a 3 per cent minimum tier 1 leverage ratio during a parallel run period until 2017 with final rules being implemented by 1 January 2018. Additional loss-absorbing conditions may be imposed on systemically important banks which work was being discussed with the FSB. The Basel Committee's 2009 quantitative impact study had confirmed that smaller banks already met the higher standards while larger banks would in aggregate have to hold additional amounts of capital.

Member countries are expected to adopt relevant national rules to begin implementation on 1 January 2013. Initial requirements would be based on a 3.5 per cent common equity, 4.5 per cent tier 1 and 8 per cent total tier 1 capital requirement. Common equity would rise to 4 per cent and tier 1 to 5.5 per cent during 2014 and to 4.5 per cent and 6 per cent by 1 January 2015. The capital conservation buffer would be phased in between 1 January 2016 and 2019. It would rise from 0.625 per cent in 2016 and increase by 0.265 per cent each year up to 2.5 per cent of risk weighted assets. Public sector capital injections would be grandfathered until 1 January 2018 with non-common equity tier 1 capital or tier 2 capital instruments being phased out over ten years beginning 2013. Such instruments would be capped at 90 per cent in 2013 and reduced by 10 per cent each year. Instruments not qualifying for common equity tier 1 would be excluded from 2013 subject to special rules for instruments treated as equity under current accounting standards and national laws. These would be subject to the same 90 per cent and 10 per cent falling cap rules. The LCR would come into effect on 1 January 2015 following an observation period beginning in 2011. The NSFR would become a minimum requirement by 2018 subject to monitoring and review during the transitional period.

Higher capital and liquidity standards had been examined by the Basel Committee long-term economic impact (LEI) working group and by the joint FSB, Basel Committee Macroeconomic Assessment Group (MAG).[10] The LEI confirmed that raising capital ratios by one percentage point above average pre-crisis levels could cut the probability of crises by 50 per cent and an estimated 1.6 per cent of gross domestic product (GDP). The MAG adds that for each percentage point increase in capital over a four-year period, relative GDP would decline by around 0.19 per cent. Lending rates would rise by 15 basis points for each percentage point increase in capital. These costs should dissipate after the transitional phase-in period with GDP then returning to path.

19.2.4. Countercyclical Capital Buffers

The Bank for International Settlements (BIS) issued a separate working paper on Countercyclical Capital Buffers in July 2010[11] where six key design features were identified. An effective scheme must identify the correct timing for accumulation and release; the buffer must be sufficiently large to absorb loss without triggering further instability; it must avoid regulatory arbitration and manipulation, be enforceable internationally; be rule based insofar as possible; involve low implementation costs; and be simple and transparent. The Basel Committee also released its own paper in July 2010.[12] The Committee agreed to adopt a building block approach to secure the four key objectives identified in its consultation document entitled *Strengthening the Resilience of the Banking Sector* in December 2009.[13] These consisted of dampening any excess cyclicality of the minimum capital requirement, promoting more forward-looking provisions, conserving capital to build-up buffers within individual banks and the banking sector as a whole to be used under stress and achieving the wider macro-prudential objective of protecting the banking sector from periods of excessive credit growth. The third objective would be achieved through the development of a capital conservation buffer which would be examined by the Macro Variables Task Force (MVTF) before the full Committee's meeting in July 2010.

The Committee agreed on a need to use capital buffers to protect the banking sector from periods of excess aggregate credit growth. The Committee accepted that this may only be required to be used infrequently, possibly only every 10–12 years. This would operate by giving effect to a buffer add-on during periods of excess aggregate credit growth where this may increase system-wide risk. These would be pre-announced by 12 months to allow banks to achieve the additional capital levels required. The add-on would generally be zero until used with an upper limit to be set by the Committee following calibration. Banks would be required to raise their capital by the amount set or restrictions would be imposed on the distribution of earnings. A degree of jurisdictional reciprocity would apply with host authorities setting initial limits which home authorities would be required to respect. The Committee's methodology converts the aggregate private sector credit (GDP gap) into the recommended buffer add-on with specific figures being set on a national basis. Additional requirements apply with regard to transparency and accountability to allow banks to understand the decisions taken by local authorities.

Five principles are set out in the paper concerning the use of judgement within the framework. Buffer decisions are to be determined by the principal objective of protecting the banking system against potential future losses where excess credit growth is associated with an increase in system-wide risk. The credit-GDP guide provides a useful first reference in taking decisions although authorities may use other means to take and explain levels. Assessments may be based on other factors including other asset prices, fund spreads and credit default swap (CDS) spreads, credit condition surveys, real GDP growth and non-financial entity data and the possibility of misleading signals. Buffers should be released promptly to reduce the risk of credit supply being constrained by regulatory capital requirements. The new buffer would only act as one instrument as part of a larger range of macro-prudential tools to be used by authorities. The Committee has accordingly agreed to adopt an infrequent, moderate and discretion-supported regime. Effective use of other continuing prudential and new macro-prudential tools may avoid the need for any counter-cyclical add-on buffers in practice.

19.2.5. Capital Absorbency

The Basel Committee issued a separate consultation paper on *Loss Absorbency* in August 2010.[14] This requires that the contractual terms on which capital instruments are issued will be allowed to be written off at the option of the regulatory authority or converted into common shares in the event that a bank is unable to support itself in private markets. This forms part of the Committee's larger package of measures on *Strengthening the Resilience of the Banking Sector*.

19.3. MARKET RISK AMENDMENT

The Committee approved a separate set of measures to strengthen the 1996 rules concerning trading book capital and the Basel II framework in July 2009.[15] Amendments would be made to the market risk framework and guidelines for the calculation of incremental risk within the trading book which would come into effect at the end of 2010. These include imposing higher requirements to cover the credit risk on complex trading activities with a new stress value-at-risk (VAR) obligation to reduce cyclicality. Certain types of securitization would be strengthened, higher risk weights introduced for securitization (referred to as collateralized debt obligations (CDOs) of asset-backed securities (ABS) with the credit conversion factor for short-term liquidity facilities to conduits being increased and banks being required to conduct more strict credit analyses of externally rating securitization exposures.

Supplemental guidance is to be included within pillar 2 including tightened standards on firm-wide governance and risk management, inclusion of off-balance sheet exposures and securitization activities, managing risk concentrations and providing incentives for banks to better manage risk and returns longer-term. The guidance also incorporates the FSF *Principles for Sound Compensation Practices* issued in April 2009 with further work being carried out by the Committee's Standards Implementation Group. Pillar 3 would also be strengthened to provide additional disclosure on securitizations, off-balance sheet exposures and trading activities which would reduce market uncertainties concerning the strength of banks' balance sheets with regard to their capital market activities. The pillar 1 revisions were to come into effect immediately with the pillar 1 and 3 changes by end-2010. The existing capital floors would be extended beyond end-2009.

19.4. LIQUIDITY

The crisis had also confirmed the need to strengthen liquidity and capital adequacy together, especially as a liquidity crisis could quickly escalate into a solvency crisis and banks had to manage their liquidity and capital resources in parallel. The Basel Committee had issued an enhanced set of global 'Principles of Sound Liquidity Risk Management and Supervision' in June 2008 with earlier guidance having been published in 2000. Revised principles were released in September 2008. A number of revision papers have also been issued by the Financial Services Authority (FSA) in the UK on liquidity[16] and by other agencies.[17]

19.4.1. Liquidity Risk Management

The Committee issued its revised *Principles for Sound Liquidity Risk Management and Supervision* on 25 September 2008.[18] The principles stress the importance of establishing a sound liquidity risk management framework that is well integrated into bank-wide risk management processes. Effective provisions must be maintained on the conduct of regular stress testing in respect of short-term and protracted institution-specific and market-wide stress scenarios with the results being used to develop robust and operational contingency funding plans. Banks must ensure the alignment of risk-taking incentives within individual business lines with their liquidity risk exposures these activities create. Institutions must actively manage their intra-day liquidity positions and risks to cover payment and settlement obligations on a timely basis under both normal and stress conditions at the same time as maintain a reserve of unencumbered high-quality liquid assets to cover a range of stress scenarios.

The paper highlights the role of public disclosure to allow market participants to make informed judgements concerning the soundness of bank liquidity risk management frameworks and individual bank liquidity positions. Supervisors must remain responsible for intervening to ensure that effective and timely remedial action is taken by banks to address liquidity risk management deficiencies. Regulated communication must also be maintained with other supervisors and public authorities within and across national borders. The principles are equally applicable within medium and large complex banks as well as smaller institutions. Implementation must nevertheless be adjusted to reflect the particular size, business nature and complexity of individual bank activity. The draft principles were issued for consultation in June 2008 with the original liquidity guidance being issued in 2000.

19.4.2. FSA Liquidity Standards

The FSA issued a consultation paper in the UK on *Strengthening Liquidity Standards* which applied to banks, building societies and investment firms.[19] The measures follow the work conducted by the Basel Committee and other international efforts. Senior management remain responsible for the management of liquidity risk. Four new policies are nevertheless proposed in connection with the creation of a new quantitative framework for liquidity risk management, a strengthening qualitative framework (using stress testing and contingency funding plans), a liquidity reporting requirement and a new approach to group liquidity management. The objective is to enhance liquidity risk management practices substantially and reconstruct business models where appropriate. The measures will also allow the FSA to assess the quality of firms' liquidity management practices more effectively. The proposals follow an earlier discussion paper (07/07).

The FSA released a further consultation paper in June 2009.[20] This follows the earlier CP08/22 and CP09/13 on the creation of a new UK liquidity regime. The latest consultation paper provides for the phased implementation of different elements of the new regime in connection with systems and controls requirements, quantitative requirements and reporting for separate classes of regulated firms including banks, building societies, branches of European Economic Area (EEA) and non-EEA banks and BIPRU investment firms. BIPRU Limited Licence and Limited Activity investment firms will only be subject to the proposed enhanced systems and controls provisions. The new liquidity risk management rules and guidance are to come into effect from the fourth quarter of 2009 with a short consultation period being adopted with regard to the transitional provisions set out in CP09/14. The paper includes a cost–benefit analysis and compatibility statement. Nine sets of transitional measures are set out in the annexes with draft Handbook text in the appendix.

The FSA published its final rules on the revised liquidity rules to be complied with by UK firms in October 2009.[21] The measures include a strengthened quantitative regime with a narrower definition of liquid assets, certain over-arching principles of 'self-sufficiency' and 'adequacy of liquid resources', enhanced systems and controls, granular and more frequent reporting requirements and the new regime for foreign branches operating in the UK proposed earlier. The objective is to enhance liquidity risk management practices within firms including through improved business models and increased competitiveness. The UK's competitive advantage was considered to require a strong perception of financial soundness of firms by counter parties. The new measures would also protect customers, counter parties and other participants in the markets as a result of defective liquidity risk management. Firms would be specifically encouraged to hold government bonds rather than other more complex instruments that could lose their AAA ratings. The additional burdens imposed would nevertheless be phased in to avoid unsettling existing bank lending patterns. The new regime would be phased in over a number of years and take into account UK and wider international developments.

19.5. REGULATORY REFORM

The Basel Committee has produced a number of other papers on related banking and regulatory reform over the last three years as part of its larger response programme. These specifically relate to bank governance, remuneration, risk and performance alignment resolution and supervision through supervisory colleges.

19.5.1. Corporate Governance

The Basel Committee issued a consultation paper called *Principles for Enhancing Corporate Governance* in March 2010.[22] This was followed by a final paper on *Corporate Governance* in October 2010.[23] The Committee had earlier published initial guidance on corporate governance in 1999 with revised principles in 2006. This reflected the principles published by the Organization for Economic Co-operation and Development (OECD) in April 2004. The objective was to assist bank supervisors and provide a reference point for the adoption of sound corporate governance practices by banking organizations. A number of corporate governance failures were revealed by the recent financial crises following the earlier guidance. The Committee has accordingly strengthened its principles especially with regard to roles of boards, board qualifications and composition, independent risk management (including the appointment of a Chief Risk Office or equivalent), the importance of monitoring risks on an ongoing firm-wide and individual entity basis, oversight of compensation systems and board and senior management understanding of operational structures and risks. Supervisors had also to assess banks' corporate governance policies and practices on a regular basis.

Fourteen specific principles were developed in the Committee's final paper in October 2001.[24] Five additional principles are imposed in relation to supervisory function (including providing guidance on expectations for sound corporate governance, regular comprehensive evaluation, consideration of other internal and prudential reports, effective and timely remedial action and cross-border co-operation). The contribution of other entities in promoting a larger environment supportive of sound corporate governance is also referred to.

19.5.2. Compensation[25]

The Basel Committee issued a statement on *Compensation Principles and Standards Assessment Methodology* in January 2010.[26] The objective was to develop supervisory approaches that promote sound compensation practices and ensure a level playing field. This provides a comprehensive tool for supervisors to ensure relevant practices in an effective and consistent manner. Supervisors will be able to assess a firm's compliance with the FSB's nine Principles for Sound Compensation Practices[27] and supporting implementation standards including the FSA's thematic review of national and firm implementation. The Basel Committee Methodology was structured in terms of effective governance of compensation, alignment of competence with prudent risk-taking and supervisory oversight and engagement by stakeholders.

The Basel Committee produced a separate paper concerning *Methodologies for Risk and Performance Alignment of Remuneration* in October 2010.[28] The purpose of the paper was to respond to recommendation 7 in the FSB Peer Review report in March 2010[29] which required the Basel Committee to examine methodologies to align to risk and performance within firm compensation schemes. The Committee's response paper in October 2010 does not contain prescriptive conditions but was intended to assist banks and their supervisors understanding risk-adjusted remuneration. The FSB had noted that good progress had been made within the financial industry with regard to governance, oversight on disclosure of remuneration practices although further work was required. Additional guidance is provided in the Basel Committee paper on methods for incorporating risk and performance into bonus pools and individual compensation packages, deferral compensation options and adjustments having regard to firm size. A number of illustrative examples are provided through the report.

19.5.3. Cross-Border Bank Resolution

The Basel Committee published a set of recommendations prepared by its Cross-Border Bank Resolution Group.[30] They follow an examination of legal and policy frameworks for cross-border crisis resolution and follow-up work on the global financial crisis. The tools and techniques for handling cross-border bank crises had not been developed in parallel with the expansion of the scope, scale and complexity of international financial transactions in recent years. The crisis confirmed gaps in intervention techniques and the absence of appropriate resolution tools in many countries. Responses had tended to be ad hoc and limited by time constraints and involved significant public support. The Committee's recommendations are intended to strengthen national resolution powers and cross-border implementation. Ten specific recommendations are made with regard to the nature of effective national resolution powers, frameworks for a coordinated resolution of financial groups, national resolution measures convergence, cross-border effects of national measures, reduction of complexity and interconnectedness of group structures and operations, advanced planning for orderly resolution, cross-border co-operation and information sharing, strengthening risk mitigation mechanisms, the transfer of contractual relationships and appropriate exit strategies and market discipline.

19.5.4. Supervisory Colleges

The Basel Committee on Banking Supervision issued a consultation paper on *Good Practice Principles on Supervisory Colleges* (March 2010).[31] The financial crisis has stressed the importance of closer international co-operation between home and host authorities. The Committee has accordingly developed a set of eight principles to promote and strengthen the operation of supervisory colleges following an assessment of current practices. These support the efforts of the G20 and FSB to strengthen international co-operation and supervision. The principles stress that the main aim of colleges is to enhance information exchange and co-operation and support the effective supervision of international banking groups. Guidance is provided on the types of information to be exchanged and different communication channels available. Collaborative work between supervisors is promoted. The principles accept that no single college structure is suitable for all banks and that a college may have multiple or variable sub-structures. The structure should be determined by the characteristics of the banking groups being supervised and specific supervisory need. The principles take into account the latest developments in policy work adopted in response to the financial crisis with colleges forming one building block in crisis management planning. Colleges will also support the identification and dissemination of information relevant to macro-prudential analysis.

19.5.5. Macro-Prudential Measures

The Basel Committee accepts the need to strengthen the resilience of the banking system more generally and to limit the damaging effects of procyclicality. Specific concerns arise with regard to the interconnected nature of systemically important global banking groups, domestic and cross-border resolution and moral hazard and 'too-big-to-fail'. Procyclical effects should be limited through the leverage ratio and stressed VAR and counterparty credit risk rules with the additional conservation and countercyclical capital buffers and application of an expected loss approach to provisioning through the work of the International Accounting Standards Board (IASB). The dangers of intra-firm contagion and systemic risk can be dealt with through higher capital and liquidity charges, contingent pre- and post-prices capital and 'bail-in' debt as well as capital loss absorbency adjustment. These represent useful reforms from within the banking sector despite the limitations on the Committee's remit and authority. As a standing committee of the G10 (G20) Governments in the banking area, the Committee is always careful not to comment on wider non-bank specific issues. These include macro-prudential oversight more generally and the conduct of monetary, competition and fiscal policy, resolution in the non-bank area and market support in extreme cases. Appropriate reforms will have to be undertaken in each of these areas to avoid future crises.

19.6. CAPITAL COMMENT AND CONCLUSION

The Basel Committee has issued over 20 papers in response to the financial crisis in almost all key areas of concern and correction. Principles for sound liquidity risk management and supervision were initially endorsed in September 2008 with the Committee announcing a comprehensive strategy to address the fundamental weaknesses revealed by the crisis in November 2008. The Committee accepted that capital standards had to be increased in March 2009 with trading book enhancements being announced in July 2009. A comprehensive response to the crisis, including relevant design principles, were issued in September 2009 with a full consultation document on proposals to strengthen the resilience of the banking sector being published in December 2009. These were accepted by the Committee's Group of Governors and Heads of Supervision in July 2010 and finalized in September 2010. The Committee has also issued other papers on compensation practices, corporate governance and cross-border bank resolution.

The revised framework represents an aggressive and comprehensive attempt to create a new minimum reserves framework for banks globally. Many of the key elements are highly ambitious although many would argue that the overall effect, and especially the extended eight-year implementation period, may dilute their overall effect and value materially. The final package of measures agreed nevertheless represents an intelligent, albeit slightly flawed, compromise between all relevant regulatory, political and wider public interests.

The final Basel III package is intended to strengthen the regulation, supervision and risk management of the banking sector. This should improve the ability of banks to absorb shocks arising from financial and economic stress whatever the source, improve risk management and governance and strengthen banks' transparency and disclosures. The micro-prudential regulation of banks is to be strengthened during periods of stress and a new macro-prudential approach adopted more generally to ensure that the sector as a whole can withstand wider risks and procyclical effects.

The key elements within the new measures are based on five fundamental reforms. Core tier 1 capital is to be more than doubled from 2 to 4.5 per cent. This is supplemented by the new 2.5 per cent conservation buffer. This provides regulatory authorities with an additional tool to limit perceived excessive dividends and bonuses which must be paid without reliance on the buffer. A further 1 or 2 per cent charge will be imposed on systemically important groups (subject to final agreement in November 2010) with national authorities also being able to impose charges of between zero and 2.5 per cent during periods of high economic growth to create a further counter-cyclical capital buffer. All of this will be supplemented by the new non-risk weighted tier 1 3 per cent leverage ratio subject to final adjustment.

The 2.5 per cent conservation buffer represents an intelligent, and almost inspired, means of limiting excessive dividends and bonuses. Regulators are already assessing banks' compensation and dividend policies in terms of risk under various codes of practice, many of which implement the Basel Committee's January 2010 methodology for compensation practices and March 2010 principles for enhancing corporate governance. The new conservation buffer conditions will impose an additional discipline, in particular, to ensure that payments are only made from surplus profits. Payment packages for senior executives and the most talented staff should otherwise be left to market agreement subject only to the additional transparency and disclosure obligations to be imposed at the national level. Remuneration in private markets should not otherwise be subject to central state direction.

The systemic buffer reflects the additional potential contingent liability that larger complex groups can create. This represents an intelligent compromise that allows authorities to impose additional capital requirements in respect of larger groups that create material systemic threats and potential liability under public support packages. Again, many authorities could have used their existing powers for this purpose but simply failed to do so until it was too late. The imposition of new systemic charges with the other initiatives already adopted, and especially with regard to pre-crisis internal resolution (UK 'living wills' and US 'funeral plans') and new post-crisis official resolution procedures, should avoid the need for any further discussion of bank levies. These are simply intended to generate income for deficit governments and obtain perceived political advantage.

The more muted and discretionary counter-cyclical buffer is also to be welcomed following all of the rancour raised by politicians and economists over the last two years. Excessive and distortive counter-cyclical effects should be avoided. Attempting to manage economic cycles and flows directly using discretionary regulatory tools may create substantial unforeseen consequences and undermine market processes beyond the possible benefits achieved in terms of perceived increased financial stability.

The new leverage and liquidity ratios will also add value following testing and final calibration. Rather than impose any ill-considered excessive new obligations in response to external pressure, the Committee has attempted to identify the most efficient and effective means of incorporating a larger non-risk weighted debt limit and minimum continuing liquidity reserve within the new framework. As with the capital ratios, this is not diluting or avoiding necessary obligations but simply ensuring that appropriate mechanisms are created that can secure their intended objectives without causing unnecessary market damage or market distortion elsewhere.

The main concern that remains is with regard to the extended eight-year implementation period which will last until 2018. Certain countries, and especially Germany, had called on the adoption of extended transitional arrangements especially to allow smaller banks to adjust their capital positions over time. This can be justified on the basis of the need to avoid any immediate increases in capital costs which may cause further damage to lending and destabilize slow global and national recoveries. The unnaturally long implementation period is arguably unnecessary and unjustifiable although capital levels will still be increased in stages during this period and national authorities can impose higher amounts at any time and especially on more systemically important institutions.

The markets generally welcomed the calibration agreement secured in September 2010 as the figures agreed to were not as penal as many had expected. Most UK, US and Swiss as well as many Asian banks would easily qualify. Further balance sheet adjustments were expected for other European and Western banks. The residual threat was that national authorities may impose substantially higher standards on a discretionary basis with market-related difficulties remaining for many banks in raising capital quickly. Deutsche Bank immediately announced a proposed EUR9.8bn (USD12.7bn) issue. The Swiss authorities also confirmed that they would impose a total 19 per cent requirement with 10 per cent common equity and a further 9 per cent in convertible contingent capital. Other complex balance sheets will have to be restructured over time as earlier hybrid instruments (such as deferred tax credits) would no longer qualify for tier 1 capital purposes. Other commentators have questioned the inability of the new rules to deal with industry size and concentration despite the tripling of capital to be generated. Others have argued that capital levels should be raised to exorbitant 20 per cent or 30 per cent levels on a non-risk weighted basis. The extended transitional period agreed will also allow many banks to recapitalize using government-injected liquidity rather than their own assets although this is an inevitable result of the stimulus provided to support growth and recovery.

It has to be stressed that low capital levels within the major global banks did not cause the crisis directly. This only became an aggravating factor once the crisis had moved from an initial tightening of credit in the inter-bank markets to a full solvency and market crisis. This also specifically only arose after the disclosed losses and bailouts at the giant US mortgage processors, Fannie Mae and Freddie Mac, and insurance company, AIG but with the Treasury's decision not to bail out the Wall Street securities house, Lehman Brothers, on 15 September 2008. Capital adequacy may then be considered to have been an aggravating rather than a direct causal factor in the crisis. Many banks' ratios were not that low and would have to have been increased very substantially and possibly to economically unsupportable levels to have protected them following the onslaught of the severe collapse in market confidence and global stock market crash and subsequent recession that occurred. Official support will unfortunately always remain necessary in the most extreme cases. The principal capital failures that arose were also concerned with trading book and market risk cover on securities activities, rather than credit risk and commercial banking, with relevant trading book capital rules having been increased by the Committee substantially under its new programme.

More serious concerns possibly arose with regard to liquidity cover although this was again not principally in terms of the amount or level but the type of reserve or cover maintained. Many institutions had relied on credit rating agencies and were holding higher-yielding AAA rated structured products which were traded over-the-counter rather than more traditional on-exchange government gilts or bonds. The nominal value of these instruments had then to be marked down substantially under mark-to-market valuation rules even without any disposals. This problem can be most easily dealt with by simply requiring banks to hold their core liquidity reserves in the form of exchange-traded rather than over-the-counter instruments. The issue of overdependence in short-term inter-bank markets is also only one of degree. Higher levels of short-term funding or other wholesale market dependence can be dealt with through arranging back-up credit lines and other alternative support facilities in the event of a shortfall. The crisis surrounding Northern Rock was wholly avoidable both before and after its demise and bungled rescue arrangements.

The major banks and markets have already adopted many of the necessary corrective actions required following the crisis. Capital levels have been increased and debt levels reduced. Credit assessments have been tightened in light of worsening credit conditions. Banks restocked their liquidity reserves at a very early stage using more traditional and safer but lower yielding government debt. The International Swaps and Derivatives Association (ISDA) has also confirmed that more complex risk models have already been adjusted to incorporate the correlation and housing market default data that was missing before and caused so much over-reliance.

It is essential to protect the natural operation and value of markets at the same time as limit potential sources of instability and wider loss. A simple balance or trade-off arises in all cases. Where banks are subject to substantially higher capital, liquidity and other regulatory costs, markets will grow more slowly and market users will be subject to higher borrowing costs and lower credit amounts. This is a complex relationship and the authorities must secure the most appropriate balance is secured between regulatory cost and economic and social benefit and advantage over time.

The new Basel III provisions represent an intelligent and balanced response to the crisis. These will not prevent further instability but they will substantially increase core capital and liquidity reserves to allow banks to withstand prolonged periods of difficulty. Future crises can only be prevented through the continued improvement of risk management and pricing, strengthened governance, the establishment of effective resolution and support facilities for all systemically important institutions and the creation of new macro-prudential oversight regimes within all major economies. Government, businesses, households and society as a whole must also learn to borrow more intelligently and manage their debt levels more safely and effectively.

Financial regulation and crisis management are evolutionary processes. We have learned substantial lessons following the crises, the severity of which has not been experienced since the early 1930s. A number of important initiatives have been taken forward at various levels to prevent further crises or, at least, to manage the instability created more effectively. A full reform agenda must be constructed including improved risk management and governance, higher capital and liquidity and substantially improved evolution in a pre- and post-crisis situation. Capital and liquidity reform only form one part of this larger objective and cannot be considered in isolation.

The Basel Committee has produced a highly credible reform package based on increased tier 1 capital requirements with supplementary conservation, systemic and counter-cyclical buffers supported by a new non-risk weighted leverage ratio and additional liquidity obligations. This is supported by the Committee's separate recommendations with regard to governance, compensation and cross-border college supervision and resolution. Relevant capital, liquidity and leverage levels will be appropriately set following impact studies and calibration exercises having regard to prevailing credit and market conditions. The most significant flaw in the Committee's new regulatory agenda remains the eight-year implementation period which reflects unfortunate political concessions and compromise. National authorities may nevertheless still impose higher levels at any time and especially as market conditions change and adjust. The Committee may also be able to agree to further amendments, including the implementation timetable, as markets recover.

This does not represent a regulatory end but the beginning of a new process of enhanced regulatory adjustment and validation. Basel II and Basel III represent significant advances on the original overly minimal Basel I capital model. It is only necessary to incorporate all of this into the new much more substantial and expansive micro- and macro-prudential oversight and control frameworks still under construction following the most devastating financial crisis in generations. This will form a core, but only one necessary, component within this larger response agenda.

NOTES

1. Please see Basel Committee, *Consultative Proposals to Strengthen the Resilience of the Banking Sector Announced by the Basel Committee* (17 December 2009). See also Basel Committee, *Strengthening the Resilience of the Banking Sector* (December 2009); and Basel Committee, *International Framework for Liquidity Risk Measurement, Standards and Monitoring* (December 2009).
2. Please see Basel Committee, *Basel II and Revisions to the Capital Requirements Directive* (May 2010), Press Release.
3. See, for example, Nout Wellink, Chairman of the Basel Committee, *Recent Market Turmoil – Implications for Supervisors and Risk Managers* (February 2008). See also Jaime Caruana, *Systemic Risk and its Management. Cross-sectional (Structural) and Time (Procyclical) Externalities Arose* (February 2010); Caruana, *Back-stopping Global Banking* (April 2010); Caruana, *The Emerging Framework for Financial Regulation and Monetary Policy* (April 2010); Caruana, *Macro-Prudential Policy: What we have Learned and Where we are Going* (June 2010); Nout Wellink, Basel Committee Chairman, *The Basel Committee and Regulatory Reform* (June 2010); Herve Hannoun, Deputy General Manager of the BIS, *Information Gaps: What has the Crisis Taught us?*; Stephen Cecchetti, BIS Economic Advisor, *Current Efforts to Enhance Global Financial Supervision* (June 2010); Claudio Borio, *Implementing a Macro-prudential Framework: Balancing Boldness and Realism* (August 2010); and Tommaso Padoa-Schioppa, *Markets and Government Before, During and After the 2007-20xx Crisis* (June 2010).
4. Please see Basel Committee, *Comprehensive Strategy to Address the Lessons of the Banking Crisis* (20 November 2008), Press Release.
5. The Basel Committee issued a statement on the work undertaken to develop Basel II in parallel with the work undertaken on the EU Capital Requirements Directive (CRD). The underlying objective is to ensure that the new standards achieve the objective of

greater banking sector resilience at the same time as promote maximum sustainable growth.

6. Please see Basel Committee, *The Group of Governors and Heads of Supervision reach Broad Agreement on Basel Committee Capital and Liquidity Reform Package* (26 July 2010), Press Release.
7. Please see Basel Committee, *Strengthening the Resilience of the Banking Sector*; and Basel Committee, *International Framework for Liquidity Risk Measurement, Standards and Monitoring*.
8. Please see Basel Committee, *The Group of Governors and Heads of Supervision reach Broad Agreement on Basel Committee Capital and Liquidity Reform Package*, Press Release.
9. Please see Basel Committee, *Group of Governors and Heads of Supervision Announces Higher Global Minimum Capital Standards* (12 September 2010), Press Release.
10. Basel Committee on Banking Supervision, *An Assessment of the Long-term Economic Impact of Stronger Capital and Liquidity Requirements* (August 2010); Macroeconomic Assessment Group, *Interim Report on Assessing the Macroeconomic Impact of the Transition to Stronger Capital and Liquidity Requirements* (August 2010).
11. BIS, *Countercyclical Capital Buffers: Exploring Options* (July 2010) No. 317.
12. Basel Committee, *Countercyclical Capital Buffer Proposal* (July 2010).
13. Basel Committee, *Strengthening the Resilience of the Banking Sector* (December 2009).
14. Please see Basel Committee, *Proposal to Ensure the Loss Absorbency of Regulatory Capital at the Point of Non-viability* (16 August 2010).
15. Please see Basel Committee, *Basel II capital framework enhancements announced by the Basel Committee* (13 July 2009). See also Basel Committee, *Enhancements to the Basel II Framework* (July 2009); Basel Committee, *Guidelines for Computing Capital for Incremental Risk in the Trading Book* (July 2009); and Basel Committee, *Revisions to the Basel II Market Risk Framework* (July 2009).
16. FSA, *Review of the Liquidity Requirements for Banks and Building Societies* (December 2007) 07/7; FSA, *Strengthening Liquidity Standards* (December 2008) CP08/22; FSA, *Strengthening Liquidity Standards 2: Liquidity Reporting* (April 2009) CP09/13; and FSA, *Strengthening Liquidity Standards 3: Liquidity Transitional Measures* (June 2009) CP09/14.
17. BIS, *Central Bank Co-operation and International Liquidity in the Financial Crisis of 2008–9* (June 2010); The Committee on the Global Financial System (CGFS) has issued a report on *Funding Patterns and Liquidity Management of Internationally Active Banks* (May 2010).
18. Basel Committee, *Liquidity Risk: Management and Supervisory Challenges* (February 2008).
19. FSA, *Strengthening Liquidity Standards* (December 2008) CP08/22. These were issued as part of the International Conference on Banking Supervisors held on 24–25 September 2008.
20. FSA, *Strengthening Liquidity Standards 3: Liquidity Transitional Measures* (June 2009) CP09/14.
21. FSA, *Strengthening Liquidity Standards* (October 2009) PS 09/16.
22. Basel Committee, *Principles for Enhancing Corporate Governance* (March 2010).
23. Basel Committee, *Principles for Enhancing Corporate Governance* (October 2010).
24. These specifically relate to: board practices (including overall responsibilities in respect of strategic objectives, risk strategy, corporate governance and corporate values as well as oversight of senior management, board qualifications, training and composition, board governance practices and structure including the role of the chairman and committees, conflicts of interest and controlling shareholders and group structures), senior management (including ensuring that the bank's activities are consistent with its business strategy, risk tolerance/appetite and board-approved policies), risk management and internal controls (including maintaining an effective system and risk management function with the relevant officer having sufficient authority, stature, independence,

resources and access to the board, effective risk identification and monitoring, robust internal communication and effective use of work conducted by internal audit functions, external auditors and internal control functions), effective board oversight of compensation system's design and operation with employee's compensation being effectively aligned with prudent risk taking, complex or opaque corporate structures (with an express board and senior management 'know-your-structure' requirement and 'understand-your-structure' obligation in respect of more complex special purpose or non-transparent structures) and disclosure and transparency (with bank governance being transparent to shareholders, depositors and other relevant stakeholders and market participants).

25. The FSB issued *Principles for Sound Compensation Practices and Implementation Standards* (30 March 2010). The Principles and Standards had been endorsed by the G20 at the April 2009 London and September 2009 Pittsburgh Summits. Substantial progress had been made in incorporating the Principles and Standards into domestic regulatory and supervisory frameworks with compensation structures having been changed accordingly. Full implementation was nevertheless far from complete with sustained efforts being required by firms and authorities to align compensation practices with prudent risk-taking. A follow-up review on compensation would be undertaken during the second quarter of 2011.
26. Basel Committee, *Compensation Principles and Standards Assessment Methodology* (January 2010).
27. Financial Stability Forum (FSF, *Principles for Sound Compensation Practices* (April 2009). The FSF was subsequently renamed the Financial Stability Board in February 1991.
28. Basel Committee, *Range of Methodologies for Risk and Performance Alignment of Remuneration* (October 2010).
29. FSB, *Thematic Review on Compensation – Peer Review Report* (March 2010).
30. See also the Committee on the Global Financial System (CGFS), *The functioning and resilience of cross border funding markets* (March 2010).
31. The Financial Stability Board (FSB) announced an initiative to promote global adherence to international co-operation and information exchange standards.

20. Basel II to Basel III: a great leap forward?

Imad Moosa

20.1. INTRODUCTION

The global financial crisis has revealed the inadequacy of Basel II and exposed its loopholes. As a result, the Basel Committee on Banking Supervision (BCBS) has come up with proposals to overhaul and reform Basel II, so that it can deal with a future crisis of the magnitude of the global financial crisis. The reforms, as Nout Wellink argues, are designed to respond to key pre-crisis shortcomings.[1] On 19 December 2009 the BCBS announced the publication of two consultative documents for review and comments: *Strengthening the Resilience of the Banking Sector*;[2] and *International Framework for Liquidity Risk Measurement, Standards and Monitoring*.[3,4] The two documents contain the details of a 'reform package' designed to 'improve the banking sector's ability to absorb shocks arising from financial and economic stress, whatever the source, thus reducing the risk of spillover from the financial sector to the real economy'.[5] The reform proposals constitute what has become to be known commonly as Basel III, a term that is not used officially by the BCBS.[6, 7]

The objective of this chapter is to evaluate the BCBS reform proposals in relation to the developments unfolding during the global financial crisis. It was claimed, at one time, that Basel II was a great leap forward compared to Basel I, but that turned out not to be the case. Here, we want to find out if the planned move from Basel II to Basel III is a great leap forward.

20.2. BACKGROUND

The initial response of the Basel II architects and enthusiasts to the crisis-triggered critique of the accord was to claim that an earlier implementation could have prevented the crisis. The Chairman of the Basel Committee, Nout Wellink,[8] once argued that Basel II 'would have helped prevent the global credit crisis from occurring' and that 'it was a misunderstanding to say that Basel II would have allowed the risky practices among banks that triggered the crunch'.[9] He further argued that Basel II would provide impetus for banks to produce 'forward-looking approaches to assessing, managing and holding adequate capital for risk'. Wellink is also quoted as saying that 'the accord is designed to combat liquidity risk and would have improved the robustness of valuation practices and market transparency of complex and less liquid products', implying that the implementation of Basel II would have gone some distance to alleviate the crisis.[10] One reaction to this statement was that 'we do not believe that the implementation of the Basel II proposal or anything that looks remotely like it would have alleviated the ongoing collapse of the market of complex structured assets'.[11] For one thing, Basel II was fixated excessively on capital adequacy, which is a 'lagging indicator of potential trouble'.[12]

Byres defends Basel II on the grounds that it was introduced in most countries at the beginning of 2008, 'long after the seeds of destruction have been sown', whereas the US was engulfed by the crisis while thinking whether implementing Basel II was a good or a bad idea.[13] This argument is valid because Basel II was never fully and uniformly implemented.[14] However, a major cause of the global financial crisis was the 'originate and distribute' model of banking that was motivated by Basel I and sustained by Basel II. Furthermore, Dolan points out that dozens of the world's largest banks, including many that (on paper) fully met Basel II capital adequacy standards, were devastated by the crisis.[15] He suggests that Basel II allowed banks to overstate their true amount of capital and understate the risks to which they were exposed. This is a sound argument, given that Basel II allows banks (at least big banks) to determine their economic (and hence regulatory) capital by using their internal models, and to judge the riskiness of assets by the 'grades' given to those assets by the rating agencies. Likewise, Blundell-Wignall and Atkinson argue that 'the Basel risk weighting approach has allowed banks to expand their leverage almost without limit for all practical purposes'.[16] Llewellyn points out that 'Basel II created incentives for banks to develop off balance sheet business and to shift credit risk', and that 'it was largely the Basel Capital Accord that induced banks to engage in securitisation and to develop credit risk shifting instruments'.[17]

Whilst it may not be the truth, the whole truth and nothing but the truth to claim that Basel II caused the crisis, it is implausible to suggest that the crisis could have been prevented or its effects mitigated by early introduction of Basel II. It is for this reason that the BCBS and Basel II enthusiasts have switched gears from defending the accord to promoting its reform. For example, Nout Wellink admits that Basel II is not perfect and that 'there are opportunities to reflect on some of the new lessons within this more adaptive capital regime'.[18] The Secretary General of the BCBS, Stefan Walter,[19] said in an interview that 'current regulatory requirements [presumably under Basel II] remain unacceptably low and will not deter a renewed race to the bottom in which financial institutions end up undercapitalised, over-leveraged and illiquid'.[20] Basel II sceptics, on the other hand, believe that a world without Basel II is a better world or at best that Basel II must undergo a major overhaul. For example, Morris Goldstein suggests that 'Basel II will need to be reworked thoroughly, not just tweaked at the margin'.[21]

In a speech to the European Parliament Committee on Economic and Monetary Affairs on 3 May 2010, Stefan Walter outlined the key elements of the BCBS reform package in the light of the characteristics of the pre-crisis financial system.[22] To put things into perspective and explain what motivated the proposals, Walter described the kind of environment that led to the crisis. He argued that the depth and severity of the crisis was amplified by a financial system that exhibited too much leverage, insufficient liquidity buffers and capital levels, and poor incentives for risk taking.[23] Specifically, Walter identified the following pre-crisis characteristics of the financial environment: (i) too much leverage; (ii) inadequate quality capital to absorb losses; (iii) excessive credit growth based on weak underwriting standards; (iv) underpricing of liquidity risk and credit risk; (v) insufficient liquidity buffers; (vi) overly aggressive maturity transformation; (vii) inadequate risk governance and poor incentives to manage risk towards prudent long-term outcomes through poorly designed compensation schemes; (viii) inadequate cushions in banks to mitigate the inherent procyclicality of financial markets and its participants; (ix) too much systemic risk, interconnectedness and common exposure to similar shocks;[24] and (x) inadequate oversight that should have served to mitigate the 'too-big-to-fail' problem.

A legitimate point to make is that these characteristics were evident while Basel II was being formulated, yet the designers of the accord were only concerned with loosely-defined capital. Basel II does not have provisions for leverage, while the calculation of the capital ratio on the basis of risk-weighted assets distorts the relation between the leverage ratio and capital ratio. Capital, as defined under Basel II, includes low-quality capital items (actually, items that should never be classified as capital). Liquidity risk is bound to be underpriced when there are no provisions in the regulation to take care of it. It is rather strange to suggest that credit risk was underpriced, given that it has been repeatedly claimed that Basel II provides the means for calculating appropriate levels of regulatory capital against credit risk (as well as market risk and operational risk). The claim that there were inadequate cushions to mitigate pro-cyclicality in financial markets is a valid point, but there is no explanation as to why Basel II was designed in such a way as to boost the pro-cyclicality of the banking industry (as a result of the requirement that the capital ratio should be calculated on the basis of risk-adjusted assets). Basel II had nothing to do with underwriting standards, maturity transformation, risk governance, and the 'too-big-to-fail' problem. If anything, Basel II provided a boost to 'too-big-to-fail' banks because it allowed them the luxury of determining their own capital charges, thus discriminating against small banks.[25]

In general terms Walter describes the reform proposals as integrating micro- and macro-prudential elements, pointing out that they are designed to be proportional to the risks of individual banks' business models. He also suggests that a significant proportion of the reforms are targeted at activities that are systemic in nature (by increasing capital requirements for trading book activities, counter-party credit risk and complex securitization). Under the reforms, he explains, systemically important banks are subject to tougher standards.[26] The proposals include five specific elements and some general qualitative objectives. These points are dealt with in turn in the following sections.

20.3. REVIEWING THE DEFINITION OF CAPITAL

The first proposal is concerned with the quality, consistency and transparency of the capital base to ensure that high-quality capital is present to absorb losses. The BCBS suggests that capital as defined under Basel II suffers from fundamental flaws, including: (i) regulatory adjustments generally are not applied to common equity; (ii) there is no harmonized list of regulatory adjustments; and (iii) weak transparency.[27] These shortcomings, according to the BCBS, 'resulted in the banking sector entering the crisis with a definition of capital that was neither harmonised nor transparent, and it allowed a number of banks to report higher Tier 1 capital ratios but with low levels of common equity net of regulatory adjustments'.

This is to be achieved by (i) making common equity (common stock and retained earnings) the predominant form of Tier 1 capital; (ii) harmonizing Tier 2 capital instruments; and (iii) eliminating Tier 3 capital. Under Basel III, Tier 1 capital will include, in addition to common equity, some subordinated equity-like debt instruments where dividend payments are discretionary. Items to be excluded from the definition of capital are goodwill, minority interest, deferred tax assets, bank investments in own shares, investments in other financial institutions, and other items. Amending the definition of Tier 1 capital is aimed at bringing it into closer alignment with 'tangible common equity', which is the concept that should be used for the purpose of measuring regulatory capital strength rather than Tier 1 capital. Under Basel II, Tier 1 capital often included items such as trust preferred and other 'hybrid' elements that, as demonstrated by the global financial crisis, exhibited less ability to absorb losses on an operating basis. In addition, the proposal calls for an explicit minimum ratio of common equity to risk-weighted assets, although it does not specify this ratio.

Redefining capital to exclude items that do not remotely represent or resemble capital is a positive move. It does not make much sense to consider goodwill as part of the capital available to absorb losses, neither does the mixing of intangible and actual capital.[28] However, redefining capital does not solve the problems associated with the calculation of the capital ratio on the basis of risk-weighted assets. The risk weights are arbitrary, and the whole system boosts the pro-cyclicality of the banking industry without solving the problem of regulatory arbitrage. More important perhaps is that the introduction of a leverage ratio makes the capital ratio redundant if both ratios, as they should be, are calculated on the basis of the same concepts of assets and capital. It does not make any sense to define capital one way for the purpose of calculating the capital ratio and another way for calculating the leverage ratio (which is the case under Basel III). And, as we are going to find out later, a risk-weighted capital ratio may not blend in well with a risk-unweighted ratio.

20.4. RISK COVERAGE

The objective of widening risk coverage is to ensure that all material risks are adequately integrated into and covered in the process of computing regulatory capital, particularly those related to trading activities, complex transactions and derivatives. This includes boosting the capital requirements for counter-party credit exposures arising from banks' derivatives, repos and securities financing transactions. The objective here is to provide incentives to move over-the-counter (OTC) derivative contracts to central counterparties (probably clearing houses) and to strengthen the risk management of counter-party credit exposures. To deal with systemic risk, more capital is to be held against the activity of trading derivatives and complex securitizations associated with systemic risk and interconnectedness, as well as inter-financial sector exposures that are more correlated.

In connection with the enhancement of credit counter-party risk coverage, the proposals also include a package of measures designed to eliminate excessive reliance on external credit ratings. Among other things, the proposals would (i) require banks to perform their own internal assessments of externally rated securitization exposures, (ii) eliminate certain 'cliff effects' associated with credit risk mitigation practices, and (iii) incorporate key elements of the code of conduct fundamentals for credit rating agencies into the eligibility criteria for external credit assessment institutions under the Basel II framework.

While expanding risk coverage is a positive move, the regulation still excludes reputational risk and business risk, which were proved to be of paramount importance (a prime source of destruction) during the global financial crisis. Again, there are too many unnecessary complications in the process of calculating capital against this kind or that kind of risk under Pillar 1. The problem that remains is that there is no way of finding a number for the level of capital that protects a firm from insolvency (particularly at the 99.9 per cent confidence level as required by Pillar 1 of Basel II).

The objectives of providing incentives to move OTC derivative contracts to central counter-parties and to strengthen the risk management of counter-party credit risk sound good but there are problems. To control the problem of counter-party risk in derivatives, a more effective course of action is to force the trading of derivatives on organized exchanges or to require a full financial back-up of transactions.[29] Regulators should learn from the lessons of the late 1990s, when Brokesley Born, the then head of the Commodity Futures Trading Commission (the US agency in charge of regulating derivatives), made some serious suggestions to regulate OTC derivatives. Unfortunately, Born's proposals (which could prevent the recurrence of an AIG-type mess) did not see the light because of opposition from Larry Summers, Alan Greenspan and Robert Rubin.[30] To claim improved risk management under Basel-type regulation is far-fetched because the Basel accords are not about risk management.

Dealing with systemic risk brings with it the problem of judging the systemic importance of individual financial institutions. The plan is to use interconnectedness and correlation as measures of systemic importance, but this is not so straightforward. Criteria other than size have been suggested for the purpose of identifying systemically important institutions as an alternative to the concept of 'too-big-to-fail', which pertains to size only.[31] These criteria include contagion, correlation, concentration and (the underlying) conditions. However, no matter which one of these criteria is used (including correlation), systemic importance boils down to size.[32]

Correlation, as a source of systemic importance, is what Thomson calls the 'too-many-to-fail problem'.[33] The underlying idea is that if risk exposures are correlated, then a group of financial institutions may become systemically important. The 'too-many-to-fail' problem requires that a group or subset of institutions be classified as being jointly systemically important. This task is not easy, although Thomson tries to assign parameters to correlated risk exposures (including the determination of what level of correlation across portfolios poses a systemic threat), asserting the importance for this purpose of risk models, stress testing and scenario analysis. Fortunately, Thomson argues, 'some large financial institutions are doing this type of risk modelling and scenario analysis for looking at their own risk profile' and that 'their work provides a good foundation for others to work from'. But the global financial crisis has exposed the weakness of these techniques, not in the least because of the fact that rare events occur more frequently than what is predicted by value-at-risk (VAR) models. VAR models are inadequate because the global financial crisis has demonstrated vividly that the financial institutions using those models turned out to be grossly undercapitalized and were hit by massive losses that should not have been experienced as predicted by the models. Even worse, financial institutions find it tantalizing to manipulate their models to produce results that make everyone happy.[34,35]

Thomson tries to identify levels of correlated risks that would give rise to systemic concerns.[36] According to him, thresholds that would make groups of institutions systemically important include: (i) the probability that an economic or financial shock would decapitalize institutions accounting, in aggregate, for 35 per cent of financial system assets or 20 per cent of banking assets; and (ii) potential for economic/financial shock to decapitalize institutions accounting, in aggregate, for 15 per cent of financial system assets or 10 per cent of banking assets. But assets are a measure of size, which means that the correlation criterion boils down to size.

Requiring banks to perform their own internal assessments of externally rated securitization exposures (while incorporating key elements of the code of conduct fundamentals for credit rating agencies into the eligibility criteria for external credit) leaves out two problems. Using internal models is like allowing the inmates to run the asylum. Using a code of conduct that credit agencies overlooked without any repercussions will achieve nothing. Credit rating agencies have been discredited and so should their code of conduct.

20.5. INTRODUCING A LEVERAGE RATIO

A leverage ratio is to be introduced as a 'supplementary' measure to the Basel II risk-based framework.[37] This proposal is motivated by the objectives of (i) putting a floor under the build-up of leverage in the banking sector, and (ii) introducing additional safeguards against model risk and measurement error by supplementing the risk-based measure with a simpler measure that is based on gross exposures. Walter[38] and Wellink[39] view the leverage ratio as a 'backstop to risk based requirements'. The numerator of the leverage ratio (capital) would consist only of high-quality capital that is generally consistent with the revised definition of Tier 1 capital set forth in the proposals. However, it is indicated that during the risk assessment and calibration process, the BCBS intends to consider whether the more appropriate measure would be total Tier 1 capital (as revised) or only the common equity component.

Leverage is motivated by the desire to maximize profit, particularly when interest rates are low. High leverage means that the effect of an adverse market movement will be amplified, causing the destruction of the underlying firm. The devastating effect of excessive leverage was quite conspicuous during the global financial crisis, so the introduction of a leverage ratio is a step forward. The Basel Committee recognizes the fact that 'one of the underlying features of the crisis was the build up of excessive on- and off-balance sheet leverage in the banking system', admitting explicitly that 'the build up of leverage has been a feature of previous financial crises, for example up to September 1998'. While Blundell-Wignall and Atkinson correctly argue that 'the introduction of a leverage ratio is likely to be the single most important reform', the problem is that the leverage ratio is regarded as being 'supplementary' or a 'backstop to risk-based requirements'. They point out that 'the leverage ratio should not be thought of as a backstop measure, given how effective the capital weighting approach has been'. They go so far as arguing for the leverage ratio to be the primary 'capital control tool'.[40]

To suggest that the leverage ratio is a supplementary tool to the capital ratio is strange, given that when a leverage ratio is in place, it implies that there is a corresponding capital ratio.[41] Leverage and capital ratios are not supplementary. Indeed they are equivalent, unless the capital ratio is measured on the basis of risk-based assets rather than total assets. While leverage is measured in terms of the ratio of assets to capital, capital adequacy is measured in terms of the ratio of capital to assets. Thus, a high capital ratio implies low leverage, and vice versa. This relationship, however, gets distorted when the capital ratio is calculated on the basis of risk-adjusted assets. Without a leverage ratio it is possible for banks to hold a small amount of capital versus the unweighted balance sheet, which, according to Blundell-Wignall and Atkinson, 'has been symptomic of a banking culture with a greater willingness to take on more risk with the taxpayer's money'.[42]

Blundell-Wignall and Atkinson argue that 'risk weighting and leverage ratio may not sit well together'.[43] Under the risk weighting approach, the minimum regulatory capital is

$$K_{RW} = 0.08[12.5(OR + MR) + \sum w_i A_i] \quad (1)$$

where OR and MR are measures of operational risk and market risk, respectively, A_i is asset i and w_i is the corresponding weight. Under the leverage ratio

$$K_{LR} = \beta \sum w_i A_i \quad (2)$$

where β is the reciprocal of the leverage ratio. Blundell-Wignall and Atkinson demonstrate that

$$K_{EW} \leq K_{LR} \quad (3)$$

which means that the leverage ratio is 'likely to be the binding constraint' because 'banks' ability to arbitrage the capital weights to reduce capital and expand leverage is very extensive'.

Furthermore, the leverage ratio is more objective, easier to calculate and more readily understandable than the risk-based capital ratio. Regulations should be based on leverage, particularly that the leverage ratio is indicative of capital adequacy. While there is substantial empirical evidence for a negative relationship between the leverage ratio and bank insolvency, there is no such evidence on how insolvency is related to risk-based capital ratios.[44] Likewise, Blundell-Wignall, Atkinson and Lee show a positive correlation between losses and the Tier 1 risk-weighted capital ratio and a negative correlation between losses and the leverage ratio.[45]

It is unfortunate, therefore, that Byres views the leverage ratio as 'an interesting development' but that it has limited benefit 'if the risk-based ratio is correctly implemented and policed'.[46] He goes as far as claiming that improper calibration (a big word for choosing the appropriate value) of the minimum leverage ratio would act as the binding constraint on normal banks in normal times.[47] This is rather strange, first because if the leverage ratio is a constraint, the capital ratio is also a constraint. It does not make any sense to advocate the use of a constraint that is difficult to measure and enhances the pro-cyclicality of the system while rejecting another effective constraint that is easy to measure, implement and police. Having seen how devastating excessive leverage can be, it is only logical to impose a constraint on the banks' insatiable appetite for leverage.

20.6. COUNTERCYCLICAL CAPITAL BUFFERS

Countercyclical capital buffers will be introduced to promote the build-up of capital in 'good times' that can be drawn upon in periods of stress ('bad times'), hence reducing the procyclicality of the banking industry. The capital buffers are designed to (i) dampen any excess cyclicality of regulatory capital; (ii) promote more forward-looking provisions; (iii) conserve capital to build buffers at individual banks and the banking sector that can be used in stress situations; and (iv) achieve the broader macro-prudential goal of protecting the banking sector from periods of excess credit growth.

At one time the Basel gurus dismissed procyclicality as a problem in Basel II. Caruana argued that a number of factors that are built into the framework are designed to ease some of the procyclicality effects.[48] The most important offset against the procyclical effects of Basel II, he argued, is the increased emphasis on effective risk management in the form of better control structures, sound corporate governance, and investment in technology, information systems and human capital. This is a rather strange argument. It does not make sense to introduce a system that is procyclical by design then claim that it has features to reduce procyclicality (which it does not have).

The procyclicality of Basel II results from the calculation of the capital ratio on the basis of risk-adjusted assets, which means that one of the proclaimed advances over Basel I (increased risk sensitivity) is counterproductive. This is why some economists argue that procyclicality can be reduced by calculating the capital ratio from total unadjusted assets. For example, it has been suggested that one way in which countercyclical elements could be introduced into regulatory capital requirements is to make capital a function of the change in assets, not the risk-weighted level.[49] Introducing countercyclicality by design sounds more sensible than suggesting a procyclical system and subsequently looking for countercyclical measures. This is what the countercyclicality proposal is all about.

In the BCBS document on countercyclical buffers, Drehmann et al. point out that capital buffers are in excess of the minimum regulatory capital specified by Basel II, held for the purpose of absorbing losses in bad times.[50] The minimum capital requirement is treated as the floor for capital at all times. One can immediately detect a number of problems in this scheme. The first is the implication that the minimum regulatory capital specified under Pillar 1 may be inadequate to absorb losses. This is strange, given that one of the proclaimed innovations of Basel II is the alignment of economic and regulatory capital and that economic capital is the magical number that protects the bank from insolvency with a confidence level of 99.9 per cent. The second problem is that no matter how capital is calculated there is no way to ensure its adequacy in the face of gigantic losses, with or without countercyclical buffers. Then who is going to do the calculation of the capital buffer: prudential regulators or banks? If regulators do the job, then so much for allowing banks to calculate their own capital, which is a proclaimed novelty of Basel II. Assigning the task to banks preserves the Basel II problem of effectively allowing banks to police themselves.

The document specifies some desirable features of an effective scheme for countercyclical capital buffers. These include the following:

1. It would identify the correct timing for the accumulation and release of the capital buffer – that is, correctly identifying 'good times' and 'bad times';
2. It would ensure that the size of the buffer built up in good times is sufficiently large to absorb losses without triggering serious strains;
3. It would be robust to regulatory arbitrage;
4. It would be 'as rule-based as possible';
5. It would be enforceable internationally;
6. It should have a low cost of implementation; and
7. It should be simple and transparent.

These desirable features make such a scheme a 'pie in the sky'. There are too many complications, and any of these features is problematical. To start with, identifying 'good times' and 'bad times' is subjective at worst and rather difficult at best. The same problems will be encountered as in macroeconomic policy, caused primarily by lags (including the recognition lag). Another problem is that the financial cycle (in terms of bank performance) is not necessarily identical to the business (output) cycle. Drehmann et al. admit that although the financial cycle and business cycle are intertwined, they are not fully synchronized at all points in time.[51] Furthermore, the task of recognizing good times and bad times requires high-quality data, which is typically unavailable for most countries. Drehmann et al. use US data because, as they put it, it is 'the country for which most data are available'. How can a scheme like this be implemented evenly worldwide?

Then there is no way of coming up with a figure for the capital buffer that will absorb losses in bad times. It is some sort of 'Mission Impossible' to calculate (basic) regulatory capital Basel-style, which makes the task of calculating capital buffers 'Mission Impossible 2'.[52] How can the scheme be robust to regulatory arbitrage when the whole of Basel II has not overcome this problem because of the risk-based asset approach? And how can the scheme be 'enforceable internationally' when the whole of Basel II is not so and cannot be so. Last, but not least, how can the scheme be cheap, simple and transparent when the whole of Basel II is complex, opaque and very expensive to implement?[53]

It is suggested that one possible scheme is to have the minimum regulatory capital to move countercyclically. The problem is that, because regulatory capital is calculated on the basis of risk-weighted assets, risk and consequently risk-weighted assets tend to increase in economic downturns. Reducing the capital ratio in bad times can be offset by rising riskiness. The same problem arises when the scheme involves setting a target above the minimum such that the gap between the two moves countercyclically. Drehmann et al. acknowledge this problem, arguing that 'the incentive for banks to retrench in bad times is linked to the amount of capital in excess of regulatory constraint, which is set in risk-weighted asset terms', but 'the impact of that retrenchment on the economy is related to the amount of capital in relation to risk-unweighted assets'.[54] They also point out that the decision to cut risk-weighted assets by altering the composition of the balance sheet towards safer investments is procyclical. The bottom line is that the banking industry is procyclical, and no-one can change this fact of life.[55] But at least we know what not to do – that is, boosting the procyclical tendencies of the banking industry, which is what Basel II does and what Basel III will also do.

20.7. INTRODUCING LIQUIDITY PROVISIONS

The objective of the liquidity proposal is to introduce a global liquidity framework that establishes minimum standards for funding liquidity risk. The provisions include the following: (i) banks must hold a stock of high-quality liquid assets that is sufficient to allow them to survive a 30-day period of acute stress; and (ii) a longer-term structural liquidity ratio to promote the funding activities with more stable sources of funding on an ongoing basis.[56] Banks can meet these standards by changing their funding profile, which makes them less vulnerable to liquidity shocks.

Regulating liquidity is a step forward because low liquidity hampers business and may induce a run on bank deposits. Nout Wellink[57] highlights the importance of liquidity by arguing that 'strong capital is a necessary but not a sufficient condition for banking sector stability'.[58] The BCBS suggests that 'a strong liquidity base reinforced through robust supervisory standards is of equal importance [to regulatory capital requirements]'.[59] Wyplosz points out that 'one of the significant lessons of the crash of 2007/08 is that the risk of an asset is largely determined by the maturity of its funding'.[60] He points out that Northern Rock might have survived with the same assets if the average maturity of its funding had been longer. Blundell-Wignall and Atkinson argue that when 'short-term wholesale liabilities fund longer-term assets [which was the essence of Northern Rock's funding strategy] failure to roll over short-term financial paper, or a 'run on deposits' can force de-leveraging and asset sales'.[61]

Harper and Thomas argue that 'when liquidity in the wholesale capital markets dries up, no level of capital may be adequate to ward off potential insolvency'.[62] Referring to the global financial crisis, they argue that 'even well-capitalised banks – including the major Australian banks – have struggled to obtain adequate funds at times during the crisis'. Likewise, Llewellyn points out that 'most banks that have failed (including many during the recent crisis) have had apparently strong capital immediately before their demise'.[63] Goldstein suggests that 'much of the crisis has been about liquidity', arguing that 'large banks in some G-7 countries have reduced significantly the share of narrow liquid assets, like treasuries, in their total assets'. The practice, according to Goldstein, has been 'just-in-time' borrowed liquidity for major players instead of an adequate reserve of own liquidity.[64] A similar view is put forward by Henry Kaufman who points out that the public perception of liquidity has changed from one based on assets (what you could sell) to one based on liabilities (ease of borrowing).[65] Goldstein attributes the unpopularity of higher liquidity requirements to the effect of limiting leverage and asset growth, thus reducing the rate of return when things are going well.[66]

Blundell-Wignall and Atkinson identify two problems in the liquidity proposal: (i) bias towards government bonds while budget deficits are large may work against lending to the private sector; and (ii) some sovereign bonds are highly risky, which may create solvency problems.[67] However, they seem to trivialize the liquidity problem, arguing that 'if banks are solvent and have adequate capital, then the management of liquidity and funding should, in principle, be left to them'.[68] By seeking high return, in the presence of a negative liquidity-return trade off, banks (particularly 'too-big-to-fail' banks) are tempted to mismanage liquidity, which may lead to insolvency. The bottom line is that in the aftermath of the global financial crisis, banks cannot be trusted to manage their own capital, leverage or liquidity.

The problem here is that the proposed liquidity provisions are rather complex in the sense that the liquidity ratios are difficult to measure. More seriously, the provisions are based on liabilities rather than assets, which is inappropriate. Instead, a simple asset-based liquidity ratio can be used to supplement the leverage ratio. A liquidity ratio may be set in terms of deposits, total liabilities or current liabilities, with a clear-cut listing of the underlying liquid assets. Another useful indicator is the funding gap, the difference between loans and deposits.

The central bank may play a big role by performing the function of a 'liquidity provider of the last resort'. Another idea is perhaps to form a fund (managed by bankers' associations/federations) to which member banks make contributions, and which would act as a liquidity provider. The same function can be performed by a government agency funded by special taxes or liquidity insurance premiums paid by banks. Some would argue that such a scheme is conducive to moral hazard and cross subsidization, but that is not the case. It will be just like borrowing from the interbank market.

20.8. GENERAL OBJECTIVES AND PROVISIONS

In addition to the specific objectives discussed so far, the following objectives are stated by Stefan Walter:[69]

- Assuring that regulation and supervision of systemically important banks is strong, forcing them to internalize the risks they create for the public at large;
- Strengthening risk governance and management, building on the Pillar 2 supervisory review process;
- Improving market discipline by enhancing Pillar 3 disclosure of risk profile and capital adequacy; and
- Promoting practical approaches to improve the management of cross-border bank resolutions.

These points sound more like rhetoric than achievable objectives. Walter seems to overlook the problems associated with Pillar 2 and Pillar 3, which have been identified in the literature. George Kaufman suggests that Pillar 2 contains very few specifics, focusing primarily on general principles and does not consider the wide variation in supervisory competence across countries.[70] If Pillar 2 is designed in part to allow supervisors to impose capital charges above the minimum required by Pillar 1, this boils down to admitting the inadequacy of Pillar 1. Then it is not clear how supervisors determine the required capital over and above the Pillar 1 minimum. Under Basel II, therefore, three tranches of capital have to be determined: (i) regulatory capital as required by Pillar 1, (ii) supplementary capital as required by Pillar 2, and (iii) countercyclical buffers as required by the new proposals. This is a triple 'Mission Impossible' that produces a number (in billions of dollars) that means nothing for all intents and purposes.

Kaufman also argues that Pillar 3 is not really about market discipline but about creating transparency and disclosure.[71] A particular criticism is directed at Pillar 3 by Lopez who suggests that the requirements for effective market discipline are not discussed in as much detail as what information on a bank's financial and risk positions need to be disclosed to the public.[72] Kaufman, on the other hand, believes that disclosure and transparency constitute a necessary but not sufficient condition for effective market discipline.[73] In any case, Sundmacher and Ford found significant variability in the quality and quantity of disclosure on operational risk. By examining the 2004 annual reports of 57 financial institutions, they reached the conclusion that there is a lack of consistency in the way operational risk information is reported, which places doubt over its usefulness for external parties.[74]

Wihlborg casts doubt on the effectiveness of Pillar 3, arguing that 'market discipline is not likely to boost the sensitivity of banks' funding costs to changes in bank risk-taking' because 'the proposal is limited to information disclosure'.[75] In this respect, the Basel Committee seems to overlook the proposition that the amount and truthfulness of information available in the market depend on both the demand for and supply of information. Without increased market discipline, they argue, 'Basel II is not likely to resolve the regulatory problem caused by explicit and implicit guarantees of depositors and other creditors of banks'.

20.9. THE TRIUMPH OF BANKS

Since the publication of the December 2009 proposals, bankers have been characteristically on the offensive, expressing concern about the proposals and claiming the typical nightmareish scenarios that they opine whenever they feel that their interests are under threat. *The Economist* reports that 'banks dislike some of the fine print and also claim that the cost of Basel III will force some of them to raise the price of loans, devastating the economy'.[76] The banks argue (and some regulators agree) that a tough reform package could impede the still-patchy economic recovery by impeding new lending. According to Masters and Murphy, a regulator once said that the liquidity rule known as the net stable funding ratio was 'ill judged' and that 'there isn't enough stable funding to meet the requirements'.[77] They suggest that changes in the definition of Tier 1 capital were frightening (for banks) and that one of the liquidity proposals, designed to prevent banks relying on short-term funding, would drastically change business models.

In its comments on the Basel proposals, the French Banking Federation argued that 'the new liquidity requirements' effects on the entire economy need to be carefully thought-through, anticipated, disclosed and accepted by stakeholders well beyond the banking industry stakeholders'.[78] This is because 'the increased costs of required term funding would need to be passed onto banks' clients or avoided in the first place by a decrease in offered loans, which means that 'in both cases, this will negatively affect the GDP growth'. The liquidity proposals 'will lead banks to massive long term borrowings, in the very same period as government needs to finance their budget deficits, ... which will be detrimental to the GDP growth'.

The Institute of International Finance, which represents more than 400 of the world's biggest banks, believes that Basel III could reduce economic growth by some 3 per cent over the next five years in the US, euro zone and Japan and cost almost ten million jobs. Other studies – done by banks, their sympathizers and supporters – show how the implementation of the reforms would have 'catastrophic effects' on the banking industry and economy at large. Nomura's banking analysts believe that the 16 biggest European banks would lose a total of EUR300 billion worth of top-quality Tier 1 capital, pushing the capital ratio from 9 to 5.3 per cent. Estimates made by the Debt Capital Markets Unit at Barclays Capital show that the 35 largest bank holding companies would be short of EUR225 billion in capital. Analysts at BNP Paribas predicted that the proposed reforms would cost European banks around EUR400 billion in extra capital.[79]

These fears seem to be confined to bankers and their supporters, as a large number of economists disagree with the conclusions of these studies. Murphy and Cohen report the results of two separate studies by the Basel Committee and the Financial Stability Board, which concluded that tightened capital and liquidity rules would have only a modest impact on world economic growth patterns if they were phased in over time, as planned.[80] For example, the studies show that a one percentage point increase in bank tangible equity capital would lead to a 0.2 per cent average decline in global output. Giles reports a pre-emptive blast by Stephen Cecchetti, chief economic adviser to the Bank for International Settlements, who said the banks' 'doomsday scenarios' were based on their assuming 'the maximum impact of the maximum change with the minimum behavioural change'.[81] According to Cecchetti, banks 'are assuming they're not adjusting their business at all to the regulatory reforms and that the result for the economy will be the worst possible'. But adjusting business is exactly what banks do not want to do, as they strive to return to the pre-crisis 'business as usual'.

Cecchetti estimates the net impact of the proposals on growth to be 'negligible and well within normal forecast errors'. In the long run, Cecchetti expects a safer banking system to provide economic benefits rather than costs. Furthermore, he gives three examples of banks over-estimating the likely effects of the new regulations: (i) banks claim that the new liquidity rules would force them to swap large quantities of high-yielding loans for low-yielding government bonds, which would have an impact on their profitability and lending; (ii) they assume that investors would demand the same returns on new tranches of equity capital when this equity would make banks more resilient, lowering risk to equity holders and the cost to banks; and (iii) the warnings of high costs are based on banks' estimates that the new rules would reduce credit growth and economic growth severely.[82]

Despite these sensible arguments, the BCBS yielded to bank lobbying, watering down the proposals after the 14–15 July 2010 meeting. The rules have been made substantially less strict than in the first draft of December 2009: one of the two liquidity proposals has been delayed for further revisions, the leverage ratio was eased and the effective dates for both were pushed away by nearly a decade. The Committee made significant changes to the definition of what banks could count toward Tier 1 capital and effectively trimmed the amount of liquid assets they would be required to keep on hand. Masters and Murphy argue that the Basel Committee moving from the December 'harsh' proposals to July's 'compromise' was 'the result of growing fears about the impact of the proposals on a nascent economic recovery than last-ditch lobbying efforts by the banking industry'.[83] However, commentators on both sides of the Atlantic see the July changes to the proposals as a big victory for bankers.[84]

As a result of the July 2010 retreat by the BCBS, banks are back in business as usual. According to calculations by Barclays Capital, big US banks should be able to meet tighter global capital requirements without having to raise substantial amounts of new equity. The 35 largest US bank holding companies will need to come up with USD115 billion in new equity or retained earnings to bring the ratio of their Tier 1 capital to risk-weighted assets to 8 per cent under the revised rules (that is, about half the USD225 billion in new capital the largest US banks would have had to raise under a tougher draft of the rules circulated in December). Similarly, Nomura analyst Jon Peace predicted that the top 16 European banks would need to raise EUR200bn (USD257bn) to restore capital removed by the reforms, down from `EUR300bn under the December rules.

It is strange, therefore, that following the 26 July 2010 meeting, the European Central Bank President, Jean-Claude Trichet, declared that 'the agreements reached today are a landmark achievement to strengthen banking sector resilience in a manner that reflects the key lessons of the crisis'. He claimed that the modified reforms 'are still rigorous enough to promote long term stability in the financial system'. One can only wonder if there is any point at all in the so-called 'reform' and 'Basel III': they are problematic schemes that have been watered down significantly. The announcement that was made on 12 September 2010 said nothing about leverage or liquidity ratios, calling instead for a 4.5 per cent Tier 1 capital and an additional buffer of 2 per cent to be implemented in 2013 and 2019, respectively.

20.10. THE WAY FORWARD

Blundell-Wignall and Atkinson correctly argue that 'some of the most fundamental problems with Basel I and Basel II have not been dealt with'.[85] These problems include the model framework, regulatory and tax arbitrage and the need for more capital. But there are more: allowing banks to use internal models to calculate regulatory capital, reliance on rating agencies, the implementation problems, and the exclusionary and discriminatory aspects of Basel II.[86] Regulation should cover banks and non-bank financial institutions because banks deal with insurance companies and hedge funds to shift promises, which enables them to raise leverage and reduce capital. Furthermore, there are no provisions in the Basel accords for resolution regimes, which leaves a lot to be desired with respect to the problem of 'too-big-to-fail'. This is why David Llewellyn suggests that 'there needs to be a Pillar 4 which would encompass intervention and resolution arrangements as part of overall regulatory strategy and regulatory regime'.[87] The most serious problem, however, remains to be the risk-based approach to the calculation of regulatory capital. For all of these reasons, John Kay[88] argues that 'the failure of the Basel Accords is not that the regime should be elaborated beyond the 4000 pages of text' but that 'the whole system should be swept away'.[89] The way forward is to rein in banks by going back to basics, using simple but effective liquidity and leverage ratios.

The question that remains is whether or not the way forward should be led by the Basel Committee, in the sense that the required regulatory changes are introduced as a Basel accord and implemented worldwide. This may not be the right thing to do because it has become quite clear that the international harmonization of banking regulation does not work. Masters and Murphy write:[90]

> As a group of central bankers and regulators responsible for reforming the world banking system sat in a Toronto conference room in mid-June [2010], hopes of a historic global agreement were fading fast. While the overall goal was to draft rules designed to prevent a repeat of the 2007–08 financial crisis, country after country began to argue for special exemptions that would benefit its domestic banks. Some participants began to disappear.

This anecdote tells the whole story. Financial regulation should be a domestic issue. For example, it is not at all clear why the US needs Basel II or Basel III following the passing of the *Dodd-Frank Act* in July 2010. The Act is a superior piece of financial regulation because it (i) sets out a resolution mechanism for the failure of financial institutions (thus it deals with the 'too-big-to-fail' problem), (ii) provides improved consumer protection, and (iii) reduces the risk arising from derivatives and private trading. What it does not do is to set rules for bank capital, but what it lacks is liquidity and leverage ratios that would make it a more effective piece of regulation.

NOTES

1. Wellink, N. (2010), *The Basel Committee and Regulatory Reform*, Institute of International Finance 2010 Spring Meeting, Vienna, 11 June.
2. BCBS (2009), *Consultative Document: Strengthening the Resilience of the Banking Sector*, Basel: Bank for International Settlements, December.
3. BCBS (2009), *Consultative Document: International Framework for Liquidity Risk Measurement, Standards and Monitoring*, Basel: Bank for International Settlements, December.
4. In the first of these two documents, it is stated that 'the prospects set out in this paper are a key element of the Committee's comprehensive reform package to address the lessons of the crisis'.
5. BCBS (2009), 'Press Release: Strengthening the Resilience of the Banking Sector Consultative Document'. Available at http://www.bis.org/publ/bcbs164.htm.
6. Cassidy, G.S. (2010), 'The Basel III Proposal Flaws', *American Banker*, **175**, 8.
7. Melloan, G. (2010), 'The Lesson of Basel's Bean Counters', *Wall Street Journal*, 24 April.
8. Wellink, N. (2008), 'Basel II Might Have Prevented Crunch'. Available at www.Bobsguide.com/cgi-bin/guide/newsExtras.
9. It was not only the banks covered by Basel II that triggered the crunch. Hedge funds, a particular insurance company and the shadowy unregulated financial system in general caused most of the damage. These are entities that the Basel accords do not cover, perhaps for convenience.
10. Basel II is about capital adequacy, not liquidity. It is about the ability to pay creditors in case of failure or enduring a significant loss event. It is only because the Basel II architects realised the hard way the hazard of ignoring liquidity risk that they decided to introduce provisions for liquidity as part of the proposed reforms.
11. Whalen, C. (2007), 'Basel II: Do Big Banks Need More Capital?' *Seeking Alpha*, 24 October.
12. Llewellyn, D.T. (2010), *The Global Banking Crisis and the Post-Crisis Banking and Regulatory Scenario*, Research Papers in Corporate Finance, University of Amsterdam, June.
13. Byres, W. (2010), *Balancing National and International Interests*, Paper Prepared for the Bond University Symposium on Global Financial Crisis: The Way Forward, 9 April. Available at http://www.apra.gov.au/Speeches/upload/20100409-Bond-University-Speech.pdf.
14. The damage inflicted on individual countries by the global financial crisis was not a function of the extent to which they had implemented Basel II.
15. Dolan, E. (2010), *Financial Reform: What is Basel III and Why Should we Regulate*

Bank Capital?, Available at http://dolanecon.blogspot.com/2010/08/financial-reform-what-is-basel-iii-and.html.

16. Blundell-Wignall, A. and Atkinson, P. (2010), 'Thinking Beyond Basel III: Necessary Solution for Capital and Liquidity', *OECD Journal: Financial Market Trends*, **1**, 1–23.
17. Llewellyn, D.T. (2010), *The Global Banking Crisis and the Post-Crisis Banking and Regulatory Scenario*, Research Papers in Corporate Finance, University of Amsterdam, June.
18. Wellink, N. (2008), *Basel II: Market Developments and Financial Institution Resiliency*, Paper Presented at the Risk Minds Asia Conference, Singapore, 4 March.
19. Davies, R. (2009), 'Q&A: Basel Committee's Walter Outlines Basel II Reform Agenda', *Risk*, 17 June.
20. This is an explicit recognition of the importance of leverage and liquidity, as well as the inadequacy of Basel II. It is also an admission that the Basel II rules did not produce appropriate capital charges despite the claim that Pillar 1 of the Accord provided rules allowing banks to determine the capital required to protect them from insolvency with a confidence level of 99.9 per cent.
21. Goldstein, M. (2008), *The Subprime and Credit Crisis*, Paper based on transcript of speech presented at the Global Economic Prospects meeting, Peterson Institute for International Economics, 3 April.
22. Walter, S. (2010), 'Basel II and Revisions to the Capital Requirements Directive'. Available at http://www.bis.org/speeches/sp100503.htm.
23. Exactly the same words were used by Nout Wellink (op cit). A better word than 'poor' to describe the incentives for risk taking is 'great' or 'effective'.
24. David Llewellyn (op cit) makes the interesting remark that while financial institutions have become rather diversified, the whole system lacks diversity, in the sense that everyone does everything.
25. Moosa, I.A. (2010), *The Myth of Too Big to Fail*, London: Palgrave.
26. Walter, S. (2010), 'Basel II and Revisions to the Capital Requirements Directive'. Available at http://www.bis.org/speeches/sp100503.htm.
27. BCBS (2009), *Consultative Document: Strengthening the Resilience of the Banking Sector*, Basel: Bank for International Settlements, December.
28. A firm that suffers a big loss event will invariably sustain reputational loss, which implies the erosion of goodwill.
29. Measures like these are not as draconian as they may sound. Regulators often resort to the prohibition of short selling, which is probably a more drastic action than bringing transparency into derivatives trading.
30. Johnson, S. and Kwak, J. (2010), *13 Bankers: The Wall Street Takeover*, New York: Pantheon Books.
31. Thomson, J. (2009), *On Systematically Important Financial Institutions and Progressive Systemic Mitigation*, Federal Reserve Bank of Cleveland, Policy Discussion Papers, No. 27, August.
32. Moosa, I.A. (2010), *The Myth of Too Big to Fail*, London: Palgrave.
33. Thomson, J. (2009), *On Systematically Important Financial Institutions and Progressive Systemic Mitigation*, Federal Reserve Bank of Cleveland, Policy Discussion Papers, No. 27, August.
34. Moosa, I.A. (2008), *Quantification of Operational Risk under Basel II: The Good, Bad and Ugly*, London: Palgrave.
35. Moosa, I.A. (2010), 'Basel II as a Casualty of the Global Financial Crisis', *Journal of Banking Regulation*, **11**, 95–114.
36. Thomson, J. (2009), *On Systematically Important Financial Institutions and Progressive Systemic Mitigation*, Federal Reserve Bank of Cleveland, Policy Discussion Papers, No. 27, August.
37. The leverage ratio has long been a key component of the US regulatory capital regime, although several elements of the current proposal differ significantly from the existing US requirements.

38. Walter, S. (2010), 'Basel II and Revisions to the Capital Requirements Directive'. Available at http://www.bis.org/speeches/sp100503.htm.
39. Wellink, N. (2010), *The Basel Committee and Regulatory Reform*, Institute of International Finance 2010 Spring Meeting, Vienna, 11 June.
40. Blundell-Wignall, A. and Atkinson, P. (2010), 'Thinking Beyond Basel III: Necessary Solution for Capital and Liquidity', *OECD Journal: Financial Market Trends*, **1**, 1–23.
41. This is why Blundell-Wignall and Atkinson consider the leverage ratio as a capital control tool.
42. Blundell-Wignall, A. and Atkinson, P. (2010), 'Thinking Beyond Basel III: Necessary Solution for Capital and Liquidity', *OECD Journal: Financial Market Trends*, **1**, 1–23.
43. Ibid.
44. Evanoff, D.D. and Wall, L.D. (2001), 'SND Yield Spreads as Bank Risk Measures', *Journal of Financial Services Research*, **19**, 121–146.
45. Blundell-Wignall, A., Atkinson, P., Lee, S.G. (2008), 'The Current Financial Crisis: Causes and Policy Issues', *OECD Financial Market Trends*, OECD, Paris.
46. Byres, W. (2010), *Balancing National and International Interests*, Paper Prepared for the Bond University Symposium on Global Financial Crisis: The Way Forward, 9 April. Available at http://www.apra.gov.au/Speeches/upload/20100409-Bond-University-Speech.pdf.
47. A minimum leverage ratio indicates maximum borrowing relative to capital. This is because the leverage ratio is measured as the ratio of assets to equity, such that a leverage ratio of x means that a bank cannot borrow more than x times equity.
48. Caruana, J. (2005), 'Implementation of Basel II', *Financial Markets, Institutions and Instruments*, **14**, 253–265.
49. Goldstein, M. (2008), *The Subprime and Credit Crisis*, Paper based on transcript of speech presented at the Global Economic Prospects meeting, Peterson Institute for International Economics, 3 April.
50. Drehmann, M., Borio, C., Gambacorta, L., Jimenez, G. and Trucharte, C. (2010), *Countercyclical Capital Buffers: Exploring Options*, BIS Working Papers, No. 317.
51. Ibid.
52. The problem of regulatory capture arising from the requirement of model validation by regulators will be reinforced.
53. The Credit Suisse Group (2001) estimated the Basel II compliance costs to average $15 million per bank for about 30000 banks worldwide.
54. Drehmann, M., Borio, C., Gambacorta, L., Jimenez, G. and Trucharte, C. (2010), *Countercyclical Capital Buffers: Exploring Options*, BIS Working Papers, No. 317.
55. In *Strengthening the Resilience of the Banking Sector* (op cit), the BCBS identifies some of the channels through which procyclicality has been amplified: (i) accounting standards for both mark-to-market assets and held-to-maturity loans, (ii) margining practices; and (iii) the build up and release of leverage among financial institutions, firms and consumers.
56. The liquidity measures corresponding to (i) and (ii) are the liquidity coverage ratio (LCR) and the net stable funding ratio, respectively. The LCR is the ratio of high quality assets to 30-day net cash outflows. The net stable funding ratio (NSFR) is the ratio of available stable funding to required stable funding. Both must be greater than one.
57. Wellink, N. (2010), *The Basel Committee and Regulatory Reform*, Institute of International Finance 2010 Spring Meeting, Vienna, 11 June.
58. Again, why is it that the focus of Basel II is capital only and that liquidity is ignored?
59. BCBS (2009), *Consultative Document: Strengthening the Resilience of the Banking Sector*, Basel: Bank for International Settlements, December.
60. Wyplosz, C. (2009), 'The ICMB-CEPR Geneva Report: "The Future of Financial Regulation"', *Vox*, 27 January.
61. Blundell-Wignall, A. and Atkinson, P. (2010), 'Thinking Beyond Basel III: Necessary Solution for Capital and Liquidity', *OECD Journal: Financial Market Trends*, **1**, 1–23.

62. Harper, I. and Thomas, M. (2009), 'Making Sense of the GFC: Where Did it Come From and What Do We Do Now?', *Economic Papers*, **28**, 196–205.
63. Llewellyn, D.T. (2010), *The Global Banking Crisis and the Post-Crisis Banking and Regulatory Scenario*, Research Papers in Corporate Finance, University of Amsterdam, June.
64. Goldstein, M. (2008), *The Subprime and Credit Crisis*, Paper based on transcript of speech presented at the Global Economic Prospects meeting, Peterson Institute for International Economics, 3 April.
65. Kaufman, H. (2009), *The Road to Financial Reformation: Warnings, Consequences, Reforms*, New York: Wiley.
66. Goldstein, M. (2008), *The Subprime and Credit Crisis*, Paper based on transcript of speech presented at the Global Economic Prospects meeting, Peterson Institute for International Economics, 3 April.
67. Blundell-Wignall, A. and Atkinson, P. (2010), 'Thinking Beyond Basel III: Necessary Solution for Capital and Liquidity', *OECD Journal: Financial Market Trends*, **1**, 1–23.
68. Northern Rock did not suffer from subprime assets write-downs or defaults on subprime loans, but it had an acute liquidity shortage. The bank went down because of illiquidity, not insolvency.
69. Walter, S. (2010), 'Basel II and Revisions to the Capital Requirements Directive'. Available at http://www.bis.org/speeches/sp100503.htm.
70. Kaufman, G.G. (2005), 'Basel II vs. Prompt Corrective Action: Which is Best for Public Policy?', *Financial Markets, Institutions and Instruments*, **14**, 349–357.
71. Ibid.
72. Lopez, J.A. (2003), 'Disclosure as a Supervisory Tool: Pillar 3 of Basel II', *Federal Reserve Bank of San Francisco Economic Letter*, August.
73. Kaufman, G.G. (2003), *Basel II: the Roar that Moused, Mimeo*, Federal Reserve Bank of Chicago, October.
74. Sundmacher, M. and Ford, G. (2007), 'Operational Risk Disclosures in Financial Institutions'. Available at http://ssrn.com/abstract=963244.
75. Wihlborg, C. (2005), 'Basel II and the Need for Bank Distress Resolution Procedures', *Financial Markets, Institutions and Instruments*, **14**, 359–369.
76. *The Economist* (2010), 'Bare-knuckle in Basel', 29 May, 11–14.
77. Masters, B. and Murphy, M. (2010), 'Banking Reform: Suspense Over', *Financial Times*, 18 August.
78. French Banking Federation (2010), *FBF Comments on the Consultative Documents Published by the Basel Committee on Banking Supervision (BCBS 164 &165)*, 16 April. Available at http://www.bis.org/publ/bcbs165/frenchbankingfe.pdf.
79. Crosland, J. (2010), 'Can We Bank on Basel?', *Investors Chronicle*, 21 May.
80. Murphy, M. and Cohen, N. (2010), 'US Banks Receive Basel II Boost', *Financial Times*, 18 August.
81. Giles, C. (2010), 'Bankers' "Doomsday Scenarios" Under Fire', *Financial Times*, 30 May.
82. Ibid.
83. Masters, B. and Murphy, M. (2010), 'Banking Reform: Suspense Over', *Financial Times*, 18 August.
84. Murphy, M. and Cohen, N. (2010), 'US Banks Receive Basel II Boost', *Financial Times*, 18 August.
85. Blundell-Wignall, A. and Atkinson, P. (2010), 'Thinking Beyond Basel III: Necessary Solution for Capital and Liquidity', *OECD Journal: Financial Market Trends*, **1**, 1–23.
86. Moosa, I.A. (2010), 'Basel II as a Casualty of the Global Financial Crisis', *Journal of Banking Regulation*, **11**, 95–114.
87. Llewellyn, D.T. (2010), *The Global Banking Crisis and the Post-Crisis Banking and Regulatory Scenario*, Research Papers in Corporate Finance, University of Amsterdam, June.
88. Kay, J. (2009), *Narrow Banking: The Reform of Banking Regulation*, London: Centre for the Study of Financial Innovation.

89. Kay (op cit) distinguishes between 'casino banking' and 'utility banking', arguing that casino banks cannot in practice be controlled by regulation and hence no attempt should be made to do so. In other words, casino banks should be allowed to regulate themselves without expecting favours from the government. The problem with this argument is that these banks may inflict collateral damage on the financial sector and the economy before their demise.
90. Masters, B. and Murphy, M. (2010), 'Banking Reform: Suspense Over', *Financial Times*, 18 August.

PART VI

Country case studies

21. The US architecture of bank regulation and supervision: recent reforms in their historical context

Dalvinder Singh

The US system of prudential regulation and supervision of banking is without doubt a complex structure – it is not centralized in a single regulator but is the responsibility of a number of separate and independent regulators. In the early periods of the financial crisis of 2007 a number of proposals were put forward for wholesale reform of the US regulatory system. These proposals were to improve the effectiveness of the regulatory structure and to simplify the financial regulatory structure overseeing the financial system in the post-*Gramm-Leach-Bliley Act 1999* (GLB) world of large complex financial conglomerates. The proposals took the form of either a twin peaks model or a single regulator model.[1] The debate about regulatory reform once again took centre stage during the recent financial crisis. This chapter explores some of the key features of the *Dodd-Frank Act 2010* and then reflects on the historical resistance to wholesale architectural reform of the system of regulation. It seems as though history has repeated itself and the status quo remains and we explore why that is the case given the severity of this financial crisis.

21.1. THE HISTORICAL MOVES TOWARDS REGULATORY CONSOLIDATION

The move towards regulatory consolidation in the banking system dates back to the 1930s and continued intermittently into the 1990s.[2] However, this has been unsuccessful due to the underlying confidence in the regulatory system that prevails, despite a number of misgivings. This issue was obviously heightened with the move in some quarters towards a single-regulator model governing the financial system, or even a single bank regulator. The multi-agency approach has advocated that competition between the regulators results in a diminution of unnecessary regulation and supervision. Alan Gart illustrates the idea of 'competing in laxity' by pointing out that some regulators lured new members with the incentive of reducing the burden of regulation.[3] Moreover, Gart highlights that competition existed between the regulators regarding, for instance, the permissible business activities they allowed their members to pursue, and gave rise to pressure to ensure the multi-regulator model is retained.[4] The most significant concern was the large number of bank failures, which undermined confidence in having such a multitude of bank regulators. This led to criticism of the rigour with which these institutions were examined. The findings of a Government Accountability Office (GAO) review highlighted a number of misgivings across the board in all the regulatory bodies; for instance, the Federal Reserve Board (FRB) failed to supervise the activities of financial holding companies sufficiently, in particular intra-group transactions.[5] Moreover, the GAO report highlighted the lack of coordination between regulators with supervisory responsibilities. It pointed to the failure of the Bank of New England as an example where the Office of the Comptroller of Currency (OCC) as the examiner of the lead bank and the Federal Reserve responsible for examining the holding company did not discover the fact that it was about to collapse.[6] The report proposed the establishment of a Federal Banking Commission and the dismantlement of the OCC and the Federal Deposit Insurance Corporation (FDIC). However, the rationale for change at the time could not provide a conclusive solution as to the future role of the Federal Reserve, given the importance attached to combining bank regulation and the implementation of monetary policy.[7] Notwithstanding the various proposals for reform, the move towards a single bank regulator never bore fruit.

The wholehearted move towards universal banking was reined in by the overarching concern about the fragility of the banking system.[8] The vulnerability of the official safety net for FDIC-member institutions (often referred to in the US as insured depository institutions) has been a major consideration.[9] The position pre-1930s was a different picture, with an active policy of allowing commercial banks to pursue securities activities.[10] The fragility of the banking system was heightened during the 1930s when thousands of banks failed and the Great Depression ensued. The policymakers at the time thought that the fragility of the banking system was exacerbated by its involvement and dealings in the securities business. Consequently, the separation of commercial bank and securities businesses, in the form of deposit-taking and lending and underwriting securities respectively, was enacted with the passage of the *Banking Act* of 1933, colloquially referred to as the *Glass-Steagall Act*. This Act also attempted to avoid concentration within the financial system by dismantling the universal banking model.[11] Subsequent research into the failures during the Great Depression called into question the premise on which the *Glass-Steagall Act* was passed, suggesting that the Great Depression ensued from the economic circumstances at the time rather than systemic failures in the conduct of bank securities business.[12] Benston contends that the abuses and conflicts of interest associated with banks involved in securities business at the time were exaggerated.[13] The *Glass-Steagall Act* was considered, therefore, to be a political reaction to mete out appropriate measures to curb the excesses of those deemed to be the culprits responsible for the Great Depression.[14] The possibility post-GLB of the unreasonable demands on the federal safety net transpired during this financial crisis in the light of the potential systemic risk that could result from part of a large financial conglomerate getting in trouble.

The key problem associated with the multi-agency approach governing banking, securities and insurance businesses is the level of communication and cooperation, and indeed competitiveness, between the regulators. This is especially the case when issues to do with one part of a financial conglomerate transcend into other regulatory domains.[15] The issue of regulatory confidentiality means that information about firms cannot be readily passed on to other interested regulatory bodies.[16] To mitigate this problem, in the banking system the Federal Financial Institutions Examination Council (FFIEC) was established at the federal level. The FFIEC is said to have been successful in setting common principles and standards, but has been reluctant to widen its scope to incorporate securities and insurance businesses to reflect the nature of the industry post-GLB.[17] While the FFEIC is a formal mechanism to coordinate efforts better between the federal regulators, other informal methods of communication also exist to alleviate day-to-day problems.[18] However, the level of competition between the regulators has led, for instance, to failures at banks being exacerbated by a lack of coordination between regulators in resolving the problems that have arisen.[19]

The issue of financial holding companies (FHCs) requires the FRB to seek the cooperation of securities and insurance regulators to assist it to supervise their activities, which can be elevated to presidential level if a crisis is serious enough. However, coordination between the regulators on a day-to-day level to supervise FHCs does pose problems, with issues such as fraud not being detected when it transcends into other financial sectors.[20] For example, a 2001 GAO report recommended better information-sharing between bank, securities and insurance regulators to eliminate the possibility of individuals working in one part of the financial services industry when they have been banned in another sector.[21] The issue of monitoring risks that emanate from other sectors has also been heightened in the securities industry. The pressure for better coordination between regulators has been emphasized at a political level post-1987 with the stock market crash and after the attacks of 11 September 2001. But according to the GAO report, while ad hoc coordination systems are in place there is no 'systematic sharing of information', and this undermines the assessment of risks that can adversely affect other areas of the industry.[22] For example, the rescue of Long-Term Capital Management (LTCM) showed how regulators were only interested in protecting the interests of their own firms' link to the hedge fund rather than dealing with issues that crossed over into other regulatory jurisdictions.[23] The GAO report highlights that 'functional specialization has drawbacks as well, including the inability to take advantage of the economies of scale and scope'.[24] This regulatory structure overseeing financial conglomerates does not mirror the way they manage their activities across the companies they have formed under holding structures. Wilmarth explains how FHCs manage their affairs, and indeed protect their reputation, in a more centralized rather than decentralized manner which does not reflect the fragmented regulatory structure, even though consolidated supervision is exercised.[25] The incremental changes adopted in GLB, such as firewalls between banks and non-banks, are not robustly supervised, calling into question their actual utility to prevent transactions between the companies in a holding structure.[26]

The strengths of the current system were clearly noted in the GAO assessment before the financial crisis with its sheer size, specialism and flexibility in the way regulation is implemented.[27] The GAO report noted the ability of regulators to be more sophisticated and innovative, rather than adopting a single approach across the system.[28] Whether it is principles- or rules-based depends on the regulators' choice of how best to oversee the activities for which they are responsible. Notwithstanding the strengths of the current regulatory system, the GAO puts forward a number of 'options' for change; these varied from adopting a single-regulator model to setting up a single body to oversee large, complex financial groups.[29] However, the introduction of GLB warrants further examination of how FHCs are regulated, possibly with the adoption of a lead regulator to coordinate the examination processes of the entities associated with the holding company. The lead regulator could act in cases when a problem arises in one particular entity to help coordinate the dissemination of information between the respective regulators.

The regulatory response to the crisis has on one level followed the historical pattern despite the early political rhetoric for wholesale architectural reform. The reforms introduced by the *Dodd-Frank Act 2010* have not adopted the initial proposals for wholesale change to the regulatory structure (with the exception of one sacrificial lamb in this case the scrapping of the Office of Thrift Supervision (OTS)) but more specific changes, which are without doubt very extensive, to improve the regulatory, supervisory, and examination of the financial intermediaries and markets. The *Dodd-Frank Act 2010* is very much a multifaceted piece of legislation with specific changes to the regulatory system but also an attempt to allow the 'appropriate federal banking agencies' (§ 2(2)) the responsibility to work out how they will adopt some of the changes. In addition to this, it also initiates a number of studies on regulatory reform, so there is a considerable amount of work for both regulatory agencies and banks and nonbanks ahead. The *Dodd-Frank Act 2010* provides significant and wholesale changes in a host of other areas, namely the establishment of the Financial Stability Oversight Council, the Federal Insurance Office, and the Bureau of Consumer Financial Protection. Moreover, the *Dodd-Frank Act* also introduces a number changes at the regulatory level in areas such as liquidation arrangements for bank holding companies and nonbank financial companies and derivatives and hedge funds. The *Dodd-Frank Act* does not change the dual banking system of state and federal charters for depository institutions and indeed the core responsibilities of the FRB and FDIC.[30] One purpose of the legislation is to 'preserve and protect the dual system of Federal and State-chartered depository institutions'.[31] In other areas the *Dodd-Frank Act* maintains the status quo with the insurance industry for example, so it remains the responsibility of individual states. It does, however, create the Federal Insurance Office under the umbrella of the Treasury which will be primarily responsible for monitoring the insurance industry and review regulation of the industry to assess the gaps which may exist.[32]

21.2. THE DUAL BANKING SYSTEM

The dual banking system consists of two formal methods of chartering commercial banks (authorizing them to undertake the business of banking): at the state level and at the federal level.[33] This is a consequence in many respects of the constitutional make-up of the US, based on both a state and a federal system of governance.[34] Historically, state-regulated banks issued their own notes. This was before the federal government intervened to introduce, at a federal level, a national currency to support its war efforts at the time.[35] The Office Comptroller of Currency (OCC) was placed at the helm of the national currency to manage it.[36] The dual banking system was a by-product of the legislation to introduce the national currency, and put an end to states issuing their own banknotes. Indeed, the expectation was that state-chartered banks would abandon their state charter for a federal charter. But the introduction of the new federal charter did not result in a mass exodus from the state system, even when a subsequent punitive tax was imposed on state banknotes to force them to change.[37] The result was two formal systems of chartering: the bank regulator in the individual state charters the state banks, and the OCC charters national banks pursuant to the *National Bank Act of 1864*.[38] But the dual banking system is not rigidly divided into two parts – a state bank could convert its charter to a national charter and vice versa.[39] According to Kenneth Scott, 'the core of the dual banking system is the simultaneous existence of different regulatory options that are not alike in terms of statutory provisions, regulatory implementation and administrative policy'.[40]

In addition to these two chartering systems, membership of the Federal Reserve and the FDIC also plays a significant role.[41] The FDIC and the FRB have prudential responsibilities to oversee the activities of their members in addition to the primary regulators.[42] National banks are required to be members of the Federal Reserve and the FDIC.[43] The FDIC has its own application process as well for insured depository institution.[44] State member banks have the option to choose to come under the jurisdiction of the Federal Reserve[45] and thus the FDIC. Membership means the banks are under the umbrella of their chartering authority, as well as the Federal Reserve and the FDIC, for the purposes of supervision and enforcement to a lesser or greater extent to fulfil their individual responsibilities.[46] For example, a national bank will be chartered by the OCC, which will have responsibility for its prudential supervision; the FDIC will have supervisory and enforcement responsibility to fulfil its obligations to the deposit insurance fund; and the Federal Reserve will have responsibility over its access to the discount window and reserve requirements.

21.3. THE INDIVIDUAL REGULATORS

The primary regulators have the main responsibility for prudential regulation. The primary regulatory bodies are the Federal Reserve,[47] the OCC,[48] and the FDIC.[49] The OTS will be abolished as of 19 October 2011 and its various responsibilities will be transferred to the Board of Governors of the Federal Reserve and the OCC.[50]

The regulation and supervision of the business of banking has evolved over a considerable period of time, most notably through legislative means codified in various places in Title 12 Banks and Banking of the United States Code (USC); this is divided into over 50 chapters, giving rise to a considerable level of complexity.[51] The responsibilities of the FDIC,[52] the

OCC,[53] and the FRB[54] are broadly speaking set out in separate chapters; these make up the 'Appropriate Federal Banking Agency'.[55] In addition, a significant proportion of responsibility is conferred on the individual federal regulators as administrative bodies separately within the Code of Federal Regulations (CFR) designating administrative powers.[56] The primary regulators have devised their own styles of regulation, supervision, and enforcement which is reinforced by the *Dodd-Frank Act*. It also allows the federal regulatory agencies to interpret the various changes it requires them to adopt as well.

The OCC is responsible for chartering and supervision of national banks. Pursuant to § 27 of 12 USC,[57] it is authorized to grant national bank charters and is responsible on an administrative level, as provided in 12 CFR s.4.2, for overseeing national banks, with powers to regulate, supervise, and exercise enforcement actions in accordance with federal laws.[58] The OCC can appoint examiners to national banks 'as often as the [OCC] shall deem necessary',[59] and these banks are required to make reports about their 'condition', regarding their financial health in terms of assets and liabilities to the OCC.[60] The OCC is also responsible for ensuring that national banks operate in a safe and sound manner, which will be explored further on in this chapter. But it must be mindful that it achieves its other regulatory goals, which are to 'promote competitiveness for national banks' and 'improve efficiency of examinations and supervision, including reducing supervisory burden'.[61] It will also pursuant to § 312(b)(2)(B)(i)(I) take on responsibility for the regulation, supervision, and examination of federal savings associations that were previously under the jurisdiction of the OTS.[62] It is also required to designate a Deputy Comptroller who will have responsibility for the supervision and examination of federal savings associations.[63]

The Federal Reserve is at the helm of the banking system in its capacity as central bank to manage monetary policy[64] and with a mandate for financial stability. It acts as a central source of liquidity and a single-note issuer.[65] The Federal Reserve puts emphasis on combining its responsibilities for monetary policy and bank supervision to gauge the prudential stability of the banking system.[66] The *Dodd-Frank Act* introduces changes to the way its credit lines can be sought by non-banks.[67] It seeks to limit such support to rescue the financial system rather than providing support to an individual institution. Moreover, the decision to lend will, inter alia, require the Federal Reserve to consider whether the security for emergency loans is 'sufficient to protect taxpayers from losses'[68] and the facility is 'terminated in a timely and orderly fashion'.[69] If support is going to be provided then the individual institution needs to be experiencing liquidity rather than an insolvency problem. In this case insolvency is determined by whether the individual institution has sought bankruptcy protection.[70] This restricts the ability of the Federal Reserve to lend to institutions that are in distress; by providing the support to the financial system it is essentially sending out a message that it is not willing to rescue individual institutions unless they pose a threat to the financial system. Liquidity to the financial system means it is primarily attempting to mitigate the impact on it rather than rescue an individual institution. The vexing issue of when a liquidity crisis is a systemic liquidity crisis so to speak that warrants action by the authorities, is also given specific attention in the *Dodd-Frank Act*. The Federal Reserve is required to undertake consultation with the Treasury and FDIC 'to determine whether a liquidity event exists that warrants use of the guarantee programme'.[71] In order to arrive at that point an evaluation of the evidence is required that such an event exists and 'failure to take action would have serious adverse effects on financial stability or economic conditions in the United States'; and action is needed to 'avoid or mitigate potential adverse effects'.[72]

The Federal Reserve has specific responsibility for supervising FHCs, bank holding companies, state chartered banks, and foreign bank operations.[73] The Federal Reserve will also take over responsibility from the OTS for the supervision and rule-making powers for savings and loans holding companies and their subsidiary.[74] The oversight the Federal Reserve exercises over the respective holding companies is deemed necessary for the purposes of gauging the groups' safety and soundness. This gives rise to a necessity to cooperate and seek relevant information from the other primary regulators rather than making duplicate examinations of a bank and its subsidiaries.[75]

The FDIC was established in 1933 after the huge spate of bank failures in the 1920s and 1930s.[76] It was set up to insure 'the deposits of all banks and savings associations'.[77] FDIC membership gives rise to a further layer of prudential supervision for the purpose of safeguarding the deposit insurance fund.[78] The FDIC is the primary federal regulator and supervisor of state-chartered banks that have decided not to become members of the Federal Reserve system, which are categorized as non-member banks.[79] Furthermore, with the abolition of the OTS the FDIC will also take responsibility for state savings associations.[80] Clearly, its most important function is the administration of the deposit insurance fund. The level of protection afforded to depositors has been increased by the *Dodd-Frank Act* from USD100 000 to USD250 000 to an individual depositor.[81] The basis of calculating the deposit insurance premium will be changed as well – based on consolidated total assets rather than deposit liabilities. This move will mean the large complex institutions will contribute more towards deposit insurance than the less risky ones.[82] This will coincide with the reforms to the FDIC minimum reserve which will increase to 1.35 by 30 September 2020.[83]

The FFIEC was set up in 1979 to assist the federal bank regulators' ability to enhance the level of uniformity and consistency in their supervisory and examination practices.[84] The move towards creating a single body to coordinate and enhance consistency between the regulators should not come as a surprise: it is designed to reduce the potential inconsistency that might arise from the fact that a number of regulators have overlapping responsibilities to oversee the activities of federally regulated banks. In addition to enhancing the level of consistency, another concern is to reduce unnecessary regulatory burdens that might arise as a result of federal regulators' actions. The FFEIC periodically publishes interagency notices on, for example, the importance of notifying and coordinating information about possible enforcement decisions taken by a federal regulator with other regulators.[85]

The *Dodd-Frank Act* will mean a new level of coordination will be required by FFEIC on a federal bank agency level to ensure consistency in the way federal bank agencies apply the new reforms. Moreover, it could also be equally called into doubt whether it can sustain its current form given that it is made up of federal bank agencies and does not include either securities or insurance regulators. The *Dodd-Frank Act* seems to better reflect the need for improved coordination and consistency of treatment of banks and non-bank activities that undertake similar financial activities and so mitigates this with a host of new measures.

The Bureau of Consumer Financial Protection (BCFP) is a new body on the federal level to regulate consumer financial products and services.[86] The BCFP will form a part of the Federal Reserve rather than an independent body and so will be classed as an Executive agency rather than a federal agency. The necessity for such an organization culminates primarily from the systemic failures to curb the 'mis-selling' of mortgages that formed part of the catalyst for the financial crisis. The BCFP will have regulatory, supervisory, and enforcement authority over those that provide financial products and services despite oversight of such banks and non-banks by the primary regulator. In order to execute its role effectively, the BCFP will have the authority to request information and examination reports provided there are assurances about its confidentiality.[87] The introduction of the BCFP will mean that the federal agencies will lose a proportion of their responsibilities to the new agency with the mandate to enforce federal consumer financial law. More specifically the Dodd-Frank legislation significantly curtails the ability of national banks and their respective regulators to exercise the pre-emption rights.

21.4. THE FRB AND THE *GRAMM-LEACH-BLILEY ACT OF 1999*

The move towards the dismantlement of barriers between banks, securities firms, and insurance businesses formally came about with the enactment of the GLB.[88] The Act's remit is not to provide for a wholesale change to the regulatory structure for the dismantled financial services industry, but to take away the barriers that had prevented financial conglomeration between banks, securities, and insurance firms.[89] The objective of the 1999 Act is to encourage the growth of financial conglomeration to enhance the efficiency of the financial system in the US. However, it does not allow the co-mingling of investment and commercial banking under the same roof, as seen in a 'universal bank' type model. The legislation in that respect is not a complete overhaul of the previous system, but only provides incremental change. It retains, in part, a functional system of regulation where financial businesses are overseen by their respective bodies: the SEC, the State Insurance Commissioner, and the state or federal regulators will respectively regulate the securities, insurance, and bank businesses.[90] But at the helm of this system is the Federal Reserve, with the responsibility of being 'lead regulator' to the financial system as a whole by acting as the consolidated supervisor of FHCs. In particular the Federal Reserve is to act as the 'umbrella supervisor for financial holding companies, and the state insurance regulators' for the purposes of coordinating supervision of FHCs that have bank and insurance company subsidiaries.[91]

The 1999 Act extends a bank holding company's scope by giving it the right to form an FHC[92] which can engage in activities of a financial nature or 'incidental to such activities' or 'incidental to a financial activity'[93] provided 'it does not pose a substantial risk to the safety and soundness of depository institutions'. The FRB in consultation with the US Treasury is empowered to decide what activities are 'financial in nature' or may be 'complementary' to financial activities.[94] The provision and the long list of activities included indicate that the idea of 'financial in nature' is interpreted broadly.[95] The restrictions on banks' affiliation with commercial businesses have been relaxed somewhat: FHCs can in certain circumstances hold shares in commercial companies for a limited period, after which they need to be divested.[96] The significant premise for the decision to extend the scope of activities in which an FHC can engage is the safety and soundness of the deposit-taking institution.[97]

The Federal Reserve is conferred formal oversight of both bank holding companies (BHCs) and FHCs for the purposes of consolidated supervision. The respective functional regulators are required to provide examination reports to the Federal Reserve.[98] It can on the findings of these reports or its own examination of the holding companies and their subsidiaries, take the necessary action to deal with their activities if they pose, inter alia, an adverse risk to the deposit-taking institution or the deposit insurance fund. The *Dodd-Frank Act* requires BHCs if they have consolidated assets of USD50 billion or greater to be under a programme of enhanced supervision and more stringent prudential standards to reduce the risks they give to the stability of the financial system.[99]

21.5. FINANCIAL STABILITY OVERSIGHT COUNCIL

The financial crisis highlighted the need to oversee macro- and micro-prudential matters so as to reduce systemic risks in the financial system. This is by any stretch of the imagination a significant task so that financial intermediaries and markets are regulated more effectively and consistently, to avoid gaps in the regulation of the whole financial system which could materialize into possible systemic risks. The primary objective of the Financial Stability Oversight Council (FSOC) is to undertake this huge task.[100] The FSOC is made up of regulators responsible for the financial system.[101] The FSOC has three primary purposes, namely: to identify risks to the US financial system from both within the system or outside for the purposes of financial stability by assessing risks that could arise from individual institutions or the activities of large interconnected banks or non-bank activities;[102] to re-establish the constructive ambiguity associated with the expectation counter-parties have that the government will bail banks or non-banks out of trouble;[103] and respond to emerging threats to the financial stability of the financial system.[104] In order to achieve its purpose it will be able to obtain information and monitor the financial markets both domestically and internationally in order to determine possible threats to the financial stability of the US financial system. It has the power to make recommendations to the member agencies for the purposes of following up on its findings. More importantly, it has the power to make recommendations to intensify the supervision undertaken by the primary federal agencies which includes, inter alia, the federal banking agencies, the SEC, the Commodity Futures Trading Commission, insurance authority, and the Federal Housing Finance Agency.[105] In exceptional circumstances the FSOC may determine a non-bank financial company poses a threat to the financial stability of the US and in such circumstances it could decide that the institution should be supervised by the Federal Reserve.[106] In order to decide whether to transfer a non-bank financial firm to the Federal Reserve the FSOC should take into account:

its leverage, off-balance sheet exposure and interconnectedness, among other factors.[107] These primarily determine whether the non-banking financial firm is 'too-big-to-fail' or 'too-interconnected-to-fail' and so requires supervision by the Federal Reserve. Moreover, the FSOC has the authority to make recommendations to the Federal Reserve regarding how it exercised authority to require that a non-bank financial company or BHC report a plan for its rapid and orderly resolution in the event of material financial distress or failure.[108]

The decision in respect of non-bank financial institutions is open to judicial review to determine whether the decision is arbitrary and capricious.[109] The fact that it has such a broad mandate does mean it could potentially be a very influential player for both banks and non-bank activities to mitigate the risks of another systemic crisis, especially with its ability to influence the intensity of supervision. This will be primarily determined by its ability to develop an independent viewpoint on matters that can withstand the viewpoints of the primary regulators and the Federal Reserve during the consultation period. Moreover, any measures it does recommend will need to be gauged against international efforts as well.

21.6. THE *DODD-FRANK ACT* IN AN HISTORICAL CONTEXT

No regulatory architecture has really come out of this crisis with its credentials intact whether it is a multi-agency or single agency model. However, the political response has been to revisit this area to alleviate some of the political pressure. The responses have been somewhat different with the US response being one of keeping the existing architectural structure in place. The underlying rationale for the US resistance to change the regulatory architecture may lay with the significant periods of US history such as the 'Progressive Era' when the 'New Deal' regulatory authorities were established which still resonate strongly today. These are in one form or another government agencies exercising its 'economic mission'.[110] With each financial crisis in the US the question immediately follows as to whether the US regulatory structure is fit for its purpose. In comparison to other jurisdictions the strength of the US federal regulatory agencies to resist such political pressure for reform is clearly evident, in light of this financial crisis and indeed subsequent crises as well. The debates and recommendations albeit well constructed never seem to sway the political will to actually change the architecture. Confidence in the federal regulatory authorities still exists rightly or wrongly that they can still protect the public interest by curbing the excesses of the financial industry and safeguard financial stability and consumer protection. The political net so to speak, of the government has extended rather than contracted with the new changes introduced by Dodd-Frank as the FRB will cover systemically important non-bank financial institutions as well which were once the sole responsibility of the SEC.

What did fail was day-to-day supervision both in the area of banking and non-banking activities and specifically in a number of areas such as capital and liquidity requirements and the lack of understanding of the systemic risk associated with structured finance, for instance. The *Dodd-Frank Act 2010* addresses many of the problems that surfaced during the financial crisis both in terms of regulatory and resolution reforms for both banks and non-banks by broadening the definition of systemically important institutions. These were gaps in financial regulation that were systemic in scope across all jurisdictions and not simply located in one single jurisdiction. Those issues require close attention rather than simply focusing on the regulatory architecture.

The establishment of the FSOC provides some degree of collective oversight between the various bank and non-bank federal authorities but this does not go as far as setting up a single authority for banks let alone for the whole financial system. This should achieve the objective of reducing the inconsistency in approach to regulation when banks and non-banks participate in the same activities. Moreover, the need for regulation of markets which previously lacked any real form of regulation should be addressed with its reducing systemic risk agenda. Whether the FSOC is a solution to ensure day-to-day supervisory cooperation between the federal regulatory authorities will need to be seen especially for those areas that transcend regulatory boundaries.

NOTES

1. See The Department of the Treasury blueprint for a modernized Financial regulatory structure, March 2008, available at <http://www.ustreas.gov/press/releases/reports/Blueprint.pdf> at pp. 13–14 and Jackson, Howell E., 'A Pragmatic Approach to the Phased Consolidation of Financial Regulation in the United States' (12 November 2008). Harvard Public Law Working Paper No. 09-19. Available at SSRN: http://ssrn.com/abstract=1300431.
2. GAO (1996), 'Bank oversight: Fundamental principles for modernizing the US structure', GAO/T-GGD-96-117.
3. Gart, A. (1993), *Regulation, Deregulation, Reregulation*, New York, John Wiley & Sons, at p. 140.
4. Ibid., at p. 143.
5. GAO (1994), 'Bank regulation: Consolidation of the regulatory agencies', GAO/T-GGD-94-106.
6. Ibid., at p. 2.

7. Ibid., at p. 6.
8. GAO (1987), 'Bank powers: Insulating banks from the potential risks of expanded activities', GAO/GGD-87-35, April; GAO (1988), 'Bank powers: Issues related to the repeal of the Glass-Steagall Act', GAO/GGD-88-37, January; GAO (1988) 'Testimony, using "firewalls" in a post-Glass-Steagall banking environment', GAO/T--GGD-88-25, April; GAO (1995), 'Testimony, financial regulation: Modernization of the financial services regulatory system', GAO/T-GGD-95-121. For examination of the regulatory structure that oversee the securities markets see GAO (1995), 'Testimony, financial regulation: Benefits and risks of merging SEC and CFTC', GAO/T-GGD-95-153, May.
9. GAO, GAO/GGD-88-37, at p. 16; GAO, GAO/T-GGD-95-121, at p. 6.
10. See Edwards, F. R. (1979), 'Banks and securities activities: Legal and economic perspectives on the Glass-Steagall Act', in Goldberg, L. G. and White, L. J. (eds), *The Deregulation of the Banking and Securities Industries*, Lexington, Mass, Lexington Books, pp. 273–291, at p. 275.
11. Shull, B. (2000), 'Financial modernization legislation in the United States: Background and implications', UNCTAD Discussion Paper No. 151, UNCTAD/OSG/DP/151.
12. Benston, G. (1990), *Separation of Commercial and Investment Banking: The Glass-Steagall Act Revisited and Reconsidered*, Oxford, Oxford University Press; White, E. (1986), 'Before the Glass-Steagall Act: An analysis of the investment banking activities of national banks', *Explorations in Economic History*, vol. 23, 33; Calomiris, C. W. (2000), *US Bank Deregulation in Historical Perspective*, Cambridge, Cambridge University Press.
13. Benston, ibid.; Senator Carter Glass contended that the abuse of the banks' powers to undertake securities business at that time undermined the safety and soundness of the banking system.
14. GAO (2004), 'Financial regulation: Industry changes prompt need to reconsider US regulatory structure', GAO-0561. Wilmarth, A. E. (2002), 'The transformation of the US financial services industry, 1975–2000: competition, consolidation and increased risks', *University of Illinois Law Review*, Vol. 2, 215, pp. 454–456.
15. A gateway for example does exist in for 'significant financial or operational' risks that may be evident see 12 USC, § 1831l, Coordination of risk analysis between SEC and Federal banking agencies.
16. GAO, n. 14 above, at p. 97.
17. GAO, n. 14 above, at p. 98.
18. Ibid., at p. 99.
19. Ibid., at p. 100.
20. Ibid., at p. 105.
21. GAO (2001), 'Financial services regulators: Better information sharing could reduce fraud', GAO-01-478T.
22. GAO, n. 14 above, at p. 109.
23. Ibid., at p. 110.
24. Ibid., at p. 113.
25. Wilmarth (2002), n. 14 above, at p. 456.
26. Ibid., at pp. 456–457.
27. GAO, n. 254 above, at p. 114.
28. Ibid.
29. Ibid., at pp. 129–132.
30. *Dodd-Frank Act:* Title III – Transfer of Powers to the Comptroller of the Currency, the Corporation, and the Board of Governors.
31. § 301(2).
32. § 502: see amendments § 313(a)–(c), in particular.
33. For an examination of the dual banking system see OCC (2003), *National Banks and the Dual Banking System*, in particular the limited powers of the state to intervene in the supervision of national banks, at p. 16; Schooner, H. M. (1996), 'Recent challenges

to the persistent dual banking system', *Saint Louis University Law Journal*, vol. 41, 263, at 267; Butler, H. N. and Macey, J. R. (1988), 'The myth of competition in the dual banking system', *Cornell Law Review*, vol. 73, 677. For a critique of the some of the limits of the dual banking system, in particular the utility of state involvement in banking regulation and supervision, see Wilmarth, A. E. (1990), 'The expansion of state bank powers, the federal response, and the case for preserving the dual banking system', *Fordham Law Review*, vol. 58, 1113, at 1239–55.

34. Redford, E. S. (1966), 'Dual banking: a case study in federalism', *Law and Contemporary Problems*, vol. 31, 749.
35. The *National Currency Act of 1863* and subsequently modernized with the enactment of the *National Bank Act of 1864*.
36. 12 USC, § 1.
37. Schooner, H. M. and Taylor, M. (1999), 'Convergence and competition: The case of bank regulation in Britain and the United States', *Michigan Journal of International Law*, vol. 20, 595, at 610.
38. OCC (2003), *National banks and the dual banking system*, in particular the limited powers of the state to intervene in the supervision of national banks, at p. 16.
39. For conversion from national banks to state banks see 12 USC, § 214(a).
40. Scott, K. E. (1977), 'The dual banking system: A model of competition in regulation', *Stanford Law Review*, vol. 30; Schooner, H. M. (1996), 'Recent challenges to the persistent dual banking system', *Saint Louis University Law Journal*, vol. 41, 263, at 272.
41. 12 USC § 1813(d)–(e).
42. 'Banking institutions and their regulators', available at <http://www.ny.frb.org/banking/regrept/BIATR.pdf>. This matrix provides a 'simple' outline of the primary regulators and membership system in the US system of regulation and supervision, deposit insurance and emergency liquidity support provided therein.
43. 12 USC § 282; Board of Governors of the Federal Reserve System (1994), *The Federal Reserve System: purposes and functions*, Washington, DC, available at <http://www.federalreserve.gov/pf/pf.htm>, at p. 12.
44. FDIC Forms, Interagency Charter and Federal Deposit Insurance Application, www.fdic.gov/regulations/laws/forms/.
45. 12 USC § 321.
46. See for instance 12 USC § 325–326.
47. See <http://www.federalreserve.gov/>.
48. See <http://www.occ.treas.gov/>.
49. See <http://www.fdic.gov/>.
50. § 312, 313.
51. For a historical account of the evolution of bank regulation at both state and federal level see Davis, A. K. (1966), 'Banking regulation today: A banker's view', *Law and Contemporary Problems*, vol. 31, 639.
52. 12 USC, Chapter 16.
53. 12 USC, Chapter 1.
54. 12 USC, Chapter 3.
55. Until 19 October 2011, 'Appropriate Federal Banking Agency' will also include the OTS. 12 USC § 1813(q)(1)–(4).
56. 12 CFR.
57. 12 USC § 27.
58. 12 CFR 4.2.
59. 12 USC § 481.
60. 12 USC § 161.
61. OCC (1996), *Bank Supervision Process*, p. 1; OCC, Comptroller of the Currency Administrator of National Banks (2005), *A Guide to the National Banking System*, Washington, DC, April, p. 3.
62. Until 19 October 2011, 'Appropriate Federal Banking Agency' will also include the OTS.

63. Revised Statutes of the United States § 327B. Deputy Comptroller for the Supervision and Examination of Federal Savings Associations.
64. *Federal Reserve Act of 1913*; Board of Governors of the Federal Reserve System (1944); *The Federal Reserve System: Purposes and Functions*, Washington, DC, available at <http://www.federalreserve.gov/pf/pf.htm>, p. 13.
65. Ibid.
66. Board of Governors of the Federal Reserve System, n. 65 above, at p. 72.
67. § 1101. *Federal Reserve Act* Amendments on Emergency Lending Authority.
68. § 1101(a)(6).
69. § 1101(a)(6).
70. § 1101(a)(6).
71. § 1104(a)(1).
72. § 1104(a)(2)(A)(B).
73. Board of Governors of the Federal Reserve System, n. 65 above, Chapter 5, Supervision and Regulation. For bank holding companies see *Bank Holding Company Act* of 1956 as amended 12 USC § 1841 *et seq.*; foreign banks, *International Banking Act 1978* as amended 12 USC § 3101, *et seq.*
74. § 312(b)(1)(A).
75. For example, FRB (2000), 'Framework for Financial Holding Company Supervision', Supervisory Letter SR 00-13, 15 August.
76. *Banking Act of 1933*, Public Law 73-66.
77. 12 USC § 1811(a).
78. 12 USC § 1811 *et seq.*
79. 12 USC § 1815.
80. § 312(b)(2)(c).
81. § 335(a).
82. § 331(b) Deposit Insurance Reforms.
83. § 334(d).
84. 12 USC § 3301–3308, in particular § 3305; for information about the Federal Financial Institutions Examination Council see <http://www.ffiec.gov/>.
85. FFIEC (1997), 'Interagency coordination of formal corrective action by the Federal Bank regulatory agencies', revised policy statement, February, available at <http://www.fdic.gov/regulations/laws/federal/rpsi.pdf>.
86. § 1011(a).
87. § 1022(c)(6)(B)(i).
88. Public Law 106-102, *Gramm-Leach-Bliley Act of 1999:* 'To enhance competition in the financial services industry by providing a prudential framework for the affiliation of banks, securities firms, insurance companies and other financial service providers, and for other purposes.'
89. Ibid, §§ 101, 103, and 104.
90. See Titles II and III GLB. For a critical analysis of functional regulation of a financial services industry where barriers are closely eroding away giving rise to financial conglomeration see, Schooner, H. M. (1998), 'Regulating risk not function', *University of Cincinnati Law Review*, vol. 66, 441.
91. Public Law 106-102, § 307.
92. It amends the *Bank Holding Company Act 1956*, § 4; Public Law 106-102, § 102.
93. Public Law 106-102, § 103 (s 4(k)(1)(A) and (B)).
94. Ibid, § 103 (s 4(k)(1)–(2)).
95. Ibid, § 103 (s 4(k)(4)).
96. Ibid, § 103 (s 4(n)).
97. In some instances a firewall is also allowed to be put in place; see Public Law 106-102, § 46, 'Safety and Soundness Firewalls for State Banks with Financial Subsidiaries' for insured state banks. In addition, to curb the risks associated with the title of 'too big to fail' for some FHCs the Federal Reserve and the Treasury are required to conduct a study into the 'feasibility' of FHCs holding 'a portion of their capital in the form

of subordinated debt to enhance the discipline within such groups by such creditors: Public Law 106-102, § 108.
98. Public Law 106-102, § 111.
99. § 165.
100. § 111. Financial Stability Oversight Council Established.
101. § 111(1)(A)–(J).
102. § 112(1)(A).
103. § 112(1)(B).
104. § 112(1)(C).
105. § 2(12).
106. § 113(a)(1). There is also power to transfer supervision of a foreign non-bank financial company to the Federal Reserve, see § 113(b).
107. § 113(a)(2).
108. § 115(d)(1).
109. § 113(e)(5)(h).
110. Moran, M. (2003), *The British Regulatory State: High Modernism and Hyper-Innovation*, OUP, 13–17.

22. An evaluation of the Canadian financial safety net during the global financial crisis[1]

John Raymond LaBrosse and James F. McCollum

22.1. INTRODUCTION

The Canadian financial sector came under some pressures during the financial crisis, but these were relatively moderate and largely imported. The Canadian banks were remarkably resilient, particularly compared to those of other major advanced countries, such as the US and the UK, and there were no institutional failures or bailouts. This performance has led some observers to suggest that Canadian public policy in this area – the characteristics of the financial safety net, including regulation, supervision and coordinating mechanisms – may provide a model for other countries.

The chapter starts with an overview of the entities that make up the financial system safety net and then describe, in Section 22.3, the coordinating mechanisms. In Section 22.4, we focus on the Canadian mortgage market and then consider the Canadian situation during the recent global financial crisis in Section 22.5. The resiliency of the Canadian system is examined in Section 22.6. In the penultimate section we propose some ways to address two important gaps in the financial safety net – a means to integrate the prospective national securities regulator into the safety net and a policy to locate responsibility for overall financial system stability within the safety net. The final section offers some conclusions.

22.2. THE PLAYERS

22.2.1. The Minister and Department of Finance

Through the Minister, the Department of Finance is the central agency that has ultimate responsibility for the overall soundness of the financial system and in resolving financial crises. The Department prepares legislation governing the financial safety net participants and measures respecting federal financial institutions and pension plans. Thus, it is the key player in setting financial sector policy.

During the recent financial crisis the federal government intervened directly in credit markets by acquiring mortgage assets from deposit-accepting institutions.[2] This was quite different from the Troubled Asset Relief Program (TARP) in the US, in that the assets were not impaired and, since the mortgages were guaranteed directly or indirectly by the government, there was no additional assumption of risk. Rather the purpose of the Canadian programme was to encourage the continued flow of credit via the banking sector to the real sector, and to reduce the probability of a negative feedback loop developing. This programme provided funds to the banks at a time when wholesale funding was very expensive and both securitized mortgage and business credit products were not selling very well.

The government also introduced a voluntary programme of insurance for inter-bank lending (the Canadian Lender Assurance Facility), in order that Canadian banks not be placed at an international disadvantage, given the introduction of similar programmes in other countries. The banks viewed the programme as overly costly and funds were not taken up. A special programme created to assist the life insurance companies was short lived and was not used.

22.2.2. Bank of Canada

The Bank of Canada is the ultimate supplier of currency and liquidity to the Canadian financial system and acts as the lender of last resort to the financial sector. While the Bank does not have a direct role in bank supervision and regulation, it does have responsibility for the oversight of systemically important clearing and settlement systems. Like all central banks, it closely monitors domestic and international financial developments through a number of channels, and provides the government with advice on the implications of such matters.

The Bank's lender of last resort function has three aspects. In the normal course of carrying out its responsibilities for the Large Value Transfer System, the Bank can supply overnight credit to direct participants through a Standing Liquidity Facility (SLF).[3] This facility provides assurance to the players in the system that they will be able to cover temporary shortfalls in settlements' balances and helps to ensure that the payments system, per se, is not a source of systemic risk. Advances are fully collateralized with assets that are acceptable to the Bank. During the recent financial crisis, the Bank made various adjustments to the facility and introduced additional facilities as precautionary measures. While the SLF was made more flexible during the crisis, it is nevertheless the case that SLF operations are part of the normal course of running the business of the Canadian payments system; as well, the modifications were used to free up collateral that could be used elsewhere and to stabilize interest rates during the crisis. This was done by lending longer than the usual overnight term, broadening the range of acceptable collateral to free up collateral for use in the system and, should it have been necessary, expanding the Bank's counterparty list to counteract liquidity hoarding.[4] The supplementary facilities under the SLF were not heavily used and some have expired.

The Emergency Lending Assistance (ELA) programme is closest to what is usually thought of as the lender of last resort function of a central bank. The Bank can provide assistance to a deposit-accepting institution that faces a liquidity problem as long as the institution is determined to be viable by the Office of the Superintendent of Financial Institutions (OSFI). The raison d'être of the ELA is to prevent a problem associated with one financial institution from spreading to other institutions. The terms and conditions of ELA borrowing are such that potential borrowers are encouraged to first look for private sector support and the facility has been rarely used.

In the event of severe or unusual stress in the financial system, a 1997 amendment to the *Bank of Canada Act* gives the Bank the authority to provide additional liquidity to the system through the purchase of a variety of securities issued by Canadian or foreign entities if, in the opinion of the Governor, such action is considered necessary to preserve the safety and soundness of the Canadian financial system. This authority has never been used.

The Governor is legislatively required to meet frequently with the Minister of Finance and there is considerable interaction between Bank officials and their counterparts within the 'Ottawa agencies'. Notably, the Governor sits on the Board of Canada Deposit Insurance Corporation (CDIC), and is a member of both the Financial Institutions Supervisory Committee (FISC) and the Senior Advisory Committee (SAC). Among the 'Ottawa agencies' only the Deputy Minister of Finance is an *ex officio* member of the Bank of Canada's Board.

22.2.3. OSFI

The Superintendent of Financial Institutions is appointed by the Cabinet and the Office is the prudential regulator of banks and other federally incorporated financial institutions, some of the central credit unions as well as private pension plans under federal jurisdiction. Additionally,

OSFI supervises provincially incorporated financial institutions on a contractual basis with some provinces. Deposit-accepting institutions account for almost 80 per cent of assets at regulated institutions and pension plans, life insurance companies close to 14 per cent, property and casualty companies 3 per cent and federal private pension plans close to 4 per cent.

OSFI supervises federal financial institutions to determine their soundness and extensive use is made of an important tool called the 'Guide to Intervention'[5] that emphasizes the independence, accountability and transparency of the prudential regulatory system. In the event that significant deficiencies are found at a regulated institution, supervisory attention is enhanced and boards and managements are required to take prompt corrective action. OSFI's mandate requires it to focus on protecting depositors' and other creditors' interests and both it and CDIC are obligated to deal promptly with problem institutions. The focus and requirements of its mandate have served to reduce the risk of a run on a bank.[6] However, with much of OSFI's efforts focused on individual financial institutions or pension plans, it monitors and evaluates systemic risks only as they may impact negatively on the institutions that it supervises.[7]

22.2.4. CDIC

As a crown agency, CDIC provides protection for deposits in banks, other federally incorporated financial institutions and some provincial trust companies. Its statutory objectives are to provide insurance against the loss of part or all of deposits, and to promote and otherwise contribute to the stability of the financial system in Canada. These objects are to be pursued for the benefit of persons having deposits with member institutions and in such a manner as to minimize the exposure of the Corporation to loss. Interestingly, CDIC, not the Bank of Canada, is the only member of the Canadian financial system safety net that has a mandate that includes financial stability. We return to this point later in the chapter.

In the normal course of events, CDIC monitors the risk level of its members, with closer monitoring for those institutions which pose higher risk as required by the Guide to Intervention. It has a strong incentive to identify problem institutions in an expeditious manner and have them take prompt corrective action. In the early 1990s CDIC developed 'Standards of Sound Business and Financial Practices' for its members based on best management practices used by the banks and trust companies; the Standards are used by OSFI as benchmarks in supervising financial institutions.[8] CDIC's differential premium system encourages its members to act in a financially prudent manner; in fact, deterioration in a member's classification carries a financial, as well as a reputational penalty.[9] CDIC has other measures at its disposal, including the ability to apply premium surcharges, impose conditions on a member in terms of the kinds of deposits that can be raised from the public and it can cancel the insurance policy of a member which would effectively prevent it from raising retail deposits.

The Corporation can provide liquidity and, if appropriate, support to a member institution through loans, guarantees and deposits provided that such actions reduce its exposure to loss. Since CDIC was established in 1967 there have been many changes to its governing legislation, as part of a continuous improvement process, incorporating lessons learned from dealing with troubled members. Recent amendments have focused on the ability of CDIC to create 'bridge banks' to enhance the provisions that were incorporated into the *Canada Deposit Insurance Corporation Act* in the early 1990s.[10] To date, neither of these provisions has been used.

22.2.5. The Financial Consumer Agency of Canada (FCAC)

The FCAC has the responsibility to promote the rights and interests of consumers of financial services in Canada. It has an interest in ensuring that financial consumers are not subject to undue risk and that financial institutions disclose sufficient information about such things as the full cost of borrowing, to facilitate informed client decision-making. It also plays an educational role, encouraging consumers to use financial services wisely and prudently, to compare costs and not to become over-extended. It does not appear, however, to have a role in informing investors regarding risks associated with securities matters and financial advisory providers which seems at odds with the name of the organization.

22.2.6. The Provincial Governments

For completeness, it should be noted that jurisdiction over financial sector matters is shared with the provincial governments. The provinces regulate credit unions and *caisses populaires*, some insurance companies, provincially incorporated deposit-accepting institutions such as trust companies, many pension funds and the securities industry. In gross terms, however, the trend has been for federal regulation given the very high percentage of total financial sector assets under federal purview.

22.3. THE COORDINATING MECHANISMS

In order to ensure the effectiveness of a financial system safety net, close cooperation and goodwill among the participants is essential. Indeed, coordination of activities along with effective information sharing and confidentiality are particularly relevant. Best international practice suggests that arrangements should be explicit and designed to avoid or minimize jurisdictional confusion and inconsistent responses. The importance of inter-relationships can be summed up, in layman's terms, by the expression 'Good Fences Make Good Neighbours'. Strong accountability regimes are essential to provide clear mandates and the right incentives to ensure that the safety net participants fulfil their responsibilities. There are a number of means that support the interaction and exchange of information which have evolved over time concerning the activities of the so-called 'Ottawa agencies'.

22.3.1. Financial Institutions Supervisory Committee (FISC)

The FISC is mainly a contingency planning committee, not a board; it was established under the *Superintendent of Financial Institutions Act* in 1987. It is chaired by the Superintendent of Financial Institutions and meets regularly to discuss financial institution supervisory issues. In addition to the Superintendent, its membership consists of the Deputy Minister of Finance, the Governor of the Bank of Canada, the Chair of the CDIC, and the Commissioner of the FCAC. It facilitates a coordinated interagency approach when it comes to supervisory issues which could affect institutional solvency, last resort lending, and deposit insurance payouts. FISC plays an important role in ensuring consistency and in coordinating efforts among the safety net players to deal with troubled institutions and in the identification of problematic situations. The FISC does not have any reporting or disclosure requirements to Parliament or to the public.

22.3.2. Senior Advisory Committee (SAC)

This is an ad hoc committee, has the same membership as the FISC, and is chaired by the Deputy Minister of Finance. It covers much of the same territory as FISC but it has a wider focus. SAC is concerned with the operation of the financial system more generally, including markets as well as institutions, international financial and exchange market policy, the efficiency of the financial system, payments and settlements matters, systemic issues, and so forth.

22.3.3. The CDIC Board

A major element of financial sector stability in Canada relates to the activities of CDIC and the understanding by the public of the role of deposit protection. CDIC's Board includes the Governor of the Bank of Canada, the Finance Deputy Minister, the Commissioner of the FCAC, the Superintendent of Financial Institutions and a Deputy, five private sector directors plus the Chair. Through the efforts of the 'Ottawa agencies', CDIC issued a by-law in the 1990s requiring member institutions to follow the 'Standards' noted earlier. The Standards form part of OSFI's supervisory activities[11] and they are used as an important element to support the CDIC risk-based differentiated deposit insurance premiums.

22.3.4. Interagency Relations

This is an informal, but important, element. The 'Ottawa agencies' are all located within a small area in the central core of the capital city and are within walking distance of one another. Moreover, there is constant communication and meetings among their respective staffs on a wide variety of economic and financial issues, as well as an interchange of personnel both at the desk officer and senior management levels. These frequent contacts promote a mutual appreciation of cross-institutional concerns and the emphasis is on inter-agency cooperation rather than competition.

The mechanisms that have been created to date have been quite effective in dealing with individual financial institution matters or problems. One important aspect that is missing, however, is a means to coordinate a response to a systemic crisis particularly when it comes, in the main, to a market situation or turmoil in a market emanating from an unregulated source. The handling of the Asset-Backed Commercial Paper (ABCP) issue is a case that we examine in Section 22.4 when we review the resiliency of the Canadian financial system.

At the international level, in recent years, staff from the 'Ottawa agencies' have been very active in the work of the Basel Committee on Banking Supervision, the Financial Stability Board, the Committee on Payment and Settlement Systems, and the Committee on the Global Financial System.

22.4. THE CANADIAN MORTGAGE MARKET

Certain aspects of housing finance in Canada have helped make the financial system very robust. While high-ratio loans (those that have an 80 per cent and above loan-to-value ratio) are quite common there is a regulatory requirement that banks can only invest in them if they are insured either by Canada Mortgage and Housing Corporation[12] (CMHC, which is a federal government crown agency) or a private sector insurer which, in turn, is back-stopped by the federal government. In the case of non-insured mortgages, banks require a minimum of a 20 per cent initial owner equity position.[13] Moreover, mortgage interest in Canada is not tax-deductible and, while there is no capital gains tax on the sale of a principal residence, there is on secondary residences. These aspects provide an incentive for homeowners to build up equity in their principal residence (since the after-tax rate of return of paying down a mortgage relative to holding interest-bearing securities is high and carries low-risk) and, compared to the US, there is less of an incentive for small investors to engage in residential real estate speculation.

Most Canadian mortgages are initiated in the banking sector and the banks have branches across the country which limits their interest in purchasing mortgage-backed securities for geographical diversification purposes. While there is such a market, mortgage-backed securities in Canada largely consist of bundles of fully insured loans and are similar to government bonds (since the mortgages underlying the security are backed directly or indirectly by the government). They are a much less important source of mortgage finance in Canada than in the US. Most mortgages are held directly on lenders' balance sheets (about one half of chartered bank loans are mortgages and mortgages account for around 35 per cent of their assets), which facilitates closer monitoring. In fact, there is no counterpart to the US sub-prime mortgage-backed security in Canada. While there was some decline in housing prices in Canada, particularly in Western Canada, there was no real estate meltdown, foreclosures did not spiral upwards and neither mortgages nor mortgage derivative instruments have posed a problem for banks.

22.5. THE CANADIAN SITUATION DURING THE FINANCIAL CRISIS

Paul Krugman asked why Iceland's meltdown made headlines but the remarkable stability of Canada's banks attracted very little attention, the suggestion being that some aspects of the Canadian system might be worthy of imitation elsewhere.[14] There are a number of reasons why the Canadian system performed so well during the crisis. Some of them relate to the operation and improvements in the financial supervisory and regulatory system and a strong macroeconomic situation which contributed to the government's healthy fiscal position before the start of the crisis, while others are connected to the make-up and approach to managing risks by the individual banks themselves. However, in hindsight, it appears that there may have been a bit of 'luck' involved, particularly in respect of the turmoil in the market for ABCP discussed in the next section.

A White Paper aimed at enhancing the efficiency and stability of the financial system was issued by the Department of Finance in 1995. That paper contained recommendations drawn from lessons learned from the failures of financial institutions in the 1980s and 1990s. One of the measures adopted was development of the 'Standards' noted earlier and they have since been incorporated into the actual business practices of Canadian banks.[15]

It is important to note that prudential regulation and supervision in Canada only allow viable banks to operate.[16] There are a number of other distinguishing factors. First, as shown in Tables 22.1 and 22.2, the capital positions of Canadian banks are higher than their international peers, they are of better quality[17] and only Canadian and US bank regulators among G7 countries impose leverage caps. Two large Swiss banks, UBS and Credit Suisse, will have their ratios reduced from 33⅓ to 25 by 2013 but those leverage ratios are still above the Tier 1 and 2 ratios of Canadian banks of 20 to 1. Tier 1 capital for US banks is also scheduled to be reduced from 33⅓ to 25.

Table 22.1. Regulatory Leverage Ratio Limits

Country	Numerator	Denominator	Maximum
Canada	On-balance-sheet assets plus specified off-balance sheet exposures[18]	Tier 1 and 2 Capital	20
Switzerland	On-balance-sheet assets, but excluding domestic lending	Tier 1 Capital	33⅓ / 25
US	Only on-balance-sheet assets	Tier 1 Capital[19]	33⅓/ 25

Note: Canadian banks have to hold Tier 1 capital of at least 7 per cent (versus 6 per cent in the US) of risk-weighted assets (RWA), and total capital of 10 per cent (versus 8 per cent in most other G7 countries) of RWA as shown below.

Table 22.2. Tier 1 and 2 Capital Requirement as a Percent of Risk-Weighted Assets

	Basel II	Canada	US	France	Germany	Italy	Japan	UK
Tier 1 Capital	4	7	6	4	4	4	4/2[20]	4
Total Capital	8	10	10	8	8	8	8/4	8

The Canadian system of consolidated supervision coupled with bank ownership of the investments dealers and the fact that the investment dealer claims on bank capital are quite small are features particular to Canada which have promoted resiliency. By contrast, the US investment banks were not subject to equivalent bank capital requirements and they needed to find protection through the creation of bank holding company structures regulated by the Federal Reserve Board. Those particular steps exposed the US financial system safety net to additional risks.

The Canadian economy was less heavily financially exposed at the start of the crisis: private and public sector balance sheets were in better shape than most countries; the Canadian mortgage market did not have a large sub-prime component and did not witness the proliferation of products and marketing practices that led to serious problems elsewhere; the prudential regulatory system in Canada was not put under the same sorts of pressures; the Canadian banking system was not unduly reliant on funding from abroad; Canadian banks were not heavily exposed to European sovereign debt; and the Canadian dollar appreciated against most major currencies. It is nonetheless important to consider some issues relevant to the resiliency of the Canadian financial system along with some longer-term issues should be taken into account in enhancing financial stability.

22.6. RESILIENCY OF THE CANADIAN SYSTEM

The Bank of Canada discontinued two of its less-used extraordinary liquidity facilities at the end of October 2009 and the authorities have been actively contributing to international work to raise global bank capital standards.[21] More recently, as financial conditions have improved, the Bank has been able to raise its target for the overnight interest rate and the Governor has signalled that further increases are to be expected.[22] At the political level, the federal government has been successful in deflecting the imposition of a global bank tax and, at home, emphasis has been on measures to reform some aspects of housing finance. On the other hand, there have been no initiatives to seek public input on lessons learned from the global financial crisis.

While it is clear that the Canadian financial sector performed very well during the crisis, there are some shortcomings when it comes to the regulatory/supervisory framework. Some of these are Canada-specific, while others are common to most countries with complex financial systems. The most striking Canada-specific deficiency is the area of securities regulation; additionally, in common with other countries, there has been insufficient attention to macro-prudential (systemic) concerns.

Canada does not yet have a national securities regulator and there is no single organization or person that can stand up and attest to the integrity of securities markets; rather, securities regulation is a provincial responsibility and there are 13 separate regulatory bodies. The system is costly, inefficient, confusing as to which commission has jurisdiction, lacks transparency and it does not give the 'Ottawa agencies' a clear window on the state of securities markets which, as in many developed markets, can be an important source of systemic risk or potential financial sector disruption.

The fragmentation of securities regulation in Canada complicates coordination with other safety net players and hampers effective contingency planning for major financial problems. The fact that there are so many players involved can result in a delay of response times – which can be critical if events are unfolding rapidly. For example, during the financial turmoil of 2008/09, it would have been difficult to halt short-selling of equities in a timely manner.

A clear example of a recent Canadian regulatory and supervisory failure was the collapse of the non-bank ABCP market, which had certain features in common with the sub-prime mortgage-backed securities market in the US. It should be noted that concerns of the Bank of Canada were voiced about the ABCP market as early as 2003.[23] Their attention focused on the lack of liquidity support for ABCP and the lack of any effort to protect retail investors.[24] No actions were taken following those warnings and in mid-2007 the ABCP market collapsed when conduits were unable to rollover maturing notes. Behind the problem was a maturity mismatch in combination with the use of overly-risky derivative instruments.

Because ABCP was considered to be commercial paper it was unregulated and not subject to prospectus requirements. The backstop providers of liquidity were offshore banks and non-bank financial institutions and, as it turned out, the wording of the various liquidity guarantees rendered them virtually meaningless. Despite the lack of transparency, the high degree of leverage, the lack of regulation and the use of unconventional stand-by lines of credit, the rating agencies gave ABCP their highest ratings. The OSFI was also drawn into the line of fire but it made it clear that it had no obligation to ABCP investors.[25] When the sub-prime crisis surfaced in the US the ABCP market in Canada quickly unravelled and there was no locus of responsibility within the 'Ottawa agencies', who were mere bystanders. Interestingly, the FCAC played no role in cautioning ABCP investors which seems at odds with the name of the organization. The non-bank ABCP was, in some sense, an accident waiting to happen and a number of factors, such as a rise in interest rates, could have triggered its collapse. Timing is perhaps where 'luck' played an important role.[26]

Quite apart from the travails of the ABCP market, once the global financial crisis was in full swing, it became clear that the financial safety net structures around the world were not adequate to the task and that there were financial risks of a system-wide nature that were not being appropriately addressed. For the most part regulation and oversight is focused on institutions (that is to say, is a given financial institution being operated in a prudent manner, does it have adequate risk-management procedures in place, and so on), rather than on markets. While this covers many of the major risks to the financial system, it does not cover them all. Additionally, the risk aversion tactics of members of the system may actually jeopardize the system taken as a whole, since they may call for actions which, when taken in unison, can exaggerate financial swings.

It would be incorrect, however, to conclude that systemic risk has been totally overlooked in Canada. Such considerations have been at the forefront in designing systemically important clearance and settlement systems, creating the deposit insurance system and mandating early intervention. It was also a major factor in enhancing the Bank of Canada's authority to provide additional liquidity to the financial system. But, certain macro-prudential concerns have yet to be adequately addressed within the current Canadian system. They include:

- institutional linkages (examples would be inter-bank lending within the global financial system, guarantees and other counterparty exposures)[27] and monitoring thereof;
- the macro-economic or systemic implications of the use of value-at-risk management systems which can exaggerate financial swings or not adequately reflect the cyclicality of margins;
- the level of margin requirements on securities transactions;
- designating in legislation which agency or Minister is truly responsible for monitoring and dealing with systemic risk and providing that body[28] with the appropriate authorities;
- closer monitoring and assessment of the risks associated with the rapid growth of new instruments (such as ABCP and mortgage-backed securities);
- an assessment of the risks associated with off-balance sheet items and whether they involve contingent liabilities;
- risks associated with over-the-counter derivatives (in particular the lack of liquidity, counterparties and standardization) and the transparency of composite financial instruments; and
- the development of tools and procedures (such as memorandums of understanding (MoU)) to help deal with imported financial disturbances.

22.7. IMPROVING THE CANADIAN FINANCIAL SYSTEM SAFETY NET BY ADDRESSING THE GAPS

A national securities law should help improve the protection afforded to retail investors.[29] With the creation of the Canadian Securities Regulatory Authority (CSRA), it is timely to consider improvements in the functioning of the evolving financial system safety net to better equip the responsible authorities with the tools they need to address systemic risk issues from wherever they emanate. As such, the head of the CSRA should be given an opportunity to join some of the so-called 'Ottawa' coordinating committees.

The most obvious body where the views of the CSRA would be useful is the SAC. However, the Minister of Finance may not want to expand that body, as it is a source of private advice and, if it were enlarged, there would be pressure to impose public reporting requirements on it; however, such a requirement would be consistent with processes being developed elsewhere.[30] The UK, for example, has created a Financial Stability Council and the US is undertaking a review of the crisis through a special Congressional commission.

It would be inappropriate for the head of the CSRA to join FISC. This is because discussions within that grouping are largely focused on issues surrounding problem institutions which are, by their nature, highly confidential. Since securities market regulators rely heavily on disclosure the head of the CSRA would not be able to participate when a problem institution is discussed at FISC.

To address governance issues more generally, and the growing number of 'safety net' agencies at the federal and provincial levels, it may be timely to create a Canadian Financial Stability Board (CFSB). A CFSB would include high level representation from the Bank of Canada, OSFI, CDIC, FCAC, CSRA, the provincial securities commissions and, given the importance of housing finance issues, CMHC. There are a number of areas that a CFSB could focus on.

The terms of reference of the CFSB should include the promotion of financial sector stability which could be supported by agreements between the 'Ottawa' agencies including the CSRA, the provincial securities agencies, and any relevant provincial Ministries. The CFSB could play an important coordinating role and undertake needed work regarding prudential issues such as:[31]

Macro Issues:

- sources of systemic risk with recommendations to the relevant agencies on how to best respond to them;

- reviewing the lessons learned from elsewhere and their possible implications for Canada;
- the development of contingency plans by all of the financial safety net players to prepare for possible financial crises;
- undertaking a study with recommendations on the use and pricing of government guarantees;
- undertaking a formal review of the lessons learned from the experiences with ABCP in Canada which could also address what should be done with the substantial amount of fines that were collected;[32]
- developing recommendations to enhance market discipline and reduce potential conflicts of interest, including a review of the role of ratings in securities legislation and how those credit rating agencies are overseen;
- reviewing the adequacy of the Canadian derivatives market with a focus on whether and how it should be regulated; and
- understanding better the exposure of Canadian financial institutions to risks due to cross-border counterparties and the transfer of risks through instruments such as credit default swaps.

Micro Issues:

- to further protect the federal government's guarantee, the *CDIC Act* should be amended to require Material Loss Reviews[33] when a member institution fails or receives any form of financial assistance;
- there should be a review of the mandate of the FCAC to better focus its role in the handling of instruments like ABCP and consumer protection issues related to financial planning;
- there should be a study of lenders' compensation policies, how they affect banks' risk profiles and whether certain pay structures should be taken into account when assessing deposit insurance premiums;
- there should be a review of the Canadian Secured Credit Facility that was used to purchase up to CAD$12 billion in securities backed by loans and leases on vehicles and equipment; and
- there should be a review of the accounting rules for financial institutions to ensure that the new capital rules align with the actual risk exposures of banks.

As a legislated committee, a CFSB should be required to publish minutes from its meetings, seek public input, expand on the contacts that the current agencies have with international bodies, and it could assist the Bank of Canada in its monitoring and analysis of the financial system. To improve accountability and transparency, the Bank's Quarterly *Financial*

System Review could be given a higher status by having it referred to a Parliamentary Committee.

22.8. CONCLUSIONS

The performance of the Canadian financial system and the response of the authorities during the recent global financial crisis have been described by at least one observer as 'boring'. Presumably this is because the financial sector did not become stressed and the safety net players did not need to engage in dramatic manoeuvres. There were no financial firm failures and actions by the authorities were precautionary in nature or designed to ensure that normal payments and credit flows were not inadvertently disrupted. Some of the facilities put in place by the Bank of Canada and Ministry of Finance were used, while others, in the end, were not needed and have expired.

The foundations for the stability of the Canadian financial system were established long ago. The last major bank failure in Canada was in 1923. While there have been bank failures since that time, they have been uncommon and limited to small, often start-up, operations. Following the failures of Northland Bank and Canadian Commercial Bank in 1984, the supervisory and regulatory system was strengthened and subsequent reforms have reinforced this.

The Canadian banks are well capitalized by international standards, lending practices have been conservative and housing sector exposure has not been problematic. The banks have a stable deposit base, are able to charge profitable fees for banking services, enjoy relatively stable share prices and they have not placed heavy reliance on securitization. Regulation and supervision are not as fragmented as in the US, there are stricter limits on bank leverage, banks are regulated on a consolidated basis and the supervisor has access to considerable information on individual institutions, most off-balance activities are subject to capital requirements, there is an effective deposit insurance system which in conjunction with prompt corrective action limits moral hazard, and there are mechanisms in place to ensure a consistent response by the relevant safety net players as well as a long history of cooperation among them.

Looking forward, with the introduction of a national securities law and the creation of the CSRA, there is an opportunity to address a significant gap in the Canadian financial system safety net and by expanding the safety net coordinating mechanisms to include CMHC. These changes would further strengthen the system. In other countries, there is an ongoing debate on how best to monitor and respond to various systemic issues which the existing safety net may not adequately address and we have noted several possibilities for remedial action in Canada such as the creation of a CFSB. Through the establishment of a CFSB there is an important opportunity to strengthen the safety net further by expanding the consultation mechanisms to include both the CSRA and CMHC and to establish an organization with a specific mandate to pursue financial stability with supporting powers and responsibilities. In accordance with good governance, a CSFB should be independent, accountable, transparent and composed of individuals with relevant backgrounds.

NOTES

1. This paper was presented by J. R. LaBrosse at the Banking Law Symposium on Managing Systemic Risk, 7–9 April 2010 held at the University of Warwick. We would like to thank David Walker, Garth McNaughton, Rodrigo Olivares-Caminal and especially Mark Zelmer and Jack Selody for their helpful comments on earlier drafts of this chapter. Any remaining errors or omissions are the responsibility of the authors.
2. In a Budget presented in 2009 the Minister of Finance announced some programmes that were administered by the Export Development Corporation and the Business Development Bank to assist the provision of credit to businesses.
3. For a description of the Bank's activities during the crisis please see http://www.bankofcanada.ca/en/review/autumn09/zorn.pdf.
4. We are grateful to Jack Selody for pointing out that the 1997 amendments to the *Bank of Canada Act* facilitated some of those actions.
5. The 'Guide to Intervention' was proposed in a White Paper issued by the Department of Finance in February 1995. It set out details on the nature of prudential regulatory actions to be followed by the OSFI and CDIC. For details on the five-stage process please see http://www.osfi.gc.ca/osfi/index_e.aspx?ArticleID=537@criteria=guide per cent20to per cent20intervention&templateID=2, accessed 2 June 2010.
6. For more details on OSFI's mandate see: http://www.osfi-bsif.gc.ca/osfi/index_e.aspx?ArticleID=3586, accessed 18 March 2010.
7. During the asset-backed commercial paper (ABCP) debacle, discussed later in this chapter, the Superintendent of Financial Institutions was questioned as to the role of OSFI in respect to the market's problems. It was made clear that OSFI had assessed the impact of the freezing of the ABCP markets on all federally regulated institutions. The Office found that very few of the institutions they oversee had material exposure to non-bank ABCP. The private pension plans that OSFI oversees also had virtually no exposure. Please see Remarks by Superintendent Julie Dickson, to the House of Commons Standing Committee on Finance, June 2008: http://www.osfi.gc.ca/app/DocRepository/1/eng/speeches/ABCP_Hearing_Opening_Statement_e.pdf, accessed 2 June 2010. There were no specifics offered on how investors could best proceed or what precautions they should take.
8. The Standards were first implemented through a CDIC by-law. That by-law was repealed in 2005 and responsibility for them was transferred to OSFI. The Standards are integrated in OSFI's guidelines and examination protocols.
9. The financial penalty is severe. There are four premium levels. When a CDIC-member moves from one level to the next level premiums double.
10. A bridge bank is a technique used by banking regulators to transition the gap between a failing bank and a continuing institution. The US has made extensive use of this technique and proposals have been developed for other countries. In the US, for example,

the authorities create a bridge bank as a temporary national bank chartered by the Office of the Comptroller of the Currency and organized by the FDIC to take over and maintain banking services for the customers of a failed bank. After a period, the FDIC hopes to implement a satisfactory acquisition by a third party. For further discussion of bridge banks please see LaBrosse, J. R. (2009), 'International Experience and Policy Issues in the Growing Use of Bridge Bank,' in LaBrosse et al., *Financial Crisis Management and Bank Resolution*, London: Informa Law, especially Chapters 14 and 19.

11. CDIC was given the responsibility to develop the 'Standards' following the failure of a number of small banks in the late 1980s. The Standards are high-level best practices that address capital management, credit risk management, internal controls, foreign exchange risk management, interest rate risk management, liquidity management, real estate appraisals, and securities portfolio management of member institutions.
12. CMHC does not report to the Minister of Finance although that Minister can exercise some control over the Corporation through its borrowing programme. While it could be considered one of the so-called 'Ottawa agencies' it does not have a seat on any of the coordinating mechanisms. This is somewhat surprising given the importance of housing finance and that the Corporation can heavily influence mortgage lending provisions such as loan-to-value ratios and premiums paid by borrowers to obtain *National Housing Act* (NHA)-insured mortgages. In recent periods it has been the Minister of Finance who has been quite vocal on such matters.
13. It is acknowledged that mortgage borrowers could borrow funds by way of second or third mortgages which can be secured against the property. As well, a significant share of mortgage financing occurs outside the regulated sector by way of arrangements between individuals.
14. See Krugman, P. (31 January 2010), *The New York Times*, op ed. column.
15. See, for example, the Royal Bank of Canada, Annual Information Form, 16 December 2003 which makes several references to the Standards. At a practical level the directing minds of a CDIC member are required to acknowledge and attest to the bank's ability to comply with the Standards. In doing so a bank's board is required to report periodically on the criteria, methods, and means to ensure compliance. Indeed, the level of insurance premiums paid by a bank is linked to a system where by CDIC categorizes each bank, according to its assessment of various quantitative and qualitative factors and criteria.
16. In Canada, the trigger to close a bank used by OSFI is 'viability' as opposed to 'insolvency', which is used in many other markets. Deposit insurers tend to support a 'viability' trigger since it should lead to greater value being left in the bank than at the point of insolvency and provide better protection to the insurer than an insolvency trigger.
17. OSFI requires that 75 per cent of a bank's Tier 1 capital be in the form of common shares.
18. Canadian specified off-balance sheet exposures include direct credit substitutes, trade- and transaction-related contingencies, and repurchase agreements.
19. US banks that meet certain criteria of strength and sophistication are subject to a 33⅓ maximum leverage ratio. All others are limited to 25.
20. The higher (lower) requirements apply to internationally active (domestically orientated) Japanese banks.
21. Bank of Canada, *Financial System Review*, December 2009.
22. Please see http://www.bankofcanada.ca/en/fixed-dates/2010/rate_010610.html, accessed 6 June 2010.
23. In June 2003 researchers at the Bank of Canada focused on the mechanics of credit risk reduction, legal risks associated with the securitization of risk reduction, disclosure issues concerning the lack of transaction details and the degree of real risk transfer. Please see Toovey, P. and Kiff, J. (June 2003), 'Developments and Issues in the Canadian Market for Asset-Backed Commercial Paper', *Bank of Canada Financial System Review*, pp. 43–49.
24. The problems surrounding the plight of the ABCP market were eerily reminiscent of the

collapse of a firm called Atlantic Acceptance, in the 1960s, which resulted in the creation of the 'Porter Royal Commission on Finance' and led to a substantial overhaul of the Canadian prudential regulatory system. The introduction of deposit insurance in 1967 was also a fallout of the Atlantic Acceptance problems.

25. See n. 7.
26. Had the ABCP market collapsed in the fall of 2008, the situation in Canada could have been much worse because the ABCP market would likely have been much larger and the timing of the collapse would have been closer to the problems of Bear Stearns and the closure of Lehman Brothers and there could have been greater spillover or contagion effects. The existence of a true 'national securities commission' could have provided greater insight into the sources of systemic issues in securities markets and provided the basis for effective contingency planning on the part of all of the financial safety net players. Also, a national body could have played a role in improving investor protection.
27. Bank of Canada researchers found that 'systemic capital allocations can differ substantially from reported capital levels and are not related in a simple way to bank size or individual bank default probability'. They also noted that 'systemic capital allocation mechanisms reduce default probabilities of individual banks as well as the probability of a systemic crisis by about 25 per cent'. Their results suggest that 'financial stability can be enhanced substantially by implementing a systemic perspective on bank regulation'. Please see Gauthier, C., Lehar, A. and Souissi, M. (January 2010), *Macroprudential Regulation and Systemic Capital Requirements*, Bank of Canada Working Paper 2010-4.
28. Logically, the mandate of the Bank of Canada should be expanded to include the promotion of financial stability but attempts to modify its mandate have proved difficult in the past.
29. With the creation of a national regulator, provincial participation will be voluntary, which suggests that regulatory arbitrage could remain a problem. Still, a national body could play an important coordinating role for the other commissions in a crisis, it could enhance the focus on issues within securities markets that may lead to instability and there is a potential to even broaden its scope to help protect sophisticated investors, which is becoming increasingly more of an issue. For details on the proposal please see http://www.fin.gc.ca/n10/10-051-eng.asp, accessed 2 June 2010.
30. The IMF has shown that the quality of regulatory governance and governance practices adopted by financial system regulators and supervisors matters for financial system soundness. For further views on this area please see Udaibir, S.D., Quintyn, M. and Chenard, K. (May 2004), *Does Regulatory Governance Matter for Financial System Stability? An Empirical Analysis*, IMF Working Paper WP/04/89.
31. In order to eliminate overlap and duplication the Bank of Canada could provide the Secretariat to the CSRA.
32. Material loss reviews are mandated in the US under Section 38(k) of the *Federal Deposit Insurance Act* when the FDIC incurs a loss greater than USD25 million or 2 per cent of a FDIC member institution's total assets at the time the FDIC was appointed receiver.
33. Material loss reviews are mandated in the US under section 38(k) of the *Federal Deposit Insurance Act* which states that when the Deposit Insurance Fund incurs a material loss with respect to an insured depository institution, the inspector general of the appropriate Federal banking agency shall make a written report to that agency reviewing the agency's supervision of the institution (including the agency's implementation of prompt corrective action provisions of section 38), which shall ascertain why the institution's problems resulted in a material loss to the Deposit Insurance Fund; and make recommendations for preventing any such loss in the future. A loss is material if it exceeds the greater of USD25 million or 2 per cent of an institution's total assets at the time the FDIC was appointed receiver.

23. Financial safety net reform in Nigeria[1]

Ganiyu A. Ogunleye

23.1. INTRODUCTION

Nigeria is the world's sixth-largest crude oil producer and the second-largest economy in Africa. Its economy, therefore, is largely crude-oil dependent and vulnerable to external shocks. Fiscal policy is driven by oil revenue and has been pro-cyclical due to price volatility. The boom period of 2004–08 witnessed huge liquidity flows which encouraged expansionary fiscal policy with attendant pressures on inflation and exchange rates. The economy had experienced boom and bust cycles which manifested in macro-economic instability.

A resilient financial safety net requires macro-economic stability; mutually reinforcing monetary and fiscal policies; effective regulation; effective depositor/investor protection and sound governance of banking institutions. To what extent has Nigeria attained these imperatives? Given its vulnerability to external shocks, maintaining macro-economic stability has been a daunting challenge to policymakers and the financial system safety net has been put to test from time to time.

This chapter focuses on the performance of Nigeria's financial safety net over the last decade. The chapter is divided into seven sections. Section 23.2 provides an overview of the financial system, while Section 23.3 discusses the regulatory framework. Section 23.4 highlights the causes of the recent financial crisis, while Section 23.5 discusses the Reform initiatives. Section 23.6 focuses on lessons learned and Section 23.7 offers some conclusions.

23.2. OVERVIEW OF FINANCIAL SYSTEM

Banking, insurance and securities are the three major components of the financial system and they are complemented by the pension industry. The system is dominated (80 per cent of total assets) by the banks which are universal-type institutions. Their liabilities are mainly short-term while a significant proportion of their deposits are sourced from the public sector. However, those deposits have tended to be volatile in nature. There is a wide spread between deposit rates which are as low as 2 per cent and lending rates which hover around 20 per cent per annum with an inflation rate at about 12 per cent. This scenario can hardly encourage savings.[2] Up to the year 2000, banking business was segmented into commercial and merchant (investment) banking. Universal banking was introduced at the end of the year 2000. In July 2004, a bank consolidation policy was unveiled with an implementation period of 18 months.[3]

23.3. THE REGULATORY FRAMEWORK

The objectives of regulation include: contributing to economic development, promoting safety and soundness of financial institutions with a view to preventing or minimizing financial crises and protecting consumers, especially depositors. The principal regulatory agencies are the Central Bank and the deposit insurer for banking business, the Securities and Exchange Commission for the capital market, the National Insurance Commission for insurance business and the National Pension Commission for pension assets. Inherent in this structure are regulatory overlaps and arbitrage opportunities for market operators. A Financial Services Regulation Coordinating Committee (FSRCC) was established to address inter-agency issues and it is supported by a memorandum of understanding to guide information sharing amongst the regulators.

23.4. CAUSES OF THE RECENT FINANCIAL CRISIS

The crisis in Nigeria was the result of both endogenous and exogenous factors. They include macro-economic instability largely attributable to huge capital flows and the lack of fiscal discipline; failure of corporate governance especially in banks; poor risk management practices; insider dealings; a substantial increase in non-performing assets; inadequate disclosure and weak supervision/enforcement by regulators.

The bank consolidation programme concluded in 2005 also contributed significantly to the financial crisis. That exercise reduced 89 banks to 25 and a number of the merged banks were not well-capitalized and lacked the synergy usually associated with such transactions. A classic case was the merger of five banks in the last week of the permissible period of 18 months without conducting due diligence on one another.[4] The consolidated banks embarked on a race for growth without developing the capacity to manage the growth. The Code of Corporate Governance and Guidelines for Developing Risk Management Framework issued by the Central Bank of Nigeria in 2006 were not adhered to.[5] Of particular concern was the frenzy of capital raising by banks post-consolidation allegedly financed with depositors' funds. Also, speculative lending through margin loans to stock brokers was rampant. As a result, the crash of the capital market impacted severely on banks' asset quality and capital base. For example, banks' non-performing loans which stood at 6 per cent of total loans in December 2008 increased to 32 per cent by December 2009. Furthermore, banking stocks which had persistently dominated trading volumes at the Nigeria Stock Exchange suffered huge losses resulting in balance sheet contractions. Paradoxically, those shares were used to collateralize the credit exposure of some banks.

In order to ameliorate these adverse developments, the Central Bank took some measures in 2008 aimed at restoring liquidity in the financial system. They included:

- forbearance for banks to restructure their capital market exposure up to December 2009;
- the timeframe of the lending window was expanded from overnight to 365 days while eligible instruments were expanded to include Bankers Acceptances, Commercial Paper and Certificates of Deposit;
- reduction of monetary policy rate from 10.25 per cent to 9.75 per cent;
- share buy-backs by banks up to 15 per cent of issued capital;
- a reduction of liquidity ratio requirement from 40 per cent to 30 per cent; and
- a reduction in cash reserve requirement from 4 per cent to 2 per cent.

While the measures taken were desirable, there was no specific directive to banks on the treatment of provisions on restructured facilities. Banks that benefited from the forbearance treated restructured facilities as performing which would have overstated their profitability. However, the stress test conducted in 2009 removed the perverse incentives.

23.5. FINANCIAL SECTOR REFORMS

The Financial Safety Net (FSN) comprises the lender of last resort function, prudential regulation, deposit insurance and the guarantor of last resort by the government. Interestingly, the reforms of the FSN over the last decade have been driven by regime changes at the Central Bank of Nigeria. The Governor appointed in 1999 introduced universal banking in 2000 while the Governor appointed in 2004 implemented a bank consolidation policy effective from 2006. The Governor appointed in June 2009 has unveiled a new reform agenda that will replace universal banking with bank fragmentation under the umbrella of bank holding companies. In effect, three successive Governors have had three different reform agendas.

While universal banking was introduced to remove competitive inequity between commercial and merchant banks and to reap the benefits of economies of scale, bank consolidation was introduced in an effort to foster the emergence of well-capitalized banks that could support economic development. Bank consolidation did not achieve its objectives partly because of the short period allowed for the consolidation, non-implementation of proposed supporting institutional framework like the establishment of an Asset Management Corporation, and the questionable capitalization process by some merging institutions.

The latest reform agenda is based on four pillars, namely: enhance the quality of bank assets; promote financial stability; enable evolution of a healthy financial sector; and ensure that the financial sector contributes to the real economy. The reform has a ten-year time horizon and its deliverables include:

- crisis containment;
- resolution of eight insolvent banks;
- establishment of an Asset Management Corporation;
- strengthening inter-agency cooperation;
- implementing bank categorization based on capital thresholds;
- implementing risk-based supervision;
- implementing consolidated supervision;
- implementing International Financial Reporting Standards; and
- restructuring the Central Bank.

The first step was to embark on crisis containment. In this regard, special examinations were undertaken on 24 universal banks jointly by the Central Bank and the Nigeria Deposit Insurance Corporation (NDIC) over the period June to September 2009. The stress tests revealed that eight banks were insolvent and illiquid and they accounted for about one-third of total assets of the banking industry. The Central Bank injected USD4 billion into those banks and appointed new management teams. It further guaranteed the interbank market transactions up to end of 2010 while the Federal Government (as the guarantor of last resort) made a declaration that no bank would be allowed to fail. These measures sustained confidence in the banking system. Meanwhile, the erstwhile management teams of the eight insolvent banks were found to have engaged in abusive and unprofessional practices and they were reported to the Economic and Financial Crimes Commission for further investigation and prosecution. Some of the cases are currently pending before the Courts.

Numerous complementary measures were taken to enhance corporate governance and improve accountability and transparency through the following measures:

- limiting the tenure of banks' Chief Executive Officers to a maximum of ten years;
- disqualifying bank CEOs from serving on the boards of their banks until three years after their tenure;
- disqualifying the Governors and Directors on the board of the Central Bank and Managing/Executive Directors and Departmental Directors of NDIC from serving on the boards of banks until five years after their tenure;
- adoption of December as the accounting year-end for audited financial statements by banks; and
- issuance of stringent disclosure requirements for banks which include non-financial risks.

While the current reforms are laudable, there are factors that could impair attainment of the desired objectives. They include:

- the jumbo 2010 federal budget which is indicative of an expansionary fiscal policy with attendant consequences for macro-economic stability;
- a delay in passage of the Asset Management Corporation Bill by the Legislature;
- the hostility of shareholders of eight insolvent banks which could frustrate early resolution;
- an inadequate legal framework for bank resolution;
- an unpredictable outcome of litigation against the Central Bank;
- developing a supervisory capacity for the array of institutions that could emerge under the new bank categorization/fragmentation policy;
- the absence of an effective consumer protection mechanism;
- the absence of on-line, real-time information and follow-up capabilities on banks' operations; and
- the absence of emergency powers for systemic crisis such as nationalization or powers to compel a merger.

The reforms also produced some unintended consequences. The stricter provisioning requirements helped banks to become more risk averse and unwilling to lend. Some preferred to place their funds with the Central Bank at 1 per cent under the standing deposit facility rather than take credit risk. Also, several banks resorted to cost-cutting measures such as freezing branch expansion and staff rationalization thus accentuating unemployment.

23.6. LESSONS LEARNED

The financial crisis underscored that no economy is immune to systemic crisis and reinforces the need for a very resilient financial safety net. Some of the lessons learned include:

Need for macro-economic stability

Macro-economic stability is critical to the resilience of the financial system safety net. The pro-cyclical fiscal policy experienced contributed to the resurgence of the financial crisis and undermined the efficacy of monetary policy instruments.

Need for financial deepening

The dearth of long-term funds makes the financial system prone to liquidity crisis and frequent liquidity crises can undermine public confidence and impair a savings culture. Apart from pension assets, priority should be accorded to the development of bond/corporate debt markets to further develop long-term financing.

Inter-agency cooperation

A regulatory structure with multiple regulatory agencies requires effective inter-agency cooperation to minimize regulatory overlaps and arbitrage opportunities for market operators.

Need to exercise enforcement powers

Some of the causes of the Nigerian crisis revealed a lack of will to exercise enforcement powers. For example, only lip service was paid to the much-trumpeted policy of zero tolerance for unprofessional/unethical practices.

Need to appreciate market dynamics

The rigid adherence to the specified period for bank consolidation undermined market dynamics. The implementation process failed to appreciate the risks inherent in rushed business combinations as reflected in the merger of five banks that was approved without needed due diligence.

Need for a holistic long-range reform

The reform agendas of three successive Central Bank Governors portend sustainability risks. Reform initiatives should be in tandem with a national economic blueprint such as the Vision 20: 2020 economic development project.

Promptness in creating enabling environment

The huge portfolio of non-performing loans of the eight intervened banks could not be resolved without an Asset Management Corporation as a resolution vehicle. The prompt enactment of the law for its operation is needed.

Need for emergency powers

The resolution of a systemic crisis requires certain emergency powers such as nationalization which is lacking in Nigeria. Protracted financial crises impair the resilience of the financial safety net.

Need for effective consumer protection framework

Apart from the explicit deposit insurance system managed by NDIC, investors and creditors do not have an effective formalized protection mechanism(s). While the Central Bank can issue consumer protection guidelines, it lacks the necessary enforcement powers. Meanwhile, the Consumer Protection Council created by law focuses on product compliance with production standards and the elimination of hazardous products from the markets. It is unable to offer assistance to financial services consumers.

Need for financial literacy advocacy

A sophisticated financial market requires well-informed (educated) clientele. Most of the victims of the liquidity crisis in the money market did not know what financial instruments qualified as deposits for deposit insurance purpose. Similarly, most of the victims of the capital market crash did not understand the inherent risks in stock trading. Instead, they invested under the illusion of continuous stock price appreciation until the asset bubble taught them a bitter lesson.

23.7. CONCLUSION

We have examined features of the financial safety net in Nigeria and the reform initiatives that were undertaken over the last decade. In doing so, we considered the causes of the various financial crisis and the regulatory responses to each of them and highlighted the four pillars of the current reform agenda initiated in 2009 by drawing attention to some factors that could hinder its successful implementation. The need for macro-economic stability as a sine qua non for a resilient financial safety net was emphasized.

We also drew attention to the importance of inter-agency cooperation in a financial safety net with multiple regulatory agencies. The need to tailor a reform agenda to national economic objectives was emphasized along with the need for consumer protection and financial literacy advocacy. Some of the lessons learned from the Nigerian experience and other developing countries in similar circumstances (and settings) can be found instructive.

NOTES

1. This paper was presented at the Symposium on Managing Systemic Risk organized by the School of Law, Warwick University, Coventry UK, 7–9 April 2010.
2. Nigeria has a large informal sector because only about 35 per cent of the economically active population has access to financial/banking services. In appreciation of this undesirable situation a Microfinance Policy was introduced in 2005 to promote synergy and mainstream the informal sub-sector into the national financial system. The policy sought to make financial services accessible to a larger segment of the populace. A liberal licensing approach was adopted which resulted in many illiquid and/or insolvent community banks converting to become microfinance banks. That licensing policy partly contributed to the financial distress of many microfinance banks.
3. The capital market crashed in the wake of the global financial crisis and market capitalization declined by as much as 70 per cent between 2007 and 2008. The downturn arose mainly from price speculation and capital flight. The insurance sub-sector is relatively small and unsophisticated. However, pension assets have grown remarkably to USD10 billion. It was hoped that pension funds would contribute to a deepening of the stock market.
4. The merger agreement had a clause which mandated a post-merger due diligence. The post-merger due diligence resulted in a sharp disagreement which warranted regulatory intervention by the Central Bank. Also, there were allegations of bubble capital in some of the consolidated banking groups. The obvious lesson learned is that business combination should be driven by market dynamics and not regulatory fiat.
5. See http://www.cenbank.org/out/circulars/bsd/2006/RBSGuidelineRevised2.pdf.

24. Islamic deposit insurance system: the Malaysian model

Khairuddin Hj Arshad

24.1. THE NEED FOR ISLAMIC DEPOSIT INSURANCE

Since the last three decades, Islamic finance has been experiencing tremendous growth and today, it has transformed into a vibrant intermediation mechanism. According to a McKinsey's 2007–08 report, Islamic assets have reached USD 750 billion and with growth rates of 15 per cent to 20 per cent per annum, the assets are expected to hit USD 1.6 trillion by 2012. The number of Islamic financial institutions globally has reached 625 in over 75 countries.

Amidst the recent more challenging environment, the continued expansion of global Islamic finance demonstrates its viability and resilience and this has drawn significant interest from global regulators and players. The role and relevance of Islamic finance in contributing to global financial stability and in support of overall global economic growth is discussed in this chapter.

Against this backdrop, there is a need to support the continuous growth of Islamic finance and further strengthen its viability and resilience. Among the key initiatives is the establishment of Islamic deposit insurance, which is a mechanism to protect Islamic deposits and maintain public confidence in the safety of their Islamic deposits in the Islamic banking institutions. Additionally, some countries are looking at deposit insurance as a catalyst to sustain and attract Islamic funds in their countries, thus helping them to spur the growth of Islamic finance and their economy.

24.2. MALAYSIA'S ISLAMIC FINANCIAL SYSTEM

Malaysia's Islamic finance started with the establishment of the Pilgrimage Fund Board in 1963 and the establishment of the first Islamic bank, Bank Islam Malaysia Berhad, in 1983. To date, there exists a comprehensive

Islamic financial system comprising Islamic banking, Islamic money market, *takaful* (an Islamic insurance concept which is based on Islamic banking practices and Islamic law), Islamic capital market and Islamic fund management.

The comprehensive system is supported by diversified players. For instance, the Islamic banking system comprises 17 Islamic banks, two Islamic windows, six development financial institutions offering Islamic banking services, four international Islamic banks and 16 international currency business units.

In addition to the robust legal, regulatory, supervisory and Shariah frameworks that set the landscape of the Islamic financial system, an Islamic deposit insurance system has been put in place to strengthen the resilience and promote stability to the Malaysian Islamic financial system.

24.2.1. Malaysia's Islamic Deposit Insurance System

Malaysia established its Islamic and conventional deposit insurance systems in September 2005. The establishment of a dual system comprising both Islamic and conventional systems was necessitated due to Malaysia's dual banking system. The system would not achieve its public policy objective of promoting the stability of the financial system if only one aspect of the banking system is covered.

Under the current system, the Islamic deposit insurance system (IDIS) operates in parallel with but separately from the conventional deposit insurance system. Both systems are administered by Malaysia Deposit Insurance Corporation (MDIC). To date, Malaysia is the only country that has implemented a dual banking system administered by one entity.

Malaysia's IDIS is an ex-ante system requiring mandatory membership. Islamic member institutions (IMIs) comprise 17 Islamic banks and two Islamic banking windows. To ensure that the IDIS is in line with Shariah requirements, the authorities have sought the endorsement of the Shariah Advisory Council of Bank Negara Malaysia (the SAC).[1]

The IDIS has been implemented on the basis of *maslahah* (public interest). *Maslahah*, which is an Arabic word, means utility, good, beneficial or advantage, i.e. something good for the public. It relates to the preservation of faith, life, intellect, posterity and property of the human beings. Islam allows a conduct or practice, among others, when there is an element of *maslahah* or public interest in such conduct or practice. Such an element could be seen in the IDIS in several ways.

Firstly, the IDIS is part of a customer protection framework that aims at protecting the public from losing the money that they place in Islamic banking institutions (IBIs) in the event of a failure, thus preventing them from facing financial difficulty and social consequences linked to economic distress.

Secondly, the IDIS instils public confidence in the safety of deposits in IBIs. This reduces the likelihood of panic among the public when there is rumour or real occurrence of an IBI's failure, and therefore, it enhances the resilience and stability of the Islamic financial system.

Thirdly, the IDIS helps to maintain the competitiveness of Islamic deposits vis-à-vis conventional deposits. This prevents regulatory arbitrage and helps to stimulate the growth of Islamic deposits and the Islamic financial system.

While the IDIS is allowed to be practised by Islam on the basis of *maslahah*, Islam requires the IDIS to be implemented in accordance with Shariah principles. This means that the IDIS must be free from the element of interest (*riba*) and other elements that Islam clearly prohibits.

24.2.2. Salient Features of IDIS

In developing the IDIS, the guiding principle is to provide equivalent protection for both the Islamic and conventional deposits.

24.2.2.1. Shariah arrangement

The IDIS is implemented based on the arrangement of *kafalah bil ujr* (a guarantee with a fee). This was agreed by the SAC as an acceptable and practicable Shariah arrangement that provides the foundation for the IDIS.

Kafalah is a contractual guarantee given by a guarantor to assume the responsibilities and obligations of the party being guaranteed should claims arise. As a consideration for the guarantee, a fee is paid by the guaranteed party to the guarantor.

MDIC adopts the *kafalah bil ujr* arrangement to define the relationship between an IMI as the guaranteed party and MDIC as the guarantor. As a consideration for the guarantee, the IMI pays a fee to MDIC in the form of an annual premium and, in the event the IMI fails, MDIC will assume the obligation of making reimbursement to the insured depositors.

24.2.2.2. Funding and premium assessment

The operations of the IDIS are funded by the premiums received from the IMIs. Premiums are assessed annually based on the amount of total insured Islamic deposits held as at 31 December of the preceding year and the IMIs' respective risk profiles under the differential premium system (DPS).

In the event that funds are insufficient to carry out its mandate, MDIC has access to Government and market funding and, when they are needed, loans are to be structured according to Shariah requirements.

24.2.2.3. Coverage

MDIC provides a separate but equitable protection for Islamic and conventional deposits. The Islamic insurable deposits include savings, demand and investment deposits and these deposits are accepted under various contracts such as *wadiah* (safe custody), *qard* (loan) or *mudharabah* (profit sharing).

With the implementation of the Government Deposit Guarantee in October of 2008, deposits held by the IMIs enjoy coverage over and above that provided by the explicit deposit insurance system and deposits held by guaranteed institutions are also protected until the end of 2010.

24.2.2.4. Management of the Islamic Deposit Insurance Fund

The premiums received from the IMIs are maintained and administered separately in the Islamic Deposit Insurance Fund (IDIF). MDIC keeps separate accounting records and prepares separate financial statements for the Islamic and conventional deposit insurance systems. There is no commingling of funds or cross-subsidization between the Islamic and Conventional Deposit Insurance Funds.

Any expenditures incurred for a specific Fund will be charged against that Fund. However, for non Shariah-compliant expenditures they will be charged against the conventional deposit insurance system only. If an expenditure cannot be identified to either the IDIF or the Conventional Deposit Insurance Fund, the expenditures will be apportioned to the respective funds based on the amount of Islamic and conventional premiums collected in the assessment year prior to the year in which such expenditures are made.

The reserves held in the IDIF can only be invested in Shariah-compliant instruments. Currently, they are invested in securities issued or guaranteed by the Government or Bank Negara Malaysia.

24.2.2.5. Payment and priority of payment

To maintain confidence in the financial system, MDIC is responsible, among other things, to protect the depositors from the loss of their deposits in the event of a bank failure. MDIC is required to reimburse insured depositors of a failed IMI quickly, and by law no longer than three months from the date of a winding-up order. All costs or losses incurred by MDIC in meeting its obligations to pay for the insured Islamic deposits are to be charged to the IDIF.

The priority of claims accorded to depositors would affect the level of resolution costs incurred by MDIC. Under the MDIC Act, the depositors will automatically subrogate their rights and interests but only to the extent of any deposit insurance payment made. In respect of Islamic deposits, the priority of payments is based on the underlying contracts of the deposits whereby the non-*mudharabah* (non-profit sharing) deposits are given priority over *mudharabah* (profit sharing) deposits. The non-*mudharabah* deposits include *wadiah* (safe custody) and *qard* (loans).

24.3. WHY PROTECT PSIA?

Profit sharing investment accounts (PSIA) is unique to Islamic banking operations. Given its distinct features, much has been debated about PSIA such as its classification as a deposit or investment and its impact on capital adequacy and liquidity requirements. In deposit insurance, the debate is as to whether PSIA should be protected by deposit insurers.

Under PSIA, the depositor and the bank share the profit from the investment of the deposit received based on an agreed profit sharing ratio. Losses arising from the investment of PSIA are to be borne by PSIA holders, except in the event of negligence or mismanagement, where the losses are to be borne by Islamic banking institution. Since the losses will be borne by PSIA holders, some argued that PSIA should not be protected under the deposit insurance system.

In Malaysia, PSIA is covered under the IDIS based on the following:

(a) Although *Mudharabah* contract does not allow an Islamic banking institution to guarantee PSIA, it does not restrict a third party guarantee, e.g. by the deposit insurer;
(b) The guarantee is only in the event of an IMI's failure, not losses in the normal course of business; and
(c) In Malaysia, PSIA forms the bulk of the total deposits in the Malaysian Islamic banking system. Therefore, protecting PSIA represents a prudential measure taken by the Government to enhance the resilience and stability of the Malaysian Islamic financial system under the principle of *maslahah* (public interest).

24.4. ISSUES AND CHALLENGES

In implementing the IDIS, there have been several issues and challenges that were addressed. Firstly, there were no guiding principles on IDIS to help in developing and implementing IDIS. To date, very few countries have implemented an IDIS and the information is not easily available. In developing IDIS, an assessment was conducted on the applicability of the conventional deposit insurance system and some modifications were made to the conventional deposit insurance system in ensuring that the IDIS is Shariah compliant.

Secondly, with the greater product innovation under various Shariah contracts, it is a challenge to determine the insurability and priority of payments for new and complex deposit products. Previously, there were only deposit products accepted under *wadiah*, *qard* and *mudharabah* contracts but now, more new and hybrid products have been introduced based on several contracts.

As mentioned earlier, DPS was also introduced for IMIs. In addition to the challenge in identifying the appropriate indicators for assessing the unique risks of the IMIs, some statistical data on the Islamic banking operations is not available.

Other issues and challenges include cross-border liquidation, liquidation of assets funded by restricted PSIA and public awareness.

24.5. CONCLUSION

The IDIS plays a vital role in strengthening the resilience of the global and domestic Islamic and conventional financial systems, especially when an Islamic financial system is an integral part of the overall financial system. Therefore, considerable effort was made to design the IDIS so that it can function effectively and complies with Shariah principles. The establishment of the IDIS also portrays Malaysia's seriousness in building a comprehensive Islamic financial system and achieving a major hub for international Islamic finance.

The current model adopted is suitable for the Malaysian system and MDIC is willing to share with other countries about the features of the model. This model has not been tested in other countries but the countries that have the interest to develop IDIS could study the model and do the necessary modification to their systems.

MDIC will continuously keep abreast and develop new guidance within the Islamic deposit insurance sector as the Islamic financial system is undergoing rapid development and transformation.

MDIC has also been entrusted to chair the Islamic Deposit Insurance Group (the IDIG), which was set-up under the International Association of Deposit Insurers (IADI). The IDIG is expected to conduct research on Islamic deposit insurance as well as issuing guidance and ultimately core principles to help policy-makers to develop effective IDIS. A discussion paper on 'Deposit Insurance from Shariah Perspective' has been completed and the IADI will be issuing it for public consultation. Another research paper will also be developed on 'Approaches in Designing an IDIS'.

MDIC has also organized seminars on Islamic Deposit Insurance for the last two years. The Seminar is part of MDIC's effort, as the Chair of IDIG, to provide a forum for discussions on Islamic deposit insurance and facilitating the sharing and exchange of expertise and information on Islamic deposit insurance issues.

NOTE

1. The SAC is the highest Shariah authority that provides views and resolutions on Islamic finance in Malaysia.

25. Managing financial risk: the precautionary principle and protecting the public interest in the UK

John F. McEldowney

. . . [T]he scarcity of money is not always confined to improvident spendthrifts. It is sometimes general through a whole mercantile town and country in its neighbourhood. Over-trading is the common cause of it. Sober men, whose projects have been disproportioned to their capitals, are likely to have neither wherewithal to buy money, nor credit to borrow it, as prodigals, whose expense has been disproportioned to their revenue.
Adam Smith, *The Wealth of Nations* (1776), p. 348.

25.1. INTRODUCTION

Financial risk management[1] has received a bad reputation through the failures of banks[2] resulting in the financial crisis of the past years. As profits increased aided by large borrowing and by 'light-touch regulation',[3] financial institutions over-exaggerated the margins of safety and the result was a financial crisis. *The Economist* concluded[4] that overall in many countries, including the UK and the US, the more that risk was calculated and mathematically calibrated the greater the opportunity arose for debt to be turned into securities, sold and held in trading books with lower capital charges than regular loans. The financial institutions' internal assessment was over-relied upon as were levels of self-regulation; with the benefit of hindsight, this seems reckless. The result has been to cast doubt on the capacity of financial regulators to regulate complex and very technical markets and to require ever more government intervention to prop up ailing banks. The economic data is clear and stark, particularly as US financial firms grew their debts to a level that exceeded the overall US economy. Similar problems appear to have occurred in the UK in the way banks were regulated. Different causes are held to be responsible for the financial crisis;[5] a failure to see the impending financial disaster;

over-reliance on risk management models that relied on recent rather than historic data; and a failure of realism aided by a culture of regulatory conservatism and inertia that was reactive rather than proactive. The regulatory system appeared mesmerized by the size of banks 'too-big-to-fail' and their interdependence. There was a failure to appreciate that the complexity in financial instruments often hid simple truths that the risks had become too great and unsustainable. Muddling through was preferred over sensible risk assessment and analysis.

This chapter focuses on a future strategy and how financial regulation must meet challenges, most notably achieving a balance between financial stability and systemic risk. The recent White Paper[6] announcing a new approach to financial regulation is considered alongside the announcement of changes to the architecture of financial regulation that places the Bank of England at the apex of financial regulation. In considering the organization of financial regulation it is important to assess how financial risk should be managed. It is argued that such risks must in the future be tempered by the precautionary principle.[7] Principles of good regulation[8] must be combined with contemporary lessons from regulatory theory.[9] There is a tension between regulatory systems that effectively expand the role of the state and those that use different forms of self regulation or light touch regulation giving primacy to the main stakeholders. Setting the balance correctly is about directing the values of good risk taking, strategic thinking and forward planning. Here the precautionary principle provides a way of approaching the taking of risk and engaging with the awareness and assessment of financial danger. It provides a clear role for government to ensure that preventive action is relative and proportionate to the identified risk. It also provides the basis for a validated system of risk assessment to protect the public interest. Applying the precautionary principle also implies tough measures for defaulting banks or on those who are reckless in assessing risk. Equally it prescribes a degree of due diligence to understand the nature of risks and take preventative steps to limit the fiscal and other impacts of banking failures.

It is argued that the precautionary principle provides an important mechanism for bridging the gap between public and private sectors in their approach to financial harm. The principle is consistent with G20 and European Commission initiatives[10] to adopt crisis prevention and crisis management strategies. The likely setting of an EU framework for crisis management in the financial sector will be greatly facilitated by the adoption of a clear framework. The precautionary principle is familiar in the literature associated with sustainable development of the environment. Its application in the financial world has been widely canvassed by Benjamin Richardson.[11] In essence, precautionary principles provide the basis of favouring prudent investment over the more risky by identifying the potential for failure together with a cost analysis of what might be at stake. It is an investor beware presumption that brings due diligence to investment strategies while retaining freedom of choice based on a calculated assessment of exposures to failure. Greater transparency of information provides a mechanism for the risk averse to gauge risk and calculate the opportunity costs. Seasoned risk takers will remain but under a precautionary principle both the regulatory authorities (the Bank of England), and individual banks will be better informed and more knowledgeable of what is at stake. Risky investments in banks will be more easily recognizable from the more reliable and the banks themselves will be in a much better position to operate regulatory controls and manage risk.[12]

In the future, the precautionary principle might become imbedded in the regulation of financial institutions and in the Government's pre-eminent role to protect the public interest. At the same time, the precautionary principle will empower managers to take risks but not behave recklessly. There is some evidence that a precautionary approach to risk regulation is already at work in many of the innovative responses to the banking crisis and in the current proposals for giving the Bank of England the primary role as the banking regulator in place of the Financial Services Authority (FSA). It is important that risk assessment be given attention in prudential supervision of the banking system.

25.2. LESSONS FROM THE FINANCIAL CRISIS AND THE FUTURE OF FINANCIAL REGULATION

Banking failures over the past few years have seen unprecedented UK government financial support for financial institutions, a response reflected in many countries. This has led to a worldwide interest in banking regulatory reform[13] as well as initiatives undertaken in the UK. The G20 noted how risk assessment was intrinsic to the future of strengthening prudential oversight:

> Substantial progress has been made in strengthening prudential oversight, improving risk management, strengthening transparency, promoting market integrity, establishing supervisory colleges and reinforcing international cooperation.[14]

The report of the Treasury Select Committee made stark reference to the perilous state of the public finances and noted: 'In the 1970s the UK banking sector had a balance sheet of 50 per cent of United Kingdom GDP; it is currently 500 per cent of GDP'.[15] In real terms the recession and financial crisis has made a dent in public finances estimated to be in the region of 5.2 per cent of national income (GBP73 billion in 2009–10). There are varying estimates that this will continue to diminish public finances by a further GBP25 billion with a less optimistic forecast of GBP50 billion. Planned government initiatives, including fiscal tightening are likely to require 5.5 per cent of national income or GBP77 billion, and there are pressures for tax revenues to rise substantially.[16] It is uncertain whether the aspirations on fiscal tightening and taxation are going to be easily met. It is clear that the financial crisis has resulted in the new coalition government engaging in an unprecedented reduction in public finance and a culling of regulatory bodies.

It is important to recognize the scale of the UK government's involvement in the banking sector because of the crisis. This includes the virtual nationalization of four major banks and the transfer of assets of two major building societies as well as lending support through bank guarantees and loans.[17] There has also been unprecedented use of quantitative easing of up to GBP200 bn from February 2009 to February 2010.[18] This has given the Bank of England a significant interest and substantial ownership of the gilts market. Thus, the government of the day has an involvement as lender, owner, regulator and customer of the banking system. Consequently, how regulation is designed and shaped is fundamental to the future of the banking system as well as critical to the protection of the taxpayers' interests. Assessing risk and more accurately establishing the boundaries of prudent management of public money has provided incentives for the better management of risk regulation in the banking sector. There is evidence of a 'precautionary' approach to banking regulation being adopted to meet the pressures of market confidence and the public interest involving new and innovatory approaches to regulation. This has led to steps to ensure that the multiplicity of functions of banking regulation are identified and addressed. Perhaps one of the first lessons of the financial crisis is that financial regulation needs to be responsive and flexible. This is underlined by the many innovative responses to risk assessment.

The UK Financial Investments Ltd. has been set up as an autonomous company that falls under a Framework Agreement, subject to regular revision, setting the relationship between the Treasury and the company. It was established to manage public support through government assistance to Northern Rock, Bradford and Bingley, Lloyds and the Royal Bank of Scotland. The government's role in the UK Financial Investments Ltd. is under the Treasury as sole shareholder and under its guidance a Framework Directive to develop a strategy to dispose of the government's banking holdings has been developed. UK Financial Investments Ltd. also manages the government's banking assets including Royal Bank of Scotland.[19] Responsibilities include an Investment Mandate to ensure propriety in the management of investments, including Directors' regulations with the aim of balancing financial decisions and political oversight.

The oversight of the management of the Royal Bank of Scotland's assets falls under an Asset Protection Scheme underwritten by HM Treasury. There is an Asset Protection Agency (APA) established by the Treasury in December 2009 to ensure good management to support the stability of the UK financial system. The Asset Protection Scheme is part of an Asset Protection Agreement whereby banks are granted asset protection. There are strong lines of parliamentary accountability through the Public Accounts Committee, oversight by the National Audit Office (NAO) and reporting obligations through the Accounting Officer. The APA has significant responsibilities for implementing the Asset Protection Scheme and to ensure that the scheme funded by the taxpayer is not required to be used.[20] Its first Annual Report published in July 2010 criticized the way Royal Bank of Scotland managed various risky assets.[21] Criticism included concerns over the quality of financial advice and asset management which resulted in estimated losses of GBP57 billion. The expectation is that the Government would not have to pay out of the Asset Protection Scheme but risks remain. Advisers appointed by the APA have sought to improve the Royal Bank of Scotland's financial management of high risk assets. The Asset Protection Scheme requires annual payments by the Bank to protect its assets.[22]

Finally, there is a Debt Management Office (DMO), an executive agency of the Treasury, established in 1998 with duties to administer two guarantee schemes, the Credit Guarantee Scheme, to guarantee bank borrowings, established in October 2008 and the Asset Guarantee Scheme, with a limit of GBP50 billion, begun in April 2009 to stimulate mortgages by offering banks some degree of creditor protection. This particular task lasted until December 2009. The main role of the DMO that remains is to sell government gilts and government debts.

Overall financial regulation is currently dependent on the tripartite arrangements consisting of the Treasury, the Bank of England and the FSA; the latter is currently the main independent financial regulator in the UK. The Treasury has primary responsibility in two matters, the overall institutional structure of financial regulation and the legislation that governs it; and informing and accounting to Parliament for the management of serious problems in the financial system and any measure used to resolve them. In exceptional circumstances where a major bank is in some difficulty, the Treasury has responsibility for the authorization of a support operation with the release of public funds.

As well, the Bank of England has four main responsibilities for the maintenance of financial stability: (1) making funds available in the market to address fluctuations in liquidity; (2) overseeing financial system infrastructure systemically significant to the UK and in particular payment systems whether based in the UK or abroad; (3) undertaking in exceptional circumstances, official financial operations in accordance with the Tripartite arrangements in the Memorandum of Understanding on financial stability: and (4) to limit the risk of problems in or affecting particular institutions spreading to other parts of the financial system.

The FSA has a primary role in financial regulation. Given the independence of each, as well as competing cultures and approaches, the relationship between each part of the tripartite arrangement was first set out in a concordat demarcating the respective role and functions of each part. Lessons have been gained from the financial crisis that transformed the role of the FSA. Under the *Financial Services and Markets Act 2000* are: authorization and prudential supervision of firms providing financial services; supervision of financial markets, securities listings and of clearing and settlement systems; continual conduct supervision in responses to firms, markets and clearing banks and operating the Tripartite arrangements.[23]

A major criticism of the FSA was an over-reliance on the 'principles based' approach to regulation making the regulator dependent on the firms' advisers and also on the application of technical and complex rules by the various regulated institutions. The application of risk management was also left to the various institutions through setting expectations as to what might be achieved.[24]

The FSA was also claimed to be 'one of the world's first unified financial services regulators,[25] formed by the merger of several earlier bodies between 1979 and 2000.[26] From its inception, the FSA was well regarded by the NAO[27] and its approach to regulation consistent with open globalized financial markets, lightly regulated and centred in London.

There had been past banking failures such as the Johnson Matthey Bank (JMB)[28] in 1984, BCCI[29] in 1991, and Barings Bank[30] in 1995, but the Northern Rock collapse had the potential to start a run on the main High Street banks and financial institutions. The failures of financial regulation, particularly of Northern Rock, contributed to a rethink of financial regulation in general. The Turner Review[31] followed recommending a strengthening of regulation and a more robust approach to Risk Management and Governance.[32] The then Labour Government strengthened the FSA through the *Financial Services Act 2010* which replaced the Tripartite Standing Committee with a Council for Financial Stability comprising the Chancellor of the Exchequer, Governor of the Bank of England and Chairman of the FSA. This was intended to strengthen the *Financial Services and Markets Act 2000*, which was amended to include a new responsibility of having an explicit financial stability objective. This includes establishing the costs to the economy of instability and of regulatory action. The FSA has an obligation to consult the Treasury when determining strategy. This is a welcome development and provides a sound basis for the FSA to make strategic decisions in collaboration with the other members of the tripartite group. The FSA is also required to establish a new consumer financial education body with a proactive role in tackling consumer awareness about finance and financial products. This will include impartial generic financial advice.[33] At the time there was a wide divergence of views about whether the new Council for Financial Stability will work or not.[34] Strengthening the FSA within the existing tripartite framework was intended to encourage the FSA to take a lead role in a more expanded and pervasive system of regulation. At the same time the experience of the run on Northern Rock exposed the weakness of Parliamentary oversight and the regulatory role of the Treasury[35] which also requires attention. It is difficult to evaluate whether the changes under the *Financial Services Act 2010* would prevent a recurrence of the financial crisis of a few years ago. It is clear that lessons have been learned and any new regulatory system that replaces the existing tripartite arrangements needs to address how improvements were made and have come about.[36]

25.3. FSA APPROACH TO MORE INTENSIVE REGULATORY REVIEW

The FSA, as an independent regulator, must act in accordance with promoting public confidence in the financial system.[37] This includes the protection of consumers of financial services and its products and in carrying out its supervision of financial markets. Market abuse or manipulation including short selling falls within the FSA's powers to undertake criminal prosecutions. This raises the question of whether criminal prosecutions should have been more extensively used in financial regulation. Sections 401 and 402 of the *Financial Services and Markets Act 2000* give the FSA similar powers to other prosecution authorities.[38] Section 401 is directed at prosecutions that specifically arise for offences found within the *Financial Services and Markets Act 2000*. For example, under section 307 of the *Financial Services and Markets Act 2000* the FSA may prosecute for making false or misleading statements – often associated with causing share price inflation and the ultimate collapse of the share market. Section 402 is broader and applies to offences outside the *Financial Services and Markets Act 2000* but where there is a need to prosecute that is related to maintaining market confidence in the public interest. The broader remit captures offences that fall within money laundering offences under Part V of the *Criminal Justice Act 1993* and related regulations. Taken together the FSA has considerable scope to prosecute especially when practices that fall under the generic term of 'market manipulation' are considered. Lacking a clear definition means that the term can cover various ways in which the capital market may be distorted or inaccurately adjusted to produce an outcome that leads to loss of investor and market confidence. The fragility of markets and their sensitivity is at the heart of the problem of setting a clear definition. At stake, however, is the idea that market efficiency is being put in jeopardy. Market abuse is also covered to include insider dealing, inaccuracy in information and its misuse. Insider dealing is also a specific offence under Part V of the *Criminal Justice Act 1993*. This has proved a controversial and difficult offence, not least for the collection of the evidence to prove it as well as for the jury to understand its complexity. The link between insider dealing and its damaging effects on financial markets is also contentious.

In addition to the criminal jurisdiction of the FSA, the FSA has a large civil jurisdiction for imposing civil sanctions under section 118 of the *Financial Services and Markets Act 2000* for market abuse. This is enforced by the FSA through its own specialist tribunal. Insider dealing falls within this jurisdiction as set out in the Market Abuse Directive[39] under the *Financial Services and Markets Act 2000* (Market Abuse) Regulations 2005.[40] The use of civil sanctions is consistent with the direction favoured by the European Union and it is also part of a wide-ranging debate on the use of civil sanctions and their application in the regulatory process in the United Kingdom.[41] As recently as 3 August 2010, the FSA fined the Royal Bank of Scotland GBP5.6 million for failing to have adequate systems in place to prevent UK financial sanctions over screening procedures to prevent money laundering. The NAO noted how important[42] civil sanctions had become to the work of the FSA and this remains today.

Initially the FSA was not active in pursuing criminal prosecutions. Only in 2005 was the first criminal prosecution against market abuse taken,[43] and this was successful. Even by 2007 there had been no insider dealing prosecutions taken by the FSA under the *Criminal Justice Act 1993*. This may have reflected a policy approach to use prosecutions sparingly or recognition of the high evidential burdens required to mount successful prosecutions. Jury trial and the complexity of financial instruments and markets may also have inhibited the use of prosecutions. Difficulties of detection are also evident in such cases. The fear of detection and the threat of criminal prosecutions may also act as a deterrent. Monitoring and surveillance are likely to be easier if the threat of criminal prosecutions is not aggressively pursued.

The banking crisis has changed the FSA's approach. Following the Turner Review,[44] the FSA adopted a more intensive supervisory model in its attempts to redress past regulatory shortcomings. The use of fines and prosecutions was intensified. *The Economist* noted: 'That year (2009) saw a big change in the level and nature of fines imposed by the FSA: GBP34.9 million (USD54.6 million) compared with GBP22.7 million in 2008 and just GBP5.3 million in 2007'.[45]

In fact the FSA is getting tougher and more vigilant. At the end of March 2010 a large investigation into insider dealing resulted in the arrest of six, amongst them employees of Deutsche Bank, BNP Paribas and Moore Capital, a large hedge fund. This accompanied large-scale penalties against a former interest rate trader at Merrill Lynch (a ban of at least five years) and the prosecution of a former stock broker at Cazenove. The FSA hired an additional 460 staff and the largest banks have been allocated 15 officials permanently stationed at the individual bank's headquarters. No one can doubt that regulation is likely to be more intense as shown by criminal prosecutions such as *R. v Rollins* and *R. v McInerney*[46] where the Court of Appeal secured an important extension of prosecution powers for the FSA to prosecute beyond sections 401 and 402 of the *Financial Services and Markets Act 2000* to include sections 327 and 328 under the *Proceeds of Crime Act 2002*.[47]

The FSA's own Business Plan 2010/11 is indicative of the robust approach planned by the FSA that includes deterrence, changing the current culture, and linking regulation and financial stability.[48] The future of criminal prosecutions depends on the development of a network of information and strategies to combat market manipulation and abuse. General market misconduct needs to be addressed through the successful prosecution of high profile hard cases and also through a public awareness and debate about strategy and how the public interest is to be protected. This debate is likely to be controversial, especially issues such as the granting of immunities in return for evidence, whistle blowing within the City and even the use of 'super-grasses' for collecting evidence. There are dangers in malicious motives giving rise to unjust prosecutions and considerable doubts about the effectiveness of such strategies[49] in the light of human rights considerations and protections afforded to the accused. There is also a debate over whether civil or criminal sanctions are to be given priority and which is likely to be most cost effective and offer adequate deterrence.

Evaluating how effective the FSA has become is difficult given the absence of an in-depth analysis before the new government announced in June 2010 its decision to transfer to the Bank of England many of the functions of the FSA and abolition of the FSA as a legal entity. The announcement was followed by a White Paper in July and public consultation. The FSA was already reforming itself and making proposals for change. The Walker Review[50] published in November 2009 makes important proposals for the establishment of Board risk committees and the appointment of chief risk officers at senior executive levels in appropriately listed banks and insurers. This is to reinforce the firm's own due diligence and to ensure more effective scrutiny at the Board level.[51] The publication of the recent White Paper is an opportunity to consider the FSA's experience and lessons gained before adopting the new approach to financial regulation. Given the FSA's history and current approach to financial regulation it is argued that this should inform any new approach to financial regulation. There are some inter-related issues.

Developing a robust approach to financial regulation especially tackling insider dealing, market abuse and money laundering must be seen as part of the difficulties confronting business crime in general. There are also lessons from other regulatory examples. The Office of Fair Trading (OFT) had limited success in this regard and the Asset Recovery Agency was merged into the Serious Organized Crime Agency (SOCA) and subsequently abolished in April 2008. The Serious Fraud Office (SFO) established in 1987 has also suffered severe criticism including judicial doubts over a US-style plea bargaining system.[52] There are also lessons to be gained from the long-running experience of the Crown Prosecution Service (CPS). It has been 25 years since the CPS was set up and it has emerged stronger after a period of intense criticism. The Revenue and Customs Prosecution was merged with the CPS in 2008 and this has pooled together considerable experience. There may be a case for integrating financial regulation within the CPS as the co-ordinating agency.[53] In the area of financial regulation experience counts and expertise needs to be shared. This is particularly important given the technical complexities of many financial instruments.

25.4. A NEW APPROACH TO FINANCIAL REGULATION

The May 2010 election has seen a radical departure from the past approach to financial regulation favoured by the previous government. Legislation is promised by mid-2011 and the White Paper[54] published in July 2010 proposes the abolition of the FSA and the restoration of the Bank of England as the primary prudential regulator. The White Paper is one of a spate of new initiatives primarily intended to address the fiscal deficit by adopting fiscal tightening across the public sector.[55] Its main

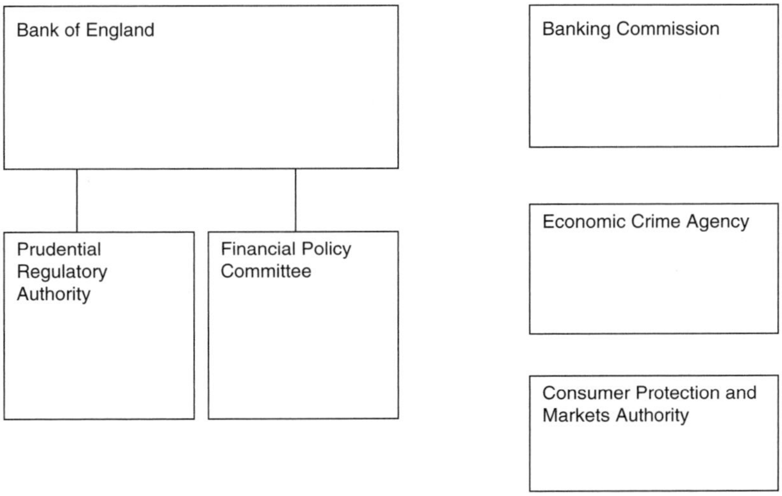

Figure 25.1. The New Banking Regulatory Scheme (June, 2010)

focus is on the institutional architecture of financial regulation rather than methodology or regulatory theory. Figure 25.1 above sets out the proposed new regulatory framework. The underlying assumptions behind the new institutional architecture of financial regulation are that the existing tripartite system has failed. The White Paper asserts:[56]

- to identify the problems that were building up in the financial system;
- to take steps to mitigate them before they led to significant instability in financial markets; and
- to deal adequately with the crisis when it did break, especially during the first part of the crisis in mid-2007.

There is a strong emphasis on institutional structures rather than an analysis of the *way* in which regulation was applied. There is also an absence of a detailed analysis of what went wrong and what succeeded and little acknowledgement that post the financial crisis, regulation has changed and adapted to past failures. Consequently the White Paper asserts that there are 'inherent weaknesses and contradictions' in the tripartite system. The main weaknesses are that the responsibilities of the FSA are in 'the hands of a single monolithic financial regulator' and this points to the wide ranging nature of the scope of regulation. The White Paper refers to the Bank of England having only nominal responsibility including, since the *Banking Act 2009*, statutory obligations for financial stability but this 'does not provide it with the tools or levers to carry out this role effectively'. Finally the White Paper criticizes the fact that the Treasury has responsibility for maintaining an overall legal and institutional framework 'but no clear responsibility for dealing with a crisis which put tens of billion of pounds worth of public funds at risk'.[57] The White Paper concludes that there is 'no single institution' 'that has the responsibility, authority and powers to monitor the system as a whole'.[58] This leaves the task of macro-prudential risk analysis as falling between the gaps of the current system.

Some of the above concerns had been addressed previously in the *Financial Services Act 2010*. Moreover section 74 of the *Banking Act 2009* has given the Bank of England the ability to make transfer instruments through delegated powers without recourse to Parliamentary debate. Section 74 also gives the Treasury considerable power to make broad regulations that might apply to address the fiscal consequences of any financial crisis consistent with the Treasury's overall stabilization powers. An additional 'catch all' power that has been highly criticized[59] is contained in section 75 of the *Banking Act* which gives the Treasury overarching powers, including retrospective effects 'where the Treasury considers it necessary or desirable for the purposes of the Order making powers of the Treasury including special resolutions'. These reserve powers suggest that at least in theory the *Banking Act 2009* might address some of the shortcomings mentioned in the White Paper.

Account should also be taken of the pro-active way in which the Treasury has managed the banking crisis. The Bank of England was given an indemnity by the Treasury in November 2008 to make available up to GBP18 billion and a further GBP60 billion in liquidity assistance to RBS and HBOS.[60] There was also a GBP250 billion Credit Guarantee Scheme available and again readily and speedily announced. The issuing of indemnities and the availability of government funds have been heavily criticized because of the lack of information and accountability to Parliament rather than the absence of adequate financial and legal powers to provide needed financial support when required.

It is now proposed that the Bank of England will be responsible for monetary policy, financial stability, macro-prudential oversight and supervision, and oversight of micro-prudential supervision. The aim is to restore to the Bank of England the main responsibility for prudential regulation and to the systemic or aggregated risks associated with the financial sector. The Bank of England will be at the apex of the system of financial regulation in the UK under a system of macro-prudential regulation aimed at addressing risk and its association with the wider economy. Doubts have remained about the Bank's ability to achieve this aim. In the past many banking failures have been attributed to problems with its capacity to predict and overview systemic weaknesses. The belief is that a central bank-focused structure for financial sector supervision is desirable because the central bank 'has a competitive edge due to their first hand exposure to markets and the depth of their staff's experience in the functioning of financial firms and markets'.[61] Within the Bank of England there will be a new Financial Policy Committee (FPC) with responsibility for preventing credit and asset bubbles and for overall financial stability. This is to be set up and be running in advance of new legislation for 2011. Financial stability is today inextricably linked with fiscal stability that the new FPC will have to work closely with the Bank's existing Monetary Policy Committee. The test of the FPC's responsibilities will be its ability to predict and provide transparency so that both the public interest is protected, the taxpayer's investment in the banks is secure and that there is financial stability. Public confidence is key and there is a promise of future legislation to ensure reporting from the FPC through the Treasury to Parliament, and the Treasury Select Committee. It could be argued that the degree of taxpayer exposure should also be linked to accountability before the Public Accounts Committee and audit by the NAO. Paradoxically the Bank of England, not known in the past for openness and transparency during periods of market vulnerability, is expected to be transparent and accountable. The requirement for transparency between the Treasury and the Bank of England will set demanding expectations which are important for the future success of the new regulatory system.

There will be several additional advisory bodies with specific responsibilities. These include, the Prudential Regulatory Authority (PRA), a legally distinct subsidiary, responsible under the Bank of England for micro-prudential supervision of day-to-day matters relating to oversight of bank safety and soundness. Its main focus is on the prudential regulation of financial firms. The PRA will have many of the FSA supervision and enforcement powers. It will have shared responsibilities in consumer matters with the Consumer Protection and Markets Authority (CPMA) which has responsibilities for investor protection, market supervision and regulation as well as the business conduct of banks and financial services.

The CPMA inherits many of the FSA's responsibilities but the main test of the CPMA will be to ensure consumer protection amidst changes in derivatives trading in the aftermath of changes in the US. The role of the Bank of England will be paramount in providing the necessary steering to negotiate the regulation of exchanges, the payment systems for derivatives and the facilities for securities and derivatives. All of which fall within the remit of the CPMA.

There is to be an independent Banking Commission under the chair of Sir John Vickers. Its task is to assess the arguments relating to 'too-big-to-fail' namely the desirability of breaking up the large banks in the public interest. This will include the structure of UK banking, the state of banking competition and the issues of how customers and taxpayers are to receive the best deal. This should be seen in the general context of a bank levy and the settling of pay and bonuses in the financial sector.

The new arrangements place a pivotal role on the Bank of England and seek to adopt a preventative stance to avoid and prevent another financial crisis. The new Banking Commission will make recommendations to guard against any undue financial risks taken by the banks. The appointment of the Independent Banking Commission includes within its terms of reference reducing systemic risk based on the different risks posed by different banks. The aim is to provide the basis for reform of the banking system, especially structural reform that promotes a competitive banking sector. It is hoped that the value of the FSA and its robust approach to regulation in evidence over the past couple of years will prove instructive for the future and lessons will be learned from past mistakes. The focus on the 'institutional architecture' of the regulatory system is potentially problematic. The key issue is not only the main functions of the regulatory bodies but *how* effective is regulation and the type of regulation adopted. The advantages of making the Bank of England the clear body with overall responsibility for regulation is that this will remove past problems of lack of clarity in responsibility. There is some continuity in the use of personnel from the previous arrangements. Lord Turner, chair of the soon to be defunct FSA, is continuing on to oversee the transition of the arrangements. The departing FSA Chief Executive is also retained as a Deputy Governor of the Bank of England.[62] There is also acknowledged difficulty within the new arrangements in distinguishing prudential regulation and the regulation of business conduct. The regulation of consumer interests is also important and recognized in the creation of a Consumer Protection and Markets Authority. This is an attempt to address one of the failures of the Tripartite arrangements.

Critics of the new proposals focus on the competence of the Bank of England to exercise sufficient and transparent regulation.[63] Regulatory tensions are bound to increase in a period of transition and this may impede progress in achieving the most suitable regulatory approach to banking. There were some encouraging signs of a more vigorous and effective FSA, but this has not been such as to change the Government's view of introducing the new arrangements. One aspect that the new proposals will have to take account of is the general strengthening of the FSA undertaken over the past two years. The lessons to be gained from those efforts should not go unnoticed if valuable insights about banking regulation are to be gained.

There is an obvious accretion of policy making within the Bank of England. This is likely to prove controversial and difficult to manage. If the Treasury was distrusted on the amount of public spending, hence the Office of Budgetary Responsibility, then will the Bank of England be trusted to steer regulatory objectives and policy making? The Bank of England's role is difficult given its past record. It also assumes that the staff when working as regulators and central bankers will know when to alert their political masters that something is going wrong before it happens. The proof of the new arrangements and the details of implementation is anxiously awaited especially in the context of whether the effectiveness of regulation will be improved.

The aim of the new regulatory system is to provide a Bank of England-led system of financial regulation that will address lessons from past failings, encourage greater transparency and more effective financial sector regulation. In the absence of new legislation, it is too early to assess the new regulatory structure. It is clear that running through the White Paper is recognition of systemic risk. The architecture of financial regulation is largely dependent on the successful approach to risk but there is the added necessity to address issues about public accountability and transparency.

25.5. THE PRECAUTIONARY PRINCIPLE AND GOVERNANCE

At the heart of the new proposals there is the complex issue of how to connect the Treasury and the Bank of England[64] in their new roles. Close cooperation is envisaged as is effective coordination and communication. There is an emerging paradox, namely how to reconcile the Treasury, as custodian of public money, to protect the interests of taxpayers, and the wider public interest, linked to financial stability and bank profitability. This applies to financial institutions as well as small firms for whom bank lending is critical. One way forward is to change not only the institutional architecture of financial regulation but also the policy underpinning the way regulation is undertaken. The dominant influence is the fiscal deficit. The unprecedented provision of vast amounts of public finance to underpin the financial markets is unique and carries an overriding duty on regulators to protect the public interest. Still further, the granting of largely discretionary powers to regulate financial institutions has directly expanded the role of the state in many tangible ways. The nationalization of banks as well as the issuing of indemnities supportive of the banking sector revealed a plethora of largely concealed and unknown powers available to the Treasury, the Bank of England and the FSA. This raises issues about public accountability and the need for Parliament to keep abreast of the rise in regulatory powers. The existing Select Committees and the NAO performed their task but were often limited by the retrospective nature of their inquiries. There are also many sources of legal powers – some originating from banking legislation and some from company law that seeks to protect the financial interests and confidentiality of company activities.

The unprecedented state involvement in financial regulation necessitates that a balance is sought between protecting the public interest and regulating the market for financial stability. One technique is to adopt a precautionary principle as an important tool to ensure sustainable financial regulation.

The precautionary principle is well known in the field of environmental law, especially as a founding principle in the development of international environmental law. The principle dates from the 1970s when it was commonly adopted to implement various international agreements as a protective strategy against pollution and to protect the environment. The basic underlying idea is that proactive prevention is to be preferred to crisis management after the event. There are a number of ways the precautionary principle might be approached in the banking field. Linked to good governance, the principle might provide a public interest responsibility that requires systems of transparency and public accountability as a check and protection of public money. It may provide a common frame of reference to support a risk awareness and risk management regulatory style. There is recognition that the problems of one bank may rapidly spread to the entire financial sector and rapidly cross national boundaries. The setting up of new bodies to replace three committees that attempted to regulate European banks, insurers and pension funds and securities[65] offers an opportunity to adopt preventative measures to limit any future financial crisis. The EU Commission and the G20 have noted the future need for 'prevention and crisis management' strategies adopting 'a tool box' of preparatory and preventative measures that road map the challenges ahead.[66] It is clear that one of the impacts of the financial crisis has been to raise questions on how the wider economy and the financial systems are best able to work together. The precautionary principle is a means of endorsing Basel III arrangements to ensure that the financial system in general is not prone to collapse due to poor management of banking risks. The precautionary principle is a means to facilitate future strategic planning consistent with responsible lending and borrowing within the EU as a whole.[67] The EU has recently set out preparatory and preventative measures; early action powers to remedy problems before they become severe, a strategy plan including implementation of recovery plans and divestment powers over activities that pose excessive risks and also resolution tools. There are proposed powers to take over failing banks or transfer risky banks or businesses to more secure institutions to enable the authorities to ensure the continuity of essential services. Road mapping future measures and ensuring an integrated approach is part of an ongoing review of the European Banking Authority due to report in 2014. Across EU member states government aid to banks is estimated to amount to 13 per cent of GDP[68] and the need for a more joined-up approach to crisis management requires integrated strategies and approaches. Putting in place new arrangements presents new challenges and to minimize risk of contagion from bad banks spreading to good ones and ensures the continuity of financial services. The conceptual framework that co-ordinates forward planning and preventative measures with the current needs of day-to-day regulation may be found in the precautionary principle. This seeks to avoid a crisis by foresight testing current decision-making through an evaluation of risk, and engaging through cross-border co-operation and the development of a co-ordinated strategy.

One of the most difficult questions is how best to understand risks and set priorities for the banking system. In response, the Treasury Select Committee[69] identified the inter-connection between sound finance; good banking and prudent risk-taking. The four elements identified are:

- Protecting the consumer;
- Protecting the taxpayer;
- Setting the appropriate correlation between risk and return; and
- Ensuring sustainable lending to the economy.

Designing the right framework will take time and effort as the role of banking is not confined to national or European levels but also internationally. It is clear that due to government protection, the Financial Service Compensation Scheme has ensured that no UK depositor in a building society or bank covered by the scheme has lost money up to the limits set by the scheme.[70] However, there is an active debate about how to ensure that savers receive sufficient incentives to save, while borrowers are able to borrow and invest. Better consumer advice and more informed analysis will undoubtedly assist. Protecting the taxpayer is addressed by ensuring that, if required, the Government should be able to give support to banks. Equally, though, taxpayers must be assured that their stake in banks is well protected and accountability as government policy is essential here and also a benchmark of good governance. In assessing the future effectiveness of the regulation of banking there is a need for a substantial review of how better risk management can be implemented. There is consensus that the debate on appropriate regulation is important as a 'fragile banking system' is regarded as unsafe and lacking in public confidence.[71] There are a number of competing views about how effective risk management might be. The current Governor of the Bank of England has doubted whether risk management is likely to be effective. Risk monitoring may be distinguished from risk management: however, he cautioned about making risk the centrepiece of bank regulation:

> In any risk activity – which we want people to engage in; we want innovation, we want the real economy to be prepared to take risks – things will happen that we cannot even easily define or imagine, let alone measure today. If that is the case the idea that you can always approach regulation in terms of saying, "We know all the risks that are being taken. We can calibrate them precisely, measure them and work out the precise capital requirement", it simply will not work. For some risks, you can behave in that way; but for other things, unexpected events will come along and the lesson from that is to create a resilient system.[72]

It is clear that despite such doubts there are different approaches to risk management. Mathematical modelling of risk is possible and can predict consequences. Making such calculations a basis for certainty is another matter. The Treasury Committee concluded that better risk monitoring is possible while risk management must take into account uncertainties. This is fundamental to the precautionary principle. The role of the government and the creation of a resilient banking system is regarded as an essential part of better banking supervision. However, there are considerable doubts that effective regulation in itself will be a panacea for the problem of the failure of a financial firm. The White Paper addresses the institutional architecture without taking into account the lessons to be gained from the FSA and the tripartite system in the aftermath of the financial crisis. Doubts remain as to how effective the new regulatory system will be if it is not clear what lessons have been learned from the past mistakes.

25.6. PROTECTING THE PUBLIC INTEREST AND ACCOUNTABILITY

The banking crisis has also highlighted the need for checks and balances for the constitutional actors. Prominent amongst the various Parliamentary procedures and committees is the role of the Treasury Committee.[73]

This Committee has undertaken important reviews of the banking crisis and taken evidence from the main regulators. The White Paper gives special mention to the need for the new regulatory structure to conform to parliamentary supervision, including through the role of the Treasury Committee. One interesting footnote is that during the nationalization of the main banks and the merger and takeover of others, notably the Lloyds, TSB and HBOS merger, the competition authorities, now the Competition Commission, did not have much comment on the mergers. Julia Black has observed how the pre-eminent role given to the Secretary of State to issue an Intervention Notice under the *Enterprise Act 2002* was pivotal.[74] The Secretary of State ruled that the merger of Lloyds,TSB and HBOS was related to the stability of the UK financial system. Contested by many shareholders unsuccessfully in the courts,[75] there was little real transparency given to the arrangements. The protection of the public interest and the Executive's determination of what may constitute the public interest through reconciling fiscal stability and financial stability is not going to be easy in the future. One suggestion is that the NAO[76] and the Public Accounts Committee (PAC) in combination may provide the relevant expertise and analysis needed to support good decision-making. The PAC has the virtue of experience in engaging with the Treasury. This is important since the Treasury's pivotal relationship with the Bank of England is at the apex of the new system of financial sector regulation. Building on the experience of past practice makes the PAC the committee of choice for ensuring that the public interest is defined by Parliament rather than the tendency at present to have it defined by the Government of the day. Proper strategic risk assessment is one that requires expertise and specialist assessment that can be provided through NAO input[77] into the oversight of financial regulation. The NAO has already developed considerable knowledge of banking regulation, not least in the problems associated with Northern Rock[78] which led to its nationalization.

25.7. CONCLUSIONS: THE PRECAUTIONARY PRINCIPLE AND FINANCIAL REGULATION

Adam Smith reminds us of the need to balance the role of 'projector' with the deterrence against 'the prodigal'. Undoubtedly the use of risk assessment is increasingly imbedded in the role of managing risk as well as monitoring risk. The culture of avoiding risk brings issues as to whether some banks are too large and that some banks may have to be made smaller to allow their credible regulation. There is a wide divergence of views on this issue especially in the light of the arguments made by John Kay before the Treasury Select Committee.[79]

Banking governance has to be considered within the context of the larger public investment made by the Government. This requires attention in terms of recognizing the need for transparency and accountability as well as an increase in public awareness and Parliamentary scrutiny.

The culture of taking excessive risks when ultimately funded by taxpayers is likely to give way to a more prudent and cautious approach. The ever present threat of a systemic regulator is also likely to make hearts beat faster and for risk avoidance, but like all human behaviour financial gambling is likely to maintain high stakes risk takers and regulators may have to look away as political fashion changes. At a minimum new legislation on financial regulation should be subject to pre-legislative scrutiny and the resulting Act should be periodically reviewed under the arrangements for post-legislative scrutiny.

The *Financial Services Act 2010* gave the FSA the lead role as the independent regulator. Various ways of strengthening the FSA including a new Council for Financial Stability were intended to improve the overall structure of financial supervision and regulation. The FSA also received new powers to cover the banks' recovery plans; settle executive remuneration and provide an increased disciplinary role and oversight over short selling. This is in addition to many consumer rights and schemes to provide compensation and redress consumer needs. There was an added step in the direction of failing institutions being able to institute Recovery and Resolution Plans (RRPs) before failure takes place.

The decision to transform the responsibilities for regulation under the Bank of England's control provides an institutional focused response to the financial problems of the past. This is a significant leap in the dark. In itself this does not meet the expectations of risk management across the financial sector nor does it fully address the question of how effective is the new regulatory system likely to be. As shown above financial regulation is best built on past experience drawing on lessons from success and failure. It is critical to the success of the new regulatory structure that the experience and achievements made by the FSA are built upon including the removal of 'light-touch' regulation and its replacement with a macro-prudential sort of regulation that attempts to make risk monitoring as distinct from risk management an operative form of oversight. The Bank of England has been set a demanding task that will require a careful balance and transparency in future financial regulatory strategy. Systems of Parliamentary accountability also need to be strengthened to ensure that the public interest is protected for both customers and taxpayers. Proper oversight and transparency are needed for fiscal stability and financial stability to be reconciled. The precautionary principle offers a credible way forward that balances market needs, against customer and taxpayers interests set under an effective framework of parliamentary accountability. It also may be the mechanism that engages with the need for an assessment in the future review of the effectiveness of policy-making.

NOTES

1. This paper was presented at the Warwick Law School Symposium: Managing Systemic Risk: 7–9 April 2010. See: Toporowski, Jan (2003), 'The Prudence of Projectors: Adam Smith's Premonition of Financial Fragility and the Origins of Monetary Policy', *Research in the History of Economic Thought and Methodology*, **22**, pp. 93–122; Schoemaker, Paul J.H. (1993), 'Determinants of Risk-Taking: Behavioural and Economic Views', *Journal of Risk and Uncertainty*, **6**, pp. 49–73; Cheffins, Brian R. (2010), 'The Stewardship Code's Achilles' Heel', *Modern Law Review* 1004.
2. Brammertz, Willi (2010), 'Risk and regulation', *Journal of Financial Regulation and Compliance*, 46.
3. Black, Julia (2007), 'Tensions in the regulatory state', *Public Law*, 58. Also see: Black, Julia (2010), *Managing the Financial Crisis – the Constitutional Dimension*, LSE Working Papers 12; Baldwin, R. (2005), *Is better regulation smarter regulation?* Public Law, 485.
4. *The Economist* (13 February 2010), *The Gods strike back: A Special Report on Financial Risk*, pp. 3–16. Also see: Lindblom, C. E. (1959), 'The science of "muddling through"' (19 *Public Administration* 78–88).
5. Treasury Select Committee, *Banking Crisis: Dealing with the Failure of UK Banks*, HC 416 Session 2008–09 paras 203–29.
6. See: HM Treasury (2010), *A new approach to financial regulation: judgement, focus and stability*, CM 7874 London.
7. The development of the precautionary principle owes much to environmental and scientific developments where it is readily applied and has become a means of testing future 'green technologies' such as Genetically Modified Organisms (GMOs). See: Wildavsky, Aaron 'Trial and Error versus trial without error'.
8. Scott, C. (2000), 'Accountability in the regulatory state', 27 *JLS* 28. Also see: Graham, C. (1995), *Is There A Crisis in Regulatory Accountability*? Chartered Institute of Public Finance and Accountancy, London.
9. BRTF, Alternatives to State Regulation (2000).
10. EU Commission sets out its plans for a new EU framework for crisis management in the financial sector IP/10/1353.
11. Richardson, Benjamin (2008), *Socially Responsible Investment Law*, Oxford OUP, pp. 190–203.
12. See: Nield, Sarah (2010), "Responsible lending and borrowing: whereto low-cost home ownership? *Legal Studies* 610. EU Commission on the Precautionary Principle COM (2000) 1 (02.02.2000.)
13. Currently being considered by the Basel Committee 12 September 2010, endorsing the capital and liquidity reform under Basel III Package proposed in December 2009. Insisting on higher capital ratios but taking account of fears of a double dip economic recession.
14. Leaders' Statement, *The Pittsburgh Summit*, 24–25 September 2009.
15. House of Commons Treasury Select Committee, *Too important to fail – too important to ignore*, Ninth Report Session 2009–10 HC 261-1 pp. 3 Summary.
16. Institute for Fiscal Studies (2010), *The IFS Green Budget February 2010* London: IFS, pp. 51–3. Also consider the Bank of England Stability Reports 2008, 2009.
17. See NAO, Maintaining Financial Stability Across the UK Banking System; Report of the Comptroller and Auditor General HC 91 Session 2009–10.

18. Black, Julia (2010), *Managing the Financial Crisis – the Constitutional Dimension*, LSE Working Papers 12.
19. Bradford and Bingley from July 2009, Northern Rock from January 2010.
20. The scheme is primarily intended to manage the GBP281 billion of Royal Bank of Scotland.
21. *The Financial Times*, 23 July 2010.
22. Royal Bank of Scotland pays GBP700 m.
23. Section 2 of the 2000 Act provides a range of statutory duties and general principles. Various regulatory objectives are set out in Section 2(2) and are aspirational in tone such as market confidence, public awareness, and the protection of consumers and the reduction of financial crime.
24. Historically, our regulatory philosophy has been defined by the 'strap line' of more principles-based regulation. This has often been misunderstood. Principles-based regulation means, whenever possible, moving from prescriptive rules to a higher level articulation of what we expect firms to do. This has the major advantage of placing on firms explicit responsibility to decide how best to align their business objectives and processes with the regulatory outcomes we have specified. See: Memorandum to the Treasury Committee's Inquiry into the Banking Crisis Ev.456 (16 February 2009).
25. See Financial Services Authority Annual Report 2008, London: 2008.
26. The FSA's annual budget is over GBP270 million with 3000 staff and responsibilities for over 30 000 firms with financial activities. One aspect of the work of the FSA is a conscious awareness of rules and procedures – detailed in an 8000-page *Handbook of Rules and Guidance* and supported by a range of disciplinary, civil and criminal penalties.
27. In the National Audit Office's Report on 30 April 2007, before the impending financial crisis, NAO, *The Financial Services Authority: A Review under section 12 of the Financial Services and Markets Act 2000* HC 500 Session 2006–07 (27 April 2007) p. 5 explained 'highly regarded within the financial services industry in the UK and internationally and its risk based approach is increasingly seen as a model to follow by other regulators'. The NAO report goes on to detail how delegated authority to dedicated supervisors provided for the 1000 largest firms the basis to develop 'an effective working relationship including senior level engagements with those firms'.
28. The Bank of England decided to rescue the JMB and offered 50 per cent of the GBP150 million of guarantees in return for bank ownership at a token amount. The various London Clearing Banks and the other four members of the gold bullion club provided the remaining guarantees. The rationale for take-over came from a fear of loss of confidence in the banking system and undesirable consequences from a knock on effect.
29. Lord Bingham (1991–2), *Inquiry into the Supervision of the Bank of Credit and Commerce International* HC198.
30. See: Sixth Report Treasury and Civil Service Committee, *The Regulation of Financial Services in the UK* HC 1994–5 332-I .
31. See generally the FSA, *The Turner Review: A regulatory response to the global banking crisis*, London: March, 2009.
32. FSA (March 2009) *The Turner Review. A regulatory response to the global banking crisis*, London.
33. See Thoresen Review of Generic Financial Advice: Final Report HM Treasury 3 March 2009.
34. The debate is set out in two useful House of Commons Research Papers: Financial Service Bill: Committee Stage Report Bill No 6 of 2009/10 Research Paper 10/04 20 January 2010 and also House of Commons Research Papers: Financial Service Bill: Committee Stage Report Bill No 6 of 2009/10 Research Paper 09/84 27 November 2009.
35. House of Commons: Treasury Committee Reporting Contingent Liabilities to Parliament 5th Report of Session 2009–10 HC 181 (22 February 2010). Here the Treasury failed in a time of emergency to inform the Chair of the Public Accounts Committee or Parliament of the failure of the Treasury's own rules on giving information on the Emergency Liquidity Assistance to Northern Rock.

36. See: McEldowney, John F. (2009), 'Defining the public interest: Public Law Perspectives on Regulating the Financial Crisis', in John Raymond LaBrosse, Rodrigo Olivares-Caminal and Dalvinder Singh (eds), *Financial Crisis Management and Bank Resolution*, London: Informa, pp. 103–132.
37. Wilson, G. and Wilson, S. (2010), 'Market misconduct, the Financial Services Authority and creating a system of "city grasses": blowing the whistle on whistle blowing', *Company Lawyer*, **67**.
38. The Director of Public Prosecutions, HM Revenue and Customs and the Serious Fraud Office.
39. Directive 2003/6/EC.
40. SI 2005 No. 381.
41. Macrory, R. (May 2006), *Regulatory Justice: Sanctioning in a post-Hampton World: A Consultation Document*, London: Cabinet Office and *Regulatory Justice: Making Sanctions Effective*, London: Cabinet Office (November 2006).
42. NAO, *The Financial Services Authority: A review under section 12 of the Financial Services and Markets Act 2000* HC 500 Session 2006–07 (27th April 2007), p. 49 noted that from 2001–02 there were an average of 200 cases each year dealing with money laundering and other breaches of the financial standards. At para. 4.63 2005-06, 17 cases involving financial penalties totalling GBP17.4 million, GBP14 million of which was for one market protection case and GBP505,000 related specifically to financial crime.
43. *R. v Rigby, Bailey and Rowley* [2005] EWCA 3487.
44. FSA, *The Turner Review: A regulatory response to the global banking crisis*, London: March, 2009.
45. *The Economist*, 27 March 2010, p. 81.
46. [2009] EWCA Crim 1941, [2010] 1 All ER 1183.
47. FSA, *Decision Procedure and Penalties Manual and the Enforcement Guide* (PS07/12).
48. FSA's Annual Review for 2008–09 reported that the FSA imposed a record GBP27.3 million in financial penalties compared to an average of GBP14 million over the previous five years with an increase in FSA investigations and inquiries.
49. Wilson, G. and Wilson, S. (2010), 'Market misconduct, the Financial Services Authority and creating a system of "city grasses": blowing the whistle on whistle blowing', *Company Lawyer*, **67**, p. 80.
50. FSA, *Effective corporate governance* (*Significant influence controlled functions and the Walker review*) (10/3) January 2010.
51. See Recommendation 23 of the Walker Review *op. cit.*
52. *R. v Innospec Ltd.* Crown Court 26 March 2010 Judgment of Lord Justice Thomas.
53. Binning, Peter (30 July 2010), 'Another bad idea', *New Law Journal*, 1059.
54. See: HM Treasury, *A new approach to financial regulation: judgement, focus and stability* CM 7874 London, 2010.
55. The Office of Budget Responsibility under Sir Alan Budd, provided an independent view of public expenditure, borrowing and the deficit in percentage of GDP. In June 2010 the Treasury published a guide to a Spending Review (HM Treasury: The Spending Review 2010, CM 7872) setting out the Government's main fiscal agenda. In this context an overhaul of the financial regulatory system took place.
56. HM Treasury (2010), *A new approach to financial regulation: judgement, focus and stability* CM 7874 London, para 1.4.
57. Para. 2.16 White Paper.
58. Ibid.
59. HL *Select Committee on the Constitution Banking Bill* Session 2008–09 HL Paper 19 and HL Paper 97.
60. Treasury Select Committee, *Reporting Contingent Liabilities to Parliament* HC 181 session 2009–10.
61. Para. 2.14 White Paper.
62. Hector Sants of the FSA has agreed to co-ordinate and supervise the new arrangements.

63. See the Treasury and Civil Service Committee (8 December 1993), *Role of the Bank of England* HC 98-I. Tomlinson, Jim (1990), *Public Policy and the Economy Since 1900*, Oxford: Oxford University Press, pp. 25–28. Lord Bingham (1991–2), *Inquiry into the Supervision of the Bank of Credit and Commerce International* HC 198 Sixth Report', Treasury and Civil Service Committee, *The Regulation of Financial Services in the UK* HC 1994-5 332-I.
64. See: Fforde, J.S. (1983), 'Competition, Innovation and Regulation in British Banking', 23 *B.E.Q.B.* 363.
65. The European Securities and Markets Authority (ESMA) provides a means to set rules to supervise the overall supervision by national supervisors. *The Economist* 6 November 2010.
66. EU Commission sets out its plans for a new EU framework for crisis management in the financial sector IP/10/1353.
67. EU Commission *op. cit.*, HM Treasury Reforming Financial Markets CM 7677, 2009.
68. Ibid.
69. House of Commons: Treasury Committee, *Too Important to fail – too important to ignore*, 9th report of Session 2009–10 HC 264-I (29 March 2010).
70. See: the *Financial Services and Markets Act 2000*. The scheme became operational 1 December 2001. It protects deposits, insurance policies, insurance broking for businesses after 14 January 2005, types of travel insurance, investment business and certain kinds of home finance.
71. Ibid. para 30–31.
72. House of Commons: Treasury Committee (29 March 2010) *Too Important to fail – too important to ignore*, 9th Report of Session 2009–10 HC 264-I, para. 50, pp.23 Q171.
73. Examples in the past are: Treasury and Civil Service Committee, Second Special Report, Banking Supervision and BCCI International and National Regulation: The Response of the Government and the Bank of England to the Fourth Report from the Committee on Session 1991–92 HC (1992–3) 248. Contemporary examples include: House of Commons: Treasury Committee (29 March 2010), *Too Important to fail – too important to ignore*, 9th Report of Session 2009–10 HC 264-I.
74. Julia Black, *Managing the Financial Crisis – the Constitutional Dimension*, LSE Working Papers 12/2010.
75. *Merger Action Group v Secretary of State for Business Enterprise and Regulatory Reform* [2008] CAT 36 (107/4/10/08).
76. NAO (27 April 2007), *The Financial Services Authority: A review under section 12 of the Financial Services and Markets Act 2000* HC 500 Session 2006–07.
77. See: NAO Report (20 March 2009), *HM Treasury: The Nationalisation of Northern Rock* HC 298 Session 2008–09.
78. NAO Report (20 March 2009), *HM Treasury: The Nationalisation of Northern Rock* HC 298 Session 2008–09.
79. House of Commons: Treasury Committee (29 March 2010), *Too Important to fail – too important to ignore*, 9th report of Session 2009–10. HC 264-I.

Index

ABCP market collapse 426
ABS (asset-backed securities) 5
accountability and TARP 75
AIFP (Automotive Industry Financing Program) 64
Alessandri, P. 30
Appelbaum, B. 337
Argentina, debt defaults 159, 165
asset-backed securities (ABS) 5
asset disposition, LCFI insolvency 287–8
Asset Guarantee Program (AGP) 62
asset loss guarantees 43
asset market programs, TARP 63
Asset Protection Scheme, UK 453
assets, banks, Canada and US 89
Atkinson, P. 375, 381–2, 386, 391
Australia, retail deposit insurance 43–4
Automotive Industry Financing Program (AIFP) 64

Bain, J.S. 182, 191
balance sheets
  effects of financial crisis, Iceland 147–8
  and government guarantees 34–6
Banco Ambrosiano Holdings 311–12
Bank Act, Canada 89
bank consolidation programme, Nigeria 435–6, 437
Bank for International Settlements (BIS) 358
bank levy, UK 111–25
  policy goals 117–25
Bank of Canada 88, 417–18
Bank of Credit and Commerce International (BCCI) 313–14
Bank of England 453–4, 460–61, 468
Banking Act 1933, US (*Glass-Steagall Act*) 340, 400–401
Banking Act 2009, UK 460
Banking Commission, UK 462
bankruptcy, corporate, US 275–6
  compared with bank insolvency 276–82
banks
  balance sheets, and government guarantees 34–6
  influence on Basel III reforms 388–91
  insolvency 236–8
    US 272–5, 276–82
  levy, UK 111–25
  recapitalization, Iceland 144–5
  resilience 354–6
  resolution regimes 195–7, 201–203
    cross-border 364–5
  system comparison, Canada and US 89–90
  and TARP 62–3
barriers to entry 182–3
Basel Committee on Banking Supervision *xi*, 25, 111, 119, 233, 245, 246, 294, 308, 310, 321, 351–5, 357–61, 363–5, 374, 381, 388–9, 391, 422
  capital and liquidity regulation 351–71
  and consolidated supervision 310–16
  regulatory reform 363–6
  Working Group on cross-border resolution 324
Basel Concordat 311–13
Basel II 374–7
Basel III 366–71, 377–92
  banks influence on reforms 388–91
  counter-cyclical capital buffers 383–5
  effects of reform 389–91
  leverage ratio 380–82
  liquidity regulation 385–7

objectives 387–8
redefining capital 377–8
risk coverage 378–80
Baumol, W. 191
BCCI (Bank of Credit and Commerce International) 313–14
BCFP (Bureau of Consumer Financial Protection) 407
Bear Stearns 317
Benston, G. 190, 401
Berlin, I. 125
Bernanke, Ben 57, 58, 201
bilateral voluntary agreements, insolvency 324
Black, F. 94
Black, J. 467
Blundell-Wignall, A. 375, 381–2, 386, 391
Bordo, M.D. 20
Born, Brokesley 379
borrower behaviour, Canada and US 90
Brady Bonds and debt restructuring, Greece 172–3, 173–4
Brady Plan 161
bridge banks 292
Brown, Gordon 112, 119, 123, 124
Brunnermeier, M.K. 17
Buchheit, L. 163
budget deficit, Greece 156
Buiter, W. 341
Bureau of Consumer Financial Protection (BCFP) 407
Bush, George W. 75–6
Bush administration and financial crisis 59–60
business conduct regulation, EU 342–4
Byres, W. 373, 382

Calomiris, C.W. 340, 346
Canada
banking system stability 81–91
and financial crisis 423–5
financial safety net 416–31
financial system resiliency 425–7
mortgage market 422–3
Canada Deposit Insurance Corporation (CDIC) 88, 419–20, 421–2
Canadian Securities Regulatory Authority (CSRA) 428
capital
redefinition under Basel III 377–8
reform, Basel Committee 354
capital and liquidity regulation, Basel Committee 351–71
capital absorbency, Basel reform 359–60
capital adequacy, Basel reform 354–60
capital buffers, countercyclical 358–9, 367–8, 383–5
Capital Purchase Program (CPP) 62
capitalization, Canadian banks 90
Caruana, J. 383
CCA (contingent claims analysis) 94–6
CDIC (Canada Deposit Insurance Corporation) 419–20, 421–2
Cecchetti, S. 389–90
central banks
Bank of Canada 417–18
Bank of England 453–4, 460–61, 468
guaranteeing banks balance sheets 34
Nigeria 436, 347
and systemic liquidity 24–5, 28
see also European Central Bank; Federal Reserve
Central Clearing Party (CCP) 26
Čihák, M. 333
Citigroup 198
City of London and bank levy proposal 113
clawbacks 298
Clegg, Nick 124
Clower, A.N. 66
Cohen, N. 309
collateralized debt obligations 11–12
Iceland 142
collateralized lending and Icelandic financial crash 143–4
collateralized loan obligations (CLOs) 11
collective action clauses (CACs) 162, 166, 169
Greece 173
compensation
Basel Committee 363–4

to foreign depositors, Iceland 145–6
competition 190–92
and market concentration 84–6
in supervisory systems 336–7
competition law, EU 248
confidence loss, Iceland 146–7
Congressional Oversight Panel for TARP 75
conservation buffer, Basel III 367
consolidated resolution 321–8
consolidated supervision 308–21
EU 310–16
SIFIs 213–16
Consumer Financial Protection, Bureau of (BCFP) 407
consumer protection 190
Consumer Protection and Markets Authority (CPMA) 461
contingent capital 28, 215
contingent claims 26–7
contingent claims analysis (CCA) 94–6
in large G7 economy 98–106
systemic 97–8
contingent liabilities and systemic risk 101–106
Continuous Linked Settlement (CLS) 25
coordination, financial sector, Canada 420–22
corporate governance guidance, Basel Committee 363
corporate reorganization 275–6
corporate resolution regimes 201–204
correlation of risk 379–80
countercyclical capital buffers 358–9, 367–8, 383–5
counterparty risk 26
CPMA (Consumer Protection and Markets Authority) 461
credit
and Icelandic financial crisis 137–43
impact of TARP 72
credit default swap markets 96
credit enhancement, Greece 173–4
credit ratings and investment decisions 8–12
crisis, impacts on Canada and US 81–4
crisis mitigating actions by deposit insurers *xxi*
cross-border fee structures 44–5
cross-border financial institutions 309–10
insolvency resolution 293–9, 321–6, 364–5
'living wills' 326–8
Cross-Border Insolvency Cooperation, Practice Guide on 324
Crouch, C. 116
CSRA (Canadian Securities Regulatory Authority) 428
Cummings, Kevin 121
currency depreciation, Iceland 148–9
currency unions 156–7

Darling, Alistair 119, 124
De Bandt, O. 30
debt, government-guaranteed, Iceland 149
Debt Management Office, UK 453
debt re-profiling 164–5
debt restructuring 161–5
Greece 168–77
Decressin, J. 333
delaying bank closure 291–2
deposit insurers, crisis mitigating actions *xxi*
Depositor Preference Act 279
depository funding, banks, Canada 89–90
DIP financing 292
Dodd-Frank Act 392, 402–403, 405, 407, 410–11
Dolan, E. 375
Drehmann, M. 383, 384, 385
dual banking system, US 403–404
dual supervisory system
EU 333–45
US 335–7, 339–40, 403–404

ECB *see* European Central Bank
Economic and Monetary Union 157
economic growth, impact of TARP 73
EESA (*Emergency Economic Stabilization Act*) 3, 60
Einstein, A. 328
Emergency Economic Stabilization Act 3, 60

Emergency Lending Assistance, Bank of Canada 418
EMU (Economic and Monetary Union) 157
EU *see* European Union
European Central Bank
  benchmark interest rate 157
  purchasing debt securities 177
European Convention on Human Rights and local law bonds 176
European System of Financial Supervisors 327
European Union
  consolidated supervision 310–16
  cross-border insolvencies 294–5
  dual supervisory system 333–45
  insolvency regime 324–6
  see also Basel Committee; Basel II; Basel III
exchange offers, Greece 171–2
exit consent 162, 166

Fama, E. 191
Farantouris, N. 254
FCAC (Financial Consumer Agency of Canada) 420
FDIA (*Federal Deposit Insurance Act*) 198, 203–204
FDIC (Federal Deposit Insurance Corporation) 274–5, 281–2, 404, 406–407
  and Bank of England, bilateral agreement 324
FDIC Improvement Act (FDICIA) 56
Federal Bankruptcy Code 198, 202–203
Federal Deposit Insurance Act (FDIA) 198, 203–204
Federal Deposit Insurance Corporation (FDIC) 274–5, 281–2
Federal Financial Institutions Examination Council (FFIEC) 401, 407
Federal Reserve 57–8, 340, 404, 405–406
  as consolidated supervisor of SIFIs 213–16
  and financial crisis 57–8
  and *Gramm-Leach-Bliley Act* 408–409
  Term Asset-Backed Loan Facility 63
fee structures across borders 44–5
Ferguson, J.M. 182
FFIEC (Federal Financial Institutions Examination Council) 401, 407
financial conglomerates
  crisis management 316–21
  insolvency approaches 321–6
Financial Conglomerates Directive, EU 326
Financial Consumer Agency of Canada (FCAC) 420
financial crises
  and Basel Committee 352–4
  and Canada 81–4, 423–5
  Nigeria, causes 435
  and sovereign debt 155–6
  and State Aid rules, EU 258–64
  and USA 57–8, 81–4
  UK 451–2
financial freedom, Canada and US 87
financial holding companies 401
Financial Institutions Supervisory Committee (FISC), Canada 421
Financial Policy Committee, UK 461
financial regulation *see* regulation
Financial Regulation, A New Approach (White Paper) 450, 458–60
financial risk management, UK 449–69
financial safety nets *see* safety nets
financial sector reforms, Nigeria 436–9
Financial Services and Markets Act 455
Financial Services Authority (FSA) 454–8, 468
  liquidity standards 361–2
financial stability, Canada and US 81–4
Financial Stability Oversight Council (FSOC) 211–12, 409–10
FISC (Financial Institutions Supervisory Committee), Canada 421
fiscal cost as trigger of insolvency reform 234

fiscal impact of Icelandic financial crash 143–50
Flaherty, Jim 121
forbearance 55–7
Ford, G. 388
foreign depositor compensation costs, Iceland 145–6
fragility, LCFIs 283–4
Frank, B. 59
FRB *see* Federal Reserve
freedom, financial, Canada and US 87
freedom to exit 186–7
FSA *see* Financial Services Authority
FSOC (Financial Stability Oversight Council) 211–12, 409–10
Furletti, M.J. 343

Gart, A. 400
Germany
  bank insolvency management reform 240–44
  Stabilization Fund 234
Giles, C. 389
Glass-Seagall Act (*Banking Act 1933*) 340, 400–401
Goldstein, M. 376, 386
Good Practice Principles on Supervisory Colleges 365
Gorton, G. 339
governance
  Canada and US 87
  and precautionary principle, UK 463–6
government
  and financial safety net, Canada 416–17
  as guarantor of last resort 32–53
  see also State Aid legislation
government deposit guarantees (GDG), Malaysia *xxii-xxviii*
  exit plan *xxiv-xxvii*
government-guaranteed debt, Iceland 149
Gramm-Leach-Bliley Act 408–409
Greece *xviii*, *xxxiv*, 34, 42, 155–65
  budget deficit 156
  debt restructuring 163–5, 168–77
  risk sharing system 159
  Stability and Growth Programme 156
Greek Drama scenario 160
Greek Tragedy scenario 160
guarantees, government-backed 32–53
  costs and benefits 36–45
  Iceland 149
Gulati, M. 163

H-statistic 85
Haldane, A. 26, 30
HAMP (Home Affordable Modification Program) 65
Hardy, D.C. 346
Harper, I. 386
Hartman, P. 30
HBOS, acquisition by Lloyds TSB 262–3
Hellenic Stability and Growth Programme 156
Hertig, G. 333
Hicks, J. 84
Hoban, Mark 112
Home Affordable Modification Program (HAMP) 65
home ownership, impact of TARP 72
household financial assets, impact of TARP 73
housing industry aid and TARP 64–5
Huertas, Thomas 328
Hüpkes, E. 324

Iceland 133–52, 318, 329, 423
  build-up of risk 137–43
  cost of financial crash 143–50
  currency depreciation 148–9
  pre-crisis fiscal position 136–7
inattention as reason for buying bad securities 7–12
Independent Banking Commission 462
infrastructure strength and systemic risk 25–6
insolvency
  avoidance 296–7
  conglomerates 319–21, 321–6
  cross-border 289–90, 293–9, 321–6
  German reforms 240–44
  LCFIs 271–300
  requirements, banks 236–8
  'too-big-to-fail' institutions 238–40
  US regimes 198–201, 272–82

inter-affiliate financing 304–305
interagency relations, Canada 422
interest rate, ECB 157–9
intermediated finance and securities purchase 12–14
internal devaluation 159
international aspects of insolvency 289–90
  see also cross-border financial institutions
International Framework for Liquidity Risk Measurement, Standards and Monitoring 374
investor behaviour, pre-financial crisis 3–15
  reasons for buying bad securities 6–14
Islamic deposit insurance system, Malaysia 442–8

Jamaica, debt re-profiling 164, 171

Kafalah bil ujr 444
Kahn, C.M. 346
Kaufman, G.G. 30, 387, 388
Kaufman, H. 386
Kay, J. 115, 116, 123, 391
Knight, Angela 117
Krimminger, M. 322, 324
króna, Icelandic, depreciation 148–9
Krugman, P. 84, 423

Labour government, taxation policy 114–15
Laffer, A. 191
Landsbanki 142, 145
large complex financial institutions (LCFIs) 282–4
  cross-border issues 293–9
  insolvency resolution 271–300
  limiting growth 209–11
  see also banks
Latvia, internal devaluation 159
Lee, P. 382
Lee, R. 333
legal aspects of debt, Greece, 168–71
Lehman Brothers 59, 99, 198, 317
lender of last resort
  Bank of Canada 417–18
  EU 341–2
  US 339–40
  see also safety nets
Lerner index 85–6
leverage capital requirements 214
leverage ratio, Basel III 380–82
levies 50–52
  UK bank levy 111–25
life savings, impact of TARP 73
liquidity
  Basel Committee 356–8, 360–61
  Basel III 385–7
  FSA standards 361–2
  measures to reduce moral hazard 28
  and TARP 68
Liquidity Risk Measurement, Standards and Monitoring, International Framework for 374
'living wills' 187–9, 194–5, 298–9, 326–8
Llewellyn, D.T 375, 386, 391
Lloyds Banking Group 262–4
local law bonds 174–6
Lopez, J.A. 388
Loss Absorbency 359–60
loss allocation, LCFI insolvency 286–7
loss of confidence costs of Icelandic financial crash 146–7
Loughlin, M. 117

macro-prudential measures, Basel Committee 365–6
Making Home Affordable (MHA) program 64–5
Malaysia
  exit from government deposit guarantee *xxii-xxviii*
  Islamic deposit insurance system 442–8
Malaysia Deposit Insurance Corporation (MDIC) *xxii-xxviii*
management and insolvency, LCFIs 285–6
Mandelson, Peter 115
market concentration and competition 84–6
market risk, Basel framework 360
Marshall, A. 191
maslahah 443
Mason, J.R. 348

Masters, B. 388, 390, 391
MBS (mortgage-backed securities) 5
McCahery, J.A. 333
MDIC (Malaysia Deposit Insurance Corporation) *xxii-xxviii*
Merton Model 94
Methodologies for Risk and Performance Alignment of Remuneration 364
MHA (Making Home Affordable) program 64–5
Minimum Standards for the Supervision of International Banking Groups and their Cross-border Establishments 314–15
money market mutual funds (MMMFs) 220–21
Mopping-Up Law 175
moral hazard 27–8
mortgage-backed securities 5
mortgage market, Canada 422–3
Mullineaux, D. 339
Mundell, R. 156
Murphy, L. 113
Murphy, M. 388, 389, 390, 391
mutualisation of losses, LCFI insolvency 289

Nagel, T. 113
Nakashima, E. 337
narrow banks 218–26
neoliberalism and bank levy 115–17
Nieto, M.J. 346
Nigeria 434–41
  financial crisis 435–6
  financial safety net reform 436–41
  financial system 434–5
Northern Rock 185–6, 255, 317

OCA (optimum currency area) 156–7
OCC (Office Comptroller of Currency) 403, 405
Oehmke, M. 17
Office of Superintendent of Financial Institutions (OSFI), Canada 418–19
optimum currency area (OCA) 156–7
originate-to-distribute (OTD) model 5
Osborne, George 112, 116–17, 118, 119, 120, 123
OSFI *see* Office of Superintendent of Financial Institutions
OTD (originate-to-distribute) model 5
overconfidence as reason for buying bad securities 7–12

Panzar, J.C. 85
Patankar, N. 16
Paulson, H.M. 59, 60, 76
PCA (prompt corrective action) 275
Peace, J. 390
pension fund losses, Icelandic financial crash 149–50
Plender, J. 116, 124, 125
plurality of bankruptcy 322
PPIP (Public–Private Investment Program) 63
Practice Guide on Cross-Border Insolvency Cooperation 324
pre-insolvency transfers 279–80
precautionary principle 450–51, 463–6
premium setting, government-backed guarantees 43–52
  cross-border 44–5
Preussen Elektra case 250
Principles for Enhancing Corporate Governance 363
Principles for the Supervision of Banks 312
procyclicality, Basel II 383
profit sharing investment accounts (PSIA) 446
prompt corrective action (PCA) 275
provincial governments, Canada 420
Prudential Regulatory Authority 461
Public Accounts Committee, UK 467
Public–Private Investment Program (PPIP) 63

rapid entry to banking sector 183–4
recapitalization, banks
  Iceland 144–5
  impact of bank levy 121
recovery allocation, international LCFI insolvency 290
Recovery and Resolution Plans (RRPs) *see* living wills
regulation
  Canada 88–9
  Nigeria 435

and systemic risk 20–21, 42
US 399–411
regulatory reform
Basel Committee 363–6
UK 458–63
Reinhart, C.M. 56, 153, 154, 156
rescue aid, EU 255–6
resolution regimes
LCFIs 204–206, 271–300
systemically important financial institutions 211–13
Resolution Trust Corporation (RTC) 56
restructuring aid, EU 254–6
Restructuring Communication, EU 260–61
retail deposit insurance 34, 43–4
Richardson, B. 450
Riegle-Neal Interstate Banking and Branching Act 209–10
risk-based premiums 43–52
across borders 44–5
SIFIs 216–17
risk-based SRCRs 214–15
risk coverage, Basel III 378–80
risk management practice improvement 27
risk sharing, Greece 159
Rogoff, K.S. 56, 153, 154, 156
Rosse, J.N. 85
Roy, R.K. 115

safety nets 32–53
Canada 428–30
EU 341–2
Nigeria 436–41
US 339–40
Santander 184
Santos, J.A.C. 346
savings, impact of TARP 73
SBS (shadow banking system) 4
SCAP (Supervisory Capital Assessment Program) 65
Scholes, M. 94
Schooner, H. 79
Schumpeter, J.A. 192
Scott, K.E. 30, 404
Senior Advisory Committee (SAC), Canada 421
shadow banking system (SBS) 4
Shariah Advisory Council of Bank Negara Malaysia (SAC) 443
SIFIs *see* systemically important financial institutions
Singer, Paul 201
Sloman Neptune case 250
Smith, Adam 449, 467
social contributions, Iceland 149
sovereign debt
restructuring 161–5
impact of global financial crisis 155–6
special purpose vehicles (SPV) 5
Special Resolution Regime (SRR) 327
SRE (systemic risk exemption) 275
SRIF (systemic risk insurance fund) 216–17
stability
Canada and US 81–4
and regulators 181–92
stability funds 52
and TARP 72
Standing Liquidity Facility, Bank of Canada 417–18
Stardust Marine case 249–50
State Aid legislation, European Union 248–64
in financial crises 341–2
stays 277–8
Steger, M.B. 115
Stigler, G. 182
Strengthening Liquidity Standards 361–2
Strengthening the Resilience of the Banking Sector 358, 374
structural complexity of LCFIs 299
Structure-Conduct-Performance paradigm 81
structured securities 3–15
sub-prime MBS investment 8–9, 10–11
Sundmacher, M. 388
supervision, EU-level 333–45
Supervisory Capital Assessment Program (SCAP) 65
supervisory colleges 365
supervisory competition 336–7
SVP (special purpose vehicle) 5
systemic buffer, Basel III 367

systemic contingent claim analysis 93–107
in large G7 economy 98–106
systemic events, mechanism 23–4
systemic risk 19–30, 235–6
capital requirements for SIFIs 214
from contingent liabilities 101–106
definition 20–22
determination 210
exemption 275
from expected losses 100–101
levies 50–52, 216–17
systemic risk insurance fund (SRIF) 216–17
systemically important financial institutions (SIFIs) 211–13
risk-based premiums 216–17
supervision 213–16
Systemically Significant Failing Institutions (SSFI) program 62

TALF (Term Asset-Backed Loan Facility) 63
Targeted Investment Program (TIP) 62
TARP *see* Troubled Asset Relief Program
taxation
Labour government policy 114–15
and neoliberalism 115–17
taxpayer protection and TARP 73–5
TBTF *see* 'too-big-to-fail' institutions
Term Asset-Backed Loan Facility (TALF) 63
Thomas, M. 386
Thomson, J. 379–80
timeliness, insolvency resolution 281–2
Tobin tax 112, 119
'too-big-to-fail' institutions *xx*, *xxvi*, 94, 105, 197, 208–27, 316, 319, 327, 329, 352, 365, 376, 377, 386, 410
resolution regimes 233–45
'too-many-to-fail' problem 379–80
trading infrastructure and systemic risk 25–6
Treasury Committee, UK 466–7
'trees of the forest' analogy 191
Trichet, J.-C. 390
Troubled Asset Relief Program (TARP) 55–77
and asset markets 63
and automotive industry 64
as crisis response 59–60
evaluation 67–75
and financial institutions 62–3
and housing industry 64–5
implementation 65–7
Turner Review 454
two-tiered bank regulation structure 218–26

UCSB (Unlocking Credit for Small Businesses) 63–4
UK *see* United Kingdom
UK Financial Investments Ltd 452–3
UNCITRAL 323–4
unemployment
costs of Icelandic financial crash 149
impact of TARP 73
United Kingdom
bank levy 111–25
financial risk management 449–69
United States
bank regulation and supervision 336–7, 399–411
banking system compared with Canada 81–91
dual banking system 335–7
Emergency Economic Stabilization Act 3
insolvency regimes 198–201, 272–6
political system 58–9
safety net provision 339–40
Troubled Asset Relief Program 55–77
Unlocking Credit for Small Businesses (UCSB) 63–4
Uruguay, debt re-profiling 165

Value-at-Risk (VAR), banks, Canada and US 82
Vickers, John 462
Volcker, Paul 210, 218, 221
Volcker liabilities cap 211
Volcker rule 218

Walker Review 458
Walter, S. 376, 377, 381, 387
Weder di Mauro, B. 51

Wellink, N. 374–5, 375–6, 381, 385
White Paper on financial regulation, UK 450, 458–60
Wihlborg, C. 388
Williams-Brown, O. 66–7
Wilmarth, A.E. 337, 343, 402
Wolf, M. 115
Wyplosz, C. 385–6